By Their Blood

"I saw under the altar the souls of them that were slain for the word of God, and for the testimony which they held"
(*Revelation 6:9*).

"These all died in faith, not having received the promises, but having seen them afar off, and were persuaded of them, and embraced them, and confessed that they were strangers and pilgrims on the earth. . . . Others were tortured, not accepting deliverance; that they might obtain a better resurrection: and others had trial of cruel mockings and scourgings, yea, moreover of bonds and imprisonment: they were stoned, they were sawn asunder, were tempted, were slain with the sword: they wandered about in sheepskins and goatskins; being destitute, afflicted, tormented; (of whom the world was not worthy): they wandered in deserts, and in mountains, and in dens and caves of the earth"
(Hebrews 11:13, 35–38).

By Their Blood

Christian Martyrs
of the
20th Century

James and Marti Hefley

A Mott Media Book

BAKER BOOK HOUSE
Grand Rapids, Michigan 49516

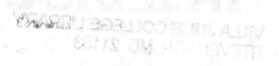

Copyright © 1979 by James C. Hefley

Reprinted 1988 by Baker Book House
and used with permission of copyright owner

ISBN 0-8010-4312-3

Third printing, June 1989

Printed in the United States of America

Library of Congress Cataloging in Publication Data

Hefley, James C
 By their blood.

 Bibliography: p.
 Includes index.
  1. Christian martyrs—Biography. I. Hefley,
Marti, joint author. II. Title.
BR1601.2.H43   272'.092'2 [B]   78-6187

CONTENTS

PREFACE

Christian martyrs! The words stir the imagination. A saint singing above flames that crackle around his stake. A believer kneeling serenely before a blood-stained block; the gimlet-eyed executioner preparing to swing his sword. A missionary bound with vines beside a bubbling pot, his eyes lifted confidently to heaven, while loin-clothed cannibal aborigines dance wildly around to the beat of booming drums.

But burning at the stake passed out of style after Reformation times. Death by the sword rarely occurs today. And only a few missionaries have ever been cooked by cannibals. Such macabre martyrdoms more often occur in the imagination of novelists.

Martyrs of the 20th century have met their earthly end in more conventional, up-to-date methods such as gunshots, bombs, banditry, debilitating prison diseases and starvation.

A second oversimplification is that Christian martyrs always die strictly for their testimony of Christ. This idea persists because accounts of martyrdom often do not include sufficient backgrounding of the events. When all the details are known, it is apparent that most Christian martyrs die in circumstances *related* to their witness for Christ. For example, five young American missionaries were speared to death in 1956 by Auca Indians in Ecuador because of the Indians' fear that they were cannibals. And nurse Mavis Pate was killed by gunfire from a Palestinian refugee camp because Arab commandos mistook the Volkswagen Microbus in which she was riding for an Israeli army vehicle. However, some Christians are killed *primarily* for their allegiance to Christ. Most martyrs to communism in China and the Soviet Union fit into this category.

So the first dictionary definition of martyr—"One who submits to death rather than renounce his religion"—cannot always be strictly applied to the violent death of Christians. The second definition—"One who dies, suffers, or sacrifices everything for a principle, cause, etc."—is more inclusive. By this delineation Lottie Moon, the heroine of Southern Baptists, who died from self-imposed starvation in China was as much a martyr as John and Betty Stam, who were brutally murdered by cold, calculating Chinese Communists.

Recognizing this, we have included many martyrs who might be excluded in some books because they did not die a violent death. At the same time we have not classified as martyrs those who died in accidents which might have happened to them in the homeland. Admittedly, the line is hard to draw here.

We have sought to provide stories of the deaths of Christian nationals where reliable information is available. This is often not the case. Young churches, developing amidst persecution, are less likely to keep records than established congregations with more time and freedom. National believers, also, because of educational and communicational disadvantages, do not document and preserve the stories of their own who have died for Christ. These stories are usually transmitted orally and later written down by educated leaders and/or missionaries. In contrast, the stories of most missionary martyrs and nationals who die with them are well attested. Books by eyewitnesses or close relatives have even been written about some of them.

We have generally restricted our time limit to the 20th century, although in giving background and introducing the martyrs of a country or area, we have usually summarized hostilities to Christianity before the year 1900. In instances of both martyred nationals and missionaries, we have also sought to understand the political, national and social forces behind great outbreaks, such as the Boxer Rebellion of China and the more recent Congo massacre.

We have organized the narrative by geographical units, with the chronological being subordinate to the geographic. Large nations such as China and the Soviet Union are treated as units within themselves, as is Nazi Germany. Smaller nations where little bloodshed of Christians has occurred in the twentieth century are encompassed in larger units and given less attention.

We have excluded the United States, Canada, Australia, New Zealand, the Scandinavian nations, and western European countries (except for martyrs of Nazi Germany). True, there have been isolated instances of martyrs dying for or in circumstances relating to their Christian witness in these "Christian" domains, but most western governments have been neutral, if not encouraging, to the advance of Christianity. There has been, in this century, no particular policy of physical persecution of evangelicals in the West, except as may have occurred in varying degrees by church–state regimes in Italy, Spain, Portugal and Greece.

We must plead imperfection and the subjectivities of our rearing and national loyalties in failures to adequately define Christian martyrdom in many instances. We are humbled at the devotion and commitment of these thousands of Christians who were willing to lay down their lives for the Cause in which they believed.

We do believe that every martyr, whether included in this classification or not, has died for a purpose within the sovereign will of God. God was there when every human life was taken—not setting up the deaths, but permitting evil men to exercise free will and to do their dastardly deeds under the temporary dominion of Satan. Yes, our God was there in grace abounding over sin, beauty growing out of ashes, victory triumphing over death, and the Church advancing beyond defeat.

With this brief preface, we now present *By Their Blood: Christian Martyrs of the 20th Century*. It represents the largest research project we have undertaken in fifteen years as full time evangelical Christian writers. A citation of assistance and sources, with accompanying bibliography, is presented at the end of the book.

James and Marti Hefley
Signal Mountain, Tennessee

MARTYRS OF CHINA

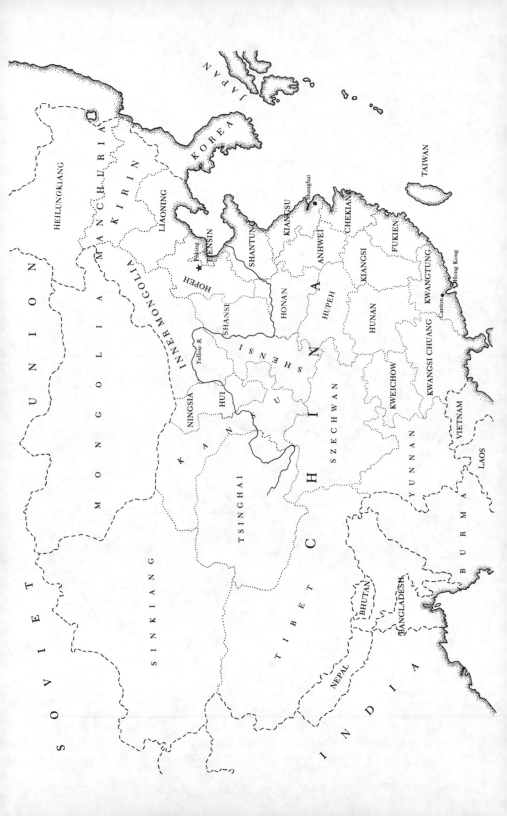

THE FURY OF THE BOXERS:
China, 1900

BY IMPERIAL COMMAND EXTERMINATE THE
CHRISTIAN RELIGION! DEATH TO THE FOREIGN DEVILS!
In June, 1900, crazed mobs bannered this terrible proclamation as they rampaged through cities of north China, looting
and burning churches and the homes of missionaries and
Chinese Christians. They were led by bare-chested fanatics
called Boxers who brandished long-curving swords and cried
for the heads and hearts of Christians and missionaries.

Item: In Manchuria, where all missionaries managed to
escape, a Chinese pastor was caught. When he refused to
deny Christ, his eyebrows, ears and lips were cut off. Still he
would not recant. His heart was then cut out and put on display in a theater. His fourteen-year-old daughter, following
the example of her father, suffered a like fate.

Item: In Shansi Province Mary Huston and Hattie Rice,
two young single women affiliated with the China Inland
Mission, strove to flee an angry mob. Miss Rice was beaten
to death by the roadside. Miss Huston, seriously injured by a
cart run over her to break her spine, died a month later.

Item: At remote Tsun-hua the Chinese Methodist pastor
was forced to a pagan temple, mocked before idols, then left
tied to a pillar. He spent the night preaching while friends

pleaded with him to recant. In the morning a thousand-strong mob descended on him and literally tore out his heart. Two Chinese women teachers who were captured, also refused to renounce Christianity. The feet of one were chopped off and she was then killed with a sword. The other—shouting to her pupils, "Keep the faith!"—was wrapped in cotton, soaked with kerosene and burned alive. One hundred sixty-three Chinese Methodists in Tsun-hua were martyrs for Christ in June, 1900. Only four or five escaped.

As the blood flowed, newspaper headlines abroad screamed:

CHINESE MASSACRE MISSIONARIES

and a shocked world asked why.

Intrigue Leads to Tragedy

The world's most populous nation had appeared to be moving from idolatrous darkness toward the light of Christianity. Converts had been doubling and redoubling in recent years, circulation of Scripture running in the millions. The China Inland Mission (CIM; now Overseas Missionary Fellowship), largest of the evangelical agencies in China, had welcomed over a thousand new workers in the past decade. Other missions were also expanding, but on a lesser scale.

Western churches spoke of China as "our largest and most promising mission field." Yet ironically, Christianity had reached China centuries before Columbus sighted America. In fact, an eighth century Chinese Nestorian church leader claimed the Magi, returning from Bethlehem, had brought the first news of the Savior.

Christianity had waxed and waned until around 1300 when Franciscans arrived and tried to dominate the Chinese church. Their actions provoked intervention by Asian Muslims who had been abiding by a truce. The aroused Muslims killed hundreds of thousands of Christians, piling seventy thousand heads on the ruins of one city. Organized Christianity was swept from Asia.

The Jesuit order came in the sixteenth century and in 1705 convinced the Chinese emperor to make China a Catholic state. A sharp rebuff came from the pope who said the emperor could not be a Christian and continue to worship his ancestors. In 1724 Christianity was banned, and hundreds of Catholic missionaries and converts were put to death.

The first Protestant missionary, Robert Morrison, went out as an employee of the East India Company in 1807. He translated almost the entire Bible into the main Chinese language, but when he died in 1834 there were only three known Chinese Christians in the whole Empire.

Western military and political pressure opened the door for the entrance of foreign missionaries in the latter half of the nineteenth century. Hundreds poured in and took up stations across the vast mysterious land.

Disease, travel accidents and violence took a heavy toll. The average life expectancy dropped to forty. The countryside rumbled with frequent rebellions against the central Manchu government in Peking. Missionaries were often caught between opposing forces, and some gave their lives. For example, an early Southern Baptist worker, J. Landrum Holmes, and an Episcopal missionary were killed while trying to intercede with rebels for the safety of their town.

Added to the rebellions was the continuing encroachment of foreign powers. By 1898 the political situation was so chaotic that young Emperor Kuang-hsu decided Christian moral and social reforms were the only hope for saving China from total foreign domination. He asked Timothy Richard, an influential British Baptist missionary, to come to the palace to help draw up the reforms. But on the very day Richard arrived, the emperor was deposed in a coup by underlings controlled by the secret Boxer Society, who feared the emperor was about to sell out the nation.

The Righteous Ones, as the Boxers were called, bitterly opposed Christianity, which they termed "the religion of the foreign devils." In a desperate effort to preserve the old pagan religions, they had established a network of secret cells across China. Initiates repeated a sacred formula until they fell foaming at the mouth, then joined in a black magic ritual that sometimes included human sacrifices to temple idols. The Boxers claimed they were commanded by "heavenly deities," and were thus invulnerable. A potion smeared on them by their priests was supposed to make them bulletproof.

Following the coup, the Boxers and their supporters installed the emperor's mentally ill aunt, Tzu Hsi, on the throne. They persuaded the empress that missionaries were stealing Chinese spirits and gouging out the eyes of Chinese children for use in their medicines. At their urging, she issued a secret order to officials in the provinces calling for the execution of all foreigners. As the nineteenth century faded, Boxer organizers fanned out across China, recruiting new members, preparing to strike when the empress delivered her edict. They moved cautiously, knowing that the great majority of local officials were opposed to violence and determined to keep law and order.

Sometimes fanatical zeal overtook strategy. In Shantung Province, for example, they captured a young English missionary, Sidney Brooks, returning from vacation on December 30, 1899. After torturing him for hours, they killed him. At his murder the foreign community demanded punishment. Two Boxers were executed for the crime and Governor Yu-hsien, a Boxer supporter, was replaced.

Throughout the spring of 1900 the fanatical Boxers agitated the populace by stirring up historic Chinese racial pride in their nation as the celestial center of the world. They fired hatred against foreign powers for forcing exploitative treaties on the country and sustaining the hated opium trade which kept millions of Chinese addicted. They fueled resentment over jobs lost through foreign building of railroads. In northern China, which had suffered crop failures for three years, the Boxers blamed missionaries and their foreign religion for the long drought. "The foreigners have insulted our gods," they declared. "Foreign blood must be spilled before our gods will send rain." The Boxers also capitalized on enmity which had developed against Catholic missionaries when the French government had actually forced the Chinese government to give Catholic prelates power equal to judges and magistrates.

Still the foreigners did not become alarmed until it was too late for many to flee. After all, many reasoned, China had always seethed with rebellions and banditry, and even so the CIM had lost only one missionary to mob violence, although other martyrdoms had occurred. Danger went with the work, the missionaries assumed, and went on about their business of preaching, teaching and healing.

The Terror Begins

In March the empress appointed the notorious, known Boxer supporter Yu-hsien governor of Shansi, the northern province where much missionary work was concentrated. In June the German and Japanese ambassadors were murdered in Peking.

The alarmed foreign community grouped in the British embassy compound and began building fortifications as Boxers paraded through the Imperial capital.

The royal edict to kill all foreigners and exterminate Christianity was given to couriers for delivery to provincial governors. Messengers to the south, however, changed one Chinese character on the decree, so that it read "protect" instead of "kill" foreigners. For this disobedience they were cut in half. But the missionaries and Christians in this area were saved, and the bloodletting was confined to the northern provinces.

One hundred eighty-eight foreign missionaries and missionary children were murdered during the Boxer wrath in the summer of 1900, all in four provinces. Most of these casualties were suffered in Shansi Province under the diabolical governor Yu-hsein. Of the 159 foreigners who died in Shansi Province, 91 were associated with the China Inland Mission.

Rugged Shansi Province is the cradle of ancient Chinese civilization. The famous Emperor Yao lived and ruled from here over the "black-haired race" eight hundred years before Abraham was born. Shansi is an inhospitable land, bitterly cold in winter and fiercely hot in summer. Topographically, it is mostly high undulating tablelands, punctuated by steep hills and sandwiched between the Yellow River on the west and a rugged mountain range on the east. Shansi was not an easy place from which foreigners could escape.

The Governor's Treachery

The bloodiest massacre took place in the ancient Shansi provincial capital Taiyuan where the gates of the walled city were closed to prevent the foreigners from escaping. Trapped in their residences were twenty-four adults and nine children, associated with the Baptist Missionary Society of England, the CIM, and the small Sheo Yang Mission which operated the Schofield Memorial Hospital in a satellite town.

The doctor for whom the hospital was named had died of typhus fever in 1883, contracted from a patient admitted by the gatekeeper without the doctor's knowledge. Shortly before his death, he had begged for reinforcements. Two medics had answered his call, Dr. William M. Wilson and Dr. E.H. Edwards. Dr. Edwards took charge of the Schofield Hospital. Dr. Wilson, who was with the CIM, operated a hospital for opium addicts in an outlying city at his own expense. To these doctors thousands of persons owed their lives.

Dr. Edwards was safely away when the crisis came. Dr. Wilson and his wife and young son were due for furlough, but had stayed on to help during the famine. Early in the summer Mrs. Wilson and son went ahead to Taiyuan for rest from the baking heat. The doctor remained to care for his patients until he fell prey to peritonitis. One of his last acts of mercy was to travel twenty dangerous miles to save the life of Pastor Si who lay severely wounded from a Boxer sword slash in his side. Before the doctor left for treatment in Taiyuan, Chinese Christians presented him with a large red satin sash, bearing the gilt inscription "God's Faithful Servant." His last letter was written on the road to Taiyuan. "It's all fog," he wrote a colleague, "but I think, old chap, that we are on the edge of a volcano, and I fear Taiyuan is the inner edge."

Besides Mrs. Wilson, two CIM single women missionaries were in Taiyuan. Jane Stevens, a nurse, was in frail health. During her last trip back to England for rest, a friend had suggested that a position in the homeland might be easier. Nurse Stevens had replied, "I don't feel I have yet finished the work God has for me in China. I must go back. Perhaps—who knows?—I may be among those allowed to give their lives for the people."

Miss Stevens had come to China in 1885. Her Taiyuan partner, Mildred Clarke, came in 1893. Upon reaching Taiyuan, Miss Clarke wrote home, "I long to live a poured-out life unto Him among these Chinese, and to enter into the fellowship of His sufferings for souls, who poured out His life unto death for us."

Of the other missionaries at Taiyuan nine were former CIM members: six had joined the small Sheo Yang Mission which operated the Schofield Memorial Hospital; W.T. and Emily Beynon were now representatives of the British and Foreign Bible Society; Alexander Hoddle was independent, operating a small Christian bookstore and teaching English to Chinese students for his support.

At the Sheo Yang Mission were T.W. and Jessie Pigott and their young son Wellesley. A friend had written of Mr. Pigott, "If ever a man lived in earnest, it was Thomas Wellesley Pigott." A man of many talents, he could fix anything. Emily Pigott, though not a doctor, was skilled at removing eye cataracts. Old China hands, the Pigotts had lost friends in an earlier massacre—four Church Missionary Society workers killed by the radical vegetarian sect in Fukien Province in 1895. Since then the Piggots had felt their time would be short in China and had worked almost nonstop. Another prophetic note had been sounded by W.T. Beynon in the ending of his 1899 report to the Bible Society: "We trust that this coming year the God of all grace will give all of us grace to be faithful."

Violence exploded in late June, 1900. Mobs roamed the streets, setting fire to the compounds of the British Baptists and the Sheo Yang group. The missionaries and a group of Chinese believers linked hands and sought refuge in the Baptist boys' school about a half mile away. After reaching the school, Edith Coombs of the Sheo Yang Mission suddenly realized she had left two Chinese schoolgirls behind, one of whom was very sick. Miss Coombs broke away and ran back to the blazing buildings to rescue them. As they were rushing out, the sick girl stumbled and fell. Miss Coombs bent to lift her and shield her from the brickbats being hurled by the mob. The mob moved in closer, forced them to separate, and drove the missionary back into the house. The mob and the Chinese girls she had tried to rescue last saw her kneeling in the flames.

The remaining thirty-two missionaries and children, along with their loyal Chinese friends, barricaded themselves in the boys' school. Day and night stones pelted the walls and doors while the group inside waited and prayed behind barricades, hoping for rescue by the provincial governor, Yu-hsien, whose palace was a short distance away.

On July 9 soldiers arrived and escorted the missionaries to the courtyard of the governor's palace where they joined twelve Catholic clergy. The missionaries, thinking they would now be saved, saw they were doomed when Yu-hsien stormed out waving his sword and shouting, "Kill! Kill!"

The governor announced that the men would die first. George Farthing, one of the English Baptists and the father of three children, stepped forward. His wife clung to him, but he gently put her aside and knelt before the chopping block without a murmur. His head fell with one stroke of the executioner's sword.

The other men were killed one by one, then the women and children. The Farthing children hung on to their mother and had to be pulled away when she was ordered to kneel. Mrs. Lovitt was permitted to hold the hand of her little boy. "We all came to China to bring you the good news of salvation by Jesus Christ," she said in a firm voice. "We have done you no harm, only good. Why do you treat us so?" In a strange act of gentleness, a soldier stepped up and removed her spectacles before she and her son were beheaded.

The priests and nuns died with equal courage. Their bishop, an old man with a white beard, asked the governor, "Why are you doing this wicked deed?" Yu-hsien answered by drawing his sword and slashing the bishop across the face.

Finally the Chinese Christians were brought forth to complete the carnage. Few escaped to report the tale of horror.

The bodies were left for the night where they had fallen and were stripped of clothing, rings and watches under cover of darkness. The next day the heads were placed in cages for a grotesque display on the city wall. Yu-hsien was without remorse and later crowed to the empress, "Your Majesty's slave caught them as in a net and allowed neither chicken nor dog to escape." The old woman replied, "You have done splendidly."

No Hiding Place

Eight British Baptist missionaries at Hsinchow, forty-five miles north of Taiyuan, heard the tragic news and decided to flee to the hills. They took refuge in caves where they were lovingly cared for by local Christians. Boxers roamed the area, seeking their hiding place. A Chinese evangelist was beaten to death for refusing to cooperate with the Boxers.

After their food supply was cut off, the missionaries received a message from the magistrate at Hsinchow offering them protection if they would return to the city. Upon arrival they were jailed about two weeks, then promised a protective armed escort to the coast. Rev. Herbert Dixon, one of the eight, told a Chinese preacher, "We are ready to glorify our Lord, by life or by death. If we die, there will certainly be others to take our place."

The Hsinchow eight set out in carts on August 8. As they were passing between the inner and outer gates of the

city, their "escort" suddenly closed around them and other
armed men sprang from hiding and brutally beat them all to
death.

Massacre at Soping

At Soping ten missionaries of the small Swedish Holiness
Union were holding their annual church conference in cooperation with Mr. and Mrs. Oscar Forsberg of the International Missionary Alliance Mission. Soping was already
seething with unrest. Boxer agitators were saying that the
missionaries had swept away approaching rain clouds with a
yellow paper broom and that the foreigners were praying to
their God that it might not rain.

According to Chinese evangelist Wang Lan-pu, who
managed to escape, a mob converged on the house where the
missionaries and Chinese Christians had barricaded themselves and began battering the door. Just as the mob burst
into the house, the missionaries and their friends slipped out
the back and ran to the city hall where they asked the magistrate for refuge. The Boxer leaders learned where they had
gone and led the mob there. The magistrate refused to surrender his charges, but to pacify the howling crowd he said
he had been ordered to send the foreigners to Peking where
they would be executed. As the mob looked on, he had his
blacksmith make manacles for five of the men. Apparently
satisfied, the crowd dispersed.

Later than night the mob came back with soldiers sympathetic to the Boxers. Sparing no one, they stoned to death
all the missionaries and their children along with Chinese
Christians who had sought refuge. They hung the heads of
the missionaries on the city wall as a ghastly testimonial to
the populace. Among the Chinese who died were the mother
and little daughter of the evangelist who escaped.

The June 29 massacre almost wiped out the tiny Swedish mission. Only two members in another province and one
home on furlough were left. The senior Swedish martyr was
Nathanael Carleson. Chinese believers had often used the
scriptural allusion to introduce him: "Nathanael, an Israelite
indeed, in whom is no guile." The youngest martyr was
Ernst Petersson. He had been in China only five months.
Four of the other eight were single women, all about thirty
years of age. Aware of the danger of serving in bandit-rid-

den north China, Mina Hedlund, one of the four, had written in her last letter, "I don't fear if God wants me to suffer the death of a martyr."

Ambushed in the Desert

The International Missionary Alliance (now known as the Christian and Missionary Alliance–C&MA) had been founded by A.B. Simpson, a far-seeing Presbyterian minister with a vision for world evangelization. At the time of the Boxer uprising, this mission had about forty Swedish missionaries on the China field. At least nineteen adults and fifteen children met violent death.

The Olaf Bingmarks and their two young sons sensed trouble when children stopped coming to their school. Friends told them stories were spreading that Mr. Bingmark was extracting the eyes of Chinese boys for use as medicine. Duly warned, they kept inside their house. A peddler named Chao, whom they had kindly received many times, betrayed them for a price. Boxers dragged them outside and attacked them with swords and stones while an artist stood by sketching the violence. The picture, as later revealed, showed the two little boys kneeling and imploring mercy.

The Chinese evangelist who worked with them was bound for ten days without food and drink. Near death, his sufferings were mercifully ended by the sword.

Miss Gustafson, a beloved missionary teacher, lived alone at another station. When warned that Boxers were coming, she fled with another Chinese evangelist. A few miles down the road she was overtaken and stoned to death. Her body was thrown into a river and never seen again.

In far northwest China seven Alliance (C&MA) missionaries and seven children tried to flee on camels into Mongolia. Robbers intercepted them and took everything, even their clothes. In the trauma two of the missionaries gave birth. French missionary priests found the fourteen and the two infants naked in the desert and subsisting on roots. The priests gave them covering and took them back to the Catholic mission station.

News came that a Boxer army was approaching. "Our way . . . is cut off," the Alliance's Carl Lundberg wrote. "If we are not able to escape, tell our friends we live and die for the Lord. I do not regret coming to China. The Lord has called me and His grace is sufficient. The way He chooses is best for me. His will be done. Excuse my writing, my hand is shivering."

Six days later he added, "The soldiers have arrived and will attack our place. The Catholics are prepared to defend themselves but it is in vain. We do not like to die with weapons in our hands. If it be the Lord's will let them take our lives."

When the Boxers attacked, the priests and two of the Alliance men, Emil Olson and Albert Anderson, tried to escape. They were captured, ordered to undress, then made to kneel for beheading. The others fared no better. The Boxers killed them with guns and swords, then set fire to the church.

Another seven Alliance missionaries with three children and four workers from other missions huddled in a chapel at Patzupupulong. Warned by the local magistrate that Boxers were on their way to kill them, the group set out for the coast. They ran into an ambush planned by the magistrate and all were killed except one of the wives. Left for dead, she was rescued and taken into the tent of a Mongol widow. However, the treacherous magistrate's wife learned where she was and sent soldiers to the tent. They murdered her in bed.

The Fatal Appointment

Most local Chinese officials were protective of missionaries. The magistrate at Fenchow in north Shansi was notably kind. Because of his friendliness, Mr. and Mrs. C.W. Price and other workers of the American Board of Commissioners of Foreign Missions invited three CIM colleagues, Mr. and Mrs. A.P. Lundren and Miss Annie Eldred, to come to stay with them during July when mob violence was at its peak. However, shortly after they arrived, the vindictive provincial governor appointed another magistrate to Fenchow. The new magistrate ordered the missionaries out of the city and assigned them an armed guard under the pretense of protection.

Apparently the missionaries expected the worst. Lizzie Atwater wrote her family on August 3:

Dear ones, I long for a sight of your dear faces, but I
fear we shall not meet on earth. . . . I am preparing
for the end very quietly and calmly. The Lord is
wonderfully near, and He will not fail me. I was very
restless and excited while there seemed a chance of

life, but God has taken away that feeling, and now I just pray for grace to meet the terrible end bravely. The pain will soon be over, and oh the sweetness of the welcome above!

My little baby will go with me. I think God will give it to me in Heaven, and my dear mother will be so glad to see us. I cannot imagine the Savior's welcome. Oh, that will compensate for all these days of suspense. Dear ones, live near to God and cling less closely to earth. There is no other way by which we can receive that peace from God which passeth understanding. . . . I must keep calm and still these hours. I do not regret coming to China, but am sorry I have done so little. My married life, two precious years, has been so very full of happiness. We will die together, my dear husband and I.

I used to dread separation. If we escape now it will be a miracle. I send my love to you all, and the dear friends who remember me.

Twelve days later, when they were out of the area, the guards assigned by the new magistrate murdered the seven missionaries.

Detour to Death

Other trusting missionaries were betrayed by Boxer-inspired Chinese claiming to be their protectors. Such was the case of six CIM workers, two married couples and two single women, returning to their Shansi stations from vacations.

George McConnell, an Irish evangelist, and his Scottish wife Belle had buried their daughter in Scotland only two years before. They had just opened three new chapels and received fifty-one new inquirers. But the preacher sensed danger in the air. He quoted from Psalm 31 in a letter, " 'My times are in Thy hand.' "

John and Sarah Young had been married only fifteen months. He was Scottish, she an Indiana Hoosier. Both had made exceptional progress in the difficult Chinese language, but they lived one uncertain day at a time. In her application to CIM, Sarah had written, "I want to be found in the battle when He comes, and I want to be an instrument in the hands of God in saving souls from death." Eleven days before her martyrdom she wrote, "The winds may blow, and the waves may roll high; if we keep our eyes off them and on the Lord, we shall be all right. . . ."

Annie King and Elizabeth Burton, Britishers, were still single and strikingly attractive. They had been in China less than two years. Previous to her departure for China, Annie had been a home missionary, helping in the "Ragged Schools" for friendless child waifs in England. "Praise the Lord, I am really in China," she wrote home. "I don't know what the future holds for me, but, whatever comes, I know I have obeyed the will of our God." And later, "Often I wish I could have come before. . . . It is so nice to be in this village, where the people trust us, and love to hear of Jesus, for whose sake and the Gospel's we have come. There are numbers of villages where the name of Jesus is unknown, all in heathen darkness, without a ray of light."

Elizabeth, also a teacher, had written, "Oh, I feel so inadequate, so weak, and yet I hear Him say, 'Go in this thy might, have not I sent thee?' Yes, He has sent me; if ever I felt God has called me in my life, I feel it tonight." Then shortly before taking the fateful vacation: "Jesus is very real to me out in this land, and I would not change my present lot in spite of loneliness and occasional hardships."

Along the road to Yu-men-k'ou the group was met by soldiers who advised them to detour off the main road for safety. "We will accompany you," they said. Nearing the Yellow River, their escorts suddenly dismounted and unsheathed their swords. "You thought we came to protect you," the captain said. "Our orders are to kill you unless you promise to stop preaching your foreign religion." When the missionaries refused to so pledge, Mr. McConnell was pulled from his mule and decapitated with a quick swing of a sword. As Mrs. McConnell and their young son Kenneth hit the ground, the boy was heard to say, "Papa does not allow you to kill little Kennie." Swords flashed and two more heads rolled on the ground. The young women embraced each other as did the Youngs. Arms swung and death came quickly. The last to die was a faithful Chinese Christian servant, Kehtienhuen, who refused to deny his faith.

A Chinese Christian friend was able to escape. He smuggled a letter out describing the killings. "Men's hearts are shaking with fear," he reported. "We cannot rest day or night."

No Mercy Shown

At Ta-t'ung on June 24 CIM missionaries, two couples and their four children and two single women, took refuge with a friendly magistrate. The official defied the Boxer mob that circled the house clamoring for the blood of the foreigners. Then orders came on the twenty-seventh from a superior, ordering them to their home. The magistrate sent them under cover of darkness with an armed guard that remained at their door. A few days later Mrs. Stewart McKee gave birth. Now there were five children sheltered in the small house, while the mob outside grew noisier.

By July 12 only two guards remained. At seven o'clock that evening an official knocked and demanded the names of those inside. They were given.

An hour later three hundred soldiers arrived on horseback in support of the Boxers. Stewart McKee went out and tried to reason with them. Instead of listening, they hacked him to pieces, then set fire to the house. In the flames and confusion, only little Alice McKee managed to escape. In the morning the mob discovered her in a cowshed and slashed the defenseless child to death.

Buried in a Baptistry

The CIM's Emily Whitchurch and Edith Searell were one of many teams of young single women serving in isolated towns. Their only protection was the goodwill of the people.

They worked in Hsiao-i, a town in south central Shansi Province, with slaves of the terrible opium trade from which western nations were profiting. "Mornings and evenings," a visiting colleague wrote of Miss Whitchurch, "she would gather the opium patients around and teach them Scripture. . . . The Scriptures were as the voice of God to Miss Whitchurch; they shaped her life, and she had confidence in their power to purify and to convert."

Miss Searell was one of the first New Zealanders to come to China. In May she had been seriously ill with pleurisy, but refused to leave her British partner and Chinese friends. On June 28 she wrote a close friend, "From the human standpoint [all missionaries in Shansi Province] are equally unsafe. From the point of view of those whose lives are hid with Christ in God all are equally safe! His children shall have a place of refuge, and that place is the secret place of the Most High."

Two days later a Boxer mob attacked their house and showed them no mercy. After the mob left, loving Chinese Christians risked their lives in order to place the martyrs' bodies in a baptistry bordered with flowers which Miss Searell had planted a few weeks before.

No Earthly Sanctuary

No missionary was safe in Shansi Province. Scores were hidden by Chinese Christians at grave peril to their own lives.

"We will stand by you til death," Chinese friends vowed to the CIM's Duncan Kay, a colorful Scottish evangelist. "And we will stay until driven out," declared Kay.

When mobs threatened, Chinese believers spirited Kay, his wife and daughter Jenny, and three single women missionaries into the mountains and hid them in caves. With their help, Mrs. Kay was able to get a letter out to her three children at the CIM school in Chefoo, which was in a safe area in another province near the coast. She described their plight:

[We are] being molested every day by bands of bad men who want money from us. Now our money is all gone. We feel there is nothing for us but to try and get back to the city; this is no easy matter. The roads are full of these bad people who seek our lives. I am writing this as it may be my last to you. Who knows but we may be with Jesus very soon. This is only a wee note to send our dear love to you all, and to ask you not to feel too sad when you know we have been killed. We have committed you all into God's hands. He will make a way for you all. Try and be good children. Love God. Give your hearts to Jesus. This is your dear parents' last request.

Your loving papa, mama, and wee Jenny.

Shortly after the letter was sent, the three Kays were killed. The three young women, hiding in another cave, survived.

Another group of CIM missionaries were hidden in caves for three weeks before being captured by Boxers. "We are in God's hands," Willie Peat, who was accompanied by his wife Helen and two daughters and two single women, wrote. "I can say, 'I will fear no evil, for Thou art with me.' " One of the single women, nurse Edith Dobson, said in her last letter, "We know naught can come to us without His permission. So we have no need to be troubled: it is not in my nature to fear physical harm, but I trust, if it come, His grace will be all-sufficient."

They received a reprieve when a magistrate intervened and ordered a guard to deliver them to the town of K'u-wu. At K'u-wu a mob threatened, and they fled into nearby mountains. From their hideout in an earthen cave, Willie Peat wrote a last letter to his mother and uncle:

> The soldiers are just on us, and I have only time to
> say "Good-bye" to you all. We shall soon be with
> Christ, which is very far better for us. We can only
> now be sorry for you who are left behind and our
> dear native Christians.
>
> Goodbye! At longest it is only "til He come."
> We rejoice that we are made partakers of the suffer-
> ings of Christ, that when His glory shall be revealed
> we may "rejoice also with exceeding joy."

Helen Peat added, "Our Father is with us and we go to Him, and trust to see you all before His face, to be forever together with Him."

They were put to death on August 30.

Australian David Barratt, a veteran of only three years, was traveling when he heard of the Taiyuan massacre. "The news nearly made me faint," he wrote a colleague.

> The Empire is evidently upside down. No "Mene,
> mene, tekel, upharsin" is written on the old Middle
> Kingdom. Our blood may be as a true center (for the
> foundation) and God's kingdom will increase over
> this land. Extermination is but exaltation. God guide
> and bless us! "Fear not them which kill," He says,
> "are ye not of much more value than many spar-
> rows." "Peace, perfect peace," to you, brother, and all
> at Lucheng. We may meet in the glory in a few hours
> or days. . . . Not a sleep, no dinner, a quiet time with
> God, then sunset and evening bells, then the
> dark. . . . Let us be true till death.

In such trusting faith the young Aussie was killed while seeking refuge on a desolate mountain.

Barratt's partner, Alfred Woodroofe, was at their station in Yo-yang when the persecution hit. The year before he had barely escaped a mob. Then he had written, "Are we called to die? The poor, feeble heart says, 'Oh, no; never.' But, to bring blessing into the world, what has it always meant?

What to the Savior? What to the Apostles? 'This is the way the Master went; should not the servant tread it still?' "

This time Woodroofe and three Chinese Christians were forced to flee into the mountains. For a week or more they slept in caves at night, retreating into remote canyons during the day. Woodroofe sent a message back to other believers in Yo-yang, stating his wish to return "so we can die together." The reply told him to remain hidden. He wrote again, describing how his feet were cut and bleeding from wandering among the rocks, but ended by quoting James 5:11: "We count them happy that endure." This was his last message. He died at age twenty-eight.

Details of how he and about a dozen other CIM workers died were not known for many months. The few who managed to slip letters out expressed similar courage and faith and wished only that the Chinese church would be strengthened through their martyrdom. Wrote Edith Nathan, who served with her sister May and with Mary Heaysman at Ta-ning: "I hope I shan't be ordered off anywhere; if my Christians are in trouble, I trust I may be allowed to stay and help. One does long for the native Church to be on the right foundation—Christ Jesus." Mary Heaysman headed her last letter, "There shall be showers of blessing." The three young women and ten Chinese believers were captured after a long and harrowing flight and put to death in a pagan temple.

Journeys of Death

In the most terrible of the flights, two parties of missionaries fled from Shansi Province to the city of Hankow in Hupeh Province a thousand miles south.

One group of fourteen included two families with six young children and four single women fleeing from the town of Lucheng. Mobs followed them from one village boundary to the next, hurling sticks and stones, shouting, "Death to the foreign devils!" Robbers stripped them of everything but a few rags. Emaciated from hunger and thirst, shoeless, barebacked in the scorching heat, desperately trying to hold up filthy, torn Chinese trousers, they staggered from village to village half alive.

The young children displayed remarkable insight and faith. "If they loved Jesus they would not do this," seven-year-old Jessie Saunders reminded her parents. Once when they took shelter in a barn, the now fever-stricken child looked up at her mother who was fanning her and said, "Jesus was born in a place like this."

A few days later Jessie's baby sister, Isabel, died from beatings and exposure to the hot sun. As Jessie grew weaker, she cried for a place of rest. Her wish was granted a week after Isabel's death. The two children were buried beside the road.

In one village attackers dragged one of the men, E.J. Cooper, into the open country and left him for dead. He somehow revived and crawled back to his family and friends. Margaret (Mrs. E.J.) Cooper began lapsing into unconsciousness. Once she whispered to her husband, an architect whom she had married after joining the CIM, "If the Lord spares us, I should like to go back to Lucheng if possible." But her beatings were too severe, and she slipped into merciful death.

On July 12 Hattie Rice collapsed in the heat. A mob began stoning her and a man ran a cart over her naked body to break her spine. Her companion, Mary Huston, shielded her body until shamefaced men came with clothing. When she was again clothed, they took her from Miss Huston to a temple and consulted their gods about her faith. When a priest announced that the gods would let her live, the men carried her back to the other missionaries on a stretcher. She died a short time later.

The survivors somehow kept moving. They crossed and recrossed the Yellow River. They were imprisoned and released. Miss Huston suffered the worst. Part of her brain was exposed from beatings received at the time Miss Rice had been fatally wounded. Her friends could do no more for her than protect her from the sun. She died on August 11. Both young women were from the United States, Miss Rice from Massachusetts and Miss Huston from Pennsylvania. Assigned to a refuge for opium addicts, they had taken nothing from China and given everything.

Shortly before Miss Huston's death, the Lucheng group had met and joined a second group. Led by the CIM's Archibald Glover, they told a harrowing story of beatings, imprisonments and miraculous deliverance. Mrs. Glover was in her last month of pregnancy. The last leg of their journey was made together by boat, allowing them to take the bodies of Mrs. Cooper and Miss Huston to Hankow for burial.

Three days after their arrival, Mr. Cooper laid his tiny
son Brainerd beside his wife. He then wrote his own mother:
The Lord has honored us by giving us fellowship in
His sufferings. Three times stoned, robbed of everything, even clothes, we know what hunger, thirst,
nakedness, weariness are as never before, but also the
sustaining grace and strength of God and His peace
in a new and deeper sense than before. . . .

Billow after billow has gone over me. Home
gone, not one memento of dear Maggie even, penni-
less, wife and child gone to glory, Edith [his other
child] lying very sick with diarrhea and your son
weak and exhausted to a degree, though otherwise
well. . . .

And now that you know the worst, Mother, I
want to tell you that the cross of Christ, that
exceeding glory of the Father's love, has brought continual comfort to my heart, so that not one murmur
has broken the peace of God within.

The Peril at Paoting

Outside of Shansi Province the worst Boxer massacre of missionaries occurred at Paoting, then capital of the adjoining
province Chihli (now Hopeh Province), where American
(Northern) Presbyterians, the CIM, and the American Board
of Commissioners for Foreign Missions had stations.

On June 1 CIM workers H.V. Robinson and C. Norman
were seized and killed by Boxers outside the old walled city.
The gates were heavily guarded, sealing off any possible
escape by the eight remaining missionaries, four children,
and the Chinese believers inside Paoting.

A story was circulated that the missionaries had poisoned the dwindling water supply in the wells. Another
rumor charged that the Presbyterian's Dr. G.B. Taylor was
extracting the eyes of children for medicine. Still another lie
said the missionaries had helped build the hated railway that
had taken jobs from cargo haulers.

The last letter out stated, "Our position is dangerous —
very. We are having awfully hot, dry dusty days and *yao yen*
[rumors] are increasing. . . . Oh that God would send rain.
That would make things quiet for a time. . . . We can't go
out and fight — we must sit still, do our work, and if God
calls us to Him, that's all. Unless definite orders come from

Peking that we are to be protected at any cost or a guard of foreign soldiers sent at once, the blood must flow. We are trying to encourage the [Chinese] brethren, but it is difficult work. A crisis must come soon—the Lord's will be done."

In this situation two friends managed to enter the city. One was Pastor Meng, the first Chinese to be ordained by the American Board's North China Mission. The missionaries begged him to leave. As a Chinese he could melt into the constant flow of human traffic and go to a safer town. "No," he vowed, "I will keep the church open as long as God allows. And after I am with the Lord, my son will keep it open."

The second arrival, Rev. William Cooper, deputy director of the CIM, had been visiting mission stations in adjoining Shansi Province and was returning to the metropolis of Tientsin on the coast. Like a Paul Revere, he had been warning missionaries at stations along the way, enabling some to escape just in time. Now he was caught.

Cooper was an old China hand, having been on the field nineteen years. A long bout with typhoid had impaired his hearing, but his spiritual senses remained strong. "One of the very few blameless lives I have ever come into contact with," declared a missionary friend. "He lived in an atmosphere of prayer," said another. "He literally drew breath in the fear of the Lord." In Paoting he joined CIM colleagues Benjamin and Emily Bagnall and their five-year-old daughter Gladys.

At the American Board station were H.T. Pitkin, Miss A.A. Gould, and Miss M.S. Morrill. Pitkin was one of the great missionary spirits of China. A classmate of Henry Luce (who later founded *Time* magazine) and Sherwood Eddy, Pitkin had served as secretary of the vigorous Student Missionary Movement before manning the American Board's mission station at Paoting.

On Saturday, June 30, the American Presbyterian Mission in the northern part of the city was attacked. Dr. Taylor went outside to plead that the missionaries had come to China only to do good. He was killed almost immediately and his head displayed in a pagan temple. After disposing of Dr. Taylor, the Boxer-led soldiers set the Presbyterian mission house on fire. One of the men, Frank Simcox, was seen walking to and fro on the veranda, holding the hands of his two sons as the flames enveloped them.

News of the martyrdom of the Presbyterians traveled rapidly to the other mission houses on the south side. The three members of the American Board, Pastor Meng, and other Chinese Christians kept a vigil through the night, writing last letters to loved ones, letters which would later be dug up by Boxers and destroyed. When morning dawned the Chinese, at the urging of the missionaries, slipped out the back door. About nine o'clock the Boxers arrived.

Miss Morrill went out to plead with the soldiers. "Kill me and let the others go," she begged. "I am ready to die for them." Her entreaty, according to the later report of one of the soldiers, touched off an argument in the crowd. Some of the older Boxers and the soldiers wanted to spare the four. The others wanted to proceed with the killing. During the controversy the missionaries were allowed to remain in their house.

The hard-liners won the dispute. Pitkin was killed defending the women. Miss Gould died of shock before the attackers could reach her. Miss Morrill was captured alive and taken to a pagan temple where William Cooper and the Bagnall family had already been taken.

Throughout Sunday they were taunted and abused as objects of sport and mockery. That evening they were taken out for execution. Mrs. Bagnall begged in vain for the life of her daughter while the cherubic-faced child with long golden curls stood by in frightened perplexity. The plea was refused, and at the captain's command they were all beheaded.

Murders in Mongolia

The dark hand of Boxer hate reached even into bleak Mongolia. Once the fountainhead of the great Mongol Empire, the high, thinly populated desert nation was in 1900 a vassal state of China. Christian work was so difficult that mission boards hesitated to send their missionaries there, and it came to be called "the neglected field."

In 1895 the Scandinavian Alliance Mission of Chicago (now The Evangelical Alliance Mission—TEAM) sent its first worker, a red-bearded Swede. Taking a cue from pioneer James Gilmour, "the apostle to Mongolia," David Stenberg clad himself in woolen Mongolian skirts, rode a camel, traveled with the nomadic shepherd people, ate their food and learned their language. Within three years he received support from five other hardy Scandinavian missionaries—N.J.

Friedstrom, Carl Suber, Hanna Lund, and Hilda and Clara Anderson. Upon finding Stenberg, they mistook him for a Mongolian.

In the spring of 1900 they heard the rumors of danger to foreigners in China. Such rumors were common and they were from far off. They gave them little consideration.

In September they embarked on a long journey. A half-day out they met a Mongol who advised them to turn back. Stenberg and the women went on under the protection of a Mongol chief. Friedstrom and Suber waited awhile, then fearing danger decided Friedstrom should search for their friends while Suber remained with the caravan. When Friedstrom did not return, Suber became alarmed and sent a friendly Mongol to investigate. He came back in two weeks with horrifying news. The chief had betrayed them. Following orders from Peking, he had sent them to a lonely spot in the desert where soldiers killed them, then preserved their heads in salt for shipment to Peking where an award was expected. Weeks later, another Mongol led Suber to the spot where the only visible remains were a blonde curl and a shoe among ashes.

The Merciless Vegetarians

The extent of the Boxer persecutions in north China and Mongolia obscured bloodshed elsewhere by other rebellious groups. The worst violence occurred at Ku-chau in south central Chekiang Province where the Kiang-san, a secret vegetarian society similar to the Boxers, had launched an anti-foreign, anti-Christian vendetta. It was in this province that CIM founder Hudson Taylor had commenced work in 1857.

Three hundred federal soldiers had been sent to calm the agitated populace and to protect CIM missionaries D. Baird and Agnes Thompson and their two young sons, Edith Sherwood, Etta Manchester, and Josephine Desmond. The protectors were a joke. They had come without arms.

"We hear all kinds of evil reports which make us fear," Thompson wrote, "but by His grace we are able to rise above all, and take hold of our God and Savior. . . . We will just 'stand still and see the salvation of God.' . . . His will be done."

The five workers were among the best the CIM had in China. The Thompsons had not taken a furlough in fifteen years. In the Ku-chau area they had established a bustling church with a strong evangelistic outreach. Almost every night, Scotsman Thompson and national evangelists held services. Mrs. Thompson was instructing eighty Chinese women twice weekly.

Nurse Josephine Desmond, an Irish American from Massachusetts, had trained at Moody's Bible Training School in Chicago under R.A. Torrey. Miss Desmond had been caring for her co-worker Etta Manchester, a New Yorker who had been in China only three years. Friends had implored her to return home. She replied: "I am willing to come home if that is what God wants. If He wants me to remain here, I will stay. I am prepared to do the will of God, whatever the cost."

At forty-six Edith Sherwood was the eldest of the single women. She had been influenced by the Thompsons to leave missionary work in Europe and come to China. A friend had called her "a center of hope and love to old and young."

Reports from Chinese Christians described the missionaries' martyrdom. A mob attacked the mission house on July 21, wounding Thompson. Edith Sherwood and Etta Manchester ran to seek help from the magistrate and arrived as he was being led to execution. Chinese friends pulled them aside just in time and directed them to a secret hiding place.

The mob succeeded in breaking down the missionaries' door that afternoon. Helpless to resist, the Thompsons, their two children, and Miss Desmond were put to death immediately. Three days later Miss Sherwood and Miss Manchester were discovered and killed.

Around the same time three other CIM missionaries were about twenty miles away, trying to reach a hoped-for haven in Ku-chau. Britisher George Ward and his wife Etta, an Iowan, had met and married on the field. The number of Chinese believers at their station in Ch'ang-shan had doubled in three years. Their companion, Emma Thirgood, was still weak from a long illness that had kept her in England for three years. She had amazed everyone by returning to China the year before.

Upon learning that the Kiang-san were in close pursuit, they decided to split into parties. Mrs. Ward and Miss Thirgood boarded a boat with the hope that they would be safer as unprotected women. They were killed at a river jetty. Mr. Ward was caught and murdered about five miles from Ku-chau.

The Fellowship of Blood

More evangelical Protestant missionaries were killed in the Boxer bloodbath than Catholic representatives from abroad. The Catholics were often able to barricade themselves in fortress-like cathedrals. Chinese casualties, however, were just the reverse. Thirty thousand Catholics perished, while only two thousand Protestants gave their lives. Many thousands more lost all their property to burning, looting mobs who systematically sought out residences of persons listed on church registers.

Stories of bravery abound.

At P'ing-tu, Shantung Province, some twenty native Christians were seized and offered escape if they would deny their God and worship the idols. When they refused, their queues were tied to the tails of horses, and they were dragged twenty-five miles to Lai-chou where most were killed.

At Ta-t'ung, in Shansi Province, where six missionaries and five children died, eighteen Chinese believers offered themselves for baptism while the Boxer storm was mounting. Five died with the missionaries a few days afterward.

At another town in Shansi, one man who at first had denied Christ later repented and told the Boxer magistrate, "I cannot but believe in Christ: even if you put me to death, I will still believe and follow Him." For this he was beaten to death, his body cut open, and his heart extracted and exhibited in the magistrate's office.

At the town of Honchau, also in bloody Shansi, "Faithful" Yen and his wife were tied to a pillar in the pagan temple. After beating them with rods, the Boxers lit a fire behind them and burned their legs raw. Although they still would not deny Christ, Mrs. Yen was set free. But Mr. Yen was thrown to the ground and firewood stacked around him. The fire was lit. After a few minutes of roasting in agony, he tried to roll out of the fire. A Boxer began to heap his body with hot ashes and coals. A soldier standing by could stand it no longer and cursed the Boxer. The Boxers leaped on the soldier and cut him to pieces. At that, the other soldiers rushed on the Boxers and chased them out of the temple. They then took the pitifully burned Chinese Christian from the fire and carried him still alive to the magistrate's house, only to see the official throw the man in a dark prison cell where it is presumed he died.

At Taiyuan, after the foreigners were beheaded, many of the Chinese Christians were forced to kneel down and drink their blood. Some also had crosses burned into their foreheads.

Here, a mother and her two children were kneeling before the executioner when a watcher suddenly ran and pulled the children back into the anonymity of the observing crowd. Taken by surprise, the Boxers were unable to find either the man or the children. They then turned back to the mother and asked if she had any last word. Dazed, she begged to see the face of the kind man who had taken her children. The man came forward in tears at risk of his life. Satisfied that the children would be cared for, the mother went to her death because she would not deny her Lord.

In the Hsinchow district, where eight English Baptist missionaries were killed, a Christian family—Chao Hsi Mao, his wife, sister, and mother—were driven to their place of execution in a large open cart. As they were pushed along they sang the hymn, "He Leadeth Me." When everything was ready, each in turn was asked to recant. One by one they bravely refused and were beheaded.

At Fang-ssu, another British Baptist station, the small church building was burned by the Boxers and the young minister Chou Yung-yao beaten nearly to death for refusing to divulge the names and whereabouts of his flock. As the mob began dragging him toward the flames, he shouted, "You need not drag me. I will go myself." He crawled into the blazing ruins. A moment later the roof collapsed over him to crown his final act of devotion to Christ.

About one hundred Chinese Christians were rounded up in the Shou-yang district, among them fourteen members of one family, and given a test of faith. A large circle was drawn on the ground and a cross inscribed in the center. To indicate their denial of Christ, all they had to do was step outside the circle. Only a few accepted this invitation. Those that stood their ground included a sizable number of teenagers. All were killed.

In a village in Shansi, another mother, Mrs. Meng, was weaving cloth on her household loom when a crowd of fierce faces appeared in her doorway. She knew who they were and what they wanted even before the inevitable question, "Will you deny your belief in Jesus?" "Wait a moment, please," she calmly replied. She stepped down from her loom and went to the closet where her family's best clothing was kept for holidays and funerals and donned her best gown. Then she walked to the door and knelt. "Now you may do as you wish, for I will not deny Jesus." A command, a flash of steel in the air, and the deed was done.

In the mountains nine Black Miao tribal Christian men, the first believers of their tribe, were called before the headman of their village on a ruse. One of the nine, sensing a trap, slipped away. Seven of the eight who appeared were seized and beheaded without trial or defense. In the days following, twenty-seven other Miao Christians were martyred and hundreds fined and forbidden to speak to one another.

In a church in Honan Province the Boxers took the rollbook and went around to one hundred homes, offering each family immunity from persecution if they would renounce their faith and worship idols. Ninety-nine stood fast. Their homes were looted, their cornfields trampled down, their farm implements stolen, their cattle driven off, and they were left destitute.

A young teacher near the Great Wall was left in charge of seventeen schoolgirls in a boarding school when the missionary had to leave. Influential people offered to hide her, but she refused to leave the girls who could not get to their homes. Hiding in fields and caves, they were hunted like wild animals. Finally they were captured and led to a Boxer temple for execution.

A Christian cook was seized and beaten, his ears were cut off, his mouth and cheeks slashed with a sword, and other shameful mutilations afflicted. He remained true.

A Chinese preacher who refused to apostatize was given a hundred blows on his bare back and then asked again to deny Christ. "No, never," the half-dead man of God declared. "I value Jesus Christ more than life and I will never deny Him!" Before the second hundred blows were completed, he collapsed and his tormentors left thinking he was dead. A friend stealthily carried him away, bathed his wounds, and secretly nursed him to recovery.

No Chinese Christian was safe from the Boxer wrath, not even the most highly educated. Dr. Wang was one of the first graduates from the Peking University Medical School.

When he and his little son were arrested, Boxers told him, "Dr. Wang, you are an educated man. We do not want to kill you, but we have no choice unless you burn incense to the gods."

"No, I cannot do that," he replied.

"We'll make it easy for you," the Boxers offered. "Get someone to burn incense in your place."

When he again refused, they offered to find him a substitute. "You will only have to go to the temple with us," they said.

"No, I will not," he persisted. "You may kill me, but I will not worship your gods in any way. There are four generations of Christians in my family. Do you think I would let this child see his father deny his Savior? Kill me if you must, but I will not betray my Lord."

They ran him through with a sword, lamenting, "What a pity to kill such a man."

The bravery of such Christians astounded the Boxers. Sometimes they ripped out the hearts of victims in search of the secret of their courage. Finding nothing but flesh, they would then remark, "It was the medicine of the foreign devils [the missionaries]."

The Bravery of Blind Chang

Of all the Chinese martyrs none died with more courage than Blind Chang, the most famous evangelist in Manchuria, homeland of the Manchu rulers of China.

Chang Shen had been converted after being stricken blind in mid-life. Before his conversion he had been known as *Wu so pu wei te,* meaning, "one without a particle of good in him." A gambler, woman-chaser and thief, he had driven his wife and only daughter from home. When he was stricken blind, neighbors said it was the judgment of the gods for his evil doing.

Chang heard of a missionary hospital where people were receiving sight. In 1886 he traveled overland for hundreds of miles to reach the hospital, only to be told every bed was full. The hospital evangelist took pity and gave up his own bed. Chang's eyesight was partially restored, and he heard about Christ for the first time. "Never had we a patient who received the gospel with such joy," reported the doctor.

When Chang asked for baptism, missionary James Webster replied, "Go home and tell your neighbors that you have changed. I will visit you later and if you are still following Jesus, then I will baptize you."

Five months later Webster arrived in Chang's area and found hundreds of inquirers. He baptized the new evangelist with great joy.

A clumsy native doctor robbed Chang of the little eyesight the missionaries had restored. No matter—Chang continued his travels from village to village, winning hundreds more, praising God when cursed and spit upon, even when ferocious dogs were turned loose to drive him away. He learned practically the whole New Testament by memory and could quote entire chapters from the Old Testament. Missionaries followed after him, baptizing converts and organizing churches.

When the Boxer fury arose, Chang was preaching at Tsengkow, Manchuria. Christians felt sure he would be one of the first targets and led him to a cave in the mountains.

The Boxers reached the nearby city called Ch'ao-yang-shan first and rounded up about fifty Christians for execution. "You're fools to kill all these," a resident told them. "For every one you kill, ten will spring up while that man Chang Shen lives. Kill him and you will crush the foreign religion." The Boxers promised to spare the fifty if someone would take them to Chang. No one volunteered. Finally when it appeared the Boxers would kill the fifty, one man slipped away and found Chang to tell him what was happening. "I'll gladly die for them," Chang offered. "Take me there."

When Chang arrived, the Boxer leaders were at another town. Nevertheless, he was bound by local authorities and taken to the temple of the god of war, and commanded to worship.

"I can only worship the One Living and True God," he declared.

"Then repent," they cried.

"I repented many years ago."

"Then believe in Buddha."

"I already believe in the one true Buddha, even Jesus Christ."

"You must at least bow to the gods."

"No. Turn my face toward the sun." Chang knew that at this time of day the sun was shining toward the temple and his back would be to the idols. When they turned him around, he knelt and worshiped the God of the Bible.

Three days later the Boxer leaders arrived. The blind evangelist was put in an open cart and driven to the cemetery outside the city wall. As he passed through the crowds, he sang the first Christian song he had learned at the hospital.

> Jesus loves me, He who died
> Heaven's gate to open wide;
> He will wash away my sin,
> Let His little child come in.

> Jesus loves me, He will stay,
> Close beside me all the way;
> If I love Him when I die,
> He will take me home on high.

When they reached the cemetery, he was shoved into a kneeling position. Three times he cried, "Heavenly Father, receive my spirit." Then the sword flashed, and his head tumbled to the ground.

The Boxers refused to let the Christians bury his body. Instead, fearful of a report that Blind Chang would rise from the dead, they forced the believers to buy oil and burn the mangled remains. Even so, the Boxers became afraid and fled from the revenge which they believed Chang's spirit would wreak upon them. The local Christians were thus spared persecution.

The Tribulation in Peking

The largest number of Chinese Christians died in the populous cities of Peking and Tientsin. Fewer died in Tientsin where a young Quaker engineer named Herbert Hoover, the future president of the United States, and other foreigners gave them refuge and the opportunity to help defend the foreign garrison against attacks by Chinese government soldiers.

But not a single missionary died in Tientsin. And only one was martyred in Peking, an Englishman known as Professor James who had been in the country since 1883. As the crisis was developing, he went out to check on Chinese Christian friends. Soldiers captured him and took him to the house of two of the leaders in the coup that had overthrown Emperor Kuang-hsu. They ordered him to kneel. The missionary refused, declaring, "I cannot kneel to anyone but my

God and King." Then he was forced to kneel upon a chain
for several hours. He was executed three days later and his
head exhibited in a cage hanging from the beam of the Tung
An Gate.

The foreigners in Peking were fast gathering in the British ambassador's compound for protection against sniper attacks. Unexpectedly, the empress' troop commander in the
capital announced a short truce to permit all the foreigners
to take shelter. American Methodist missionaries begged
their ambassador to wait for seven hundred Chinese Christian girls who were unprotected in their mission school a
mile away. "We appeal to you in the name of humanity and
Christianity not to abandon them," the missionary said. The
ambassador felt the risk was too great. Missionary Frank
Gamewell then warned that "our Christian nation will never
live down your decision." Gamewell and his colleagues could
only go back and distribute money to students and faculty
and instruct them to hide wherever they could.

After the foreigners were safely behind the walls of the
British compound, the Boxers and their fanatical supporters
struck. The tragedy they inflicted was described by Dr.
George Ernest Morrison of the London *Times* who was
caught in Peking:

As darkness came on the most awful cries were
heard in the city, most demoniacal and unforgettable,
the cries of the Boxers—*Sha kuei-tzu* [kill the devils]
—mingled with the shrieks of the victims and the
groans of the dying. For Boxers were sweeping
through the city, massacring the native Christians
and burning them alive in their homes. The first
building to be burned was the chapel of the Methodist
Mission in the Hatamen Street. Then flames sprang
up in many quarters of the city. Amid the most
deafening uproar, the Tung-tang or East Cathedral
shot flames into the sky. The old Greek Church
in the northeast of the city, the London Mission
buildings, the handsome pile of the American Board
Mission, and the entire foreign buildings belonging to
the Imperial Marine Customs in the east city burned
throughout the night. It was an appalling sight.
. . . On June 15th rescue parties were sent out by
the American and Russian Legations in the morning,
and by the British and German Legations in the after-

noon, to save if possible native Christians from the burning ruins. . . . Awful sights were witnessed. Women and children hacked to pieces, men trussed like fowls, with noses and ears cut off and eyes gouged out. Chinese Christians accompanied the reliefs and ran about in the labyrinth of network of streets that formed the quarter, calling upon the Christians to come out from their hiding places. All through the night the massacre had continued, and Boxers were even now shot red-handed at their bloody work. As the patrol was passing a Taoist Temple on the way, a noted Boxer meeting place, cries were heard within. The temple was forcibly entered. Native Christians were found there, their hands tied behind their backs, awaiting execution and torture, some had already been put to death, and their bodies were still warm and bleeding. All were shockingly mutilated. Their fiendish murderers were at their incantations burning incense before their gods, offering Christians in sacrifice to their angered deities.

Several hundred Chinese Christians did reach the besieged foreigners and worked heroically digging ditches and fortifying the walls against Boxer attacks. As the first shells burst over the walls, Chinese children could be heard singing, "There'll be no dark valley when Jesus comes." Finally in August an international rescue force, marching from Tientsin, reached Peking and broke the siege. By this time the Chinese Christians were reduced to eating leaves. Arm and leg bones protruded through their skin, and they were too weak to cheer their rescuers.

The empress was overthrown and fled Peking in terror. Many of her advisers committed suicide. The victorious foreign expeditionary force allowed a caretaker government to take over. Now the Boxers became the hunted, and thousands were killed by foreign and Chinese troops. The mad governor of Shansi Province was beheaded.

The Last Boxer Martyr

Meanwhile, the CIM missionaries who had been beaten on long marches were being cared for in hospitals. Mrs. Glover gave birth to the child she had carried on her thousand mile trek. But tiny Faith Edith lived only ten days.

Mrs. Glover helped plan the burial service, choosing one of the CIM's favorite hymns which begins, "Hark, hark the song the ransomed sing." After the burial, Mrs. Glover's health improved and she was moved to Shanghai. There she took a sharp turn for the worse and began sinking fast. Late on the afternoon of October 24, she picked up the lines of "Jesus, Lover of My Soul" which her husband had been singing by her bedside. In a remarkably clear voice she sang,

Leave, ah! leave me not alone,
Still support and comfort me.

At four the next morning she was with Christ.

She was the last of the Shansi missionary martyrs to die. As her coffin was lowered, her husband, two sons who had been away at school, and missionary and Chinese friends sang the hymn she had sung so many times to her children at bedtime:

Sun of my soul, Thou Savior dear,
It is not night if Thou be near.

Afterwards her husband had inscribed on her headstone two praise notes appropriate to all the martyrs of the Boxer uprising:

THE NOBLE ARMY OF MARTYRS PRAISE THEE.
IN THY PRESENCE IS FULNESS OF JOY.

The Power and the Glory

The Boxers had inflicted the most severe blow ever dealt to the modern Protestant missionary movement launched by William Carey. A total of 135 missionaries and 53 children had been killed—100 from Britain and Commonwealth nations, 56 from Sweden, and 32 from the United States. Of this number, 79 were associated with the CIM and 36 with the C&MA, the societies which suffered the greatest losses. Many China watchers thought Protestants were finished in China. Chinese believers, they said, are rice Christians and the native church will fade away. They further predicted that missionaries would never again be welcome in China.

The doomsayers were wrong on all counts.

When the rebellion was over, an assessment showed that the Chinese church had been battered but had never bent. For example, the Methodists in Foochow met after the missionaries had departed and agreed they would continue their educational and evangelistic work, even if they never received another missionary or dollar of mission money.

When peace and order came and the missionaries returned, a delegation of twelve men came from a village to ask for a Christian preacher. "We want to know more about your religion. We will support the minister and provide him a place to live and a building in which to preach."

At Taiyuan the remains of the slain missionaries and Chinese Christians were carefully gathered up and buried in the Martyr Memorial Cemetery. Later a Martyr Memorial Church was opened at the spot where Miss Coombs had been burned to death while trying to rescue two of her Chinese students. A memorial stone, on which was inscribed the names of the Taiyuan martyrs, was placed on the porch of the new church.

At Paoting, where two hospitals were built as memorials to the slain missionary doctors, the commander of the Chinese Second Army Division, General Wang, came to the Presbyterian mission and requested Christian teachers to come to instruct his men in the gospel and biblical morality.

Powerful, soul-cleansing revivals surged across north China. Missionaries confessed sins of arrogance, pride and ill feeling toward their co-workers and asked forgiveness. Chinese pastors and church leaders confessed failures to their flocks. Kinsmen who had been long estranged made tearful reconciliations. Prodigals came and knelt at their parents' feet and begged forgiveness. Many parents asked their children for forgiveness. The Methodist's Bishop Cassels recorded:

Scoffers might call the work by an evil name; unbelievers might laugh at the unusual scenes; hard hearts might for a time resist the influence; but those whose eyes were opened and whose hearts were touched, felt indeed that now, if never before, they had been brought into touch with the powers of the other world, and with the mighty working of the Spirit of God.

Protestants more than doubled during the six years following the massacres. In 1901 one missionary in Kiangsi Province reported twenty thousand converts.

Throughout China there was mass interest in Christianity. It was well-known that most Christians, Chinese and foreign, had not demanded indemnities for loss of life and destruction of property as other foreigners had. Hudson Taylor, director of the missionary society which had suffered most, asked CIM workers to show to the Chinese "the meekness and gentleness of Christ, not only not to enter any claim against the Chinese Government but to refrain from accepting compensation even if offered." In Shansi Province, where the greatest damage had been wreaked, newly appointed officials appointed Baptist missionary Timothy Richard to help make post-Boxer adjustments. Richard suggested that a large sum be set aside as an indemnity, not to be paid foreigners but to found in Taiyuan a Chinese university. He believed this would help dispel the ignorance and superstition which had enabled the Boxers to gain support from the populace. The proposal was accepted and another English Baptist missionary was appointed the first principal.

Chinese church leaders more than matched the spirit of the missionaries. Even those who had lost loved ones exhibited remarkable restraint and forgiveness. Chen Wei-ping, pastor of the Asbury Methodist Church in Peking, had lost his minister father and mother and sister to crazed Boxers in Yen-ching-chou. His father had been beheaded, his mother and thirteen-year-old sister hacked to pieces as they clung in each other's arms. When invited by the government to submit a claim, Pastor Chen replied, "We are not in need. We do not want payment." Instead he requested his bishop to "Appoint me to Yen-ching-chou that I may preach the message of love to the men who killed my loved ones." The bishop consented.

The families of the missionary martyrs were equally forgiving. Sherwood Eddy, the missionary statesman, told a student missionary convention in Kansas City about visiting the parents of Mrs. E.R. Atwater in Oberlin, Ohio. She, her husband, and their four children had been killed by soldiers who had pretended to be their protectors. Recalled Eddy, "They said, in tears, 'We do not begrudge them—we gave them to that needy land; China will yet believe the truth.' "

Sending churches were challenged by missionary and Chinese speakers fresh from China to embark on a crash program for evangelizing China. Yale student Fei Chi-hao told another student missionary convention, "My parents are now wearing the martyr's crown in the 'Home above.' It is my ambition to follow in the footsteps of your missionaries and carry back the blessed message to my people." Then he challenged the students about China's immediate needs. "We need colleges and universities, railroads and factories," he said. "But the thing that we need most, just now, is Christianity. The Christian religion is the only hope and salvation of China."

Such appeals brought wave after wave of new missionaries to China and millions of dollars for evangelization and education.

The Boxer martyrdoms in China bore fruit for decades following. Thousands upon thousands came to Christ as a direct result of the slaughter of Christians in 1900. Some had been direct observers of persecutions and could not, as Saul of Tarsus in witnessing the stoning of Stephen, forget the bravery and dedication of those who had died.

One of the most notable was Feng Yu-hsiang, the soldier who watched the murders at Paoting. In 1913, as a major, he professed faith in Christ at an evangelistic meeting led by John R. Mott in Peking. Afterwards he testified, "I saw Miss Morrill offer her life for her friends. And a missionary walking with his sons on a veranda in calmness and peace while flames rose to envelop them. I could never forget that."

Feng Yu-hsiang became China's most famous "Christian General." He won hundreds of his officers to Christ, forbade gambling and prostitution in his camps, and had his men taught useful trades.

The results were much less spectacular in Mongolia where the Scandinavian missionaries had given their all. But their successors were confident. Said Mrs. A.B. Magnuson:

Looking back on our work in Mongolia it seems dark, having borne little fruit, but I lift my eyes upward to Him who can look deeper and farther than we can look and does not judge simply by the outward appearance as we do. He can change and transform all things and no work for Him is in vain. We believe there will be some saved souls from Mongolia in the great blood-washed multitude before the throne of the Redeemer. "They that sow in tears shall reap in joy."

The defeat of the Boxers and their Imperial backer marked a turning point in China's history. The feudal Manchu dynasty was soon overthrown and the Chinese Republic founded under the leadership of Sun Yat-sen, a Christian whose life had once been saved by a British missionary.

The new generation of Chinese looked to the "Christian" West for education and technical aid. Protestant missionaries were invited to start universities in every major city. By 1911 most Chinese political leaders were Protestants, including Sun Yat-sen. One official even suggested that Christianity be made the state religion.

NO ARK OF SAFETY:

China in the Following Decades

The Boxer defeat opened China to greater evangelization, but it did not mark the end of violence. Scores of missionaries and thousands of Chinese Christians were martyred in the line of duty during the next half century. Most were killed by mobs, dread diseases, Japanese bombs and bullets, and Communist assassination squads—all before the Red scourge enveloped the Celestial Kingdom and cut off communication with Christianity abroad.

Superstition and ignorance continued to spur the dark horse of death. In the summer of 1902 a cholera epidemic swept parts of north China. Thirteen children died at the CIM's Chefoo school where missionaries sent their school-age youngsters. One was the son of Boxer martyrs, Mr. and Mrs. Duncan Kay. Missionaries at their stations were working to save thousands of Chinese when a rumor was circulated that they were spreading the epidemic with their poison (medicine). In Chen-chou, Honan Province, two CIM members, J.R. Bruce of Australia and R.H. Lowis of England, were attacked by a fear-ridden mob and murdered as a result of the rumor.

The Doctor's Devotion

Anti-foreign mobs continued to lengthen the trail of blood of the Christian missionaries, who were not ordinary foreigners but humanitarians of the highest order. Dr. Eleanor Chestnut, an orphan girl from Waterloo, Iowa, is an example. An orphan raised by a poor aunt in the backwoods of Missouri, she skimped and starved to get through Park College, dressing in castoffs from the missionary barrel. Determined to be a medical missionary, she lived in an attic and ate mostly oatmeal while attending medical school in Chicago. To earn money she nursed the aged. She was nurse to Dr. Oliver Wendell Holmes in his final illness.

After studies at Moody Bible Institute, Dr. Chestnut was appointed by the then American Presbyterian Board to China in 1893. She started a hospital in Lien-chou, Kwangsi, the province adjoining Hongkong. She lived on $1.50 a month so that the rest of her salary could be used to buy bricks. Her Board learned what she was spending on bricks and insisted on repaying her. She refused the sum offered, saying, "It will spoil all my fun."

While the building was under construction, she performed surgery in her bathroom. One operation involved the amputation of a coolie's leg. The surgery was successful, except that the flaps of skin did not grow together. Eventually this problem was solved and the man was able to walk with crutches. Someone noticed that Dr. Chestnut was limping. When asked why, she responded, "Oh, it's nothing." One of the nurses revealed the truth. The doctor had taken skin from her own leg for immediate transplant to the one whom nurses called "a good-for-nothing coolie," using only a local anesthetic.

When the Boxer uprising began Dr. Chestnut was one of the last missionaries to leave. She returned the following spring. On October 28, 1905, she and other missionaries were busy at the hospital when an anti-foreign mob attacked. She slipped out to ask for protection from Chinese authorities, and might have escaped had she not returned to help her fellow-workers. Her last act was to tear strips from her dress to bandage a wound in the forehead of a boy in the crowd. She was killed along with Rev. and Mrs. John Peale and two other missionaries.

Martyrs during the Revolution

In the decade after the Boxer defeat China wobbled chaotically toward Revolution. The medieval Manchu dynasty was dying. New leaders were rising and demanding a democratic form of government built on ideals they had learned from western missionaries. One revolutionary leader, Huang Hsing, declared, "To Christianity more than to any other single cause is owed our revolution." Yet in the turbulence of the fighting that culminated in the establishment of the Chinese Republic in 1911 missionaries were among those who suffered the most from bandits and mobs.

One of the first to die was Miss Christine Villadsen of the Scandinavian Alliance Mission. She was killed by bandits while trying to protect Chinese Christians at Shao-shui.

Ironically, supporters of the old Manchu dynasty sought refuge with missionaries in many cities. At Taiyuan, Shansi, the daughter of the Boxer governor who had ordered the murder of missionaries there in 1900, was given protection by British Baptists.

It was well known that many leaders of the Revolution had been educated in mission schools. Yet extreme elements in some areas of China were determined to vanquish foreigners, including missionaries, along with the Manchus.

The ancient city of Sian, southwest of Taiyuan, was the old capital of the Chinese Empire and had been a center of Manchu power. CIM missionaries had been twice driven out before Scandinavian Alliance missionaries located there. The work grew, churches were started, and a boarding school for children of the mission was built in a south suburb, beyond the wall of the city.

The missionaries knew that the anti-Manchu and anti-foreign Ancient Society of Elder Brothers had hundreds of secret members in Sian. Though they were assured by national revolutionary leaders that they would be protected, E.R. Beckman, director of the school, and W.T. Vatne, a young teacher, were worried. When they discussed their situation, Beckman's oldest daughter Selma overheard and cried, "Let's go home."

Rumors of an impending attack spread throughout the area in early October, 1911. In this same month the churches in Sian were stirred by a remarkable revival. A young evangelist prophesied, "There are many evil men in this city, and something terrible will happen. Pray earnestly to the Lord."

On Sunday, October 22, Beckman was conducting services in a south suburb when he heard a military command and the sound of running feet. A messenger brought a note from his wife, imploring, "Hurry home." Beckman was stopped several times by soldiers, but finally reached the children's home.

That night the missionaries and the children crowded onto the veranda of the second floor. They could see pillars of fire in the distance—the wall of Sian was under attack.

Around midnight a mob massed at the gate in the high stone wall that protected the mission school. While the residents watched, soldiers torched the gate. They would be inside in a matter of minutes.

Beckman and Vatne got a rope to help the children over the back wall. Vatne went first, then Beckman helped his oldest daughter Selma over. The director had just put another child on top of the wall when shots rang out and his daughter screamed. Unable to help Vatne and Selma, he tried digging a hole in the wall at another spot. Then he heard shouts and timbers falling. The mob was through the gate.

Beckman, his wife Ida, and the six remaining children took shelter in a room of a small outbuilding. They could hear people running about and could smell smoke from more fires. "Find the foreigners! Kill them!" the intruders were shouting.

Mrs. Beckman tenderly took her youngest daughter, four-year-old Thyra, from her husband. She kissed the child and whispered, "I must say goodbye to you, my darling." Then she handed her back to her father.

Moments later their hiding place was discovered. They all dashed out, trying to run through the crowd milling around the yard. Beckman, carrying little Thyra, became separated from his wife and the others. Oblivious to blows from the fanatics who saw him, he rushed through the gate and ran into a grove of trees on the south bank of a large pond. Hearing voices behind him, he jumped in and waded to the middle of the pond where he and his child huddled in the thick vegetation which had grown out of the shallow water.

For the next three or four hours he remained there with his daughter in his arms. The little girl never uttered a sound. Finally the voices ceased and he saw flickering torches disappearing in the distance.

The morning star appeared. He feared that with the coming of day the mob would be back to search the pond. Holding little Thyra tightly, he cautiously waded to the north bank and crept through some bushes. Skirting a military camp, they reached a mission station hours later. Father and daughter were numb and exhausted, but otherwise in good health.

He was told that his wife, his middle daughter, and four other children had been killed while trying to break through the mob. But what of the teacher and Selma? Three days later he learned they had escaped and taken shelter with a Chinese family. Fanatics discovered them and a mob gathered demanding that they be given up. They tried to run and were slashed and beaten to death.

Revolutionary leaders made profuse apologies when told about the tragedy. This did little to console the grieving four-year-old. "Your momma and sisters and the others are with Jesus" Mr. Beckman kept assuring. Finally she asked, "Are they with *our* Jesus?" He nodded. "Then I will see them again."

Beckman took his daughter to Sweden for rest. There she developed diphtheria and hovered close to death. He and other Christians prayed and miraculously, she lived. Years later she married a missionary and served in China. She now lives in retirement in Woodstock, Illinois, awaiting the time when she will see her loved ones again.

Tragedies in the Twenties

The political future of China was decided in the 1920's. World War I weakened the European powers. Fueled by biblical ideas of freedom, China's new leaders began pressing for release from the foreign treaties that had milked the nation's resources for decades. Britain and the United States, which had the most missionaries in China, refused to give up the special privileges which were so profitable. Resentment flared against citizens of these countries living in China. Not since the time of the Boxers were missionaries in such great danger.

New philosophies and theologies from the West also helped to erode Chinese confidence in Christianity. A new wave of so-called missionaries from mainline Protestant denominations came teaching evolution and a non-supernatural view of the Bible. Methodist, Presbyterian, Congregationalist, and Northern Baptist schools were especially hard hit. Bertrand Russell came from England preaching atheism and socialism. Destructive books brought by such teachers further undermined orthodox Christianity. The Chinese intelligentsia who had been schooled by orthodox evangelical missionaries were thus softened for the advent of Marxism.

The crucial year was 1923. The United States and Britain again refused to give up their special rights in China. Sun Yat-sen, the Christian president, was facing a growing revolt in the south. Forth came the Soviet ambassador. His government, he pledged, would give up its treaty rights and help unify the country. Communism would not be established in China, he further promised.

On the last day of the year, President Sun announced, "We no longer look to the Western Powers. Our faces are turned toward Russia." The door was open for Communist agitation and infiltration that would inflame feelings against "imperialists" (missionaries and other western nationals) and their "running dogs" (Chinese Christians and employees of westerners).

Martyrs to Bandits and Kidnappers

Disorders and rebellions continued. In June, 1920, William A. Reimert, a missionary educator, was murdered by bandit soldiers. In December, 1921, the C&MA's W.H. Oldfields was kidnapped by brigands in Kwangsi Province. In 1922 Dr. Howard Taylor and four other CIM missionaries were seized by bandit soldiers, but were subsequently released. In August, 1923, F.J. Watts and E.A. Whiteside of the English Church Missionary Society were murdered by robbers in Szechwan Province. A few months later four American Lutheran missionaries were captured in Hupeh Province, and one, B.A. Hoff, died of injuries after his release. In 1924 George D. Byers, an American Presbyterian, was killed by bandits in Hainan Province. A few months later the anti-foreign Red Lantern Society murdered Mrs. Sible, a Canadian Methodist, at Ch'eng-tu. More kidnappings and murders followed, including the killing of several national Bible Society colporteurs.

A vast spiritual harvest paralleled the violence. For example, in Kweilin, capital of Kwangsi Province, thousands of new converts were baptized by Christian and Missionary Alliance missionaries. Three times the church sanctuary had to be enlarged. The foundation of the third building was laid during a period of near anarchy while bullets from battling military factions zinged over the construction site. C&MA

missionary Cunningham was supervising the work when hit by a fatal shot. His life and the lives of other missionaries and national church leaders were part of the price of the spiritual reaping.

The violence continued to escalate. Kidnappers no longer sent sliced ears as warnings, but killed their victims immediately if demands for ransom were not met. The anti-foreign spirit, kept high by Communist agitation, was so strong that local military and civil authorities often looked the other way when attacks were made on missionaries and even on Chinese Christians.

The Blood Keeps Flowing

President Sun Yat-sen died in 1925. His party split apart, factions fighting among themselves. China became even less safe. Six more missionaries died, among them the beloved Bishop Cassels. Before his death he had written, "We came in the steps of Him who was despised and rejected of men. Perhaps this is one of the lessons we have to learn at a time when extraordinary and bitter hatred is being stirred up against us."

In 1926 the British Navy, in a show of force, sailed up the Yangtze Gorges and bombarded the populous city of Wan-hsien. Hundreds of Chinese were killed. Anti-foreign passions flamed so high that hundreds of Chinese churches severed relations with foreign mission boards. Marshall Feng, the famed Christian general, went to Moscow to study communism.

The year 1927 was the worst since the Boxer violence in 1900. Mission hospitals and schools had to be closed in the interior of China. Missionaries were ordered to evacuate to the coast or return home. In that year the Protestant force dropped from sixty-five hundred to four thousand.

Crossing deserts and high mountains, missionaries were again easy prey for bandits and undisciplined troops. In one incident bandits attacked three CIM American missionaries, Mr. and Mrs. Morris Slichter, their two children, and Miss May Craig. They were traveling under military guard to a railway station in Yunnan Province. When the bandits opened fire, the guards fled leaving the missionaries unprotected in a rice field. Heedless of cries for mercy, one bandit fired at Mrs. Slichter who was holding her three-year-old daughter Ruth in her arms. The bullet passed through the child's head and ripped a gash across the mother's left wrist. Another robber stabbed Mr. Slichter in the back. He fell dead without a sound. These bandits raced on in pursuit of the guards. Others coming up behind paused only to rob Mr. Slichter's body and snatch Mrs. Slichter and Miss Craig's glasses before running on.

When the battle was over, the robbers returned and carried the dead and living off to their village. Little Ruth had died a few minutes after being hit. Eight days later Chinese soldiers attacked the village. The robbers, dragging their three captives, scattered into the hills under a hail of bullets. At daybreak the bandits regrouped and decided to leave Miss Craig with a letter to the soldiers warning that if they continued to follow, Mrs. Slichter and her son would be killed. The soldiers called off the chase, but returned to the village and seized the bandit leader's family as a ransom for the release of the two Americans. The exchange was made.

In remote Kansu Province Dr. George King, director of the Borden Memorial Hospital, was the only physician for a thousand miles. Young Bill Borden, heir to a fortune and a scholar–athlete graduate of both Princeton and Yale, had died in Egypt while studying Arabic in preparation for missionary service among the Muslims of northwest China. One quarter of his estate had been left to the CIM and had been used to build the hospital.

Dr. King did not want to leave his post, but since he was a strong swimmer and proficient in Chinese, his help was needed in evacuating thirty-seven missionaries and twelve children by goatskin rafts down the Yellow River. They were attacked by bandits along one remote stretch. Fortunately, the current was strong enough to allow them to escape. Then a few miles down the river they became stuck on a sand bar. Twelve hours in the water, tugging at the rafts, sapped the doctor's strength. When all but one of the rafts had been freed, he slipped into a nasty current. "Can you make it?" someone called. "I don't know," he replied, and slipped under, never to be seen again.

Chinese Christians Were Not Spared

For every missionary who died directly or indirectly because of the violence, at least ten Chinese Christians lost their lives. One was Y.C. Liu, a promising scholarly young preacher in Szechwan Province. He was on his way to his ordination ceremony in a CIM–related church when kidnapped by bandits. His body was later found in the woods. Another Chinese Christian from the same area was the former incense-maker, Ho. After hearing the gospel, Ho had invited missionary C.M. Tan and his Christian brother-in-law to the destruction of his idols. A man of few words, he became known for his warm smile and willingness to tackle any task in the church. While on a trip to sell cloth, he was stopped by brigands, robbed, and killed. Left to mourn were his wife and three young children.

Besides the bandit peril, Chinese Christians continued to be targets of anti-foreign and anti-Christian societies. Traveling Bible and book salesmen were especially in danger. One was seized in Kiangsi Province, his books were confiscated, and his hands tied. He was ordered to run through the streets, calling out, "I am also an imperialist, a slavish dog of the foreigners." Instead he proclaimed at the top of his lungs, "I am a slave of Jesus Christ!" They did not kill him on the spot, but threatened to do so if he ever dared sell another Christian book. How long he lived after this is not known. Another Chinese Christian in Yonanchow, Hunan Province, was grabbed by Communists and charged with being a "running dog of imperialists" for disseminating the teachings of Jesus. When told he was worthy of death, he begged the opportunity to pray. A Communist instantly struck off his hand. "Lord Jesus, receive my spirt," the Christian shouted in a loud voice. A second blow with the sword and he was dead.

The Nationalist armies now pushed north and conquered the upper Yangtze Valley. With the fall of Nanking on March 27 many foreigners, including missionaries, were murdered. Many others escaped. Pearl S. Buck, daughter of missionaries and later to become a world-renowned novelist, hid in a peasant hut. A Southern Presbyterian doctor was pushed into a hospital coalbin by his loyal staff. After the danger had passed, he crawled out, sooty but safe.

The Red Peril

Chiang Kai-shek purged the Communists from his armies and reversed Sun's policy of friendship with Russia. In 1928 the long civil war began between Chiang's Nationalist armies and the Communists under Mao Tse-tung. Vastly out-

numbered by Nationalist troops, the Communist armies retreated to the far northwest. But infiltrators and guerrillas
remained hidden in the dense population.

Undaunted, the CIM called for two hundred new workers in 1929 to serve in dangerous areas. "It will involve the
most tremendous conflict [with Satan] which we have ever
undertaken," said the CIM director. Within the next few
months eight more missionaries were killed, thirty captured
and held for ransom, and twenty of thirty-two CIM stations
looted. The price of serving in China remained high. In 1930
three missionaries of the Finnish Free Mission Society,
Misses Cajander, Ingman and Hedengren were killed by
Communist outlaws. Altogether, during 1930, the Communists killed an estimated one hundred fifty thousand Chinese
in Kiangsi Province and burned one hundred thousand
homes. One and a half million Chinese fled the province in
fear.

When Chiang Kai-shek declared himself a Christian the
next year, missionaries and Chinese church leaders became
direct targets for Communist hostility. Propagandists nailed
up posters announcing such charges as, "The church is the
headquarters of murderers and incendiaries," "The missionaries have love in their mouths and hate in their hearts,"
and "Christians are traitors to China." Other posters urged
Chinese, "Drive out these missionaries who are making
slaves of us." To the testimony of one CIM missionary in
Kiangsi Province that he was not afraid to die because "I
know I will go to Heaven," a Communist answered, "Let
him go to Heaven. We will have one less missionary in
China to cheat the people."

Missionaries urgently warned their home offices and
government officials in western countries of the Communist
threat to China. But the West paid no heed and continued to
enforce profitable trade concession treaties with China.

Muslim Marauders

The decade of the thirties began with terrible famines and
plagues added to Communist guerrilla activities and other rebellions in many cities. In Minchow, Kansu, the Assemblies of God lost one hundred fifty school children out of
five hundred students in a plague. Next, bandits attacked the
town, seizing citizens by force and torturing them until they
gave up their valuables. Hundreds were burned and beaten.

Many Christians among them died. The bandits had hardly left when thirty thousand rebellious Muslims marched in and took control. Their leader made his headquarters in the front yard of the Assemblies mission house. The Muslims looted, burned, raped and killed at will for eighteen days. When missionary W.W. Simpson tried to have a worship service, a brute on the Muslim General's staff seated himself on the platform. As Simpson spoke about the coming of Christ into the world, the Muslim made motions with his sword of cutting off the missionary's head. Surprisingly, the missionary was spared.

The brutalities were even worse in Tsinchow, Kansu Province. A Muslim army captured the town in May, killed twenty-seven hundred natives in three days, took over a thousand young women captive, and turned the CIM girls' school into horse stalls.

Afraid of What?

In October, 1931, widower Jack Vinson, a beloved Southern Presbyterian missionary, was captured by bandits while visiting rural churches in Kiangsu Province. A government force, loyal to Chiang, pursued the kidnappers and surrounded them in a small town. The bandits offered the missionary freedom if he would persuade the force to withdraw. Vinson agreed only if they would release other captives. The bandits refused and tried to shoot their way out. In the melee many bandits were killed, and the survivors fled with Vinson. However, the missionary could not run because of recent surgery. One bandit shot him, then another ran up and cut off his head.

The daughter of a Chinese pastor was among those rescued by government troops. She recalled having heard a bandit tell him, "I'm going to kill you. Aren't you afraid?" She said Vinson had replied simply, "Kill me, if you wish. I will go straight to God."

Jack Vinson was the first Southern Presbyterian martyr in China. A colleague, E.H. Hamilton, was inspired by his courage to write a poem that was widely printed and became an encouragement to other missionaries and Chinese believers in constant danger.

Afraid? Of What?
To feel the spirit's glad release?
To pass from pain to perfect peace,

> The strife and strain of life to cease?
>   Afraid — of that?
>
>   Afraid? Of What?
> Afraid to see the Savior's face
> To hear His welcome, and to trace
> The glory gleam from wounds of grace?
>   Afraid — of that?
>
>   Afraid? Of What?
> A flash, a crash, a pierced heart;
> Darkness, light, O Heaven's art!
> A wound of His a counterpart!
>   Afraid — of that?
>
>   Afraid? Of What?
> To do by death what life could not —
> Baptize with blood a stony plot,
> Till souls shall blossom from the spot?
>   Afraid — of that?

Victory Day for the Stams

John and Betty Stam, new CIM missionaries in hazardous Anhwei Province were among those strengthened by "Afraid? Of What?" They had met at CIM student prayer meetings at Moody. Betty, a gifted poet, had been raised in China of Presbyterian missionary parents and felt God's call to return there. John, of Dutch immigrant ancestry from New Jersey, was also drawn to the land where, as he said, "a million a month pass into Christless graves."

At that time the CIM was calling for a vanguard of single men to serve in dangerous Communist-infested areas. Even though this could mean not marrying for several years, if at all, John was willing to go. Chosen to give the Class Address for the Moody Class of '32, he challenged,

> Shall we beat a retreat, and turn back from our high
> calling in Christ Jesus; or dare we advance at God's
> command in face of the impossible? . . . Let us
> remind ourselves that the Great Commission was
> never qualified by clauses calling for advance only if
> funds were plentiful and no hardship or self-denial
> involved. On the contrary, we are told to expect tri-
> bulation and even persecution, but with it victory in
> Christ.

Since Betty was a year ahead of John in school, she went to

China first. Assigned to Anhwei Province, she was delayed in Shanghai when the veteran CIM missionary in Anhwei, H.S. Ferguson, was captured by bandits and all the women missionaries had to leave. Ferguson was never seen alive again.

So she was in Shanghai when John arrived and after a year they were given permission by the CIM director to be married. "Truly, God seems to go out of His way to make His children happy," John wrote his parents after the wedding. They were even happier when Helen Priscilla was born in September, 1934, in a Methodist hospital far up the Yangtze River.

Communist activity was said to have subsided in Anhwei Province, and they were assigned to do evangelistic work in the town of Ching-te. The district magistrate assured, "There is no danger of Communists here. I will guarantee your safety."

A few weeks later Communists did attack and the magistrate was one of the first to flee. The Reds were quick to go to the Stams'. Betty served them tea and cakes while John tried to explain their peaceful intentions. When they finished their tea, the visitors politely said, "You will go with us."

At the direction of his captors, John wrote CIM that the kidnappers wanted $20,000 ransom. "The Lord bless and guide you, and as for us, may God be glorified whether by life or by death." He told the Communists, "I do not expect the ransom to be paid."

The Reds abandoned Ching-te, taking their captives with them. On the trail they discussed killing the baby to save trouble. An old farmer protested, "The little one has done nothing worthy of death." "Then you will die for her," the leader retorted. "I am willing," said the farmer. He was killed on the spot.

They stopped in the town of Miao-shou and ordered John to send another letter demanding the ransom. The postmaster recognized him and asked, "Where are you going?" "We don't know where they're going," John replied, "but we are going to heaven."

A short time later they were painfully bound, stripped of their outer garments, and quartered in a house. The next morning, still bound, they were marched through the town. As they moved along, the Communists shouted ridicule and hate slogans and called the people to the execution.

The procession stopped in a pine grove at the top of a hill. Suddenly the town physician, Dr. Wang, a Christian, ran to the prisoners and pleaded for their lives. He was dragged away to be killed.

John was asking mercy for the doctor when ordered to kneel. The executioner swung his sword and the young missionary was gone. Betty quivered momentarily, then fell beside him. Another swing and they were together with God.

The "Miracle Baby"

The next day a Chinese evangelist named Lo arrived. The Communist soldiers had left, but the townspeople were too terrified of Communist spies to talk. Finally an old woman pointed to a vacant house and whispered, "The foreign baby is still alive." Lo found the baby lying warm and snug on a bed and took her to his wife. Then they recovered the bodies of the parents and lovingly wrapped them in white cotton for burial.

The bravery of the evangelist and his wife shamed the townspeople and they gathered to hear his funeral sermon.

You have seen these wounded bodies, and you pity
our friends for their suffering and death. But you
should know that they are children of God. Their
spirits are unharmed, and are at this moment in the
presence of their Heavenly Father. They came to
China and to Miao-shou, not for themselves but for
you, to tell you about the great love of God, that you
might believe in the Lord Jesus and be eternally saved.
You have heard their message. Remember, it is true.
Their death proves it so. Do not forget what they
told you — repent, and believe the Gospel.

After the burial Evangelist and Mrs. Lo tenderly carried little Priscilla in a rice basket a hundred miles through dangerous mountains to the home of another CIM missionary, George Birch. Along the road they had asked Chinese mothers to nurse the child. Birch promised to care for her until his wife returned. Tucked away in the baby's clothing was ten dollars hidden by the mother for food.

When Mrs. Birch arrived, the couple arranged for the tiny orphan to be taken to its mother's parents, Dr. and Mrs. Charles Scott, at their Presbyterian station in Chi-nan, Shantung Province. Dr. Scott said of his daughter and son-in-law: "They have not died in vain. The blood of the martyrs is still the seed of the church. If we could hear our beloved children speak, we know from their convictions that they would praise God because He counted them worthy to suffer for the sake of Christ."

The report of the Stams' martyrdom and the survival of the "miracle baby," as Priscilla was called, was widely publicized in the United States and Britain. Hundreds of letters came to the parents of the young couple and their mission. Many contained large gifts. Some writers volunteered to go as replacements. At Moody and at Wilson College, where Betty had also attended, there were student prayer meetings. A biography was published and quickly ran through nine printings. Noting the impact, a CIM missionary in China wrote Betty's parents, "A life which had the longest span of years might not have been able to do one-hundredth of the work for Christ which they have done in a day."

Martyrs to Disease

More missionaries died in China from dread diseases than from violence. The C&MA, for example, lost ten missionaries to smallpox, typhus, dysentery and malaria from 1900–24, while losing only two workers to afflictions common in the homeland. The larger CIM mission lost many more to dread diseases. Missionary doctors were most vulnerable to diseases such as smallpox, cholera and typhus because they were often involved in fighting epidemics.

Dr. Arthur Jackson was a living legend in Manchuria where he was director of a Presbyterian hospital. When the bubonic plague struck, he worked day and night trying to save as many lives as possible. In the midst of the epidemic he caught the plague from patients and died. Thousands attended a memorial service where the viceroy, not a Christian himself, gave the eulogy. "The Chinese government has lost a man who gave his life in his desire to help," he said. Then he followed Chinese custom and addressed a prayer to the departed missionary doctor.

O spirit of Dr. Jackson, we pray you to intercede for the twenty million people of Manchuria and ask the Lord of Heaven to take away this pestilence, so that we may once more lay our heads in peace upon our pillows. In life you were brave, now you are an exalted spirit. Noble spirit, who sacrificed your life for us, help us still, and look down in kindness upon us all.

Another killer disease was typhus fever, marked by eruption of red spots, cerebral disorders and extreme prostration. Without treatment, victims usually died or were left with permanent brain damage. Typhus claimed two of China's most renowned medical missionaries.

Dr. Gaynor of the Quaker Friends' Mission provided a hospital and refuge in Nanking for officials and relatives from the deposed Manchu dynasty. In 1912 the Quaker physician contracted the disease from patients and died.

Dr. Whitfield Guinness, chief of the CIM hospital at Kaifeng, caught typhus while treating Chinese soldiers during the chaotic year of 1927. He was critically ill when anti-foreign mobs began forming to attack the hospital. Friends carried him to the railway station and shoved his bed into a crowded boxcar for evacuation to Peking. Two nights in the jolting, swaying, unventilated car proved too much. He died shortly after reaching the capital.

Many other missionaries were struck down by diseases they would not have contracted at home. The Scandinavian Alliance Mission lost four workers in the year 1930 alone. One of the four, Mary Anderson, had worked alone in a dangerous bandit-infested area for thirty-four years. But while the bandits respected her, the dread fever did not.

The multi-talented J.O. Fraser—preacher, linguist, musician, and engineer—came to Yunnan Province in 1910 and mastered the difficult Lisu language. Developing his own "Fraser Script," he devoted himself to translating Scripture into the tribal dialect. In 1916 the Lisu began turning from their demon worship to Christ in large numbers. Sixty thousand were baptized in a two year period. The Lisu church continued to grow and became one of the largest tribal Christian bodies in the world. Then in 1937, in the peak of life, the "apostle to the Lisus" came down with malignant malaria while on a trip in the mountains and died.

Shine On, Lottie Moon

Famine, the result of floods and drought, was the greatest destroyer of all. The loss of life in China in the first third of the twentieth century would have been infinitely greater without emergency relief programs funded by Christians in the United States and Britain and administered by missionaries. In 1906 one Christian periodical, *Christian Herald*, raised and forwarded $450,000 in gold. Upwards of two million lives were saved. Many impressed Chinese came to the missionaries, asking, "Tell us about your religion."

Too often the money was not available from home, and missionaries were helpless to prevent mass starvation. They had only their own small salaries for purchasing food. Some hastened their own deaths by going without.

The most celebrated martyr to hunger was Lottie Moon, a household name among Southern Baptists today. Each Christmas Southern Baptist women in thirty-five thousand American churches gather an offering in Miss Moon's name for foreign missions.

Born and reared in Virginia Baptist aristocracy, Lottie Moon was self-willed and rebellious through most of college. Surrender to Christ was not easy. Of her conversion she said, "I went to the service to scoff, and returned to my room to pray all night."

Her younger sister Edmonia went to China first. Charlotte went to Cartersville, Georgia, to teach. There she sought out destitute families for whom she bought clothing from her own purse. One morning the pastor spoke on the text, "Lift up your eyes, and look on the fields; for they are white already to harvest." At the close of the sermon the young teacher walked down the aisle and declared, "I have long known God wanted me in China. I am now ready to go."

She joined Edmonia in 1873 at Tengchow in northern Shantung Province. Edmonia was later compelled to leave China permanently because of poor health. Charlotte gave herself without reserve to her teaching and evangelistic work and to pleading for new workers from the homeland. She sometimes struck sparks in letters to her Board. "It is odd that a million Baptists of the South can furnish only three men for all China," she wrote once. "Odd that with five hundred preachers in the state of Virginia we must rely on a Presbyterian minister to fill a Baptist pulpit [here]. I wonder how these things look in heaven. They certainly look very queer in China—but the Baptists are a great people, as we never tire of saying in our associations and conventions, and possibly our way of doing things is best!"

When more men finally were appointed, the decision was made that women should not share policy making with them. Miss Moon promptly submitted her resignation over the issue and officials backed down.

In 1887 she was preparing to leave for furlough when two Chinese men arrived. They had walked 115 miles to seek a teacher. There was no one else to send, so she went. This was the year when she suggested that Southern Baptist women designate a week of prayer and offerings for missions the week before Christmas. "I wonder how many of us really believe that it is more blessed to give than to receive," she challenged.

She was now facing persecution and hatred for being a foreigner. Frequently she was called "Devil Old Woman." After receiving a death threat, she underlined this sentence in her copy of *Imitation of Christ:* "Thou oughtest so to order thyself in all thy thoughts and actions, as if today thou wert to die."

She survived through most of the Boxer Rebellion before agreeing to evacuate to Japan for a few months. In 1911 came the Revolution, followed by famine. The Chinese churches did all they could. Miss Moon regularly gave a large part of her salary. She wrote to the Southern Baptist Foreign Mission Board again and again. Each time the reply was negative. The Board was heavily in debt and could hardly pay missionary salaries. Not one cent had been budgeted for famine relief.

She wrote a nephew, begging him to speak with his pastor about a local church offering. She told of mothers eager to give their children away and warned that "unless help comes from one to three million must perish from hunger. One penny a day up to the next harvest will save a life. How can we bear to sit down to our bountiful tables and know of such things and not bestir."

The famine worsened. Her appeals to the homeland continued to receive no response. She drew out the last of her savings from a bank in Shanghai to send to relief workers. "I pray that no missionary will ever be as lonely as I have been," she wrote in her bank book.

Fellow missionaries began noticing that she was behaving strangely and appeared befuddled. They sent for a doctor. One look told him she was starving to death. Indeed she had vowed to eat no more so long as her Chinese friends were starving.

Gentle hands gave her nourishment and put her on a ship for home with a missionary nurse escort. Enroute, the ship stopped at Kobe, Japan. There on Christmas Eve night,

1912, she lapsed into unconsciousness. The nurse saw her lips move and bent to catch the name of a Chinese friend. Her frail, thin, almost transparent hands were moving, clasping and unclasping in the Chinese fashion of greeting. She was saying goodbye to old friends. Or was she saying hello? Finally her hands grew still, her breathing stopped, and she was in the heavenly company.

After cremation (required by Japanese law) her ashes were delivered to Virginia and buried under whispering pines. At the head of her grave her family placed a marble stone with the inscription:

LOTTIE MOON 1840–1912

FORTY YEARS A MISSIONARY OF THE SOUTHERN

BAPTIST CONVENTION IN CHINA

"FAITHFUL UNTO DEATH"

Her home church hired an artisan to design the figure of a beautiful woman in graceful, flowing garments, walking through a field of lilies, one hand clasping the Word of God to her heart, the other holding high a blazing torch. On this he inscribed in gold lettering:

GO YE, THEREFORE, AND TEACH ALL NATIONS

Back in China her Christian friends erected their own memorial stone:

A MONUMENT TO BEQUEATH THE LOVE OF

MISS LOTTIE MOON

AN AMERICAN MISSIONARY

THE CHINESE CHURCH REMEMBERS FOREVER

But her greatest memorials have been the numbers of young Christians who have been challenged by her life and the annual week-of-prayer-offerings taken in thirty-five thousand Southern Baptist churches every year for foreign missions. In 1976 the collection amounted to almost thirty million dollars.

Martyrs in War

A new and dangerous period of world history had begun in the thirties. China was at center stage and again the Chinese church and Christian missionaries were caught in the violent vortex. Many heralds of the cross gave their lives.

In 1930 the Shinto zealot Baron Tanaka became prime minister of Japan. Tanaka reasserted *hakko-ichiu* — "the whole world under one roof." Japan's destiny, he vowed, was to bring the world under the rule of Shintoism, as personified by the Japanese emperor, worshiped as the Imperial incarnation of the Sun Goddess.

China was then reeling from epidemics, famines, communist terror and factional wars. Taking advantage of the weakness of Japan's long-time traditional enemy, Baron Tanaka and other war lords seized two northern provinces and demanded that China give independence to five other northern provinces. To buy time in his fight against the Communists, Chiang agreed. Then the Communists scored a dramatic coup. They kidnapped Chiang and forced him to sign a truce.

The Japanese launched an all-out attack in 1937 and by 1939 had conquered most of populous eastern China. American missionaries warned their homeland of Japan's global intention. But the United States refused to intervene and even continued selling war material to Japan which was used to bomb innocent civilians.

During the Boxer uprising and the other anti-foreign rebellions that had followed, it had not been safe for missionaries to be on the street. The situation was now reversed. Foreigners were given safe conduct, for Japan did not want to provoke intervention from abroad.

Undisciplined soldiers looted, raped and killed as they desired. Thousands of Chinese girls were gang raped, then killed for sport. Traveling missionaries sometimes came across trembling Chinese men sitting by the roadside. Their story was always the same: Japanese soldiers had driven them from their homes, keeping behind their wives and daughters. The only safe place was with foreigners. When soldiers were about, mission schools, hospitals and homes were jammed with Chinese women and girls.

Both Japanese and Communists persecuted Christians, although the Japanese were careful about disturbing a church when missionaries were around. Apart from missionaries, Chinese church leaders were fair game. In Shansi Province thirteen Christian leaders were rounded up at one time and shot. In mountainous tribal areas Communist guerrillas continued killing Christians as they had before the Japanese occupation.

Patriotic Chinese Christian leaders refused to kowtow to the invaders. One of the most notable was Dr. Herman Liu, the first Chinese president of the Baptist University of

Shanghai, who held the Ph.D. degree from Columbia University. He headed up refugee work in occupied Shanghai.

The Japanese put him on their blacklist. Many attempts were made on his life. He was sent flowers with notes of warning. The gate leading to his home was dynamited. Poisoned fruit was delivered to his home—he discovered the poison just in time.

Friends begged him to flee, but he refused, declaring, "I will remain as the Lord can use me here. I will not desert."

On the morning of April 8, 1938, Japanese soldiers shot him to death in front of his home, where he was waiting with his young son for a bus to take him to his office. His friends tearfully held his funeral while a crowd of five thousand waited outside the church, unable to get in. On a cross over his grave was inscribed:

HERMAN LIU, CHRISTIAN MARTYR AND PATRIOT.

Still the Chinese church was unbent. One woman told CIM missionaries: "My house has been burned twice and nothing is left. Four of six relatives there are dead, including my brother who was branded with a hot iron. My daughter-in-law was shot before my eyes and my only grandson has died from exposure. But I will not let go of Jesus Christ."

Missionary work in China became more hazardous after Pearl Harbor. In areas already under control hundreds were seized and placed in internment camps. Missionaries in unoccupied areas of China had to evacuate as Japanese armies moved closer. Many got out just in the nick of time by hastily arranged five-hundred-mile flights by the U. S. Air Transport Command over the dangerous Himalayan "Hump" to Burma. There were numerous accidents. In 1944 the CIM alone lost three missionaries in plane crashes.

During this second phase of the war, thousands of Chinese Christians perished or lost all their property. In some regions entire church congregations vanished. Nevertheless, between 1937 and 1945, evangelicals in China increased from six hundred thousand to seven hundred fifty thousand.

The Real John Birch

John Birch is one of the most remarkable martyrs of this period. Unfortunately, his service to China has been all but forgotten in the controversy over the political organization named after him.

Born in India of missionary parents, Birch graduated at the head of his high school, college and seminary classes. He went to Hangchow in 1940 under the World Fundamentalist Baptist Missionary Fellowship and immediately demonstrated an unusual proficiency in learning the language and adapting to the culture. Within a year he was slipping through Japanese occupation lines and preaching in villages where missionaries had not dared to go since the war began.

After Pearl Harbor the Japanese ordered his arrest. But he had fled to Shang-jao in Kiangsi Province from which he and four Chinese preachers sustained national churches for several months. Because Shang-jao was still in "free" territory, he became a conduit for American funds sent to missionaries stranded in Shanghai.

As the war progressed, he became a one-man rescue unit, helping missionaries and Chinese preachers evacuate before advancing Japanese. In one operation called "Harvey's Restaurant" he arranged for sixty missionaries and children to be flown out to safety. In another he rescued Colonel James Doolittle, the most celebrated American flier shot down during the war.

He asked to join the American Military Mission as a chaplain. Instead he was commissioned a captain in intelligence and told he could preach all he wanted. He became a legend. He was the only American who had the complete trust of the Chinese Army and could go anywhere. His commander Colonel Wilfred Smith said later, "John influenced more as a military officer than he did as a missionary."

But he never saw himself as anything but a missionary. "I'm just making tents," he wrote his father. "When the war is over, I'll be ready to welcome the others back."

His announced intention to remain in China after the war may have led to his death. He was sent to convince hold-out pockets of Japanese in north China that the war was over. Communists, under the guise of "agrarian reformers," were then entrenched in north China, awaiting the opportunity to resume their war of conquest. Birch and his team were intercepted by a column of Chinese who were not supposed to be there. "Let us take you to our commander," they offered. Warned by his lieutenant that he might be walking into a trap, Birch decided to go. "It doesn't make any difference what happens to me," he said, "but it is of utmost importance that my country learn now whether these people are friend or foe." His body was found the next day, punctured and slashed by bayonets.

Chinese friends tenderly wrapped his body in white silk. He was buried in a Chinese coffin with full military honors, several missionaries and Chinese pastors looking on. On his stone they placed the inscription:
HE DIED FOR RIGHTEOUSNESS.
Only the barest details of his death were released to his family by the State Department. In the amoral game of diplomacy Communists were never blamed. There were at the time Red sympathizers ensconced in high places in the United States government. It was also later disclosed that the decisive United States atomic bombing mission had been carried out with the aid of essential weather bulletins from Mao Tse-tung's Communists in north China.

Why was John Birch killed? The best speculation is that the Chinese Reds did not want him around as a missionary after the war.

Martyrs of Red China

The West was blind to the Red tide washing across China. But the old China hands who returned to their mission posts soon saw the handwriting on the wall. The Soviets had declared war on Japan in the closing days of the war—to grab Manchuria, some thought. The Chinese Marxists had helped the Americans defeat the Japanese in China and gained valuable experience in guerrilla warfare. All during the war they had been subverting and plotting to take over the government.

Meanwhile, the opportunities for evangelism seemed never greater. Most churches had either held their own or actually grown during the years of war and Japanese occupation. Missionaries and national church leaders began reopening hospitals and schools and launching evangelistic crusades.

The euphoria was short-lived as Communist propagandists began stirring up old hatreds against Americans. Communist armies launched new attacks. Banditry intensified, making travel as dangerous as ever.

In December, 1947, Evangelical Covenant Church missionaries at Hankow became concerned about their colleagues in Kingchow which was in imminent danger of being taken by the Communists. On January 7 Dr. Alexis Berg, Esther Nordlund and Martha Anderson left by transport truck to consult with their friends. Some of the passengers, worried about a bandit attack, had hired an armed guard.

About two in the afternoon as they were traveling through deserted hilly country, a shot rang out. The driver stopped immediately and one of the guards fired a shot to scare off any small group. More shouts and more firing— then about sixty armed men appeared. The guard fled.

The bandits advanced on the passengers and ordered them to get off the truck and to give up their valuables. The missionaries were also forced to give up their coats and shoes. Dr. Berg asked if he might keep his passport. At that one bandit cursed and slapped his face. The doctor handed the passport over. A passing bicyclist was stopped. When he hesitated to give anything up, the bandits shot him dead.

They then left by scrambling up a nearby hill. Part way up, four turned around and returned.

"Shall we kill these foreigners?" the leader asked. Then looking at Dr. Berg, he demanded, "Are you Americans?" When Dr. Berg did not reply, the bandit snarled, "Americans are the worst of all. They have done China much harm." Then he shot Dr. Berg through the head.

When the shot was fired, Miss Anderson burst into sobs. The bandit leader responded, "She must be a relative of his," and immediately shot her also. By this time some of the passengers were kneeling, pleading with the bandits to stop killing. The four consulted briefly among themselves, then turned toward Miss Nordlund. "Yes, you may kill me, too," she said. Then she was shot. None of the other passengers were killed.

The killers left. But the frightened passengers insisted that the driver take them on and leave the bodies by the roadside. The bodies were later recovered and taken to Kingchow. The missionaries there sorrowfully dressed the bodies and placed them in coffins. They were taken back to Hankow for a final service and buried in the International Cemetery among the graves of scores of other departed missionaries who had given their all for Christ in China.

The Communist armies kept advancing. By 1949 the conquest was all but complete. There was much hand wringing and finger pointing in the West. It was said "fuzzy" liberals and hidden Communists in the United States government had blinded the Americans until it was too late to rescue Chiang. There was less quibbling over other factors, such as corruption in the Nationalist government, runaway inflation and student unrest. Later even the liberals had to concede they had been duped while the Communists had followed their game plan to victory.

The Communists sought to destroy the old Confucius order of family loyalty and morality and level the social system. Millions were killed for nothing more than owning property and paying respect to parents. How many Christians died in the secret genocidal purges will never be known.

Not wanting to inflame world opinion, the new "People's Republic" pursued a more wily strategy against Christianity. First they got rid of most of the missionaries, not by execution but by cutting ties between East and West. They charged that Christianity as it existed was too closely tied to western imperialism and colonialism. Missionaries were suddenly without jobs, property and financial support. For example, the CIM, still the largest mission, had served in China eighty-five years. By 1953 it did not have a single worker in China nor a piece of furniture to call its own. The schools, hospitals and all properties of the CIM and other foreign missions were confiscated.

Taking a lesson from history, the CIM changed its name to Overseas Missionary Fellowship, began accepting Asian workers on a par with Westerners, established headquarters in Singapore, and began work in East Asian countries.

By 1950 only a scattering of missionaries remained in China. Some had welcomed communism as a partner to Christianity and were outright propagandists for the regime. The others were holdouts, determined to stay until they were forcibly removed, imprisoned or killed. Along with the Protestants were not a few Catholic diehards who died in prison.

The Communists had a step-by-step plan for dealing with the immovables: false accusations, planting of evidence, arrest, showcase trial, imprisonment, interrogations and torture until the victim signed a confession, then if life remained, release of the shattered mind and body to authorities in Hongkong.

Many faithful evangelists and pastors were arrested, never to be heard from again. One was Pastor Wang Shih-kuang, who was conducting a morning service at Ch'in-hsien in northwest China when Communists entered. The venerable preacher had apparently been expecting arrest. Raising his hand, he said simply, "This is God's service. Kindly remain at the back until we have finished." The Communists complied.

When the service was over and the soldiers came forward, Pastor Wang had only one last request. "Permit me to change clothes first." They understood. When a Chinese believes death is upon him, he wants to be dressed in his best garments. A few minutes later Pastor Wang reappeared, properly dressed, for his trip to jail. His fate was never known. The bodies of those who died in prison were usually released with the cause of death cited as disease, accident or suicide.

Indomitable Bill Wallace

The diabolical brutality of twisted Marxist minds is no better illustrated than in the treatment given a Baptist bachelor surgeon from Knoxville, Tennessee.

The quiet and devout Wallace joined the staff of Stout Memorial Hospital in Wuchow in 1935. A veteran missionary on board ship had told him that during the first half century of Protestant work in China, only one missionary had reached age forty. Wallace surpassed that by only three years. He steadfastly refused all marriage prospects. One hopeful said after a short acquaintance, "Marriage to Bill would be bigamy. He's married to his work."

The first incident occurred when he returned from language school to find the other missionaries had departed in fear of an advancing bandit army. He simply pulled the Chinese staff together and went to work. An American ship anchored in the nearby river. The captain sent an officer to remind the young surgeon that he could not be responsible for his safety even if he stayed overnight. "Tell your captain," Wallace said, "that he was not responsible for my coming here in the first place and he does not need to be responsible for my staying here."

The Japanese could not bomb him out during their war with China. He stubbornly remained during World War II until Wuchow officials decided the city must be evacuated.

Then he put the hospital on water by transferring staff and equipment to a barge. When enemy planes roared overhead, he had the tugboat captain pull the floating hospital into one of the many large caves along the riverbank.

After VJ Day he set up shop again in the old building at Wuchow and for four years operated in peace. Then the Communists took over. One by one his missionary colleagues had to leave. Finally only he and nurse Everly Hayes remained. Local Communists tried to impose a crippling tax. Wallace said he could not believe the new People's Republic would so handicap an institution of mercy. Local citizens rose up and demanded exemption. It was granted.

The Korean War was on and Communists in Wuchow mounted a "hate America" campaign. But the only "American dogs" and "imperialist wolves" remaining in the city were Dr. Wallace and Nurse Hayes, and Wallace was renowned as the finest surgeon in south China. The propaganda campaign fizzled.

One pre-dawn morning more than twenty Communist soldiers came to the hospital gate claiming to have a sick man. When the gate was opened, they rushed to the doctor's house. "We hide nothing," Wallace protested. "Our only work is healing the suffering and sick in the name of Jesus Christ."

A planted pistol was excuse enough to arrest and jail the doctor for espionage. From his cell Wallace preached to peasants brave enough to come within hearing.

At a mock trial his prosecutors waved a paper they said was his signed confession. What they had gotten from Wallace was only a brief, factual biographical summary. After he had signed it, they had typed in the confession. Citizen accusers were asked to come forward. To the prosecutor's embarrassment, no one moved. No matter. At a prearranged signal, hired stooges stood to deliver false testimony.

The missionary doctor was convicted, sentenced to prison, then marched through the streets to the main prison. His hands were tied and he wore a placard bearing obscene charges. Along the way he was shoved by a guard, and he fell badly hurting his hand.

The next days were a nightmare of almost hourly interrogations accompanied by charges of medical incompetence, murdering and maiming Chinese, performing obscene operations, and immoral conduct with nurses. Once he was forced to pose holding a radio aerial for a picture to prove the spy conviction.

Near the end of one brutal day in February, 1951, one of the Catholic missionaries asked from a nearby cell how he was holding out. "Trusting in the Lord," came the weak reply. His prison mates often heard him crying out in agony. It was also learned later that he wrote short Scripture verses, affirmations of faith, and denials of guilt on pieces of paper which he stuck on his cell walls and repeated to prepare for the next grilling.

The questioning continued, the pressure unrelenting. He became delirious and lapsed into crying spells.

Perhaps in fear of punishment for not succeeding, his guards used long poles to jab him into unconsciousness. The next morning they ran along the cellblock yelling, "The doctor has hung himself." They showed the Catholic priests where he was hanging from a beam and asked them to sign a statement attesting to his suicide. They would only state that they found him hanging.

Nurse Hayes and the Chinese hospital staff, who had been held under house arrest, were asked to claim his body. Miss Hayes noticed that his eyes were not bulging nor his tongue swollen, the usual features which would indicate hanging. But his upper body was a mass of bruises.

These devoted friends took his body to a cemetery. The Communists permitted no service and required the mourners to leave immediately after his body was lowered into the grave. But the Chinese could not be cowed. Defying the Communists, they returned and erected a shaft over his grave pointing heavenward. On the shaft they inscribed the Scripture which they felt described the motivation of his life:

"FOR TO ME TO LIVE IS CHRIST"

When Everly Hayes was released and returned home to tell the story, the head of the Southern Baptist Foreign Mission Board commented: "The Communists thought they were rid of him; instead they immortalized him." So true. *Bill Wallace of China*, by Jesse Fletcher (Broadman Press), had multiple printings. A film was made. Scores of young men and women committed their lives to missionary service. Said a Christian and Missionary Alliance missionary friend, "There have been and there will be many martyrs, but few can so glorify Him in death as Bill did."

The Fiery Trials of Chinese Believers

Chinese Christians and church leaders having close connections to President Chiang's Nationalist government were among the first targets of a Communist purge. Some were killed. Others managed to flee with Chiang's staunchest supporters to Taiwan.

One who escaped was Dr. Chen Wei-ping, who had been a Methodist pastor for over fifty years. In 1900 he was pastor of the First Methodist Church of Peking when the Boxers spilled their rivers of blood across north China. His church and home were burned, but he and his wife and young child escaped. His parents and brother and sister did not. Later Dr. Chen had been told the gruesome story of his family's murder. He had borne the memory for almost fifty years. Now, with the Communist takeover, he too was willing to die for Christ. But leaders of the defeated government begged, "Come with us. We need you more." He went to Taiwan and became Chief of Chaplains in the Nationalist Army. Later he became pastor of the Shih Ling Church which President and Madame Chiang regularly attended.

Many thousands of Christians stayed behind, telling departing missionaries and fleeing Chinese friends, "We ask only that you pray for us as we remain to face the storm."

The storm broke on Catholics more suddenly than Protestants. The Reds tried to induce the Catholic clergy to set up an independent Chinese Patriotic Church but met stiff resistance. A crackdown resulted, and hundreds of priests were imprisoned. Before 1952 about one hundred Chinese clergy died in jail. In 1952 over two hundred perished. By 1954 an additional four to five hundred priests had joined these martyrs. Not until 1958 was the puppet church established, and then it was denounced by the Pope. Most of the remaining opponents of the new church were put in prison.

The Marxist regime had more success with Chinese Protestants. In 1950 Chou En-lai persuaded a few leaders to draft "the Christian Manifesto," affirming loyalty to the government and opposition to "imperialism, feudalism, and bureaucratic capitalism." Chinese "volunteers" were then fighting in Korea. The anti-foreign spirit for past western ag-

gressions remained strong. With support from liberal churchmen, some trained in liberal American seminaries, three
hundred thousand Chinese Protestants signed the Manifesto.

The next tactic was the "Resist-America, Aid-Korea,
Three-Self-Reform Movement" (self-support, self-government,
and self-propagation), followed by the organization of a
unified Chinese Christian Church with officers from Three-
Self Committees. All denominational structures were dismantled. Services were allowed only in authorized church
buildings at announced hours with a government monitor
present. By 1958 only a dozen of two hundred churches in
Shanghai were open; in Peking only four of sixty-five still
held services.

From the beginning of the Red takeover there had been
Christian resistance. In Manchuria a Christian leader protested indiscriminate killing. He was dragged into a People's
Court and accused of numerous crimes against "the people."
The judges ordered spectators to march by him, each to hit
him with a club until he was beaten to death. But the people
refused, declaring, "He's a good man."

Changing tactics, the judges promised that if he renounced Jesus he would be set free. "Which do you choose—
Jesus Christ or Communism?" they demanded.

"Jesus! Jesus! Jesus!" he shouted back.

Then they took him to the river bank for execution.
Along the way he sang, "Jesus Loves Me" and the Twenty-
third Psalm set to Chinese music. He asked to pray, and
they granted him permission to kneel briefly. When he stood
up, he was shot in the back. But instead of falling on his face
to grovel in the dust as victims usually do, he fell backwards, as if he were falling into the arms of Jesus. The entire
community was reportedly stirred by his testimony.

In Shansi Province, scene of bloody Boxer massacres,
many evangelists and pastors were martyred. In one instance, a preacher was tortured, then told he could go but
dare not preach again.

"No, I cannot do that," he replied. "I cannot obey you."

Furious, the official shouted, "Then you must die, you
miserable lout."

"I am not the one who is poor and miserable," the
preacher replied calmly, and he began preaching to the man.
He was shot without further delay.

There was widespread resistance to joining the puppet
National Christian Church. This resistance was concentrated

in the communal Jesus Family and the Little Flock house churches. Neither had direct connections with missionaries. Thousands of Chinese participants in the house churches of these groups were killed or imprisoned. Best known in the West for his books was Watchman Nee, leader of the Little Flock. He was imprisoned in 1952 and lived until June, 1972.

A deceitful calm came in 1957 when many political prisoners were released and Mao Tse-tung proclaimed as state policy, "Let all flowers bloom and all schools of thought contend." This was taken as an invitation to speak up. Some church leaders charged the Three-Self Movement with taking away their political rights. One churchman called the lack of personal freedom under the government "intolerable." The veteran evangelist Chia Yu-ming told theological students that the "mark of the beast" as revealed in Revelation was membership in the Communist Party. Another faculty member at this seminary displayed a poem that challenged atheism:

> I say, God is; you say No;
> Let's see who will suffer woe.
> You say, No God; I say you're wrong;
> We'll see who sings Salvation's Song.

The bloom faded. Most of those who had been released from prison when the deceitful invitation was announced were rounded up and put back in jail. One of these was Henry H. Lin, who had previously been arrested in 1957. Before that time he had been president of the Baptist University of Shanghai, succeeding Herman Liu, a martyr to the Japanese. President Lin languished less than two years in prison. According to a report, he was given a higher release when he died in a jail near Nanking early in 1960.

Too late the critics learned they had been tricked. The Communists now knew who the resisters were and began hauling them into court for crimes against the state.

In one city fifty-two pastors, evangelists and leading laymen were put on trial and pressured to make confessions. During the procedure, Communist supporters were invited to display their loyalty by slapping, pulling the hair and spitting on the accused. The inquisition continued for seven days and the last two nights. On September 7, 1958, one pastor collapsed and died. He was rolled up in a reed mat and dumped in a grave before his widow knew he was dead. When she asked permission to move the body to their home burial ground, the Communists jeered, "You Christians are going to heaven. Why do you worry about burial?" As a result of this pastor's death, seventeen of his co-defendants denounced Communist injustice and were immediately sentenced to long terms of hard labor under inhuman conditions.

Astute China observers believe that similar trials occurred all over China, leading to imprisonment for thousands of Christian leaders. Communist secrecy insures that the records will never be publicized.

But thousands more were absorbed into the Communist plan with little murmur. They came largely from the leadership of denominations included in the national union church (Methodists, United Church of Christ or Congregationalists, Presbyterians, and others). They had been conditioned for the Communist appeal by liberal theology professors who themselves were largely trained in the United States.

Protestant liberalism, deemphasizing and demythologizing miracles and biblical authority, introduced the powerful but crippling secularism into Chinese Christianity. Yale's late distinguished Professor in Missions and Oriental History, Kenneth S. Latourette, termed "the secularizing movements issuing from alleged Christendom and the essence of the Christian Gospel as seen in the apparent weakness of the incarnation and the cross" as the most important factor in the reverse suffered by Christianity in Communist China. More important than the association of China missions with western imperialism, Latourette said.

The Chinese Church Refuses to Die

What of Christianity today behind the bamboo curtain?

In recent years hard news of the state of Christianity in China has been scarce. There were a million baptized Protestants and around three million Catholics at the time of the Communist takeover. Journalists and other visitors report seeing only a few showcase churches still open and these are sparsely attended. Unauthorized meetings of three or more persons are illegal. The "president" of the Nanking Theological Seminary admitted in 1977 that he had had no students in five years.

Relatives outside the bamboo curtain occasionally get news of their loved ones. Franklin Liu, for example, a Baptist educator in Hongkong and the son of martyred Herman Liu, heard that his mother remained under house arrest in Pe-king, his brother was in a labor camp in Manchuria, and his sister was allowed to teach mathematics in Shanghai. That news was several years ago and their fate is now unknown.

But letters to the Far Eastern Broadcasting Company in Manila, stories from refugees trickling into Hongkong, and reports from Chinese allowed to visit relatives inside China suggest that cell churches are thriving in some areas. Among a population of thirty thousand in an area near the coast, three thousand believers are said to be meeting in small house churches. But sources for this report also say that plundering Red Guards during the height of the Cultural Revolution destroyed almost all Bibles in the district.

David Adeney, dean of OMF's Discipleship Training Centre in Singapore and a veteran China watcher, tells in *Christianity Today* (18 November 1977) of a Hongkong resi-dent who visited his relatives and found almost all of them still professing Christians. Relatives told him many had been baptized in 1976 and numbers of young people were seeking Christ. These were being warned that the cost of com-mitment could be great. The times and places of house church meetings were constantly being changed to avoid a crackdown. Nevertheless, leaders continue to be arrested and sent to labor camps. At one meeting worshipers "strongly sensed the presence of the Spirit of God and the love of Christ." At the conclusion of the meeting, five visitors stood and announced they had been sent to make arrests. Now they too wanted to believe. They were then instructed to kneel and confess their sins and receive salvation in Christ.

Adeney tells of another Chinese Christian who came to Hongkong with his five-year-old daughter to visit his father. He had left his wife behind in an area where Christians feared to confess their faith. He recalled that he and his wife sometimes prayed together in bed, but had been afraid to tell their child for fear she would tell in kindergarten and bring trouble upon them.

Adeney further reports news of a powerful revival in one section of China. In this area five hundred Christian leaders associated with Watchman Nee were arrested. The news-bearer said that five of eleven who came from his village were sent to a remote spot from which only one returned. Three died of extreme cold and hard labor. One was shot be-cause of his continued witness. But in 1976 revival swept the area and four to five thousand were baptized in secluded places.

Has a New Era Begun?

The most astounding news came in late 1978 when President Jimmy Carter and Chinese Vice Premier Teng Hsiao-p'ing announced establishment of diplomatic relations between their two countries. Immediately afterwards, wall posters appeared in major Chinese cities calling for more democracy and friendship to the West. The Chinese government began signing contracts with American corporations for tourist hotels, airline service, and technological assistance. Train car loads of Coca Cola were shipped from Hongkong to major Chinese cities for Chinese New Year celebrations.

The first wave of American tourists visiting large Chinese cities in 1979 reported almost no sign of Christianity. One small group did locate a Protestant worship service in downtown Peiping and boosted the crowd of worshipers to seventeen. Chinese scholars and journalists touring the United States told readers back home that religion was very important to westerners.

What is the future for Christianity in earth's most populous nation (now almost a billion) where more martyr blood has undoubtedly been shed than anywhere else in modern times? If the rapprochement between China and the West continues and blossoms, millions of Chinese will be exposed to Christianity in the 1980's and beyond by tourists visiting China and student exchange programs in both countries. How deep this will penetrate and how far the communist government of China will allow the gospel to spread are matters of prayer concern for Christians.

Perhaps the best answer can be found on a charred page from the New Testament, recovered by a Chinese Christian after Red Guards had burned his Bible. Standing out were these words: "Upon this rock I will build my church; and the gates of hell shall not prevail against it."

MARTYRS OF
JAPAN AND KOREA

CHINA

MANCHURIA

U.S.S.R.

HOKKAIDO

SEA

OF

JAPAN

Pyongyang

KOREA

Seoul

J A P A N

HONSHU

Tokyo

SHIKOKU

KYUSHU

RYUKYU ISLANDS

PACIFIC OCEAN

"LET NO CHRISTIAN COME":
Manchuria and Japan

Conflict between Christianity and the national Shinto religion was inevitable in Japan and its occupied territories. The Japanese emperor was regarded as the divine incarnation of the Sun Goddess. Shinto tradition said she was born from the right eye of the male creator and was the grandmother of the first emperor. Each successive emperor had been her living incarnation.

Shintoism was weak when the first Christian missionaries, Roman Catholics, arrived in the sixteenth century. For a while they met with enormous success. They baptized one hundred fifty thousand converts in thirty years and had almost made Japan into a papal state with a full-blown inquisition when Shinto devotees of the Sun Goddess raised an army and struck back. In 1638 the Shintoists massacred thirty-seven thousand Catholics in one city.

Throughout the Empire this inscription was posted: "So long as the sun shall warm the earth, let no Christian be so bold as to come to Japan; and let all know that the King of Spain himself, or the Christian's God, or the Great God of all, if he violate this command shall pay for it with his head." For the next two hundred fifty years special police squads hunted down suspected Christians and tested their loyalty to the emperor by demanding that they step on a crucifix. Those who refused paid a dire price. Some were burned to death, others buried alive.

A trade treaty with the United States opened the door for Protestant missionaries in 1859. Protestant success brought renewed Shinto reactions. Between 1868 and 1873 some two thousand Christians died in prison. Then in a turnabout, evangelical Christianity flowered again under the leadership of keen Japanese believers. By 1884 many Japanese leaders, having viewed the changed lives of national Christians and social and industrial advance in "Christian" America, were suggesting that Japan be declared a Christian nation.

Again there was a resurgence and counterattack from Shintoism. The first persecutions of the twentieth century occurred in occupied Korea and Manchuria.

The Manchurian Martyrs

The great Manchu dynasty that ruled China for so long had come from Manchuria. In 1905 the province was divided between Russia and Japan, Japan occupying the southern half.

Presbyterian missionaries had won thousands of Manchurians to Christ. There was a strong network of churches when the Japanese took control and ordered reverence and submission to the emperor as the incarnation of the Sun Goddess. The Christians of Manchuria were willing to obey civil authority, but they would not reverence the emperor as a deity. When this became known, Japanese soldiers marched on Christian villages, burning homes and massacring hundreds.

Dr. S.H. Martin, a Canadian Presbyterian doctor, interviewed survivors from the Manchurian village of Norabawie and filed this report to his mission board in Toronto:

> At daybreak . . . Japanese infantry surrounded the main Christian village, and starting at the head of the valley, burned immense stacks of unthreshed millet, barley and straw, and then ordered the people to vacate their homes.
>
> As each son and father stepped forth he was shot, and though perhaps not dead, heaps of burning straw were placed over them. If they struggled to escape the flames, they were bayoneted. The Japanese soldiers then set fire to the houses. . . .
>
> I have names of, and accurate reports of, thirty-two villages where fire and willful murder were used — in one village the dead numbering 145. I saw the ruins of a house which was burned with women and children inside. At Sonoyung four men were stood up near an open grave and shot. . . .

Later Manchurian Martyrs

Small shrines were required to be installed in church buildings. Evangelist Kim, a Presbyterian minister steadfastly
preached that no one could have two Masters—he must
choose between the emperor or Christ. He was arrested, tortured and released seven times. The eighth time he was
given the famous "water cure." While he was stretched out
on a bench with his head hanging back, water was poured
from a kettle down his nostrils. Near strangling and half insane, he finally consented to sign a paper signifying his approval of Shinto shrine worship. After his release, he was
racked with remorse. He went to Presbyterian missionary
Bruce Hunt and confessed that he had lied.

"What will you do now?" the missionary asked.

"I must write back to the police station and say that I
do not approve of shrine worship. I expect they will arrest
me again."

This time, according to the later recollection of Presbyterian missionary John Young, Kim was kept in a cramped
cell until he was too weak to stand. Believing he was about
to die, the police called a friend to get him. The friend took
him to the home of Dr. and Mrs. Roy Byram, missionaries of
the Independent Board for Presbyterian Foreign Missions. He
regained his strength and began preaching again. His ninth
incarceration was the last. He died in prison in 1943.

Another courageous Manchurian Christian was Miss An,
a Sunday school teacher. When a close friend was arrested in
the spring of 1940, Miss An went to the police station hoping to secure her friend's release. Instead she was questioned
about her loyalty to the emperor and imprisoned. By November she was critically ill. She was released and taken to the
mission dispensary, jaundiced and little more than skin and
bones. A few days later, as Dr. Byram was entering her room,
she suddenly rose up and declared, "I go into the presence of
my Father." Then she fell back on her bed and died.

Manchurian martyr Mr Ni, Young relates, was a country
evangelist and worker in secret schools where believers were
educating their children free from Shinto influence. He too
was arrested, and steadfastly refusing to compromise, later
died in prison.

Japanese Militarists Prepare for War

Christians in Japan were prominent in business and society.
Rabid Shintoists worked to undermine moderates in govern-

ment who had not been anxious to enforce the rule of emperor worship. In 1929 the Shintoist champion, Baron Tanaka, became prime minister. He revived the ancient Shinto crusade to bring the "whole world under the Shinto roof." The fanatic militarists began planning for war.

Japanese educators were ordered to state that participation in the ceremonies was tacit acknowledgment that the emperor was Supreme Lord, and that "no god should be reverenced above the emperor." The educators asked for time to apply persuasion. They believed that missionaries and national church leaders would now cooperate on the basis that all religions are good.

The Liberal Compromise

At this time liberal theological currents from the West were flowing into Japan's seminaries. Leading Japanese pastors were repeating the catchwords of prominent western theologians: the Bible is not infallible; Jesus was only a great teacher of ethics; the sum of Christianity is the Sermon on the Mount; Christians should respect and draw from the teachings of other great religions. From these positions, it was an easy step to accede to the militarists' demands.

The conservative evangelical minority refused to compromise. They quietly ignored the militant promotion of Shintoism and prayed that police would not interfere with the education of their children.

Two Brothers Who Refused to Bow

Then in 1933 two brothers, eleven and twelve years old, in Ogaki, Japan, refused to accompany their class on a trip to the Grand Shrine of Ise to worship the Sun Goddess. The boys were backed up by their parents and members of the Mino Mission Church. Mobs threatened to destroy the church. Patriotic rallies were held in pagan temples, and posters were displayed throughout the area, declaring: "Stand against the Mino Mission" and "Protect the Structure of Japan." The leading national newspaper headlined:

THE MINO MISSION REFUSES TO RECOGNIZE ANY
OTHER GOD THAN THE GOD OF THE BIBLE.

The boys were not harmed, but pressure increased on Christian schools. In one school police ordered that a stained glass picture of Christ be covered with a curtain while a Shinto pledge of reverence was read before a picture of the emperor.

Parts of the Bible and hymns speaking of Christ as Supreme Lord were banned from churches. Small shrines were even installed in church buildings. Ministers who refused to cooperate were jailed. Dissident church organizations were dissolved.

Prelude to Pearl Harbor

In October, 1941, while America continued to sleep, Dr. and Mrs. Roy Byram and another missionary were arrested by the Japanese. The charges: propagating a religion opposed to State Shintoism and holding that Jehovah God and not the Sun Goddess, as incarnated in the emperor, was the supreme God and Savior. In the trial held before Japanese judges and military officers, the missionaries were questioned about their beliefs regarding the return of Christ. The central question was: "Do you teach that divine emperors of the divine Rising Sun nation will also have to recognize Christ as Lord of all at His return?" The missionaries were uncompromising. The judges finally decided to defer judgment for two years. When this verdict was announced, spectators in the courtroom began saying, *"Choi upso, choi upso,"* meaning, "There is no crime. They are not declared guilty."

On December fifth the three missionaries were taken before the provincial governor and lectured sternly. "All the world will soon know that the Sun Goddess is the God of Japan," he told them. Thirty-six hours later Japanese warplanes bombed Pearl Harbor, touching off World War II.

The "Schizophrenic" Martyr

Before 1941 the Shinto government had not taken direct action against western missionaries in Japan. This policy changed a few months before Pearl Harbor. In October, 1941, two Irish Plymouth Brethren workers, R.G. Wright and John Hewitt, were arrested. Wright was put in a cell with street thieves and given food so dirty he could not eat it. Hewitt was in a separate cell, but later in the day Wright heard him preaching to his cellmates.

They were permitted to go home that night with the promise to return early the next morning for questioning. For the next five days they were grilled by relays of interrogators about their thoughts on the deity of the emperor, Christians bowing before shrines, spirits dwelling in shrines, and the Bible's teachings about such Shinto ideas. Then they were released.

Wright was subsequently put on board a ship supposedly

bound for the United States. The ship was at sea when the
Japanese attacked Pearl Harbor. With America and Japan
now officially at war, the captain turned back to Yokohama.
Fortunately, police records on Wright were not available in
the Yokohama district. He was interned with other missionaries and repatriated in 1942.

Hewitt did not fare so well. He was locked in Sugama
Prison on December 8, the same prison where the victorious
Allies would later incarcerate Japanese war criminals. About
January 15 he was transferred to Tokyo's insane asylum
without notification to his Japanese Christian friends.

Finally his Buddhist neighbor was notified to make prep-
arations for his funeral. A child overheard and got a message
to two women missionaries who had not been interned.
They and a third woman found Hewitt lying on the floor in
a pauper ward. Weak and emaciated, he could only whisper,
"Praise the Lord! " The women later learned that the police
had inquired if foreigners had come to see Hewitt. The or-
derly had said no. The women returned and took turns
spending time with him. That night he died. After a Buddhist funeral was held, the women wangled permission from
the police for a Christian funeral conducted by one of the interned missionaries.

After the war Wright was able to get the medical report
on his martyred friend. It said that Hewitt was schizophrenic
but not dangerous, and that he was heard singing hymns under his blanket. Also found with his records was a tract on
which Hewitt had scrawled Ephesians 5:11,12: "Have no fellowship with the unfruitful works of darkness, but rather
reprove them. For it is a shame even to speak of those things
which are done of them in secret."

The Sufferings of Japanese Pastors During World War II

Hewitt was the only Protestant missionary to die in Japan
during the war. That minority of Japanese Christians who
refused to bow at the shrines and acknowledge the emperor
as supreme Lord fared much worse than the interned missionaries. They were branded traitors for honoring the "religion
of the enemy." Scores of unyielding pastors were jailed and
questioned mercilessly by teams of interrogators.

The largest mass arrest occurred on July 26, 1942, when
forty-two Pentecostal pastors were rounded up by civil police. They were charged with teaching that when Jesus re-

turned, every knee would bow to Him. The police correctly assumed this meant the emperor would have to bow to Christ as his superior.

Toyozo Abe, the general affairs chairman of the group, refused to sign an incriminating statement and was imprisoned for 288 days. During this time he saw the sun only twenty minutes. He was not put on trial until July, 1944, when he was tried with twelve other leading pastors. He and five of the twelve were sentenced to three years in prison and the others given lesser terms. In other proceedings over fifty additional Pentecostal preachers were given long prison terms. Two of these died in jail, two succumbed after release, and several others emerged with health broken by torture and long confinement.

Thankfully the war ended in 1945, preventing any more Japanese Christian martyrdoms.

Japan After the War

General Douglas MacArthur, Supreme Commander for the Allied Powers, saw clearly the danger in racist Shintoism. One of his first acts was to declare separation of church and state "to prevent misuse of religion for political ends, and to put all religions, faiths and creeds upon exactly the same legal basis." MacArthur also denounced "the doctrine that the emperor of Japan is superior to the heads of other states because of ancestry, descent or special origin," or that the Japanese people and the islands of Japan were superior to other peoples and lands for the same reasons. Shinto teaching was excised from textbooks.

The humiliation of defeat and their emperor's admission that he was not divine threw the Japanese people into mental confusion. "The problem now is a theological one," MacArthur declared. He proposed that America send ten million Japanese Bibles and ten thousand missionaries to meet the challenge. American church bodies did send two thousand missionaries along with great quantities of reconstruction aid.

Prominent members of the emperor's household even asked for Bible instruction from missionaries. The Federal Council of Churches in New York was asked to recommend a woman Bible teacher for the crown prince. The Council sent one who did not believe the biblical doctrine of redemption.

Sparked by the preaching of Jake DeShazer, an American serviceman who had been captured and ill-treated in Japanese prisons during the war, and by the conversion of Mitsuo Fuchida who had led the attack on Pearl Harbor, thousands of Japanese professed Christianity. But the uptrend in conversions continued only five years, then began steadily dropping. Japanese Christians today number less than one percent of the population.

In more recent years Communists and other radicals have made political gains while Christian influence has been slipping. There may yet be another age of martyrdom in this ancient stronghold of pagan Shintoism.

THE LAND OF MORNING CALM:
Korea

A Korean proverb says: "He that is born in the fire will not faint in the sun." Perhaps this explains why Indiana-sized South Korea with 34 million people is today the most Christianized nation in Asia and the Christians of Korea are among the most loyal, devoted followers of Christ in the world. Prayer meetings are routinely held at four and five o'clock before the people go to their work. It is not unusual for one third of a congregation to spend Sunday afternoon evangelizing their neighbors. Nor is it extraordinary for Korean Christians to offer up their most precious possessions sacrificially. One farmer who had nothing else gave his ox, and returned home to pull his plow himself.

Korea, like other Asian nations, is steeped in antiquity. Korean legend carries back to 4300 B.C. The earliest recorded date is 1122 B.C., when five thousand Orientals rebelled against Chinese rule. They fled to the mountainous peninsula that is now Korea and organized the new state of "Morning Calm." For the next three thousand years the "Hermit Nation," as it was called, was a punching bag for China, Mongolia, and Japan. Not until 1876 did Korea emerge from isolation when Japan forced a trade treaty on it. Treaties with other nations followed, and by 1900 all of Korea's ports were open to western commerce.

There can be no accurate accounting of Korean Christian martyrdom in the twentieth century. Thousands died during the long Japanese occupation from 1910 to 1945. Many more were undoubtedly murdered by Communists in North Korea after the country was divided at the close of World War II. And at least five hundred pastors were killed during the savage Korean War of the early 1950's.

A "Missionary Manual"

In the early nineteenth century Korean diplomats at Peking had met missionaries and brought back the Catholic faith to Korea. In 1835 Catholic missionaries began secretly entering the country. The new faith spread rapidly despite frequent persecutions led by Buddhist priests. In 1846 the Korean Catholic hierarchy and ten thousand communicants were savagely put to death by bitter anti-foreign religionists. A great fear spread across the land. Koreans did not dare even whisper the names Jesus or Mary.

The signing of a trade treaty between Korea and the United States in 1882 opened the door for Protestants. The first missionaries were medical doctors, appointed by the Northern Presbyterian Board. Evangelists and educators followed quickly after.

The pioneer missionaries adopted in 1890 a developmental policy suggested by Dr. John L. Nevius, a visiting missionary from China. The Nevius method, far advanced for that day, called for complete self-support and control by the national church. Churches were to be started in homes and led by tradesmen pastors. Nationals were to build whatever church buildings they could afford. Missionaries were to train Korean leaders and medical specialists at the behest of the church. The Korean evangelical church was thus guaranteed a solid footing.

By 1907 Korea was the missionary marvel of that time with over one thousand self-supporting Presbyterian churches serving an evangelical community of one hundred twenty thousand. That year an evangelical revival of Pentecostal proportions swept across Korea. Church after church witnessed mass prayer meetings, confessions by backsliders and conversions of hardened sinners. Thousands were empowered by the Spirit to face a coming trial by fire unmatched even by the Boxer scourge in China.

Shinto "Evangelism"

In 1910 Japan forcibly annexed the country as a colony and set out to convert the Koreans to Shintoism. The Koreans rebuffed the Shinto missionaries and continued turning to Christianity in great numbers. The Japanese responded by arresting the most prominent Korean Christians on a charge of conspiring to murder the colonial governor. Three were tortured to death. Nine were exiled without opportunity to protest in court. Trials were held for 123 others on June 28, 1911, in the district court of Seoul. Some of these had signed confessions under torture which they later repudiated. None were permitted to produce witnesses who could have testified to their innocence. On September 28, 106 of the accused were sentenced to prison terms of five to ten years.

Documented evidence of the Japanese plot was provided western nations by Presbyterian missionaries. Smarting from heavy foreign criticism, the Japanese released all of the prisoners except six. They offered to let these go if the American Presbyterian Church would confess its guilt and beg the Japanese government for clemency. The Presbyterians flatly refused. Embarrassed before the world, the Japanese released the remaining prisoners in 1915 under the pretense of Imperial clemency.

A Policy of Strangulation

The persecutors now tried to strangle the Korean church in less obvious ways. "Educational Ordinances" prohibited religious instruction in mission schools. Classes at mission schools had to be conducted in the Japanese language and daily reports prepared under a Japanese supervisor. No new Christian schools could be opened without government permits, and no minister could preach without a license. Permits were almost impossible to obtain. Many old schools had to close because of alleged violations of nit-picking regulations.

Fiery Trials

Resentment against heavy-handed Japanese rule boiled over in an independence demonstration in March, 1919. Koreans took to the streets in major cities, crying for freedom. The most influential leaders were Christians.

The Japanese retaliated with brute force. Churches and mission schools were burned. Travelers were stopped at roadblocks and asked their religion. Those confessing Christ were killed on the spot. Thousands of pastors, Bible women and other church officers were rounded up like cattle and herded into smelly, freezing jails. Christian nurses attempt-

ing to help the injured were arrested. One pastor was imprisoned because he refused to stop praying for the sick.

Christian men, pressured to sign confessions, were tortured in indescribable ways. As Nathaniel Peffer reported it
in an effort to arouse the world's conscience:

Men and boys were trussed and suspended from the
ceilings so that their weight hung on the shoulders.
Thus they were raised and lowered til unconscious.
They had their fingers pressed over red hot wires.
Their naked flesh was lacerated with sharp hooks
and seared with hot irons. Toe nails were torn from
the flesh with pincers. Men were placed in a tight
box and then screwed up. They were tied up, their
heads forced back, and hot water or a solution of
water and red pepper poured down their nostrils.
Slivers of wood were shoved far under their finger
nails. They were flogged until they had to be taken
to hospitals, where big slabs of gangrenous skin had
to be cut off. In many cases they were flogged to
death. And some kinds of tortures were unprintable.
This was not done once or twice, but repeatedly for
days and nights, hours at a time, until the victim confessed, whether he had anything to confess or not.
There are cases where men have said yes to anything, ignorant even of what they had admitted.

Women and girls were not tortured so severely, but they
were beaten and humiliated. Knowing the sense of shame
Korean women feel about exposure to men, the Japanese
stripped them naked in the presence of men who shouted
obscenities. They had to appear in the courtroom nude, and
then were pronounced guilty.

A twenty-one-year-old Christian girl from Pyongyang
gave Presbyterian missionaries this signed statement of her
experience:

I was arrested on the streets of Pyongyang the 3rd of
March and taken to the police station. There were
many others, both men and women. They asked us if
we smoked, if we drank, and if we were Christians.
Soon all were let out with little or no punishment,
with the exception of twelve Methodist women, two
Presbyterians and one Chundokyo woman. Three of
the Methodist women were Bible women. They
stripped all of the women naked in the presence of
many men. They found nothing against me except

that I had been on the street and had shouted, *Mansei*. They beat me until the perspiration stood out all over my body. Then they said, "Oh, you are hot," and then threw cold water over me. Then they stuck me with the lighted ends of their cigarettes.

My offense was considered very little compared with those who made flags, or took part in the independence parade. Some were beaten until they were unconscious. One young woman resisted having her clothes taken off. They tore off her clothing and beat her all the harder. After four days we were taken to the prison. Here we were packed in a room with men and women. One day an old man was beaten until he died. One of the Bible women was chained next to him. She asked to be moved, but they compelled her to watch the dead body all night. One of the Bible women not only had her hands bound, but had her feet put in stocks. They would not allow us to talk or pray. They made vile and indecent remarks to us.

All this was done by the Japanese. Though there were Korean policemen in the room they took no part in the beating or in the vileness. The Japanese know the Bible and blaspheme the name of Christ, and asked us if there was not a man by the name of Saul who was put in prison. They asked us most of all as to what the foreigners had said and were most vile and cruel to those who had been with the missionaries, or who had taught in the mission schools. Some of the girls were so changed that they did not look like human beings.

Protests from Abroad

By this time the Japanese had driven out foreign businessmen by trade discrimination. Only missionaries were left in the remote areas where the worst atrocities occurred. In the larger cities, where diplomats were stationed, the Japanese tried to hide their heinous deeds under the cloak of law and order.

The reports reached the mission boards at the same time Japanese delegates at the peace conference concluding World War I were pretending to defend human rights. Some church papers headlined the atrocities. Others ignored it. Said the *Christian Advocate:* "It is the duty of humanity to hold the Japanese Government to account for the horrible deeds which have been perpetrated upon the unresisting Koreans." The *Philadelphia Presbyterian* declared: "The groans of these innocent people have ascended to Heaven, and it is time that Christian nations entered their protest, and the mission boards, who either condone this violence or fail to protest against it, are already condemned."

For awhile the Japanese tried to block the bad news at its source by hiring two hundred thugs from Japan to terrorize the missionaries. Many missionary homes had to be guarded every night. Two American women were beaten by soldiers without even citing a cause. One missionary teacher, Rev. Ely M. Mowry of Ohio, was sentenced to six months at hard labor for "harboring criminals" — five of his students.

The missionaries hung on. Finally, after scathing eyewitness stories appeared in the *New York Herald* on June 16, 1919, the Japanese promised "reforms."

Repression Before and During World War II

The reforms lasted barely a decade. The new Japanese militarists in power brought fresh repressions in the thirties. Korean church leaders who had studied in the United States were placed under house arrest. In 1937 Christian schools were ordered to have their students worship at a shrine of the Sun Goddess. As in Japan, Christians were divided over the issue. The more liberal Methodists acceded, claiming the rites were more patriotic than religious. Presbyterians closed their schools rather than comply. The Japanese ordered some churches to require members to worship before a Shinto shrine before coming to church. Those that failed to obey were imprisoned. In 1939 all foreign missionaries were ordered to leave.

After Pearl Harbor more restrictions were imposed. Use of the Old Testament was forbidden in worship. The New Testament was censored to exclude all references to Christ as Lord and King. Christian families were pressured to give their children Shinto "baptism." Many church buildings were confiscated. Clergy were drafted for war work.

The Red Menace

Announcements that Japan had surrendered brought Koreans pouring into the streets shouting, *"Iayu haebang Mansei! Hurrah for our freedom and independence!"* Christians sang with fervor hymns that had been banned, such as "All Hail the Power of Jesus' Name." For the first time in thirty-five years they were free to worship and witness as they pleased.

Not for long. Soviet troops remained in North Korea, forcing a division of the country into Communist and free zones. In 1948 two separate governments were established, and Communist persecution began in the north where Christianity was strongest.

Upwards of 5 million refugees fled the "socialist paradise" for the south where a Christian, Syngman Rhee, was president. After the curtain closed, the blood of Korean martyrs again began to flow.

Thousands upon thousands of faithful Christians are believed to have been killed or herded into forced labor camps. As in Communist China, iron censorship and banishment of non-Communist foreigners prevented the free world from ever knowing the extent of the bloodletting. Only a trickle of escapees lived to describe the horror.

Murders in Communist "Paradise"

One was Chulho Awe, a mining executive who traded the highest professional honor in North Korea for the life of a fugitive when he declined to join the Communist Party. In *Decision at Dawn* (Harper & Row, 1965), Awe tells of slipping back to Pyongyang, the capital, to see how his Sangjung Presbyterian Church had fared. He found furniture smashed, pews toppled over, files strewn over the floor. A choir member led him to an execution ground outside the city where corpses were stacked like cordwood. In the stack they found the bodies of the pastor and the ruling elder.

The Incredible Love of Pastor Son

Communist troublemakers infiltrated South Korea, sparking local rebellions in which many Christians died for their faith. Two of those martyred were Tong-In and Tong-Sin, the sons of Pastor Son, the minister of a Presbyterian church near Soonchum.

Tong-In, the eldest, had been thrown out of school by the Japanese for refusing to worship at a Shinto shrine. After World War II, he had gone back to high school where he was elected president of the campus YMCA. In October, 1948, a wild Communist uprising exploded in the area and young Communists seized the school. A nineteen-year-old Marxist pointed a pistol at Tong-In and ordered him to renounce Christ. Tong-In replied with the gospel message, pleading for the Communist to accept Christ.

Suddenly Tong-Sin, the younger brother, rushed up. "Shoot me," he shouted, "and let my brother live."

"No," objected Tong-In, "I am the elder. If you must kill someone, shoot me."

The Communist killed them both. When Pastor Son was brought to identify their bodies, he said only, "Their shining faces are as lovely as flowers."

The uprising was quickly put down and the murderer of the two brothers caught and put on trial. Pastor Son found him with his hands tied behind his back, awaiting the death sentence. He hurried to the military authorities. "Nothing will bring back my boys now, so what is to be gained by killing this one. I am willing to take him and try to make a Christian of him so he could do for God what Tong-In and Tong-Sin left undone."

The military officers were momentarily stunned. Finally, they reluctantly agreed to the proposal and Pastor Son took the murderer of his boys home.

The young Communist's parents were overcome with gratitude. "Let us feed and clothe your daughter in return," they begged. The pastor's sixteen-year-old daughter was hesitant to go. But after her father told her, "It is the best Christian witness you can make," she agreed.

The Martyr Who Died Twice

Another martyr to the Communists during this time was Sung Du, a young Christian teacher. Before World War II, Sung had disappointed the missionaries by yielding to Japanese pressure and worshiping at the shrines. Five years after the war ended, missionary Arch Campbell ran into the teacher's younger brother and asked what had happened to Sung Du. "Oh, he repented before God with bitter tears," the young Korean said. "He promised God that he would die before denying the faith again. And he kept his promise. He died twice."

Campbell requested an explanation. The younger brother, Sung Ho, explained that Sung Du had gone to seminary and prepared for the ministry. After being ordained, he had taken a church near Suyang-Ch'on. Then the Communists came and put him to work as slave laborer in a mine.

Because he refused to work on Sunday, they beat him so badly they thought he was dead. "They carried my brother out and threw him in the river," Sung Ho lamented. When they turned away, some of his church members jumped in and pulled his body out. They took him back to the village and were preparing for his funeral when they found he was still alive. Many months later he was well enough to preach again.

"But then the Communists came back and arrested him again. This time they shot him and made sure he was dead. So he died twice to make up for the time when he was unfaithful."

Brave Pastor Im

On June 23, 1950, the North Korean Communists invaded the south and pushed the South Korean Army and a few American soldiers to the southeastern tip of the peninsula. The United Nations pronounced the invasion aggression and authorized UN member nations to help defend South Korea. In slow, bitter fighting, UN forces drove the Communists back into North Korea where the Chinese Communists entered the fighting. The result was a cease-fire agreement fixing a buffer strip at the thirty-eighth parallel just north of Seoul.

One of the many prisoners freed during the UN advance into North Korea was Pastor Im. He had a heartbreaking story to tell. When the Communists first took over, he said, they had ordered the pastors to insert Marxist propaganda into their sermons. Those who refused were pulled from their homes at night and beaten. Some were never seen again.

The day of Pastor Im's testing came. "If you do not teach what we say, you will die," a Communist official warned.

"You may destroy my body, but not my soul," the brave preacher retorted.

"If you do not care for yourself, then think of your family. They will be killed also."

Pastor Im hesitated. Then he said, "I would rather have my wife and babies die by your gun and know that they and I stood faithful than to betray my Lord and save them."

The preacher was taken away and kept in a dark prison cell for two years where he was never allowed to shave or change clothes and was fed only a bowl of slop each day. He kept up his courage by reciting Bible verses he had memorized long before. One verse that gave him comfort was John 13:7: "What I do thou knowest not now; but thou shalt know hereafter."

When the UN troops arrived in September, 1950, Pastor Im was put with Communist prisoners by mistake. They refused to believe that he was a pastor. "All you Communists lie," they said.

Accepting the situation as God's will, he began witnessing to the Communist prisoners. Many were converted. Months later American missionaries, who had stayed in Korea as chaplains, heard about the prison camp preacher and investigated. They obtained permission for him to organize evangelistic services in prison camps all over South Korea. By the summer of 1951 thousands had accepted Christ. Upwards of twelve thousand were rising each morning for dawn prayer meetings. But Pastor Im never saw his family again.

Forgiveness Beyond Measure

Another who lost his family was Kim Joon-gon. The first Christian in a Buddhist family, Kim was persecuted by the Japanese for refusing to worship at a Shinto shrine. When World War II ended, he came out of hiding and enrolled at the Presbyterian seminary in Seoul. When the Communists attacked in 1950, he took his wife and young daughter and fled to Chunnam Island where his parents lived. There he was trapped again when Communists took over the island.

He lived from day to day while Christians were being arrested and martyred around him. In October, 1950, he was arrested and accused of friendship with American missionaries "who came to make Korea a colony of the United States." When Kim denied this, the Communists dragged him to a place where several other Christians lay dead and naked. Still he refused to make false charges against the missionaries or deny his Lord.

They allowed him to go home. That night his wife showed him the white clothes which she had prepared for their expected martyrdom. Then she prayed that they might be prepared to die.

About two o'clock in the morning the Communists came for Kim, his wife and his father. They were taken to a "people's court." There an angry crowd shouted "Christians!

Capitalists!" The louder the people screamed, the harder the Communist soldiers beat them. Kim's father died first, begging, "Have pity on my son," as he fell. Kim's young wife fell next, crying, "Goodbye, I'll see you soon in Heaven." Finally Kim sank to the ground unconscious.

Kim revived as dawn was breaking. Tears stung his eyes as he looked on the bruised, still bodies of his dead wife and father. He noticed that the ropes which had bound his hands were loose—from the beating, he believed. Wriggling free, he managed to stumble to the house of a woman he knew.

Instead of hiding him, she called the Communists. One advanced toward him with a long sword. "I have killed 300 Christians. Kim Joon-gon will be number 301."

"No," the woman suddenly screamed. "Not in the house. Kill him outside."

Kim was pushed outside where his accusers debated about pushing him over a cliff into the sea. As they argued, a group of villagers came up the road crying. They had heard about the violence and begged, "Don't kill him. He has taught us only good." While the Communists hesitated, a troop ship appeared on the horizon. "Americans!" one shouted. "Go to headquarters immediately." With that the soldiers took off running, leaving Kim to escape death again.

Twenty days later South Korean troops captured the island and rounded up about a hundred Communists, including the ones who had killed Kim's wife and father. At a quick trial Kim told of the killings. But when the South Koreans prepared to execute them, he asked that mercy be shown. "Spare them," he said. "They were forced to kill."

"But they killed your wife and father," the South Korean commander said. "Why do you want them to live?"

"Because the Lord to whom I belong would have me show mercy."

At Kim's behest and because President Syngman Rhee had said Communists who repented should be forgiven, the captives were freed. News of what Kim had done spread across the island. Repentant Communists came to hear him preach and many accepted Christ.

The following year Kim took his little girl to the mainland where he served as principal of a high school and pastored a large church. In 1957 he received a scholarship to Fuller Theological Seminary. There he met Dr. Bill Bright, founder and director of Campus Crusade for Christ. He returned home to head up Campus Crusade's work in South Korea.

The Costly Harvest

The Korean War devastated both north and south. South Korea was left with four million refugees, tens of thousands of orphans and widows, and some twenty thousand amputees. One third of all church buildings were destroyed. Around five hundred pastors were dead. There was hardly a Christian family that had not lost a loved one. Most families had little more than the clothes on their backs and a flimsy hut in which to sleep.

In this darkness the grace of God shone brightly. Fresh reinforcements of missionaries arrived. One was Bob Pierce who, seeing the bereft widows and orphans, founded World Vision, due to become the leading evangelical care organization of the next quarter century. "Let my heart be broken with the things that break the heart of God," resolved Pierce.

The resilient Korean church, tempered by decades of persecution, astonished the world by its sacrifice and evangelistic zeal. All across the war-ravaged country Korean believers gathered in bombed out churches for prayer and praise meetings at four in the morning. Today 1.5 million South Koreans — one out of every twenty-two — are Protestants. That proportion of Christians makes South Korea the most Christianized country in Asia. The evangelistic response has no precedent. An estimated 3.2 million attended a five-day Billy Graham Crusade in 1973 in which eighty-one thousand registered "decisions for Christ." A year later three hundred thousand came for training in witnessing and discipleship by Campus Crusade for Christ. More recently, a consortium of evangelical missions from fourteen Asian countries established the Missionary Research and Development Center in Korea for training and sending out ten thousand additional Asian missionaries over the next twenty-five years.

South Korea is "white unto harvest." Ninety percent of the population, including President Park Chung Hee, claim no religion. Park Chung Hee, who rules as a dictator, has strongly backed evangelism and Bible distribution. But he has imprisoned several prominent clergymen who have called for political and social reforms.

Most Korean Christians, however, consider North Korea the far greater threat. With American troops withdrawing, the South Koreans fear another attack from the militant Marxist enemy just twenty-five miles from Seoul. Should South Korea fall to the Communists, the blood of Korean martyrs in the past may well be only a rivulet compared to the torrent that will then flow.

MARTYRS OF
SOUTHEAST ASIA

A HARD BUT OPEN FIELD:
Thailand

Ancient Siam. Pagodas and bells. Enchanting land of mystery. Never burdened with colonial rule, Thailand is led by one of the oldest royal monarchies in the world. Thai means "free." Of Mongol descent, Thais are notably friendly and peaceful.

Although officially Buddhist, Thailand has long been a western political ally and admits missionaries. Dutch missionaries were the first, in 1828. They were followed by British, French and German representatives. Yet Christian work was agonizingly slow. Presbyterians waited nineteen years to baptize their first convert. Congregationalists gave up without baptizing a single Thai after eighteen years.

The reluctance of Thais to accept Christ stemmed mainly from family and community pressures. To convert to a foreign religion was seen as mockery of the national heritage. The traditionally friendly Thais did not object, however, to the social work of the missionaries.

One of the first believers was Nin Inta, a Buddhist scholar of Chiengmai Province. He accepted Christ after missionary friends foretold an eclipse a week before it happened.

When Nin Inta's conversion was followed by seven others, the governor of Chiengmai took action. Two of the seven, Noi Su Ya and Nan Chai, were arrested. When they confessed to having abandoned Buddhism, a death-yoke was hung around their necks and a small rope passed through their ears and hung over the beam of a house. After being tortured all night, they were asked if they wished to deny Christ and return to Buddhism. "We do not," they said, and bowed in prayer. The death sentence was pronounced, and they were taken to the jungle and clubbed to death.

The hostile governor died; his successor was less harsh. More converts were baptized.

The next crisis occurred when two Thai Christians asked to be married by missionaries without first participating in the traditional feast to evil spirits. Relatives appealed to the magistrate, but he forbade the marriage. The missionaries promptly sent a petition to the king in Bangkok, who responded with a proclamation of religious liberty in 1878.

Since that time there has been little official persecution of Christianity in Thailand. The Thai church has grown steadily, though not spectacularly. Today the Protestant community numbers about one hundred fifty thousand and receives aid from some four hundred missionaries.

Tribal Christians Die

Much of this growth has taken place among thirty spirit-worshiping tribes in north and south Thailand. And it is among these tribes that Christians have been martyred for Christ in the twentieth century. As in China, most have been victims of banditry, terrorism and border skirmishes.

Documentation on killings of tribal Christians is hard to come by. In one of the worst known incidents, in May, 1955, Burmese soldiers intruded across the border—looking for fleeing Chinese soldiers, they claimed. When they discovered a box of Scripture portions in a Lahu village which they thought was Chinese literature, they shot and killed a missionary's language teacher and one of two Lahu preachers in the village. The frightened tribespeople moved away.

"The Lord Giveth and the Lord Taketh Away"

The first missionary casualties were recorded in 1952. In April, Paul and Priscilla Johnson of the C&MA were conducting services in the village of Ban Dong Mafai, some fifteen miles from their station at Udorn, Thailand. Attendance had been good. One man had accepted Christ and two others had been baptized. On that fateful Friday, the eighteenth, Priscilla had seen seven village children pray to receive Christ.

The evening services were being held under an open

shelter. The Johnsons' two youngest children, ages five and two, were sleeping in a nearby Thai house. Their seven-year-old was in the C&MA school for missionary children at Dalat, Vietnam. Priscilla was playing the little pump organ and Paul leading the song service. Three hymns had been sung and one of the local Christians was leading in prayer when gunshots shattered the calm.

Priscilla was hit in the chest by shotgun pellets. She ran a short way to a clump of banana trees where she collapsed and died. Paul was hit in the abdomen and fell to the ground but remained conscious. "Give us your gun and valuables," the bandits demanded. Paul had no gun, of course, but they took his watch, camera and keys to the Land Rover. Then they proceeded to the house where the Johnsons were staying and looted their baggage while the two frightened children looked on. The nine or ten armed bandits got the Land Rover started but could not find the brake and finally ran away on foot.

Paul, still conscious, somehow gave instructions in starting and driving the vehicle to a local man who had never driven before. They went directly to the Thai Army hospital where Paul was given the best emergency treatment available.

The news spread quickly. Government officials, upset and concerned, brought gifts and apologies. The next day R.M. Chrisman, a missionary colleague, arrived. He took custody of Priscilla's body, and arranged for the care of the children and the evacuation of Paul to a better hospital in Bangkok. The first words he heard Paul say were, " 'The Lord giveth and the Lord taketh away. Blessed be the name of the Lord.' "

The doctors in Bangkok performed an emergency colostomy and gave blood transfusions. For three more days Paul hung between life and death, conscious much of the time. Early Wednesday morning, April 23, he sang with a clear voice a prayer for his fellow workers and Thai Christians left behind: "Bless Them, Lord, and Make Them a Blessing." A few minutes later he lapsed into unconsciousness and died.

The deaths of Paul and Priscilla Johnson deeply moved the growing missionary corps, many of whom had only recently evacuated from Communist China. Priscilla and Paul, both Minnesotans, had been in Thailand only five years, yet they were loved by hundreds. "We will have to wait until the resurrection to understand why this hap-

pened," commented A.C. Snead, then director of the
C&MA's foreign work. "Now let us trust and go forward in
Christ's name with greater courage, effort and zeal than ever
before."

An "Extraordinary" Christian

The next missionary martyr in Thailand was Lilian Hamer, a
cheerful young woman with close cropped brown hair who
was not "one whit afraid" in the remote tribal area where
she served as a nurse.

Lilian was a member of the China Inland Mission,
which with many China evacuees, was easily the largest
missionary agency in Thailand. An English girl, she had been
working in a cotton mill when converted in a Methodist
youth meeting. "I wanted to be an extraordinary Christian,"
she said later.

Stirred by the martyrdom of John and Betty Stam
[see pp. 56–59] Lilian felt a call to China. By the time she had
completed nurse and midwifery training, World War II was
on and the CIM could not take her. Finally in 1944 she got
to China under the auspices of the British Red Cross and
was accepted by CIM after the war ended. She was appointed
to a missionary hospital in Tali, China, where she was
drawn to the poor and neglected hill tribespeople who came
to the hospital for treatment. When forced out by the Communists, she willingly accepted the assignment to serve with
the Lisu tribe in Thailand.

Living conditions in her new area were hard and rigor-
ous. She was always on call for the sick. She struggled with
opium addicts and prayed for demon worshipers. Although
she dropped exhausted at the end of a day, her sleep was
frequently disturbed by tribespeople dancing around a
"spirit" tree for hours on end. But when a friend wondered,
"Must you really give all your life to this?" she replied, "The
Lord Himself faced the cross because He could not give less
than all."

Sometimes she had a missionary partner; often not. In
1959 she was living at a new location known as "demon
people." One night a cobra got into her room, a symbol of
the enemy she faced. She battled the snake with a stick and
won. In her last report she quoted from an old poem: "The
handles of my plough with tears are wet. The shears with
rust are spoiled. And yet, and yet, My God! My God, keep
me from turning back."

On the morning of April 18 she decided to go down to the plain. She walked with two Thais, but along the way they stopped and she went on ahead. A short way on she followed the trail between two trees. As she passed, a figure stepped from behind one and confronted her with a sawed-off shotgun. A few minutes later the carriers came upon her body, slumped against a tree. They noticed that before dying she had managed to cover her feet—a last gesture of identity with the people.

Today there is a small bamboo and grass church only two hundred yards from the tree where Lilian Hamer's blood reddened the earth. The whole countryside knows the spot where she died. The tribespeople. The headman. The old witch doctor who planned the killing. And the tribal believers who walk by her grave on their way to worship the God for whom she laid down her life.

"Except a Corn of Wheat . . . Die"

Roy Orpin heard of Lilian Hamer's death shortly after telling his parents, "I've been accepted by OMF [Overseas Missionary Fellowhip, fomerly China Inland Mission]. Maybe I'll leave my bones in some foreign country."

Orpin, a New Zealander, was engaged to marry a young Englishwoman he had met at the New Zealand Bible Training Institute in Auckland. Both had been deeply moved by reading about the death of John and Betty Stam and by the more recent martyrdoms of five young Americans in the Auca jungle of Ecuador [see pp. 569–577]. They were married in Thailand, April 27, 1961. At the reception they sang a duet, "Calvary," the last stanza of which seemed to hold special meaning:

> So much more may we united
> Bear Thy Name to men oppressed,
> Break to them the Bread of Calv'ry
> Bless their souls as we are blessed.

After a short honeymoon, Roy took his bride, Gillian, to the shanty house he had prepared in the Meo tribal village of Namkhet. They arrived at night to find the house a shambles. Both had lived in tribal villages for a few months before their marriage. They made the best of the bad situation and settled down for the night. The next morning they ate their first meal off an upside-down pig trough.

Violence escalated in the area during their first year of

marriage. They heard of three Thai opium traders being robbed and killed while begging for their lives. Roy stumbled across the bodies of two more murder victims while hiking to another village. Fearing for his safety and that of his now-pregnant wife, he said, "I had no peace until I remembered II Corinthians 10:5, 'Make every thought captive to obey Christ.' What havoc uncontrolled thought can play."

As Gillian's time approached, they decided to move to Bitter Bamboo, a village where a few struggling Christians desperately needed instruction and encouragement. Gillian went to a regional town where there was a missionary hospital while Roy worked on the new house and moved their household goods. As he was making his last trip before leaving to join her, three young robbers suddenly appeared and demanded his valuables. When he had emptied his pockets, they told him to go on. When he was a few steps away, they shot him in the back.

Critically wounded, he was rushed to a government hospital. Gillian came and sat by his bedside from Wednesday through Saturday when he worsened. "Say for me the chorus 'Jesus! I am resting, resting,' " he whispered. Slowly, her lips close to his ear, she recited,

> Jesus! I am resting, resting
> In the joy of what Thou art;
> I am finding out the greatness
> Of Thy loving heart.

"How good God is," the young missionary whispered again. A little later his kidneys failed and he was dead at age twenty-six.

The funeral was on May 20, less than thirteen months after their wedding. A few days later little Murray Roy was born. After a short recuperation, Gillian returned to live with two single women missionaries who had shared the White Meo work.

The timing of Roy's death seemed symbolic of John 12:24: "Except a corn of wheat fall into the ground and die, it abideth alone: but if it die, it bringeth forth much fruit." The Meo were then planting their grain. A few months later came a bountiful harvest, both in the fields and in the hearts of Meo tribespeople. Twelve families expressed their intention to follow Jesus and to burn their pagan charms.

Minka and Margaret

A dozen more years passed before the next missionary martyrdoms occurred in Thailand. The war from Vietnam spilled over into Laos and Cambodia. Communist terrorists were now operating in north Thailand. In south Thailand Muslim "liberation" groups fought frequent hit-and-run battles with Thai police. Adjoining Malaysia had become an independent Muslim nation in 1955. The Muslim activists in south Thailand were demanding independence for four predominantly Muslim provinces or annexation to Malaysia where conversion of Muslims was forbidden.

Two veteran OMF nurses, Minka Hanskamp and Margaret Morgan, ministered to lepers in this troubled southern area. Part of their job involved washing the feet of patients, cutting away rotten flesh, and tending to ulcerated sores emitting a nauseating stench.

Minka, a six foot Hollander, had grown up in Dutch controlled Java where her parents were missionaries. While interned by the Japanese during World War II, she had worked in a prison camp hospital. After the war ended, she moved to New Zealand where she volunteered for missionary service. She entered Bible school at age thirty-four and was accepted by OMF two years later in 1958.

Her partner, Margaret Morgan, came from a Welsh mining village and took nurse's training at the Bristol (England) Royal Infirmary. Two years younger than Minka, she began serving in south Thailand in 1965.

Every two weeks the two nurses traveled to the town of Pujud to hold a leprosy clinic. On April 20, 1974, the day of Minka's sixteenth anniversary with OMF, they were called aside by strangers who said they had come to take them to treat some sick patients in the mountains. At first the nurses did not realize the men were terrorists. Margaret suggested that Minka accompany them while she continued the clinic. They were gruffly ordered to pack up their medicines and get in the waiting car.

Ten days later the area OMF representative, Ian Murray, received two letters. One was from Minka and Margaret stating they were in the hands of the "jungle people," and they were well and "still praising." The second letter was from their captors. The Muslims demanded that OMF pay a half million dollar ransom and that the society write an official letter to Israel, protesting denial of Palestinian rights. Mis-

sion policy since China days had been never to pay a ransom
for kidnapped members. To have done so would have put a
price on every missionary's head. The missionaries could not
meet the second demand because it was against mission policy to become involved in political issues.

A meeting was set up between Thai officials, Ian Murray
and representatives of the kidnappers. Murray stated that
OMF was in Thailand only for religious purposes and that
the missionaries worshipped the One Creator God, as Muslims did. "He is a God of mercy and forgiveness, as well as a
God of judgment," he added. "He wants to forgive you, but
that depends upon your response to Him." The spokesman
for the group listened politely, but agreed only to speak to a
higher-up in behalf of the captives.

A few days later a police unit was ambushed in the area.
Thai military activity was intensified. Then word came that
the Muslim gang had no quarrel with OMF but with the
United States and British governments for supporting Israel
against the Palestinians. They demanded that the "Christian
world stop any support to Israel against the Palestinian
people."

Introduction of these demands brought international
publicity. Thai military pressure increased. The occasional
letters that had been coming from the nurses assuring that
they were all right stopped. Conflicting rumors spread. One
story said they were kept in chains. Another reported they
had been shot.

Early in March, 1975, a Malay came forward to confess
that he had shot them. The gang, he said, had argued over
their fate. The chief had concluded that to keep the respect
of underlings they should shoot the missionaries. The informer said the nurses had been calm when told they were
to die, saying only, "Give us a little time to read and pray."
"They were good people," the man added. "Good."

The missionaries did not want to believe the story. But
doubts were dissipated on March 20 when news reached
them that the skeletons of two women had been found in
the jungle. One was tall enough to be Minka and there were
identifying dentures and bits of clothing and hair. Both had
been shot in the head and had been dead five or six months.

The remains were recovered, positively identified, and
buried May 15. The funeral was attended by hundreds of
Christians and many Buddhists and Muslims as well. Many

sobbed openly. A former bandit killer testified before the mourners that he had become a Christian after Minka had taken his ulcerated foot on her lap to treat it. A leprosy patient recalled how Minka and Margaret had tenderly taken him from a little shack where he had been quarantined from his village and cared for his sores. After the funeral, the missionaries and native preachers received more inquiries about Christianity than ever before in the difficult southern provinces.

Death on the Trail

Banditry and political terrorism continued in the more remote tribal areas of Thailand. Some missionaries moved in closer to population centers while others chose to remain in isolated hill stations.

Peter and Ruth Wyss worked with the Akha people, one of the least advanced tribes in the north, while their three children remained in school in their native Switzerland. In March, 1977, they received a visitor from home. Samuel Schweitzer, a Christian businessman, had made a trip to Japan and arranged a stopover to see OMF work in Thailand. His parents had served before retirement with CIM in China.

Schweitzer spent several days with Peter, helping prepare a house in a village for two single women missionaries. They had much in common. Among other things, both were forty-two and both had three children. On the afternoon of March 15, the businessman figured how much money he would need for the trip home and gave Peter his remaining traveler's checks and currency. Peter took this as an answer to his prayer for aid to the salaries of tribal pastors. Then after telling Ruth, "We'll be back soon," they left for the final trip to the new house.

Ruth became concerned when they did not return by the following afternoon. But, as she testified later, "The Lord gave me John 14:15–18 and with these words also a deep peace came into my heart that I could only praise Him for all the good things He had put in my life."

Still expecting them to return, she did not fix breakfast herself the next morning. Schweitzer was due to leave for the regional airport later that day.

The day wore on and finally she and a missionary friend, who had providentially happened along, set out by jeep to discover what had happened. They found Peter's motorcycle at the place where he always left it before beginning the climb to the new house. Part way up the path they met two tribesmen. One said he had seen Peter's body. The tribesmen tried to keep Ruth from going, but she was adamant and ran ahead to the spot. Schweitzer's body was discovered nearby.

The murders had to be reported to the police. Then Ruth had to endure long hours of questioning. She knew of no reason why her husband and his friend should have been killed, unless their assailants had meant to rob them. After that she had to tell tribal and missionary friends and prepare for the funeral. "Yet even in those darkest moments," she recalled later, "the words sounded through my mind: 'I will send you another Comforter' and I knew that He was right there with us, although it was still impossible to comprehend what had happened."

Following the funeral, Ruth Wyss flew home to Switzerland to be with her children. There she began working on curriculum for the Akha Bible School, expecting to return to Thailand within a few months.

Preparing for the Worst

Since the murders of Peter Wyss and David Schweitzer, there have been no other missionary killings in Thailand. However, many Thais have been killed by Communist guerrillas and in clashes with Cambodians. Some of these were likely Christians.

With Communist governments now in adjoining Laos and Cambodia, Thai Christians are not optimistic about the future of their country. Some churches are memorizing the whole New Testament, with books assigned to individuals. As one missionary said, "It's not a question of 'if the Communists take over,' but 'when.' When this happens, the Christians will be ready."

THE BOOKS ARE STILL OPEN:
Vietnam

Vietnam is now only a bad memory for most westerners. Americans would like to forget the dragon-shaped country in Southeast Asia where over fifty-six thousand Americans died. The terrible war which ended in a Communist victory has obscured the suffering and martyrdom of Vietnamese Christians and foreign missionaries. Their sacrifice is the least known story of Vietnam.

Since 1911, when the C&MA's R.A. Jaffray established a base at Da Nang, evangelical Christians have never known a time in Vietnam when they were not persecuted. First it was the haughty French colonial government which confined Jaffray and his colleagues to the large cities. This proved to be a blessing in disguise, for the missionaries then sent their first converts to evangelize the towns and countryside. Indigenous congregations sprang up from Hanoi to the Mekong Delta.

When Japanese invaders swept across Indochina (Vietnam, Laos and Cambodia) in 1941, most missionaries refused to leave and were placed in internment camps. Many evangelical pastors went underground and continued to serve their flocks despite threats from the new imperialists.

Peace came only briefly at the close of World War II. A new phase of war began in 1946. Ho Chi Minh and his Viet Minh Communist guerrillas launched their war of "libera-

117

tion" against the French who had returned in 1945. The fighting lasted eight years and ended with French withdrawal from Vietnam and partitioning of the ancient country along the seventeenth parallel (DMZ).

Christians Were Caught in the Middle

Not one C&MA missionary died in Vietnam from hostile action during the French–Indochina War. Most of the missionaries were Americans who were considered neutrals by both sides. But tens of thousands of Vietnamese died along with thirty-five thousand French soldiers.

The Vietnamese evangelicals were caught in the middle and often held suspect by both sides. The result was a trail of martyrs' blood up and down the country, among them the following documented examples:

Item. Pastor Phan Long and three deacons were shot by French soldiers and their bodies thrown into the Bau Rau River near Da Nang.

Item. Nguyen Van Tai, pastor at Ma Lam in central Vietnam, was chased and shot by Communist Viet Minh guerrillas on the road between Phan Thiet and Ma Lam.

Item. Nguyen Thien Thi, pastor of Thanh Qui Church in central Vietnam, and his wife and son were seized and bound by the Viet Minh in the home of a layman, then led into a field and executed.

Item. Trinh Ly, a pastor near coastal Nha Trang, was murdered by French soldiers at the Nha Trang railroad station. Later his wife was shot near Dalat.

Item. Mr. So, a zealous layman at Phong Thu, was killed by French soldiers while on his way to church with Bible in hand.

Item. Tranh My Be, pastor at Choudoc, south of Saigon, was seized by the Viet Minh and buried alive standing up. The shock killed his wife.

Scores of other pastors and laymen were killed. Many churches were burned and bombed. Christians who left their homes and fled to the jungles returned to find their household belongings stolen. Of pastors in one area it was said, "When they have not clothes enough they curl up on a heap of straw. One of them has only a coat and a Bible left, but keeps on living with his flock."

After the French admitted defeat, peace again proved illusionary. The Communists in North Vietnam placed restrictions on Christian activity. Thousands fled south. The Communist Viet Minh resurfaced in the South as Viet Cong and began terrorizing villages in the countryside. Headmen who refused to pay tribute and cooperate were killed. Christians suffered not so much because of their religious affiliation but because they had strong moral principles and abhorred violence.

Kidnapped Missionaries

The war heated up. The United States government began a slow escalation of military assistance to South Vietnam. Missionaries, concerned that their purposes not be misunderstood, proclaimed their neutrality at every opportunity. Whenever possible, they drove cars marked with the identification of the Tin Lanh National Evangelical Church. Still they knew that the danger was great and inevitably some would pay a terrible price for serving in a war zone.

By early 1962 the Viet Cong were strongly established in the central jungle highlands around the provincial capital of Banmethuot, once considered a tiger-hunting paradise by Asian royalty. The C&MA ran a leprosy hospital twelve miles outside Banmethuot where pitifully afflicted tribesmen came to receive treatment. The five missionaries serving at the hospital knew they were exposed to danger from the Viet Cong, but did not believe the Communists would rile the people by an attack on the hospital.

Archie Mitchell, the newly appointed director of the hospital, had seen firsthand the horrors of war while a pastor in Washington State. On May 5, 1945, he and his wife took four Sunday school youngsters on a picnic in the back country. One of the children came across a mysterious looking object. Archie's warning shout came too late. The boy poked at the object and a Japanese balloon bomb, blown across the Pacific by trade winds, exploded with a roar. The children and Mrs. Mitchell were all killed. The pastor had been protected by a tree. Two years later he married Betty Patzke, the older sister of two of the dead children. They went to Vietnam as missionaries.

Dr. Ardel Vietti, the no-nonsense, spaghetti-loving doctor, had been raised in South America and Texas. While in high school in Houston she saw two girls bow their heads in the lunchroom. Curious, she bluntly asked why. The incident led to her conversion. A summer after medical school spent with a Wycliffe woman translator among Mexico's disease-plagued Chol Indians aroused her compassion for the less fortunate. She went to Vietnam in 1957 and moved into the central highlands where ten to thirty percent of villagers were afflicted with leprosy.

Dr. Ardel was assisted by Ruth Wilting, a slender, brunette missionary nurse from Cleveland, Ohio. From Vietnam she had once written home to worrying relatives: "Keep in mind two verses that the Lord gave me recently: Joshua 1:9 and Isaiah 26:3. No matter what, God's way is the best way and I know I'm in the center of His will. None of us here are afraid of the future. We live each day as it comes."

The fifth adult was young Dan Gerber, only twenty-one, a Mennonite farm boy from Ohio who was serving in his church's program for conscientious objectors to the draft. His assignment was to help tribal workers at the leprosarium grow better crops. His main side interest was Ruth to whom he was engaged.

May, 1962, brought a heavy load of patients. The Mitchells were settling into their new home. Ruth was busy making her wedding dress.

On the morning of the thirtieth Archie Mitchell found three bridges burned and trees blocking the road that led into Banmethuot where the C&MA had a tribal Bible school. A crude sign at one spot warned: "FIX THIS BRIDGE AND OFF WILL GO YOUR HEAD." Archie got Dan and his tractor. "They don't mean missionaries," he said. "They know we're only here to help."

About sunset Dan and Ruth went for their usual evening stroll. A short way from the hospital they were surrounded by a group of black pajama-ed Viet Cong. The guerrillas tied Dan's hands and ordered Ruth to return to the hospital. She ran back and found another group of VC's holding Betty Mitchell and her children. Archie was led back to where Dan was held. Another group of guerrillas called Dr. Ardel from her bed where she was resting her badly ulcerated leg. They took her to join the men. Others piled medical supplies into the hospital's pickup truck. Then after warning Betty and Ruth to stay inside for the night and not to leave until sunrise, they picked up their three captives and roared away into the night.

Fortunately, the kidnappers had left a Land Rover. The next morning the women and children made the trip into Banmethuot to alert the missionaries at the Bible school there. Missionary Bob Ziemer notified the local commander of the U.S. Special Forces and within hours hundreds of South Vietnamese soldiers, accompanied by American advisors, mounted a search and rescue operation. Once they got close enough to the abductors to see them going over a hill. But intelligence sources advised that the guerrillas had been reinforced and a battle would cost many lives. Reluctantly, the search force pulled back.

C&MA leaders in New York began a diplomatic offensive. They contacted Red Cross organizations in surrounding countries. They asked representatives of the Viet Cong in Cuba and Algeria to intervene. They sought help from Russia, Switzerland and the International Control Commission appointed to supervise the "neutrality" between North and South Vietnam. Every effort proved fruitless.

Death on the Highway

Missionary linguists with the Wycliffe Bible Translators were now moving into tribal locations. The international organization founded on the faith principles of the old China Inland Mission was committed to translating Scripture into over two thousand Bibleless minority languages, over thirty of which were spoken in South Vietnam.

Elwood Jacobson, a Minnesota farm boy of Norwegian descent, was typical of the intrepid Wycliffe pioneers. He had been challenged for full-time Christian service by Dawson Trotman, founder of the Navigators, a ministry that emphasizes Scripture memorization and training young Christians to be "spiritual reproducers." Two statements from Trotman haunted Elwood: "If the dying seed of Adam can produce such a race as mankind, what can living seed—the Word of God—produce?" And, "Nothing is yours until you give it away. Giving is the essence of love." One Thursday after seeing a Wycliffe film, he wrote in his diary, "I wonder if this is the thing for which God is preparing me? May You lead me in Your chosen path."

The "chosen path" led Elwood to Wycliffe's Summer Institute of Linguistics, to marriage to Vurnell Newgard, a brown-haired nurse he met through Inter-Varsity Christian Fellowship, and ultimately to Vietnam. A quiet, studious man, he had calculated well the dangers in the war-torn country. Of the German martyr Dietrich Bonhoeffer, Elwood once had written Vurnell: "He had to make the decision . . . whether he would remain in Nazi Germany or escape. He remained and paid for his witness with his life. Life is so short and there are so many things to be done that we really need to choose between the better and the best."

Elwood and Vurnell arrived in Saigon with a new baby, Kari. There they met a young Filipino, Gaspar Makil, whom Elwood knew from Wycliffe's jungle training camp. Gaspar was the first Filipino Wycliffe member.

Gaspar had fought with Filipino guerrillas against the Japanese in World War II and once helped rescue an American missionary from a prison camp. After the war he studied engineering at Southern Methodist University in Dallas, where he was influenced by Inter-Varsity Christian friends "to submit my life to total abandonment to Jesus Christ, that He might lead according as He pleased." Later he wrote his sister Emma, "I do not pray for long life this side of the grave. How you live that life is the thing that matters, not how long. That life is Christ's." Gaspar also attended Moody Bible Institute, where he met and married Josephine Johnson, a black girl with deep conviction. Shortly after their arrival in Vietnam, Josephine doubled their family by giving birth to twins, Thomas and Janie.

While waiting for his and Vurnell's assignment, Elwood was "Mr. Fix-it" at the Wycliffe group house in Saigon. No job was too menial for him. "Every work has its place," he wrote in his diary, "and there is time for all that God wants us to do." So it was natural for Elwood to drive the Makils to their location near Dalat where Elwood intended to help another translator with a language survey. Vurnell and baby Kari went along, making seven in the Land Rover. The date was March 4, 1963.

Sixty-six miles out of Saigon they came upon a roadblock. Assuming at first it was a South Vietnamese army checkpoint, they got out and showed identification. Their suspicions were aroused when the "soldiers" began taking things from their vehicle.

Suddenly a truck loaded with real government soldiers rolled into view. A warning shot zinged overhead. More shots rang out around the Rover. Elwood was shot in the head by a Viet Cong and died almost instantly. Gaspar was also killed. His twin son and daughter were wounded. Vurnell, Kari and Josephine escaped unharmed.

The VC's vanished into the woods. The government soldiers rushed Josephine and her two babies to a first aid station from which they were taken to a hospital. Little Janie died at eleven o'clock that night. Her brother, who had received a bullet in the thigh, recovered.

News of the attack on the unarmed missionaries brought quick apologies from the Viet Cong. "We thought they were government workers. We didn't know they were missionaries," VC agents told people in surrounding villages.

An avalanche of letters poured in on Wycliffe. Young people wrote of making deeper commitments to follow Christ. A South Carolinian said, "He [Elwood] gave his all for Christ. The Lord Jesus has been showing me how necessary it is for me to give my all to Him."

Both widows remained in missionary service. Vurnell later married another Wycliffe member and continued in Vietnam. Josephine transferred to Wycliffe's Philippine headquarters in Bukidnon Province and took charge of preschool children for busy translators who were accomplishing what she and Gaspar had dreamed of doing.

Christians Buried Alive

Two years of escalating war passed. Christians in remote tribal areas suffered most. For example, the language helper of Wycliffe members Dick and Sandy Watson, and a native evangelist were seized by the Viet Cong and buried alive. The Communists charged in propaganda that the two had been serving as "American imperialist agents."

Viet Cong terrorists made travel a nightmare. Still the missions refused to retreat. Southern Baptists, Mennonites, World Evangelization Crusade, World Vision and the World Relief Commission were now substantially involved. Most missionaries were Americans, but representatives from Canada, Australia, Germany, England and other countries were there as well.

Ambush at the Pass

Curly-haired John Haywood went on ahead of his Swiss fiancee, Simone DuBois, to help with the World Evangelization Crusade's (WEC) orphanage and Happy Haven Leprosarium at Da Nang. John had served in Britain's Royal Army Medical Corps, then worked in London's Bermondsey Medical Mission where he had met Simone. He was one of the hardiest in the Vietnam missionary corps, often disregarding personal danger to accompany Dr. Stuart Harverson to remote tribal villages where they confronted exorcisers who charged the sick for making sacrifices to appease demons. "I am not out here for thrills," John wrote home. "I have a job to do, and I can best do it while I am alive. There are just not enough hours in the day for the work I have in hand."

Terrorism became more personal to John when the Viet

Cong slipped a bomb into the bathroom of his close WEC friends, Roy and Daphne Spraggett, at isolated Cam Phuc. The bomb exploded at midnight, hurling Roy and Daphne to the floor. Daphne was not seriously injured and their two-year-old daughter was not hurt at all. Roy suffered a broken collar bone, damaged hearing and serious burns. When he heard about the bombing, John went to salvage what he could of the couple's belongings. Then he drove to Saigon and stayed with Roy day and night in the hospital for more than a week.

John and Simone were married on a golden May day in 1965 in Da Nang. They honeymooned in Hongkong where they studied three months at the British Leprosarium. When they returned to Vietnam, John took over as director of WEC's Happy Haven Leprosarium.

The war continued to escalate. Trips to and from the leprosarium, located at Marble Mountain outside of Da Nang, became more hazardous. But John and Simone were happy and looking forward to the birth of their first child.

On January 8, John kissed Simone and left in the WEC Volkswagen Microbus for the old Vietnamese capital of Hue where he was to pick up a load of pigs and chicks for the leprosy patients. He either failed to notice or ignored a risk factor—the Microbus had just been repainted and new lettering had not been inscribed to identify it as belonging to a mission hospital. It is known that he reached the famed high "Pass of the Clouds" that overlooks the foaming China Sea, and fell in behind a convoy of South Vietnamese army trucks loaded with rice. There was an ambush. American Marines later found his bullet-ridden body in a metal culvert running under the road.

Gordon Smith, the senior missionary who had married John and Simone, preached the funeral. "Jesus said, 'I am the resurrection and the life,'" the veteran WEC worker quoted. "He promised, 'He that believeth in me, though he were dead, yet shall he live.' John is not dead. He is alive, and one blessed day we will see him again." Three days later Jacqueline Edith Haywood was born.

The Approaching Crisis

The war kept worsening. By 1967 soldiers were dying on both sides at the rate of a thousand a week. The highland cities of Dalat, Pleiku, Kontum and Banmethuot, with concentrations of missionaries and churches, were surrounded by roving Communist armies. Yet not a single missionary had left because of the danger.

Stories kept filtering through the jungle that Dr. Ardel Vietti, Archie Mitchell and Dan Gerber were still alive. A tribeswoman told of seeing a group of Viet Cong with two white men and a white woman. The white woman had asked her for a Bible. Allied soldiers had captured a VC hospital and found prescriptions which they said only an American doctor could have written. C&MA headquarters had tried every possible diplomatic channel. Still no word. Not even an admission from the Viet Cong that they had captured the three.

Ruth Wilting and Betty Mitchell had moved into the C&MA compound on the outskirts of Banmethuot. Tribal nurses kept the jungle leprosarium open and came to the mission station for supplies. The missionaries dared not venture to the hospital.

Betty Mitchell and her four children left for a long overdue furlough late in 1967. In December and January Viet Cong activity in villages around Banmethuot picked up. Many nights the missionaries fell asleep to the pounding of heavy artillery.

The large Raday tribal church next to the missionary homes and across the highway from the Bible school was jammed every Sunday. There were conversions every week along with many funerals of villagers killed by Communist attackers. Even babies were machine-gunned.

The holidays passed. The missionary children who had been home on vacation returned to the C&MA school which had been moved from Dalat to Malaysia.

The Massacre at Banmethuot

January 30, the eve of Tet, the Vietnamese New Year, the "year of the monkey"—the signal for unprecedented Communist attacks from the DMZ to the Delta coast. Thousands upon thousands died in suicide charges. In city after city missionaries huddled in bunkers only yards away from the fighting. Amazingly, no missionaries died, except in one place—Banmethuot. Here occurred the most terrible missionary massacre of the war.

Ten missionaries began Tet at Banmethuot. Ruth Wilting roomed with Betty Olsen, another nurse who had come to help in the medical work. Born of missionary parents to Africa, Betty had been only sixteen when her mother died.

The years immediately following were confused for her. She rebelled in school and irritated missionaries by her attitude. On one visit back to Africa she was asked to leave by the missionaries.

Though she had announced her intentions to go to the mission field, she felt constantly defeated. Her conscience bothered her about things for which she'd asked over and over for forgiveness. Marriage prospects dimmed. Depression increased until she was contemplating suicide. In a desperate move, she made an appointment at the church she was attending in Chicago to talk with a young youth counselor. He agreed to talk only if "you really want God's best for your life." Betty said she did. As Betty recalled later:

> He showed me that I was bitter toward God about the way He had made me. I realized I didn't like myself and in rejecting myself, I had rejected God's handiwork. He asked, "How can you serve God if you aren't satisfied with the way He made you?"
>
> He showed me from Scripture how God had prescribed exactly how I was to look, even before I was born. He explained how God could make His strength perfect in bodily weaknesses and how He was not finished working on me yet. I realized then that God's goal was to develop inward qualities in me so that I would reflect the beauty of Christ.

This interview and others with Bill Gothard, who later developed the famous Basic Institute of Youth Conflicts — "based largely on the questions Betty Olsen asked," he says — turned the red-headed nurse in a new direction. She became a warm, caring person and in a few years was accepted by the C&MA for Vietnam.

The nurses shared a house on the Bible school grounds. Ed and Ruth Thompson, veteran transferees from Cambodia, lived in one of the three Italian-style villas in the main compound across the highway. They were studying the Vietnamese language in Banmethuot while a house was being built in Quang Duc where they intended to work with tribespeople who had once lived in Cambodia. Ed was famed as a tiger hunter. At six foot three, he towered over the diminutive tribespeople who affectionately called him, "The Giant."

Bob and Marie Ziemer lived next door to the Thompsons. Ohioans, they had been in Vietnam twenty-two years. Once, while home on furlough in Toledo, Bob had been asked to take the pastorate of his home church, one of the largest in the C&MA. "No," he said. "God wants me in Vietnam. We're needed more there." Bob was now just about completed with his translation of the New Testament into Raday language and was also teaching in the Bible school.

Leon and Carolyn Griswold, father and daughter, occupied the third house. Leon had attended the C&MA's Nyack College in 1919 and talked of becoming a missionary. Growing family and business commitments kept him and his wife from going. "Go in our place," they encouraged Carolyn. "We'll pray for you and maybe visit sometime." Carolyn, a willowy brunette secretary, reached Saigon in 1953 and became the belle of the foreign community. Her single girl colleagues called her *le papillion*—"the butterfly." Upon moving to Banmethuot, she became immediately popular with tribal teenage girls who constantly came to her for beauty hints. Meanwhile, Carolyn's parents moved from New York to retirement in Florida. After her mother died, her father volunteered to help with office work at Banmethuot and came to live with his daughter in 1966.

Hank and Vange (Evangeline) Blood, the other two missionaries at Banmethuot, were members of Wycliffe. Hank and his brother Dave, both civil engineers from Oregon, had come to Vietnam for Wycliffe in 1951. Dave and the Wycliffe girl he had married, Doris, were working among the Chams, who spoke one of the oldest known languages in the world. Hank and Vange were assigned to a Mnong-speaking group near Banmethuot. Viet Cong pressure had forced them to move into a Raday tribal settlement which adjoined the C&MA Bible school. Shortly before Tet, Hank returned to the Mnong village for a short visit. While there he escaped marauding Viet Cong by hiding in a pigpen. Back with Vange, he wrote his widowed mother, "I have a feeling the Lord is going to do something special."

Monday evening of Tet week, the Banmethuot missionaries went to bed with the distant pop–pop of firecrackers set off by the celebrants, sounding in their ears. About one in the morning the pops grew louder—artillery and small arms fire. About 3:30 the Griswolds heard loud raps on their door. They opened it to be confronted by Communist soldiers who ordered them upstairs. A few minutes later the house blew apart in a violent explosion.

There was nothing the others could do. The missionaries were caught in a crossfire between Communist attackers and government soldiers. Bullets whined between the houses.

After daylight the Thompsons and Ziemers saw three or four Vietnamese tanks in front of the tribal church shooting at Communists.

Ignoring the danger, Bob and Ed ran to the Griswold house and began pulling away wreckage. They rescued Carolyn, still alive but unconscious, and carried her into the Ziemer house. When they got to her father, he was already dead. The firing slackened, allowing Ruth and Betty to cross the highway and join their C&MA co-workers. The nurses determined that Carolyn's right leg was broken and she was in shock.

Later in the morning they saw a United States Agency for International Development agriculturist friend, Mike Benge, approaching in a jeep. "Go back! Go back!" Ed shouted. The warning came too late. The missionaries watched helplessly as Viet Cong ran from hiding places and ordered Mike down into the tribal village.

Tuesday night and Wednesday was more of the same. The C&MA people huddled in the Ziemer house. Once, with bullets flying around them, the nurses ran to the clinic behind the church for medicines and blood plasma for Carolyn. The Bloods remained in their house in the village below.

Wednesday night they saw two North Vietnamese soldiers blow up the Thompsons' house. Fearing that the Ziemer house would be next, the C&MA missionaries took refuge in an open garbage pit in back. Carolyn was left lying in a servant house.

At dawn Ruth and Betty tried another run to the clinic for more medicines. Instead of returning, Betty tried to start a car hoping to get Carolyn to a hospital. Communists closed in and took her to a house in the village where they had other captives.

The Ziemer house suddenly exploded. North Vietnamese swarmed over the grounds. Bob Ziemer jumped from the garbage pit and ran toward the soldiers, hands in the air. They riddled his body with bullets. Ruth Wilting came running toward the bunker amidst a hail of bullets. She fell mortally wounded into the pit, crying, "Lord, help me, so I can help the others." The Communists advanced on the makeshift bunker. Ed Thompson lifted his huge hands, crying, "Mercy! Mercy!" The attackers opened fire. He fell across his wife, also mortally wounded, in a last desperate effort to shield her body.

Only Marie Ziemer and Carolyn Griswold were still alive. Marie was bleeding profusely on her left side. The Communists ordered her out of the hole. They then bound her wounds and took her to a house in the village filled with about fifty prisoners. Here were Betty Olsen, Pastor Ngue of the Raday Church, Hank and Vange Blood and their young children, and about fifty other tribal captives. Shortly, Marie and Vange were told they and the Blood children were free to go. Vange had only time to kiss Hank goodbye before he and Betty and the Raday captives were marched away.

Marie and Vange staggered up the hill with the Blood children. They were met by a Raday church leader who took them and Carolyn, barely alive, to an area hospital. From there they were flown to a hospital in Nha Trang where Carolyn died seven hours later.

The martyrdom of the Banmethuot Six triggered an avalanche of deepened commitments to Christ from families and friends. In one of the many memorial services, Dr. Nathan Bailey, president of the C&MA, said it all to students at Nyack College:

> The missionaries at Banmethuot were not drafted.
> They chose to be there and stay there. They were all
> veterans. The romance and the glory of the mission-
> ary call had long since departed. They had lived in
> the midst of war for many years. They had watched
> three of their comrades being led away into the
> jungle, never to be seen again. They knew they were
> vulnerable. They chose to be faithful, even unto
> death.

The Mystery of the Captives

The Communists pulled back into their jungle enclaves. They had suffered severe losses, while winning a psychological victory through the western media.

Shattered missionary residences were rebuilt, churches sieved with bullet holes repaired. C&MA missionaries cabled their home constituency:

> MORALE HIGH. CHURCH–MISSION RELATIONSHIP
> EXCELLENT. OPPORTUNITIES COUNTLESS.

Five missionaries were now in captivity. The latest, Betty Olsen and Hank Blood, were presumed to be in the company of agriculturist Mike Benge and the captured tribesmen. In the weeks following Tet a steady trickle of tribal escapees found their way back to Banmethuot. One was Pastor Ngue and he reported Betty, Hank and Mike to be in reasonably good condition.

The following few months brought fewer confirmed reports of the three, then silence. There was no solid news of the 1962 captives either, though Betty Mitchell, who had returned to Banmethuot from furlough, refused to give up hope that her Archie was alive. The loved ones of the other captives kept believing.

Meanwhile, persecution of tribal Christians continued unabated in the highlands and other remote areas where missionaries could no longer live. Escapees trickled into refugee camps telling of mass kidnappings and in some places massacres.

Miracles Among the Tribes

Suddenly, revival! The fresh moving of the Spirit began on a Friday morning in December, 1972, in the History of Revival class at the C&MA Biblical and Theological Institute in Nha Trang. A student had completed a report on the recent revival in Indonesia. Then he surprised everyone by falling to his knees and calling for revival in Vietnam. By noon all 177 resident students were on their knees praying. Missionary Spencer Sutherland noted that "scores of students" confessed their sins, then "asked that hands be laid upon them for the filling of the Holy Spirit. He came, sweeping through the room, reproving, filling, and giving gifts to many."

The revival spread to over a hundred churches when the students went home for the holiday break. At devastated An Loc, Pastor Dieu Huynh led 1,086 tribespeople to Christ. At Banmethuot a missionary reported "miraculous events, such as healings, angelic choirs, visions, one documented raising from the dead, and a number of enemy sightings of soldiers in white guarding Christian villages." In one church eight hundred backslidden believers cried in repentance. Four hundred of their neighbors were converted.

One Captive Comes Home

The awakening continued alongside more kidnappings and killings into 1973. Then came the cease-fire agreement which resulted in withdrawal of all the American troops from Vietnam, followed by the release of all the American prisoners which the North Vietnamese would admit having.

Friends and families of the five unaccounted-for missionary captives scanned the lists with growing concern. There was only one familiar name. Mike Benge, the agriculturist who had been captured with Betty Olsen and Hank Blood at Banmethuot in 1968, was alive and well.

Mike was flown with other prisoners to Clark Air Force Base in the Philippines for debriefing. There he met Vange Blood and told her how Hank had died on a mountain about five months after capture from malnutrition and pneumonia. "His last thoughts were of you and the children," he recalled. "He hoped you would continue working on the Mnong translation."

Vange managed a wan smile. "That's why we're here at Wycliffe's Philippine base. It's slow, hard work, but I'll finish it."

"And he mentioned Tang, his language assistant."

Vange smiled again. Tang, Hank's only convert in nine years of work in Vietnam, had become a great evangelist in the villages around Banmethuot, leading thousands to Christ.

In Wheaton, Illinois, Mike met Betty Olsen's sister, Marilyn. Betty had helped him bury Hank, he said, and had survived three more months. "She suffered terribly," Mike recalled with difficulty. "She died from starvation and dysentery two days after her thirty-fifth birthday." He swallowed hard. "She never showed any bitterness or resentment. To the end she loved the ones who mistreated her."

C&MA leaders quizzed Mike in a Washington hospital about the 1962 captives. Had he heard anything? "Everywhere I went, I asked about them. No one knew anything, or if they did they wouldn't tell me."

A Matter of Time

An uneasy calm now hung over Vietnam. The American troops were gone. Almost three hundred evangelical missionaries remained. Over half belonged to the C&MA and Wycliffe. The missionaries and national church leaders were not fooled by the North Vietnamese. They knew the Communists would complete the conquest when Vietnam began to fade from world attention. It was just a matter of time.

March, 1975. Betty Mitchell was still in Banmethuot, serving the people, awaiting news of Archie. Wycliffe members Carolyn and John Miller and their five-year-old daughter LuAnne lived close by. The Millers were translating for the Bru tribe, a people that had suffered terribly from Communist terrorism. Two more C&MA families were their neighbors, Dick and Lillian Phillips and Norman and Joan Johnson. The Phillips were long-time Asia veterans. Dick had been interned by the Japanese during World War II. They barely missed being in Banmethuot during the Tet offensive.

The tribespeople knew that North Vietnamese soldiers were all around Banmethuot, building supply roads, bringing in heavy weapons. They expected the first offensive to start along the coast. They were surprised when the enemy attacked Banmethuot first.

This time no missionaries were killed at Banmethuot. But all were captured and taken on a long and harrowing journey to Hanoi. At every stop Betty asked about her husband Archie, Dr. Ardel Vietti and Dan Gerber. Nobody would admit to knowing anything.

From Banmethuot the Communist juggernaut rolled south. Military leaders panicked and fled. Behind them came miles and miles of pitiful refugees, hoping somehow to escape the Red peril. Saigon was a madhouse as Vietnamese fought to get out with Americans. The missionaries tried to get out the Christian leaders they feared would be marked for death—especially those who had studied the Bible and theology in the United States. Many had to be left behind.

The following October 29 the 1975 Banmethuot missionary captives were released in Hanoi to United Nations officials and flown to Bangkok, Thailand.

Vietnam Under Communism

What of South Vietnam under communism since? Happenings bear a remarkable parallel to events in China after the Red conquest there. Virtually all foreign missionaries who sought to remain were forced out within a year. They were told that the Vietnamese church no longer needed their help. Church educational and social ministries were taken over by the government and evangelistic activity discouraged and hindered. Religious services were confined to existing church buildings.

As of 1978 about sixty Protestant pastors and around two hundred Catholic priests are reported to be in prison. One priest is accused of plotting against the government. Counterfeit money and weapons were displayed as evidence, evidence which is generally believed to have been planted and the arrest made as a warning to others reluctant to fall in line.

Resistance to the Communists is said to be strongest in

tribal areas where one third of the evangelical community of around four hundred thousand live. Refugees report that twelve leaders from the Banmethuot Raday church have been arrested. It is not known if any have been killed. There are also reports of baptisms and revival in some areas.

The books are still open in tragic Vietnam. There will doubtless be many more martyrs in this land that is only a bitter memory to the West. As a church elder said at Che Reo as the North Vietnamese were advancing: "How many times can you die? My life is in God's hands."

"LAND OF A MILLION ELEPHANTS":
Laos

Laos, fabled "land of a million elephants," is a little larger but less populated than Minnesota. It was once the center of a great Buddhist kingdom, later a part of French Indochina, then an independent nation; and since 1975, following South Vietnam's fall to Red control, a Marxist state.

"His Love Inflames Me"

As in Vietnam, evangelical Christianity came late to Laos. The pioneers were Mr. and Mrs. Gabriel Contessee, sent by Swiss Brethren. While a young architectural student, Gabriel had been invited by an English biscuit maker to study for the mission field at Livingstone College in London. There he learned of 25 million people in Indochina without a single messenger of the gospel.

Gabriel and a companion reached Saigon on September 4, 1902, and proceeded up the Mekong River. Fifty-nine days later they completed the last leg of their journey by dugout canoe. "His love inflames me," Gabriel wrote his mother, "preparing me for this service."

Slowly the two foreigners became accepted by the local people as they learned the language from a Buddhist monk. They baptized their first convert, a sixty-year-old man, on Easter Sunday, 1905.

When reinforcements arrived, Gabriel returned to Switzerland to marry Marguerite Johnson, a girl he knew only by correspondence. He brought her back to Laos, and they started a school.

A cholera epidemic, which had started in Tibet, swept into Laos. Thousands died. Many more fled to the forest in terror. The missionaries, refusing to flee, plunged in to help alleviate the suffering. Marguerite was the first to become ill, then Gabriel. Quinine, the standard remedy, could only slow the disease. Gabriel, not yet thirty, scribbled his last testament: "I am violently ill. I am ready to go. Thank you, Jesus, for saving a sinner such as I." A few hours after he died, Marguerite succumbed. They were buried side by side in the corner of a field.

The Christian Missions in Many Lands, as the Brethren work is known in English, grew to over one thousand members. The Bible was translated into Lao, and a leprosarium was opened.

The Terror Begins

The C&MA entered the country in 1929 and began working among both Laotians and tribal aborigines. In 1950 a mass movement of tribal peoples toward Christianity culminated in four thousand conversions. Three years later Vietnamese Communists invaded the little country and the reign of terror began.

Hardship and persecution fueled the growth of the Laotian church. Overseas Missionary Fellowship, Southern Baptists, and Missionary Aviation Fellowship sent workers. World Vision mounted special relief efforts to alleviate the terrible suffering of thousands of villagers forced from their homes by Communist insurgents. Thousands of Laotians gave their lives in resisting communism. But in the crazy-quilt, all-in-the-royal-family political and military struggle that included a Communist faction, missionaries remained untouched.

In 1968 North Vietnamese Communists launched a fresh invasion. They were repelled with United States help. In 1971 South Vietnamese forces with United States air support cut off the Ho Chi Minh Trail, the road used by North Vietnam to supply its troops in South Vietnam. Two years later came the cease-fire and a false peace in which the Communists pretended to stop fighting.

Two Die, Two Escape

The missionaries were not fooled, but the force of about fifty missionaries stayed. There were constant Communist violations, and finally in October, 1972, the first missionary murders occurred.

The incident happened at Keng Kok, a town of about three thousand in northern Laos. Mr. and Mrs. Leslie Chopard of the Brethren mission had started work here in 1965. By 1972 they had four new associates assisting them in evangelization, literacy, agricultural aid, construction projects, and care of tubercular patients. The newcomers included two single men and two single women. Canadian Lloyd Oppel had come from the University of British Columbia to help with construction workers. Sam Mattix, a native of Washington State, had training in tropical medicine. Beatrice Kosin, also from Washington, was an experienced school teacher and her partner, Evelyn Anderson, a registered nurse from Michigan.

In the early morning hours of October 28, 1972, North Vietnamese soldiers advanced into Keng Kok and surrounding villages. The Chopards managed to flee into the jungle. The young women lived in the section of town first overrun by the Communists and had time only to hide under their beds. They remained concealed in their locked house while North Vietnamese roamed the neighborhood searching for them for two days before they were discovered.

News of their capture quickly reached the leaders of the local Lao Brethren assembly. The Laotians risked their lives by going to bargain for the missionaries' release. The negotiations were unsuccessful. The two American women were shot and dumped in their house, then the house was set afire.

About 5:30 A.M. on the day the women were captured, Lloyd and Sam were warned that the Communists were coming. They tried to flee but ran into a contingent of North Vietnamese. By six o'clock they were tied to fence posts by the side of the road. When the sun rose higher, a man began digging a hole between them—a hole shaped like a grave. Were they to be buried alive?

They saw a Christian man, Mr. Pi, bicycling towards them. Sam began singing, hoping Pi would realize they were all right and go away. When he greeted them several times, they pretended not to know him. Finally he put his hand on

Lloyd's shoulder and said, "God be with you, brother." Then after doing the same to Sam, he rode off.

A half hour later he returned with two other Lao Christians. They boldly began challenging the Communists: "Why did you take these men captive? They're Christians. They run the Jesus Hospital. They don't carry guns."

At first the soldiers appeared to pay no attention. Then they moved in with guns pointed. The Lao believers simply knelt down near the missionaries. One embraced Sam. Another wrapped his arms around Lloyd. They prayed and wept together. A North Vietnamese officer came up and ordered the Laotians to leave. They tried to reason with him. He cocked his gun and shouted, "Go! Go!" Only then did they walk away.

After darkness fell, the Canadian and the American were pushed into a truck. A little ways on they were put out and then marched for forty days to Hanoi where they were imprisoned with American G.I.'s. They were released a few days later with the American prisoners.

The familiar pattern of pressure and persecution followed the Communist takeover of Laos. Missionaries were ordered out. Foreign support funds were cut off. "Uncooperative" Laotians were sent to "reeducation" camps. Christian activity was confined to religious services inside recognized church buildings. Excuses were found to close some of the churches.

Yet escaping refugees indicate that the Lao believers, though scattered, remain true to Christ. The number who have died or been imprisoned is unknown.

DICTATORSHIP OF DEATH:
Cambodia

The recorded history of Cambodia goes back to A.D. 100. From A.D. 802 to the 1400s the Buddhist Khmer "God-Kings" ruled over a great empire from their capital at Anghor Wat, a city of dazzling temples. Catholic missionaries entered in the sixteenth century, but by 1970 there were only one thousand Catholics in the country. The C&MA began work in 1923 and was the only Protestant mission in the country until 1960.

Chief of state Prince Norodom Sihanouk ordered all North American missionaries out in 1965 after South Vietnamese planes bombed Viet Cong forces fleeing into Cambodia. National pastors were jailed for preaching without authorization. Two French Alliance missionary couples were the only missionaries allowed to live in Cambodia during this period.

General Lon Nol's coup in March, 1970, brought the Americans back. The following month President Nixon sent American troops into Cambodia to drive the Communists from the sanctuaries which Sihanouk had permitted. Student anti-war leaders reacted by touching off mass demonstrations on United States college campuses, forcing the end of the American incursion.

The campus activists proclaimed their beliefs from safe campus havens. C&MA and OMF missionaries proved their compassion by moving their families into the ravaged country. Assisted by food and medicine shipments from World Vision, the missionaries and leaders of the small Khmer evangelical church launched one of the most significant ministries of mercy in modern times. Cambodian officials responded by granting permission for World Vision to build a Christian hospital which would be operated by C&MA missionaries—an unprecedented action in the almost-solid Buddhist country.

The Harvest Comes

In April, 1972, Cambodian evangelicals took the bold step of renting a thousand-seat auditorium for a week's evangelistic crusade led by Stanley Mooneyham, president of World Vision, ignoring warnings of a possible Buddhist riot or Communist bombing. They were not sure the auditorium would be filled. But two hours before the first meeting hundreds were gathered outside the gate. Every seat was taken, and many left disappointed.

Mooneyham preached and asked those who wished to accept Christ to stand up. About two-thirds of the audience stood. He thought they might have misunderstood, so he explained more carefully the Christian message. When he gave a second invitation, about five hundred immediately came to the front.

More Cambodians became Christians that week than in the past thirty years. Among them were government officials, diplomats and educators. More prominent Cambodians accepted Christ in the months following. One was Men Ny Borinn, president of the national Supreme Court. "I feel like I have become a torch, and I want to go around lighting candles," he said. Another was the author of the Cambodian national anthem.

Before the nation fell to the Communists, the Cambodian church was one of the fastest-growing churches in the world. From three hundred believers in 1970 the church multiplied to an estimated ten thousand in 1975. In Phnom Penh three congregations multiplied to twenty-six during this time.

Cambodia Falls

The church kept multiplying until missionaries foresaw the entire nation turning to Christ if the Communists could be held back. But after the United States Congress forbade further American participation in the war, the little country was doomed. The enemy took over much of the countryside and encircled and blockaded land and water entry into Phnom Penh. Supplies could be brought in only by air as the Communists tightened the noose.

Most of the twenty-five missionaries remained long past the time they were urged to leave by their embassies, some until the last possible moment. They bade their Cambodian friends goodbye, expecting to see them again only in heaven.

Genocide!

The Communist Khmer Rouge took over Cambodia on April 21, 1975, renaming the nation "Democratic Kampuchea." "Dictatorship of Death" would have been more appropriate. Reliable estimates by world news organizations say that at least two million Cambodians may have been killed in purges. Marxist leaders predict another three million may be liquidated to complete the building of their "pure society." This in a country the size of Oklahoma with only seven million population at the time of the Red "liberation." In ratio of murders to population, Hitler, Stalin and Mao Tse-tung must take a bloody back seat to the Cambodian Marxists.

The Communists clamped strict censorship over the country. Still the world got the story from refugees able to escape into Thailand and from a few outsiders allowed to remain in the country. Over a million Cambodians were driven out of the capital, including some twenty-five thousand hospital patients. Thousands died by the roadside. Refugees reported entire villages emptied of people taken out to be shot, stabbed to death or bulldozed alive into mass graves. Every educated person in the country and every soldier above the rank of private was put to death. Family units were broken up, Bibles confiscated, prayer forbidden. The survivors were told that the new Angka "organization on high" was their only source of true wisdom for the future.

Eyewitness stories of the massacres were printed in *Time, Newsweek* and other respected journals. This time there were no peace marches against bloodshed in Cambodia. Most of the ones who had protested so vociferously against the United States "invasion" were as silent as the graves in which over a million Cambodians were buried. Missionaries and others who knew personally many of the Cambodian martyrs could only weep as they moved among the few

Cambodian refugees who had managed to escape into Thailand.

It is probably correct to assume that most of the ten thousand Protestant believers counted in Cambodia before the fall have been martyred. Among these are twelve Cambodian Gideons, who distributed a million Scripture portions before the Communist takeover.

"Pray for Cambodia"

More than a year after the fall of the capital, Phnom Penh, the widow of Chhirc Taing, a colonel in the defending army and an important church official, received a letter written by her husband before his execution. He told of the meeting of the Cambodian church leaders when they knew their position was indefensible. Together they had read John 13 and then washed each other's feet and quietly talked about the future, realizing they were about to die. In his last words to his wife who was safe in Scotland studying, the lay leader pleaded, "Tell Christians around the world not to forget to pray for Cambodia."

This need for prayer continues since the 1979 invasion of Cambodia by Vietnam and the fall of the Pol Pot government. The new government may be less repressive but is certainly communist and antagonistic to Christianity.

MARTYRS OF SOUTH
AND CENTRAL ASIA

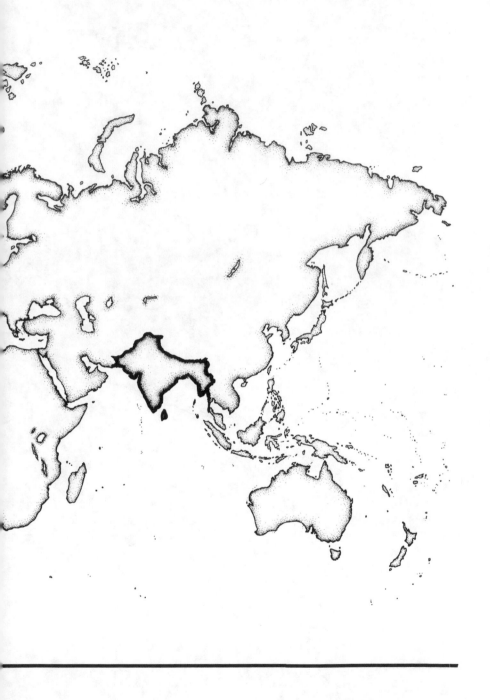

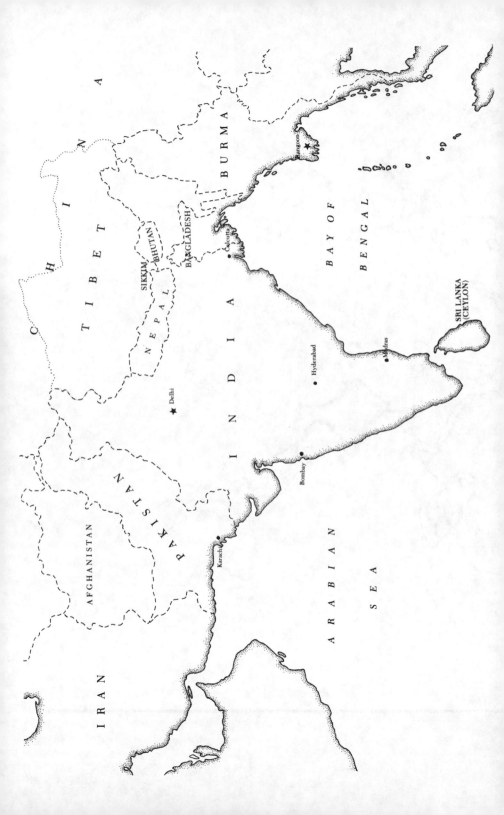

ROOF-OF-THE-WORLD:
Tibet

Tibet—remote and foreboding. Mysterious roof-of-the-world kingdom of high mountain plateaus and hidden valleys. Even before it became a vassal state of Communist China in 1951, Tibet was one of the most resistant nations to the gospel in the world.

Antoine de Andrade, a Portuguese Jesuit, was the first Christian missionary to enter the Buddhist kingdom. Eight years later in 1634, he was dead with symptoms of poisoning. A few others tried to introduce Christianity into the isolated Buddhist kingdom during the next century. Most paid with their lives. Finally in 1745 the last mission station, run by Capuchin friars, closed and no further attempts were made until the nineteenth century.

In 1898 two Dutch missionaries, Dr. Susie Carson Rijnhart and her husband, set out for Lhasa, the capital from which the Dalai Lama, the Buddhist head of state, ruled. Mr. Rijnhart and their baby were murdered along the trail. Dr. Rijnhart somehow escaped and after weeks of wandering through the high Himalayas reached a mission outpost across the Chinese border, wearing dirty sheepskin clothes and almost black from exposure. Upon arriving home, she was asked if it would not be a cross to return to Tibet. "No," she replied. "It would be a cross not to return."

Chain Reaction

Dr. Rijnhart's story became one of the most stirring missionary sagas of the early twentieth century. She later married another missionary, and they returned to Tibet and established a church of baptized nationals—the first evangelical church in Tibet.

The challenge of her story raised up a small force of new recruits. Dr. Zenas Loftis, from a church in Nashville, Tennessee, volunteered "for the most difficult field in the world where the need is the greatest." When he reached the foot of a high snow-covered mountain in Tibet, he saw the grave of a martyred missionary. Unable to sleep that night and heeding a premonition, he rose in the middle of the night and wrote in his diary, "Sleep on, thou servant of the Living God, if it be Thy will that I, too, should find a grave in this dark land, may it be one that will be a landmark and an inspiration to others, and may I go to it willingly if it is Thy will."

Dr. Loftis was soon in the midst of a smallpox epidemic. His own vaccination did not hold. On the second day of treating patients he caught both smallpox and typhus. In six weeks he was dead.

The announcement of his death at his home church drew a quick response. Young Dr. William M. Hardy declared, "I'll go and take his place." Dr. Hardy was joined by more missionaries and the Tibetan work grew rapidly. A number of Tibetans were converted as a result of Dr. Loftis's death.

Forced Out by Bandits

The intensifying of banditry in the area forced the missionaries out. Efforts continued at China border stations from which missionaries made daring forays into the country where no official would guarantee their safety. Three more bodies, all missionary children, were buried beside Dr. Loftis in the cemetery which the missionaries called "God's Acre."

Dr. Albert Shelton, another missionary doctor in Tibet during the early twentieth century, tried for years to get a message to the Dalai Lama, requesting permission to build a hospital in Lhasa and to train young Tibetans in medicine. Finally a friendly governor agreed to forward the letter. The ruler responded in the only communication he had ever had with a missionary, "I know of your work and that you have come a long way to do good. I will put no straw in your way."

Political difficulties with China and banditry prevented the hospital from ever being established. Dr. Shelton was captured by bandits and held for 71 days before he managed to escape.

Never Give Up

Finally there were no Protestant missionaries residing in Tibet and only one remaining on the China–Tibetan border. This was William E. Simpson, the twenty-nine-year-old bachelor son of one of the four remaining missionaries serving in rugged western China.

Associated with the Assemblies of God, Simpson had arrived with his parents in the bleak border country when he was a year old. He grew up with the Tibetans and Chinese, ate their food, spoke the local languages, and braved their hardships. He faced tragedy when his baby sister died and later when his mother died on a trip home. After education in the United States, he returned "home" to Tibet, knowing well the risks and privations involved in missionary work on the border.

Marriage for young Simpson was out of the question. One year he traveled thirty-eight hundred miles on horseback, planting the gospel seed among Tibetans. He won the friendship of Tibetan rulers and was permitted to lease a plot of land for a mission station in Labrang, Tibet, where other missionaries had tried and failed to establish permanent work. From Labrang he became a familiar figure riding among wild herdsmen and sharing with them his message of love. He spent many nights under the stars in their camps. One Christmas the only presents he received were fodder, fuel and a few pears from a Tibetan.

His converts were few, but he pressed on. At the end of one lonely, exhausting trip, Simpson wrote the Assemblies' Foreign Mission Department:

> All the trials, the loneliness, the heartache, the weariness and pain, the cold and fatigue of the long road, the darkness and discouragements, and all the bereavements, temptations and testings, seemed not worthy to be compared with the glory and joy of witnessing to this "glad tidings of great joy."

His escapes from robbers were legendary. Once he faced down a bunch of bandits demanding ransom. "I will surrender nothing," he declared. "Go and leave us in peace." The brigands glared at him for a few moments, then fired several scattered shots and rode off.

He refused to leave during murderous rampages of Muslim fanatics along the border in 1928. Sixty miles from Labrang the Muslims massacred every person living in a city of fifty thousand. "Our hearts go out for the sufferings of all these people," he wrote home. "We try to help as we can, but what can we do among such stupendous needs?"

On June 25, 1932, as William Simpson and a Russian traveler were moving some baggage to Labrang, a horde of Muslim army deserters swooped down upon them. The American and the Russian were killed instantly. A Chinese tax collector who was traveling with them escaped to notify Simpson's father and direct him back to where the mangled bodies lay. As the father was picking up his son's mutilated body, he noticed a Sunday school paper smeared with blood lying nearby. The printed words, "IN REMEMBRANCE OF ME," seemed a fitting testimony of why the young missionary had died.

The Zeal of Sundar Singh

Another zealous missionary to Tibet in the early twentieth century was Sundar Singh, the world famous Indian evangelist. The son of a wealthy landowner of the fanatical Sikh Hindu sect, Singh was reared to be a Hindu priest. In 1904 at age fifteen he became a Christian after having a vision of Christ. His family pronounced him "dead." A relative tried to poison him.

Singh became close friends with Charles Andrews, a noted evangelical English missionary. He studied the Bible intensely and took a vow of poverty. He was known to pray four hours at a time and fast for days. Once he tried to fast for forty days after the manner of Christ. He traveled to Europe, America, Australia and various Asian countries, preaching to large audiences. His books were translated into numerous languages.

Beginning in 1912 he evangelized several months each year in Tibet, Nepal, and other regions along the Himalayas. In 1929 he made his last trip to Tibet and disappeared. How he died remains a mystery.

A Closed Land

After Sundar Singh's disappearance and William Simpson's martyrdom, only an occasional missionary ventured into Tibet. The foreboding land remained closed to any type of permanent Christian work. When the Communists sent in a brutal occupation force in 1951, there were probably no more than a few hundred Christians. Most of these were likely killed in the genocidal Marxist purges that snuffed out the lives of hundreds of thousands of Tibetans.

The Tibetans surviving today under Communist tyranny are said to live in virtual slavery. Thousands of refugees have trekked into India. Among them is the Dalai Lama, Buddhist leader of the Tibetans, who was recently presented a translation of the New Testament in the Tibetan language. Missionaries and national Christians in India have reported a sprinkling of converts among the refugees, and it is presumed some of these are filtering back into their homeland.

FAMINE, DISEASE AND RIOTS:
India

The story of Christian sacrifice in India, the world's second most populous nation, is not nearly so tragic or violent as in China.

Modern Christian missions began when William Carey and his family arrived in this vast country in 1793. India was then a part of Britain's vast colonial empire, and British commercial interests did not welcome the Careys. But the British government protected them and later arrivals.

The British did not give up India until 1947 when Mahatma Gandhi's non-violence campaign finally succeeded. Before leaving, the British carved the land into two nations — Hindu India and Muslim Pakistan — in an attempt to halt religious wars between Hindus and Muslims. The two countries both elected to remain in the British Commonwealth and agreed that violence against Christians and other religious minorities should be strictly prohibited. Disease, not violence, took a heavy toll of missionary lives before and after the British occupation.

A Disastrous Famine

John F. Frederickson served with the Scandinavian Alliance Mission in Ghoom, India. Shortly before 1900 he began translating the Bible into a Tibetan language. One of his

early converts was a Tibetan monk named Jjeurah who became his chief language assistant. By the year 1900 Frederickson and Jjeurah had completed portions of Scripture, a
hymnbook, and a reader in the Tibetan tongue.

In 1900 a disastrous famine swept the area. Frederickson
was appointed to administer his mission's relief program. In
one operation he rescued around a hundred starving children,
then transferred them to the care of other missionaries. He
worked strenuously until he came down with dysentery. He
died on September 5 while praying for his wife and daughters
and the masses of starving children who had so little hope.
When the children he had saved heard about his death, they
said, "Two have died for us, Jesus and Sahib [Frederickson]."
Many of these children grew up to become stalwart Christians. And like so many other missionaries who lost their
spouses on the field, Mrs. Frederickson continued to serve in
India.

Mountains of Death

In 1907 Jesse Brand went as a young bachelor to serve in the
disease-ridden Chat "Mountains of Death" in southern India.
He returned to England on furlough to tell of a deadly plague
epidemic. Fleas on rats, he explained, would jump from dead
rats to other bodies, often human beings. Having had only a
year's medical training, he had done all he could, but still
many of his fellow workers had died.

One who heard him speak was Evelyn Harris, the belle
of a fashionable London suburb. She went to India as a missionary and subsequently fell in love with Brand. They were
married in 1913 and spent their honeymoon among the desperate people they wanted to serve.

By 1927 they had given medical assistance to over
twenty-five thousand people. During one year Jesse had
preached over four thousand times in ninety villages.
Churches had sprung up in many of these communities.
Jesse had studied law to determine the rights of the poor
people who were being exploited by rich landowners and
money lenders from the more fertile plain at the foot of the
mountains. He had organized a cooperative credit society so
the small farmers could borrow money at five per cent instead of the customary thirty-five per cent paid to the money
lenders. He had persuaded government officials to build
thirty miles of bridle paths through the hills. The poor

people had been paying a road tax for years without receiving a cent of benefits. He had arranged for unemployed people to get jobs building the paths.

Both he and Evelyn had suffered from the dread disease of the Mountains of Death, malaria, yet they had never allowed the fever to slow down their work. In 1928 Jesse had the worst attack. In late May and early June he kept working while his fever ran from 100° to 104°. On June 9 he preached on the text, "Arise, shine, for your light is come." Two days later he was making his usual rounds when his temperature jumped to 106°. The missionary doctor applied conventional remedies for malaria—he had never treated a case of blackwater fever. Day by day Jesse grew worse as Evelyn sat beside him watching his flesh become dry and yellow and his blood drain away. On the fifteenth, just at sunset, she saw him quietly slip into the presence of the Lord. As the news spread through the mountains, a great wail resounded from village to village, for he was beloved by thousands, both Christians and Hindus.

They buried him as they would one of their own. His body was wrapped in a Hindu mat and carried on the shoulders of four men to a hillside grave. Then after a simple service, the men dragged a huge stone a half mile and pushed it to the head of his grave. Part of the long inscription which they carved said: "He delivered up his life to the Lord on behalf of the people."

Evelyn Brand never remarried. She lived to see one of their children, Paul, become one of the foremost missionary surgeons of the world, the pioneer in performing successful rehabilitative surgery on the hands and feet of lepers. In her later years "Granny" Brand became a world famous legend on her own. With only the aid of walking sticks, she climbed the mountains. On one trip she injured her knees in a fall. Less than three months later she was buried beside her long-departed husband.

The Continuing Hostilities

Indian Christians have suffered far more than missionaries in the twentieth century. Many have been disowned by their families. In northern India hundreds were killed in riots directed against British troops and certain missionaries closely identified with the colonial regime.

The greatest Christian advances have been made among the Nagas and other tribal peoples of northeast India with a background of pagan animism. In the 1920's over a hundred thousand were baptized under the direction of American Baptist missionaries.

The Hindu majority of India resented and feared such a large conclave of Christians in one area. After independence, there were incidents of discrimination. It seemed to the tribespeople that they had merely exchanged one colonial government for another. An influential missionary had already encouraged the Nagas and their kinsmen to think of organizing their own nation. A Christian tribesman formed a revolutionary government. The alarmed Indian government banned all foreigners from the area and sent in troops.

The hostilities have continued for thirty years with many killed on both sides. As a further complication, reports persist that Chinese Communists are supplying arms to the Christian rebels and promising to help establish a Naga nation. The unrest has spread to predominantly Christian tribes along the borders of Bangladesh, Burma, Laos and Vietnam. There is a tight news blackout on all fronts. No one really knows how many Christians have died in the fighting. Nor is there likely to be any intervention by the United Nations or big powers because of the delicate issues involved. World diplomats pretend that the fighting does not exist.

MUSLIM—HINDU WARS:
Bangladesh and Pakistan

When Pakistan was part of India and the British Empire, missionaries and their converts were protected by the colonial government. A referendum held in 1947 revealed two predominantly Muslim parts of the old colonial empire. These two sections became East and West Pakistan. When their borders were announced, one of the greatest cross-migrations in history began, as almost six million Muslims fled to Pakistan from India and about four million Hindus entered India from Pakistan. Thousands died in the rioting and fighting that accompanied the mass movement. India's beloved "apostle of non-violence," Mahatma Gandhi, was killed trying to stop the fighting.

Mission work established before the separation from India continued in Pakistan. Religious freedom was guaranteed, but Christian teachers were forbidden to give religious instruction to students of another religion attending mission schools. In some isolated areas Christian witnessing was resisted and missionaries viewed with suspicion.

Florida-sized, river-laced East Pakistan was the smaller, more thickly populated of the two sections of the country. It was richer in natural resources, but less developed industrially. The people were short and dark-skinned, and spoke the poetic Bengali tongue. The western section was peopled by tall, light-skinned, long-nosed Punjabis who spoke mainly the Urdu and Sindhi languages.

A Tragic Mystery

British Baptist missionaries had gone to East Pakistan in 1795 when it was still the state of Bengal. But it was not until the 1950's that the southeastern foot of the amoeba-shaped country was entered by the Association of Baptists for World Evangelism (ABWEY).

This jungle stretch along the hilly borders of India and Burma was an unevangelized gap between territories covered by the two great pioneer missionaries of South Asia, William Carey and Adoniram Judson. It was populated by Bengali Muslims and Hindus, plus hill tribespeople related to India's Nagas.

In the center of this area, still frequented by Bengal tigers and elephants, an ABWEY team led by a distinguished missionary surgeon, Dr. Viggo Olsen, built the best equipped hospital in East Pakistan. Along with the medical ministry, a tribal school was started and Bible translation and literature distribution begun.

One of the key translators and educators was Harry Goehring, who had once aspired to be a forester. Harry was studying at Byran College in Tennessee when God spoke to him about full-time Christian service through Ephesians 3:8: "Unto me, who am less than the least of all saints, is this grace given, that I should preach among the Gentiles the unsearchable riches of Christ." He described his commitment and longing to serve his Lord in a poignant poem, "What Is Life To Me?" The last three stanzas read:

> What is life to me, Lord,
>   Unless for Thee to die,
>   Retain not one small want of mine,
>   Just on thy Grace rely;
>   Thy faithfulness to me, Lord,
>   Is all that I will need,
>   To shed my blood in service
>   Of planting precious seed.
>
> Oh, this is life to me, Lord,
>   To daily bear Thy cross,
>   To daily have Thee search my heart,
>   To daily burn all dross,
>   To daily bring to Thee, Lord,

All burdens, griefs, or cares,
To daily walk in childlike trust
Through Satan's tangling snares.

Oh, Christ, The Everlasting God,
The Bread of Life to me;
The Living Water from above,
The Rock to which I flee,
In Thee is found all joy of life,
For by Thy Grace and Love,
Life here for me is one great task —
Reflecting God above!

Harry married a fellow Bryan student, Nancy Goodman. Stirred by a challenge from Dr. Olsen, they began language study for East Pakistan. They arrived in 1963 and within a year Harry had a booming tribal Bible school going and was beginning to translate Scripture into a tribal language. His January, 1965, prayer letter to home supporters brimmed with optimism. "The Lord is good," he said in summary. "May He find us yielded to His molding hand this new year."

Early in June he was studying in Colossians about the sufferings of Christ. He had recently led a tribal chieftain to Christ, and at the time was sensing the powers of Satanic darkness more than ever before. "I wonder," he mused to his wife Nancy, "what it is going to take to bring some of these people, so hardened in sin and superstition, to Christ."

Two days later Harry Goehring's kidneys stopped functioning. The missionary doctors diagnosed acute kidney infection and cabled their home office for money to send the Goehring family to Chicago where the young missionary could receive artificial kidney treatment. The next day they cabled that he was better and might not have to return home. The following morning his heart began failing. They applied every possible remedy, but finally he gasped, "Let me go!" In a moment he was dead.

A chemical analysis showed that his kidneys had failed not from an infection but from a poisonous substance. How had it gotten into his body? They examined every possible source and found no answers.

Scores of Bengalis and tribespeople came to his funeral. More people were challenged when Nancy returned to the United States and witnessed of Harry's faith. Several volunteered for foreign mission service, some offering to take

Harry's place in East Pakistan. Later Nancy married a close missionary friend, Russell Ebersole, who had lost his wife to cancer. They are serving today in the Philippines.

Bloody Bangladesh!

In 1971, six years after Harry Goehring died, East Pakistan rose in rebellion against callous discrimination by West Pakistan. In one of the bloodiest "small" wars of history over three million Bengalis in the east were killed—mostly innocent civilians—and some three hundred thousand women savagely raped Nazi-style.

The Hindu minority in East Pakistan was a special target of Muslim Punjabi soldiers from the west. The Hindus scrawled crosses on their homes so the Punjabis would think they were Christians. Many begged Christian missionaries to baptize them and give them shelter.

About 320 missionaries, almost equally divided between Protestants and Catholics, were in East Pakistan when the war started. The missionaries were sympathetic to the Bengali cause. Some risked their lives in "smuggling" relief supplies and medicines to endangered Bengalis. Although some had narrow escapes, no Protestant missionaries were killed. Three Catholic workers were not so favored.

Italian Father Mario Veronese came out with his hands up when he saw West Pak soldiers coming into his hospital, the Red Cross symbol on his arm clearly visible. The invaders shot him in his tracks, then ran into the hospital, shooting at frightened staff members. West Pakistani officials later apologized and claimed it was a mistake.

Another Italian priest was beaten to death with a tire iron after he served tea to West Pak soldiers at his hospital.

A third padre, Holy Cross Father William Evans, was pulled from his boat by West Pak soldiers while on his way to church service. They shoved him into a ditch, slashed him with bayonets, shot him twice, then kicked his body into the river.

Despite their neutral status, upwards of a hundred Bengali Christians were later martyred. At Bogra in the far north, a band of West Pak sympathizers burst into the home of a respected Church of God teacher. Utpal Biswas was too sick to flee and get his family away. They killed him, his wife, two sons and a daughter who served as a nurse at the nearby Church of God hospital. South of Bogra, West Pak troops invaded Rangamati village, tossing torches into flimsy, dry huts. Occupants fleeing the flames were lined up and executed in the light of the flames. Sixteen Christians perished. Similar atrocities were inflicted in other villages.

The tides of war quickly changed after India entered the war and cut West Pakistan's tenuous supply lines. Within days East Pakistan had become newly independent Bangladesh.

But not without a terrible price in the destruction of property and the loss of life. Thirty million Bengalis were destitute. Many were in imminent danger of starving to death. While the victors sought revenge from neighbors who had collaborated with West Pak soldiers, Christian relief organizations fed the starving, built houses, dug wells, and healed the sick and wounded. A Muslim cabinet member of the new government observed that "only the Christians [one-fourth of one per cent of the total population of seventy million] are fulfilling the commandments of their Holy Book."

In the years since disbandment Bangladesh has been plagued by unstable governments as well as by disease and hunger. The brave band of missionaries and the Christian minority of one-half of one per cent of the population continues to serve.

NO MASS MURDERS:
Nepal, Sri Lanka and Burma

THE MYSTERY OF NEPAL

No western missionary is known to have given his life for Christ in Nepal, an independent buffer Hindu state between China and India where scores of mountain climbers have died trying to scale Mt. Everest and other peaks. Foreigners were not even allowed to enter this mecca for mountain climbers until 1950. Christian social, educational and medical workers are permitted today only if they pledge not to evangelize. The Wycliffe Bible Translators, which had seventy members working in eighteen Nepalese dialects, were asked to leave in 1976.

There are said to be only five or six hundred Nepalese Christians among a population of ten million. These few either were evangelized illegally within the country, or became believers while outside the country. The Nepalese constitution states explicitly that "no person shall be entitled to convert another person to his religion." Because of this law Prem Pradham, a Nepalese converted while serving in the Indian army, has served time in seven jails. An unknown number of other Nepalese believers have been imprisoned for evangelizing. Many have been disowned by their families.

There are no records of Nepalese who may have died in prison or from other persecutions. Any such incidents would

have been hidden before 1950 and would not be reported today by the controlled press.

SRI LANKA

Christian martyrs are unknown in Sri Lanka (formerly
Ceylon), the island nation off the tip of India. The little West
Virginia-sized country was ruled for almost four centuries by
three European powers in succession — Portugal, Holland and
Britain. Each promoted its own language and national branch
of Christianity. Around 1800 over half of the population professed Christianity.

Since its independence from Britain in 1948, an anti-
Christian spirit has been rising. Militant Sinhalese Buddhists
promote Sri Lanka as the "Promised Land" for members of
their sect living abroad. Their brand of Buddhism, they say,
is the patriotic national faith and Christianity is the tool of
colonialists. Many professing Christians have returned to Buddhism, including a former premier. Today only eight per cent
of the fourteen million inhabitants claim to be Christian.

A hard core of fervent evangelicals, missionaries and nationals are evangelizing vigorously. Sri Lanka law permits individuals to change their religion. They are opposed by the
Buddhists and Communist agitators bent on creating conflict. There may be trouble and martyrdom ahead.

SUFFERING AND DEATH IN BURMA

Burma is another South Asian country which has avoided
blood purges of Christians during the twentieth century.

Shaped like a kite with a tail, this Texas-sized predominantly Buddhist country was first visited by Armenian
Christians in 1612. In 1685 two French Catholic missionaries opened a small hospital, only to be murdered four
years later for spreading Christian doctrine. Protestant missions began in 1813 when Baptists Adoniram and Haseltine
Judson arrived. Judson was arrested as a spy and thrown into
the death prison at Ava. After months of torture and suffering in a squalid cell, he was asked by a jailer, "How bright
are the prospects of your mission now, O foreign animal?"
Judson answered, "As bright as the promises of God, my
friend."

Judson survived twenty-one months in the filthy jail and
upon release moved to Rangoon. His wife died in 1826 from
a combination of tropical diseases. Judson then married the

widow of a colleague who had given his life for Burma. He subsequently lost this wife and several children to the ravages of the Orient. Judson persisted. At his death there were seven thousand Christians and 163 missionaries in Burma. By 1900 the Baptist community had grown to almost one hundred thousand, due largely to a "people" movement among the Karen tribe.

Both the missionary force and the national Christian body kept growing in the early twentieth century. There were only scattered, localized acts of violence against Christians.

The Widow's Plea

One tragic incident involved a young Karen doctor who came to help an American Baptist missionary, Dr. Albert Henderson, at the Taunggyi Hospital that served the Shan tribe. For eighteen months all went well. Then one night the Karen physician was called to aid a woman who had been severely injured by her drunken husband. As he was dressing her wounds, the husband suddenly returned and tried to finish the job. While trying to protect his patient, the doctor was killed by the madman.

When the Shan ruler ordered the murderer executed, the Christian doctor's widow rushed to the palace and begged that the man be spared. Drink, she said, had made him insane. The ruler granted the request.

"He Showed Us God"

Dr. Henderson had been in Burma since 1893. He had laid six colleagues to rest in the little cemetery at Taunggyi. In February, 1937, he returned from visiting a sick colleague to find a typhoid epidemic raging in the town. His two associates away, he drove himself day and night to help the sick and dying. One morning his wife Cora noticed he was flushed. She quickly took his temperature and found he had a high fever. Further diagnosis indicated that he too had contracted typhoid.

A medical missionary from another station and his nurse wife came and fought two weeks to save Dr. Henderson's life. Finally he awoke from the coma and smiled at his wife. "It's all right, dear, I'm going home," he whispered. Then he closed his eyes and slipped away peacefully.

Thousands came to his funeral—Christians, Buddhists,

Hindus and tribal animists, loin-clothed tribespeople and members of royal households. One old man sobbed, "He was our beloved father. He showed us God by the way he lived."

Closed to Missionaries but Still Open for Christ

Japanese troops occupied Burma during World War II. They succeeded in cutting the Burma Road, over which scores of missionaries had escaped from China. But the Japanese were too busy fighting and keeping order to mount an anti-religious crusade.

After the war Burma reverted to colonial status in the British Empire, then in 1947 became an independent state. From 1947 to 1950 the country was wracked by revolts from Communists and rebel Karen tribesmen. Like their tribal cousins in northeast India, the Karen people wanted an independent state. The central government finally did agree to a separate Karen state within the nation. Many Karen tribespeople were killed in the uprising. They died in the political struggle and not because they were Christians.

In the 1960's Burma was spared the agonies of Vietnam, Cambodia and Laos, by adopting a stance of strict neutrality and maintaining tight control over dissidents. The country is ruled today by a one-party socialist government. Burma is now closed to missionaries, but national churches are permitted a wide latitude. The largest body, Baptists, reported 305,252 members in 1976.

Burma, Nepal, and Sri Lanka remain relatively calm. But the calmness in any of them could be swiftly whipped into a storm if Christians became more aggressive in evangelism and large masses began turning to Christ.

MARTYRS OF THE
ASIAN PACIFIC ISLANDS

PACIFIC

OCEAN

PHILIPPINE

SEA

PHILIPPINES

Manila

SOUTHEAST ASIA

MALAYSIA

Singapore

BRUNEI

MALAYSIA

BORNEO

S U M A T R A

I N D O N E S I A

J A V A

C E L E B E S

TIMOR

PAPUA
NEW GUINEA

AUSTRALIA

INDIAN

OCEAN

CANNIBALISM AND DISEASE:
Indonesia, Papua and Surrounding Islands

"We crept over the spine of the ridge and looked straight down on the naked savages feasting on enemies they had slain in battle. Suddenly we heard a rustle in the grass. Turning in fear, we saw two painted faces staring at us. We had found the cannibals and now they had found us."

Furloughing missionaries, in the nineteenth century, from the Asian Pacific islands kept congregations on the edge of their pews with such hair-raising tales of narrow escapes from fierce cannibals. They brought chills by telling of martyrs speared to death and eaten by cannibal islanders. They roused young people to their feet, resolving to fill the martyrs' shoes.

Overdrawn? Perhaps missionaries did often omit from their home talks such positive factors as native honesty, willingness to share and simplicity of life, and did neglect to draw attention to the equally savage crimes of so-called civilized peoples. But cannibalism was indeed rampant. One Fiji chief had 872 memorial stones to mark the number of human beings he had eaten. And infanticide was common. Some tribes killed up to two-thirds of their children after birth. And it was very true that missionaries were more likely to be martyred or die of a tropical disease than live out a normal lifetime. In New Guinea there were once more missionary graves than native converts.

Approach to Indonesia

Missionaries and traders sailed into the vast Pacific behind the legendary Captain Cook, whose voyaging tales stirred the imagination of Europeans and Americans. The traders came to extract riches and slaves from the green "spots of paradise"; the missionaries to Christianize and civilize the myriads of dark-skinned, almost-naked natives who lived in superstition and fear of animistic spirits.

Laying between the west coast of America and the eastern shores of Asia, the islands were grouped into three main chains. Polynesia (many islands) was scattered across five thousand miles of ocean from Midway in the north to New Zealand in the south. Micronesia (small islands) dotted the ocean south of Japan. Melanesia (black islands) lay in the southwestern Pacific and was largely populated by people of black skin. New Guinea, the world's second largest island, was in Melanesia. It is this chain of islands – Melanesia – particularly New Guinea and the Asian island group now federated as Indonesia, that gave rise to the most spine-tingling tales.

The smaller islands and the coastal regions of the larger land masses – New Guinea, Borneo, Sumatra and Java – were evangelized in the nineteenth century. Consequently, most Christian martyrdoms of the nineteenth century occurred on the smaller islands while twentieth century casualties happened in more remote interiors of the large islands.

"Martyr Isle"

Because of the number of missionaries killed there, one small island in the New Hebrides chain of Melanesia, Erromonga, came to be known as "Martyr Isle."

The first two martyrs were John Williams and James Harris. They landed on Erromonga in 1839 and were speared to death for a cannibal feast. Twenty-five of Williams' converts from Samoa volunteered to take his place. Several were killed and the rest fled after a year of hostilities.

In 1857 two Presbyterians from Nova Scotia, Mr. and Mrs. George Gordon, made a try. All went well until traders stopped and touched off an epidemic of measles. The natives rose in vengeance and killed the Canadian couple.

James Gordon went to carry on his brother's mission and was soon joined by James McNair, a Scot. McNair lived only two years, and Gordon was killed two years later by an islander who imagined the missionary had cast a death spell on his child.

When the news of Gordon's death reached Nova Scotia, Mr. and Mrs. Hugh Robertson applied for service on Erromonga. The violence ended when they arrived, and by 1880 there were hundreds of Christians.

In memory of those who died, a "Martyr's Church" was built at Dillon's Bay where John Williams and James Harris had been killed. A monument listed the names of all the missionaries who had died, with this testimonial:

They hazarded their lives for the name of our Lord Jesus. Acts 15:26.

It is a faithful saying, and worthy of all acceptation, that Christ Jesus came into the world to save sinners. 1 Timothy 1:15.

By 1900 the small Pacific islands had a larger percentage of Christians in their populations than had the United States or Great Britain. The missionaries and early indigenous church leaders were honored with almost worshipful respect. On the island of Aneityum, for example, this inscription was placed on a tablet in a church that seated 1,000:

IN MEMORY OF JOHN GEDDIE
When he landed in 1848 there were no Christians here; when he left in 1872 there were no heathen.

Into New Guinea

The first twentieth century missionary martyr in the Pacific was James Chalmers. The son of a Scots stonemason, Chalmers was challenged in his teens when his pastor read a letter from a missionary in Fiji describing the power of the gospel over cannibals. The minister finished in tears, then looked over his spectacles and said, "I wonder if there is a boy here who will by-and-by bring the gospel to the cannibals?" Young Chalmers vowed he would be a pioneer.

Some ten years later, January 4, 1866, Chalmers and his bride Jane sailed on the *John Williams*, named for the martyred missionary. After surviving a shipwreck, the two were put ashore on the island of Rarotonga. "What fellow name belong you?" a native called to him. He answered, "Chalmers." The native declared, "Tamate," and ever after he was known by that name among the island people.

There were already Christians at Rarotonga. As soon as

other missionaries arrived, the Chalmers turned down a furlough and headed for virgin New Guinea. "The nearer I get
to Christ and His cross, the more do I long for direct contact
with the heathen," he wrote. They soon reported, "Several of
our new friends wear human jawbones on their arms." Once
Mr. Chalmers was surrounded by a mob of painted bandits,
demanding tomahawks and knives or else they would kill
both him and his wife. "You may kill us, but never a thing
will you get from us," he declared. The surprised leader left,
then came back the next day to apologize. Chalmers extended a gift of friendship and they were friends thereafter.
Invitations to feasts began coming. They accepted some, but
declined those where human flesh was served. Jane Chalmers was once offered the gift of a portion of a man's chest,
already cooked.

The strain soon showed on Mrs. Chalmers. Two years
after coming to New Guinea, she went to Sydney in Australia for rest. There she died in 1879. Upon receiving the
sad news, Chalmers told his friends, "Let me bury my sorrow in work for Christ, with Whom my dear wife is. Some
of our teachers have suffered and lost their wives, and with
them I must be."

By 1882 Chalmers could report "no cannibal ovens, no
feasts, no human flesh, no desire for skulls," in the area
where he worked. He had become so well known and
beloved that when he visited neighboring islands residents
invited him to speak in heathen temples that were lined
with the skulls of people they had sacrificed and eaten. Often
he and his assistants would preach all night and at the conclusion, the congregation would declare, "No more fighting,
Tamate, no more man-eating; we have heard the good news
and we shall strive for peace."

Again he was urged to take a furlough. "No," he said, "I
would rather risk climate and savages, than sea and land
traveling." Finally in 1886 he did go and received a hero's
welcome in London. He returned to the Pacific two years
later with a new wife.

He kept pioneering along the New Guinea coast and
among nearby islands. In 1900 he lost his second wife after a
fourteen-week illness. He comforted himself in "the sweet
will of God," and said, "I cannot rest with so many thousands of savages without a knowledge of God near us." To
an invitation to spend his last years in England, he replied,

"I am nearing the bar, and might miss resting amidst old scenes, joys and sorrows."

On April 4, 1901, the old salt sailed to Goaribari Island where there were few believers. Three days later, on Easter evening, his ship anchored off the end of the island. Armed natives paddled out and swarmed over the vessel. Chalmers promised to go ashore the next morning and they left. Shortly after dawn they returned. Another missionary named Tomkins decided to go with him.

The crew waited all day. When the missionaries did not return, the captain dispatched a search party. The searchers were told a grisly story.

Upon coming ashore, Chalmers, Tomkins, and the few native Christians had been invited into a building for a feast. As they entered, men knocked them to the ground with stone clubs. The attackers then cut off their heads and hacked their torsos into pieces for cooking the same day.

The murders of Chalmers and Tomkins shook Europe and America. No missionaries had been lost in the Pacific to cannibals for several years. Scores of young men and women were stirred to volunteer.

Death Almost Certain

The new missionaries found that their biggest foe was rampant disease. Among ten Methodists who went to New Guinea, not a single one was living twenty years later. Some perished from malaria and other tropical scourges. Others returned home, broken in health. The German Lutheran Neuendettelsau Missionary Society, which established in New Guinea the largest Protestant mission society in the South Pacific, lost the most. But between 1900 and 1940 this mission baptized thousands of converts and trained hundreds of native evangelists to go into more remote areas of the large unmapped island.

The Dutch East Indies

The going was just as tough in Java, Sumatra, and Borneo, now part of the Republic of Indonesia, but then known as the Dutch East Indies. In northern Sumatra two early American pioneers to the large Batak tribe were killed and eaten. The early corps of native evangelists among the Bataks suffered because of resentment felt against the Dutch colonialists who had controlled the East Indies since 1623. Several were killed for embracing the religion of the hated foreign bosses. Bapa Gabriel, a young Bible teacher in Kabandjahe, was dragged to a river for execution. "Allow me only to pray," he asked his captors calmly. They were so surprised by his courage that they released him.

Independence movements, led mostly by Muslims, mushroomed through the 1920's and 1930's. Christianity, in the minds of the people, was the Dutch religion. They noted that the Dutch gave preference to Reformed Church missionaries from the homeland. The Dutch colonial government was not enthusiastic about other missionaries moving into the uncharted interior.

"General" Jaffray's Strategy

In 1928 the C&MA's R.A. Jaffray came from Vietnam to map plans for the spiritual conquest of "the unreached areas of the Dutch East Indies."

He set up headquarters at Makassar, the largest city of the Celebes (now Sulawesi), a large island group betweeen Borneo and New Guinea. Like a commanding general, he pored over maps and planned strategy. He was also a good diplomat and soon had the trust of Dutch officials.

His first big move was to start a Bible school for Chinese, Malays and converted "wild men of Borneo." As fast as students were trained, he sent them back to their own people. By 1934 he could report "no less than 4,347 souls" who had accepted Christ and destroyed their idols.

Jaffray got more excited when a young Dutch flier, J.F. Wissel, discovered in central New Guinea a cluster of lakes which had a large native population. He made a quick trip to Java for talks with Dutch officials about beginning work in the newly named "Wissel Lakes" area. The officials received him warmly.

In 1938, at age 64, Jaffray made a trip to coastal New Guinea, and gathered every scrap of information available about the tribes around the lakes. Then he rushed to the United States and alerted his Alliance constituency.

Mission to the Stone Age

Back in the Celebes, Jaffray selected two of the C&MA's most promising young strategists, Russell Diebler and Walter M. Post, to make the first survey trip. At the last minute Post was unable to go. Diebler went ahead anyway, taking ten native carriers into the rugged highlands where no missionary had ever gone. After a long arduous journey he reached the lakes and met Kapaukus "a most backward people, living still in the Stone Age." The natives were friendly. Diebler decided they would be the key to reaching other lost tribes.

He returned to the coast and made a second exploratory trip with Post. Then they went back for their wives. By 1940 they could report a thousand Kapaukus listening eagerly to the gospel.

"If We Die, We Will All Die Together"

Jaffray was due a furlough home. Rest did not concern the old warrior, even though he was past retirement age. He wanted to excite the constituency about the new opportunities in the Pacific and recruit more workers. Diebler left the Kapaukus to take over the station at Makassar.

Jaffray stayed no longer than necessary. To suggestions that he remain in the States he snorted, "Never. I'm just putting on new tires." His friends did not argue with him. They knew that when he set out to do something, there was no turning him back. After all, in answering a call to the mission field, he had turned down the opportunity to succeed his wealthy father as publisher of the *Toronto Globe*. Jaffray also smelled the war coming. "I don't want to get caught in the United States or Canada when war breaks and be unable to get back to the field."

The "commander" reached Makassar the day before Pearl Harbor. The Japanese occupied the city two months later. Jaffray and the other missionaries had advance warning but chose to stay. "If we die, we will all die together," Diebler told the Bible school students.

"God Takes the Best"

The five C&MA missionaries at Makassar—Dieblers, Jaffrays, and Canadian Ernie Presswood—were permitted to move to a mountain rest home. Five weeks later Japanese officers came and ordered Diebler and Presswood to accompany them back to the city. Because of his age they allowed Jaffray to remain with the women in the rest home until they were moved in December to a small camp nearby.

Diebler and Presswood were interned with about a hundred Dutchmen in an overcrowded police barracks. "It will be only one night," one of the officers promised. The "one night" for Diebler lasted a year and a half, and for Presswood three and a half years.

During their captivity the men were served only two cups of poorly cooked rice and one bun each day. A Bible student who saw them later reported, "They were so thin. It was enough to make a person weep."

In September the two men were moved to the large Parepare camp where there were other missionaries. For a while they were permitted to hold Sunday worship services at the nearby war prisoners' camp. One memorable sermon was based on James 4:14, "For what is your life? It is even a vapor, that appears for a little time, and then vanishes away."

In the spring of 1943 Jaffray was brought to Parepare. He was given a small room in the hospital and allowed to take walks with Presswood and Diebler.

Diebler's greatest sorrow was the separation from his wife Darlene. They had been married only three years when the war broke. Before that they had been apart for about a year while he was preparing the entry into the Wissel Lake area. Presswood had buried his wife three years before in the jungle after only two years of service together.

In August Diebler came down with dysentery, not unusual in the camp, and had to be hospitalized. Then he became suddenly worse. Presswood later recalled, "I had prayed so fervently for Russell, but toward midnight the Lord convinced me that I should no longer pray for him. I surrendered him to our Savior." Diebler began calling for his wife and died a few hours later. The Japanese permitted a funeral which all the interned missionaries attended. "God takes the best," a grieving Catholic priest said. Months later a Dutchman confided to Presswood that he had trusted in Christ at the service.

"So Hard to Be Brave"

Darlene Diebler did not learn of her husband's passing until three months later. Not until the end of the war, almost two years later, was she able to convey her grief to her parents. "I can't put on paper the heartache that has made me so much older," she wrote.

> I only know about his passing what others have told
> me. He was unconscious the last few hours, the doc-
> tor told me, who attended him, and he kept calling

for me. And to think I was only three hours by car
from him and couldn't be there. The first night I
thought I'd go crazy with grief but God—how precious He has become to me! The heartache is still
there, but the terrible hurt has left me. . . .
I took dysentery, tropical malaria and beri-beri all at
once. For six weeks I lived on salt-free rice porridge.
How often that verse came to me, "The Lord is my
Shepherd, I shall not want." I can't write what we
suffered there, but through personal intervention of
our Jap Camp Commander, we were finally released
after having been told we were to be beheaded as
spies—but they forgive us this time! Enough said. . . .
After Russell's death and during those weeks in
prison, I turned quite gray. O Mummy dear, it is so
hard to be brave. I did so love Russell.

A Missionary Statesman Dies

The young widow also reported that after the war turned
against the Japanese and Allied planes began bombing in the
area, the prisoners were jammed in trucks like cattle and
transported 156 miles into the jungle to a camp of grass
huts. Jaffray's health had been failing and here he became
much worse. He died on July 28, only a few days before
peace was declared.

Said Dr. A.C. Snead, the C&MA Foreign Director, of
Jaffray:

The Christian and Missionary Alliance and the
Church of Christ throughout the earth have lost an
intrepid pioneer, a great missionary statesman, and a
man so filled with the love and grace of God that his
whole being—body, soul, and spirit—was devoted
utterly to Christ and His service.

Bayoneted to Death

Besides Diebler and Jaffray, four other C&MA missionaries
perished in prison camps in the Dutch East Indies, and two
others died afterward.

Pilot Fred Jackson and Mr. and Mrs. Andrew Sande had
reached east Borneo just before Pearl Harbor. Jackson
replaced George Fisk, the first C&MA pilot, who had gone
home on furlough. The Sandes, who had an infant son, were
also new workers in the already fruitful east Borneo field.

Thousands of Dyak tribespeople had renounced cannibalism and were seeking baptism from missionaries and graduates of the Makassar Bible School.

For several weeks Jackson flew mercy missions at the request of Dutch officials, ferrying sick and wounded to hospitals. When the Japanese took control of the air, he hid the plane and joined the Sandes at Long Nawang where the Dutch had a military base. Here the missionaries lived in a house at the edge of a Dyak Christian village.

All was peaceful until August 19, 1942, when some Dyaks reported foreign soldiers moving around the base. The Dutch officers apparently did not believe the report, for they took no steps to fight or flee. Early the next morning the Japanese attacked when the Dutch were taking infantry practice with unloaded guns.

The Japanese rounded up sixty-nine men, including the two male missionaries, for questioning. Jackson and Sandes were kept under close guard but not mistreated during the following week. The women and children were detained separately.

Near the end of August, all of the European men were taken out one by one and bayoneted to death. Two months later the women and children were also brutally murdered.

No "Situation Ethics"

When the Japanese invaded, John Willfinger and Mr. and Mrs. Richard Lenham of the C&MA fled deep into the Borneo jungle and took refuge with Murut Christians. A bachelor Bible translator, Willfinger had been anticipating his upcoming furlough and a reunion with his fiancee when the war came. The Lenhams were also working on the translation of the Murut Bible.

In July, 1942, the trio heard that the Japanese had captured a party of Europeans. They moved to a village in north Borneo. Here they learned that Jackson and the Sandes had been imprisoned.

They anticipated that the Japanese would learn their location. On September 19, a courier came to the village with a list of names of people for whom the Japanese were searching. Their names were on the list. The messenger warned the tribespeople that they would be severely punished for trying to hide any of the wanted persons.

"Stay. We will take you where you cannot be found," the Murut Christians begged.

The three missionaries mulled over their future. Finally they told the Muruts, "You would have to lie to the Japanese. We would rather go and surrender than cause you to be disobedient to God's word."

Willfinger explained their decision in a "whomsoever-receives-this letter."

> We feel that we could have successfully hidden, but
> at the risk of involving those Muruts who have been
> kind to us, and are desirous of hiding us. But we
> cringed at the thought of this. Therefore we have
> decided to go to the enemy, trusting God as to the
> ultimate results.

He added the addresses of his loved ones, asking the receiver to "kindly send my love to my family and sweetheart."

The three decided to separate. Willfinger wanted to visit several tribal churches in east Borneo before surrendering. The Lenhams took the precious Bible translations and struck out for a Japanese post further north. Several days later they walked into a Japanese camp and were immediately interned. Mrs. Lenham managed to conceal the Gospel of Mark, often hiding it in wet clothes on the clothesline when the women's quarters were searched. Mr. Lenham kept Matthew until a guard discovered it. After they were released at the end of the war, he found the translation in a pile of trash. Both Gospels were subsequently published by the British and Foreign Bible Society for the Murut church.

Willfinger completed his last missionary journey and gave himself up for imprisonment. He was executed on December 28. At war's end his Bible was recovered. Inside the cover he had inscribed a poem which indicated the power of his commitment:

> No mere man is the Christ I know,
>   But greater far than all below.
> Day by day His love enfolds me,
>   Day by day His power upholds me;
> All that God could ever be,
>   The man of Nazareth is to me.
>
> No mere man can my strength sustain
>   And drive away all fear and pain,
> Holding me close in His embrace
>   When death and I stand face to face;
> Then all that God could ever be
>   The unseen Christ will be to me.

Below the poem he had written, "Hallelujah! This is real! "

When the war ended, the circumstances of John Will-finger's death were unknown. Ernie Presswood set out to get the facts after his release. He recovered the body of his colleague and arranged for final burial in a cemetery just off the Borneo coast. Presswood died a short time later and was laid to rest in a Pacific grave.

Still the toll of prison martyrs was not to end for the C&MA. Word came that another internee, Grace Dittmar, had succumbed from privations suffered while trying to escape from Sumatra.

Nine More Die in New Guinea

There were many other prison camp martyrs besides the seven C&MA missionaries. In Papua (eastern New Guinea), the Anglican bishop, when ordered by British authorities to leave, broadcast this message to his staff:

> We must endeavor to carry on our work in all circumstances, no matter what the cost may ultimately be to any of us individually. . . . We could never hold up our faces again if, for our own safety, we forsook Him and fled when the shadows of the passion began to gather around Him in His spiritual and mystical body, the church in Papua.

The bishop and eight of his staff were killed in concentration camps.

A New Nation Is Formed

The end of the war brought a resurgence of independence movements in the Dutch East Indies. Sukarno and Muhammed Hatta, founder of the Indonesian Nationalist Party, immediately formed a provincial government. After four years of bitter Dutch resistance and much bloodshed, the United Nations intervened. The Dutch agreed to withdraw, and in 1949 the world's fifth most populous nation, Indonesia, became a reality. The vast island archipelago included Borneo (now Kalimantan), the Celebes (Sulawesi), Java, Sumatra and Timor. Western New Guinea (Irian Jaya) did not come under Indonesian control until 1963.

Many American servicemen who had seen duty in the Pacific were eager to return with the gospel. Some had evidence of missionary work firsthand when they were hidden by friendly, Christian natives after being shot down. Independent youth-oriented Christian movements—such as Youth for Christ, The Navigators, and Inter-Varsity Christian Fellowship—were firing up the ex-servicemen and other young people for missionary service. At the same time old mission societies were revving up for new challenges, and new independent evangelical organizations were on the runway eager to takeoff.

The Fateful Journey of Erickson and Tritt

A Salvation Army couple, imprisoned by the Japanese, was urging The Evangelical Alliance Mission (TEAM), formerly the Scandinavian Alliance Mission, to send workers to tribes in newly independent Indonesia. Walter Erickson, a young theology student, had asked TEAM for appointment to New Guinea. Erickson had visited the south coast while serving in the U. S. Coast Guard during the war and had traveled to the Wissel Lakes. He could not forget the tribespeople he had met.

Erickson accepted appointment to Indonesia, hoping to enter New Guinea later. He reached Java on a student visa and was warned by the American consul to leave immediately because of dangerous political disturbances. He went instead to the Dutch consulate and procured a visa to western New Guinea.

Erickson conferred with C&MA, Unevangelized Fields Mission and Missionary Aviation Fellowship personnel already there. They suggested that TEAM locate in untouched "Bird's Head", an area on the end of the island half the size of Illinois and teeming with unreached tribes. Erickson wangled Dutch permission for a quota of ten missionaries.

Erickson had already made several surveys when Edward R. Tritt, his first reinforcement, arrived. On September 10, 1952, the two set out on foot with five native carriers for the remote Kebur and Karoon regions. MAF's single plane had crashed a year before, killing the pilot, and there was no flight service available.

On October 17 Erickson and Tritt's mutilated bodies were found near the Ainim River. Tritt had died at the place of attack. Erickson had crawled to a cave where he succumbed. Investigation by Dutch police resulted in a confession of murder by the missionaries' carriers. The hired tribesmen had not wanted to go further for fear of being killed by the unknown tribespeople. The missionaries wanted to press on. While the missionaries slept, the carriers attacked and slashed them to death with machetes.

Stirred by Sacrifice

The sacrifice of Erickson and Tritt stirred students at Columbia College in South Carolina to raise funds for an MAF airplane that would reduce the danger of future surveys. None of TEAM's volunteers preparing for New Guinea, including Tritt's fiancee, Beulah Staph, canceled their plans. She had been at the home office switchboard and had been the first to hear the news.

The martyrdom of the New Guinea pioneers triggered a flurry of new applications for missionary service. Vernon Mortenson, then responsible for TEAM's recruiting program and now the mission's general director, told the Erickson–Tritt story at the Highland Park Baptist Church in Chattanooga. Afterwards a couple came to him and said they felt God was leading them to New Guinea. Mr. and Mrs. Ronald Hill later joined the TEAM force in the new field. By 1965 there were forty-seven TEAM missionaries in the Bird's Head area, and by 1969 they reported 4,280 baptized believers among former head-hunting tribes.

Meanwhile, other C&MA missionaries had returned to the Kapauku people around the Wissel Lakes area where the Dieblers and Posts had pioneered before the Japanese invasion. They enrolled hundreds of young people in village schools conducted by Indonesians trained at the Makassar Bible School. The first graduates began carrying the gospel to more distant villages of their own tribe.

Tokens of Death

Suddenly, on November 4, 1956, a mob of tribal elders attacked the mission station at Obano where a school was located. They were bent on driving out all the foreigners, but eleven missionaries and four Indonesian workers had left the day before. However, they succeeded in killing the Indonesian teacher, Mr. Lesnussa and his family and a Christian carpenter. They also burned the houses and school and destroyed a C&MA plane.

Before leaving, they cut fingers from the teacher's and the carpenter's hands and sent them to villages in the area, inviting elders there to join the revolt. Only three responded. Shortly, the Dutch government sent in police and crushed the uprising.

Two reasons were suggested for the outbreak of hostility. The elders believed an epidemic among their pigs had been caused by evil spirits displeased over the presence of the foreigners. Second, and more likely, the older Kapaukus saw that they were losing their influence in the villages to the young evangelists.

The crushing of this rebellion marked a dramatic upswing in conversions around Wissel Lakes. The Kapauku church more than quadrupled, from twenty-three hundred to ten thousand, in four years.

"Cannibal Valley"

The missionaries at Wissel Lakes knew of an even more remote valley, first seen by an American scientific expedition in 1938. It was reported to be a tropical Shangri-la of breathtaking beauty, surrounded by high mountains and populated by the most ferocious cannibals of New Guinea. R.A. Jaffray had dreamed of entering this valley through which the Baliem River flowed. After the war C&MA workers had made survey trips near the valley. Then in 1951 Jerry Rose and three Dutch officials crossed a rugged plateau at about twelve thousand feet and descended into the remote region. They were on the trail for sixty-seven days and along the way their guide was killed with arrows. Afterwards Rose moved his bride into the valley.

Rose was married to Darlene Diebler, the widow of Russell Diebler. She became the first white woman to live among the Danis, the principal tribe of the valley. The Danis were cannibals. One of their funeral customs required the chopping off of fingers and bits of ears from relatives of the deceased to be eaten by other mourners.

The C&MA missionaries had their own amphibious plane and by 1955 two other couples had joined the Roses.

The Danis were friendly and it appeared the missionaries were making headway when hostilities flared. The three men were attacked while on a routine medical mission to a village and had to run for their lives. Lloyd Van Stone took an arrow in his left thigh which proved not to be a serious injury. A much bigger setback that same day was the crash of the C&MA plane into the side of a mountain overlooking the valley. Pilot Al Lewis was killed instantly. Only a few days previous he had predicted, "I believe it is going to cost much to open this field, but I am ready to pay the price."

The First Dani Martyr

The Baliem Valley missionaries remained, although at times they needed all the spiritual strength they could muster. Hardest was watching the bloody battles between nearby villages and cannibal feasts of the victors which followed.

In 1957 the men were attacked again while on a scouting expedition to the hitherto unreached Wosi Valley. They ran and escaped without harm.

By this time the word of God had taken root. Newly trained Dani evangelists were going to distant villages where no gospel messengers had ever gone.

In 1961 the C&MA's Tom Bozeman and Dave Martin, a visitor from the Regions Beyond Missionary Union, made a trip to a new mission outpost in a deep gorge. They arrived on Saturday night in time to help two Dani preachers, Selanuok and Alikat, prepare for the Sunday service. Before retiring, Selanuok told them that enemies on the hillside intended to kill the Christians in the village. They prayed and committed the threat to the Lord.

The next morning three hundred villagers were chanting praise to God when Selanuok whispered to the missionaries, "The enemy warriors are coming today to kill me." They again prayed with him. A few minutes later Bozeman looked up and saw a long line of scowling warriors filing down the hillside. They carried spears and bows and arrows. Someone shouted the alarm. The Christians huddled together. "Keep singing! Keep singing!" the Dani preachers cried.

The attackers bounded into the clearing, leaping and shouting war cries. The worshipers scattered in all directions, looking for places to hide. Several men charged Selanuok. One threw a spear. "Jesus! Jesus!" he cried and fell. He was the first Dani Christian martyr.

The missionaries reached the woods and sprinted up a trail. From the village they could hear the shrieks of the wounded and dying. Behind them they could hear men in pursuit. They reached the crest of a ridge and heard voices above. "This way," Bozeman shouted, as he led Martin down a side trail leading toward the river. By this stratagem they escaped.

"The Enemy Is Upon Us"

Meanwhile, missionary work in the long Baliem Valley continued despite the danger. In 1957 Australian Baptists occupied the north end. By 1962 they had won several hundred converts. On September 30 a large force of pagan Danis launched war on about sixty villages in the vicinity of the Baptist mission station. They burned fifty villages and killed scores of Christians. One of the martyrs was heard to tell another as attackers approached, "Pray my brother, pray, the enemy is upon us. If we die we ascend to be with Jesus."

It was customary for defeated villagers to flee to another area. But the survivors announced to the local Australian missionary, "We will stay. We need you and you need us. We will rebuild." And they did.

In 1966 Stan Dale, an Australian member of the Regions Beyond Missionary Union, was hit by five arrows while trying unsuccessfully to save two Yali Christians from death. In September, 1968, Dale and colleague Phil Masters were ambushed on the bank of the. Seng River. Their bodies were found riddled with arrows from warriors of the Yali tribe.

The High Cost of Serving

The cost continued high. On December 31, the MAF plane crashed in the area. Pilot Meno Voth, along with Mr. and Mrs. Gene Newman and three of their four children were killed. The Newmans were also with MAF. The one survivor, ten-year-old Paul Newman, was only slightly injured. He wandered into a tribal village and was given shelter by some of the same Yali people who had killed Masters and Dale.

By this time there were almost twenty thousand baptized believers in the interior jungles of western New Guinea. The Yali work prospered. Hundreds turned to Christ, including many of the murderers of the martyrs.

Tribal evangelists padded along the rugged trails, opening up new territory in New Guinea. Before leaving home they chanted a vow of commitment: "We are ready to be killed for You, to drown or be crushed in a landslide in Your service. You died for us. Your servant Paul went through great tribulations for You. We are ready to suffer for You." Eight were crushed to death by a landslide in the Wusak Valley in 1969. Their Christian friends responded: "Because our blood has been shed in the Wusak it has become our land, and we will continue to take the gospel there."

The Miracle in Indonesia

Western New Guinea came under Indonesia's jurisdiction in May, 1963. At this time the Indonesian Communist Party, a

million-and-a-half strong and with strong backing from Red
China, was laying plans to take over the populous new country. Early in the morning of October 1, 1965, the Communists struck. The scheme was to murder eight top army generals under the pretense of catching them in the act of
staging their own coup. The Communists would then begin
a mass annihilation of their enemies all over Indonesia, including Christians.

Miraculously, two of the generals escaped. When the
plot was exposed, anti-communist rioting swept the country.
In the ensuing bloodbath, Muslims killed upwards of four
hundred thousand Communists. One of the generals emerged
as the power in a hard-line anti-communist regime. The new
government required every citizen to accept the principle
that the nation was built on the foundation of belief in a
"Divinity." Evidence of acceptance was adherence to a recognized religion.

There followed a mass turning to Christianity, unprecedented in modern times, marked by hundreds of acclaimed
miracles. Within two years the Indonesian Bible Society
counted four hundred thousand new believers. In 1974 the
largest evangelical group on the Indonesian island of Timor
claimed six hundred fifty thousand members.

Because of the dramatic turn, there have been only minor localized hostilities against Christians in the Indonesian
islands since 1965. In one instance a Chinese missionary,
Miss Lo, was presumably murdered by ax-wielding bandits in
west Borneo.

Buried Alive

In eastern New Guinea, now independent Papua, the same
pattern has prevailed. Recent missionary casualties there
have resulted from a landslide and a plane crash. In March,
1971, Walter and LaVonne Steinkraus, Wycliffe missionary
linguists, and their two daughters were buried under a landslide that swept down upon a Tifalmin tribal village. Thirteen months later five Wycliffe members and two tribal language assistants perished in the crash of a Wycliffe Aztec
plane, the first Wycliffe fatalities in years of flying over the
most hazardous terrains on earth.

The Challenge Ahead

Excluding islands belonging to other nations, Indonesia today
includes 13,677 islands stretching over three thousand miles

from the Indian Ocean to the South Pacific. Indonesia in population is now the fifth largest nation in the world, with almost 140 million people. It is classified ninety per cent Islamic, but Indonesian Muslims have proven to be more open to the gospel than Muslims in the Middle East and North Africa. Over two thousand tribal groups inhabit Indonesia. Many of these are without a New Testament. The Wycliffe Bible Translators have mounted a full scale advance to meet this need.

Many heroes of the faith of past generations gave their lives to establish the first beachheads for the gospel in this paradise of islands. They are among the "cloud of witnesses" now cheering believers on.

"RIGHT TO PROFESS, PRACTICE, PROPAGATE":
Malaysia and Singapore

Malaysia, a former British possession, is situated on two land masses—the finger-like peninsula south of Thailand and the northern coast of Borneo. A constitutional Islamic monarchy governs twelve million Malays, Chinese, Indians and Pakistanis. The constitution guarantees every person "the right to profess, practice, and propagate his religion." But evangelization of aborigines and persons under eighteen is strictly forbidden. Christian missionaries are also barred from certain "New Villages" which are totally or majority Muslim.

No missionary martyrs have been reported in modern times, but government pressure continues strong. Around one hundred eighty missionaries are now registered. A few others have recently been expelled or been refused the renewal of work permits. One of the latter tells of officials coming to his school almost every week and threatening to "take all of us to jail if we continued. Nothing happened but the constant harassment made our lives miserable." This former missionary "knows of" Malaysian Christians who have been imprisoned and not heard from for months or years. One, he says, was recently released after converting to Islam.

An Oasis in Singapore

The 224-square-mile island of Singapore, population 2.3 million, was federated with Malaysia until 1963. The evangelical minority of Singapore enjoys complete religious freedom for worship, education and evangelism. Because of its openness, neutrality and strategic location, Singapore has become a training center for Christian nationals from other Asian countries.

Missionaries and national leaders wish that all Pacific countries were as open as Singapore.

THE REPUBLIC OF CHINA:
Taiwan

The large cucumber-shaped island off the coast of mainland China was lost by China to Japan in 1895 and not regained until the end of World War II. When mainland China fell under Communist control, two million Chinese followed Chiang Kai-shek's government to the island. Today it is officially known as The Republic of China, but more often is called Taiwan or Formosa. Besides the mainland Chinese, there are three other distinct groups in the island country: (1) Nine mountain tribes comprising about two hundred thousand people; (2) Hakkas, who migrated generations before from the mainland, and numbering about eight hundred thousand; (3) Taiwanese, numbering over six million and making up the majority.

Before 1950 the Presbyterians were the only Christian denomination in Taiwan. Because of Japanese opposition, no missionaries worked among the mountain tribes before World War II. The Japanese were sorely afraid of these "wild" headhunters and built a 360-mile fence around the tribal territory. The few Japanese settlements in the mountains remained under constant alert. In one attack 134 Japanese heads were taken.

The mountain people were officially off limits to all but Shinto missionaries. However, a few Japanese Christian workers were given tacit permission to work around the fringes. The pioneer was Inoue Inouke, a young Japanese believer whose father had been killed by the headhunters. Inoue was allowed to do only medical and educational work near the fence. On March 10, 1912, he wrote in his diary:

> Mr. Ito had been brought to me badly wounded by savages' attack. I quickly did my best to keep him alive, and I think he is hopeful. I heard that there were eight other Japanese killed this morning.
>
> I sincerely hope and pray that one day these people will hold the Bible and the hymnbook in their hands, instead of these swords to kill people.

"You Will Not Obey Orders"

During World War II the Japanese troops publicly announced they would massacre all Christians on the island if American troops landed. A minority of church members asked that their names be stricken from the rolls to avoid being placed on an official death list. The rest stood firm. Fortunately there were no landings and a blood bath was avoided.

The worst persecution during war time was heaped upon a small minority of tribal Christians. Some were arrested, beaten, and imprisoned as spies.

Wiran Takko, an ex-drunkard who had become a preacher, was conducting a midnight clandestine meeting in the mountains when the police suddenly appeared. He and his listeners were beaten severely for believing in the "American God." Once released, Takko went back into the mountains.

At another meeting he predicted that Japan would lose the war to the United States which would then liberate the tribespeople. Again he was arrested and beaten, this time so savagely that he was thrown out for dead. A tribal Christian carried him home and cared for him until he regained consciousness. The third time he was kept in a wooden cage for a year. Once released, he went right back to preaching. The sergeant who arrested him declared, "You will not obey orders, so we will have to kill you." While a grave was being dug, the sergeant asked, "Are you ready to die?" Takko replied, "Yes, yes, I'm ready." The sergeant was so shaken that he released him again.

Takko survived, but another Christian hero named Saka Tani did not. Police broke all of his ribs and every bone in his hands and feet. Upon regaining consciousness, he was beaten again, so severely that he died.

Pastor Wu Tien-shih asked his widow if she planned to avenge his death. "No, we should love our enemies," she said. "This is the order of the Lord."

The end of World War II brought liberation and rapid evangelization of the mountain tribes. Within fifteen years the Presbyterians had sixty thousand baptized believers in the hills.

The Mad Cook

The only American missionary to die from violence in Taiwan was Miss Gladys Hopewell, a Southern Baptist who was found strangled in her apartment on March 11, 1973. A Kentuckian, she had previously served in China before the Communist takeover and later in Thailand. She came from Bangkok to pioneer Baptist student work on Taiwan and had been at the student center the afternoon before her death.

Ten days later the body of a Chinese cook was discovered on the roof of Miss Hopewell's apartment building. Beside him police found an empty insecticide bottle. The cook's wife had worked for Miss Hopewell and he had been sought as a prime suspect. The police decided that he had killed the missionary in a fit of madness and later in remorse committed suicide.

No Christian worker is known to have been killed in Taiwan since this incident. There are now almost six hundred missionaries on the island. Southern Baptists, with eighty-nine workers, are the largest mission. Many of the missionaries, like Miss Hopewell, previously served in mainland China.

The Call of the Martyred Pioneers

The Taiwan Protestant community of around one hundred seventy-five thousand, including the mountain tribal believers, continues relatively small. The challenge of evangelizing the mostly Buddhist Taiwanese majority remains as a symbol of the larger job to be done in all the isles of the Pacific where so many have given their lives to pioneer the gospel.

OPEN DOOR
FOR MISSIONS:
The Philippines

The vast Philippine archipelago of 7,107 islands (only ten per cent inhabited) forms a triangle reaching from Indonesian Borneo in the south to Taiwan in the north. With 44 million people, the Philippines is the only nominally Christian nation in Asia. This is because it was a Spanish possession for some three hundred years until ceded in 1898 to the United States as part of the settlement of the Spanish–American War. In 1946 the nation became independent, but American influence has remained strong. This has produced an open door for missions. Today eighty-nine independent and denominational agencies are represented by about twelve hundred workers. Wycliffe Bible Translators is the largest with about one hundred fifty linguists and support personnel.

In culture, however, Filipino people are akin to other Pacific groups. There are three main families: the aboriginal mountain Negritos (about thirty thousand), the Indonesians, and the Malayans who are regarded as ancestors of the majority of the Filipino people.

The first Protestants had to meet underground. One of their early converts, a Catholic Dominican friar, was put on trial, defrocked and exiled to Spain. After the Philippines became an American possession, Catholic persecution virtually ended. However, many missionaries succumbed to the diseases of the tropics, including the first C&MA worker, who died of cholera in 1902.

The Philippines was hit hard by Japanese occupation and Allied bombing in World War II. The death toll ran high. About eighty per cent of all church properties were destroyed.

The Mystery of Rufus Gray

Rufus Gray was among a group of Southern Baptist missionaries from China interned in the Philippines. He and his wife had been attending language school when the Japanese overran Peking.

Soon after arriving in the Philippines Gray was taken in for questioning. His wife and friends never saw him again, nor was his body ever recovered.

His hobby was photography and he had taken hundreds of pictures in Peking. The Japanese may have assumed that he was a spy.

A Family Is Strafed to Death

Thousands of foreign civilians were imprisoned in the Philippines. The actual treatment of missionaries varied from one command to another. Some were permitted to hold services in the camps. Some were closely confined. Some in large cities who pledged cooperation with Japanese were allowed to live in their own houses and carry on a limited ministry.

As in the Dutch East Indies, the Japanese demanded that missionaries located in remote places come out and surrender. An American sergeant saw a family of five walking down from the mountains waving a white flag. A Japanese Zero spotted them and opened fire, killing the whole family. The sergeant helped bury them. He recalled that one of the little girls was still clutching a rag doll.

The Hopedale Massacre

American (Northern) Baptists suffered the greatest loss of missionaries in the Philippines during the war. Eight of their nineteen workers surrendered and were imprisoned for the duration. Twelve, including the ten-year-old son of two of the missionaries, fled into the mountains on the island of Panay and tried to carry on a ministry among rural villagers.

The twelve set up camp in a mountain-top clearing called Hopedale. The sanctuary was in deep, thick woods and was reachable only by a narrow, winding trail. Here they were joined by eight or ten other Americans, businessmen and engineers who had been caught in the area after Pearl Harbor.

"We live in a grass hut with bamboo floor," James Covell wrote. "The people around supply us with plenty to eat, and we have a good spring . . . the Japanese came very close one day in February (1942) and we have moved out thrice to hide. . . . Our prospects for freedom and seeing you all (relatives) are most uncertain. . . ."

They worshiped in a chapel in "a beautiful, deep, dry gorge with giant trees growing in it." Every Sunday, except when the Japanese came near, they had a congregation of around one hundred—mostly other Americans who were hiding out in the region. The missionaries took turns conducting the services and baptizing those who made professions of faith in Christ. When the missionaries felt it was safe, they made evangelistic visits to nearby villages. One of the twelve, Dr. Frederick W. Meyer, was a surgeon, and he continued to carry on a ministry of healing. "Bed patients are scattered all over the jungle," he wrote. "Plenty of long hikes keep me thin but happy."

Dr. and Mrs. Meyer, from Connecticut and Wisconsin respectively, were serving their fourth term. Dr. Meyer, a graduate of Yale Medical School, had been honored by the highest officials in the Philippines for his devotion to the poor. Both he and Mrs. Meyer were talented musically. Mrs. Meyer had taught music at Central Baptist Philippine College. Dr. Meyer had developed choirs at stations where he had clinics.

James Covell, a graduate of the University of Chicago, was from Pennsylvania and his wife Charma was from Ohio. Educators, they previously served in a poor section of Yokohama, Japan, and had been forced to leave in 1939 by the Shinto war lords.

Dr. Francis Howard Rose was also a Chicago alumnus and his wife Gertrude held the master's degree from Columbia University. They had taught at Central Philippine College. Dr. Rose wrote, "My religion means only so much as what I am. And by so much, that is, by my way of life alone, may I teach religion which really counts—or I will not teach it at all."

Erle and Louise Rounds, the fourth couple, were graduates of Berkeley Baptist Divinity School. They were traveling evangelists to the mountain tribespeople. Their older son was in high school in Manila at the beginning of the war and was interned at the Santo Tomas Camp with other missionary personnel. Their younger son, Erle Douglas, was with them on the mountaintop.

Erle Rounds had written in one of his last letters before Pearl Harbor,

We are living in interesting times over here, and I believe the missionaries are going to see real persecution before the thing is over. . . . But it is one of the greatest privileges I can think of to be here as a missionary. . . . We hope to see you all again, but, if we should be denied that blessed joy, we can meet again in the land which is fairer than day. May we strive harder to be worthy of the world which God has given us and of that other land made possible through our Lord Jesus Christ. . . . May God keep a clean wind blowing through my heart.

Jennie Adams, from Nebraska, had served for twenty years as Superintendent of Nurses at Emmanuel Hospital where Dr. Meyer was on the medical staff. She had led many of her nurses to Christ and considered her Bible class the most important course in nurses' training.

The tenth missionary was Signe Erickson from Pennsylvania, a graduate of Moody Bible Institute and Columbia University. A teacher, she had worked in the Missionary Training School. On weekends she visited isolated mountain villages and slept on the floor of crude huts.

Dorothy Dowell, from Colorado, had been principal of the Baptist Missionary Training School. She was adept at getting letters to missionary friends in the Santo Tomas Internment Camp where the Rounds' son and the Meyers' son were being held. She used code words and signed herself "Dad." The boys knew this stood for the initials of her name. In 1942 she left the mountain to visit Christians in distant villages. She returned just before Christmas, 1943. She had terrible arthritis and had to crawl on her hands and knees the last part of the journey.

Erle Rounds had also been away visiting Filipino churches. He wanted to spend Christmas with his wife and son, and arrived back at the clearing about the same time.

Several months before, Japanese troops in the area had learned where the missionaries were and had decided not to molest them. A fresh Japanese detachment was not so compassionate. They surprised the American Baptists late in December, 1943, and lined them and five other Americans up for execution.

The Covells could speak Japanese fluently and pleaded eloquently that they be imprisoned instead. The soldiers were reportedly touched, but said they had to carry out orders from their superiors. The missionaries asked for time to pray and were given an hour. Then they were all shot.

The War Ends

After the war ended spiritual tides rose in the victorious West. Missionaries and chaplains home from internment camps had gripping stories to tell. One U.S. Army chaplain, Robert Preston Taylor, who survived the horrors of the Bataan Death March and three and one-half years of prison camp, was one of those who found his wife had remarried. The previous January she had been told by some other released prisoners that he had died. Taylor was later named Air Force Chief of Chaplains.

Tribal Christians Are Poisoned

Excluding the missionaries who died in Japanese prison camps, there have been few martyrs in the Philippines in modern times. In 1965 the spiritual leader and two other members of the Cotabato Manobo tribal church were poisoned after the local witch doctor had predicted that all Christians in the tribe would die. The tiny tribal church kept growing and three years later forty two new believers were baptized.

Shot on the Highway

The most recent known casualty was Nolan Williams, a missionary with the Far Eastern Gospel Crusade, the third largest mission in the islands, with eighty-four workers. His death illustrates the dangers of serving in troubled areas where justice is often lacking.

A husky, blond outgoing man, Williams was traveling with two Filipino pastors in June, 1972. They had stopped for refreshments at another pastor's house and were a block or two away when an unmarked red sedan passed and without warning cut them off. Two men in civilian clothes jumped out. One told Williams, "I want to speak with your driver." The missionary sensed that the man might be some kind of official and asked, "Why, what's he done?" Instead of answering, the man pushed forward, insisting, "I want to talk to him." At the same time the other man circled around. The spokesman advanced. Williams stood in his path. Suddenly he swung, hitting the missionary under the eye. Williams grabbed his wrists to keep from getting hit again. "Shoot him!" the attacker shouted to his henchman who opened fire. The missionary fell to the ground critically wounded.

The two men apparently realized the seriousness of what they had done. They put the wounded American into their car and sped to a hospital. Williams died there about an hour and a half later.

An investigation by fellow missionaries revealed that the stranger who had given the fatal command was one of two police chiefs in a nearby town where opposing political factions were squabbling over authority. The mission pressed criminal charges. At the trial the "police chief" denied knowing the man who had fired the fatal shot. Despite testimony from the two pastors who were eyewitnesses, both men were acquitted.

The Fruit of the Committed

At the time of the shooting, Williams' wife was teaching a Bible class. They were discussing John 12:24: "Except a grain of wheat fall into the ground and die, it abides alone: but if it die, it brings forth much fruit." She felt afterwards that the verse was prophetically related to her husband's death.

Shortly after the incident, a Baptist missionary friend in the area was stopped by a young Filipino. "May I study the Bible with you?" he asked. The Filipino, Nard, recalled that he and the slain missionary had met on a train four years before and struck up a conversation. "See, here is a letter he wrote me, hoping that we could meet again."

Nard soon became a Christian and is now a pillar in the local Baptist church.

The Risk Takers

Political unrest continues in some areas of the Philippines, particularly on the island of Mindanao. In one incident rebels killed ten students at a Catholic school which had recently been used as a headquarters for government action against the dissidents. In another instance two Wycliffe women translators were kidnapped and held by rebels for several days, then released without harm.

Some Protestant and Catholic church leaders blame the government for waging a war of repression against social action groups. They point to several pastors who have mysteriously disappeared.

What is certain is that many evangelical missionaries and Filipino Christian workers are serving at considerable personal risk.

The islands and peninsular land masses of the vast Asian expanse are not as mysterious or exotic as they seemed at the beginning of this century. The gospel has been advanced at the cost of hundreds of martyrs' lives to tropical diseases, aboriginal violence, and wars. Hundreds of thousands of believers from tribes which once practiced cannibalism and other barbarities now "... hail the power of Jesus' name" and live in peace.

And yet the high mission of Zion is far from complete. It will not be until every human ear in the Pacific shall hear the good news that "God so loved the world, that he gave his only begotten Son" for them. The completion of this task will not be easy and without sacrifice. There will doubtless be many more names added to the Pacific "book of martyrs."

MARTYRS OF
NAZI GERMANY

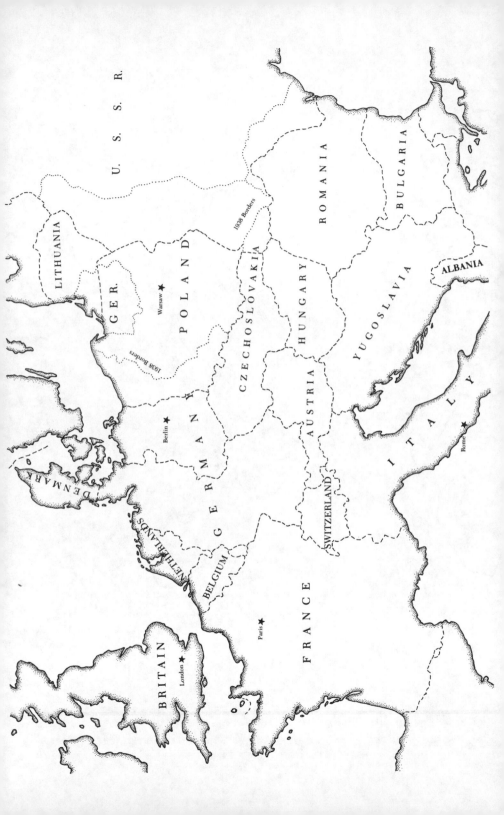

IN THE LAND OF
MARTIN LUTHER:
Nazi Germany

In the year 1927 a young Dutch theological student, Willem ten Boom, wrote in his thesis at a German university that a terrible evil was taking place in the land of Martin Luther. German theologians were tearing the Bible apart, he said, reducing it to a collection of myths and debunking the supernatural by the new method called "higher criticism." German philosophers were talking of breeding a glorious new Aryan super race which would not be contaminated by Jews or weaklings.

Harvest of Hatred

Eighteen years later the world would see the results of this modern paganism called nazism and recoil in horror. Millions of Jews, old people, citizens of conquered nations, Allied and Axis soldiers, and brave German resisters would be dead. Many among the latter would be German pastors and lay leaders who, having failed to convince their fellow countrymen and the world of the dangers of nazism, had joined the internal resistance in a futile attempt to topple a government gone mad.

Destined for Martyrdom

Above them all one name would stand out, Dietrich Bonhoeffer, of whom a prison medic would say, "In the almost fifty years that I worked as a doctor, I have hardly ever seen a man die so entirely submissive to the will of God."

As we follow Bonhoeffer along his road to martyrdom, we shall see how the monstrous Nazi evil grew and how other brave Christians came to walk the path leading to imprisonment and death.

Bonhoeffer, a handsome blond youth, was thoroughly German, from heel-clicking to a stiffly bowing handshake. He came from one of Germany's best families; his father was a distinguished psychiatrist. Although his family were only nominal Lutherans, he had a passion for finding the meaning of life. In the humiliating years following World War I, Germany was two-thirds Lutheran and one-third Catholic. Baptists and other free-church Christians comprised only a minute fraction of the population.

Born in 1906, Bonhoeffer was only thirteen when German workers and troops revolted against continuing the First World War. The revolution hastened the end of the war and led to Germany becoming a democratic republic. But then the democracy fell prey to postwar inflation, economic depression and political chaos. When Adolf Hitler's National Socialist Party came to power on a law-and-order and prosperity platform, Hitler quickly tossed out the constitution and created a dictatorship.

How Hitler Managed the Clergy

Although Hitler used religious language, he was a closet atheist. He wanted to keep in the good graces of the Catholic and Lutheran hierarchies. His deception was astonishingly successful. In 1933, the year his Nazi party rode roughshod over all parliamentary opposition, the German Lutheran bishops proclaimed: "We German Protestant Christians accept the saving of our nation by our leader Adolf Hitler as a gift from God's hand." They affirmed "unanimously our unlimited fealty to the Third Reich and its leader." In this same year Hitler signed a concordat with the Vatican guaranteeing religious freedom for German Catholics.

The question frequently has been asked, how could German church leaders have been so blind? Among Catholics it was a matter of submission to authority, even though many clergy were frightened by the specter of nazism. Among Lutherans it was an erosion of spiritual authority, the result of years of debunking the Bible in church universities and seminaries, and of a corresponding lapse into dreary formalism and decadent institutionalism.

Bonhoeffer, An Evangelical Prophet

Not all had bowed the knee to Baal. The brilliant young Bonhoeffer had, at age twenty-one, opposed some of his professors in his doctoral thesis. Bonhoeffer contended that the "essential nature" of the church could only be understood "on the basis of the gospel" and not by sociological reasoning.

Nor did Bonhoeffer agree that philosophy and theology were complementary disciplines. He held, with theologian Karl Barth, that man was irredeemably sinful and self-centered and could never discover truth through his own thought. Theology, Bonhoeffer said, is rooted and grounded in God who chooses when and how to reveal himself to man. Bonhoeffer further said that personal revelation must be experienced in "direct recourse to Christ" through the Church, which is Christ in community.

Before Hitler's ascension to power, Bonhoeffer spent a year at Union Theological Seminary in New York. Union was then caught up in the cynicism and reaction of Protestant modernism which utilized the methodology of German higher criticism in the classroom. "Union students," the perceptive Bonhoeffer wrote, "intoxicate themselves with liberal and humanistic expressions, laugh at the fundamentalists, and basically they are not even a match for them. . . . I never heard the Gospel of Jesus Christ . . . of the cross, of sin and forgiveness, of death and life (while) in New York . . . only an ethical and social idealism which pins its faith to progress."

At the same time a friend in Germany warned Bonhoeffer of a "great tragedy for our church and nation." The new nationalism of Hitler, his friend said, was "combined with a new heathenism that parades in Christian dress." The church was being made subservient to race, nation and culture.

Bonhoeffer soon returned to Germany and confronted the liberals in his church head on. "The question," he argued, "is not whether we still have a use for God in advanced society. God and the Church exist. They are questioning us. Are we ready for God to use us?"

The Theologian Becomes a Christian

Shortly after this, Bonhoeffer surrendered himself fully for God's use. He could now say, "I believe that the Bible alone is the answer to all our questions . . . that is because in the Bible God speaks to us." Bonhoeffer, as he reports, "had already preached often . . . (and) seen a great deal of the church . . . (but) had not yet become a Christian. . . . Then something new entered, something which . . . has changed my life and turned it upside down."

On January 31, 1933, the day after Hitler was named Chancellor of Germany, Bonhoeffer spoke over Berlin radio on "the concept of leadership." He posed these questions: Is the demand for a strong leader the expression of Germany's volatile political situation or is it to meet the requirements of youth? When is leadership healthy and genuine and when does it become pathological and extreme? He was cut off the air in mid-speech.

The Purge Begins

Four weeks later Communist saboteurs burned the Reichstag (parliament building)—a gift to Hitler. The next morning the fuehrer announced restrictions, "for the protection of nation and state," against free speech and free press, formation of societies, calling of public meetings, privacy of the mails and other communication systems. He also proclaimed governmental right to search houses and to restrict personal property beyond previous limits.

On April 1 the government called for a boycott of Jewish shops. Bonhoeffer's ninety-year-old grandmother walked resolutely through the cordon of storm troopers and Nazi youth that stood in front of her favorite store which was operated by Jews, did her shopping, and walked out without being stopped.

The next order demanded a purge of all Jews and part Jews from German civil service. Another order forbade church appointments of ministers with Jewish blood.

The "Aryan restrictions" hit Bonhoeffer like a thunderbolt. His twin sister, Sabine, was married to a Jew, and one of his closest Lutheran pastor friends, Franz Hildebrandt, was Jewish.

The Lutheran Church Split

Hitler further moved to control the Lutheran church by appointing Ludwig Muller, a clergyman loyal to the government, as his deputy for ecclesiastical affairs. Muller tried to interfere with a committee writing a new constitution for German Lutherans. The committee all but ignored him. Bonhoeffer and a group of reformers calling themselves the "Confessing Church," who refused to exclude non-Aryans, pushed through the election of one of their own as the new national bishop. The government and its loyal clergymen, known as "German Christians," refused to recognize the new constitution and national bishop. The church split.

"We deplore," declared Bonhoeffer, "that state measures against Jews in Germany have had such an effect on public opinion that in some circles the Jewish race is considered a race of inferior status. . . . We protest against the resolution of . . . synods which apply the Aryan paragraph of the state to the church, putting serious disabilities on ministers and church officers who by chance of birth are non-Aryan, which we believe to be a denial of the explicit teaching and spirit of the Gospel of Jesus Christ."

On July 23, three days after Hitler signed the concordat with the Vatican, a national referendum was held in the Lutheran churches. The vast majority voted in favor of the "German Christians" as their official leaders.

The reformers refused to accept this and formed their own Free Synod. They met the next year at Barmen and declared that they represented the true Protestant church of Germany as envisaged by Luther. They subscribed to a confession of faith drawn up by Karl Barth. They proclaimed that "Jesus Christ, as He is testified to us in Holy Scripture, is the one Word of God which we have to hear and to trust and obey in life and death."

Hitler made no immediate move to suppress the rebel minority. He was too busy consolidating his political rule, tightening the screws on other dissenters, and whipping up the youth for a war. And all the while, the majority of German Lutheran pastors were praising him for maintaining law and order and bringing the nation closer together.

Bonhoeffer, representing the Confessing Church, went abroad to alert other Lutherans to the perils of nazism. "There is no way to peace along the way of safety," he told the Lutheran World Alliance, "for peace must be dared . . . battles are not won with weapons, but God. They are won where the way leads to the cross."

The First Arrests

In the fall of 1934 the first arrests were made of Confessing Church leaders. On October 6 Bishop Theophil Wurm of Wurttemburg was placed under house arrest. A week later Bishop Meiser of Bavaria was confined to his home by armed guard. Their colleagues responded by calling a second Free

Synod, which rejected the official German Church and set up an independent government for the Confessing Church under a National Council of Brothers. They asked congregations "not to accept any directions from the existing 'German' church government or its agencies and to withhold cooperation from those who continue to give obedience to this ecclesiastical regime." They urged acknowledgement of "the rule of the Confessing Church and its institutions." Scores of Lutheran congregations became affiliated with the new church. The Nazi government, fearing a rebellion, withdrew the guards around the homes of the two bishops.

Bonhoeffer was appointed to set up and direct one of several new theological schools for the Confessing Church. In the fall of 1935 he began classes in a commodious old country house outside the small village of Finkenwald. The first students refurbished the house themselves and Bonhoeffer provided his personal library for their use. Bonhoeffer maintained a stiff, almost monastic regimen. Each day began and ended with a half-hour of common prayer, with arduous Bible study and theological disciplines in between. Bonhoeffer was a hard but warm taskmaster. He would not tolerate spiritual mediocrity or sloppy study habits, and constantly reminded the students that they were bonded together in love and commitment for "outgoing service."

"We have to fight for the true church . . ."

Bonhoeffer now took a harder line against the German church. He refused an invitation to participate in an ecumenical meeting because representatives of the official church would be there. "We have to fight for the true church against the false church of antichrist," he explained. "Fighting in this faith we derive no small power from considering the fact that we are fighting for Christianity not only with regard to the church in Germany but in the whole world. . . . All churches," he warned, "may be attacked by the very same power one day or another."

At the next Free Synod he detected that the Confessing Church was softening. He protested that the real issues had been ignored. Not one speaker had defended the church's freedom to teach Biblical truth; no protest had been made against a requirement that German citizens take an oath of loyalty to Hitler; and nothing had been said about increased discrimination against the Jews. Forty-eight churchmen, including Pastor Martin Niemoller, joined Bonhoeffer in signing a circular calling upon pastors to stand firm and "submit to the sole rule of our Lord Jesus Christ." The Nazi government, however, was encouraged by the "cooperative spirit" at the Synod and began assiduously courting moderates in the Confessing Church. The new minister of church affairs was successful in soliciting representatives of both the Confessing and the older church to participate in a national committee. Bonhoeffer was incensed. "Between church and pseudo-church there can be no cooperation," he thundered.

The dispute hurt the Confessing Church. Among those departing was one of Bonhoeffer's top students. Undeterred, Bonhoeffer encouraged his former students, who were now pastors, not to compromise. "If we persevere in prayer," he advised in a monthly circular, "then we can have confidence that the Holy Spirit will give us the right words at the time when we need them, and we shall be found faithful."

The government took advantage of the confusion to pass a "Fifth Emergency Decree." Unauthorized church groups were forbidden to appoint and ordain clergy, announce policy, spend money taken in collections, call synods and train theologians. Bonhoeffer's school and the other new seminaries were now illegal. At Finkenwald Bonhoeffer assembled his students and suggested that any who wished to, could leave. None did.

The young pastors who looked to Bonhoeffer as their spiritual guide stood firm. In 1936 one was arrested, Johannes Pecina, the minister at Seelow. The seminary immediately sent a replacement. When he was arrested, a Finkenwald student was sent.

Other Brave Christians Speak Out

Early in the summer of 1936 the Prussian Council of Lutheran churches issued a memorandum to Hitler. The paper, handed in at the chancellery, criticized the oppressive law against the Confessing Church and the discrimination against Jewish Christians. The government tried to suppress the charge but copies were circulated and read aloud by eighty per cent of the pastors in the Confessing Church. Also published in European newspapers, it aroused criticism of Hitler abroad.

Hitler and his Nazi henchmen were incensed over the leak. The Gestapo began an immediate investigation. Werner Koch, a student at Finkenwald, and Ernst Tillich, nephew of theologian Paul Tillich, were arrested along with Friedrich

Weisler, an employee of the Prussian Council of Lutheran Churches. Koch and Tillich were interned in a concentration camp. Weisler, because he was Jewish, was tortured and beaten to death.

From this time until 1945 there was never a time when some of Bonhoeffer's present or former students were not in prison. The seminary body lived in danger every minute. "We accept every day as a gift from God," said Bonhoeffer.

The Nazis Ridicule the Divinity of Christ

In 1937 the official church was jolted by a speech from Hitler's minister of church affairs. Hans Kerrl told the chairman of the Lutheran Church committees that "belief in Christ as the Son of God" was a "laughable . . . dogma of the past." Hitler's national socialism was the reality of the present, he said. Wilhelm Zoellner, superintendent of the church and chairman of all the controversial church committees, resigned in protest.

The Nazi government now stopped pretending to be a Christian order and began enforcing the Fifth Emergency Decree with fervor. Pastors ordained in the Confessing Church were declared to have no status. The illegal seminaries were ordered closed. Informers took notes of announcements and sermons in churches. Offerings in the Confessing Churches were seized and delivered to the government's Ecclesiastical Finance Department. Large numbers of pastors were arrested. Among them were five top leaders of the Confessing Church who went on trial for violating the Fifth Emergency Decree. Eight members of the Prussian church council were also arrested. One pastor, Paul Schneider, was seized in his parish for imposing church discipline on Nazi party members. Two years later he would die in the Buchenwald concentration camp.

Bonhoeffer and Eberhard Bethge, a member of the seminary staff at Finkenwald, went to Berlin to talk with their friend Martin Niemoller. Niemoller, who had commanded a submarine during World War I, was a leader of pastors in the Confessing Church. They arrived to learn that Niemoller had just been taken away by the secret police. They tried to escape out the back way and ran into a Gestapo officer who ordered them back into the house. For seven hours Gestapo men searched the house, then told Bonhoeffer and Bethge they were free to leave.

The Brave Church Choir

When they left, Mrs. Niemoller was alone, not knowing when or if ever her husband would return. After a while she heard singing. Tiptoeing over to the window, she saw the women's choir of her church underneath. They had heard of their pastor's arrest and had come to sing to her.

Franz Hildebrandt, Bonhoeffer's close Jewish Christian friend, took Niemoller's pulpit and defiantly made "illegal" announcements. He also used church collections for church support. Hildebrandt announced a service of intercession for the imprisoned pastor on August 8, 1938. Members arrived to find the church blocked by police. Instead of returning home, they began a march of protest. Some two hundred fifty were arrested, including Hildebrandt.

When Bonhoeffer heard about the incident, he knew Hildebrandt, because of his Jewish ancestry, was in great danger. Through his influential family, Bonhoeffer obtained the preacher's release. Hildebrandt shortly after escaped to England.

While the World Slept

Bonhoeffer, who earlier had traveled to England to warn Lutheran leaders of the serious church situation, could not understand why the world was not alarmed. The concentration camps were filling up with Jews and dissenters. Hitler was conscripting German men for military service and building an air force and a submarine fleet. Germany now had six hundred thousand men under arms, a grave violation of the Versailles treaty that had been signed at the close of World War I. Some European countries had protested, but Britain had overlooked the transgression. Hitler had already sent troops into demilitarized districts west of the Rhine River to the French border, also in violation of Versailles. In March, 1938, Hitler ordered German troops into Austria, a betrayal of his own earlier promise. That fall the Nazis took part of Czechoslovakia. This aggression was ratified by Britain's Chamberlain in the infamous Munich agreement.

Who Cares for the Jews?

The world was now aware that three hundred fifty thousand Jews in Germany and two hundred twenty thousand in Austria were in deadly danger. In July a conference was held by representatives of thirty-two nations to determine how they might help. Nazi officials were invited and were present as observers.

The first two days the diplomats argued over which nation's representative should chair the conference. The United States diplomat got the job. They spent only one afternoon listening to representatives of Jewish refugee organizations; some were given only five to ten minutes to describe the terror of Nazi persecution. One cited a new school reader that had just been published in Germany, which asked children: "Remember that the Jews are children of the devil and murderers of mankind. Whoever is a murderer deserves to be killed himself." Another told of Jews being whipped and tortured during the day in Buchenwald, while at night a loudspeaker shouted: "Any Jew who wishes to hang himself is asked first to put a piece of paper in his mouth with his number on it, so that we may know who he is."

The German government was still willing to deport its Jews. But who would take them? Nation after nation gave excuses. Catholic Brazil would accept only immigrants with a valid Christian baptismal certificate. Britain feared that a mass of Jewish refugees might "arouse anti-Semitic feeling." However, the American representative said his country would take 27,730, the maximum number acceptable under its immigration laws.

The door was all but slammed shut when the delegates voted that only Jews who could pay their transportation would be accepted. The conference had already been told that no Jew could leave Germany or Austria with more than ten reichsmarks — less than five dollars! At the request of the South American delegates, the conference voted to remove from the final resolution any "contentious allusions to Germany." Nothing was accomplished.

Hitler responded by scolding the nations for "oozing sympathy for the poor tormented people," while remaining "hard and obdurate when it comes to helping them." He told the South African defense minister, "We shall solve the Jewish problem in the immediate future . . . the Jews will disappear."

After Jews were prohibited from leaving the country, the Bonhoeffers helped Dietrich's twin sister and her Jewish husband escape to Switzerland.

Meanwhile, Bonhoeffer's seminary had moved to a secret hideout in a country parsonage. Many students were in prison. There was as yet no order out for Bonhoeffer's arrest, but police had been instructed to arrest him if he came to Berlin on church business.

Plotting to Depose Hitler

Bonhoeffer, his family and other influential Germans who opposed Hitler were certain that a European war was inevitable unless the mad fuehrer could be deposed or perhaps assassinated. Bonhoeffer's psychiatrist father, along with Hitler's chief of general staff and other key resisters, began planning a coup. A secret report on Hitler's mental condition was prepared by Dr. Karl Bonhoeffer and other psychiatrists. The plan was to seize the fuehrer, bring him before a citizen's court and accuse him of making irresponsible war. The psychiatrists would pronounce him criminally insane and unfit to continue in office. The seizure was to take place in Berlin on September 29, 1938, during a visit by British prime minister Neville Chamberlain. The plan went awry when Chamberlain, who knew of the resisters' intentions, flew to Munich.

There had been other fruitless attempts to rid Germany of its mad fuehrer. There would be more in the future.

Dietrich Bonhoeffer was not sure what he should do. He was no pacifist, but to fight for the Nazis seemed morally indefensible. He went to England and then to New York where he was offered the position of pastor to German Christian refugees. "The only thing that makes me hesitate . . . is the question of loyalty to my people at home . . .," he wrote a friend.

Hitler kept pressing. In March, 1939, his army occupied the remainder of Czechoslovakia, then seized territory from Lithuania. In April, Italy, with which Germany was bound in a pact, moved into Albania. Chamberlain's policy of appeasement was now an obvious failure. When Hitler demanded a strip of territory across Poland to link Germany with East Prussia, Britain announced it would support Poland if it resisted attack. On September 1, German troops invaded Poland. Two days later Britain and France declared war on Germany.

Bonhoeffer Returns to Face the Storm

Bonhoeffer's American friends kept urging him to remain in New York. But the young theologian's face was set. In July, 1939, having boarded ship, he wrote, "I . . . made a mistake in coming to America. I must live through this difficult period of our national history with the Christian people of Germany. I will have no right to participate in the reconstruction of Christian life in Germany after the war if I do not share the trials of this time with my people."

With a small group of students, remnants from his illegal seminary, Bonhoeffer secluded himself in a rough-hewn hunting lodge deep in the Pomeranian forest. He was there when the first stories of German brutalities and genocide in Poland began seeping back to the German civilian population.

The Christians' Dilemma

Bonhoeffer and his Christian brothers faced an agonizing decision: Should they join the cloak-and-dagger, kill-and-be-killed resistance to Hitler that was desperately trying to topple their own government and end the war, or should they continue much as before, secretly teaching and witnessing and encouraging Christian living? They concluded that they should do all they could to hasten the downfall of Hitler. It was better to "consent to the bad," Bonhoeffer said, "knowing full well that it is bad, in order to ward off what is worse. . . ." From this time on Bonhoeffer and his friends were active among the conspirators working for the defeat of Hitler. They were propelled by the conviction that Germany was being led by "criminal adventurers" who had inflicted "shocking bestialities . . . especially towards the Jews," and who could not possibly win the war militarily.

The Nazi juggernaut rolled on. Within nine months Belgium, Holland, Denmark, and Norway were all in German hands. On the day France surrendered, Bonhoeffer and his colleague Bethge were in a cafe in East Prussia. When the news came over the radio, people all around them began shouting and raising their arms in the "Heil Hitler" salute. "Put up your hand," Bonhoeffer whispered to Bethge.

At first, Bonhoeffer's pretended loyalty to the government did not deceive the Nazis. For "subversive activity" he was ordered not to speak in public and to report regularly to the Gestapo. Powerful persons in the resistance got the report order lifted. They then arranged a change of residence and assigned Bonhoeffer to a group involved in rescue operations and passing on secret information.

Bonhoeffer's "Cover"

The key leaders of the resistance were ensconced in the government's counterespionage department, known as the *Abwehr*. They cleverly assigned Bonhoeffer to a counterespionage unit, thus giving him a cover for his real work.

All through 1941 and 1942 Bonhoeffer traveled back and forth to Switzerland and Norway talking to world church leaders, declaring forthrightly, "If we claim to be Christians, there is no room for expediency. Hitler is antichrist." Bonhoeffer's hope was to open up communications with Britain for peace negotiations and for plans for the future of Europe.

Another plan was now in the making to assassinate Hitler. Bonhoeffer agreed to take part, but wanted sufficient warning so he could break his relationship with the Confessing Church. "I can never again serve as pastor," he said, "if I am to participate." The plan did not succeed. Other assassination plans followed and were also unsuccessful. In the meantime Bonhoeffer was active with the *Abwehr's* Operation U7, helping Jews escape into Switzerland.

Arrested Without a Warrant

Amazingly, the *Abwehr* was still not suspect, but Bonhoeffer continued to be watched. On April 5, 1943, the chief investigator for the air force and a Gestapo official confronted the young theologian at a friend's house. They said simply, "Come with us," and took Bonhoeffer away in a black Mercedes. Without a trial or an explanation, he was thrown into Tegel Military Prison.

Bonhoeffer was put in the most isolated cell on the top floor. He was allowed neither newspapers nor the customary exercise break. Scraps of food were shoved through the door and guards were prohibited from talking to him. It was six months before a warrant was delivered for his arrest. His comforts were prayer and his Bible, which he had been allowed to keep.

Although attempts on Hitler's life continued, still Bonhoeffer was not tied to the resistance. In prison he was now allowed to correspond and to receive monthly visits from his family and fiancée Maria. "We have been engaged for almost a year, and have not been for a single hour alone together," he lamented.

He put his inmost thoughts in writing, confessing to struggles, weariness and doubts. But he could say, "I believe that we ought so to love and trust God in our lives, and in all the good things that He sends us, that when the time comes we may go to Him with love, trust, and joy." And: "Through every event, however untoward, there is access to God."

More Arrests and Executions

In the fall of 1943 the Gestapo uncovered a secret file outside Berlin that implicated the core of the resisters in the government's *Abwehr* counterintelligence department. They were imprisoned but not executed. Information was more important to the Nazis than vengeance.

Ironically, these arrests came as the war was turning against Hitler and his Axis partners. It would go on for two more terrible years while the German resisters suffered in prison. Besides the Lutheran pastors, there were also a substantial number of Catholic priests in the jails and camps who bravely resisted the Nazis when their hierarchy was looking the other way.

Bonhoeffer was moved to the cellar of the Gestapo prison in Berlin's Prinz Albrecht Strasse. His family and fiancée were forbidden to see him and he was seldom permitted to write. His brother Klaus and two of his brothers-in-law, Rudiger Schleicher and Hans Adam von Dohnanyi, both lawyers, were now also in prison. All three would summarily be executed.

Maria's Search

Allied bombing intensified. Troops advanced towards Berlin from east and west. On February 7, 1945, twenty of the most important prisoners in Prinz Albrecht Strasse were loaded into trucks. Bonhoeffer's vehicle went to the dread Buchenwald. After he had been taken away, Maria came to the Tegel Military Prison, hoping to see him. When told he was gone, she left in the bitter weather, traveling along the line of Nazi retreat, asking about him at every concentration camp.

The special prisoners of Bonhoeffer's group were sequestered in the cellar of an old yellow house on the fringe of Buchenwald. Among them was one foreigner, Payne Best, a member of the British secret service captured at the border of Holland. By Easter Sunday, 1945, the prisoners could hear American guns. Their waiting, for life or death, would not be long now.

The Death of a Martyr

One morning they were herded into a van and driven towards the southeast. Unknown to Bonhoeffer, a Nazi official was following behind with an order for his execution.

The next Sunday, April 8, they stopped at a schoolhouse. At the prisoners' request, Bonhoeffer held a brief worship service. He chose as his texts Isaiah 53:5: "By his stripes we are healed," and 1 Peter 1:3: "Blessed be the God and Father of our Lord Jesus Christ, which according to his abundant mercy hath begotten us again unto a lively hope by the resurrection of Jesus Christ from the dead."

The service ended when a harsh voice called, "Prisoner Bonhoeffer, come with us." Bonhoeffer was taken to Flossenberg Prison. That evening he and several other prisoners were formally condemned.

Years later the prison doctor wrote, "Through the half-open door of a room in one of the huts I saw Pastor Bonhoeffer still in his prison clothes, kneeling in fervent prayer to the Lord his God. The devotion and evident conviction of being heard that I saw in the prayer of this intensely captivating man moved me to the depths."

About 5:00 A.M., an escort came for an admiral and two generals who were among those charged with trying to overthrow the government. They were taken from their cells and told of the verdict.

Bonhoeffer was soon removed to join the other condemned men. They were marched to the place of execution and told to strip. One last time Bonhoeffer knelt to pray. Then he stood up. Shots pierced the stillness of the woods. The most famous Christian martyr of World War II was dead.

Three weeks later Hitler and Eva Braun, the mistress he had just married, swallowed poison. Hitler's aides burned their bodies after dousing them with gasoline. Seven days after this Germany surrendered.

It was June before Maria learned that Bonhoeffer was dead. On July 27 his aged parents accidentally heard the sad news. They happened to tune in to a memorial service from London and heard a German saying in English, "We are gathered here in the presence of God to make thankful remembrance of the life and work of his servant Dietrich Bonhoeffer, who gave his life in faith and obedience. . . ."

Tally of the Dead

After the war ended, the dreadful tally of casualties began. Germany alone had suffered 8,156,000 military casualties, including 2,916,000 dead. Two hundred thousand aged or incurably ill Germans had been sacrificed to experiments in euthanasia. Every known German Jew or person of Jewish ancestry had been killed or deported. Thousands upon thousands of German Christians had been imprisoned or executed for protecting Jews or otherwise opposing Hitler's program. One of the ministers who had survived was Martin Niemoller. These were only the German victims of Nazism. In the occupied countries two hundred thousand gypsies, almost six million Jews, and thousands more Christians had perished.

Many Christians in the occupied countries had died protecting Jews and for opposing other Nazi occupation policies. The toll was especially high in Eastern Europe. Large numbers also gave their lives in France, Belgium, Holland, Norway, Finland, and elsewhere.

The ten Boom Story

Best known is the story of Holland's ten Boom family as related by ageless Corrie ten Boom in her best selling book, *The Hiding Place*. The ten Booms were devout members of the Reformed Church of Holland. Owners of a watch shop in the town of Haarlem which had been in the family since 1837, they were respected pillars of their community.

As early as the 1930's they became aware of the discrimination against Jews in Germany. Letters to Jewish suppliers came back marked, "Address Unknown." Twisting the radio dial, they often caught the raucous, screaming voice of Hitler preaching Aryan supremacy.

Corrie's minister brother, Willem, who had studied in Germany, was the first member of the family to help Jews fleeing from Nazi persecution. After Germany occupied Holland, he became active in the Dutch underground which sheltered Jews, helped prisoners escape, and sabotaged war installations.

With Willem and sister Nollie married and their mother dead, Corrie and sister Betsie now lived with their father above the shop. Their first Jewish fugitive was a Mrs. Kleermaker. Her husband had been arrested and her son gone into hiding. The Gestapo had ordered her to close the family clothing store and she was afraid to go back to her apartment above it. She had heard that the ten Booms had befriended a Jewish neighbor. Mr. ten Boom assured her, "In this household, God's people are always welcome."

Two nights later they heard a furtive knock and opened the door to admit their second and third guests, a frightened elderly Jewish couple. With three boarders, food was a problem. The underground came to the rescue with forged ration stamps.

The Secret Room

As Jews continued to come, the ten Booms became concerned about informers and the Gestapo. Their house was three stories, but small and narrow. If a raid occurred, where would their Jewish guests hide?

The underground sent a "building inspector," who was actually one of Europe's most famous architects, to design a secret room next to Corrie's bedroom. At the sound of a warning buzzer all guests were to run to "The Hiding Place," from which came the title of the book.

The ten Booms had seven permanent Jewish guests and others for shorter times. But the Germans saw only an elderly watchmaker living with his two spinster daughters above his small shop.

Their rigid Dutch Reformed morality made it hard for them to deny having any guests when seven Jews were closeted in the hiding place. Corrie, Betsie and their father managed. But when sister Nollie was caught at home with a blonde stranger, she blurted out the truth, "She is a Jew." Both women were arrested.

The Raid

Corrie was in bed with the flu on the fateful morning of February 28, 1944. Hours before, a member of the underground had passed word that another member had been arrested and would likely be tortured to reveal information. A raid could occur at any time.

This morning a man came into the shop asking for money to get his wife released from prison. "It's a matter of life and death," he pleaded. "We've been hiding Jews." Corrie sent the visitor to the bank with a note telling a bank official to give him money.

The man was an informer. A few minutes later the Gestapo burst into the shop, shoving, slapping, bullying their way past the sisters and their father. They took the three ten Booms away, but never found the secret room and the seven Jews hiding there. All seven subsequently escaped and six survived the war.

Father ten Boom Dies

Sister Nollie and brother Willem were released from prison. But Corrie and Betsie were not. In May they received word that their aged father was dead. After becoming ill in his cell, he had been taken to the municipal hospital in the

Hague. There was no bed available when he arrived and he had died while waiting in the corridor. Hospital workers had buried him in the paupers' cemetery.

The sisters found strength in their hidden Bible, in prayer, and in one another. They determined to love their captors, no matter what. When Corrie was called in for interrogation, she remembered that Jesus had been called before inquisitors. "Show me what to do," she implored.

"Look at Jesus Only."

Corrie and Betsie were moved to Germany, ahead of advancing Allied troops, and quartered in the notorious womens' extermination camp at Ravensbruck. They were forced to work eleven-hour days, digging and shoveling dirt in the prison yard. Betsie became weak and began coughing blood. When she faltered, the guard slashed her across the chest and neck with his crop. "Don't look, Corrie," she whispered. "Look at Jesus only."

The prisoners were permitted worship services in their crowded barracks. At every meeting a crowd of thin, sad-faced women gathered around Corrie and Betsie to hear the sisters read from the Bible. One read the Dutch text and the other translated aloud in German. Other interpreters then passed the precious words along the aisles in French, Polish, Russian, Czech, and other languages. These evenings were "little previews of heaven," Corrie later wrote in *The Hiding Place*.

When the prison became overcrowded, the sickest were taken out for extermination. But when Betsie was unable to stand, Corrie and another Dutch woman were allowed to carry her to the prison hospital. Unable to reach a doctor, they finally carried Betsie back. Two orderlies came for her and took her to a hospital bed. "Corrie, people can still learn to love," Betsie whispered as she was dying.

Corrie was released a few days later. After a short stay in the hospital she was allowed to go home. Ringing in her ears was Betsie's reminder, "We must tell people, Corrie. We must tell them what we learned. . . ."

"Tramp for the Lord"

For over thirty years Corrie, now in her eighties, has been telling their story. In 1959 she revisited Ravensbruck to honor Betsie and almost one hundred thousand other women who died there. She learned that her release had resulted from a clerical "error." The following week all women her age had been exterminated.

Her travels have taken her to over sixty countries on both sides of the Iron Curtain. Another book, *Tramp for the Lord*, describes these adventures. "God has a divine pattern for each of his children," she wrote in this book. "Although the threads may seem knotted . . . on the other side is a crown."

Corrie ten Boom's books have made her brave Dutch family heroes to millions of people living today. They typify thousands of other ordinary Christians in Germany and the occupied countries who died standing for Christian principles and caring for their Jewish neighbors.

The Martyrs Have Not Been Forgotten

Dietrich Bonhoeffer has been revered by every class of seminary students since his martyrdom was made known. Today, over thirty years after the war's end, no other modern martyr arouses more respect and reverence among young theologues than this intellectual and spiritual giant who died rather than compromise his convictions. Other German pastors and priests who died, along with those who survived Hitler's concentration camps, are less known, but in the German Lutheran and Catholic churches, their bravery will not soon be forgotten.

The "Confession" by German Christians

In 1945 the survivors of the German resistance met at Stuttgart with representatives from sister churches in other countries which had suffered mightily at the hands of the Nazis, to proclaim a "confession of guilt." They implored God's forgiveness that they had not prayed more faithfully, believed more intensely, witnessed more courageously, and loved more devotedly. The Germans, as new leaders of the Evangelical Church in Germany, confessed their solidarity with the guilt of the German nation for crimes against humanity. At the same time, high Nazi war criminals were solemnly pleading not guilty in the war crimes' court at Nuremberg.

Hitler's Greatest Folly

There are many lessons to be learned from the Nazi era to ensure that the martyrs did not die in vain. One is that no earthly power can stamp out Christian faith or eliminate the search for meaning. Small independent Protestant churches are growing rapidly in West Germany and have sent hundreds of missionaries to other lands.

A symbol of the continuing power of the gospel of Jesus Christ is revealed in the last request of German soldiers, surrounded by counterattacking Soviet troops in Stalingrad. Their last wireless message voiced the plea, "Send us Bibles." German planes responded and flew over enemy lines to drop precious copies of the Book of Books.

MARTYRS OF THE
SOVIET UNION AND
EASTERN EUROPE

TRUE FAITH
GROWS STRONG:
The Soviet Union

The trail of martyrs' blood now leads us northeast across the broad expanse of the Soviet Union, which sprawls over eleven time zones in Europe and Asia. It also covers Eastern Europe as well since after the fall of Nazi Germany near the end of the Second World War, most of Eastern Europe came under the domain of the Soviet Union as the "iron curtain" was pulled shut.

The background for martyrdom in the Soviet Union and Eastern European communist nations is different from most of the countries previously covered. The populations were "converted" centuries before by "Christian" armies marching from the West. The powerful church establishments which developed tended to see dissent as heresy and as a threat to society. Evangelicals and other religious minorities were, therefore, persecuted even before the conquest by communism. For a few years after the rise of communism, the minorities enjoyed relief from persecution while the Marxist rulers were killing and imprisoning leaders of the old national church who refused subservience to the state. Then the Marxists enacted a set of controls designed to confine the activities of the minorities to private worship inside their sanctuaries at times approved by the government. When multitudes refused to comply, particularly evangelicals, the Marxist rulers began to enforce their laws. Depending on the times and the severity of local persecutors, believers were fined, banished to Siberia, imprisoned, or in some instances killed. The persecutors maintained that punishments were not for religious reasons but for crimes against the state.

In the drive to stamp out religion, the communist leadership sought to avoid dramatic executions. They feared that violent killings of Christians would shock world opinion and that the example of the martyrs would spur church growth. Consequently, most resistant pastors and lay leaders were either exiled to barren wastelands, where their influence was restricted, or confined to prisons until they were broken in health and spirit. Even though death may occur years after he is released, a believer who dies as a result of the horrors of a communist prison is no less a martyr than one who is beaten to death or shot by a firing squad. Understanding this, we will have a broader view of the meaning of martyrdom in the Soviet Union and Eastern Europe.

As recent as 1972, for example, members of the Evangelical Christian and Baptist Church Council in the USSR included in their plea to UN Secretary–General U Thant these testaments of evangelical leaders:

"... N. Khmara was tortured to death in prison ..."

"I. A. Afonin, a member of the Action Group and father of nine children, died in prison at age 45, in July, 1971."

"P. F. Zakharov, after insults and torture in prison, died at the age of 49."

"S. T. Golev, a member of the Council of Churches, elderly and ill, has spent about 20 years in bondage. At present he is virtually condemned to death in prison for his nationwide work for the Council of Churches."

These are only four among the multitudes of Soviet Christians who have suffered in the so-called benevolent socialist workers' paradise. According to the official record, they did not die for their faith, but for disobeying the laws of the "people." These laws were never devised or administered by the majority, but by an atheistic bureaucracy intent on reducing religious beliefs to the ashes of legends and myths.

Evangelical Persecution Before Communism

We have heard so much of communist persecution that it is hard to imagine a time in the Soviet Union when evangelicals were persecuted by other powers.

Before 1917 the imperial tsarist government was aligned with the hierarchy of the Russian Orthodox Church. Persecution of evangelicals began around 1875 following a powerful revival among German immigrants which had produced a string of strong Baptist churches. It persisted until 1917 when the Communists took power.

Many Baptists, a term used for all evangelicals, lost their jobs even though they were excellent workers. Some were exiled and died far from home. Baptist marriages could not be registered since only official church weddings were legal. Thus children of "unlawful" unions were considered illegitimate and were denied many educational privileges. In some instances, children were actually taken away from Baptist parents who left the Russian Orthodox Church.

The Death of Pastor Kisil

The great majority of Orthodox Christians did not endorse kidnappings or killings. The violence occurred only in scattered communities and was usually instigated by intolerant fanatics.

In the province of Yekaterinoslav on May 19, 1914, Baptists in the village of Vasilkov were at prayer when a well-known Orthodox extremist named Rakhno entered. "Stand up!" he shouted to Pastor V. P. Kisil. The kneeling pastor arose to see who the intruder was. Already the madman was hurtling forward, dagger in hand. Before Pastor Kisil could defend himself, the blade was in his heart. The fanatic turned and ran to the Orthodox church for protection. Nevertheless he was arrested by local police.

Russian Evangelicals Welcome the Revolution

Most evangelicals were simple tradesmen and farmers. When the Bolsheviks seized power, they could not foresee where communism was leading. They knew only that the nation was in deep economic trouble and was plagued by corruption in government. They cheered reforms promised by the Communists. The evangelicals especially warmed to a statement quoted from Lenin: "Each person must have complete freedom not only to observe any faith but also to propagate any faith. . . . None of the officials should even have a right to ask anyone of his faith: this is a matter of conscience and nobody should dare to interfere in this field."

Marx also appeared to agree tacitly that the state should not interfere with religious belief. The ideologists of communism saw religion as a symptom, not a cause, of deep disorder in society and human consciousness. Religion, Marx felt, was a drug, an opiate, which primitives had invented to dull pain and misery, much as the royalty of Europe took opium as an analgesic. In the new world of communism, he predicted, the comrades would find fulfillment in liberating the earth from exploitation by the royal houses and wealthy capitalists. Religion would come to have no meaning and wither away.

When Lenin became the first communist dictator of the Soviet Union, he apparently discarded his earlier view. Members of the ruling class, he decided, were using religion as an instrument of oppression. Religious bodies, therefore, must be tamed or destroyed in order to assist the inevitable process of evolutionary change.

Catch-22's in Communist Law

Two months after taking power, Lenin had the Council of People's Commissars declare separation of church and state. At first glance the decree seemed similar to church–state legislation in other countries, including the United States. Every citizen was free to profess the faith of his choice or none at all. But there were a number of clever qualifications which, in effect, tilted the scales in favor of atheism.

Freedom of worship was permitted only when it did not affect public order and interfere with the rights of Soviet citizens. Local authorities could decide when to take necessary steps to preserve order and the public interest.

Religious education was forbidden in both state-operated and private schools and was restricted to special schools of theology. Citizens could only teach and study religion privately.

Religious associations could not own property.

Marriages, births and deaths were to be officially recorded as civic acts of the state on registers entrusted to the proper secular offices. Religious records were invalid.

Martyrs of the Russian Orthodox Church

The Orthodox Church, which in the previous century had sought to suppress the growing evangelical movement, fought back against this oppression. The newly elected patriarch announced the excommunication of "avowed or secret enemies of Christ." The Communists who had been baptized into Orthodoxy were not named, but it was obvious they were the subjects of the decree. They began a propaganda attack, and warfare soon erupted between supporters of the Orthodox Church and the state. Violent clashes occurred in several cities. Communist-inspired crowds burned Orthodox churches and pillaged monasteries. Clergymen and laymen were brought to trial for crimes against the state. Eleven were condemned to death in Moscow.

In January, 1918, Communists began attacking Orthodox churches in the Ukraine. On the evening of January 23, they broke into the Petchersky Monastery and killed hundreds of Orthodox priests. The Orthodox Church later claimed that over two thousand priests and some fifty bishops were killed or deported.

The main target in Kiev, the largest Ukranian city, was Metropolitan Vladimir. At age seventy he was the oldest hierarch in the Russian church. A widower who had lost his wife and only child to illness, he was known for ministries of charity and was one of the most beloved churchmen of Russia. At 6:30 P.M. five men dressed as soldiers entered his house. They pushed the old priest into a bedroom where they twisted the chain of his cross around his neck and demanded money. Then they took him to a waiting car and drove outside the gates of the monastery to a small clearing. When they stopped, he asked, "Is it here you want to shoot me?"

"Why not?" one of the abductors said with a curse. "Do you expect us to stand on ceremony?"

"Will you grant me permission to pray before I am shot?"

"Be quick about it!" he was told.

Lifting his arms to heaven, the old man prayed aloud, "O Lord, forgive my sins, voluntary and involuntary, and accept my spirit in peace." Then he blessed his murderers with both hands, murmuring, "God forgive you."

Four shots rang out and he was dead.

Also in January, 1918, the new communist government decreed that all church treasures now belonged to the state and that precious stones and metals must be sold to help alleviate the suffering caused by a growing famine. The ruling Orthodox patriarch told his clergymen to surrender all nonconsecrated items, but not to give up bejeweled garments and gold and silver chalices used in liturgies. He asked that collections be taken to pay the government the cash value of the liturgical objects. The Communists responded with a

propaganda barrage that the hierarchy was too greedy to
make available the means for feeding the hungry. This provoked more attacks on Orthodox churches and monasteries
and more killing of clergymen.

"I Will Lift Up My Eyes Reverently to God"

In Petrograd (now Leningrad), Metropolitan Benjamin joined
with the Communists on a committee called "Help to the
Starving." He asked clergymen to raise cash offerings and
contribute from church treasuries on a voluntary basis. His
appeals helped tremendously.

The Communist Central Committee in Moscow, fearing
that the voluntary gifts would raise the prestige of the
clergy, ordered their Petrograd comrades to confiscate church
valuables instead of accepting them by donation. They further published a letter from twelve self-proclaimed clergymen denouncing the arrangement in Petrograd.

The church valuables were confiscated and Metropolitan
Benjamin was arrested and put on trial with others. After
several false witnesses had testified and conviction appeared
obvious, his defense attorney begged the tribunal of judges,

Do not make a martyr of the Metropolitan. The
masses revere him, and if he is killed for his faith
and his loyalty to the masses, he would become
much more dangerous to the Soviet power. The
immutable law of history should be a warning. Let it
remind you that true faith feeds and grows strong on
the blood of martyrs. Would you risk giving more
martyrs to the restless people?

The presiding judge asked the Metropolitan to speak for
himself. The clergyman first expressed his sorrow at being
called "the enemy of the people . . . . I am a true son of my
people," he said. "I love and always have loved the people. I
have dedicated my whole life to them." Then he proceeded
to speak in behalf of his codefendants.

"Tell us more about yourself," the judge interrupted.

"About myself? What else can I tell you? One more
thing perhaps; regardless of what my sentence will be, no
matter what you decide, life or death, I will lift up my eyes
reverently to God, cross myself and affirm: 'Glory to Thee,
my Lord; glory to Thee for everything.' "

The verdict for Metropolitan Benjamin and the other
defendants was guilty. The sentence: death before a firing
squad.

Before the execution they were shaved of their long

beards and dressed in rags so the executioners would not know they were killing clergymen. Just before the guns cracked, one of the priests, Father Serge, prayed aloud, "O Lord, forgive them for they know not what they are doing." Metropolitan Benjamin merely crossed himself and whispered a prayer before falling under the hail of bullets.

More Orthodox Martyrs

Russia was now in the throes of a full-scale civil war between the "Whites," who defended the old order, and communist "Reds." By 1921 more than twenty million people had died in fighting, in epidemics and of starvation. Had not an American relief commission, directed by Herbert Hoover, given emergency help on a mammoth scale, millions more might have died.

As the Reds conquered, they closed more Orthodox churches and arrested clergymen. Among other Orthodox clergy put to death during the early years of communist rule in Russia were Bishop Germogen of Tobolsk, Bishop Nikodim of Belgorod, and Bishop Makary of Viazma.

Bishop Germogen and some other prisoners were taken away on a steamer. After they were well underway, guards began ripping off the prisoners' clothing and throwing the prisoners one by one into the Tura River where they drowned. When they came to Bishop Germogen, he prayed aloud. "Hold his jaw!" the commissar shouted. A fist silenced the old man's prayers. Then an eighty-pound rock was tied to his bound hands and after several swings to and fro, he was tossed into the river.

Bishop Nikodim of Belgorod had taken no sides in politics, but in his sermons he had condemned violence, robberies and murders, while asking his flock to follow the teachings of Jesus. His sermons enraged local Communists. Commandant Saenko, famed for killing hundreds with his own hands, arrested the Bishop. A furor arose among the people, forcing Saenko to return the Bishop to his residence. On that same day Nikodim preached another sermon against violence. He was rearrested by Saenko who declared, "The clergy are ruining the revolution." A priest's wife pleaded for the Bishop's freedom. Saenko shot her himself and ordered the Bishop's execution. Nikodim was disguised in a military overcoat and taken into a dark corner of the prison yard to be shot. Saenko knew that the soldiers would not perform the execution if they recognized the Bishop.

Bishop Makary of Viazma was a learned theologian and

powerful preacher. Local Communists first staged a fight at the door of his church so they could kill him when he came out to settle the dispute. Instead the Bishop remained inside and preached a powerful sermon. In the pretended melee one of the Communists was killed by mistake.

After this failure, they had the Bishop and thirteen other clergymen arrested and falsely charged with organizing a White Volunteer Army uprising. Before dawn, the fourteen doomed men were taken to a deserted spot and lined up with their backs to a freshly dug pit. As an executioner moved to the first in line preparing to shoot him through the forehead, Bishop Makary whispered, "Go in peace." The gun fired and the priest fell backwards into the grave. The Bishop comforted each of his colleagues in this manner. Finally he stood alone. The stars were now fading and the eastern sky was alight. The executioner lifted his gun, then hesitated and lowered his hand. His face hardened. He clenched his teeth. He lifted his hand again and fired. The Bishop, who had been serenely gazing into the brightening sky, tumbled backwards to join the others.

Throughout this period, 1917–1929, the Russian Orthodox Church, because of its power, influence and connections with the old tsarist regime, was the main object of the Communists' war on religion. At the beginning of the period there were over fifty-four thousand Orthodox churches and more than thirty-seven thousand parochial schools. All of the schools were closed or transferred to state jurisdiction. There is no accurate record of the number of churches closed or of the number of clergy and lay leaders killed, just as there is no accounting of the millions of civilians brutally murdered by Communists during this time. Today only an estimated seven thousand Orthodox churches remain.

Extermination of the Catholic Church

Next to the Russian Orthodox Church, the Latin-rite Catholics suffered most under Lenin's rule. When the Communists came to power, about 1.5 million Roman Catholics lived in the territory of the old Russian empire. Most were of Polish, Lithuanian, Belorussian [White Russian], German and French origin. Before the 1917 Revolution, Roman Catholics were suspect to most Russians because of their allegiance to the foreign Vatican. After the Revolution their churches, schools and priesthood were virtually wiped out. Key leaders were arrested and given long prison sentences or sent to remote labor camps. Many died from disease and malnutrition in the camps. Some were executed.

Contrasting figures tell the grim story of Russian Catholics. In 1917, 980 churches; in 1934, only three "showcases" open. In 1917, 912 priests and monks; in 1934, only ten remaining. In 1917, 504 schools and institutions; in 1934, none.

The much smaller body of Eastern-rite Catholics (Uniates) was also virtually annihilated. Other religious minorities with hierarchal structures were substantially dismantled.

How the Free Churches Fared

The Baptist groups flourished from 1917 to 1929. Because they lacked an organized superstructure and were mostly of the working class, the Communists either did not fear them as a counterrevolutionary force, or perhaps felt that, given enough time, the Baptists would slough off their religious lives and become active participants in the new order. For whatever reasons, Russian Baptists were not the target of a general persecution during this period. Under communism, they actually had more freedom to evangelize than under the Orthodox tsarist regime. However, some of the more aggressive evangelists ran into trouble.

The Case of Cornelius Martens

Raised in a German Mennonite colony, evangelist Martens was one of the most prominent Baptist preachers during the 1920's. Early in that decade he and five other believers were arrested by Communists for holding open-air meetings. They were imprisoned with seventeen men who were condemned to die. Martens and his fellow Christians felt they were due to be executed also. Nevertheless, they remained cheerful and prayed and read the Scriptures aloud before their fellow inmates in a common cell.

Early one morning guards called out seven prisoners to dig a large grave. The ground was frozen and every swing of the pick was like hitting concrete. Weakened by hunger, some of the diggers collapsed with exhaustion. Finally, after they had dug only two feet below the surface, the officer sent them back to their cells.

Shortly before midnight, guards came to the cell again. "Lie on your faces!" the commander shouted. When the prisoners fell flat, the officer pointed to one. "Kill him." His hands were bound and he was tied to the window. Then he was shot to death in the presence of his companions. One by one, men were taken off the floor and shot in this fashion. Some had been converted by the preacher and his friends. They died praying. Finally, as abruptly as they had appeared, the commander and his men withdrew, leaving Martens alive, but shaken.

About a week later Martens was taken to the office of the local Communist Party boss. "Take off his clothes," the official ordered two men.

"Don't trouble yourself," the preacher said. "I shall undress. I don't fear to die, for I shall be going home to the Lord. If He has decided my hour hasn't come, you can't do me any harm here."

The Party boss flew into a rage. "I'll prove to you that your God will not deliver you out of my hands!" He lifted his revolver to shoot. His finger froze on the trigger. Three times he tried to fire the gun and failed. His face reddened and his body quivered until it seemed he would have a heart attack. Finally, he lowered the gun and asked a minor official, "What is this man condemned for?" The official replied, "He is a Baptist. Can't you see God is fighting for him?"

Martens began putting on his clothes. "May I now go home?" he asked.

"Go and never show yourself here again!" the frightened Party leader shouted.

A month later police picked up Martens again. Again, in a dramatic way, God spared his life and Martens escaped. The evangelist fled to the rugged Caucasus Mountains where he preached from village to village. His meetings throbbed with spiritual power. Many of the converts were Communists. One cried, "I've been responsible for the murder of thousands of innocents. I will never take up the sword again. Jesus has forgiven me." He was expelled from the Party. In another village five converted Communists were driven out by Party zealots and others were imprisoned.

Conversions occurred everywhere Martens preached. In one meeting a man shouted, "For thirty-five years I've been teaching atheism, poisoning the minds of thousands of students. Is there any hope for me?" Martens shouted back, "Yes, do as Paul did and you will find peace." The professor fell on his knees and cried, "Lord, what would you have me do?"

In 1923 Martens was arrested again. This time it was for preaching to children. After being in solitary confinement for a month, he was told, "You'll be free if you tell us what ministers are receiving money from the people." Martens shot back, "I'm no Judas, but I will not be silent about Christ." He was put back in jail and told he would be banished to Siberia. A few days later he was suddenly released with the order to leave the area. Later it was learned that his release came because of complaints about Soviet religious persecution from the British archbishop of Canterbury and other religious leaders abroad.

Evangelist Martens moved into new territory. In one village he had baptized thirty-three people when the Red army suddenly appeared. Communist soldiers took one person from each of the fifty homes in the village, then ordered everyone out to see the execution. Late that evening the villagers saw the condemned persons standing in a row. Three of the newly baptized, two men and a woman, stood at the end of the line. "Fire!" the officer in charge ordered. One of the believers fell. The other two believers fell down with the rest of the condemned villagers, feigning death. "Bayonet them," the commander now ordered. The woman was killed, but the surviving man was only wounded. He later crept away, though he was crippled for life.

Once again, the indomitable Martens survived. He kept preaching for several more years. He was threatened, but never killed, perhaps because the Communists feared that he would be more damaging as a martyr. The government finally gave him a foreign passport and permitted him to leave the country.

The "Peace" Ends

While Cornelius Martens was staying one step ahead of his persecutors, most other Soviet evangelical preachers were left alone. During this period they kept up contacts with the Baptist World Alliance and the American–European Fellowship. The latter organization supported "home" missionaries in the USSR and published evangelistic reports and letters from Russian believers in a publication called *Harvest Field*.

In many areas the Communists boosted Baptist work. In 1927 Party leaders promised financial backing for a unique "Evangelsk" (City of the Gospel or Sun). But as the project developed, Party officials became alarmed and withdrew backing. They feared the possibility that the planned city — laid out with hospitals, church schools, and houses, amidst parks with fruit trees, all with a religious basis — might be a success. The dream ended when the Soviet drive for collectivization of land began.

The "golden decade" of Russian evangelicals ended in 1929. The year before leaders had reported to the Baptist World Congress in Toronto exciting new developments and prospects for greater successes. The following year most of them were either in prison or in exile.

Tightening the Screws

This new attack on religion was undergirded by a Law on Religious Associations decreed in 1928. Under the following specifications a Communist official could find a reason to arrest almost any Christian:

A religious group could hold activities only after registering with a government committee for religious matters. Registration was often denied on flimsy pretexts.

The registration committee could remove any members it desired from the executive body of a religious society.

Religious groups could not organize activities or classes for children, young people and women. Sunday school classes, sewing and prayer groups, reading rooms, libraries, excursions and children's playgrounds were also forbidden.

Clergymen were restricted to areas in which members resided and could only preach in designated prayer buildings that had to be leased from the government.

Voluntary offerings could only be collected to maintain prayer buildings and premises and to pay clergy salaries.

Under these and previous laws, organized religion was practically shut down in the Soviet Union and thousands of known church leaders were imprisoned. This time the evangelicals did not escape.

Harvest Field reported eyewitness accounts of the terrible suffering now prevailing. In 1930 a believer wrote:

Chapels in all of Russia have been taken from the believers by the thousands. . . . The banished are "fetched" at night without previous notice and are . . . placed in cattle cars. . . . The sick are carried out in their beds. The old and the children die enroute.

> . . . Many of our brethren have ended their
> thorny path in Arctic regions. Where there are believ-
> ers, there spring up small groups, and baptismal ser-
> vices are held by night. There are Christian workers
> who look for a still greater spiritual awakening in
> Russia. Is the day of labor in Russia really over, in
> regard to spiritual works, and has the night set in?

Under the Iron Heel of Stalin

Lenin was dead and the dread Stalin in power. The country
was now officially the Union of Soviet Socialist Republics
(USSR), originally comprised of Russia, Belorussia, Trans-
caucasia and the eastern Ukraine. The eastern Ukraine had
been forcibly annexed by a brutal communist invasion while
other world nations refused to intervene. Other "republics"
were annexed in the twenties. More would be swallowed up
in the thirties and forties to make the USSR the largest
nation on earth.

Stalin had become Party Secretary in 1922. In 1929 he
became Premier as well and gained iron-clad domination
of the communist apparatus. He began stepping up efforts
to industrialize the nation and collectivize all farm land.
He increased his secret police, clamped tight censorship
over all publications, and enlarged the system of concentration
and forced labor camps which had been established earlier.

The next twelve years of Stalinism were brutal beyond
description. Millions died in blood purges and famines
created by manipulations of food supplies. Hundreds of thousands were sent to prison camps from which they never
returned. They were jammed like cattle into unheated,
unventilated railway cars. On every car was the inscription:
VOLUNTARY SETTLERS FOR SIBERIA.

The Penalty for Believing

In village after village residents were called to mass meetings
and confronted with the question: "Are you with the godless
[the Marxists] or the believers?" Those who signified that
they stood with the believers were marched to central loading places and shoved into cattle cars for shipment to Siberia.

A survivor described a trip of horror for a missionary
who translated the diary into English for *Harvest Field:*
At Omsk ten thousand believers and others were

brought on five hundred sledges . . . in temperatures forty degrees below centigrade.

Priests, preachers, and ministers of other denominations were driven thus, but the majority were innocent peasants . . . . The first night was spent under the open sky. Many of the aged and women and children froze that night. Others had frozen hands, feet, or faces. There were screams and sobs that cannot be described. One father . . . could not stand it any longer. Snatching a rifle from a Red soldier, he shot his family and himself.

The howling of the wolves awaiting their prey was terrible to hear. In this way we marched four days. The dead were not buried but the wolves devoured them. Only on the tenth day did we arrive at our destination. Snow and interminable forests surrounded us. Many never reached the place, especially the children. The erection of barracks was begun. The food was unfit to eat . . . . The dying were not cared for nor taken away — we did not know what became of them.

Daily we turned to our Savior. Those who had no hope in Christ sank into a state of depression.

Faith that Overcame

The wife of a prominent pastor who was later martyred, managed to smuggle out this account of following her husband on another forced march:

For almost three months I followed him from town to town, from prison to prison. Once I drew near to a very long line of banished men, possibly a thousand. . . . Thin and haggard, pale and exhausted, they tried to keep in line. Some of them fell, but they were drawn forward by force. Beside them walked their wives and children, heartbroken, but not permitted to help them in any way. The men carried on their shoulders small bundles containing their few belongings.

The road led up a mountainside. I thought of our Savior climbing up Calvary's mountain. All the time I was scanning every face, trying to find my poor husband. At last, just as we came to the station, I caught a glimpse of him in the crowd. He looked very, very sick and had to be supported by a guard.

He saw me, too, and raised his eyes to heaven, giving me an unspoken message that I would meet him there. Just at that moment, he was roughly pushed by a Red guard into a railway freight car. Of course, I could not be admitted to see him.

Can you imagine the scene on that station platform with hundreds of women and children sobbing convulsively and wringing their hands in distress, some of them falling to earth in a dead faint? I ran from the place as from a cemetery, for I felt sure that I would never again see my husband on earth. It was only the Lord who gave me strength to bear the awful grief. Praise be to the Lord!

When I returned home, I knew that my next real danger was the loss of my children. The government had threatened to take them from me . . . . I was ordered not to leave my home, and was taxed 500 rubles because my husband was a presbyter [church leader]. Now we are awaiting confiscation of our goods because we can't pay the tax.

We are expecting every day to become beggars or prisoners, but we thank the Lord that we are free from any fear. We thank Him for everything.

After some time, word came that my husband went to be with the Lord. With my husband gone and my children constantly threatened, of course I had rather be in a place where God is worshiped and where the teachings of the schools are different. Sometimes it seems to me that the believers in Russia will have to face the arena of the early Christians.

A short time later *Harvest Field* received word that this pastor's widow had joined her husband in heaven. Exactly how she died and what happened to her children is not known.

Massacres in the Ukraine

During the Stalin era all of the Soviet Union was a prison of fear where no one could be sure of tomorrow. The Ukraine, where Stalin's police killed or took away millions, suffered the worst.

The Ukranian horror began when millions of farmers were ordered to report to city factories to help the progress of industrialization. To feed the swollen urban population,

Stalin clamped impossible agricultural quotas on Ukranians who had been allowed to remain on their farms. The quotas were set deliberately high to ensure widespread famine. The farmers were required to turn over to the government up to eighty per cent of their production. For most this was impossible, so lying became a way of life. For example, a family that was required to turn in three hundred eggs a year for each laying hen would hide some of the hens when inspectors came around. Devout Christians could not readily lie and were, therefore, likely to miss their quotas.

For them, as well as those caught cheating, the dread NKVD [Soviet secret police] came in black cars, often in the middle of the night. Many were herded into river barges which were then sunk. Others were shipped to labor camps and did not see their families again for years, if ever.

Minister Martyr

Pastors in the Ukraine and elsewhere were special targets for the NKVD and other police. The story of young Pastor Arseny is dramatically related by S. Prokhanoff in his book *In the Cauldron of Russia: 1869–1933*, published by the All-Russian Evangelical Christian Union in 1933.

Prokhanoff recalls that the young man first visited him in Leningrad in 1932, announcing, "The Lord has called me to preach the gospel in Siberia." This was at a time when millions of political prisoners were being shipped to Siberia. Prokhanoff promised to help with prayer and support.

Arseny went to a city in central Siberia. Upon his arrival he was told the atheists were arranging a series of antireligious debates. "I will go there and defend the faith!" he immediately responded.

For three nights he spoke with such eloquence that he was frequently interrupted by applause. At the end of the debates he was given an ovation.

The next day an atheist visited his landlady. "Tell Arseny not to come any more to our debates. Otherwise something will happen to him."

The landlady informed the preacher early the next morning. He listened gravely, then said, "Whatever may happen, I will go to the debates and will fulfill my duty."

Eyewitnesses reported that he spoke with special power and his face shone like that of an angel. The audience gave him a resounding ovation as the debates closed. When the applause died down, three young men came and took him away.

The next morning Christian brothers found him dead in the snow near the railway station. They noted that he was in a half-kneeling position with his New Testament in his hands. He had been shot while praying.

Letters from "Hell"

During this time of repression, perhaps unequaled since the persecutions of Christians in the first century under the mad Emperor Nero, letters continued to leak to friends outside the Soviet Union. Some of those published in *Harvest Fields* indicate the heartbreak and agony of the Russian people under Stalin.

> A woman wrote the Russian Missionary Society:
> Save, oh save us! Have pity on us! Women, young women, and children are being arrested and hundreds sent into exile. Men are sent to other places. (March 2, 1930)

> A church leader reported:
> We have divided into groups of ten. In case one is shot or imprisoned, the next in rank steps into line. One of our pastors who stood for Christ in a Communistic gathering was watched and followed by the secret police. While he was preaching in his own pulpit, they entered and arrested him. Later our congregation received a note saying, "If you wish to find the body of your pastor, go to a certain cemetery." We found him shot dead with his Bible on his breast. They had offered him a large reward if he would renounce Christ, but he chose death with Christ. (November, 1931)

> Another Russian evangelical wrote to a missionary:
> Our conditions here are becoming worse and worse, and we are facing death. We have absolutely nothing to eat. My husband is in bed, suffering from swollen legs because of starvation. Sometimes we get a little something to eat and we mix it with grass, trying to satisfy our hunger. People are falling down from starvation like sparrows in the frost. (December, 1933)

Only eternity will reveal the depth and extent of suffering among evangelicals imprisoned by the Stalinist regime because they chose to obey God in matters of faith rather than man. Many died in prison or in Siberian exile. Some, incarcerated during the late twenties and thirties, are possibly still alive today in the terrible camps. The stories of two dynamic leaders serve to illustrate the bravery and sacrifice of those who died.

Terror in the Labor Camps

Nikolai Odintsov, born in 1870 and ordained in 1909, was the best known Baptist preacher of his time. He preached in the mountains of the Caucasus, in bustling Moscow, in historic St. Petersburg, and in far eastern Russia where churches were hundreds of miles apart. In 1926 he was elected chairman of the Federal Baptist Union and in 1928 was a delegate to the World Baptist Congress in Toronto. He was editor of *The Baptist* in 1929 when that journal was closed by the government.

That same year the Baptist Bible School and the local and Federal Baptist Unions were forcibly shut down. Then Odintsov's closest assistant was arrested. The veteran preacher, teacher and journalist felt he would be next. Quoting from the Apostle Paul's farewell statement to the elders of the church at Ephesus, Odintsov told his associates, " 'Bonds and afflictions await me. But I do not consider my life of any account as dear to myself, in order that I may finish my course, and the ministry, which I received from the Lord Jesus, to testify solemnly of the gospel of the grace of God' " (Acts 20:23,24; *New American Standard New Testament*).

His arrest did not come until the night of November 5, 1929. A co-worker arrested with him reported that he vigorously defended the word of God in bouts with questioners. After serving a three-year sentence in Yaroslavl prison, he was exiled to the village of Makovskoye in remote eastern Siberia. His wife visited him there in 1937 and reported to the believers at home that he was very weak physically but strong in spirit. He sent greetings to his brothers and sisters in Christ and anticipated that he would soon be with the Heavenly Father. "He often said to me," Mrs. Odintsov told them, " 'I want to go home.' "

The following year he was placed in an unknown prison. He died there soon afterwards. Some of his letters from prison live on. In one long epistle he wrote, in part:

I shall not describe the terrors which the prisoners
are experiencing, as that is a matter for a specialist–
historian or a simple honest man. I shall say only
one thing: there is no terror like it! Can one imagine
the bestial look of the hand-picked convoy escorts,

who, making use of the right granted them, can
shoot sick men who collapse and hunt down with
vicious dogs the prisoner who falls on the road? . . .

My body is tired and weak, my work for the
Lord here in the camps is unbearably hard, and the
repressions I suffer often hold me for long periods on
my bare plank bed, which represents my bed of ease.
. . . I have grown weak in body, but not in spirit.
Jesus, the Lord, upholds me. . . . Nothing atheistic
has adhered to me. "I have fought the faith." I have
refused to betray God. "Henceforth there is laid for
me a crown of righteousness, which the Lord, the
righteous judge, will give me on that day" (II Timothy 4:8). I have always avoided every injustice. With
this my earthly life will be finished. . . .

What else will there be? The Lord knows! Eternal glory to Him! Rejoice, dear brothers and sisters,
as I REJOICE! Your brother . . . to the end of his days
has not forgotten you all. May the name of our God
and of his Son our Lord Jesus Christ be blessed and
glorified. Amen, Hallelujah!

Peter Vins

Peter Yakovlevich Vins, a minister of the gospel during the
1930's in Siberia and eastern Russia, was the first of three
generations to be imprisoned for the sake of the gospel. Vins
was participating in the assembly of the Russian Baptist
Union in Moscow in 1930 as a representative of Baptists
from the eastern part of the USSR when he was first
arrested. Advised by the secret police to back the candidacies
of two "ministers" chosen by government agencies to be
members of the administrative board of the Russian Baptist
Union, Vins had refused.

The government candidates were elected anyway. One
later proved himself to be a traitor when he helped the government shut down the Baptist Union. In that time the
churches were plagued by many apostates whom Communists maneuvered into leadership positions with the purpose
of destroying Christianity from within.

Peter Vins was arrested and, after three months of investigation, sentenced to three years in the Svetlaya Bay labor
camp. His two-year-old son, Georgi, had just begun to talk
and often prayed, "Jesus, bring Daddy back."

Peter was released in 1933 and a year later, when his

passport was restored, moved to the town of Omsk where the Baptist church had been closed. After working all day, he would visit believers at night, encouraging and strengthening them from God's Word, and teaching them to minister to fellow members of Christ's body who were suffering. Though all meetings, including those in homes, had been forbidden, by 1936 there were one thousand believers in Omsk.

Because of his activity among the believers at Omsk, it was inevitable that Peter would be arrested and tried again. This became the pattern of his life during these years. Believers all over the Soviet Union were in the same predicament. Forbidden to assemble for worship, they could only minister to one another through prayers and home visitation, and in sharing of material goods. Arrests continued; thousands more were taken away to the camps.

After a new wave of arrests began in Omsk, little Georgi Vins noticed his parents cutting a Gospel into parts and sewing sections into a coat collar lining and into trousers. He knew the departure of his beloved father was again at hand.

A Family's Last Look

This time the father was put in a cell on the fourth floor of the Omsk prison. The family took parcels for him to the prison gate. For awhile they were able to walk along the streets that surrounded the prison and see him waving his arms from a window. Noticing workmen building boxes over the windows on the lower stories, they knew this pleasure would shortly be taken away. One day they arrived and saw that the workmen were close to Peter's window. They stood and looked lovingly for a long time at the familiar figure waving to them from above. Then the workmen closed the window and they were left only with the memory of the wave of his hand and the faint outline of his face.

Lydia Vins and young Georgi never saw him again. Mrs. Vins made repeated inquiries about his fate. Finally she was told he had been sent to a closed camp for socially dangerous people for ten years. Prisoners at that camp were denied the privilege of correspondence so they had no further contact with him. They subsequently learned that he had died on December 27, 1943, at the age of forty-five. After his death, Mrs. Vins continued filing petitions that his case be reconsidered. Finally on Christmas Eve, 1963, a new hearing was held in the Omsk regional court, and Peter Vins was declared posthumously rehabilitated.

Why Persecution Eased

In 1939 Stalin signed a nonaggression pact with Adolf Hitler. Then, in a series of brutal, imperialistic moves, the Soviet Communists forcibly annexed neighboring Latvia, Lithuania, Estonia, the western Ukraine, the eastern half of Poland, and even a slice of territory from little Finland. Western democracies did nothing.

In 1941 German armies suddenly attacked the Soviet Union. Russia entered the war on the side of the Allies. Facing a long siege, Stalin ordered his underlings to stop persecuting the churches and to court the support of church leaders in the name of national unity. When the war ended, the nation was so weakened that unity continued to be pursued. Cooperative church leaders were permitted to travel abroad to world church conferences. Moscow needed them to combat claims in the West of religious persecution in the Soviet Union and to soften criticism of postwar communist takeovers in eastern European countries as well as communist spying and infiltration in other nations.

Khrushchev's Crackdown

Wily Nikita Khruschev took power in 1956. When he denounced Stalin as a despot and took a softer line in foreign policy, Christians hoped that persecution in the Soviet Union might be over. Then suddenly in 1959 the Khrushchev government initiated a new wave of repression against the churches in order to demonstrate to other communist powers that the Soviets had not betrayed the world communist movement. A target date of 1980 was set for the eradication of all religion in the country.

Once again the government-controlled press began attacking church leaders. Old laws were again rigidly enforced. Clergy were forbidden to instruct children, and youth under eighteen were ordered to stay away from churches. Some laws, which had seemed unrelated to religion, were applied to Christians. Most common was the so-called antiparasite law, which related to persons whose work was considered socially unfit by government officials. This law was used against full-time religious workers.

During the next five years ten thousand more Russian Orthodox churches were closed to services and the buildings taken over by the state for public use. Under pressure from the government, a rump synod of Orthodox bishops issued new *Regulations* forbidding Orthodox priests to serve on parish councils. In separate government actions communist sympathizers were named to parish councils by local communist committees under existing laws. Priests who refused to follow desired propaganda lines were fired. Three objecting Orthodox bishops were sent to prison. Another objector, Metropolitan Nikolai of Krutitsy, president of the Council of the Orthodox Church for Foreign Relations, was dismissed from office. Shortly afterwards he died mysteriously.

The Pochaev Monastery Massacre

The worst single atrocity against Orthodoxy during this time occurred on November 20, 1964, when the KGB and other police attacked the Pochaev Monastery. A later protest filed by the Spiritual Council of the Monastery to the Supreme Soviet [national legislature] of the USSR gave this report:

> They broke into cells, removing the doors, seized the monks and rampaged through the churches and living quarters of the monastery. The following were arrested and sentenced: priest–monks Valerian Popovich and Vladimir Soldatov and priest–deacon Gavriil Uglitsky. Monk Mikhail Longchakov, because of his age, was accorded the "indulgence" of confinement in a mental hospital instead of being imprisoned . . . . Many [monks] had to go into hiding in conditions of considerable difficulty in order to evade further arrest and imprisonment . . . . Many others died prematurely and passed on to eternal life before their time. Yevlogi died after torture outside the monastery, as did Abbot Andrei and a number of others. Some who remained alive lost their good health.

Communist Strategy Against Evangelicals

The government applied a similar strategy against Baptist evangelicals. Although details are still not known, it can be logically presumed that Party officials persuaded certain leaders of the All-Union Council of Evangelical Christians and Baptists in the USSR to issue regulations designed to check the growth of evangelicals.

What cannot be disputed is that in 1960 a group of church leaders, claiming to represent the All-Union Council, met without authority from the member churches, and adopted a set of *New Statutes* for church life and mission. The *Statutes* were then expanded upon in a *Letter of Instruc-*

tions mailed to all senior clergymen. When the *Statutes* and the *Letter* were presented in churches, thousands of evangelicals raised a loud cry of alarm.

The *Statutes* were similar to the *Regulations* imposed upon Russian Orthodoxy. They served to tighten state control over church affairs. Not only were children under eighteen to be excluded from worship, but baptisms of older young people, eighteen to thirty, were to be reduced. Evangelistic preaching was to be discouraged and "unhealthy missionary tendencies" restrained. There were even restrictions on where and when services could be held, who should preach, and who should give public prayers. A church choir could perform only in its own church building. Only the organ and the harmonium, and in some instances an upright piano, could be used in worship. Most threatening of all, only congregations whose registration had been recognized by civil authorities could belong to the All-Union Council.

The loudest cries came from pastors who had served time in prison and from relatives of evangelicals still incarcerated or who had died for their faith. They asked, "Is this to be the result of our suffering for Christ?"

The authors of the new rules never explained their actions. Two theories circulated. One was that the Baptist leaders saw the storm coming and acted to protect the churches from severe persecution. The second, and most widely believed by objectors, was that the authors had acted primarily in their own self-interest. Communist officials had warned, so the story ran, that if they wanted to keep their positions and church buildings they must slow the growth of the evangelical movement. Whatever the motives, it appeared that the government had dealt a heavy blow against evangelicals by making it seem that their own leaders were signing the death warrant of the churches.

The Evangelical Rebellion

Any death notice was much too premature.

The first effect was to unite a wide range of Baptists and other evangelicals in fresh opposition to government "interference" in the private affairs of citizens. Georgi Vins, son of martyred Peter Vins; Alexei Prokofiev; Gennadi Kryuchkov; and other recognized leaders formed an "action" committee and met secretly in Moscow. They declared their opposition to the newest antireligious policy, accusing the leaders of the All-Union Council of cooperating and conniving with the atheist regime and excommunicating the members of the Council who had signed the *Letter of Instructions.* They established a new Council of Churches of the Evangelical Christians and Baptists. They called for a church congress composed of elected representatives of all congregations in the USSR, both registered and unregistered.

The schism was now official. Hundreds of churches withdrew from the All-Union Council to support the new organization. Many simply split. Factions loyal to the Council continued as "registered" congregations. Dissenters became, in effect, outlaw churches.

A New Wave of Arrests

A government crackdown, reminiscent in some localities of Stalinism, began on the leaders of the new group and on the unregistered churches. The first arrested was Alexei Prokofiev, who had served time before for "organizing illegal Baptist sectarian groups and preaching libelous sermons against the Soviet way of life." Among other things, he was charged with " 'washing' [baptizing] a group of boys and girls in icy water, one of whom, Anatoli Shatsky, a young laborer, developed a severe mental illness." In 1962 Prokofiev was sentenced to a ten-year prison term.

Tortured to Death

Among the cities especially hard hit was Kulunda in western Siberia. There the target was an "illegal" Baptist congregation which communist officials had refused to register. This meant they could neither legally assemble nor obtain a building for their services. They could not meet outside in the bitter cold, so they met secretly in private homes.

Though they could not openly evangelize, they had private ways of witnessing. One convert was Nikolai Khmara. At forty-five he was transformed from a chronic drunk to a glowing believer. He became such an active witness that within six months he and three others were arrested for religious activities and for failing to conform to the *Statutes* of the official All-Union Council. He was sentenced to three years imprisonment. His pastor received five years. Two weeks later his dead body was returned to his wife. Burn marks were on his palms, toes, and the soles of his feet. A sharp instrument had punctured his stomach. His legs and ankles were swollen and his whole body was covered with bruises. A rag was stuffed in his mouth. His wife removed it and stepped back. His tongue had been cut out. Plainly, he had been tortured to death.

The persecution in Kulunda and other localities convinced the "reformed" Baptists that another purge was in process. Yet they would not give their persecutors victory. They banded together in prayer and mutual support and launched an action unprecedented in the Soviet Union.

The First Organized Crusade for Human Rights

Six weeks after Nikolai Khmara's brutal murder, Georgi Vins, Gennadi Kryuchkov and others convened, without government permission, the first All-Union Conference of Baptist Prisoners' Relatives. Georgi Vins' mother, Lydia Vins, took the leading role. This conference in 1964 was the first organized movement to crusade for human rights in the communist world. It was organized before Aleksandr I. Solzhenitsyn's epochal *Gulag Archipelago* was published in the West and before the broader campaign for human rights was begun by Soviet political dissidents.

The Conference members disseminated a list of 170 Baptist prisoners serving sentences for charges relating to faith and conscience. They carefully pointed out the injustices involved in each case. This information was printed secretly and copies were sent to government leaders and to international organizations and other interested groups abroad. They also noted that the imprisoned Baptists had 442 dependents, many of whom were without material support. The plight of these dependents, they said, was twofold: one, the Soviet communist system provided no social assistance for dependents of prisoners. They had to work or starve. Two, it was extremely difficult and often impossible for relatives of known prisoners to obtain jobs. In fact, some of the prisoners' wives had been discharged after their employers learned the fate of their husbands.

The Conference of Prisoners' Relatives did not expect Moscow to respond with a sudden outburst of charity. Rather, they anticipated that Soviet officialdom would launch a vigorous counterattack and attempt to disprove the embarrassing revelations.

The Continuing Crusade

The believers had always helped one another. Now with the compiling of names and needs, an organized relief ministry was begun with more fortunate believers contributing and giving encouragement to the families of those in prison and to parents who had lost their children to communist tyranny. At the same time they continued to distribute evidence showing that Soviet laws on religion were despicably discriminatory against Christians and other Soviet citizens with religious faith.

In 1965 the Conference sent a letter to Leonid Brezhnev, then the chairman of a committee that was drafting a new federal constitution. They explained how Soviet antireligious legislation contradicted Lenin's original appeals for church–state separation and the right of believers to practice and propagate their faith. They said that the main deviation was the notorious religious law of 1929 which preceded the great persecution of Christians under Stalin. But this appeal was also ignored.

Demonstrating for Freedom

Kryuchkov and Vins sent other letters without success. Finally they organized an unprecedented demonstration before the Communist Central Committee building in Moscow on May 16, 1966.

At the appointed time 500 Baptist representatives from churches in 130 towns moved into the building courtyard. Several leaders presented letters at the main doors. The petitions called for official recognition of the Council of Churches of the Evangelical Christians and Baptists, a stop to governmental interference in church affairs, a release of imprisoned believers, and the granting of rights for Soviet citizens to teach and be taught religious faith. The leaders asked to see Leonid Brezhnev, now chairman of the Central Committee. But they were permitted only to leave their petitions with the receptionist at the door. They then returned to the courtyard to keep a vigil with their brothers and sisters through the rest of the day and night. The next morning about a hundred members of the Moscow Baptist Church, a licensed congregation, joined them. There was no violence, just quiet waiting.

The Government Responds

During the morning, detachments of soldiers and KGB security officials took stations around them to prevent talk with passersby. Around noon an official came out of the building and announced that ten leaders could come in. The rest, he said, should go home. The leaders stepped through the door.

The crowd stayed. "Pray for our brothers," someone shouted. As heads bowed and prayers ascended, the number of curious onlookers outside the ring of police grew.

Suddenly a fleet of empty buses converged and began pushing into the crowd. Then the police attacked. Swinging bottles, sticks, and other weapons, they began striking at the people and pushing and shoving them into the buses. The believers linked arms in a human chain and began singing a hymn, "For the Evangelical Faith." Their singing could be heard above the shouts and blows of the police. But they were finally herded aboard the buses and driven away to various jails in Moscow.

The government was embarrassed at what had happened. The incident would be reported in foreign newspapers, damaging the humanitarian image of Soviet communism which propagandists had been trying to build up. The decision was made to deal with the leaders once and for all.

Ten were already in custody. Others were rounded up. Then on May 19 Georgi Vins, one of the most wanted, and another believer quietly walked up to the receptionists' desk at the Committee's building and announced that they had been sent by their Council of Churches to learn what had happened to the protesters. As they were leaving, police grabbed them.

Still more Baptists came to the Central Committee headquarters. By May 22 the news was all over Moscow, and foreign correspondents were waiting outside. The police became more discreet in making arrests.

But it was a different story at the service of the church in Kiev which Georgi Vins pastored. Because they had been unable to get a license, the people were meeting in some woods by a railway junction. For three years Kiev police had left them alone. On this Sunday they were surrounded by hundreds of police who waited until near the end of the service. Then they plunged forward, seeking to chase the worshipers into the woods so passengers on passing trains would not witness the commotion. About thirty were arrested. The majority were kept in custody only a few days, but Georgi Vins and Gennadi Kryuchkov were put on trial.

The courtroom was packed when the trial began. The principal charges were organizing the May protest in Moscow, publishing and distributing unauthorized literature, and organizing religious instruction for children.

The prosecutor pointed to the glorification of suffering

of believers in the literature as evidence that the preachers had rebelled against Soviet laws and even consorted with foreigners for overthrow of the government. "Kryuchkov and Vins," he said in conclusion, "are well aware of the ideology that dominates our society — one that has nothing in common with religion. Yet, in spite of our ideology and in spite of what is taught in the schools, they go and organize religious instruction for children."

The two Baptists defended themselves vigorously and used their opportunities for testimony to recite instances of persecution and discrimination. Vins freely admitted that he was responsible for the literature in question. After giving their defenses, both preachers were permitted to give final addresses. Said Vins in part:

I consider myself fortunate to be able to stand here
and testify that I'm charged as a believer . . . I do not
see you, Comrade Judge, Comrade Prosecutor and all
here present as my enemies; you're my brothers and
sisters in the human race. When I leave the courtroom, I shall pray to God for you there in my cell,
asking that he should reveal his divine truth to you
and the great meaning of life.

This evoked great shouting and laughter among the Communist spectators. After a final address by Kryuchkov, both men were sentenced to three years imprisonment in "special regime" camps.

But the imprisonment of Vins, Kryuchkov and other Baptist leaders did not break up the movement as the communist government had hoped. Though Georgi Vins' wife Nadezhda was left with four young children and lost her job as a translator, the protests continued with lists of prisoners kept up-to-date (names; charges; dates of trials and sentencing; locations of prisons, etc.).

A Mother Goes to Prison

On December 1, 1970, Georgi's mother, Lydia Vins, was arrested while in the house with her grandchildren. Put on trial in a Kiev court, the aged woman gave a vigorous recital of persecutions by Soviet authorities against believers. When the judge decreed three years in a labor camp, her daughter-in-law Nadezhda threw her a bouquet of violets. When the police brought her out to a police car, she had to be supported to keep from falling. Believers stood courageously in the street and sang,

For the faith of the Gospel,
For Christ we shall stand up,
Following his example,
Ever onward, onward after Him.

The battle rages, the flame is hot,
And places shake and sway,
Raise higher the banner
of Christ the Victor.

Sufferings in the Seventies

Persecution in the seventies has continued to center on believers from unregistered congregations. There have been more arrests, prison sentences, and "kidnappings" of children from religious families. In each instance, Soviet prosecutors carefully cite alleged law violations during the charades which Communists call trials.

With increased publicity abroad about human rights violations in the Soviet Union, the Soviet government has become sensitive to world opinion. The government does not want martyrs. Communist bureaucrats know that the sudden, violent killing of a pastor, if known to the press, will be headlined in major western cities. Still, violent deaths have occurred, perhaps more as a result of rash acts by lesser officials than as government strategy.

The "Suicide" of Pastor Moiseyevich

Ivan Moiseyevich had once predicted, "I must die for the faith." In 1974 he was in poor health and living in forced exile in cold Siberia. Though a medical commission recommended that he should be returned to a warmer climate, communist bureaucrats blocked his transfer. In January, 1975, his family received a telegram reporting his death. His sons and several close friends flew to the Siberian town of Nyagan where his body had been embalmed. They were met by an official who claimed Moiseyevich had hung himself.

His family reported in the *Bulletin* of the Council of Baptist Prisoners' Relatives:

> Knowing our father's powers of endurance and his
> deep faith in eternal life, we did not believe that he
> had done it himself . . . . We tried to discover who
> saw him last . . . but we were unable to because the
> two men who shared a room with our father had suspiciously disappeared, no one knew where, although
> we tried for the next two days to find them.

Their suspicions increased when they examined the body and noted that his hands and his legs below the knees were almost black, and his face white. They wangled permission to ship the body home to Odessa by air freight. But because of bureaucratic stalls, they were unable to leave for two weeks. Police were waiting when they landed and kept constant watch over the coffin. Twenty–five minutes after they reached the dead man's house, a group of communist doctors arrived and ordered that the coffin not be opened. The travelers were told by neighbors that Communists had been watching their house almost every night for the past two weeks.

The body was transferred to a new coffin on February 13 in the presence of relatives and three of the doctors. The relatives wanted to examine the body for marks of violence, but the doctors refused, claiming that an epidemic might result. When relatives and friends began filing by to view the body, the doctors kept hurrying them along. Afterwards the room was closed so no one could look at the body.

A thousand mourners gathered for the funeral. The services were accompanied by a church band and evangelical hymns while communist functionaries looked on sourly. One of the sons spoke about his father's life and death. Altogether eight sermons were preached.

After the burial, local police continued to harass the martyr's family. Early in March his eldest son, Pyotr, age twenty-seven, died suddenly in the night from a heart condition.

"Summonses to the authorities continue both in the family of Ivan Moiseyevich and in the church," the Council noted at the close of their report. The report continued:

> But praise God that the spring countryside and our
> beloved work on the land, together with our prayers
> to God, help us all to bear the cross laid upon us. We
> are convinced, beloved brothers and sisters, that as
> we believe in the power of the cross of Christ, so the
> Lord will manifest his power in us through him.
> Please, beloved, pray for the continuing life of our
> church and for the sorrowing family of Ivan Moise-
> yevich. "Grace be with all who love our Lord Jesus
> Christ with love undying. Amen" (Ephesians 6:24).

The Strange Case of Private "Vanya"

Another martyr of the seventies was Private Ivan "Vanya" Vasilevich Moiseyev. The parents of Vanya were told that he had died from drowning. His coffin was delivered to them welded shut. A communist officer attended the funeral to see that the lid remained closed. Despite the officer's protests, the parents insisted on seeing their son's body. A crowbar was passed through the crowd. The officer fled in fear. When the coffin was opened, the family saw their son's bruised, blackened face and body. He had been stabbed, burned, and beaten – tortured to death.

Investigators from the Council of Baptist Prisoners' Relatives carefully compiled evidence from Vanya's letters home, a tape recording he had made, and the testimony of soldiers who had known him. They soon pieced together what had actually happened.

Vanya's crime had been praying and witnessing. His first punishment was to stand outside in the cold for five days without food. When he refused to be quiet about his faith, he was ordered to stand for twelve straight nights in subzero weather. He survived this.

Determined to break him, his commanding officer, Colonel Malsin, tried interrogations, beatings, and prison. He could not be broken. He was put on trial for attending unregistered religious meetings during recreation time, and for distributing literature containing falsehoods and slander against the Soviet Union. "I have one higher allegiance," he testified, "and that is to Jesus Christ. He has given me certain orders, and these I cannot disobey."

The court sentenced him to prison. He was taken back to jail and beaten repeatedly. Colonel Malsin finally sent him to the dread KGB. The "treatment" they administered in a soundproof room ended his life. His murder was later confirmed by Colonel Malsin. Ill and stricken by remorse, the officer told Vanya's parents, "I was present when your son died. . . . He died hard, but he died a Christian." The true circumstances of his death are recorded in a book titled *Vanya*, by Myrna Grant.

Vanya's family has received many letters testifying of the spiritual impact of his martyrdom. Typical was this statement from a discharged soldier: "Our dear brother will be in our hearts eternally. He suffered much torture, but he was faithful to Christ to the end. He left us an example of how to strive for the crown of Christ."

An Analysis of Persecution in the USSR

The martyrdom of the preacher and the soldier indicate that violence against believers has not ceased in the Soviet

Union. But these and other killings, along with less violent persecution, do not mean that believers all over the Soviet Union are the victims of such oppression. Peter Deyneka, Jr., director of the Slavic Gospel Association, notes that imprisonments and beatings are "basically limited to areas where tourists do not go. In trying to woo third world nations, the Soviets are attempting to show more humaneness in places where visitors do go."

Deyneka is one of the most knowledgeable persons in the West on Christianity and communism in the Soviet Union and Eastern Europe. The Slavic Gospel Association, which his father, an immigrant from the Ukraine, founded, includes about 210 workers who are active in radio broadcasting and the printing and distribution of Bibles behind the Iron Curtain. He cautions that "while sensational stories of martyrdoms and imprisonments are true, the majority of Soviet evangelicals are able to carry on their worship and witness in meaningful ways." But he adds:

> Persecution in the Soviet Union is not just imprisonment. Every Christian there experiences psychological, economic, and educational pressure. One of the most fearful pressures which all Christian parents face is the possibility that their children will be taken away. Some children are taken away and put in atheistic orphanages because of stringent Christian teaching in their homes. Because of this every Christian mother wonders every day if it could happen to her children. This psychological pressure is real. The Communists use these and other experiences to keep Christians on edge with nervous tension.

Helsinki and Detente

The 1975 Helsinki Agreement, calling for guarantees of human rights, which the Soviets signed in exchange for *de facto* recognition from the West of their hegemony over Eastern Europe, has resulted in no relief for Soviet evangelicals. A report from Keston College, an English school specializing in study of religious life in the Soviet Union and Eastern Europe, cites an appeal made in 1976 as an example of pleas which have gone unanswered by Soviet authorities. This appeal, sent to Kosygin and Brezhnev with copies forwarded to the UN and other international agencies, states, "agreements on human rights (signed in Helsinki) are not implemented in practice. You freed criminals under the amnesty, but you did not extend it to believers, although they were also eligible for release." The appeal cites a long list of human rights violations, including the torture and beatings of prisoners which sometimes result in death; job discrimination against believers; removal of children from homes for "ideological reeducation; and breaking up of church services. The appeal reports how "in the village of Vysokovo in the Kharkov region, KGB official Zotov pushed past women who were kneeling in prayer, to the pulpit. When one believer said, 'You're behaving indecently,' Zotov replied, 'You'll be crawling on your knees to me.' "

The Continuing Vendetta Against the Vins Family

Among those arrested in 1977 was young Peter Vins, son of Georgi Vins and grandson of his martyred namesake. Young Peter was tried for "parasitism" in a courtroom packed with KGB officers. Family members had difficulty gaining entry to the courtroom and two of the accused's sisters were knocked down during a scuffle. Three of his friends, who were to testify in his behalf, were arrested and detained during the trial.

After being sentenced to a year in a labor camp, the young believer was allowed by Soviet custom to address the court. He thanked his lawyer and family. He recalled KGB threats made the previous February about his activities with the Helsinki Committee monitoring groups. He said his conviction was a result of those threats. "My way is a special one," he concluded. "It is that of my grandfather, my father, my grandmother, and my mother."

While in prison, young Vins was beaten severely. He was released on January 6, 1978, as "physically unfit for work." Then after visiting his father, Georgi Vins, in a labor camp in Siberia, he was rearrested for "parasitism." The following June 10 Georgi Vins was reported to have been "brutally beaten" and placed in an underground isolation cell. His condition is not known at this time. Because of world-wide publicity and many foreign demands, including a resolution from the United States Congress, that he be released, the Soviet government may permit him to join relatives in Canada.

Communist Blindness

The Soviet Communists will only fool themselves if they think that getting rid of the Vins family and other believers will halt the growth of the underground church. They are apparently blind to what history teaches about persecution of Christians.

Though bathed in blood, schooled in suffering and smothered by regulations from an oppressive atheistic government, the church of true believers in the Soviet Union will not only survive, but will triumph above the ashes of the ideology that marked it for extinction.

THE STRUGGLING, GROWING CHURCH:
Eastern Europe

As goes the Soviet Union, so goes Estonia, Latvia, Lithuania, Bulgaria, Czechoslovakia, Hungary, Poland, and East Germany. Moscow claims the first three—Estonia, Latvia, Lithuania—as constituent republics of the Soviet Union, but their annexation by the Soviets in 1940 has never been recognized by most of the free world. Thus in this book they are treated as separate national entities. The remaining five are political satellites of the Soviets. Three other Communist East European countries—Romania, Yugoslavia, and Albania—pursue a political line independent of the Soviets.

In a secret agreement made in 1943 at Teheran, Churchill and Stalin decided that, after World War II, Central Europe would continue in the democratic western sphere, whereas Eastern Europe would be under the auspices of the Soviet Union. America's Roosevelt opposed this tradeoff, as did his successor Truman, but the Churchill–Stalin pact prevailed. Thus all of Eastern Europe was virtually surrendered to the ideology of despotic Marxism, allowing the people no voice in their future.

Religious faith is viewed as an enemy to be vanquished. The ultimate intention—to stamp out faith and produce a generation of pure Marxists. Meanwhile, the governments must contend with the churches that maintain a grip on much of the population. Although they seek to contain

259

church growth and curtail church influence, these governments do permit temporary accommodations with powerful religious establishments, so long as the power of the state over life and conscience is explicit in the constitution. No religious group or individual, however, can be allowed to act against the best interests of the state. The constitution may call for separation of church and state, but the state is always prosecutor, judge, and jury over the activities of the church.

In the present stage the state avoids any religious martyrdoms that would arouse world opinion. Imprisonment of religious dissenters is acceptable, but the charges are always nonreligious in nature. The illusion of religious liberty under communism is to be perpetuated. The effect of this policy has been the persecution of believers and resistant churches, resulting in the martyrdom of many professing Christians.

LITHUANIA—MARTYRS BEFORE COMMUNISM

The greatest persecutions have occurred in the three Baltic countries now claimed by the USSR. Lithuania, bordered by Poland, is the southernmost of the three.

Most Lithuanians were converted to Catholic Christianity in the fourteenth century. For the next four centuries the land was self-governing and was a bulwark of Catholic faith. Then from 1792 until 1915 the little country suffered under Russian rule.

The tsarist government closed all Lithuanian Catholic convents and monasteries and shipped thousands of priests and nuns to Siberia, where many died as martyrs. Determined to stamp out the spirit of the conquered nation, the Russians suppressed the Lithuanian language. Any Lithuanian heard talking in his mother tongue was punished. Desecration of Catholic churches by Russian occupation forces provoked frequent riots. Thousands of civilians died in the two worst occurrences, in 1830 and 1863.

Russian and German Brutalities

Germany occupied Lithuania during World War I. Near the end of the war the country again became independent and remained free until communist troops invaded in 1940. After a mock election, the Soviets proclaimed Lithuania a Soviet Republic of the USSR.

The Soviets attacked religious institutions which had been revived during the period of independence. They seized Catholic schools, churches, and other church property. Thousands of Lithuanians were arrested, including most of the country's religious and political leaders, and deported to labor camps in the Soviet Union. When Germany turned on the Soviets and marched into Lithuania, the Russians massacred 5,740 Lithuanian prisoners. Among them were fifteen priests.

The German occupation was no less cruel. About two hundred thousand Lithuanians, Jews and Catholics, died in concentration camps in Lithuania and Germany.

Cruelties under Communism

The Soviets recaptured Lithuania in 1944. During the next dozen years some three hundred thousand Lithuanians were either killed or exiled to Siberia and other parts of the USSR. Families were broken up—fathers were sent to one concentration camp, mothers to another, and children were separated from both parents.

Between 1945 and 1956 almost every priest in Lithuania was ordered to submit to interrogation at one of 480 "centers of terror" set up across the country. Soviet Communists demanded that each priest sign a "loyalty" oath to spy on his own parishioners, make reports to the police, and help organize a puppet church independent of the Vatican. Clerics who refused were either shot or shipped to Siberia.

Since Stalin's death, persecution has been less savage, but Lithuania remains under the heel of tyranny. "Uncooperative" bishops and priests continue to be exiled or put under house arrest. Smaller, scattered congregations of "reform" Baptists have been treated more harshly, with scores of pastors being arrested and imprisoned.

The Student Revolt

In 1970 Catholic students became desperate. That year several young university staff members, known to be pro-Lithuanian, died mysteriously. Students who suspected murder drew lots to decide who would commit suicide in an effort to draw world attention. Romas Kalanta, only twenty, received the "honor." He poured gasoline over himself in a crowded city park and died in agony. The city of Kaunas was plunged into chaos. Riots and fights erupted, with crowds of young people shouting "Freedom for Lithuania." Three more self-burnings followed, two by men in their sixties. The Soviet press played down the uprising and called young Kalanta mentally unbalanced. The UN and western world powers did nothing.

Two years later a memorandum, signed by 17,059 Lithuanian Catholics, was sent to UN Secretary–General Kurt Waldheim, begging the UN to intervene. The paper noted:

Social ills such as crimes by juveniles, alcoholism and suicides have increased ten times during the period of Soviet power. . . . Divorces and the destruction of unborn babies have also reached a dangerous level. The further we move away from the Christian past, the more the terrible consequences of compulsory atheist education come to light and the wider the spread of the inhuman way of life deprived of God and religion.

The Communists reacted to this plea by ordering state-appointed Catholic bishops and pastors to sign a pastoral letter condemning those irresponsible Lithuanian Catholics involved. The letter was to be read in place of the sermon in all Catholic churches on Sunday, April 30, 1972. Two Communist officials attended each church and made notes. Some priests read the whole letter, but many either did not or omitted major portions. Several read a protest letter denouncing "this shameful document that will take our church down the same road as that of the Russian Orthodox Church."

The protesters were accused of dividing the church. "Who is really dividing the Church in Lithuania?" they countered in a petition.

Is it the 17,000 believers who signed the memorandum? No! They are not getting involved in matters of dogma or discipline. Is it a crime and a division in the unity of the Church to demand catechisms and prayerbooks, that priests be not jailed for teaching the catechism to children, that displaced bishops be allowed to work and that seminaries accept all who wish to enter? We deeply believe that those doing the dividing are those who are aiding the enemies of the Church and of God against those Catholics who are fighting for their rights, and those who publish dubious "pastoral letters."

We have had enough of these Monsignors who spread the "truth" about the Lithuanian Catholic Church by means of the atheist radio and press. We have also had enough of the kind of bishops who publish such "pastoral" letters. . . . Help us with your prayers and tell the world that we want at the present time only as much freedom of conscience as is permitted by the Constitution of the Soviet Union. We are full of determination, for God is with us.

Silence from the Vatican

The brave resisters hoped for support from the Vatican. They were bitterly disappointed. *America* magazine reported a sorrowful Lithuanian priest as saying, "We hoped that at this time the Holy Father would at least have wished us a Blessed Easter in Lithuanian. But even at this time, as in the past, we heard the [Vatican] radio sending greetings to the Russians, our oppressors. . . . What have we done to be abandoned in this way?"

Lithuania, with only three million population, remains no less a captive nation today. The United States and several other free countries still do not recognize Soviet sovereignty over the embattled little country where so many Catholic martyrs have perished for their beliefs.

LATVIA AND ESTONIA — PAWNS OF MOSCOW

The story of religious persecution and martyrdom in these two small Baltic countries is tragically similar to the Lithuanian experience, except that fifty per cent of Latvia's 2.3 million people and seventy per cent of Estonia's 1.3 million population were Lutheran according to the religious census taken in 1971.

Like Lithuania, Latvia and Estonia have ancient cultural, linguistic, and religious identities. Both were occupied by tsarist Russia in the eighteenth century, regained their independence at the end of World War I, and were annexed by the Soviets through mock elections in 1940. Since annexation, thousands of Latvian and Estonian Lutherans have died as a result of imprisonment in Siberian labor camps.

Martyrs Among Baptists

Both countries also have sizable Baptist minorities. Baptist work was initiated in Latvia in 1860 when a visiting German Baptist challenged a group of seekers to study believers' baptism in the New Testament. Nine of the seekers became convinced and journeyed to the German city of Memel to be baptised in a Baptist church there. By 1875 there were thirty-five Baptist churches in Latvia with twenty-two hundred members. As Baptist work continued to grow, Latvian leaders became active participants in the Baptist World Alliance. During Latvia's period of independence, 1918–1940, many prominent foreign Baptist preachers visited the small country and preached in the large church at Riga. Estonia has likewise been a fertile field for the Baptist witness.

Under communism, thousands of Latvian and Estonian Baptists have also been deported to Siberia where many have died. Some have returned home broken in health after years of confinement. Baptist churches in both captive nations, legal and illegal, are reported crowded despite the government restrictions which prevail across the Soviet Union. In the city of Tallinn, Estonia, Baptists have been permitted to meet in the Lutheran cathedral.

In Latvia and Estonia the light of the gospel continues to shine in the darkness imposed by communism. All the atheist crusades, discrimination, and persecution emanating from Moscow cannot put it out. The martyrdom of a myriad of Christian believers has not been in vain.

BULGARIA—THE MOST "RUSSIAN" OF THE SATELLITES

A mountainous, Tennessee-sized country on the Black Sea, Bulgaria is not officially a part of the Soviet Union. But it is often called "Little Russia" because its rulers adhere so slavishly to the Soviet system. The dreary tale of suffering and martyrdom for religious faith under Marxist dictatorship continues here.

Bulgaria is also deeply rooted in Christian tradition and influence. The Bulgars adopted Christianity as their state religion in 865 A.D. When Christendom split in 1054 between East and West, the Bulgarian church sided with the Byzantine-rite Eastern Orthodox Church. Later the Bulgarian church became a distinctly national movement. Today eighty-five per cent of the population of 8.5 million holds some Orthodox identity. The remaining Bulgars who profess Christian faith are divided among Roman Catholics, Arminians, Pentecostals, Baptists, and smaller groups.

For almost five hundred years—from around 1400 to

1876—Bulgaria was under Turkish control. In 1876 a nationalist revolt provoked bloody massacres by Turkish soldiers. Russian troops intervened to defeat the Turks, but other European powers forced a withdrawal and Bulgaria remained in the Turkish empire. Full Bulgarian independence did not come until 1908.

How the Communists Came to Power

Bulgaria fought on the side of Germany in World Wars I and II, but remained at peace with the Soviet Union until near the end of the second great war. In 1944 the Soviets formally declared war to justify the entry of Red troops into Bulgaria. Backed by the Red soldiers, local Communists seized power.

There, as elsewhere, the Communists made great democratic pretensions. "Free" elections, as supervised by the Soviets, were a bitter joke on the Bulgarians. This is well illustrated in their policies towards the churches. From 1944—1948 the churches were all but ignored by the new rulers. Marxist officials were busy consolidating their power, setting up a constitution modeled after the Soviet one, repairing war damages, and polishing the new Bulgaria's image for world propaganda purposes.

Martyrs to Stalinism

In 1948 the repression began, reflecting a Stalinist trend all across subjugated Eastern Europe. The puppet Bulgarian government forced the leader of the Bulgarian Orthodox Church to resign, then pressured the ruling Orthodox Synod to take a procommunist line. In 1949 state officials prodded the Orthodox clergy to hold special services in honor of Stalin's seventieth birthday. Pastors who objected or failed to follow instructions were arrested and sent to labor camps.

In this same year a new law put all church activities and appointments of clergy under the control of the state. The theological faculty at the University of Sofia was compelled to add Marxism to its curriculum. More Orthodox pastors were arrested and put on trial. Some were executed.

Persecution of smaller church bodies was even more severe. All churches with connections to denominations outside Bulgaria were ordered shut down. Only after these churches cut links with their foreign brethren were they allowed to resume worship services.

Also in 1949 fifteen prominent leaders of Baptist, Pentecostal, Methodist and Congregational churches were arrested and charged with high treason, espionage, unlawful foreign exchange transactions and attempts to undermine the government. The government press claimed that all made "confessions of guilt" and, after being sentenced to terms ranging from one year to life, thanked the judge for such "mild punishment." Protests were lodged with western governments and in the General Assembly of the United Nations, but to no avail. The only response of the Marxist regime was to make more arrests. Among others taken into custody were the Roman Catholic Bishop of Nikopol, Monsignor Eugene Boslov; the head of the Catholic seminary at Plovdiv; and two other priests. It is assumed that all four were executed.

Tortured for His Faith

As in the Soviet Union, arrested Bulgarian church leaders were convicted of "political" crimes and incarcerated with the general run of prisoners. "We [pastors] were described as 'instruments of imperialism,'" explains ex-prisoner Harlan Popov in his book *Tortured for His Faith*. The communist bosses also took stringent measures to destroy journals kept by believers about their prison experiences and about deaths of fellow inmates. Consequently, specific Christian martyrs among the thousands who died in Bulgarian prisons and labor camps have been hard to identify.

Baptist pastor Popov, a converted atheist, was picked up at his home in 1948 and taken to the local secret police station for a "little questioning." After interrogation, he was escorted to a cell block where a prisoner had scrawled a quotation from Dante over the cell door, "All hope abandon, ye who enter here."

Two weeks later Pastor Popov was put on a death diet and subjected to around-the-clock nonstop interrogation. Three questioners worked eight-hour shifts. Each time he denied spying, he was hit on the side of the head. After ten days of beatings and starvation, he saw reflected in a window

. . . a horrible, emaciated figure, legs swollen, eyes like empty holes in the head, with a long beard covered with dried blood from cracked, bleeding and hideously swollen lips. . . . In that moment of total, crushing hopelessness, I heard a voice as clear and distinct as any voice I have ever heard in my life. It said, "I will never leave you nor forsake you. . . ."

The presence of God filled the Punishment Cell and

enveloped me in a divine warmth, infusing strength
into the shell that was my body.

Popov spent eleven years in Bulgarian prisons. On the walls
of the cells were scratched the longings of former inmates.
Above another door he noticed an old Latin proverb, *"Dum
spiro spero*—as long as I breathe, I hope."

The prisoners developed a crude telegraph code. One tap
on the wall stood for "A," two taps were "B," and so on
through the alphabet. Pastor Popov used the telegraph to win
men to Christ. One prisoner who had accepted Christ
through Popov's witnessing fell near him while they were
constructing an embankment around the island. Popov tried
to carry him back to the barracks but collapsed after a few
steps. The new Christian died where he lay.

When Popov was released, he was given a "Resident's
Permit" to live in Sofia, the capital. He boldly started illegal
prayer meetings and Bible classes in an old woman's small
apartment. Later he felt compelled to escape to the free
world to tell people about the plight of the underground Bulgarian churches and to rejoin his family who had been
allowed to move to Sweden. Through the prayers of many
Christians all over Bulgaria, Popov was granted a passport.
Thirteen years and two months after his arrest, Popov was
reunited with his wife and children.

In the years since, he has preached to thousands of free
world believers, raising money to smuggle Bibles to believers
across the borders of Iron Curtain countries and pleading for
prayer and concern for those suffering for Christ under communism. Says Popov:

I have spoken around the world on behalf of the
Underground Church. I have often asked, "Who here
has prayed for the suffering Christians of the Underground Church." Always the answer is almost no
one. It is a shame on the conscience of all free Christians. We from Communist lands are your brothers
and sisters in Christ. We are one body in Christ. . . .

My people accept the suffering. They understand
this is their cross. But they don't understand why
their brothers and sisters in the free world seem to
have forgotten them—even in their prayers.

Bulgaria Today

The Bulgarian communist regime continues as one of the
most oppressive governments in the world. No Bibles or

Christian literature can be imported, although the Orthodox Church was allowed to print twenty thousand New Testaments a few years ago and evangelicals have been able to obtain some of these. The Orthodox Church is allowed a small measure of autonomy, but no church leader can expect to oppose antireligious laws and remain at his post. All church bodies have communist-approved leaders. A communist newspaper claims that two–thirds of the adult population have dropped their religious affiliation. This may be true of the Orthodox Church which was characterized by widespread indifference and spiritual laxity before the communist takeover. However, the number of Protestant evangelicals, despite the persecution and discrimination which they face daily, is reported to be growing.

HUNGARY—A LESSON IN BETRAYAL

Hungary. The name sparks memories of a tragic, futile uprising against communist rulers in 1956 when civilians courageously fought Soviet tanks with little more than their bare hands while the UN and free world nations refused to intervene. After overwhelming Soviet armed might put down the popular revolution, leaders of the revolt were executed.

Hungarians, like Bulgarians, never chose communism voluntarily. About one–third smaller than Bulgaria, Hungary lies in the heart of Eastern Europe. The state was founded in the ninth century, Christianized about two centuries later, and fell under Turkish domination in 1526.

The Protestant Reformation swept in during the latter years of Turkish rule. By 1700, when Austria captured Hungary, Hungarian Protestants outnumbered Catholics a thousand to one. A counterreformation reversed this movement to the extent that by 1800 two–thirds of the population was Catholic. This ratio prevailed in 1919 when Hungary gained independence. Two months later a communist dictator seized power, but Romanian troops intervened and a non-communist government was restored.

Tightening the Communist Noose

Near the end of World War II, Soviet troops moved in behind fleeing German soldiers and remained. In November, 1945, free elections were held under Allied supervision. The anti-communist slate of candidates won handily. Communist contenders received only seventeen per cent of the vote.

However, a Communist was given the powerful post of Minister of the Interior. From this point on, Hungary became a classic study of communist strategy. In the next election the cunning Marxists joined a coalition of other socialist groups. After the coalition won, the Communists moved into key jobs. In the 1949 elections only a single list of candidates appeared on the ballot, all approved by the Communist Party. The new president and prime minister were professing Christians, but the real power was in the hands of Secretary Matyas Rakosi, a ruthless Communist. Within a short time Hungary was completely subservient to the Soviet Union.

Brave Cardinal Mindzenty

While they were tightening the political noose, Hungarian Communists pursued a skillful policy against the churches. The Catholic hierarchy staunchly opposed the encroachment of the Communists. In 1947, seven hundred priests were imprisoned. When the state nationalized all church schools in 1948, the Hungarian Roman Catholic primate Cardinal Jozsef Mindzenty defiantly excommunicated the government ministers responsible for the new law and ordered all church bells tolled in protest. Mindzenty was arrested in December and charged with conspiracy. He denied the charge and declared, "I shall never resign my office." He also warned the Hungarian people beforehand "that any confession I may be forced to make" should not be believed.

After Mindzenty's arrest, some lower members of the hierarchy were forced to sign an agreement making the church subservient to the state. The following August a new Soviet-style constitution was adopted, separating church and state and guaranteeing "freedom of speech, of the press and of association, as long as this freedom does not interfere with the interests of the working masses." As in the Soviet Union, communist officials were empowered to define such interference.

The Protestant Compromise

Leaders of the Lutheran and the Hungarian Reformed churches, the country's two largest Protestant bodies respectively, were more amenable to communist policies. They signed agreements with the government in 1948 which in effect put them under state watch while allowing them to worship in church buildings and homes, hold Bible classes in homes, conduct evangelistic meetings, develop charitable institutions, and organize religious instruction in state schools.

The government pledged to continue to pay church subsidies. Certain Protestant clergy were even permitted to travel to the West to serve on committees of the World Council of Churches. Under this arrangement favored Hungarian Protestant leaders spoke loftily of "the servant church ministering to the people directly." The compromise was initially praised by theologian Karl Barth and many other foreign churchmen from denominations belonging to the World Council. By 1951, while the Hungarian government was pushing a vigorous antichurch campaign in public education, Barth had changed his opinion. Addressing the Hungarian church leaders, he warned,

> You're at the point of making an article of faith of
> your agreement with communism, of making it part
> of the Christian message. . . . You're at the point of
> wandering into an ideological Christian wonderland.
> . . . How can you claim in your propaganda that
> socialism is a heaven on earth . . .?

Barth suggested that they "rethink" their "theology radically." In future years the presence of the Hungarians and cooperative church leaders from other Red satellites would keep the WCC from listing flagrant communist transgressions in lists of world human rights violations.

Rebellion Within the Church

Other voices inside Hungary were now being raised in dissent. During the early 1950's, a "Confessing Church" was formed within the Reformed Church of Hungary by dissident pastors and laymen. They charged that the "serving church" had become a "servile church" to government policy. Like the Reformed Baptists of the Soviet Union, they declared that government had no business interfering with the internal affairs of churches. They were joined by many Lutherans, Methodists, Baptists, and other members of small, free church groups. Church leaders loyal to the government responded with diatribes charging them with dividing the churches of Hungary. Many of the dissenters were dismissed from their church jobs. Action from the government was more severe. Dismissed pastors were arrested for vagrancy and for presiding over "unlicensed" churches.

Hungarian society was now in the grip of Stalinization. Communist spies were everywhere. Executions were common. In the schools study of the Russian language was obligatory. History books had been revised to give the Party line on recent events. Teachers and pupils had to stand up each time Stalin's name was uttered. School choirs were forced to sing cantatas to the Soviet tyrant. His name was spelled out in rhythmic shouts in school assemblies. And yet the compliant churches were allowed to teach classes on religion in the public schools.

There was no letup after Stalin's death in 1953. Hungarian Party boss, Matyas Rakosi, seemed determined to prove to Moscow's new leaders that he alone could be trusted as their proconsul in suppressed Hungary.

We Shall No Longer Be Slaves

The economy went from bad to worse under bureaucratic mismanagement. Then in the summer of 1956 hope arose that the standard of living might be improved when a report spread that rich uranium deposits had been discovered in the Mecsek Mountains. This anticipation was demolished when it was revealed that the Hungarian puppet government had signed a secret agreement with the Soviets, giving Moscow the exclusive right to mine the uranium for a ridiculously low compensation. Soon Soviet technicians began arriving. This was the fuse that ignited the frustration and resentment of the people. Six thousand young people, most of them students, surrounded the uranium and coal mines. The Russians drove them away.

But the revolution against Soviet colonialism was on. In Budapest crowds gathered to sing the Hungarian anthem, "Lord Bless the Hungarian." They waved flags as they repeated the refrain:

> By the Hungarians' God
> We swear
> That we shall no longer be slaves!
> Never! We swear! Never!

The unorganized uprising spread spontaneously and rapidly. The government resigned. Imre Nagy, a previous premier who had been ousted by Soviet-backed Communists, was restored to office. Political prisoners, including Cardinal Mindzenty, were freed. "This struggle for liberty is unexampled in world history," the prelate declared.

Leaders of the Confessing Church had supported the revolution from the beginning. Church leaders who had cooperated with the Communists were now embarrassed. Bishop

Laszlo, speaking for the Reformed Church of Hungary, broadcast a confession "with repentance that the church submitted itself to the pressure of the political power more than it was compelled to do, and because of this, it has also caused harm in carrying out its spiritual aims. . . . God bless those who are sowing justice and love."

Moscow obviously had been caught by surprise and stood embarrassed before the world. Revolutionary leaders had announced that they were not trying to outlaw communism. They wanted only to replace the Moscow-approved dictatorship of one party by a parliamentary and democratic government which would have an independent national policy.

Already Moscow had been jolted by the independence of Yugoslavia and rumblings of rebellion in Poland. The Soviets had not acted against either country. Of this the Hungarian revolutionaries were well aware. They also believed that the free world would come to their aid if Moscow attacked in force.

Suddenly the Soviets moved. Hundreds of powerful tanks rolled into Hungary with jet planes screaming overhead. Behind the planes came thousands of troops as the Red Army swept into Budapest. The freedom fighters were all but helpless before the invaders' armor and planes. At best they had only a few submachine guns and rifles captured from Russian soldiers, and some homemade grenades. It was a pathetic sight. Clusters of young people hung on to the Soviet tanks. Women lay down on the pavement and tried to stop the armored advance. Some Russian soldiers cried when they were given orders to kill helpless civilians. The gutters ran red with blood and many streets were turned into cemeteries.

The Hungarian patriots appealed to the outside world for help. The United States and British governments condemned the Soviet action but did nothing more. In the UN Security Council, a resolution to "censure" the Soviet Union was vetoed by the Soviet delegate.

The UN—A Paper Tiger

A request for action was put before the UN General Assembly. As the delegates assembled, the desperate Hungarians sent a final appeal:

To all UN members and delegates:

In the coming hours you will decide about the life or the death of this nation. While your sons are at peace and happy, we sons of the Hungarian nation are falling under the cruel fire of Soviet tanks and bombers. Our country has been attacked from abroad. We turn to you. You are our last citadel of hope.

Exercise the opportunity which your nations have given you and save our country from destruction and slavery. We are asking for immediate and effective help. Save us from further bloodshed and give us back our neutrality. Show that the UN can carry out its will, and thus achieve that our country again be free! We appeal to your conscience and call on you to act immediately. . . .

The UN Assembly voted — against opposition from the Soviet bloc — to conduct an investigation of the tragic events in Hungary.

Return to Oppression

Within days a government, captive to Moscow, was installed under the protection of the Red Army. When it was apparent that the fight for freedom was lost, thousands of refugees fled across the Austrian border. Cardinal Mindzenty took asylum in the American legation. Many other church leaders were not so fortunate. They were arrested and some were executed along with others who had dared to lead the fight for freedom.

The old leaders of the churches, which had been deposed by the Confessing Church and supportive groups in other Christian bodies, were put back in office. Once again Christians were free only to attend "registered" churches. Pastors of unregistered congregations were liable to arrest and imprisonment.

Faith Is Alive and Well

The hard oppression continued for the next twelve years. Then in 1968 long-time Communist Party leader Janos Kadar began loosening the strings. He was forced to act by a faltering economy and by the strong, unbreakable spirit of the Hungarian people. He was also forced to admit that religious faith was likely to remain alive in Hungary much longer than communist planners had anticipated.

Hungary today is still tightly encased in the Soviet political orbit. But pragmatism reigns in government management of the economy and relations with the churches. Under the new Economic Mechanism, profits are permitted at various levels under state management. Many small businesses are allowed to operate. The result is one of the highest standards of living in any communist country.

Tensions between the Hungarian government and the churches have relaxed, particularly since Cardinal Mindzenty was allowed to leave the country. The churches are crowded and growing. Many Protestant churches operate bookstores or booktables on their premises. Forty thousand Bibles have been printed inside the country since 1975. And in 1977 Evangelist Billy Graham was officially invited by the Council of Free Churches to preach in Hungary—a first for Graham in a Soviet-bloc country. His interpreter was Dr. Alexander Haraszti, a physician who had fled with his family following the ill-fated 1956 revolution. Without advance newspaper publicity, a crowd of around fifteen thousand gathered on a hillside overlooking the Danube River to hear Graham's first sermon. Thousands raised their hands to signify their desire to commit their lives to Christ.

This does not mean that Hungary is free. Nor does it guarantee that there will be no more martyrs. The old laws are still on the books; the government is still communist; the eye of Moscow has not dimmed; and many Hungarian Christians still refuse to conform to government demands for registration of churches.

CZECHOSLOVAKIA — WHERE MARTYRS' BLOOD FLOWED

Prague. City of churches and old world enchantment. Capital of modern Czechoslovakia, of which a medieval princess reportedly said as she looked along the bend of the River Vltava, "I see a city whose glory shall reach the stars."

Here in Old Town Square a statue of Jan Hus, the martyred "Morning Star of the Reformation," still stands as an eloquent reminder and symbol of the blood of Czech martyrs who have died defending the faith that sets men free. Not far away is the spot where a statue of the hated Stalin was pulled down and destroyed by angry Czechs in 1968—a symbol of the modern Czech feeling toward Soviet communist masters.

Over six centuries separate Hus, whom the Communists have cleverly fictionalized as the leader of a peasant rebellion, and the brave Czech reformers of today. Many are still alive in communist prisons. The spiritual faith of Hus continues to burn brightly in their hearts.

Nazi Horrors

In 1918 the Czechs of Bohemia and Moravia merged with neighboring Slovakia, newly freed from Hungary, to form the modern state of Czechoslovakia. The Czechs and Slovaks experienced only twenty years of freedom. In 1938 the Western European powers met at Munich and gave Hitler's Germany the green light to move on the small nation.

During World War II the people were at the mercy of the Nazis. The nation was broken in two, with the Slovak State ruled by a puppet government led by a Roman Catholic priest who followed the wishes of his Nazi overlords. Before the war was done, over two hundred fifty thousand dissenting Czechs and Slovaks were dead.

The Teheran Death Warrant

In 1943, during the midst of the war, the Czech government-in-exile under Eduard Benes, signed a twenty-year treaty with the Soviet Union. Unknown to the Czechs, that same year Roosevelt, Churchill, and Stalin conferred at Teheran to coordinate plans for ending the war and to divide Europe into two spheres of influence.

Hopes were high for Czech democracy as the war neared an end. Fearful of Soviet intention, Benes became exultant when, in April, 1945, the American army crossed the Czech border from the west and an agreement was signed to govern relations between the Allied commander and Czechoslovakian authorities. "Thank God! Thank God!" he exclaimed to his secretary. Then he rushed to tell his wife, "Patton is across the border!"

But to the deep disappointment of Benes and other Czechoslovakian patriots, Patton's army was halted on higher orders so the agreement previously made with the Soviets could be kept. The world did not know it then, but the Teheran Conference had sealed Czechoslovakia's doom.

Another chance came in May when Czech patriots seized the German-controlled radio station in Prague and appealed for help. The Americans were only sixty miles away;

the Soviets one hundred twenty. Again the Americans paid homage to Teheran and held back. Four days later the Red Army "liberated" Prague.

Dreams of Freedom Fade

After six years of suffering, the Czechs and Slovaks saw their dream of freedom fade once again. Cunningly, skillfully, Moscow orchestrated the capture of another satellite while the free world did nothing. The stage was now set for the most severe persecution of Christians since the Protestant Reformation—worse than the sufferings inflicted during the Nazi occupation.

Czech Communists were already embedded in the Benes government. Pretending to be democratic patriots, they were under the direct command of Moscow. In secret orders from the Soviets dated July, 1943, and issued through the Central Committee of the Communist Party of Czechoslovakia to "tested comrades," their instructions called for

the proletariat . . . (to) fight openly and in the underground, alternately and simultaneously, in the name of its own class struggle for the defeat of nazism, for an armed revolutionary uprising of the Czech laboring people, for a victorious revolution, for the destruction of the political power of the bourgeoise and social fascists, for the placing of this power in the hands of the workers and thereby preventing the materialization of a peace in the Czech lands dictated by the capitalists abroad.

"The supreme revolutionary goal," the orders concluded, "is the establishment of a Czech Soviet Republic and its attachment to the Union of the Soviet Socialist Republics."

Communist Treachery

Moscow's plan permitted President Benes to set up a new government on a "constitutional basis" and to pledge that "constitutional liberties" would be "fully guaranteed; particularly freedom of the individual, of assembly, association, expression of opinion by word, press and letter, the privacy of home and mail, freedom of learning and conscience and religion."

It was all hollow mockery. Several members of President Benes' government–in–exile were arrested when they arrived in Prague from London. Benes himself was allowed to assume the office of president while under constant surveillance. His communications with other loyal Czech leaders was severed. A "national" radio broadcast by the president was heard only in the immediate vicinity of the station.

The Communists also took over the trade unions and influential departments of government. Democratic newspapers were crippled by the refusal of union members to deliver paper. The Reds sabotaged the 1946 elections by pushing through a clever law that allowed a citizen's name to be stricken from electoral lists by the mere accusation of their having collaborated with the Nazis. Around three hundred thousand names were so removed, with notices given only three days before the election. After the voting, most were restored upon appeal.

Boosted by this subterfuge, the Communists garnered thirty-eight per cent of the vote. Many Czechs, especially in rural areas, voted communist because of fear of the Red Army. Rapacious Red soldiers, whom Stalin called "no angels," had raped and pillaged at will in the countryside. Only Czechs showing evidence of Communist Party membership or support were shown mercy. Still, the Communists kept up a mask of nationalism and even piety. At Christmas, 1946, they hypocritically attended church.

Foreign Minister Masaryk's Suicide

The patriots awoke too late. In 1947 Foreign Minister Jan Masaryk left for negotiations on a new treaty with Moscow. While there he was forced to break Czechoslovakia's remaining links with the West. Upon returning to Prague, he told a friend, "I left for Moscow as Minister of Foreign Affairs of a sovereign state. I am returning as Stalin's stooge."

The following February the Communists forced the resignation of fourteen noncommunist government leaders and in effect took over all major government functions. A month later it was officially announced that Foreign Minister Masaryk had committed suicide by jumping from a high window. Masaryk's friends found this hard to believe, as did free world leaders. The event was cloaked in mystery suggesting communist duplicity. The likeliest suspect for his murder, Major Augustin Schramm, was himself killed. Others who were connected with Masaryk also died or disappeared under unexplained circumstances.

Tragedy followed upon tragedy. President Benes had

once said, "I believe that peaceful cooperation [between communism and democracy] is possible." Now he told a trusted aide, "I know them, these people in Moscow. You overestimate their intelligence and their farsightedness. I overestimated them too. . . . At bottom they are only fanatics. Their whole policy is a provocation to war. . . ." Benes then refused to sign a new constitution modeled after the Soviet document and resigned because of "illness." Within three months he was dead.

In the next election the voters had no choice. There was only a single list of candidates. All were sponsored or approved by the Communist Party.

Lying to the Churches

The rubber-stamped government promised Czech churches that the state would not damage the good relationship between church and state. The Catholic archbishop of Prague, Josef Beran, thanked them for this promise, then pointed out the damage that had already been done. Church real estate had been confiscated and religious instruction abolished in the schools. Most Catholic publications had been shut down and religious books were subject to censorship. Priests and nuns had been removed from nonchurch positions.

In June, functionaries drafted harsher laws against Czech churches. The Catholic Church was the most visible target. State commissars were appointed in every Catholic diocese to take over church organizations. A small schismatic Catholic faction, The Peace Movement of Catholic Clergy, led by three turncoat priests, was set up to solicit Catholic backing for the government.

Catholic Defiance

The Catholic hierarchy suspended the traitorous trio from their church offices and ordered all priests to keep out of politics. A pastoral letter protesting the new government regulations was sent to all churches.

Archbishop Beran gave one of his last public addresses at the monastery of Strahov. "I do not know how many more times I shall be able to talk to you in the future. . . . Whatever may happen, do not believe that I have capitulated. I come before you and swear that I shall never sign an agreement of my own free will which violates the laws of the Church." Police moved in to "protect" him against the wrath of opponents. A communist official assumed the responsibilities of his office. Though under house arrest, he still managed to smuggle out a letter to his flock that said in part, "He who refuses to betray God cannot be a traitor to his country and to his people." The brave archbishop never regained his position as the Catholic primate of Czechoslovakia. When the Vatican elevated him to cardinal, the government permitted him to go to Rome for the ceremony, then refused to let him back in the country. He died in Rome still adamant against communist policies in his native land.

In Czechoslovakia the government demanded that all Catholic clergy sign a loyalty oath to the nation. The bishops refused to take the oath, but advised their priests to do so and add the qualification: "If it is not in contradiction to the laws of God and of the Church, and to human rights." The government further sought to control the Catholic clergy by making the state their employer. The bishops instructed the priests to accept salaries only with the proviso: "I declare that I am ready to accept the salary because it is the law of the State. But with this acceptance of the salary I do not make any promises which are against my priestly conscience or against the laws of the Church. I declare that the spiritual affairs of the Church and the complete freedom of my priestly activities are more important than the material security of my personal life."

The communist answer was to replace most of the intransigent bishops with puppets, close most Catholic seminaries, drive monks and nuns from monasteries and convents, and imprison many Catholic clergymen. The "action" priests were kept as a front to persuade the outside world that Catholics were not being persecuted in Czechoslovakia.

A Bishop Becomes a Plow Animal

In the smaller (585,000 members) Eastern Catholic (Uniate) Rite Church, a communist-instigated "rump" faction declared that their church would affiliate with the Russian Orthodox Church under leadership from Moscow. For opposing this assimilation, the legitimate leader Bishop Gojdic, and nearly one hundred priests were imprisoned. Bishop Gojdic and some of his fellow prisoners were forced to serve as plow animals in the prison fields. Gojdic died in prison in 1960.

The Communists followed the same ploy with the next three largest church bodies respectively—the Czechoslovakia National Hussite Church, the Slovak Lutheran Church, and the Evangelical Church of Czech Brethren. Strict controls were clamped on church activities. "Cooperative" clergy were given special appointments and encouraged to attend international church conferences. Some were elected to important committees of the World Council of Churches.

The small, independent free churches were subject to the same laws imposed on church bodies. Among the pastors imprisoned was Henry Prochazka, a Baptist. Sharp protests against his incarceration and sufferings moved the officers of the World Council of Churches to request his release. Broken in health, he was freed to die at home.

Churchmen Try to Tame the Communist "Bear"

Most of the "cooperative" church leaders could not be called communist. Some made concessions with the rationale that they could better serve their people in limited ways than not at all. Some genuinely, though naively, hoped that communism could be transformed into "Christian" socialism.

The leader of the Czech conciliators was Josef Hromadka, a clergyman–theologian of the Evangelical Church of Czech Brethren. In 1918 he was influenced by American socialists in the world-wide Student Volunteer Movement to believe that socialism was the best political expression of the gospel. While in exile during World War II, he taught Christian Ethics at Princeton Theological Seminary. In 1948 he was one of the founders of the World Council of Churches at Amsterdam. In his home country he welcomed the communist rise to power. He assured alarmed friends that atheists could be converted.

Hromadka did not convert any atheists, but he did persuade some government officials to slightly ease pressures on churches during the terrible 1950's. He was more successful at promoting Christian–Marxist dialogue, an effort which excited some liberal theologians in the West.

The hopes of Hromadka and other Christian socialists rose after the death of Stalin, fell with the Soviet invasion of Hungary, then rose again after the fall of Khrushchev.

The Dubcek Experiment

The Czech economy was now in the worst shape ever. The people were restive and desperate for change. Reformers in the Czech Communist Party decided to act boldly. Early in

1968 the old-guard Stalinists in the government were replaced by younger, more humane men. Alexander Dubcek,
the new Communist Party boss, introduced "socialism with
a human face." A new government cabinet promised dramatic political and economic reforms.

Censorship was abolished. For the first time since the
Soviet takeover Czechs were free to express themselves.
Communist newspapers published exposures of past cover-
ups by old-line Party leaders. The most sensational story
dealt with the mysterious death of young Jan Masaryk. A
leading scholar called for a full investigation to establish if
indeed he "was the first victim on the road to totalitarian
dictatorship." The official Czech Communist Party organ
Rude Pravo (Red Rights) editorialized a few days later,
"There is very serious cause to suspect murder [by] Beria's
Gorilla." At the time of Masaryk's death, Beria was head of
the Soviet secret police.

The churches were also given new freedoms. Ministers
could preach over the radio. Open-air gospel meetings were
permitted. The new opportunities for evangelism brought
thousands of new converts into the churches. The puppet
fronts which had controlled the churches were discredited.

Hromadka and his friends were ecstatic. This was what
they had been working for. Christians could influence Marxists, they said.

In 1961 the Czech Christian Socialists had founded an
All-Christian Peace Assembly in Prague. Held again in 1964,
the Assembly attracted many Western ecumenists. Many of
the speakers at this Assembly were critical of Moscow.

Under Dubcek's "new face" the Assembly met in 1968.
The left-leaning ecumenists were on a mountaintop of expectancy. Many anticipated that the spirit of the new Czechoslovakia would spread. Some implied that Christian socialism could bring about the reign of God on earth.

The "Bear" Could Not Be Tamed

They soon came crashing down to earth. It was Hungary all
over again. In August, Soviet, East German, Polish, Hungarian, and Bulgarian troops, led by Soviet tanks and supported
by massive Soviet air power, invaded and occupied Czechoslovakia. The liberal reforms were reined in. A half million
Czechs were purged from the Communist Party. As a warning to other satellite states, the Kremlin proclaimed the

"Brezhnev Doctrine," claiming the right of the Soviet Union to intervene forcibly in any "socialist" country to protect the "people" from seditious forces within or without.

Dubcek was replaced. "I am dishonored and defense-less," he said in a letter smuggled into Italy. When he complained about harassment by the secret police he was denounced as a traitor.

Dying of a Broken Heart

Josef Hromadka and the Christian Socialists were devastated. "I am not able to express the depth of our disappointment, our grief, our feelings of outrage, and even betrayal," he told friends from the Christian Peace Assembly. Nazi enemies "always declared quite openly their intentions toward us," he said, while the Soviets claimed to be "our friends and allies."

Another crushing blow followed when the Soviets forced the dismissal of Hromadka's close friend, Dr. J.N. Ondra, from the leadership of the Christian Peace Assembly, and made the Assembly subservient to Moscow's line. Hromadka, the man who dreamed of changing communism from the inside, died a few days later of a broken heart.

After World War II, the Soviets had closed the door slowly, but painfully, on Czech freedoms. This time, the masters from Moscow slammed the door suddenly and tightly. The old clergy fronts of procommunist clergy were restored to power. Key pastors and lay church leaders who had supported Dubcek's reforms were arrested and jailed for attempting to subvert communist rule. Twenty-five of the thirty-six Baptist ministers in Czechoslovakia were reported to be among these.

The majority of Czechs refused to bow. A sociologist interviewed fourteen hundred people and found over seventy per cent still professing Christian faith. Ninety per cent of three hundred eighty-six students polled said they were "religious."

"The Truth of God Will Prevail . . ."

Despite the arrests of many colleagues, the Association of Protestant Clergy demanded that Soviet troops withdraw. A spokesman was quoted in *Time:* "A great spiritual struggle looms ahead." But "the truth of God will prevail even if for a time it is defeated."

The persecution of Czech Christians has continued unabated since the Soviet clamp down. The open dialogues between Christian Socialists and Marxist atheists have been stopped. In January, 1973, Prague Radio charged that Marxist–Christian dialogue was an effort to weaken the Marxist position in favor of clericalism. Future discussions were forbidden. Communists who had dialogued with Christians in the past were labeled "renegades."

In 1971 leaders of the Evangelical Church of Czech Brethren who asked for amnesties for Christians in prison for their beliefs, were arrested. In 1973 three more pastors from this denomination were tried and sentenced for "antistate agitation." Others have been defrocked by state officials.

In contrast to pre-takeover statements that communism and religion could coexist, the official Czech Party journal declared in April, 1972, that there "could be no room for religion in a socialist state." Religion "would be contrary to the ideological principles of Marxism-Leninism." Accordingly, in 1973 the communist rulers instituted a system of "socialist rites" intended to replace church ceremonies at baptisms, marriages and funerals.

News from Czechoslovakia is now tightly censored. Michael Boudreaux, one of the world's foremost authorities on religion in communist lands, calls the situation "terrible." Many Czech Christians, imprisoned for their beliefs, have undoubtedly died in prison or have had their health impaired for future service. To die in prison or as a result of sufferings from incarceration is not a dramatic martyrdom. But it is just as real as the death of Jan Hus whose spirit remains alive in oppressed Czechoslovakia today.

CATHOLIC POLAND—NATION OF DEATH

More people have died as martyrs to freedom and faith in Poland than in any other European country, excepting the Soviet Union. Over six million Poles died under the Nazi occupation during World War II. Many priests and pastors were among them. After the communist takeover, thousands more were imprisoned or killed by communist police and officials. Yet today no Eastern European nation is more stubbornly resistant to foreign tyranny than the beleaguered Poles. The Marxist rulers have been thwarted again and again in attempts to completely communize Poland. For example, seventy-five per cent of the land remains in private hands. And the Catholic faith is so strong that by official government policy a Pole can belong to both the Communist Party and the

Catholic Church, something which is not tolerated in any other state linked militarily to the Soviet Union.

Next to Italy, Poland is the most Catholic country in Europe. Over thirty-four million Poles, ninety-five per cent of the population, are Catholic. The next largest religious body, the autonomous Polish Orthodox Church, has 460,000 adherents. Eastern-rite Uniate Catholics number 200,000; Lutherans report 95,000; and the Polish National Catholic (Old Catholic) Church claims 25,000. There are smaller numbers of Methodists, Baptists, Calvinists, and other Protestant communions. Jews are reduced to a minority of around five thousand. In 1939 there were 3.4 million. Of these, only ninety thousand survived the genocidal slaughter by the Nazis and most of them emigrated to Israel.

A Nation Was Baptized

Poland's Catholic legacy dates from 966 when the state's first ruler Mieszko I professed faith. Following his command, the entire population of the new nation was baptized. In the centuries following, Poland continued as one of the most tightly knit Catholic countries in the world. Today, the most common greeting in the Polish countryside is still, "Blessed be Jesus Christ." And Cardinal Stefan Wyszynski, the Catholic primate of Poland, the most powerful man in the country, is the only churchman in Eastern Europe who can make the national Communist Party boss blink.

From 1772 to the end of World War II Poland was divided under Prussian, Russian, and Austrian control. A Polish republic was formed in 1918. Pianist Ignace Jan Paderewski served as the first prime minister.

The Tragedy Begins

The modern tragedy of Poland began on August 23, 1939, by the stroke of a pen when Hitler's Joachim von Ribbentrop and Stalin's Vyacheslav Molotov signed the Nazi-Soviet Pact, dividing Poland between the two totalitarian powers. Eight days later the Nazis staged a Polish "provocation" and invaded Poland from the west. The Russians moved in from the east the same month.

The Communist attackers executed fifteen thousand Polish army officers and deported another 1.7 million Poles. Many of the latter were sent to Russia and trained in communist strategy, then sent back after the war to aid in the capture of Poland.

The Nazi Death Camps

After the break between Stalin and Hitler, Nazi armies swept across Eastern Europe and deep into the USSR before being turned back. Because of its proximity to Russia, intense nationalism, and large Jewish population, Poland was turned into a vast death prison. Names of such death camps as Auschwitz and Treblinka are still sounds of terror to Polish survivors.

Catholic priests numbering 3,644 and an unknown number of Protestant ministers died in Polish concentration camps or were shot to death near their residences. Those in the death camps were forced into the gas chambers along with the laymen. In labor camps they were used like work animals. When no longer able to work, they were killed. At the Oswiecim Camp, which held thirty thousand prisoners, prison laborers were not expected to survive over six weeks. In this camp Jews and Catholic priests were given the hardest job. They were harnessed daily to huge rollers designed to smooth out walkways within the compound. Many fell in their tracks and were roughly pushed out of the path of the rollers to await the corpse collectors.

One hundred twenty priests were incarcerated in the Dzialdowo Camp. The oldest was eighty-three-year-old archbishop Antoni Julian Nowowiejski, the bishop of Plock. Because of his position, appeals were made to high authorities for his release; but he was never permitted to go free. He died there in May, 1941.

Dying for Another

Many clergymen died trying to protect fellow inmates. One of the most celebrated Catholic martyrs is Father Maximilian Kolbe. While in Auschwitz, he was an inspiration to hundreds of unfortunates. One day the names of some prisoners scheduled for execution were called out. One of these pleaded that he was married and had children. Hearing this, Father Kolbe stepped forward and asked if he could take the condemned man's place. "Since you're so stupid to ask, you may die," the commandant declared. The courageous priest was shoved into an underground cell and left to starve. During his last days, prisoners heard him praying and singing.

Communist Betrayal

During this time of awful suffering, a free Polish government-in-exile awaited the liberation. In 1943 the shadow government was jolted by a report that the Germans had discovered a mass grave of over ten thousand Polish army officers killed by the Soviets at the beginning of the war. The Russians denied the killings, but the evidence was so convincing that the Poles broke relations with Moscow.

After the tide of war turned against Germany, Soviet troops, motorized by American aid, swept back into Poland from the east. Under Soviet auspices a provisional Polish government of both Communists and non-Communists was set up at Lublin. The Red Army suddenly halted on the way to occupied Warsaw. The commander sent a message to the Polish underground in the capital, advising, "Rise up against your oppressors. Liberation is near." Thousands of Poles swarmed out of their hiding places to attack the Germans with makeshift weapons. The result was a massacre, followed by a brutal German reprisal. In an orgy of destructive rage, the angry Germans nearly leveled the capital and murdered thousands of helpless men, women and children in cold blood. All the while, the Red Army waited at a safe distance.

As the war ground to an end, Soviet strategy proceeded on course. The great Allied powers attending the Yalta Conference called for elections in liberated Poland. Under Allied pressure, the leaders of the Polish government–in–exile joined the Lublin group. Meanwhile, the Soviets had skillfully infiltrated the remnants of the Polish army. Polish officers, who had been taken to Russia at the beginning of the war for training, were put in key posts under the direct command of Soviet authorities. Poles accused of helping the Germans became the object of a massive witch hunt.

In the national elections, it was Czechoslovakia all over again, but on a larger scale. Shortly before the election, a half million voters and ninety–eight noncommunist candidates were accused of collaboration with the Nazis and temporarily disqualified. Additionally, there was massive fraud in the vote count. The official results naturally showed a majority for a left-leaning coalition.

The die was cast for the betrayal of Polish liberties. Members of the opposition minority were so intimidated that some fled the country. Those who remained were imprisoned or killed. A rule of Stalinist terror covered Poland. By 1949 even the blindest Communist apologist in the West could see that the chains of Stalinist Russia had replaced the bonds of Hitler. That year the Polish Communist Party boss, Wladyslaw Gomulka, was imprisoned for the "crime" of nationalism. The Soviet's Marshal Konstantin Rokossovsky took over as minister of defense and commander in chief of the Polish army. Sovietization became plainer every day. A new constitution made Poland a "people's democracy" after the Soviet model. Polish foreign policy was meshed with Moscow.

The Communists set out to destroy the influence of the Catholic church. Prominent laymen were put under secret police surveillance. The Catholic charity organization, Caritas, was dissolved to keep the church from helping its poor. Regular church attendance became grounds for dismissal on jobs. Communist policy in Poland, as in other satellites, was to destroy the loyal leadership of the churches and support "patriotic" clergy who would spout Moscow's line. In Poland the communist-approved "patriotic" Catholic clergy belonged to the Pax Association. Pax had permission to publish a daily paper, a privilege denied other Catholic organizations. Pax was noticeably more Stalinist than even the Communist Party and included many former fascists in its membership.

Cardinal Wyszynski's Challenge

The Catholic primate of Poland, Cardinal Wyszynski, was not cowed. Before World War II he had warned Polish politicians of problems which Communists would later exploit, notably high unemployment and huge agricultural combines which paid peasants slave wages. Wyszynski, however, did not see himself as a political leader. "I am no politician, no diplomatist, and no reformer," he said in a pastoral letter. He felt the first responsibility of the clergy was the spiritual care of his flock.

So, in 1950 he signed an agreement with the communist government promising to do nothing to hinder the "building of socialism" in exchange for the government promise of freedom of religion, freedom of the church press, and uninterrupted religious instruction in public schools and government institutions. He was criticized by anticommunist prelates abroad for this. The ink was hardly dry when the regime began breaking its promises in wholesale fashion. The cardinal reacted immediately. "We gave an irrefutable proof of the church's good will," he thundered, but "nothing has changed in the government's attitude. . . . (This) may be a normal method for Soviet justice, but it certainly shocks those whose ideas of justice are Polish."

Power and Perfidy

The communist response was to increase persecution. Eight bishops and up to two thousand priests were imprisoned. "Patriotic" priests were given back their parishes. The crowning blow came on September 29, 1953, when Cardinal Wyszynski was arrested. Promised his freedom if he would renounce his position as head of the Polish Catholics, he refused.

The pressure against Polish Catholics continued unabated. Perhaps the strangest case of communist opposition to religion came in a fishing village on the Baltic Sea. A Party member repented and confessed his sins on his deathbed. His parish priest gave him a Catholic funeral. When local officials learned about this, they retaliated against the decedent's family by confiscating all the black market goods he had been permitted to hoard as a privilege of Party membership.

The Communists had less trouble with other church bodies. The Orthodox Church had a traditional pledge to uphold "the just state." Bishops who protested that the Polish Communist state was not just were banished or imprisoned. Puppet clergy were found to replace them. Eastern-rite Uniate Catholics were denied any legal status. Adherents were forcibly uprooted from their villages and resettled where they would have less influence.

Polish Lutherans and Calvinists hardly put up a fight against government restrictions. They were heavily influenced by theologian Karl Barth, who had not yet been convinced that communism was out to destroy Christianity, and by soft-liners in the World Council of Churches. Methodists, Baptists, and other small, free church groups were too few and powerless to matter with the Communists. So long as they kept to themselves, the hirelings of Moscow paid them little attention. Only those who made a forthright stand for Christian principles at their place of employment or in community meetings were singled out for persecution.

The turning point came in 1956. In February Nikita Khrushchev exposed the crimes of Stalinism. In March the Soviet–installed dictator of Poland, Boleslaw Bierut, died during a visit to Moscow. The two events sent shock waves across the USSR's largest satellite. With dictator Bierut gone, there was no one to cap the well of exploding anti–Stalinist resentment sweeping Poland. Young Communists were disgusted with the corruption of their seniors. Factory workers were dismayed by declining wages and food shortages. The churches, particularly the Roman Catholic Church, had taken all the oppression they would tolerate.

The Confrontation

Spontaneous riots and rebellions broke out, first at Poznan then spreading to other cities. Communist bosses tried discussions, then negotiations, then threats—all in vain.

The Polish army was still under the command of Marshal Rokossovsky, a sovietized Pole. He asked the deposed Gomulka for advice. "Go ahead, if you want to start a massacre," Gomulka reportedly said. "But you'll get no support from others in the Party." Rokossovsky began mobilizing for battle. A Soviet division crossed the border from the east and joined six others already in Poland. Russian warships chugged close to the Baltic coast.

In the midst of a dangerous stand-off, Khrushchev and other Kremlin leaders flew to Poland without an invitation or advance announcement. Warsaw controllers kept their plane in a holding pattern for thirty minutes. By the time they landed, Khrushchev was in a rage. "You're traitors! Traitors!" he shouted. "We shed our blood for this country and now you want to sell us out to the Americans and the Zionists." Khrushchev finally agreed to sit down and talk with a hastily assembled delegation of Polish Communists. When one man spoke to him in Polish, Khrushchev bluntly demanded in Russian to know who he was. "I am Gomulka," he replied. "The one you put in prison for three years."

The Reds Pull Back

Khrushchev blustered on past midnight. When he stopped, Gomulka made the Polish demands. Fearing a nationwide insurrection that could bring all of Eastern Europe into rebellion, the Russians made concessions they had given no other satellite. The march of Soviet troops on Warsaw would stop. The USSR would not control internal Polish affairs. Soviet secret police would get out of Poland. Persecution of the churches would stop. Forced collective farming would cease.

Russian–Polish trade relations would be reappraised. The hated Marshal Rokossovsky and most of his Russian army advisers would leave. But Poland would remain in the Warsaw Pact and stand with the Soviets against the western alliance.

Gomulka again became Poland's top Communist. One of his first acts was to free the Catholic cardinal. Most restrictions on the churches were lifted. Communist Party members could attend church if they wished. Gomulka even publicly praised some pastors for emphasizing hard work and self-discipline.

In 1957 Gomulka told Poland's Communist Central Committee the facts of life: "Our party cannot, as part of its policy, apply administrative pressure to bear on believers without taking account of the fact that the former conflict with the church set millions of believers against the people's government and estranged them from socialism."

In 1970 riots over government-imposed increases of food prices shook the country. Polish police and troops put down the revolt, but Gomulka was forced to resign. Similar riots occurred in 1976. Edward Gierek, the new Party head, took a lesson from 1970 and cancelled most of the price increases. Also in 1976 some communist leaders proposed constitutional amendments that would have made it a crime to "use religion for political ends." Durable Cardinal Wyszynski saw the potential danger of communist flexibility in defining "political ends." He publicly denounced the proposal. It was never adopted.

The Communist-Catholic Stand-Off

So two great powers in Poland today, the Communist Party and the Catholic Church, abide by a truce. But the Polish Catholics and other Christian bodies are not deceived about the ultimate objectives of anti-Christian Marxism. Haunted by memories of both Nazism and Stalinism, they remain vigilant. Too many Poles—Catholics, Protestants and Jews—have died or gone to prison at the behest of tyrants.

Poland is the least enslaved of the Soviet satellites in Eastern Europe. There are forty Catholic and Protestant theological seminaries compared to only five in all of the Soviet Union. The small evangelical churches which preach experiential, new-birth salvation, are growing. There is an adequate supply of Bibles. Gospel broadcasts can be taped in state recording studios in Warsaw. Some churches have been granted land by the government on which to build. For a communist state, it is a strange turn of events.

EAST GERMANY—COMMUNISTS VERSUS LUTHERANS

Although Communist policy goals against religion are no different in East Germany than elsewhere in the Soviet bloc, the situation faced by Communists coming to power in East Germany was different than in Poland. East Germany was not a recognizable national entity at the end of World War II. Shortly after victory, the Soviets and other Allied heads agreed on a plan to govern Germany together, rebuilding it as a democracy while stamping out all vestiges of nazism. Consequently, the defeated country and its capital, Berlin, was divided into four zones of occupation—American, British, French and Soviet.

The Soviets never intended to cooperate in this plan. They immediately began installing German Communists in government. They blocked every Allied proposal for a unified Germany. They rejected United States aid for their zone. They tried to force the western nations out of West Berlin and starve the two million inhabitants of the western-controlled sections of the city into accepting communism. But the Allies launched a huge airlift and the blockade failed.

Facing Soviet refusals to release East Germany, the West authorized a German assembly to write a federal constitution. On May 30, 1949, the constitution was approved and the three western zones combined as the Federal Republic of (West) Germany. That same year the Russians announced that their zone would be the (East) German Democratic Republic.

East Germany's economy was directed from Moscow. Production lagged woefully behind West Germany. A large portion of manufactured goods and farm products were shipped to the Soviet Union under the guise of war reparations. As in other satellites, the result was rapidly rising inflation and food shortages.

In East Germany the Lutheran Church was the established religious body, claiming over half of the population. Many Lutheran pastors and lay leaders had shared Nazi prison cells with Communists. The German Communists could not discredit them with the brush of fascism. The Lutherans also had ecclesiastical ties with West German Lutherans and with the World Council of Churches. The Communists had to be careful not to tarnish their peace-loving image.

The Red rulers arrested thousands of pastors and laymen, but overlooked the top echelon of church leaders. They promoted a front of "fellow travelers" — churchmen who attempted to demonstrate that socialism was the fulfillment of Christian ideals. Such preachers and writers were ignored by other clergy and laymen, and mocked by young Christians.

Communism and Christian Youth

Members of the Lutheran Christian Youth Groups, who wore a small silver cross in their buttonholes, were taunted and abused by Communist youth. In June, 1952, the Christians gathered in Lubbenau for a regional youth congress and were told they could only meet in a church. No church in the vicinity could possibly hold them all. The harassment also included orders forbidding local families to provide sleeping quarters for more than two guests. The meat which the organizers had brought for meals was even confiscated. The government declared the Youth Groups illegal. When school opened, Christian students were singled out for bullying. Many were told by teachers, in front of a Party or police official, that they must either withdraw from the Youth Groups or be expelled. Some gave in, but most stood firm. Two thousand were expelled in a few weeks.

A new wave of arrests sent fifty church workers to prison. Communist rowdies disrupted church services. Church property was seized on a variety of pretexts. More Christian youth were expelled from school.

A Red Retreat?

The march of "democratic socialism" continued on other fronts. Surviving remnants of noncommunist political parties were purged. Food ration cards were withdrawn from all house owners, private businessmen, and independent tradesmen. Prices of unrationed food were raised sharply. Resentment boiled. A steady stream of refugees had been flowing into West Berlin since the Communist takeover. Now the stream became a torrent.

When Stalin died on March 5, 1953, East Germany seethed in crisis. In a dramatic about-face, the government capitulated to the Lutheran Church. The state would guarantee the Church's independence. Christian youth expelled from school would be readmitted. The cases of Christian prisoners would be reviewed. Property would be returned. The next day the Party's Politburo announced a halt to socialism. Hand-wringing and finger-pointing became prevalent among the comrades. The people of East Germany began to hope again.

Then the government tried to raise work production quotas and lower wages. Thousands of workers walked off their jobs in protest. Said one spokesman, "We want to live like humans — that's all we ask." The laborers of the "workers' paradise" marched and sang. They threatened a general strike, called for the government to resign, and demanded free elections. The answer was Soviet tanks and troops. When western nations refused to help, it was obvious that the uprising was over.

Living and working conditions improved to a degree; but the people remained discontented. By 1961 almost 3.5 million had fled to the West. The labor force was down sharply. That year the Communists built their concrete and barbed wire "Wall of Shame" between East and West Berlin, making escape almost impossible. Nevertheless, desperate East Germans kept trying. A few reached freedom, but most were arrested or shot down in cold blood by Communist border guards.

The Price of a Truce

East Germany today is not Czechoslovakia. The constitution says, "Every citizen . . . has the right to profess a religious creed and to carry out religious activities." The hitch is that religious worship and work must be "in conformity with the constitution and legal regulations of the German Democratic Republic."

The state and the established Lutheran Church have reached a stand-off. The church has separated from the Lutheran Church of West Germany. But East German Lutherans are allowed to carry on business as usual with fewer restrictions than in most other Soviet satellites. The Lutheran Church continues to operate twenty–two hundred social service institutions, including fifty–four hospitals. No other church in Eastern Europe is allowed such wide ministry outside church walls. Through a church tax system, the government funnels money for support of Lutheran clergy. Theological students may choose between government-supported seminaries, where Marxism is a required course, and private schools. The Lutherans also have a radio broadcast every Sunday. But the radio preachers and scripts must be approved by communist officials. One sermon on sin was rejected on the grounds that it undermined the optimism on the perfectability of man in a socialist society. Thirty–one Lutheran church magazines are also censored.

Roman Catholics, numbering 1.3 million, are the second largest religious body. Allowed to run their own affairs in return for political silence, the East German hierarchy seldom ever praises or complains about a state policy. On the other hand, no priest has joined the Berlin Conference of European Catholics, the "front" which supports the communist line.

Neither Lutherans nor Catholics are growing. Lutheran baptisms have fallen ninety percent in the last twenty years. Many large, city church sanctuaries are only sparsely attended. Why the decline? Observers cite dead formality in the churches and secularism among the people, not communism. If the drop continues, the Lutheran Church will no longer be a bulwark against the communist state by the end of the twentieth century.

"Free" Churches Are Growing

The one bright spot is the Federation of Evangelical Free Church Communities. Mainly Baptist and Methodist, these small evangelical churches, comprising about one per cent of the population are increasing. Conservative in theology and aggressive in evangelism, they are not dependent on state subsidies.

Martyrs? Not in the immediate future, unless there is a drastic change in the world balance of power or a return to Stalinism in the Soviet empire. Communist intention is to let the East German churches die by attrition while a new generation of Marxists are being trained in the universities. To help make this possible, university admissions officers are denying the applications of almost all Christian students.

But this has been the policy in the Soviet Union for over a half century. The Soviets have not succeeded in stamping out authentic faith. Nor will their East German allies accomplish this in the land of Luther, Bach, and Handel.

YUGOSLAVIA — A COMMUNIST MAVERICK

It is a mistake to think that because Yugoslavia is a neutral "socialist" country, friendly to the West, that Christians have not been persecuted there. It is also a mistake to blame all the persecution on Communists, for more professing Christians were killed before the communist takeover than afterwards. And it is wrong to assume that "Christian" blood was shed solely because of religious faith.

A mountainous, Wyoming–sized country, Yugoslavia runs a thousand miles along the Adriatic Sea and is bordered by seven other nations. It was created in 1918 by unification of ancient Serbia, Croatia, and other smaller kingdoms. The "marriage" of Serbia and Croatia was ill-conceived by the planners of the new Europe, for their peoples had feuded for centuries. That Serbians were members of the Serbian Orthodox Church and Croatians were Roman Catholics, seemed to accentuate the bitterness between the two peoples.

The Serbs were Christianized in the ninth century and by the fourteenth century had become the most powerful nation in the Balkan peninsula. Then their empire broke up and for some five hundred years the Serbs were brutally oppressed by Muslim Turks. The Serbian nobility was annihilated and their lands given to Turkish military commandants. The Christian peasants were treated little better than slaves.

After the Turks left in 1878 the Serbs were buffeted by regional wars and did not regain independence until 1913. The following year Serbian nationalists assassinated the heir to the Austrian throne, setting off World War I.

Croatia also became Christianized in the ninth century. From 1091 to 1918 the Croatians were ruled successively by Hungary, Turkey, France, and again by Hungary. They resented being forced into a union with the Serbs from whom the first king of Yugoslavia came. In 1929 a Croatian terrorist organization, the Ustashi (rebels), was formed to fight for separation. Croatian independence finally came in 1941, shortly before the German invasion.

The Serbian Massacre

At this time more than two million Serbs were living in Croatian territory. Ante Pavelic, the leader of the ruling Ustashi, proclaimed his loyalty to the Catholic Church and declared a crusade against the Orthodox Serbs. One of his officials declared that the new capital, Banja Luka, would have to be "thoroughly cleansed of Serbian dirt."

In many Serbian communities every person was killed. The massacres were brutal beyond description. Some Ustashi used hammers to break the skulls of their victims. They cut off arms or legs of many while still alive. They pulled out the eyes of some and threw the defenseless victims into caves. In more merciful executions, the Ustashi placed Serbs in single file, one behind the other, and killed as many as possible with one bullet. One of the leaders of the Ustashi delivered forty pounds of human eyes to the Croatian fascist dictator Pavelic. In the ancient city of Dubrovnik (Ragusa), Ustashi leaders were observed strolling on the streets, wearing large belts adorned with Serbian ears and noses. Thousands of Serbian corpses were seen floating in the Sava River, with some tagged "Visa for Serbia." In western Croatia five to six hundred Serbian men, women, and children were packed into a Serbian Orthodox Church. Maddened Ustashi slaughtered every last one with guns, daggers, and sledge hammers while local officials stood in the choir loft giving orders. When they finished, the church was set on fire.

Before the genocidal purge began, one Croatian resolved, "We shall convert one-third and melt them into Croats, expel one-third, and kill one-third." His prediction came close to being fulfilled. In less than a year 350,000 Serbs were killed; 300,000 deported; and some 250,000 converted to Catholicism in mass baptisms by Ustashi Catholic priests.

Among the Serb martyrs were three Orthodox bishops and 220 priests. The Serbian Orthodox Metropolitan in Zagreb, Monsignor Dositey, had been tortured by the Bulgarians in World War I. The Ustashi Croatians beat the Monsignor almost to death, then expelled him to Belgrade where he died from the injuries. Monsignor Platon of Banja Luka was thrown into a pond and prodded to death. Monsignor Sava was murdered by garroting.

In Croatia, all Serbian Orthodox churches were destroyed or closed. Works of art were slashed and burned. Churches were turned into stables, barns, or warehouses.

As the massacre was ending, German troops invaded both Croatia and Serbia. Within two weeks all of Yugoslavia was in Axis hands. Puppet governments were quickly installed in both Croatia and Serbia. The German invasion and the spread of war elsewhere prevented the massacre from receiving world attention.

Resistance to Nazism

Resistance movements quickly formed. The pro-Soviet Croat Partisans were led by Josip Broz Tito, a Communist. The Serb Chetniks fought under the leadership of Colonel Draza Mihailovic.

The occupation regimes patterned their oppression after the Nazi tyranny and brutality already imposed on Poland. Jews were exterminated and thousands of Catholic and Orthodox civilians dragged off to concentration camps. Serbs and Croats suspected to be anti-German were hung in public squares. A proclamation called for the killing of one hundred Serbian civilians for every German life lost in the occupation.

After twenty-six German soldiers were ambushed near the city of Kragujevac, German troops rounded up twenty-six hundred Serbs from every walk of life—priests, doctors, lawyers, workmen, and even high school boys. They were ruthlessly mowed down with machine guns. Some of the boys were holding their schoolbooks when they fell. In another city six thousand Serbs were slaughtered in similar fashion.

For awhile Hungarian troops occupied part of Serbia. Some of the Hungarians rivaled the Nazis. They swept through some villages, capturing teenage girls for transport to military brothels. When fathers in two towns reacted violently, the Hungarians executed the entire Serbian population in both communities. Even the Bulgarians, who sided with Germany, massacred the population of whole villages which were suspected of concealing resisters.

At the start of World War II there were only ten thousand Communists in the federated republics known as Yugoslavia. They rallied behind Tito, the Soviet-approved leader of the Croatian resistance movement. During most of the war the western Allies helped both the Croat and Serb resisters. Thanks to clever Soviet propaganda and diplomacy, the Croats, under Tito, were favored by western leaders near the end of the war.

How Stalin Deceived Churchill

Stalin, in effect, captured Yugoslavia at the Teheran Conference. He and other Communists convinced western leaders that Tito's Croatian Partisans best represented the people of Yugoslavia. The prime minister of the Yugoslav government-in-exile, Dr. Bozhidar Purich, tried to convince Churchill that a communist minority dominated the Partisan movement. Churchill conceded that Tito was a Communist but felt nationalistic elements would keep him from assuming power. The British prime minister said he had documents proving that Chetnik leaders had collaborated with the Nazis. Churchill did not know that this "proof" had been planted by communist agents.

After the war ended, the communist takeover of Yugoslavia continued on course. Tito and his comrades, at Soviet direction, took over a coalition government. Secret police terrorized the people. Propagandists flooded the country with communist literature. Over three hundred thousand Yugoslavs were removed from the election rolls on false charges of helping the Nazis. In the 1945 "free elections" Tito got ninety per cent of the vote. A purge of "undesirable" (anti-communist) elements began. *Time* magazine (September 16, 1946) estimated that two hundred thousand were liquidated. Among those tried and executed as a "war criminal" was the brave Serbian freedom fighter, Colonel Mihailovic.

A Falling Out Among Comrades

To Moscow's disappointment, Tito refused to follow certain Soviet directives. The Communist Information Bureau (Cominform), dominated by Moscow, expelled the rebellious Yugoslav comrades for "revisionism." Stalin expected the people to quickly overthrow Tito and accept a more subservient leader. But Tito outfoxed Stalin and remained in power. The 1948 break forced Tito to declare neutrality and look to the West for protection and aid.

Tito and his comrades were no less communist. However, they were divided over policy towards the churches. The liberals argued that religion was a private matter and should not be opposed except when it stepped out of its domain. If religious practice were limited to religious affairs and rites, eventually the churches would die, they reasoned. Other Communists demanded a harder line and a strict interpretation of religion's role. The two sides agreed to a constitution that called for religious freedom while forbidding the "abuse of religion for political purposes."

Pastors Are Beaten by Mobs

This compromise constitution did not prevent persecution. Harassment of churches and clergy was most intense from

1945 to 1953. Many priests (Catholic and Orthodox) and pastors among the small, free church minority were beaten by mobs. Crude pressures were put on Christians not to teach their children their beliefs. Young men found it difficult to attend seminaries. Some clergymen were arrested and put on trial, but always on political charges such as collaborating with the Nazis, inciting intolerance, and helping "enemies of the people."

The most famous defendent was Catholic archbishop Stepinac of Zagreb. Because he was anti-Communist, he was accused of helping the Nazis and participating in the forced conversion and slaughter of Orthodox Serbs. Actually Bishop Stepinac had condemned the 1941 massacre of Serbians by Croatian Catholics. He had also opposed the Nazis. But he was convicted and sentenced to sixteen years' imprisonment.

In 1953 Tito ordered a stop to the worst of the persecution. In a speech he said that physical attacks on clergy and believers were illegal and a shame to citizens of a socialist nation. That same year a new law was passed giving churches legal recourse for defending their rights in court. There have been no great persecutions in Yugoslavia since. Churches and seminaries remain open. Bibles can be printed in the country.

Now in his mid-eighties, Tito remains firmly in power. His leanings toward the West have not kept him from clamping down on dissidents. He and other Yugoslav Red leaders are worried about a growing nationalist spirit among Croats, Serbs, and other minorities. In 1972 Serbian Orthodox Bishop Vasilije of Zenica was sentenced to thirty days in prison for "hostile propaganda." Also in 1972 a Dominican Catholic priest, Father Franjo Kovacevic, was arrested for soliciting money from citizens of his town for restoration of the local church. And a nun was sentenced to three months for "spreading lies." She had prophesized the fall of the Yugoslav communist government.

Opportunity for Evangelism

Today, the greatest enemy of Christianity in Yugoslavia is not communism, but indifference. Only ten per cent of the Roman Catholic population is said to attend church, and in some areas only one per cent of the Serbian Orthodox.

Among Protestants, however, the story is different. Pentecostals, with around ten thousand members, are growing;

and Baptists, with thirty-five hundred members, are thriving. And in 1976 a new Protestant seminary was opened with financial aid from World Vision and the Billy Graham Evangelistic Association.

Yugoslav's one hundred fifty thousand Protestants enjoy the most freedom in Eastern Europe. They can preach the gospel freely, so long as criticism of the government is avoided. Billy Graham and other Westerners are allowed to visit and preach. Religious radio programs are taped by pastors for broadcast over Trans World Radio.

But the Yugoslav government remains communist and devoted to atheism; and Tito's rule cannot last much longer. The future is uncertain.

ALBANIA — PUBLIC WORSHIP IS A CRIME

The human spirit does not soar in Albania, land of the "Sons of the Eagle (Shqiptar)." The Maryland-sized mountain country, bordered by Greece, Yugoslavia, and the Adriatic Sea, is the most repressive police state in Eastern Europe. It is also the poorest. In this predominantly Muslim nation, Stalinism still reigns. Government leaders denounce the Soviet Union for tolerance of religion. No church or mosque is known to be open in Albania. No public expression of religion is allowed. Since World War II, any Albanian clergymen who have not escaped have been martyred, imprisoned, exiled to collective farms, or converted to communism.

Executed for Baptizing a Child

The last known martyr was Father Shtjefen who was first sentenced to death in 1945 on a charge of spying for the Vatican. His sentence was subsequently commuted to life imprisonment, and eighteen years later he was released. He served as a parish pastor for a short time; then when the Marxist government ruled all religious practices illegal, he took a clerk's job in a cooperative. For defending the destruction of his church with his fists, he was returned to prison where he carried on his ministry secretly. In 1973 a woman prisoner begged him to baptize her child. The baptism was discovered. Charged with "subversive activities designed to overthrow the State," he was executed by a military firing squad.

After his death the official Vatican newspaper *L'Osservatore Romano* published an article decrying the sad fate of Roman Catholic Christianity in Albania:

Places of worship either no longer exist or have been transformed into dance halls, gymnasia or offices of various kinds. . . . The church of the Stigmatine Sisters has become a lecture hall, the one of the Institute of the Sisters is used as the headquarters of the political police. The national sanctuary of Our Lady of Scutari, "Protectress of Albania," has been pulled down. On its ruins there now rises a column surmounted by the red star.

Albania in History

Albania, like other East European captive nations, has a storied past and the legacy of a valiant struggle for freedom.

As ancient Illyria, it was engulfed by the Roman Empire in 167 B.C. Christianity came early to the mountain province, but the mountainous tribes were never really conquered for Christ. Albania was successively a part of the Byzantine, Serbian, and Turkish Ottoman empires. Under Turkish rule seventy per cent of the population (now about 2.6 million) became Muslims through coercion or economic bribery. Many of these took only a Muslim public name, while retaining their Christian name for private use.

Another Red Coup

Albania was independent for only twenty–seven years, from 1912 to 1939, when it was invaded by Italy. When the small country was liberated, Albanian Communists, under orders from Moscow, followed the same game plan as Communists elsewhere in Eastern Europe. Pretending to be national patriots, they gained control of a coalition of political parties, the National Liberation Movement. They branded anti-Communists as fascist collaborationists, deceived the West into thinking there would be free elections, then evoked a terror campaign. The coalition received over ninety per cent of the vote. By the time the West realized what had happened, the Communists, under Enver Hoxha, had turned Albania into a police state subservient to Stalin. United States Secretary of State John Foster Dulles could only say, "The tragic plight of the Albanian people is a matter of deep concern."

Before the Red takeover, Protestant evangelical groups had made practically no headway in Albania. The last religious census (1945) showed approximately seventy per cent Muslim, twenty per cent Orthodox and ten per cent Roman Catholic.

Stalin's Albanian devotees pursued a familiar strategy toward religious groups. They enacted a law requiring religious communities to develop among their members the feeling of loyalty toward "the people's power" and the People's Republic of Albania. This same law gave the government veto power over the election of heads of religious communities. The new state rulers forbade religious instruction to young people. They steered the Albanian Orthodox Church into the arms of Russian Orthodoxy. They ordered all other religious groups to break ties with foreign links and superiors. This separated the Catholic Church from the Vatican. All pastoral letters and sermons were subjected to censorship and all religious publications stopped. Finally, in 1966, the Communists confiscated and closed all churches and mosques and forbade religious expression.

The World's First "Atheist Nation"

After the Sino–Soviet split, communist Albania sided with China on grounds that the Soviets had become soft on Marxism. The closing of the country's 2,169 churches and mosques was part of a "cultural revolution," China style, in which bands of young hoodlums were turned loose to terrorize the population. The Albanian Communists claimed that their youth had "created the first atheist nation in the world."

Relations with the Soviets have remained broken. In 1974, First Secretary Hoxha declared, "We will never reconcile with them, will never make friends with them, we will always be their enemies." After Mao Tse-tung's death, China began to be viewed with suspicion. In 1977 Albania called on China to remove its hundreds of technical experts.

The Red Record of Martyrdom

From 1945 on, clergymen and lay leaders were arrested and tried on various charges. In May, 1945, Monsignor Nigris, the Catholic nuncio in Albania, was charged with fomenting anticommunist feelings and was deported to Italy. In 1946 Catholic archbishop Nikolla Vincene Prenushi of Durres was sentenced to twenty years in prison. He died soon afterwards under mysterious circumstances. Most other Catholic bishops have been "liquidated." In the spring of 1971, only fourteen Catholic priests, among 203 priests listed in 1939, were known to be alive. Twelve of the fourteen were in concentration camps and two in hiding. One of the latter two is believed to have been arrested and charged with "theft of corn cobs" in 1973.

The worst year was the 1966 cultural revolution. The first targets were churches and monasteries. At Shkoder the Catholic Franciscan monastery was set afire. Four monks were killed. The rest were forced to stand in their underwear and watch the building burn. Then they were driven through screaming mobs of Albanian "Red Guards" and taken to prison. At the city of Fier, Red Guards stormed the Catholic church. They broke and trampled upon priceless treasures and crosses, chopped the pews to pieces, then beat and abused the resident priests.

The Orthodox clergy were generally less resistant. The stubborn ones among them were also imprisoned and some executed.

Albania today is one of the most isolated communist bastions in the world. Outsiders do not really know the state of Christianity there. The only encouraging signs come from articles in communist publications which concede that the regime is still struggling to stamp out religious belief.

ROMANIA – DEATH, BUT NOT DESPAIR

Room Four in Romania's Tirgul-Ocna Prison was known as the "death room." When Abbot Iscu, the saintly head of a Lutheran monastery, was put there, no one had yet left alive. With him was a motley group of dying men. Vasilescu had been the overseer of a slave gang working on the ill-conceived Danube–Adriatic canal project. Filipescu, an old socialist, kept up hope that the Americans would come and set the prisoners free. Bucur, a police sergeant, kept raging that the doctors had put him in the room to satisfy their personal hatred. There was also General Tobescu, a former chief of police; Moise, a Jew; two communist guerrilla refugees from Greece; Valeriu Gafencu, a member of the Iron Guard who had been in prison ten years; a farmer named Aristar whose nightly prayer was, "God smite the Communists"; Badras, who had given refuge to a Romanian nationalist fleeing from the secret police; and Richard Wurmbrand, a Lutheran pastor. Some of the prisoners were near death from beatings. Some suffered from tuberculosis and other illnesses brought on by years of maltreatment and torture.

Memories of Horror

In his weakened condition Abbot Iscu recalled for his fellow prisoners the terrible slave camps at the canal project where thousands had died from communist brutality. The canal had been forced on Romania by the Soviets who wanted a more efficient means of transportation to drain the satellite of its farm produce. Engineers who warned that the Danube would not supply sufficient water for both the canal and its irrigation tributaries were shot as "economic saboteurs." Moscow's planners said it must be built.

The abbot had been in one of the penal colonies strung along the canal route. Each of the twelve thousand prisoners in his string of barracks had been forced to move eight cubic meters of earth a day by hand. They pushed wheelbarrows up steep grades while guards rained blows on them from behind. Disease was rampant. Many men froze to death. Often, prisoners hoping to be shot deliberately ran into the forbidden area around the camp.

Christians were put in a so-called "Priest's Brigade," the abbot recalled. "If one of us so much as made the sign of the cross, or closed his eyes to pray, he was beaten." There was never a day of rest, no Christmas, no Easter. The Lutheran clergyman admitted that under the pressure, some had turned informers. One was Andrescu, an Orthodox priest, who reported a young Catholic priest, Father Cristea, for closing his eyes in prayer. "The political officer called Cristea out and asked if he believed in God. Cristea replied, 'When I was ordained, I knew that thousands of priests had paid for their faith with their lives. I promised to serve God, even if I had to go to prison or die. Yes, lieutenant, I believe in God.' "

"What happened to Father Cristea?" one of the men in Room Four asked softly.

"He was locked for a week in the place where you stand and never sleep; then beaten. When he again refused to deny his faith, he was taken away. We never saw him again."

Forgiveness for the Dying

It happened that Vasilescu had been the overseer of Abbot Iscu's brigade. A common law criminal, he had been promised special privileges for assuming this position. "It was join the torturers or be tortured," he told his prison mates. "A part of his training had been to shoot cats and dogs, then jam steel spikes into the heads of animals still alive. In the room of the dying he now listened to Abbot Iscu's whispered prayer and heard his words of comfort.

Vasilescu was also dying. Guilt-stricken, he confessed to Pastor Wurmbrand the terrible punishments he had inflicted on the abbot. The Lutheran pastor assured him that God's forgiveness knew no limits. But Vasilescu could find no peace. One night he woke up gasping for breath. "Pastor, please pray for me. I'm going," he rasped. He dozed, then woke again, and declared, "I believe in God." Then he began to cry. Abbot Iscu had overheard. He asked two prisoners to move him to Vasilescu's bed.

"You were too young to know what you were doing," the abbot told his former torturer. "I forgive you. And if I and other Christians can forgive, surely Christ will forgive, too. You have a place in heaven," he assured.

That night both died. Richard Wurmbrand, the only member of the group who survived, wrote later in his shocking narrative of prison life, "I believe they went hand in hand to heaven."

The Sufferings of Richard Wurmbrand

Wurmbrand's books—translated into forty-five languages—are among the most shocking indictments of communism ever published. Arrested for engaging in an underground ministry to both Romanians and Soviet soldiers after the close of World War II, Wurmbrand was imprisoned and tortured for fourteen years. He was subjected to the worst tortures imaginable. He describes one experience:

> A hood was pulled over my head and I was forced to
> squat with my arms around my knees. A metal bar
> was thrust between elbows and knees and set
> between trestles, so that I swung head down, feet in
> the air. They held my head while someone flogged
> the bare soles of my feet. Each blow sent an
> explosion of agony through my whole body. Some
> fell on my thighs and the base of my spine. Several
> times I fainted, only to be revived by buckets of icy
> water. After each drenching a voice would say that if
> I gave just one of the names they wanted, names of
> secret enemies of the state, the torture would stop.
> When at last they took me down from the spit, I had
> to be carried to my cell, my feet a mass of dark red

pulp. (From *Christ in the Communist Prisons*, p. 38).

During his long captivity Wurmbrand led many men to Christ, some through tapping a secret code on the walls. He saw scores of other clergymen, including some informers, and a number of former high officials in the Romanian government. Some of these were Communists, deposed and imprisoned in purges.

Wurmbrand's Testimony

Wurmbrand was released once, in 1958. After resuming his underground work, he was rearrested in 1959 and sentenced to twenty-five years in prison. In 1964 a general amnesty provided for his freedom. He was in danger of a third arrest when Norwegian Christian friends paid $10,000 to the Romanian Communist authorities for his release. He subsequently came to America and in testimony before the United States Internal Security Subcommittee in May, 1966, bared his body above the waist to show the scars from his captivity.

Wurmbrand has been criticized for attacking Romanian religious leaders, particularly Orthodox prelates who accommodated themselves to Marxist restrictions. But his descriptions ring with authenticity and his courage in resisting inhuman treatment cannot be denied. And the repression of Christianity by Romanian Communists is well-documented by many others besides Wurmbrand.

A "Roman" Nation

Oregon-sized and located on the southeastern tip of Europe, Romania is the only European country which traces its ancestry and language back to the Romans. The Romanian language is closely related to Latin, the official language of the Roman Empire.

Christianity came to Romania as early as the fourth century. In the ninth century, the Romanian church joined in the Byzantine defection from Rome. The Romanian Orthodox Church has since been the establishment faith of Romania and today claims ninety per cent of the country's twenty million people.

In centuries following, Romania, like other East European nations, became a pawn of European politics and wars. For almost four centuries the region belonged to the Turks. The Turks ruled Romania through vassal Greek Orthodox Christian princes, so Islam made no real inroads in Romania.

Persecution of Baptists in the 1920's

Romania became independent in 1877 under a monarchy closely allied with the Orthodox Church. The next three largest Christian bodies, Roman Catholic, Hungarian Reformed, and Lutheran were benignly tolerated because of their size. Baptists and other small evangelical groups were severely persecuted. The worst persecution occurred in the 1920's when many Baptist churches were confiscated and pastors imprisoned. During this harsh Fascist period, no Baptist worship services, burials, or weddings were permitted. The oppression eased from 1928 to 1937, then during 1938 and 1939 all Baptist churches were closed. Pressure from the Baptist World Alliance brought relief.

"Cleanse Your Hands, You Sinners"

Freedom for Romanian evangelicals was short-lived. Under Stalin's pact with Hitler, Romania was divided among Russia, Bulgaria, and Hungary. The fascist Iron Guard movement tried to involve the Orthodox Church in political terrorism. Premier Armand Calinescu, the leading Iron Guard opponent, was murdered. The night before, nine Orthodox fanatics had kept a prayer vigil lying across a cold church floor, their bodies forming a cross. Hitler's protege, General Ion Antonescu, seized power and ruled behind a young figurehead king.

Nazi and Orthodox fanatics ran amuck. Iron Guard agents kept a constant check on churches of minority groups. One Sunday, Wurmbrand noticed a group of strangers in the green shirts of the Iron Guard slip quietly into the back of his church. He saw revolvers in their hands and thought he might be preaching his last sermon. He spoke on the hands of Jesus—how they had fed the hungry, healed the sick, and been nailed to the cross. Then he raised his voice so the intruders could hear clearly. "But you. What have you done with your hands? You are killing, beating, and torturing innocent people. Do you call yourselves Christians? Cleanse your hands, you sinners!"

The Nazi agents waited with guns drawn as the congregation filed out. Wurmbrand surprised them by slipping behind a curtain and running through a secret exit to a side street. They ran forward, shouting, "Where's Wurmbrand?" But he had escaped.

Hitler's legions swept across Europe and invaded the Soviet Union. Thousands of Romanian evangelicals were murdered or herded into concentration camps with Jews. Wurmbrand's wife was Jewish. Her entire family was arrested. She never saw them again, but later met and forgave the man who issued the orders to kill them. Wurmbrand himself was arrested, beaten, and imprisoned by the Nazis three times. When the war ended, he was well equipped to face communism.

Communists Court the Clergy

A Moscow-guided communist minority gained control of a coalition of Romanian political parties. They took over the government through "free" elections and forced the monarchy to abdicate. The Soviets had another satellite.

Communist Party boss Gheorghe Gheorghiu-Dej moved to win the support of the Orthodox clergy. Gheorghiu-Dej had been raised in a devout Orthodox home. During imprisonment under the Nazis, he had discussed religion with many incarcerated Christians. He escaped shortly before the Russian soldiers arrived pushing the Nazis west, and would have been killed by the Nazi dictator had not an Orthodox priest given him shelter.

Gheorghiu-Dej spoke at a meeting of Orthodox priests, which Wurmbrand attended as an observer. He assured the Orthodox clergy of his willingness to forgive and forget their subservience to nazism. The state, Gheorghiu–Dej promised, would continue to pay clerical salaries from tax revenues. Communism and Christianity, he declared, could complement each other. All persons would enjoy complete liberty of conscience in the new Romania. Most of the audience cheered, and a spokesman promised that they would cooperate with the state.

Sabrina Wurmbrand was seated beside her pastor–husband. "Go and wash this shame from the face of Christ!" she demanded of him. Wurmbrand pleaded that he would probably be taken away. "I don't need a coward," she replied. Wurmbrand asked permission to speak. The organizers invited him forward, apparently anticipating a unity speech from the representative of the Swedish Church Mission and the World Council of Churches.

Wurmbrand began by saying it was the duty of pastors to glorify God, not fleeting earthly powers, and to support the eternal kingdom against the vanities of the day. As he continued, someone suddenly began to clap. The clapping erupted into waves of applause.

"Stop! Your right to speak has been withdrawn," the Minister of Cults, a former Orthodox priest, ordered.

"My right to speak comes from God," Wurmbrand declared. He kept speaking until his microphone was disconnected. From that time, Wurmbrand's days of freedom were numbered.

The Romanian Communists proceeded on course. Many properties were nationalized. A new government department, the Ministry of Cults, became responsible for paying clerical salaries and confirming appointments to church offices. Father Justinian Marina, the priest who had sheltered Gheorghiu-Dej from the Nazis, was made an Orthodox bishop and control of the church was put in his hands.

The Martyred Bishops

Party leaders now demanded that Roman and Greek Catholics break with Rome. The Greek Catholics, numbering 1.5 million, were ordered to merge with the Orthodox Church. Their monasteries and seminaries were closed and parish churches delivered to the Orthodox Church. The Romanian Catholic hierarchy paid a terrible price for protesting. All six bishops were arrested. Four of the bishops subsequently died in prison. Fifty priests were killed, two hundred disappeared, and four hundred were imprisoned or put in forced labor camps. A minority of Orthodox priests protested against the forced assimilation of Greek Catholics. They were treated in the same ruthless fashion.

Article 27 of the communist-devised 1948 constitution specified: "Under state control the Romanian Orthodox Church is autonomous and unified in its organization." Between 1958 and 1963 Orthodoxy felt the hot breath of this control. Some fifteen hundred priests, monks, and laity were arrested. Half the Orthodox monasteries were controlled and two thousand monks forced into "useful work."

The Split With Moscow

A falling out between Soviet and Romanian Communists led to an easing of the repression. The Soviets wanted Romania to become an agricultural reserve for the Communist bloc. The infamous canal project was vital to this plan. The Romanians were bent on industrializing.

In 1964 Gheorghiu-Dej asserted that each Communist country had the right to shape its own economic program without outside interference. The following year, under Nicolae Ceausescu, Gheorghiu-Dej's successor, Romania adopted a constitution that called for complete independence.

In pursuing economic independence, Romania invited trade from western nations. During the late sixties, Bucharest entertained French president Charles de Gaulle and United States President, Richard M. Nixon to the annoyance of the Soviets. Romania's leaders further declared the country neutral in the quarrel between China and the USSR and declined to support the Russian invasion of Czechoslovakia. Nevertheless, in deference to the possibility of Soviet intervention, Romania continued its military ties to the Warsaw Pact of communist forces.

Romania's interest in the West is plainly economic, not political. The present regime is as ruthless against opponents as previous governments. The machinery for controlling the churches remains intact, although violations are often overlooked. The policy of relaxation is pragmatic. Romania's communist bosses want good relations with the West. And they are quite aware that religion in Romania is not withering away. In fact, President Ceausescu has publicly conceded that Christianity "might still be around for centuries."

Foreign visitors are impressed by crowded churches in the major cities. Orthodoxy remains, in effect, the establishment church of the country. Roman Catholicism, which refuses to provide statistics for the Ministry of Cults, is obviously flourishing. The government does not officially recognize the Catholic Church, but tolerates its existence. The largest Protestant church in Romania is the Hungarian Reformed Church, with seven hundred thousand members of mostly Hungarian ancestry. It, too, continues strong.

Free Churches: Struggling and Growing

The fastest growing bodies are the free churches which historically have suffered the most persecution. Baptists, Pentecostals, and Adventists are growing rapidly.

The Baptist World Alliance reported 637 Romanian congregations with 164,000 members in 1978. Romanian Baptists have almost tripled since 1935 and are today the third largest Baptist body in Europe, behind only England and the Soviet Union. Twenty thousand new members were baptized in a recent year.

Romanian Baptists, however, struggle over the same issue which has split Baptists in the Soviet Union: whether or not to accept government controls. Reformers, such as Josef Ton, hold with Soviet prisoner Georgi Vins that each congregation is autonomous and the state has no right to tamper with the worship and organizational life of churches and the consciences of believers. Ton claims church growth was stifled by compromises made by Baptist leaders in the 1950's. Under the watchful eye of the government, the Romanian Baptist Union approved pastoral changes, paid pastors from a central treasury, ordered standardization of worship services, and even cleared the names of new believers asking for baptism.

Ton keeps bringing international attention to official persecution of Romanian Baptists. He says the fining of some Baptists for hooliganism and vandalism was insulting, since they were only meeting for worship. He also complains of Baptists being fined for singing "illegal religious songs" from the official Baptist hymnal, and of discrimination against Baptist children in schools. For such stands, Ton is highly unpopular with the government and with some of his colleagues who prefer a live–and–let–live policy as regards government restrictions. But because of Ton's ties with Baptists abroad, he has not been arrested.

So long as Romania remains economically independent of Moscow and desirous of trade and interchange with the West, the ambiguous relationship between the churches and the government is likely to continue. Should Romania's political situation worsen, the blood of martyrs will likely resume flowing.

THE PERSECUTED SPEAK

Two powerful messages come from the Christians in Eastern Europe who would rather die than compromise or surrender their faith, and who live in uncertainty of what the next day may bring.

One message is addressed to believers in the free world: don't take your freedom for granted. Use opportunities which are denied us to obey Christ's commission for world evangelization. Be aware of communist plans and strategy to enslave the world. Don't be beguiled by communist talk of peace, good will, and cooperation in coalition politics. Learn from the communist successes in Eastern Europe. And pray for us, while helping keep the world abreast of human rights violations which are inherent in the communist struggle for the dominion of faceless state bureaucracies over the conscience of individuals.

The second word is presented to the communist leadership: you have not and will not produce a "new man" through your ideology. You mistakenly assume that man is perfectible and will become honest and altruistic in a system working for economic equality. The record shows that members of communist societies act like sinful individuals elsewhere: greedy, proud, full of vice and selfishness. Your prisons demonstrate this. Yesterday's party functionary is today's criminal. The back-stabbing and string-pulling that is rampant in every communist bureaucracy is further proof that there is no salvation in materialism.

You have assumed that matter is all that matters. That man is flesh and bone, a creature of instincts and desires, devoid of eternal spirit. You have seen that man cannot live by bread alone, that he hungers for the presence of God; that he cannot find meaning in life apart from God's presence and direction.

You have discovered that your ideal of the new man is best exemplified by the Christian believers. They are honest, chaste, disciplined, unselfish, and hard-working; while the serfs of your system lie, cheat, steal, and seek release in alcoholism.

You will never change the world's social order with communist man. The world can only be changed by new men in Christ. It is these new men and women whose blood you have taken in your futile quest for Utopia. Recognize this, repent, and look to the Savior for forgiveness and the power to live righteously before the last door closes before you forever.

MARTYRS OF THE
MIDDLE EAST

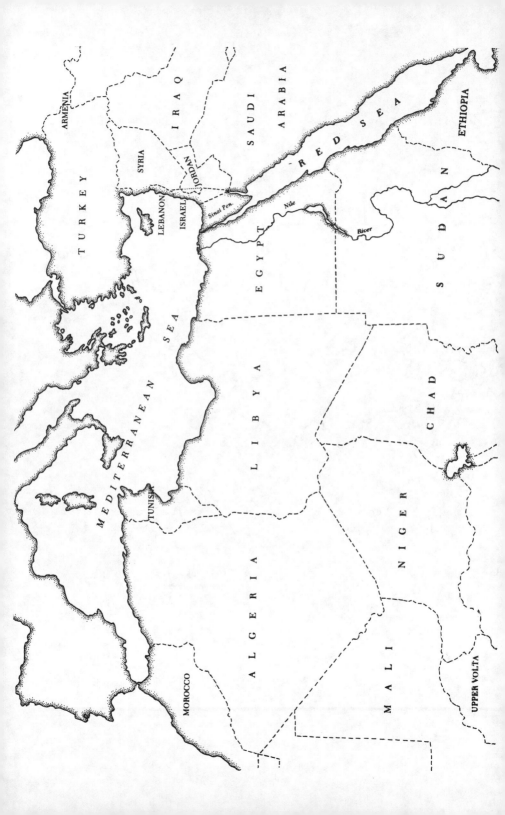

TROUBLED LANDS OF THE BIBLE:

The Middle East

The First Christian Martyr

"And when they had driven him out of the city, they began stoning him, and the witnesses laid aside their robes at the feet of a young man named Saul. And they went on stoning Stephen as he called upon the Lord and said, 'Lord Jesus, receive my spirit!' And falling on his knees, he cried out with a loud voice, 'Lord, do not hold this sin against them!' And having said this, he fell asleep" (Acts 7:58–60; *New American Standard Bible*).

Stephen was the first of many thousands who would perish in the land of the Bible that extends from present-day Turkey south across the ancient land of Canaan and into North Africa. The history of the early church courses with the blood of Christian martyrs who died rather than acknowledge the divinity of Roman emperors.

When Christianity Became Respectable

With the conversion of the Emperor Constantine in the fourth century, Christianity became, in effect, the official religion of the Roman Empire. Entire ethnic and national groups converted. The new respectability resulted in enormous growth, but at the expense of true spirituality. "Christian" soon became a status of birth and political affiliation. From that time to the present, the persecution and

317

killing of "Christians" in the Middle East must be seen from three perspectives: (1) persecution of evangelical Christians by official church bodies aligned with political and nationalistic forces; (2) persecution of believers by Muslims who see Islam as encompassing the total social, political, and religious order; (3) persecution and pressures by Jews.

THE ARMENIAN MASSACRES

Armenia, regarded as the first nation to accept Christianity, was converted early in the fourth century. A desert and mountainous country, the ancient land was sandwiched between the Russian, Turkish, and Persian empires. It was often made a buffer state for these and other rival civilizations.

In the nineteenth century Protestant evangelical missionaries brought the gospel to the Armenians with stirring freshness. This precipitated an evangelical renewal movement within the staid old Armenian church. The patriarch became alarmed and banned Bibles and books imported by the missionaries. Several evangelical Armenian leaders were imprisoned. From their prison cells they asked their supporters to continue working for reforms from within the established church.

At that time much of Armenia was under a Turkish–Muslim government. The Turks distrusted the Armenian church hierarchy and sympathized with the evangelicals, although conversion of a Muslim to Christianity was punishable by instant death. This law was suddenly lifted in 1856 and complete religious liberty declared. The evangelical movement took on new zeal. Scores of Muslims became Christians. Among them was the secretary to the ruling sultan. The opportunity proved to be short-lived. In 1864 the Turkish government began rounding up and sentencing to prison, Muslim converts to Christianity.

Turkish fears of an Armenian uprising continued. From 1895 to 1896 government soldiers killed up to one hundred thousand Armenian civilians. Then in 1915, under the cover of World War I, the Turks accused the Armenians of helping Russian invaders and launched a genocidal action that ranks as one of the most terrible barbarities in history.

In the spring an attempt was made to kill every Armenian within Turkish borders. Lawyers, doctors, clergymen and other intellectuals were rounded up and charged with subversion. Many had their heads placed in vises and squeezed until they collapsed. April 24 was the day set to kill the rest of the Armenians. Thousands of children were pushed alive into ditches and covered with dirt and sand. Many more Armenians were stoned or hacked to death. Some had their jaws ripped apart. Women and girls, some as young as twelve were stripped naked and raped before being slaughtered. Some persons were branded on the chest and back with red-hot iron crosses. Evangelicals died alongside members of the established church.

As many as six hundred thousand may have died on that fatal April 24, the day still observed as Memorial Day by the descendants of the Armenian survivors. When the Turkish soldiers saw they could not kill all of the Armenians in a single day, they began driving the crowds into the desert. Those who fell by the wayside were killed. Only the strongest escaped into Russian territory where American relief camps had been set up.

The Meaning of the Cross

One of those who escaped was a young girl of eighteen who stumbled into an American camp.

"Are you in pain?" a nurse asked when she arrived.

"No," she replied, "but I have learned the meaning of the cross."

The nurse thought she was mentally disoriented and questioned her further. Pulling down the one garment she wore, the young girl exposed a bare shoulder. There, burned deeply into her flesh, was the figure of a cross.

"I was caught with others in my village. The Turks stood me up and asked, 'Muhammed or Christ?' I said, 'Christ, always Christ.' For seven days they asked me this same question and each day when I said 'Christ' a part of this cross was burned into my shoulder. On the seventh day they said, 'Tomorrow if you say 'Muhammed' you live. If not, you die.' Then we heard that Americans were near and some of us escaped. That is how I learned the meaning of the cross."

On November 29, 1920, Armenia was annexed by the Soviet Union. Soviet policy was to allow ethnic minorities to maintain their religious rites and customs. Because Armenian Christianity was compliant and moribund under Soviet rule, little persecution was experienced. At the same time, most Armenians felt safer under the Soviets than the Turks.

The Bible today is said to be unintelligible to most

Armenians in the Soviet Union. However, William Cameron Townsend, founder of the Wycliffe Bible Translators, and his wife Elaine are enlisting translators for preparing translations of the Bible into modern Armenian dialects. The Townsends have traveled extensively through Soviet Armenia developing friendships with Armenian church leaders and communist officials for this purpose.

CONFLICTS IN LEBANON AND SYRIA

The dominant church in Lebanon is the Maronite Church, named for John Maron; a church leader who, in the seventh century, led a break from the official Roman Catholic Church over a doctrinal dispute about the nature of Christ. The Maronites were brought back into the fold of Rome in the twelfth century by Catholic Crusaders from Europe.

Evangelical work in Lebanon began in 1819 with the arrival of two missionaries of the American Board of Commissioners for Foreign Missions. Today there is a large body of Presbyterians in Lebanon, as well as in adjoining Syria, plus churches affiliated with the Baptists, the Christian and Missionary Alliance, the Church of the Nazarene and other groups.

Thousands of Maronites have been killed in clashes with Druzes and Muslims. In 1860 the Druzes, an offbeat sect of Islam, killed hundreds of Maronite Christians, arousing a military response from Catholic France. French troops took control of the area which comprises present-day Lebanon and Syria.

Under a government of like faith, the Maronites became the dominant religious group in Lebanon and Syria. Evangelical missionaries were allowed broad liberties in spreading the gospel, but Maronites who became evangelicals were persecuted. Usually this persecution involved banishment from home and community and loss of employment. Occasionally a convert was imprisoned on a trumped-up charge. A few were killed.

"Kiss the Coals!"

One of the most notable Lebanese converts to evangelical faith in the early twentieth century was Asaad Shidiak, a Syrian, and former secretary to the Maronite patriarch. The astounded patriarch first tried persuasion, then offered the convert the bribe of promotion, and finally threatened him with excommunication. When Shidiak remained stedfast, angry relatives had his marriage annulled and asked the patriarch to deal with him severely. The patriarch had him thrown into jail where he was later chained before an icon and a pot of burning coals. "You may choose to kiss the icon in token of repentance or kiss the coals!" he was told. He pressed the burning coals to his lips, and then with scorched and blackened lips was returned to his cell.

The torture continued. Finally they built a wall around him in his cell, leaving only a small opening through which he could breathe and reach out for food. There, after prolonged suffering, he passed into the presence of God.

Lebanon's "Unholy" Civil War

After Lebanon and Syria declared independence in 1943, Maronite persecution of evangelicals eased. The new Muslim government of Syria put tough restrictions on missionaries, but Syrian believers enjoyed more freedom than they had under French Catholic colonialists. Since the establishment of the state of Israel, Syrian evangelicals have been under more stress. Some have been accused of disloyalty to their country. One was reported to have been hung in Damascus as a spy. "Syrian Muslims believe that local evangelicals are allied with American evangelicals in support of the state of Israel," a missionary explains.

Lebanon, after World War II, prospered and became known as the "Switzerland" of the Middle East. The population percentage was divided about sixty–forty between the Maronite Christian majority and the Muslim minority. Both groups shared power in a coalition government. But because of an Islamic prohibition against Muslims charging interest, the Maronites, through their banking interests, came to dominate the economy.

In the 1970's the balance of power in Lebanon began shifting towards Muslims. Because of a higher birth rate, the Muslims had become a slight population majority. They sought more economic and political power without success. They sympathized with the Palestinian refugees ensconced in United Nations' refugee camps in southern Lebanon and gave material aid to Palestinian guerrillas. The Maronites were less sympathetic to the Palestinians.

In 1974 beautiful Lebanon exploded in a bloody civil war that resulted in vast property damage, thousands of casualties, and ultimately Syrian intervention. Evangelical missionaries and Lebanese believers were horrified at the bloodshed. Many felt that the Muslim cause was the more just. "It wasn't a holy war between Muslims and Christians," a Baptist woman missionary insists. "It was caused by corruption among rich Maronite Christians."

Prayer Amidst Death

Night after night evangelical believers and missionaries huddled in their homes while war between the political factions raged around them. Many inspiring stories and testimonies of God's protection are related in *Flowers From the Valley of Terror*, a book published by Baptist Publications in Beirut.

Wrote Chassan Khalaf, an instructor at the Arab Baptist Theological Seminary in Beirut:

We spent many long sleepless nights. . . . How the building shook and swayed from the force of the blasts, and how the shrapnel rained on the balconies of our apartment, falling like hailstones on a tin roof. From time to time we heard cries of distress from neighboring buildings or the siren of an ambulance speeding by, carrying the injured. And in the mornings we saw the death notices filling the walls of the narrow streets and new pictures of those who died in battle the night before. . . .

In this atmosphere of dryness and death the only soothing factor was a prayer meeting that we held by turns every night in various homes. We met around the Lord Jesus, listening to a reading from His words and pouring out our hearts before Him in thanksgiving and intercession and petitions for help. God the Father of our Lord Jesus Christ showered these meetings with a deluge of mercies and kindnesses and assurances of His care for His children. Fountains of hope exploded in the deserts of our hearts, and praises flowed out of our mouths to the Father of mercies and the God of all comfort. How we were encouraged when we would remember that we had brothers in neighboring Arab countries and in the world who were praying for us continuously. We felt that we were members of one body with them. If a member of that body suffers pain his brother feels it with him.

"Under the Shadow of the Almighty"

Many evangelicals narrowly escaped death during the 1974–1976 Lebanese war. Baptist missionary Nancy Hern, for example, was standing at her front door when a bullet, two-and–a–half inches long, smashed against the concrete beside the door. The bullet was designed to strike on its nose and explode into sharp fragments, but it hit the house sideways, saving Mrs. Hern from injury and possibly death.

Robert Haddad, a young Baptist factory worker, twice escaped death in unusual ways. The first instance happened on a Friday afternoon after he tore up a pornographic picture placed on his machine by a fellow worker. The worker threatened him with death.

"If you kill me," young Haddad replied, "I will be transported to the glories of heaven; but if you die, where will you go?" Then he added, "Jesus loves you and wants to save you, so surrender your heart to him before death comes and we will be together in heaven." At that moment the quitting bell rang.

"On Monday, I will kill you with my gun," the man vowed.

"I will be here and the Lord Jesus will be with me," the evangelical declared.

Young Haddad arrived the following Monday morning and saw his fellow workers crowded together. They had all known about the threat the previous Friday and he thought they were talking about what was going to happen to him. When he came nearer, one shouted, "Do you know what happened to the man who threatened you?"

"No, I don't," Robert replied, "but I thank the Lord that He is with me."

"Well," the other worker said, "the Lord loves you. That man who threatened to kill you on Friday went to his house and dropped dead." Robert then took the opportunity to move in closer to tell all his workers about God's love shown in Christ.

The factory was only about three hundred meters from Robert's house; however, the road was extremely dangerous because of its location between two warring armies. One day his mother warned him not to go to work, but he said, "The Lord will keep me." He prayed with her and went ahead. When he reached the street, guns began firing around him. Suddenly he was confronted by an armed commando.

"From where are you coming and where are you going?" he asked.

"I am coming from my home, as you can see, and I am going to my work," Robert replied.

The armed man then asked if he were carrying any

arms. "Yes, I have a weapon in my bag," Robert told him. The man quickly opened the bag and found only a bottle of drinking water and some food.

"Where's the gun?" he demanded.

Robert smiled and pulled out a New Testament. "This is the weapon."

"Are you mocking me?" the man snapped angrily.

"No, but I am a believer in Jesus Christ and his Book is my weapon."

"Don't mention that name," the man ordered. He took out his revolver and put his finger on the trigger. "I'm going to kill you."

The young Lebanese believer kept his calm. "My weapon is stronger, because the word of God will come out of it and enter your heart. If you believe in it you will live forever. The Lord gave me the opportunity to tell you about Jesus, the Savior, who loves you."

Again the man shouted, "Don't speak this name!" Robert saw his finger tighten on the trigger and prayed for God to intervene.

Suddenly the man smiled nervously. "Are you strong?" he asked.

"In Jesus Christ I am strong," Robert replied.

"Then push my hand down!"

Robert pushed down on his arm but could not move it. Then the man abruptly turned and ran away.

"Don't be afraid," Robert called. "Jesus loves you." But he kept running and never looked back.

A few days later Robert heard about a fighter who had told his comrades of meeting a man who believed in Christ. "He was a real Christian," the fighter reportedly said. "I wanted to kill, but my hand was paralyzed and I could not."

Many other Lebanese evangelicals also had narrow escapes. The wife of a Church of the Nazarene pastor in Beirut was standing beside a wall combing her little girl's hair when a bullet missed her head by inches. Another pastor was sprayed with cement chips from a bullet which slammed against a wall only inches away. His church was in an area of heavy fighting, but he kept it open for worshipers and persons seeking shelter.

The miracle was that there were so few evangelical casualties. A Baptist lay church worker was killed near Beirut. A Baptist theological student was hit in the head by shrapnel. His injury proved not to be serious and he recovered.

However, hundreds of evangelicals lost their homes and household possessions.

"TOLERANT" EGYPT AND JORDAN

Among the Arab countries of North Africa and the Middle East, Lebanon has the largest proportion of "Christians" among its population. However, the largest Christian minority group in the Middle East is the Egyptian Coptic Church. With around three million members, the Coptic Church dates its origin to the first century when John Mark, the author of the second gospel and Paul's sometime missionary companion, reportedly established a congregation in Alexandria. There is also a sizable Coptic Evangelical Church established by Presbyterian missionaries in Egypt. Other large constituencies are the Assemblies of God (over ten thousand reported believers and the Free Methodist Church, as well as smaller evangelical groups. Although some Copts complain of economic discrimination from the Muslim majority, believers in Egypt have escaped serious persecution during the twentieth century. Extremist Muslims recently tried to get a law passed making conversion from Islam a capital offense. President Anwar Sadat became alarmed and prevented passage.

King Hussein, ruler of the staunchly pro-Western kingdom of Jordan, is also vigilant against religious persecution. Hussein, a Muslim, claims lineal descent from the prophet Muhammed, but he sends his children to the Southern Baptist school in the Jordanian capital of Amman.

PERSECUTIONS IN "CLOSED" ARAB COUNTRIES

Other Arab countries tell a different story. With few exceptions during recent years, evangelical missionaries have been unable to enter as Christian workers in Syria, Iraq, Saudi Arabia, Kuwait, the two Yemens, Oman, Qatar, the United Arab Emirates, and the North African Arab nations of Morocco, Algeria, Tunisia, and Libya. The two hundred or so full-time foreign "missionaries" residing in some of these countries are there as teachers, nurses, doctors, and practitioners of other secular occupations. Their freedom to witness to Muslims varies from country to country.

Libya and North Yemen (San'a') are perhaps the most difficult. Southern Baptist medical workers in North Yemen, for example, are forbidden by the Muslim government to hold public services or to directly evangelize patients. In Libya four young evangelists from the United States were imprisoned for distributing Arabic gospels. After special appeals, the Libyan ruler, Colonel Muammar al-Qaddafi, issued a personal command ordering their release and deportation.

Evangelical agencies have found radio broadcasts and Bible correspondence courses effective in reaching many Muslims in "closed" countries. One evangelical worker now sends follow-up training cassettes to "home fellowships" in thirteen Arab countries. Another wrote one hundred twenty correspondence students in a North African country, asking, "Would you like for us to visit and teach you more about Christ." Eighty-six said yes.

The operators of the evangelical correspondence schools are extremely reluctant to give details of their outreaches. They decline to identify any of their students. They will only speak in confidence to trusted persons about Muslim believers in Christ who have been banished from their families and countries for public profession of their new faith. A few have been jailed, but in recent years none are known to have been martyred.

Islam's Policy Towards Christians and Jews

Still, it is incorrect to assume that Muslims have, or have ever had, a policy of killing Christians or Jews. While occasional acts of violence have been perpetrated against Christians by Muslim extremists, the historic attitude of Islam toward "people of the Book" has been one of toleration. Muslims often point to the traditional covenant given by Caliph 'Umar, a Muslim leader of the seventh century, to Christians and Jews when Muslim soldiers captured Jerusalem. "They shall have freedom of religion," he pledged, "and none shall be molested unless they rise up in a body. . . . They shall pay a tax instead of military service . . . and those who leave the city shall be safeguarded until they reach their destination. . . ." Indeed, Jews fared better under Islamic rule in the Middle East between 700 A.D. and 1250 A.D. than under despotic popes in "Christian" Europe. However, it should be noted that Muslim tolerance in conservative Muslim nations does not include freedom to evangelize Muslims.

The Muslim Challenge

Muslims now number almost seven hundred million and rank as the greatest unevangelized block of non-Christians in the world. With financial backing from Arab oil money, Islamic missionaries are moving across Africa, Asia, and into traditionally Christian Europe and the Americas, winning new converts.

Evangelical missions of today admit that past strategies in reaching Muslims have met with little success. Some mission leaders believe that one mistake has been to demand that Muslim believers come out of their cultural settings and into a western church environment. Says Donald McCurry, coordinator of a 1978 evangelical conference on Muslim evangelization: "We're taking a hard, new look at the problem of culture change. We're finding that ninety-five per cent of what we Christians do is because of our culture, and not Christianity. The way we dress. The positions in which we pray. The buildings in which we worship. Things like that."

One concept being considered is a "Messianic mosque." "Jewish believers in Jesus may worship in a 'Messianic synagogue,' " observes McCurry, a veteran missionary to Muslims. "Why can't Muslim believers have a worship in harmony with their forms?"

NO MARTYRS IN ISRAEL

In 1977 the Orthodox block introduced an antimissionary law into the Israeli Parliament, stating that anyone offering "material inducement" to persuade an Israeli citizen to change his religion is liable to a $3,200 fine and five years in prison. Furthermore any Israeli converting to a non-Jewish faith for material benefit could be jailed for three years. A woman objector noted that official records showed only seventeen Israeli Jews converting to Christianity during the past two years. (Messianic Jews say there are many more unannounced believers.) "There was no need for such drastic action," she said. The head of the Israeli Secularist League termed the proposed law a "charter for persecution." Resident Christian missionaries vigorously protested. But the bill passed.

However, both before and after the well-publicized antimissionary law that has hurt Israel's image among Christians in the West, there have been no known Christian martyrs to Judaism in Israel. Nor are there expected to be any in the future. Israel is closely tied to the democratic West. Violence against Christians by religious fanatics will not be tolerated by the government.

Martyrs in War

But many Christians have died in the wars between the Israelis and the Arabs since the establishment of Israel as a political state in 1948.

For years before 1948 there had been fighting between Arab residents of Palestine and Zionist Jewish settlers. Many Jews, Palestinian Muslims and Christians, and British occupation soldiers were killed. After the British announced in February, 1947, that they would turn Palestine over to the United Nations in 1948, the fighting escalated. Trained Jewish soldiers, immigrants from over fifty nations, sought to increase Israeli holdings before statehood was proclaimed. Palestinian resisters fought back. No one was safe.

Hilda Anderson was one of a small band of Christian missionaries who bravely remained to minister to both Arabs and Jews. Miss Anderson, a native of Sweden was a twenty-year veteran. "I don't feel it's right for me to run away from these people," she said. "It would be failing them in the time they need me most."

Miss Anderson worked and worshiped in a small Christian church in Jerusalem. The trip from her home on the Mount of Olives required that she cross both Arab and Jewish territory. Arab defenders had warned her several times not to enter Jewish territory, but she refused to stay closeted in her home. "I'm needed," she said. "I must go." One Sunday morning, early in 1948, she made the customary trip. She was killed as she was returning home, presumably by a sniper.

Death in Jesus' Hometown

At Nazareth, Southern Baptist representatives, working mainly with Arabs, had established a strong church and day school. Augustine Shorrosh, a shoemaker, was one of their first converts. He was the first evangelical in his family. After his conversion his wife and several other family members accepted Christ as their Savior. He became a zealous tract distributor and lay preacher in Nazareth and surrounding communities. After a time of testing, the missionaries began paying him a small salary so he could devote more time to Christian work. Some thought he might one day become an influential pastor.

The shoemaker-turned-preacher boldly witnessed to Jews and Muslims alike, ignoring threats against himself. One day he was on a train distributing tracts and Gospels to the passengers. Muslim fanatics became angry and turned on him. "Dog! Blasphemer!" they shouted. They forced Augustine to the back of the railroad car where one man grabbed a long-handled ax that had been placed on the wall for emergencies. The fanatics advanced menacingly toward him.

"Peace, my brothers, peace. I mean you no harm," he pleaded. But the man with the ax and the other fanatics kept coming. Augustine saw that his only hope was to get off the train. He leaped sideways and fell among the rocks.

Sometime later he came staggering home to his wife and four children. He fell on a mat and lay there for days. The missionaries came, but they could do nothing. They thought he must have suffered brain damage. After the wound healed, he became irrational. Augustine was finally admitted to a Lebanese hospital for several months where he seemed to recover. He returned home and settled down for a while until he grew worse and had to be committed to the penitentiary in Acre because of the lack of hospital facilities in Palestine. He was still in prison when the final struggle began for the establishment of Israeli statehood.

In one of the battles between the Syrians and Jews, the Shorrosh family was forced to flee into Jordan. There they heard that two cousins had been killed by the Israeli soldiers and that the Jews had rented their house to another family. But the worst blow came when a new refugee brought sad word that Augustine Shorrosh had been killed in the battle of Nazareth while trying to get home to his family. He did not know what had happened to Mr. Shorrosh's body.

The Miracle of Anis Shorrosh

The news was especially devastating to fifteen-year-old Anis Shorrosh. He wanted to get a machine gun and slip across the Jordan to kill as many Jews as possible before he was gunned down. But no arms were available and he could only seethe in frustration and hatred. Finally he ran into the desert and lay down amid the hot rocks, vowing to remain there until he died. He lay there all night and most of the next day. His vision was now blurred and his tongue swollen. He longed for a drop of cool water. Suddenly he thought, "This must be how the rich man in hell felt when he begged Lazarus to bring him just a drop of water." The young Palestinian's mind was reeling, but he was still sane enough to realize that he did not want to go to hell, for he knew that he had never truly asked the One who had been raised in his hometown to forgive his sins.

Summoning all the strength he could muster, he ran home and fell into the arms of his anxious mother. After taking food he fell into an exhausted sleep. Upon awakening he grabbed his mother's Bible and spent the entire day reading. At last he bowed in submission to Jesus and found peace.

Several months later Anis took a lab assistant job at the Baptist Hospital in Ajlūn, Jordan. The missionaries there saw promise in him and arranged for a scholarship to a Baptist college in Mississippi. After graduation he went on to New Orleans Baptist Seminary. Today he is a full-time evangelist and the most renowned Palestinian preacher in the world.

In recent years the son of Augustine Shorrosh has led many groups of Christian pilgrims on Holy Land tours. Always, he has returned to his hometown of Nazareth where his family's home is still rented out by Israeli officials. His most unforgettable trip was in 1971. As is customary, he sat next to the Jewish tour guide on the bus. When they were nearing Nazareth, the guide casually remarked, "I was a captain in the tank force that occupied Nazareth back in 1948."

Anis froze. Had he heard correctly? "What did you say?" he asked the guide.

"I was a captain in the force that took Nazareth."

Sounds seemed to explode in Anis' brain. He could hear again the screams of wounded and dying neighbors and the terrifying explosions. Praying as he struggled to control his emotions, Anis declared, "My father was killed in the battle of Nazareth."

The blue-eyed Israeli tensed in fear.

Still trying to overcome the feelings for revenge that he thought were long buried, Anis repeated, "Yes, my father was killed. And by all the tradition and tribal laws of my people, it is my duty to avenge his death."

Then an overwhelming love seemed to roll over Anis, and with a voice that seemed not to be his own, he solemnly declared, "But because Jesus Christ of Nazareth has forgiven my sins, I forgive you."*

*The inspiring biography of Anis Shorrosh is told by the authors in *The Liberated Palestinian* (Victor Books, 1975).

Episcopal Victims of War

In the years since Israel became a state, thousands more Jews, Christians, and Muslims have been killed in three succeeding wars and numerous raids by both sides. Many of those killed have been innocent civilians. For example, Presbyterian archaeologist James L. Kelso reported that during the 1967 Six-Day War, Israeli soldiers shot up the Episcopal cathedral and smashed down the Episcopal school for boys so their tanks could get through to the Arab-controlled "Old City" in the heart of Jerusalem where the Temple Mount is located. "At Ramallah a Christian (Arab) city near Jerusalem," Kelso further noted, "the Episcopal girls' school was shot up, and some of the girls were killed."

Nurse of Gaza

Only one evangelical missionary is known to have been killed in the 1970's. This was Miss Mavis Pate, a dedicated forty-six-year-old Southern Baptist missionary nurse, serving in Gaza. A short, dark-haired woman with an infectious smile, nurse Pate had only been a full-time missionary eight years.

She had served on the famous hospital ship S.S. Hope on its maiden voyage to the South Pacific in 1960–1961. At her missionary appointment service in 1964, she recalled, "God has his way to deal with us, and with this obstate one, it required that he send me approximately halfway around the world and leave me there for about a year, to see the need that existed and to help point out to me my part in meeting that need. ... On the basis of that ... I made the commitment to foreign mission service."

She served first in East Pakistan (now Bangladesh) and Thailand. In 1970 she was transferred to the Baptist hospital in Gaza to serve as operating room supervisor and director of the nursing school. Here on the narrow strip captured by Israel in the Six-Day War of 1967, she and other missionaries were in one of the most dangerous areas of the world. The staff frequently heard gunfire around the hospital, and victims were often brought in for emergency treatment.

Nurse Pate was especially touched by the plight of the three hundred sixty thousand Palestinian refugees living in camps on the narrow segment of land. Total population of Gaza, including the refugees, was then four hundred twenty thousand. She visited homes in the refugee camps and shared her faith in Christ. Her prayer list in one of her first letters home included the request, "that we all may be truly surrendered to his will, willing tools in his hand, channels for his blessings, more Christlike than manlike."

Sunday evening, January 16, 1972, Nurse Pate left with missionary Ed Nicholas and his three daughters on the short trip to Tel Aviv where the girls were enrolled in school. She went along to refill some oxygen tanks for the operating room, and to drive a new car back to Gaza. They left the hospital just after 6:00 P.M. traveling north in the hospital's Volkswagen Microbus. There was little traffic at this time because of the danger of commando attacks from refugee camps along the highway. But the missionaries felt their neutrality would be respected.

Just outside the Jabalya camp, hidden Palestinians opened fire with automatic weapons, spraying the side and back of the Microbus with fifty rounds of bullets. Ed Nicholas was wounded in the leg and side. One of his daughters caught a piece of flying shrapnel in the foot. Miss Pate was hit in the head and several other places.

Israeli soldiers patrolling nearby heard the shooting. They rushed the Americans to an Israeli first-aid station. From there Ed Nicholas and Mavis Pate were flown by helicopter to the regional medical center in Beersheba for special treatment. Miss Pate lived for about three hours after the attack and died while doctors were working on her. Nicholas and his wounded daughter recovered.

News of the tragedy brought an immediate outpouring of sympathy and sorrow. Israeli Defense Minister Moshe Dayan came from Tel Aviv to offer assistance. Israeli television presented a five-minute editorial in Arabic and an interview with missionary doctor Jean Dickman. Dr. Dickman gave a clear testimony of the assurance that followers of Christ had in such a tragedy. And in Gaza scores of Palestinian Arabs came to the hospital expressing sorrow and regret at the accident. It was generally felt that the Microbus had been mistaken for an Israeli army vehicle.

At the funeral on Tuesday morning in the church at the hospital compound, the sanctuary overflowed with Arabs, Jews, United Nations relief workers, embassy representatives, fellow missionaries and newspersons. Miss Pate was laid to rest in a quiet garden area on the hospital grounds.

The Meaning of a Life Laid Down

An Arab student nurse wrote a poetic tribute. "She went, but just her body. For she still lives in our spirits. She planted the seeds of hard work, honesty, and faithfulness in us and these seeds will become the trees of love and peace."

The Executive Director of Nurse Pate's mission board assessed her death from another perspective. Said Baker J. Cauthen in a eulogy,

> We know how urgently a missionary nurse is needed, and how radiantly a life like this shines forth in its Christian testimony. We recognize, however, that the Lord of the harvest knows more than we do about the affairs of his work. He sometimes sees fit to let his choicest servants seal their testimony by laying down their lives in the line of duty, and out of it God has a way of bringing sustained advance in the work of his kingdom.
>
> Her silent grave will be a permanent witness to the high calling of God. Missionaries will look at it and remember the great extent to which missionaries go in order that the love of Christ may be shared. Non-Christian people will look at it and be reminded of the love of God that sent the Lord Jesus into the world for our redemption, and has continued sending his messengers forth to make that redemption known.

Meanwhile, the ministry of love and reconciliation by Christian missionaries and nationals goes on in the troubled Middle East. The work continues to be slow and the responses varied.

Why Christians Remain at their Posts

Take the cases of two young Muslim Palestinians treated at the Baptist hospital in Gaza before Mavis Pate's death. One was treated first for acute appendicitis and dismissed. Two weeks later he was back in the emergency room. Several fingers had been blown off and shrapnel had literally torn out his eyes. He belonged to a commando group and the bomb he had been making had blown up in his face. Noted Dr. Merrill D. Moore in sadness: "During the entire time he was in our hospital, nothing changed his feelings of hostility and anger. This boy will bear forever in his body the stigma of hatred. His hands will never function except as claws, and he will never be able to see again. We had an opportunity to alter his life with the saving, healing love of Jesus Christ, but he refused to respond."

Another young Arab was involved in a much less serious accident at his work. The end of one finger was cut off and the skin was stripped back. He came to the hospital where he was given loving treatment and released.

Two years later a newly-hired male nurse walked up to Dr. Moore. "Do you remember me?" he asked the missionary. It was the youth who had lost the end of his finger. He explained that while he was a patient, he had seen something in the lives of the nurses that made him want to be a nurse. During his time of study he came to a saving faith in Christ through the witness of Miss Pate and another missionary. Since her death he has become one of the hospital's outstanding graduates, both as a medical professional and as an active witness for Christ.

This is how Dr. Moore contrasted the response of the two young Arabs: "One is a bitter young man filled with hatred for the world. The other is an outstanding nurse full of joy and confidence because he faces the future in Jesus Christ. He is now the head nurse of a cardiac unit at a major hospital in a large city in the United States."

It is a testimony like this that keeps Christians serving in the troubled lands of the Bible.

MARTYRS OF SUB-SAHARAN AFRICA

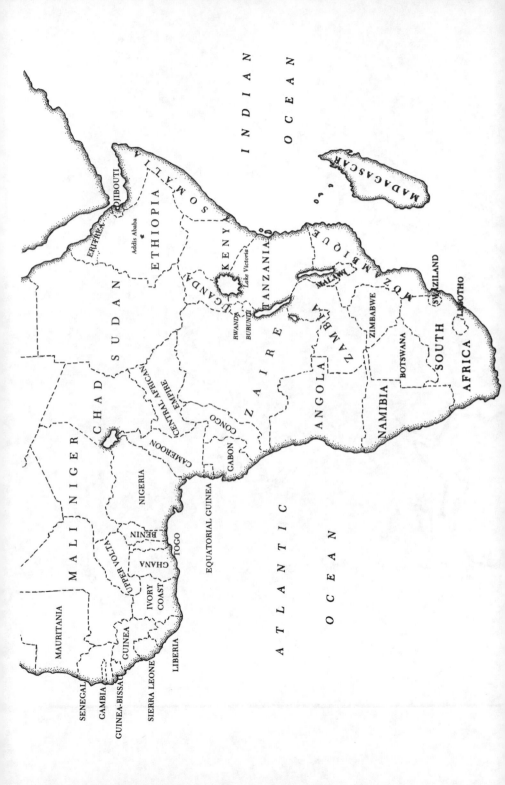

THE WHITE MAN'S GRAVEYARD:

African Missions in the Nineteenth Century

Called the Dark Continent in the nineteenth century because Americans and Europeans knew so little about Africa, this second largest continent on planet earth was also known among missionary societies as "the white man's graveyard" because the average life expectancy of a missionary was only eight years. "Our God bids us first build a cemetery before we build a church or dwelling-house," wrote an early missionary, "showing us that the resurrection of . . . Africa must be effected by our own destruction."

Faithful unto Death

Twenty missionaries died at the London Missionary Society's central African station before the twentieth convert was baptized. A book published in 1902 listed 190 martyrs from ten North American missionary societies who succumbed to disease since 1833. A sampling from the Missionary Society of the Protestant Episcopal Church reveals the life span of fourteen missionaries.

Miss Isabella Alley	1 year
Rev. J.C. Auer	21 years
Miss Phebe Bart	4 months
Miss Martha D. Coggeshall	3 months

Mrs. C.C. Hoffman	3 years
Rev. C.C. Hoffman	16 years
Rev. H.H. Holcomb	1 year
Rev. G.W. Horne	2 years
Rev. E.J.P. Messenger	3 months
Rev. Launcelot B. Minor	7 years
Mrs. Catherine L. Patch	2 years
Mrs. Jacob Rambo	2 years
Rev. Robert Smith	3 months
Dr. T.R. Steele	6 months

Nothing deterred the early pioneers of the gospel. Wrote Willis R. Hotchkiss:

> I have dwelt four years practically alone in Africa. I have been thirty times stricken with the fever, three times attacked by lions, and several times by rhinoceri; but let me say to you, I would gladly go through the whole thing again, if I could have the joy of again bringing that word "Savior" and flashing it into the darkness that envelops another tribe in central Africa.

No Turning Back

Johann Ludwig Krapf, the German Lutheran firebrand who opened up East Africa, and his bride Rosine were commissioned by the Church Missionary Society to stake out a route for mission stations from Ethiopia south along the eastern coast to the island of Zanzibar. After being driven out of Ethiopia, Rosine gave birth to a premature daughter. The child, named Eueba, meaning "a tear," lived only a few hours and was buried under a tree beside the trail.

Two months after they reached mysterious Zanzibar, Mrs. Krapf delivered a second child. This time both mother and infant died. After burying them in a single grave, the sorrowing father wrote the director of his mission:

> There is now on the East African coast a lonely missionary grave. This is a sign that you have commenced the struggle with this part of the world; and as the victories of the church are gained by stepping over the graves of her members, you may be the more convinced that the hour is at hand when you are summoned to the conversion of Africa from its eastern shore.

Krapf pressed on. While trying to build another station, he was attacked and robbed, his workmen were scattered and killed, and he was driven into the jungle. Reduced to eating ants, he began again. The station which Krapf finally established on Zanzibar became the main nineteenth century base of operations for Protestant missions in East Africa.

Krapf and a new colleague, Johannes Rebmann, crossed to the mainland and advanced across the wilds of what is now known as Kenya and Tanzania. They discovered Africa's two tallest peaks, Mts. Kilimanjaro and Kenya. They heard of a great inland sea (Lake Victoria) and surmised correctly that the sources of the Nile and the Congo rivers would be in this area. Krapf and Rebmann's advances triggered a vast sweep of scientific explorations, which in turn resulted in a great missionary movement into the very heart of Africa. Krapf himself envisioned an "Apostle Street" of mission stations stretching the length and breadth of the vast continent, each main station to be named after an apostle. "This idea I bequeath to every missionary coming to East Africa," he said. "Though many missionaries may fall in the fight, yet the survivors will pass over the slain into the trenches and take this great African fortress for the Lord."

Do or Die

Krapf's counterpart in southern Africa was Robert Moffatt, who had arrived there in 1816 at the young age of twenty. Moffatt had been preceded in 1799 by John T. Vanderkemp of the London Missionary Society who worked among the Hottentots and Bushmen. Joined by another missionary, Moffatt pushed north into Botswana, the land of the wild Tswanas.

The natives promptly set upon the invaders and robbed them of their few possessions. When the missionaries did not leave, the angry chief and his choicest warriors marched on their camp. The chief glared as he pointed in the direction from which they had come. "You will go! Now!"

"Our hearts are with you," Moffatt declared, gazing steadily into the chief's eyes. Suddenly Moffatt bared his chest. "If you choose, your warriors may drive their spears to my heart. When you have killed me, my wife will know that the hour has come for me to depart this life."

The chief stood in awe-struck silence. Then he looked at his warriors and murmured, "These men must have ten lives when they are so fearless of death. They have something to tell us."

Robert Moffatt served fifty-three years, translating the Bible into the Tswana language, establishing a strong national church, trekking into virgin territory to plant outposts for new missionaries. During his one furlough home, Moffatt described to young Dr. David Livingstone how he had often seen rising in the morning dawn, the smoke of a thousand villages where the gospel had never been preached.

The Legendary Livingstone

In 1841 Dr. Livingstone joined Moffatt, and later married Moffatt's daughter Mary. Livingstone's journals were snapped up in England. His descriptions of great jungle rivers, mountains and lakes, hitherto unknown to the outside world, fired the imaginations of European and American adventurers. His depictions of jungle tribesmen, bound to demonism and witchcraft, who had never heard the name Jesus or heard a word of scripture in their own languages, stirred Christians of all denominations. His eyewitness accounts of the slave trade provoked controversy all across the so-called civilized world. He begged the leaders of Christian Europe and America to heal this "open sore of the world" by passing laws and sending missionaries and traders to open up the African interior to Christianity and legitimate trade.

Livingstone's sympathies for oppressed Africans were met with jeers. The English-educated classes in particular tended to scorn blacks as pitiful inferiors. The British *Anthropological Review*, in 1866, called his ideas sentimental rubbish and the ramblings of a "poor, naked mind bedaubed with the chalk and red ochre of Scotch theology, and with a threadbare, tattered waistcloth of education hanging around him." Livingstone overcame his critics and became the most honored man of his time. But he paid the price in the loneliness of his kind. After burying his wife under a towering baobab tree beside the Zambezi River, he wrote,

> I loved her when I married her, and the longer I lived with her I loved her the more. . . . Oh, my Mary, my Mary! How we have longed for a quiet home. . . .
> Surely the removal by a kind Father means that he rewarded you by taking you to the best home, the eternal one in the heavens.

The Case of the Skeptical Reporter

For months nothing was heard of Livingstone, and speculation grew that he had been felled by disease or killed by hostile tribesmen. In 1871 the *New York Herald* sent famed foreign correspondent Henry M. Stanley in search of the legendary missionary doctor. "Take what you want, but find Livingstone," the publisher instructed.

After nearly eight months of search, Stanley caught up with the great man in the village of Ujiji near Lake Tanganika. Awed, Stanley could only murmur, "Dr. Livingstone, I presume." To which Livingstone modestly replied, "I am thankful to be here to greet you."

Stanley's saga of the search became a best seller. The result of Stanley's encounter is an even better story. The fabled correspondent wrote:

> For four months and four days I lived with him in
> the same hut, or the same boat, or the same tent,
> and I never found a fault in him. I went to Africa as
> prejudiced against religion as the worst infidel in
> London. To a reporter like myself, who had only to
> deal with wars, mass meetings, and political gather-
> ings, sentimental matters were quite out of my prov-
> ince. But there came to me a long time for reflection.
> I was out there away from a worldly world. I saw
> this solitary old man there, and I asked myself, "Why
> does he stop here? What is it that inspires him?" For
> months after we met I found myself listening to him,
> wondering at the old man carrying out the words,
> "Leave all and follow me." But little by little, seeing
> his piety, his gentleness, his zeal, his earnestness,
> and how he went quietly about his business, I was
> converted by him, although he had not tried to do it.

Livingstone lived only a year and a half after Stanley found him. His black employees found him at 4:00 AM on his knees, dead, his candle still burning. They buried his heart in Africa and later escorted his body to England where the remains were interred in Westminster Abbey.

Stanley picked up the torch, appealing for missionaries, exploring new territory (he was the first white to cross central equatorial Africa), and organizing tribal groups into colonies under European rule.

The Cost of Conquest

Stanley's appeal for missionaries to serve in Uganda brought engineer Alexander Mackay and seven other workers with the Church Missionary Society to Uganda in 1875. Stanley had not minimized the danger in his appeals. Mackay told the directors of the CMS upon departing: "Within six months you will probably hear that one of us is dead. When the news comes do not be cast down, but send someone else immediately to take the vacant place."

Within three months one was dead. Within a year two more had perished. Within two years Mackay was the only worker left alive in the field. For twelve years Mackay beat off fevers and tribal attempts on his life, and saw many of his converts martyred. In 1890 he died of a tropical fever on the same bed where a colleague had died.

Pioneer work in West Africa was no less costly. In 1795 the English Baptist Missionary Society adopted Sierra Leone as its second mission field (the first was India, under William Carey). They sent out two men. One died within a few months and the other was unable to continue the missionary life. The mission abandoned the work.

Sierra Leone had been chosen by British abolitionists as a haven for freed slaves and was well known in England and America. Other mission agencies sent workers. But of twenty-six men and women who went there before 1816, sixteen died along with several children. Of twelve new workers who arrived in 1823, six died that year and four others were in African graves before the end of the next year. By 1826 only fourteen of seventy-nine missionaries who had gone to West Africa during the previous twenty-two years were still alive. The port of Freetown—named for its population of freed slaves—became known as the "gate to the white man's graveyard."

Henry Palmer is an example of these pioneers. He had come home from the battle of Waterloo to marry a minister's daughter. They offered themselves to West Africa. Three months after arriving, Palmer was dead from malaria. His pregnant widow did not flinch. She wrote: "He who cannot ever [fail], whose love to his people can never fail, has seen fit to take my beloved husband to himself. Can I reply against God? I cannot. I will not." Three weeks later her child was born and lived only a few minutes. Six days later Mrs. Palmer was buried beside her husband.

Missions and Colonialism

These nineteenth century missionaries have been showered with calumnies by twentieth century armchair critics who prattle of paternalism and robbing Africans of human dignity. Granted, the missionaries were influenced by the thinking of their time—that white Europeans and Americans were at the apex of civilized greatness, a goal toward which non-whites should aspire. And true, it was the policy of

European traders, colonists, administrators, and missionaries to keep Africans in their "place"; however, the missionaries were not in Africa for spoils, but to proclaim the transforming love of God. Their commitment carried them into continual danger and almost always guaranteed a greatly shortened lifespan.

The great majority of missionaries fought with Livingstone for the eradication of slavery. Even the most paternalistic saw the degraded black tribesmen as people worthy of God's love. A few boldly called for equality in a time when many white Christians believed blacks had been consigned to servanthood under the curse placed on Noah's grandson Canaan.

In 1899 for example, Bishop Tucker of the Church Missionary Society, who spent twenty-two years in Uganda and walked twenty-two thousand miles, proposed a constitution for the Church of England in Uganda that would have put blacks on an equal par with whites in teaching and pastoral posts. His proposal, however, was rejected by his white colleagues.

Most did believe that colonialism was a good thing and aided the expansion of their respective homelands. John Mackenzie, a colleague of David Livingstone, promoted the expansion of the British Empire over regions which Livingstone explored. When British legislators balked at assuming more responsibility, Mackenzie went home and lobbied the House of Commons. Later the editor of the powerful *Pall Mall Gazette* wrote, "Hereafter he will live in the annals of our empire as the man who . . . saved Africa for England."

However, the German missionary Krapf, and some others, staunchly opposed colonialism. "Do not think," Krapf wrote,

> that because East Africans are "profitable in nothing
> to God and the world" they ought to be brought
> under the dominion of some European power, in the
> hope that they may bestir themselves more actively
> and eagerly for what is worldly and, in consequence,
> become eventually more awake to what is spiritual
> and eternal. On the contrary, banish the thought that
> Europe must spread her protecting wings over East-
> ern Africa, if missionary work is to prosper in that
> land of outer darkness.

Krapf's view did not prevail. Once the European powers realized the vastness of Africa's natural resources, they competed militantly for more territory.

The European Powers' Division of Africa

In 1884 representatives of Britain, France, Belgium, Portugal, Germany and Spain convened the Conference of Berlin to iron out contentions over land claims. Around the conference table they agreed on boundaries. The division of tribal territories in such a way that one tribe was in the domain of one colony and the other tribes came under the jurisdiction of another, sowed the seeds for many bitter conflicts which continue today.

Maps of Africa were colored red for Britain, green for France, yellow for Belgium, brown for Portugal, orange for Germany and purple for Spain. Most African territories dwarfed their European owners. Belgium's area was seventy times larger than Belgium.

The European powers made their tongues the official languages of their respective territories. Portuguese was spoken in Angola and Mozambique, English in Nigeria and Uganda, French in the sprawling Belgian Congo, and so on.

Varieties of Government

Policies of governing differed from one territory to another. Britain, which controlled the largest population, ruled through a few select white officials and allowed tribal chiefs to retain wide powers. Britain also advocated higher education and the training of leaders. Thousands of young Africans were sent to Britain and the United States for college. However, British policy was not uniform in other ways. In British West Africa there was no color bar and whites could not purchase land. British East Africa, with richer soil, was strictly segregated and whites were permitted to buy all the land they wished. This policy would later lie at the roots of the Mau Mau uprisings in Kenya when many Christians were killed.

France claimed over twice as much land as Britain, more than four million square miles. The French practiced assimilation with the aim of making the Africans Frenchmen. French Africans were citizens of France and could send representatives to the Senate and National Assembly in Paris. There was no official color bar.

Portugal went further than France in tying African territories to the homeland. Angola and Mozambique were considered provinces, not colonies.

But whites held the power and purse strings in both French and Portuguese Africa. And their policies of assimilation meant that Africans wishing to earn full rights must learn the official language and follow the ways of the conquerors, including the Roman Catholic religion. Protestant missionaries were often excluded from African possessions of France and Portugal. And native Christians were frequently persecuted.

The Belgians were the most paternalistic. They treated the Congolese as welfare clients by helping to improve their standard of living, while refusing to train native leaders. No Congolese could vote. Belgian colonists could cast ballots only in municipal elections.

The Germans were the most authoritative. Germans customarily required blacks, Arabs, Indians, and any other non-European subjects to salute militarily when a European or American passed by. A young Englishman wrote his parents from Zanzibar in 1886 that Germans "walk the streets with the air of conquerors, taking any fruit that they want without paying for it and raping any women that they see." This was not true of all Germans in Africa, but it suggests German haughtiness toward their captive people.

But whatever their differences, the European powers pursued the common goal of extracting all the wealth they could from Africa. Africa was rich in ivory, gold, diamonds, rubber, palm oil, and many other desirable commodities, not the least of which was cheap human labor. The colonial powers had good pickings for decades.

Perils of Success

The missionaries, in helping to open Africa to foreign trade and colonialism, ultimately sowed the seeds of defeat for European domination of Africa. Black Africa enjoyed the largest percentage of conversion to Christianity of any nonwhite area of the world. Mission schools educated a greater ratio of Africa's population than anywhere else. Newly literate and spiritually enlightened Africans yearned to be free. As Ndabaningi Sithole, a black leader in present Zimbabwe/Rhodesia, put it: "The missionary . . . laid explosives under colonialism." A younger African said it differently: "Africans found that the Bible begins with Genesis and ends with revolution."

Although most African leaders of the twentieth century were educated in mission schools, some were also indoctrinated in secularism, communism, and strange cults.

But by fair means and sometimes foul, almost fifty independent nations now occupy tumultuous black Africa, seventeen claiming independence in the year 1960 alone. There were only four in 1951 — Ethiopia, Liberia, Libya and South Africa which was governed by a white minority. And the end is not yet in sight. There have also been numerous wars and uprisings, not a few of which have been aggravated by communist meddling.

All of this has come at dreadful cost to human life. Hundreds of thousands have died during the past three decades, including many missionaries and African Christians caught up in the deadly crosscurrents of violence. It is their stories which are told in succeeding pages, along with the accounts of a lesser number who have been martyred in other ways during this tumultuous twentieth century.

THE SUDAN, ETHIOPIA, SOMALIA:

Northeast Africa

THE SUDAN—"DESOLATION OF DESOLATIONS"

The worst fate a nineteenth century British civil servant could suffer was being sent to the Sudan. One European traveler called it "a desolation of desolations, an infernal region, a howling waste of weed, mosquitoes, flies, and fever, backed by a groaning waste of thorns and stones—waterless and waterlogged. I have passed through it, and have now no fear for the hereafter." Yet the Sudan, extending along the upper Nile from Egypt to Uganda, over three times the size of Texas and the largest country in modern Africa, was considered important in Britain's sphere of influence.

Ethnically Sudan was then, and is now, two nations. In the more advanced north, two-thirds of the population was comprised of Arabic-speaking Islamics, descendants from mixed marriages of brown-skinned Nubians and blacks. Beyond a great unexplored marsh, the south was populated by nomadic black animistic tribes who spoke a variety of unknown languages.

The Nubians claimed descent from Cush, grandson of Noah, further asserting that the Ethiopian whom the evangelist Philip had baptized, had come from a city north of Khartoum, the capital of the Sudan. (In Greek, the language of the New Testament, "Ethiopian" meant only "burnt face.")

But it was not until the sixth century that the Nubians were converted by Byzantine Catholic emissaries. Islam sprang up in the Middle East later and by the fourteenth century the faith of Muhammed had replaced nominal Christianity. Catholic missionaries returned in 1848 when the Sudan was under Egyptian rule with aid from the British.

Debacle of the Dervishes

In 1881 a Muslim fanatic named Muhammed Ahmad proclaimed himself al-Mahdi (The Divinely Guided One) and led a revolt of dervishes against the Egyptians. He captured key towns in the vicinity of Khartoum and made the European residents his slaves.

Many of the European men were brutally slain by the Mahdi's dervishes. For example, they cut off the hands of a Greek consul, then sliced off his head. And they slit the throat of an Austrian tailor before his horrified wife and children. His only crime—making the sign of the cross.

They spared most of the women, prodding them into corrals like cattle. There, the robes of many women still dripping with the blood of their husbands, they were chosen as concubines and servants by the Mahdi and his top officers.

Islam or Death

Over a score of Catholic priests, brothers, and nuns were captured. After being condemned to death, they spent all night in prayer. Just before dawn they saw a dazzling comet with a long golden tail streaking across the clear desert sky. It reminded them of the Star of Bethlehem and they took it as a sign of divine protection. But the dervishes called it the "Star of the Mahdi." About 9:00 AM they were led before a mass of dervish warriors and ordered to bend their heads for the death blow. Suddenly they heard shouts and hoofbeats. The Mahdi was riding up on a mammoth white camel. "Bring the foreigners to me," he commanded. When they reached his presence, he looked down and announced, "May Allah lead you into the way of truth."

The Mahdi took them under his personal protection and gave them the choice of death or converting to Islam. Each declared, "Death!" He tried to dissuade them and when this failed, he ordered them to be quartered in an aide's hut. Later he convened a council to deliberate their fate. When it was brought out that it was against Islamic law to kill captive priests who had not offered violent resistance, the Mahdi and the council conceded that they could live.

The next months were horrible beyond description. The camp was appallingly filthy. Dead animals rotted in the narrow spaces between the huts. Black clouds of flies swarmed everywhere and the food was squalid. Within a month two nuns and a lay brother died. The survivors could only sew their corpses into mats and drag them to the door of the hut. No one was willing to help the "Christian dogs." Days later they finally persuaded some black slaves to drag the remains away.

Father Joseph Ohrwalder, the leader of the group, was regularly called before the Mahdi for religious discussions. Each time he refused to profess Islam. After one heated session, the Mahdi dismissed him and announced that the nuns would be taken as slaves. The nuns were forced to march across the burning sands. Upon arriving at their destination they were further tortured. One was hung from a tree and the soles of her feet beaten so hard that her toenails later dropped out. But they were never sexually violated.

Gordon — "Savior of Sudan"

Meanwhile, the Mahdi's dervishes advanced on Khartoum where Britain's General Charles Gordon represented Egypt in the governor's palace. Gordon, the most famous British soldier of the time, was a devout Christian and a social reformer. "Boldly and humbly study the Scriptures," he advised his aides. "God's dwelling in us is the key to them; they are a sealed book as long as you do not realize this truth which is sure and certain whether you feel it or not. . . . Die now and you will never die. . . . God's indwelling is all in all the great secret." General Gordon had seen caravans of Arab slave traders returning from the southern Sudan with slaves. More than once he had picked up children abandoned by the traders along the route. Many Sudanese lovingly called him "the father and savior of Sudan." He abhorred slavery and estimated that twenty-five thousand Sudanese were killed each year by the slavers. He disdained wealth and pomp. Though the Egyptians fixed his salary at fifty thousand dollars a year, he refused to accept more than ten thousand dollars.

When Gordon learned that the Mahdi's dervish army was on the march, he dispatched a request for reinforcements from British garrisons in Egypt. It should be noted here that Gordon, in defiance of his government's orders, had refused to evacuate Khartoum even though it was still possible until late in the siege. Before help could arrive, the Mahdi and his warriors entered the city on January 26, 1885. When they came into the governor's house, Gordon put on his uniform and went downstairs to meet them. "Where is your leader?" he called. The dervishes did not answer. Against the Mahdi's express orders, a spear was thrown striking Gordon in the chest. He fell forward as other blows rained upon him.

Two days later the British Relief Expedition came steaming up the Nile. Upon seeing that Khartoum had been captured, they turned their ships around in retreat.

Ironically, the Mahdi's rule was brief. Less than six months later the Mahdi was taken ill and died on June 22, 1885, at the age of forty–one. His successor was Abd Allah, who in trying to maintain the expansionist momentum into Ethiopia and Egypt begun by the Mahdi overestimated the support of the Egyptian peasantry and underestimated the strength of his enemies. Then drought swept the Sudan and food supplies vanished. Thousands starved to death.

By 1891 half of the European prisoners were dead. One of the last to die was a nun, Sister Concetta Corsi, who succumbed to typhus. Later that year Father Ohrwalder and other missionary survivors escaped to Egypt. Seven years later the British came back and under General Horatio Herbert Kitchener ended the rule of the Mahdi's successors.

Harvest in the "Desolation of Desolations"

At this time known as the Anglo-Egyptian Sudan, the country was again opened to Christian missionaries. The Church Missionary Society, the United Presbyterian Mission (also known as the Upper Nile Mission), and the Sudan United Mission all established stations during the next fifteen years in areas defined by the colonial government.

The first Protestant convert was not baptized until 1916. After that, growth was rapid and by 1940 tens of thousands of Sudanese, principally southern tribesmen, had become Christians. The "desolation of desolations" was proving to be one of the most fertile mission fields in the world.

The Birth of the Sudan Interior Mission

In 1935 the Italians invaded Ethiopia and in 1937 expelled workers with the Sudan Interior Mission. SIM had been born in the lifeblood of three pioneers who had attempted in 1893 to open a route between Lagos, Nigeria in West Africa, northeast to Lake Chad. At that time all of north central Africa was known as the Sudan, hence the name Sudan Interior Mission.

The first of the three, Walter Gowans of Toronto, Ontario, Canada, was captured by a tribal king on a slave-raiding expedition. After escaping, Gowans became ill and died from the dread fever. A black man buried him in a cornfield on November 20, 1894. Thomas Kent of Buffalo, New York, also ran into slave raiders and came down with the fever. He was buried by missionaries of another society in the town of Bida on December 8, 1895. Rowland Bingham, also of Toronto, had stayed behind in Lagos to receive mail and supplies. After rallying from an attack of the fever, he finally struck out for Ogbomosho, where he planned to open a preaching-station. Not until late January, 1895, did he learn the fate of his companions.

Bingham went on to found the Sudan Interior Mission, which today has over eight hundred missionaries serving in ten African countries, and is affiliated with over twenty–five hundred congregations numbering over a million Africans.

After being forced out of Ethiopia, SIM workers settled among the barbarous Dinka, Uduk, and Maban tribes in southern Anglo-Egyptian Sudan. Entrapped in demonism and animism, these tribespeople actually buried twins alive at birth. "Twins have the evil eye," the people explained. Missionaries Malcolm and Enid Forsberg helped protect the first Uduk twins ever allowed to live. They named them Borgay and Thoiya, meaning "Praise" and "Prayer."

No Hiding Place

The SIM stations in Sudan were around sixty miles from the Ethiopian border and hundreds of miles from any military target in Ethiopia. Guerrilla warfare against the Italian invaders was continuing in Ethiopia, but the missionaries felt safe in Sudan.

On June 17, 1940, two planes flew over the Doro station in a rainstorm. The five SIM missionaries at Doro did not know whether the planes had become lost in heavy clouds or were going some place to bomb. "We don't know what is ahead of us," wrote Mrs. Kenneth Oglesby, "but we do know our God is above us and he will watch over us."

About a month later an Italian plane bombed Kurmuk, a Sudanese town close to the Ethiopian border. "Nick" Simponis, a Greek SIM worker in Kurmuk on business, was hit in the stomach by a small piece of shrapnel. He returned safely to his station at Chali. A few days later Dr. Robert Grieve, a new medical missionary stationed at Doro, came to Chali to treat the Greek's wound. He had walked thirty-five miles, leaving his pregnant wife Claire at home. Dr. Grieve extracted the fragment of shrapnel and returned to Doro.

On the morning of August 23 the Grieves, Oglesbys and Miss Zillah Walsh saw planes pass over. They did not believe the planes would return, but just in case, Grieve and Oglesby unfolded a large American flag. They heard the roar of motors again. "Blanche, come and hold the flag while I get the number of the plane," Oglesby called to his wife.

Seconds later the earth shook around them as the bombs exploded. The Grieves and Kenneth Oglesby fell. "Oh, Bob, I'm dying," Claire Grieve moaned. The doctor never answered. Kenneth Oglesby managed to reach the medic's side and found him dying.

The planes circled and came back. Mrs. Oglesby tried to run and it seemed one of the bombers tried to follow her. Both she and Miss Walsh dropped into high grass as more bombs exploded around them. Kenneth Oglesby took shelter under a tree. While they huddled in fear, one of the planes strafed a nearby village.

In a moment the planes were gone. Miss Walsh and several tribesmen carried Claire Grieve into the clinic. Kenneth Oglesby and others brought the doctor. He had been hit in eight places, with one wound in his forehead large enough for a man to put his thumb inside. Mrs. Grieve was bleeding profusely from a hole in her back. Her spinal column was apparently broken and they could not stop the bleeding. "Let me go be with Bob," she murmured. When Miss Walsh asked if she wanted to send her loved ones a word, she gasped, "Tell them my choice is to see Him (Jesus) face to face." Then she began praying for the salvation of the tribespeople. A little later she asked her friends to sing the hymn "Face to Face" at her husband's funeral. A half hour after that she slipped away.

Kenneth Oglesby was also hit in the back. His wife had received shrapnel in about thirty-five places. Miss Walsh was not injured. They estimated that eighty-nine bombs had been dropped on the mission property.

The Oglesbys recovered. The United States government protested vigorously to the Italian government. Eventually the Italians replied, denying their planes had been in the area.

The following February, Blanche Oglesby was forced to bed. Her husband suspected yellow fever, a disease she had been supposedly innoculated against two or three weeks before. After five days her heart gave out and she joined Bob and Claire Grieve in heaven.

There were no more bombings. The tribal churches grew rapidly, and the ministry of the SIM workers and other missionaries was expanded. By the time of Sudanese independence in 1955, they had established an orphanage for unwanted twins and many schools and dispensaries. Two of their most promising young people were "Praise" and "Prayer," the first twins they had rescued.

Missionaries Are Expelled

Even before independence there was trouble between northern Sudanese Arabs and southern tribal blacks. The southerners could not forgive the northeners for slave-raiding expeditions in the past. The northerners blamed the missionaries for keeping this hostility alive. They noted that the missionaries had included the history of the slave trade in their school curriculum. After guerrilla attacks began on northerners in power, missionaries were blamed for aiding southern rebels, interfering in politics, and working against the unity of Sudan. Another contention was that the missionaries were undermining the Islamic faith. Impartial observers said the missionaries were not guilty. Before independence, they said, tribal feuding in the south and enmity against the north had been waning because of Christian influences.

The fighting escalated into full-scale civil war between the government, composed mostly of northerners, and southern Anya Nya (meaning "the venom of the Gabon viper") rebels. All mission schools were nationalized, Friday replaced Saturday as the day of worship, and severe restrictions were put on the activity and movement of missionaries. Finally, in 1964, the Muslims in power expelled all missionaries, 503 Catholics and 104 Protestants. The missionaries left behind the graves of sixty-four colleagues, most of whom had died from diseases peculiar to the harsh Sudanese environment.

Communist Intervention

An ominous new presence entered the war on the side of the north. Soviet advisers flew support missions. Soviet arms, supplied through Egypt and Algeria, were shipped via the Nile. Sudanese pilots went to Moscow for training.

Despite numerous incriminating reports, the Soviets denied intervention. In one instance a missionary pilot from the Congo landed across the Sudanese border in Juba by mistake. At the airfield he met two Soviet pilots who proudly showed him the interior of their helicopter. When local authorities realized who the visitor was, they hustled the missionary back to his plane.

All of the facts added up to one conclusion: for the first time, Russians were fighting and bombing Africans.

Christians Perish in Sudanese Genocide

Armed with Soviet arms and supported by Russian advisers, the north was overwhelmingly superior to the south. Over a half million southerners died by guns, bombings, starvation and disease. The Sudanese government claimed this was an exaggeration.

Numerous atrocities inflicted against Christians were recorded:

A southern Catholic priest, Father Bagriel Dwatuka, was whipped while he hung from a rope, then salt was rubbed into his wounds. He and others who were whipped were made to say "thank you" at the end of each whipping.

Pastor Gideon Adwok, who served a thriving church in the upper Nile region related to the Sudan Interior Mission, was charged with aiding the rebels. His accusers claimed that he had used church money for helping tribal fighters. He was killed without being given an opportunity to defend himself against the charges.

Southern Christian schoolboys who protested cruel treatment by Arab teachers were rounded up by soldiers and some had their teeth pulled out by pliers. Reports came from other schools telling of southern native teachers and students being killed.

Educated southerners, many of whom had studied in mission schools, were imprisoned and tortured. At one prison metal balls were used to push eyes out of heads to get confessions. In another torture, red chili pepper was dumped into a bag, then the victim's head was forced into the bag and held there until his eyes were inflamed and he could no longer breathe. Other victims reported having flesh sliced off their bodies. Some had their flesh roasted with hot irons.

Southern Sudanese civil servants and political leaders were special targets. Paul Debior, a southern Sudanese Christian, had served in public office for over twenty–five years. He was murdered by soldiers in his own home.

Almost every Christian house of worship in the south was destroyed. The most notorious incident was the reported massacre of a Christian village, Banja, on the Sudan–Congo frontier, July 26, 1970. Survivors told a Norwegian journalist that a Sudanese military patrol had burst in on the people while they were at prayer. They tied up the pastor with his hands behind his back. Then the soldiers scoured the village, killing everyone they saw. The rest were kept in the church, tied to chairs with thick rope. The commander reportedly told them, "We're shooting you in your church. Let your God come and save you." Then the soldiers emptied their guns on the helpless people and the building was set afire. Only fourteen persons in the village managed to reach a hospital to tell the story. The Norwegian heard their stories and took a television photographer to the scene to record the grisly evidence.

Protests of this and other mass killings were sent in vain to the United Nations.

The Russians Are Checkmated

The Soviets overplayed their hand. In 1971 Sudanese officials, led by President Jamar Nimeri, protested that the Russians were foisting manufactured goods on Sudan at prices one-third above the world market. They also blamed the Russians for a drop in industrial growth, fifty per cent below expectations.

On July 19 a group of Sudanese Communists, with alleged Soviet support, overthrew President Nimeri. But within three days Nimeri, with Egyptian help, regained power. Before the coup, the plotters had been seen saluting Russians. Now that they were out, their Russian allies denied any involvement. At the same time, to save face with Communists elsewhere, the Russians condemned the executioners of the deposed communist rebels.

President Nimeri consolidated power in a national referendum and worked out a unity agreement with the south. The government promised that Sudan would not be an Islamic republic. The south gave up the cause of secession. A southern Christian, Sayed Abel Alier, was named vice president. President Nimeri then made overtures to the West and invited back the missionaries. Next he booted out the Soviet military advisers and sent half of the Russian embassy staff packing. As a crowning rebuff to the Soviets, he requested military aid from the United States.

To Sudan with Love

The missionaries came back in 1972 to find the south devastated. Besides the heavy loss of life, over a million southerners had taken refuge in the bush; of these, two hundred thousand had fled to neighboring countries.

The mission agencies and Sudanese churches launched a vast relief effort. Most groups worked through the Commission for Relief and Rehabilitation under the umbrella of the Sudan Christian Council. The Sudan Interior Mission joined with several other faith mission groups in forming ACROSS (Africa Committee for the Rehabilitation of Southern Sudan). Aid soon began arriving from Christians all over the free world.

With seventeen million struggling people, the Sudan is potentially rich in agriculture, oil and other products. The spiritual possibilities are even greater in a land that is still only five per cent Christian. In appealing for relief aid, Dr. Kenneth Tracey, head of ACROSS, said, "If we can demonstrate genuine Christian concern to the people of Sudan now, who knows what may open up for Christian missions in this area."

EMPIRE OF ETHIOPIA – THE FUTURE LOOKS GRIM

It is possible that more Christians have died in the twentieth century in this ancient, fabled land than in any other nation of black Africa. Yet Ethiopia has the longest history of political independence and is the only country in black Africa with a Christian heritage. Today, both the historic Ethiopian Orthodox Church and the vigorous evangelical congregations are struggling against a militant Marxism that threatens to spread to neighboring countries.

Until 1974 Ethiopia was ruled by a line of monarchs claiming descent from King Solomon and the Queen of Sheba. Most modern historians disagree, holding that the ancestors of the Ethiopians came across the Red Sea from Saba (biblical Sheba) many years after the queen's death, conquered the black Hamites, and established the kingdom of Axum (present Ethiopia). The Axumites were converted to Christianity in the fourth century and established a national church under the ecclesiastical jurisdiction of the Coptic Church of Alexandria. For the next fifteen hundred years the Ethiopians remained landlocked and "slept ... forgetful of the world, by whom they were forgotten," according to historian Edward Gibbon.

Mad Emperor Orders British Missionary Flogged

The first foreign missionaries in the nineteenth century were hardly welcomed. Johann Ludwig Krapf and his wife were driven out. Britisher Henry Stern was flogged and imprisoned at the personal command of Emperor Tewodros II (Theodore), whose mad homicidal acts provoked British retaliation. Theodore subsequently committed suicide.

Ethiopia's feudalistic class structure became known to the outside world. The Amharas, members of the established church, ranked at the top. Comprising only a quarter of the population, they owned vast tracts of land and held thousands of slaves. The Gallas, numbering fifty percent of the people, toiled as peasants. Most of the rest of Ethiopia's people, the wild tribes, had never seen an outsider.

The Swedish Evangelical Mission began the first Protestant work among the Gallas. The Swedish missionaries were forbidden to evangelize members of the established church, the Amharas. This mission carried on alone for almost sixty years until in 1920 the United Presbyterians opened their first station. The Sudan Interior Mission (SIM) arrived in 1927. It would become the largest and most influential foreign work in Ethiopia and would suffer the first martyrs.

Tribal Worship of Satan

SIM missionaries found the tribespeople steeped in ignorance and barbarism. The wild Wallamos, for example, worshiped Satan. On the first day of the year they held a ceremony which resembled the Jewish Passover but really was a sacrifice to the devil. A sacrificial bull was killed and the meat divided among the members of a family clan. The bull's blood was sprinkled on the doorposts of the house, and a spot of blood was smeared on each person. The ceremony ended with the head of each household on his knees, hands outstretched, praying to Satan. Then everyone ate the meat raw.

The wealthiest persons among the tribe owned slaves. If a slave owner felt he had enough children, he would order all newborns produced by his servants buried alive.

The hostile tribal witch doctor called the first SIM workers "four-eyed people" because one missionary wore glasses. He warned his people that the foreigners would eat the Wallamos and send their blood back to their own country.

World War II Begins in Ethiopia

By 1930 the killing of newborns by slave owners, the practice of slavery, and other inhumane customs were under attack by the Ethiopian government. Emperor Haile Selassie I, who ruled under the title His Imperial Majesty, King of Kings, Elect of God, and Conquering Lion of Judah, introduced the country's first written constitution in 1931. He was trying to modernize the country when Ethiopia was invaded in 1935 on trumped-up charges invented by Italy's fascist dictator Mussolini. Italy had invaded Ethiopia before, suffering a humiliating defeat in 1896. It had been the first time an African country had ever defeated a European power. Mussolini was now determined to avenge the defeat and evoke world respect for his government.

The poorly armed Ethiopians fought back valiantly, but they were no match for Mussolini's legions. In May, 1936, Addis Ababa fell and the disorganized Ethiopian army retreated into the mountains, robbing, raping, and burning, while Italian bombers roared overhead.

For almost a year the American and British embassies had been telling missionaries to leave. Many had, but the SIM contingent remained in the tribal areas. They recognized that government security had become a leaky umbrella. Bandits threatened travelers on every road. Tribal hostilities kept escalating. "At ground level the outlook isn't so good," SIM's Raymond Davis wrote in his diary, "but thanks to God, our citizenship is in heaven, and He is still on the throne. What's next?"

The First SIM Martyrs

The next day, May 15, news came that two SIM missionaries, Tom Devers and Cliff Mitchell, had been killed in the Kassi Desert west of Addis Ababa. Mitchell's wife and child and Dever's fiancee were already in Addis Ababa. Fearing that their loved ones were in danger, the two men had been on their way there with a large group of Amharas when ambushed by two hundred fierce Arussi tribesmen. Tribal custom required a male Arussi to emasculate another man as proof of his manhood. The missionaries and Amharas had been killed with spears and then mutilated.

Allen Smith, the last missionary to see Mitchell and Devers alive, wrote a moving tribute to the two martyrs. He recalled that Mitchell had been translating the Gospel of John into the Gudgi dialect:

> When the Italian bombers visited Yirga Alem, Cliff never took refuge in our bombproof shelter without bringing with him his manuscript of John and his Bible. I have seen him, when the planes were almost overhead, run into the house to fetch the manuscript, fearing that firebombs would be dropped and the precious papers thus destroyed. The work was almost completed when he left Yirga Alem, and he took it with him on the tragic journey to Addis. . . .
>
> I have heard him speaking of Christ by the bedside of a dying Darassa — to a company gathered in a Gudgi hut — before high Amharic officials — to Greek traders. He had a message that was positive, and its never-changing theme was "Believe on the Lord Jesus Christ and thou shalt be saved."
>
> Tommy Devers was one of the joyful type. In some ways he reminded me of Peter. He was irrepressible and bubbled over with the joy of the knowledge of sins forgiven, and of a Mansion on high where the King reigns in glory. . . . No native ever heard an unkind word from Tommy. They loved him.

Mitchell's wife and Dever's fiancee were not harmed in Addis Ababa. Their response to the sad news was best expressed by Mrs. Mitchell:

> There are times when one's faith is at stake, except that God graciously turns our eyes from the greatest sorrows in this life unto Him, the Author and Finisher of our faith, and we realize all that is entailed by the words, "My flesh and my heart faileth, but God is the strength of my heart and my portion forever."

Mitchell and Devers were the first SIM martyrs, but they were not the only missionaries to die as a consequence of the Italian invasion. Dr. Robert Hockman, of the American United Presbyterian Mission, had remained to help the Red Cross. He died while attempting to remove the detonator from a bomb.

God's Multiplication Table

The Italians advanced into the tribal areas and demanded that the SIM missionaries leave. On the day before their departure, April 16, 1937, the missionaries to the Wallamos met with the native believers for a final time of fellowship around the Lord's table. When the missionaries had come in 1928 there was not a single Wallamo believer. After nine years, there were only forty–eight. They cried and prayed together and embraced one another. Then early the next morning the army trucks came to take the twenty–six SIM missionaries and seven children to Addis Ababa for evacuation. As the trucks pulled away, the missionaries looked back at tribal believers waving tearful goodbyes. "We knew that God was faithful," Raymond Davis wrote later in *Fire on the Mountains* (Zondervan), "and that He was able to preserve what He had begun among the Wallamos. But still we wondered—if we ever came back, what will we find?"

The world did not know it then, but the invasion of Ethiopia had marked the first stage of World War II. Ethiopia was also one of the first countries liberated from fascism. British forces, supported by Ethiopian nationalists, drove the Italians out and on May 5, 1941, exactly five years to the day of his departure, Emperor Haile Selassie reentered Addis Ababa.

The country did not reopen immediately for the missionaries to return. But SIM's Laurie Davison, who had served in the Sudan during the Italian occupation, got back by joining the British Army. In Addis Ababa he was put in charge of an Ethiopian soldier repatriation camp. There he encountered Wallamo soldiers eager to return home.

Eventually Wallamo Christians heard that some of the missionaries had returned to the capital. A group of church elders walked hundreds of miles to see Davison and his wife. There were now thousands of Wallamo Christians, they said.

In 1942 Dr. Rowland Bingham, the only survivor of the three founders of SIM, came to arrange for the reentry of missionaries. Soon after securing the necessary government permissions, he suffered a heart attack and died.

July 4, 1943, was a happy day in Wallamo country. That day hundreds of believers gathered to welcome the missionaries back. After the worship service, messengers left to summon leaders of more Wallamo churches to meet with the missionaries for a three-day conference.

The conference throbbed with joy. A rough tally showed the Wallamo church had grown from forty–eight to eighteen thousand while the missionaries were away. But the growth had come through a period of awful sufferings.

The Seed of the Church

The Italians had tried to stamp out the church. Hundreds of Wallamo believers who refused to kiss crucifixes extended by Italian Catholic priests had been jailed. On one occasion fifty Wallamo leaders had been clapped in prison. Each received one hundred lashes and one was given four hundred. None of the leaders could lie on their backs for months. Three of them died.

Certain Amharas, whom the Italians used to administer the tribal areas, had done their share of persecuting the evangelical believers. An Amhara lieutenant governor named Dogesa, had ordered Wandaro, a zealous Wallamo preacher, to stop evangelizing. Wandaro merely replied, "I will suffer for my Savior."

The Amhara official then ordered Wandaro to have his congregation tear down their church and await the coming of soldiers. They complied. Dogesa arrived with the soldiers. "Sing the song the missionary taught you," he demanded. The Wallamos sang about the coming of Christ to take them to a place where there would be no more trouble or pain. The singing only made the governor furious. He ordered all of Wandaro's church members jailed.

He released everyone the next morning except Wandaro. He took the pastor to the marketplace and shouted to the people. "See, the preacher is bound. His church is broken down. Don't go there again."

"Listen everybody," Wandaro shouted loudly. "Believe on Jesus for salvation. This rope on me is not the final rope."

Dogesa called on the townspeople to beat the pastor up. Bystanders rained blows upon Wandaro, but not enough to kill him. The governor sent Wandaro back to the jail. Again he was lashed and beaten. Between every lash of the whip, Wandaro preached. Wandaro was beaten several more times while his family and friends stood by helplessly. For a year he was held in prison. Wallamo Christians brought food and clothing to him and the other church leaders. Their love for the prisoners deeply impressed the guards and other observers.

When Wandaro was finally released, hundreds of Christians welcomed him home. And when Dogesa asked Wandaro to help harvest his ripened grain, a hundred singing Christians swarmed into the field. Dogesa and his friends marveled at such faith and love.

Dogesa then arranged a meeting with an Orthodox Coptic priest. "We will hear from both you and the priest," he told Wandaro. But before the meeting could take place, Dogesa collapsed in his home and died.

A Prison Miracle

Toro, another leader in the Wallamo church, stayed in hiding for six months before being captured. He was a special target of the Italians, for his church had grown to over a thousand members during the occupation.

He was given forty lashes with the hippo-hide whip. An Italian officer, wearing hard, hobnailed boots, jumped on his chest until his rib cage was nearly crushed. Tossed in prison, he lay immobile and scarcely able to breathe. There he saw a vision of Jesus and heard Him say, "Do not be afraid. You are my child."

After a slow recovery, he was released from prison. He resumed preaching and was arrested again. This time he and other church leaders were stripped naked in the marketplace, shoved face down in the mud, and lashed over one hundred times. Back in jail he was taunted by the Italians: "Where is your God who can deliver you from us? You'll never get out of here alive." Barely able to speak, Toro gasped his conviction that God would deliver Him "if He chooses — and if not, He has promised to take me to heaven to be with Him there."

Later Toro and the other believers were praying together when a fierce thunderstorm burst above their prison. The wind literally blew off the iron roof of the prison. Cascading torrents of water slammed against the mud walls, melting them from the foundation. The prisoners had no restraints. Most of the non-Christians escaped. The frightened jailers were sure that the storm came in answer to the believers' prayers. "Ask your God to withhold His anger," they begged Toro, "and we will release you." The storm dissipated. The jailers kept their word.

The Book of Acts in Ethiopia

Postwar Ethiopia was still a troubled country. Bandit hordes continued to roam the back country. In remote areas only the local laws of the tribes prevailed.

The Wallamos were now sending out missionaries to distant villages where the gospel was unknown. Two of those who answered a call from God were a husband and wife team, Omochi and Balotei. They had only one small child, having lost their first-born to illness at age three.

They left their home village and took only their animals and the few possessions they could carry. Climbing steep, stony mountains and fording deep, swift streams, they finally reached their destination after two weeks. The hut which Omochi had built on an earlier trip, was waiting for them. After three weeks, Omochi had to return to their home village on business. The morning Balotei expected him back, he was killed by roving bandits.

The elders at his home church heard first. They dispatched a messenger to break the news to his wife. Before they arrived, Balotei was awakened by a voice asking, "What would you do if your husband did not return?" She replied, "Lord, he belongs to You and I am Yours. You can do what you wish with your own."

"He is not coming," the messenger replied sadly. Balotei walked resolutely back into her hut. She knelt and prayed for guidance.

The news that the evangelist had been killed spread rapidly through the village. It was tribal custom for neighbors to weep profusely at the occasion of a death, jump high in the air, and throw themselves to the ground. The villagers came to Balotei's hut to show their sympathy by such mournings. As each group came she asked, "Why are you weeping?" Each replied, "Because your husband has been killed." And each time Balotei replied calmly, "I have already told you of One who died for you. Not once have you wept because of His death for you. Why do you now weep for my Omochi? He didn't die for you. Jesus did." Through this many heard the gospel.

After a few days elders from her home church arrived and urged her to return home. "No," she declared. "When

God called Omochi, He called me too. I will stay until God tells me to leave." She became one of the Wallamos' most effective tribal evangelists.

During the 1950's and 60's the Ethiopian tribal churches doubled and redoubled in size. There were occasional incidents of banditry, but no large-scale persecutions. The rich spiritual harvest, the stability of the Selassie government, and Ethiopia's strong prowestern stance caused western mission groups to give Ethiopia top priority. By 1972 almost six hundred Protestant missionaries were ministering in the country of less than thirty million population.

Persecution of Pentecostals

Evangelistic campaigns among Amharic Copts were still frowned upon, although educational, medical, and agricultural ministries were welcomed in communities where the established Coptic Church prevailed. Trouble came only when zealous evangelicals tried to convert Copts to a more personal faith. In 1972 *New York Times* correspondent Thomas A. Johnson reported some fifty full gospel Pentecostal churches were closed and four hundred eight members arrested on charges of belonging to an illegal organization. Their heads were shaved and one, a convert from Islam, died while in custody. A few months later the Finnish Pentecostal Church was closed by police, and a British evangelist was arrested on the same charge of proselytizing Copts.

A Kidnapping and a Killing

The biggest political trouble spot was the northeastern province of Eritrea where a guerrilla war for Eritrean independence was heating up. The Eritrean guerrillas first ignored foreigners. Then in early summer, 1974, perhaps to grab world attention, Eritrean nationalists seized an American oil company helicopter. Landing near the American Evangelical Church hospital in Ghinda, they kidnapped a pregnant missionary nurse, Mrs. Deborah Dortzbach, 24, of Freehold, New Jersey. They shot a single Dutch nurse, Anna Strikwerda, to death, apparently because she resisted capture. Mrs. Dortzbach's sponsors, the Orthodox Presbyterian Church, speculated that she was taken to provide medical assistance to the guerrillas. She was released after several months.

Another Disciple Named Peter

Other Christian lives were lost through isolated acts of hostility. Peter Isa, an Ara tribesman, had been won to Christ at age nineteen by a Wallamo evangelist. He attended the SIM Bible School at Bako and married a fellow student. After graduation in 1973 the couple went to the spirit-worshiping Bunna tribe. They faced hostility from the beginning. Some Bunnas seemed afraid of the gospel they brought. Others mocked their efforts. After three and a half years the Bunnas began to accept them. A few even became Christians.

Peter frequently left his wife and children at home to make trips to distant villages. On one trip in November he stopped at the mountain home of people he knew. He shared lodgings with a Bunna stranger. The next morning the stranger said he was going the same way as Peter. Spear in hand, he accompanied Peter down into the valley.

Two young herdsmen watched them from a high meadow. The boys saw the Bunna grab Peter by the shirt and attempt to take his small packet of food and medicine. Peter pulled back, the stranger cold-bloodedly plunged his spear into Peter's abdomen, then drew a knife and slashed his throat. The attacker stripped the body of clothing and walked away.

Word spread rapidly. Several young Bunnas gathered to dance and sing in celebration of the killing of the Ara preacher. Missionary Charlie Bonk notified the police. He found the body and buried it where it lay.

Peter's young wife wept uncontrollably when she first heard what had happened. Her youngest child, she told the missionary, had stood in the doorway each morning, announcing, "Daddy! Here comes my daddy!" Then the mother gained her composure. When neighbors arrived, she told them, "I am sitting with God. My heart is at rest."

There were seventeen other evangelists in the area. Bunna believers begged them to stay. They did. Two more families of Christian workers arrived in Bako to take Peter's place. "When I heard that Peter had been killed," said one of the new evangelists, "I was afraid to come. But God's voice continued to tell me to preach to these people. So here I am."

A Good Samaritan Is Murdered

During the 1970's Ethiopia was also hit with severe droughts. Hundreds of thousands of people starved to death.

One of the short-term workers who came to assist the career missionaries in famine relief was Dr. Douglas Hill, a twenty-six-year-old bachelor from Australia. Dr. Hill worked with two Canadian nurses, Judy Fraser and Mary Amalia, among the Somali people in the hot Ogaden Desert. They treated emaciated children, fed the starving, brought many who were dehydrated from intestinal diseases back from the edge of death, and set up mass inoculations. They traveled in the stifling heat from one desert village to another, working almost from dawn to dusk, then camping out at night.

A vibrant Christian, the Aussie medic was on a three-week stint. He had only five days to go when he and the nurses and Muhammed, a native helper, pulled into the remote little settlement of Merkman. As in other places, the entire village turned out to welcome them.

They had stopped, but the motor was still running when a mad Muslim came charging through the welcomers with a knife. An instant later Dr. Hill was lying on the ground, bleeding. In the confusion the assassin got away. Dr. Hill, whom the veteran Mary Amalia described as "one of the finest Christians I ever met," was dying. A village woman had placed her shawl under his head and now stood over him weeping. "You came in peace," she wailed. "We said peace to you. And now you are dead."

Somehow the nurses got his body in the Land Rover and headed toward the town of Bokh, an hour's drive away over a desolate stretch of gravel road where there was a small Ethiopian army base. Enroute, a rear wheel came loose. They stopped, jacked up the vehicle, and tightened the lugs. Farther on, the motor stalled. They ground the starter, checked possible trouble spots, and even tried pushing. Exhausted from the debilitating heat, they prayed: "Please, Lord, make it start." Mary hit the starter once more. The engine rumbled into life.

They reached Bokh. But their friend was dead. "Perhaps the Lord is going to reap a great harvest among the Somali people," Mary said in reflection. "The good seed had to be planted. Pray the Lord of the harvest for messengers who will follow in Doug's footsteps."

Communists Seize Power

The unrest in Ethiopia increased. The Eritrean rebellion grew worse. On September 12, 1974, a coalition of Ethiopian army officers overthrew the government. They deposed Haile Selassie, ending his fifty–eight years of rule, arrested two hundred of the emperor's closest associates, and announced a "war on feudalism." Selassie, who had been confined to a three-room mud hut in the army barracks, was allowed to return to the palace, where he died the following year.

A one-hundred-twenty-man military committee, led by Lt. Gen. Aman Michael Andom, took power. General Andom was deposed in short order on November 23, 1974, and many of his supporters were executed. The new leader, Brig. Gen. Teferi Benti was installed November 28, 1974. On February 3, 1977, General Benti was killed by members of his junta, and on February 11, 1977, a new government headed by Lt. Col. Mengistu Haile Mariam emerged. Colonel Mengistu took on dictatorial powers and proclaimed the formation of a Soviet-style "People's Democratic Republic."

The Eritrean rebellion was now a full-scale civil war. Missionaries and national church leaders worked in constant danger among the tribes, who still raided and plundered as their ancestors had for thousands of years.

An Evangelist Is Ambushed

The wild Bodis were among the most hostile. In 1975 Bodi warriors had launched raids on tribal churches, destroying fifteen houses of worship and killing hundreds of Christians.

The SIM missionaries and church leaders from the Wallamos and other tribes prayed for workers to enter Bodiland. The risk was great. The Bodis were six feet tall and adept with spears and machetes. A killer always mutilated the body, then smeared himself with the victim's blood to increase his reputation as a fighter.

In August, 1975, missionary Dick McClellan led the first trek into Bodiland, visiting five villages. When the team returned, one of the evangelists, Teka, said God had called him to take the gospel to the Bodis.

Teka, about forty, was from the Dime (Dee-may) people who lived in the rugged mountains of southwest Ethiopia. He had been raised an animist, worshiping ancestors and making sacrifices to evil spirits through witch doctors. At one time the Dimes had numbered twenty–five thousand. By Teka's time, disease and tribal wars had reduced them to two thousand. A harsh landlord kept many of these in a state of near slavery.

Teka's first two wives and his child died from fevers. Bereft of their companionship, he was enveloped by a wild passion to fight the Bodis. He was anxious to revenge the raids which Bodis had been making on Dime villages.

About this time, in the 1950's, stories of a new teaching swept through the mountains. Teka was told of a Divine Savior, more powerful than Satan, evil spirits, and death. There was a book of life. Teka wondered and hoped. But when the landlord and the witch doctor sternly warned against listening to the foreign teachings, Teka tried to think of other things.

The 1960's brought more Bodi raids and scourges of yellow fever and anthrax. Thousands of people died. Large herds of cattle were wiped out. Teka almost died of the fever. When he finally recovered, his cattle were struck by the deadly anthrax. He cried out in despair. The spirits gave him no solace.

In 1970 he heard that the witch doctor had renounced the spirits and joined the Jesus people. When the witch doctor brought a preacher named Daniel to Teka's village, Teka listened and became the first convert. He matured rapidly. He attended Bible school. He led his mother, his sister and younger brother to Christ. He helped SIM missionaries establish an outstation in Dime country and helped build an airstrip for Missionary Aviation Fellowship planes to land on. The missionaries were not surprised when he became the first Dime evangelist to answer the call to take the gospel to the Bodis.

He and a Wallamo preacher lived in a Bodi village for six months. They joined Dick McClellan and another evangelist in an evangelistic tour across Bodiland. They walked hundreds of miles, taking the gospel to thousands who had never heard. The missionary was always struck by Teka's direct and simple prayers. "O Lord Jesus," he would pray, "here I am, I'm praying." The last prayer Dick heard him pray was: "Lord, when will I see you? I want to stand before you. You are my life, my only joy."

On December 24, 1975, Teka left on a trip by himself, promising to be back in time for the Ethiopian Christmas, January 7. He carried only his Bible, a gospel booklet with pictures, a water canteen, and a package of razor blades which he planned to trade for food.

January 7 came. No Teka. The missionaries and other evangelists began a search. "Have you seen the man with the Book, the one who tells everyone about Jesus?" they asked.

Finally they traced Teka to a cluster of villages called

Gura. Young men reported seeing him leave there one morning after drinking some milk. He was bound for another village, but never arrived. Teka's friends searched along the trail, but never found his body. They were sure now that he had been killed, probably shot and then mutilated and his body hidden.

Dick McClellan told Teka's family, then traveled to Sodo for the annual tribal church conference with Christians of the Walayta tribe. When he told Teka's story and gave the challenge for evangelists to unreached peoples, sixteen responded.

When Dick returned to Bodi country, he found eighteen new believers, and a new evangelist—Teka's younger brother.

Advancing by Blood

Evangelical Christianity kept advancing in Ethiopia. But the killings also continued.

One of those slain in 1977 was Tesfaye Argew, a convert from the Orthodox Amharas. His family and neighbors had cast him out for accepting the evangelical faith. He found a place with tribal Christians, married a young woman of the Goojee tribe, and trained for the ministry in the SIM-related Dilla Bible School.

Tesfaye and his wife, Kibabush, went to an unevangelized Goojee village, even though he was warned that the Goojees there would probably kill him because he was an Amhara. His wife was then one of the few Goojee converts to Christ. The majority were still animists and prone to raiding and pillaging other tribes around them. Goojee wives proudly wore a coin in their ears to indicate their husband's reputation as a murderer.

Tesfaye and Kibabush and their two small children settled in a tent. They opened a school for village children and Goojees began affirming their belief in Christ.

Their third child, a baby girl, was born on August 19, 1977. Nine days later Goojees from the village were involved in a fight with government forces. Tesfaye and his family tried to flee to a safer place until the trouble died down. Along the road, a strange Goojee sprang from the bushes. He killed Tesfaye and mutilated his body.

Kibabush screamed and ran in terror, carrying two of her children, and holding on to the hand of the oldest, a five-year-old boy. The murderer's teen-age son caught the boy, and killed and mutilated him according to the custom of his tribe. Kibabush hid in the woods with her babies for two weeks. It was two more weeks before the missionaries learned what had happened.

Another War — More Communist Tyranny

Meanwhile, war broke out on another front. For over seven hundred years neighboring Somalia and Ethiopia had quarreled over the Ogaden desert region. In July, 1977, Ogaden guerrillas, supported by Somalian planes, launched a major campaign to take control of the Ogaden and annex it to Somalia. The guerrillas advanced rapidly until the Soviet Union and Cuba intervened on the side of Ethiopia. The Soviets sent massive military aid and advisers and the Cubans sent troops. Somalia responded by canceling its "treaty of friendship" with Russia, ordering six thousand Russian advisers out, and breaking diplomatic relations with Cuba.

Inside Ethiopia the Soviet- and Cuban-supported Mengistu regime embarked on a reign of terror. Up to one hundred fifty assassinations and executions occurred each day. The new Marxist government passed out guns to civilian supporters so they could join in the murder of political opponents. Military officers began using dynamite for mass killings to save bullets. At one point the Swedish Save the Children Federation reported that a thousand children had been massacred and their bodies left in the streets to be ravaged by hyenas and vultures.

In short order Ethiopia expelled three hundred United States consular and trade officials and shut down United States aid agencies. Western news correspondents were also ordered out of the country.

Bandits Kill Veteran Missionary

The government made no overt threats against foreign missionaries, but strong pressures were applied to make their work difficult. The greatest danger for the foreign workers seemed to be in frontier areas. On March 21, bandits attacked the SIM station at Kelafo, near the Somali border, and robbed and assaulted the missionaries. Ethiopian police intervened and after a siege of several hours succeeded in driving the bandits away. The missionaries were given sanctuary by local authorities and then evacuated out of the area.

Five days later in the middle of the night, the same bandits attacked the refugee center at Godi where United Presbyterian missionaries were staying. Dr. W. Don McClure and his wife Lyda and their son Don had left the station a few days earlier because of fighting in the area. They had returned in a mission plane to pick up some of Dr. McClure's belongings when the attackers closed in. The senior McClures had been in Ethiopia almost fifty years and were among the most admired foreigners in the country. Dr. McClure was both an agriculturist and theologian and was then director-treasurer of the Refugee Relief work in Ethiopia, treasurer of the All-Africa Relief Center, and a teacher in the Orthodox Church's seminary. With the McClures were an Australian couple, Graeme and Pamela Smith, and a number of Ethiopian Christian workers.

The bandits knew the three foreign men by name and ordered Graeme Smith in the Somali language to get five thousand dollars from the safe. The Australian did not understand and when he made no move to comply, the invaders ordered him and the McClures outside to be shot.

A moment later the women heard shots. Dr. McClure died instantly. His son managed to run into the bush. Graeme Smith was hit in the chest and fell to the ground. One bandit saw him move but did not fire, perhaps because he thought the movement was a reflex action. Children and nurses were now screaming and in the confusion and darkness bandits began firing at one another. Finally they ran away.

Graeme Smith was conscious, although a bullet had passed through the mid-section of his body. He managed to crawl into the house where the frightened women and children waited. They stayed until daylight, then the Australian staggered outside to search for Don McClure. When he could not find him, they all piled into the station's Land Rover and drove to the clinic. While they were there, Don arrived. He could hardly believe Graeme was still alive. The younger McClure said he had seen the Australian shot and had started to run as they fired at him. He tripped and a bullet whistled over his shoulder, leaving only powder burns. He had dug a hole in the desert and hid until daylight.

Later that morning Dr. McClure was buried in a simple coffin on the compound. That afternoon the survivors flew to Addis Ababa and from there were evacuated out of the country.

Missionaries Are Forced Out

Other missionaries had harrowing experiences during the terrible year of 1977. Dr. Samuel R. J. Cannata, Jr., a Southern Baptist missionary doctor, was held for questioning for several weeks in Addis Ababa by government officials. Ona Liles, superintendent of the evangelical Good Shepherd School in Addis Ababa, was detained for five months on a fictitious charge that the school owed back income taxes.

Most missionaries were gone by the end of 1977. Mission leaders cited political turmoil and "insurmountable restrictions" on their work.

After the missionaries left, a Lutheran mission leader from Germany was allowed to visit Addis Ababa. He returned home to report about ten per cent of the population of the capital living behind prison bars in "appalling conditions." The Rev. Johannes Hasselhorn, mission secretary of the Evangelical Lutheran Church of Hanover, also stated that the country's Marxist rulers were employing torture and that "priests and other church workers are hunted down like dogs." The Ethiopian Church, with which Lutheran missionaries had worked, he said, was unable to make plans "even five minutes in advance," because its members can never predict "what might happen tomorrow."

The "Gates of Hell Will Not Prevail. . . "

At this time the future of Ethiopia looks grim from a human perspective. But the missionaries forced to leave are remembering another time, during the Italian occupation, when the Ethiopian church grew by leaps and bounds.

It is already happening. As this was being written, a report came from SIM that twenty thousand more Ethiopians have come to Christ within the past few months.

SOMALIA – WILL MISSIONARIES RETURN?

Somalia is one of the twenty-five poorest nations in the world. Most of its 3.3 million people are undernourished nomads who lead their herds across vast stretches of hot, dry land in search of water and pasture. They live in small, beehive-like huts that are covered with animal skins and matted grass.

But to big-power strategists Somalia is a prize. Slightly smaller than Texas, the ancient country is draped around the "Horn of Africa," controlling the mouth of the Red Sea and approaches to the underbelly of oil-rich Arab states. The Soviet Union has coveted Somalia and until 1977 the country was considered in the Russian camp. Soviet backing of Ethiopia in the war with Somalia over disputed territory suddenly made the Russians *personae non gratae*. Now it is feared that the Marxist government of Ethiopia, with Soviet and Cuban backing, may find a pretext to invade Somalia and reclaim lost bases.

Religiously, Somalia has long been a stronghold of Islam and one of the most difficult places in the world for Christian missionary work.

For sixty years, 1875–1935, the Evangelical National Missionary Society of Sweden provided the only Protestant presence. After 1880 there were two Somalias, the north controlled by Britain and the south by Italy. When the Italians used their colony as a staging ground to invade Ethiopia, the Swedish missionaries had to leave.

The Italians lost their investment in World War II, then received it back under a ten-year United Nations trusteeship in 1950. The UN agreement specified freedom of religion. The door was reopened to missionaries.

The Eastern Mennonite Board of Missions and Charities began educational and medical work in 1953. A year later SIM workers arrived and soon opened two hospitals and three clinics.

Encounter with Bandits

One of the SIM missionaries was a five-foot-one-inch woman doctor, Jo Anne Ader. Dr. Ader had become a Christian through Inter-varsity Christian Fellowship meetings during her last year of medical school. Before coming to Somalia she had worked just across the border at a mission hospital in Kelafo, Ethiopia. On one trip back she and a nurse were stopped by fifty armed bandits.

"Get out," the leader barked, pushing his rifle inside the Land Rover. The other bandits gathered around. Suddenly a tall brigand appeared to recognize Dr. Ader. In the next instant he pinned the leader's arms behind his back. "Get in your vehicle and drive fast!" he ordered the missionaries. The doctor and nurse did not hesitate. As they sped away, they recited from Psalm 23: "Yea, though I walk through the valley of the shadow of death, I will fear no evil: for thou art with me."

The missionaries had more to fear from certain fanatical Muslim sects. They constantly harangued the government about the Christian missions. Finally the government yielded to pressure and ordered the Mennonites to cease all activities in the spring of 1962. The Mennonites were accused of committing "suspicious acts harmful to the prestige of the Muslim religion." Government officials investigated the charges and gave the mission permission to resume work on July 5.

Attack by a "Holy Man"

Eleven days later the Mennonites were registering Somalis for English night classes in Mogadiscio, the capital. Without warning, one of the "students" pulled a razor-sharp dagger from his clothing and stabbed Canadian Merlin Grove. When the missionary's wife, Dorothy, ran in from their adjoining quarters, the assassin turned on her and stabbed her repeatedly as she fell to the ground. All the while, the three Grove children, ages ten, eight, and six, looked on numbly.

Merlin Grove died almost instantly. Dorothy was rushed into emergency surgery. Pulled back from the brink of death, she remained on the critical list for many days. The assassin was caught and identified as the leader of a Muslim sect. He had come from prayers in the mosque to kill the people he believed were enemies of God. He was put on trial and sentenced to prison.

The Groves had sold their farm in Markham, Ontario, and had been in Somalia less than two years. They had won only four Somalis to Christ. When Dorothy recovered, she was asked if she still felt it worthwhile to witness to Muslims. "What value do you place on a soul?" she replied quietly.

The Government Cracks Down

The next year the government declared illegal the propagandizing of any religion other than Islam. The mission schools were told they could continue only if the Koran was taught instead of the Bible. Confronted with this ultimatum, the missions closed their elementary schools. But missionaries continued to hold Bible classes in their homes and to teach English and typing at night. Two years later SIM personnel reported "each week finds new ones turning to Christ." No church was ever organized, but a Somali Believers Fellowship of about seventy-five was established. Five young men went to Bible school in other countries to prepare to evangelize their own people.

One Believer's Ordeal

Most of the believers paid dearly for their Christian commitment. Musa Sheikow, for example, had been told by his parents never to return home. He crossed the border to attend Bible school in Ethiopia, then returned to work at the SIM dispensary at Bulo Burti and to witness to his people.

Reports of his witnessing reached the police. They shadowed him for five months, trying to catch him "preaching." Their opportunity came when a visitor to Musa's home told the authorities that Musa had in his house a booklet, "How to Lead a Muslim to Christ." The police seized Musa at the dispensary where he was treating patients and ordered him to accompany them on a search of his house. They found the incriminating booklet and arrested him on a charge of trying to destroy the national religion.

News of his arrest spread fast. Six hundred Somalis came to hear his trial. "You are charged with being a Christian," the judge began. "What do you say to that?"

Musa stood erect in the dock and spoke loud enough for everyone to hear. "It is true, your Worship. I am a follower of Jesus Christ, whether you imprison me or kill me!"

The crowd rumbled in anger. "Jail him!" someone shouted.

The judge deliberated, then gave his verdict: "Because you have confessed Christianity, and you have been found with this book, and you have been reported propagandizing, I hereby sentence you to six months imprisonment or five hundred shillings fine." Musa did not protest. Instead he thanked God for the opportunity to witness.

Because he could not pay the fine, he was put in solitary confinement. Inside the main prison was a fanatical Muslim sheik, imprisoned for fighting another clan leader. The sheik and the other prisoners decided to "humiliate this infidel" by assigning him to clean the latrines the first day. Musa faithfully complied, then shocked them by volunteering to clean the toilet again the next day.

The provincial governor heard that a man had gone to prison for confessing Christ. He came to see Musa. "Are you crazy?" he asked.

Musa witnessed to him. The governor was so impressed that he ordered Musa taken out of solitary. He also told the guards to provide Musa with medicine to treat the sick prisoners.

Somali society is divided into clans that are required to pay a ransom for members in trouble. Musa's clan sent a delegation to explain why they could not help him. "If you had killed somebody, we could pay the penalty [one hundred camels to the victim's clan]. If you had stolen a man's household goods, we could get you out. But we can't absolve you from this crime. It hasn't ever been done." They left shaking their heads.

The sheik imprisoned for fighting had remained unfriendly. One day he mentioned to Musa that he would like to hear the news but couldn't read the newspapers. Musa offered to read to him. The sheik's attitude slowly changed. "Musa," he said one day, "you are in jail for a good cause. When I get out, I will pay your fine."

The sheik kept his word. Musa returned to the dispensary and saved his wages to pay back the sheik.

Only Two Hundred Believers Remain

The missionaries continued with their Bible studies and evening schools until 1969 when the democratically elected president was assassinated and a military junta seized power. The new rulers dissolved the National Assembly and announced a swing toward "scientific socialism." The missionaries were told to wind up their work.

The Mennonites left. SIM kept a skeleton staff in the capital until 1974. The missionaries left an estimated two hundred believers in Somalia. How they have fared is not known. With Somalia's turn away from the Soviet Union, it is hoped that some missionaries may be able to return.

FOURTEEN NEW NATIONS:
Former French Africa

Thirteen independent nations in one year, 1960: Republic of Chad, People's Republic of the Congo, Kingdom of Benin, Republic of Ivory Coast, Republic of Mali, Islamic Republic of Mauritania, Republic of the Niger, Republic of Senegal, Republic of Togo, Malagasy Republic (Madagascar), Republic of Upper Volta, Central African Empire, and Gabon. A fourteenth country, the Republic of Guinea, had been expected to be in the group, but had broken ranks and declared independence two years before.

All were former possessions of France, which had ruled a great arc of almost three million square miles stretching from the westernmost side of Africa at Dakar across a vast hinterland to the border of Sudan. Except for Madagascar and for the steamy coast and equatorial region, this French empire was a vast but thinly populated area sandwiched between the Sahara and the rain forest. In recent years the Sahara has been pressing south and the land has been tortured by devastating drought and famine the like of which Africa has never seen before.

Muslim Power

The religious variances are also greater here than in the southern half of Africa. The northern area is almost totally

Muslim. The southern part is animist and Christian, mostly Roman Catholic. Mauritania, where no Christian missionaries are known to work, is practically one hundred per cent Muslim. Senegal, which is ruled by a devout Roman Catholic, is nearly ninety per cent Islamic.

For these nations independence and separation from the mother country came easier than some others in central Africa because there were fewer whites. There was no official color bar. The people had French citizenship and could send representatives to the French National Assembly in Paris. France's DeGaulle—perhaps because of the bloody war for independence in Algeria—did not drag out negotiations. He asked each colony to vote on its status after independence. A "yes" vote meant they wished to remain in the French "community" with France responsible for foreign relations and national defense. A "no" meant the colony preferred to break all French ties. Only Guinea, which was led by avowed Marxist Sekou Toure, voted no and declared immediate independence.

Still, most of these nations were plagued by problems after independence. Chad, for example, had only two persons with legal training and not a single doctor. Most of the violence resulted from palace rebellions and from guerrilla warfare by northern Muslims trying to take control of their respective countries. The Muslim guerrillas are reportedly armed and financed by radical Arabs from Libya and Algeria, which are, in turn, backed by the Russians.

There has been less Protestant missionary activity in French Africa, both before and after 1960, than in areas formerly controlled by the British and Belgians. Work in predominantly Muslim areas has been difficult and in some places impossible, particularly since France preferred Catholic missionaries. However, since independence, most of these countries have welcomed evangelical specialists in education, medicine, and agriculture, and some have admitted evangelists and church builders. Today there are around nine hundred foreign evangelical workers in former French Africa.

Fewer twentieth century Christians have been killed in these former French possessions in connection with their faith and witness than in nations further to the south. In most of these countries no Christian martyrdoms are known to have occurred. The exceptions are Chad, Guinea, the Congo Republic, Madagascar, and Mali where several pioneer workers died from tropical diseases.

REPUBLIC OF CHAD – TROUBLE BREWS

Before the 1970's the only outsiders who cared much about Chad were the French and about sixty missionaries and their supporters. French generals who served in Chad when it was a part of French Equatorial Africa would say, "The power that controls Chad can control Africa." They saw the great flat basin – supporting only about two million people but twice the size of France and sandwiched between the Sahara and the African rain forest – as a critical land area in north central Africa. The mission supporters were interested in Chad for another reason. It was one of the most fruitful fields in Africa.

Mr. and Mrs. Victor Veary, for example, went to Chad in 1926. In forty–two years their leadership, and that of later colleagues, produced 258 self-governing and self-supporting churches, 168 chapels and other meeting places, and a total of 42,000 evangelical believers with average Sunday attendance of 62,000. The Vearys came to Chad under the North American branch of the Sudan United Mission. The other large mission in Chad, Baptist Mid-Missions, began work in 1925 and also built up a large body of believers.

A "Christian" President

Most missionaries associated with the Evangelical Alliance Mission (TEAM) and Baptist Mid-Missions rejoiced when Chad became independent in 1960. The first president, N'Garta (formerly Francois) Tombalbaye, was a professing Christian. He credited his conversion to a Baptist missionary and had taught in a Baptist elementary school before entering politics. A few old-timers counseled caution. Tombalbaye, they remembered, had once been disciplined by his home congregation for "unchristian behavior." There was also concern over the lack of educated leadership.

Tombalbaye came from the Sara tribe, numbering one fourth of the country's population. The Saras and other tribes in the south had a background of animistic spirit worship. Residents of the northern desert were Muslims and spoke a Chadized version of Arabic. Antagonism between south and north had run strong for centuries. For one thing, southerners had not forgotten that northern Muslims had once hunted slaves in the south.

The new government was hardly installed when rebel activity began in the north. President Tombalbaye moved quickly to establish dictatorial powers. Then to appease nationalists, he launched an "authenticity" crusade. Step one called for the replacement of all "Christian" names with African names. The capital, Fort Lamy, was given the tribal name, N'djamena, meaning "leave us alone." Muslims were allowed to retain their Koranic names, but the rebellion continued. Then, on top of that, a terrible drought began in 1968 which lasted over six years. The drought killed thousands of Chadians, destroyed their herds of cattle and dried up vast areas of pasturelands.

Tombalbaye survived several attempts on his life. In 1973 he arrested and imprisoned his army commander on charges of plotting his overthrow.

A Return to Paganism

Suddenly, in a presidential decree, he announced step two in the "authenticity" campaign. All tribesmen, he said, must submit to "Yondo," the old pagan initiation rites that called for sacrifices to ancestral spirits, circumcision, and an animistic "rebirth." The secret ceremonies also involved floggings, facial scarring, mock burials, drugging, and gruesome tests of stamina, such as crawling naked through a nest of termites. The president said it was for the sake of national unity.

Enforcement was centered in Christian villages where the Baptist missionaries had concentrated their efforts. Some said Tombalbaye's special target was the church that had excommunicated him when he was young.

The Cost of Courage

Reprisals upon Christians who refused began immediately. Houses were ransacked, lives threatened. The children of some Christians were forcibly taken to initiation camps. A courageous pastor who refused to let his sons go was shot. The son of an evangelist who had helped translate the New Testament into the Sara language was reported killed.

Baptist Missionaries Expelled—Churches Close

President Tombalbaye was reportedly furious. He blamed the Baptist missionaries for whipping up opposition. Six Mid-Missions' families and six single workers were arrested and expelled for "subversive activities." Some were given only five minutes to leave their homes. Thirteen Baptist pastors were also detained and all Baptist churches and schools in the Sara area closed. The TEAM missionaries had also advised believers not to submit to the rites. They were left alone, indicating that the president was conducting a personal vendetta against the Baptists. Meanwhile the president continued to profess to being a Christian. However, he stated that while the blood of Christ atoned for sin, the initiation rites completed the cleansing.

The Persecution Worsens

After the Baptist missionaries left, the persecution intensified and spread to congregations related to TEAM. Tombalbaye set up a state church under the name, Evangelical Church of Chad. The top officials were two pastors who had been disciplined by Baptists. In one area government officials ordered the dismissal of the leading pastor without consent of the people. Regional political committees were set up, which included a pastor in each district, to enforce the pagan initiation. The committees also directed self-accusation meetings where punishment was meted out on the spot. "Comrade" replaced the title "Monsieur." Chinese and Russian Communists were seen in the capital.

Evangelicals outside Chad were now alarmed. The Association of Evangelicals of Africa and Madagascar investigated and authenticated at least fifty martyrs. Some Chadians estimated hundreds had perished rather than obey the government order.

Christian Protestors Suffer Agonizing Tortures

One evangelist who objected to the rites was jammed into a tall, narrow tom-tom drum. The skin was sewn back over the drum and a hole cut in the side to feed him. He was kept alive in the confining space for almost three weeks before he died.

A pastor was fastened in stocks and had all his fingers broken. He sent thanks to his fellow Christians for their love and said that he expected to die "any day now." Many others were put in stocks, beaten, or killed simply because they refused to drink chicken blood offered to idols, or to be subjected to fetish practices.

A number were buried alive with a leg exposed above the ground as a warning to others. Some were buried with their heads left above ground and exposed to heat and insects. Neighbors were told they would get the same punishment if they dug the victims up.

The Fate of the Persecutor

The persecutions continued into 1975. Then on April 13, soldiers, acting under the command of dissident army officers, stormed into the presidential palace and killed the president. The acting army chief of staff, Brig. Gen. Noel Odingar, immediately announced that the military had taken over the country. General Odingar and other officers blamed the Tombalbaye regime for provoking animosity between tribes and for the useless spilling of blood. Brig. Gen. Felix Malloum, a southerner, was named the new head of state.

The change in government brought relief to the persecuted Christians. The expelled Baptist missionaries returned. Confessions were made by pastors and other Christians at church meetings.

The president of the Evangelical Church in Chad, Reverend Jeremie N'Djelardje, resigned in an emotionally charged General Assembly of the Church in January, 1976. He specifically asked forgiveness for asking the missionaries to keep quiet when the question of initiation came up, for instructing church leaders to resist only until they were faced with the possibility of death, and for failing to give the strong, courageous leadership that had been needed during the persecution.

A New Threat from Militant Muslims

But the rebellion of northern Muslims did not stop. Libyan planes flew in arms purchased with oil money to the northerners. In June, 1978, the rebels advanced to the capital. It appeared that Chad was headed for a Muslim takeover, after which the country would be proclaimed an Islamic republic, with the Christian missionaries expelled and severe restrictions slapped on all church activities.

Before any of this could happen, France intervened to save the government. Fifteen hundred French paratroops landed in the capital and drove the rebels out. They remained to guarantee the stability of the government.

The future of troubled Chad is uncertain.

REPUBLIC OF MALI—"FROM HERE TO TIMBUKTU"

Romantic, fabled Timbuktu was the ultimate destination for nineteenth century adventurers. The first missionaries who tried to reach the Muslim citadel in the semi-desert of what is today the heart of Mali, were Catholic "White Fathers."

Three priests began trekking toward the city in the year 1876. Years later a band of ostrich hunters found their mutilated bodies in sand dunes some distance north of Timbuktu. Ten years later, they might have survived. In 1883 French soldiers defeated the great chief Samory, one of the most cruel and vindictive black despots ever to rule in Africa. From this time the barren, almost treeless land, larger than Texas and California combined, became known as French Sudan.

The Cost of Missionary Commitment

In 1890 nine Christian and Missionary Alliance missionaries sailed for the French Sudan. They hoped to reach the untouched tribes in the broad Niger River Basin that bisects present Mali. They got no farther than Sierra Leone. Within six months five of the nine were dead from tropical diseases. During the next thirty years over thirty graves symbolized the costly advance.

As it happened, workers of the Gospel Missionary Union were the first to penetrate the region. They arrived in 1919. Finally in 1923 the C&MA opened a station at Sikasso, a largely Muslim town with four tribal groups. Other C&MA workers arrived in the territory of the more remote Habbe tribe around Sangha. They were too late for thousands of Habbes. A few years before, a famine had swept the tribe and many had died.

The Power of Prayer

Soon after the C&MA missionaries came, another drought began. The tribespeople prayed to their fetishes in vain. Finally they went to the mission station and asked the foreigners if praying to God in Jesus' name would bring rain and save their crops. The missionaries spent two hours in prayer and an hour later the rain fell. Forty Bible school graduates and hundreds of other Habbe believers in eighty-five towns was the ultimate fruit from this miracle.

Sikasso was a more difficult field. In 1931 three of the four missionaries there died from yellow fever. When the news reached the United States, a siege of prayer for the Senufos tribespeople began. In the village where two of the martyrs had worked, twenty young men decided for Christ.

Missionaries worked unhindered until national independence in 1960. The first president, Modibo Keita, socialized Mali's economy and cozied up to the Soviet Union and communist China. Mali's economy went into a tailspin and the governing Sudanese Union Party split between communist and French factions. Mali's army, acting under Lt. Moussa Traore and fearing the swell of Chinese-trained militia, overthrew the president in 1968. The country has had closer ties to France since and the work of missionaries has been easier.

From 1968 to 1974 Mali was caught in the devastating drought that cut a swath across sub-Saharan Africa. Threefourths of the cattle in the country died. Hundreds of people starved to death and seven hundred thousand Tuareg tribespeople fled to other countries. Christians in the West provided aid.

In 1977 political turmoil and demonstrations provoked President Traore to declare martial law. About ninety missionaries continue to serve in the poverty-stricken and politically unstable country.

REPUBLIC OF GUINEA – REIGN OF TERROR

The extent and causes of persecution of Christians in Marxist Guinea are hard to assess.

In the 1950's Guinea was seen as the most promising of the French colonies. It had a small but influential and educated minority, rich mineral resources, and ports to the sea. The Oregon-sized country which half-moons around smaller Sierra Leone was primarily Muslim, but open to missionaries who had reached only a tiny fraction of one per cent of the people. Yet astute observers saw trouble brewing. Guineans had long memories of the European slave trade and exploitation of Guinea's natural resources. The dominant political party was controlled by Marxists who had been indoctrinated by French Communists. Sekou Toure, the party leader, had also visited Warsaw and Prague. He held Marxism to be the best hope for Guinea's future.

When Guinea rejected membership in the French community, France cut off all aid. Communist diplomats and trade officials poured in. Within a short time Guinea signed away seventy per cent of its agricultural exports. It appeared that the Soviets had their first satellite in Africa.

Political and Religious Repression

Toure's Party rode roughshod over the political opposition. Cuban-style militia suppressed dissent. Major industries were nationalized. The mass media became a government mouthpiece. Membership in the Party became the basis of personal identification rather than tribe, clan, and religion.

The Party began a debunking campaign against tribal religious practices. Some tribal religious leaders committed suicide. Others were poisoned.

Christian activities were curtailed. Mission schools were nationalized. A mission radio broadcast was cut off the air. Yet the Christian and Missionary Alliance, which had entered the country in 1918, was allowed to keep missionaries in the country.

Because of critical food shortages, inflation, and faltering production in industry and agriculture, Guinea asked western nations for economic aid. Toure continued to rely on communist countries for military aid, but refused to be Russia's cat's-paw. He played the communist field, seeking help from Russia, China, Romania, and other Marxist countries. He remained nonaligned in world politics.

A "Reign of Terror"

An attempt to overthrow the Toure government in 1970 and again in 1976 led to large-scale purges. In 1977 the International League for Human Rights appealed to the United Nations to stop the "reign of terror" in Guinea. The League claimed the Toure regime had imprisoned and tortured thousands of persons and forced more than two million Guineans to flee to other countries.

Are there Christian "martyrs" among these? Not in the sense that they have been persecuted explicitly for their faith. But many Christians have likely died for choosing not to follow Marxist policies.

PEOPLE'S REPUBLIC OF THE CONGO — INTRIGUE

This small, hot New Mexico-sized country straddles the Equator and lies across the Congo River from much larger Zaire (formerly the Belgian Congo). Unlike Guinea, Muslims in the People's Republic of the Congo number less than one half of one per cent of the population. The remaining ninety nine plus per cent are divided about equally between Christianity and tribal religions. Roman Catholic missionaries, working under French protection, have had fantastic success. Protestant missionary societies have paid more attention to Zaire. The exception is the Swedish Evangelical Covenant Mission which has built up an evangelical constituency of over fifty thousand. More recently, the United World Mission has also been able to enter this troubled country.

But like Guinea, Christian martyrs are hard to classify here. There has been no national vendetta against Christians; however, many Christians have died in political rebellions and purges.

Around 1900 much blood was shed by brutal overseers of foreign companies granted concessions by France. Shocking reports reached Europe, prompting the French government to appoint a commission of inquiry. The findings were so upsetting and bloodcurdling that the government refused to publish them. But Paris did change some policies.

Catholic Reformers Are Executed

The abuses continued. In 1927 Andre Matsoua, a Congolese Catholic teacher, organized an aid society to lift Africans to equal status with the French. French administrators saw the society as a political threat. Matsoua and other leaders were put on trial. Several were executed. Others were exiled or imprisoned. Matsoua died in prison in 1942. Many Congolese refused to accept his death and continued to believe that he was in Paris negotiating with Charles de Gaulle and would return to liberate them from French rule.

France gave the Congolese French citizenship. This helped, but the mysticism of Matsoua continued to pervade the country.

A Catholic Priest Becomes President

Matsoua's successor was Fulbert Youlou, a Congolese Catholic priest. When he ran for a seat in the French National Assembly, the Roman Catholic bishop in the Congo ordered Catholics not to vote for him. Youlou lost this election, but rapidly gained power and was elected the first president when the French Congo gained full independence in 1960. Fierce rioting resulted and in 1963 the priest was deposed.

A Marxist Coup

His successor Alphonse Massamba-Debat lasted five years before being overthrown by Major Marien Ngouabi. The new president established a one-party Marxist state. The little country became a communist stronghold and in 1975–1976 served as a staging center for Cuban troops fighting in the Angolan civil war.

Ngouabi was killed by assassins on March 18, 1977. Four days later members of his family killed the Catholic archbishop of Brazzaville, the capital, in reprisal. Shortly after this the previous president confessed to plotting Ngouabi's death and was executed.

An eleven-man military junta took over and declared themselves supreme over the Marxist political party and the government. One of their first acts was to restore diplomatic relations between the Congo and the United States which had been broken twelve years before.

The political upheavals and other problems cloud the future for Christianity in the Congo Republic.

MADAGASCAR—ANOTHER MARXIST TRIUMPH

The Malagasy Republic, as Madagascar is officially known, is a large underdeveloped island lying off the southeast coast of Africa. It is slightly smaller than Texas, has a population of around eight million, and is forty per cent Christian.

The Madagascar evangelical church has been bathed in the blood and sacrifice of martyrs. Missionaries from the London Missionary Society arrived in 1818. Within a few weeks five members of the first two families to arrive died of tropical fevers. Declared David Jones, one of the survivors: "I am determined to continue. Madagascar is a noble field of service."

"Bloody Mary of Madagascar"

Madagascar was then governed by a monarchy that favored the missionaries. In 1828 the reigning king died. One of his twelve wives seized power, murdered all rivals, and began a reign of terror that brought her the name "Bloody Mary of Madagascar." Queen Ranavalona I, as she titled herself, attacked the infant church with a fanaticism akin to the Emperor Nero. She stopped baptisms, banned Scripture, closed churches, ordered the European missionaries out, and forbade her subjects, except those in her employ, to learn to read and write.

In 1835 she presented the following charges against Christians:

1. They despise the idols.
2. They are always praying.
3. They will not swear, but only affirm.
4. Their women are chaste.
5. They are of one mind with regard to their religion.
6. They observe the Sabbath as a sacred day.

Suspected Christians were arrested. Sixteen hundred pleaded guilty to the queen's charges. Those who refused to worship the idols to which the queen prayed were chained in dungeons or killed. To the frustration of the mad ruler, for every Christian put to death, a score of new believers sprang up to take their place.

For a few years the Christians enjoyed peace. Then on March 28, 1849, nineteen Christians from influential families were condemned to death.

Dropped Over a Cliff for Christ

Fifteen of the group were to be hurled over a high cliff into a rocky ravine one hundred fifty feet below. The idols were taken to the top of the cliff and as each victim was lowered a little over the precipice, the demand was made, "Will you worship your Christ or the queen's gods?" Each answered "Christ." As the ropes were cut, the martyrs plunged downward, some singing as they fell.

Only one of the fifteen was spared, a young girl who was declared insane and sent to a distant village. She lived to establish a large church in the community and to win her relatives to Christ.

The New Queen Becomes a Christian

The martyrdoms continued until 1861 when the persecutor died. A successor declared herself a Christian, opened a palace church, and proclaimed Madagascar a Christian kingdom. That year the Madagascar church spiralled upward from thirty-seven thousand to two hundred fifty thousand. A sanctuary for the palace church was built. The queen ordered the following inscription for the cornerstone:

> By the power of God and grace of our Lord Jesus, I, Ranavalomanjaka, Queen of Madagascar, founded the House of Prayer, on the thirteenth of Adimizana, in the year of our Lord Jesus Christ, 1869, as a house of prayer for the service of God, King of Kings and Lord of Lords, according to the word in sacred Scriptures, by Jesus Christ the Lord, who died for the sons of all men, and rose again for the justification and salvation of all who believe in and love Him.

Jesuit Rampage

For almost three decades the church was blessed by peace and growth. In 1896, after a series of wars, French troops took over the peaceful island and Madagascar became a French colony. A wave of Jesuit missionaries followed the troops. Captive to Catholic thought at the time, they saw Protestants as enemies and incited a terrible persecution.

Mission property was confiscated and seven hundred churches were destroyed. The Jesuit rampage continued unabated until the Paris Evangelical Society persuaded the French government to stop the vendetta.

More evangelical missionaries arrived in the twentieth century and the church continued to grow rapidly. A resistance movement against the French, supported by many Protestants, sprang up. In 1947 armed warfare erupted. Before the rebellion was crushed by the French, thousands had died.

Another Marxist Victory

For twelve years after independence French settlers dominated the economy. In 1972 and 1973 riots raged across the island. This time minority tribes of African descent were protesting the government's effort to force all the people to accept the language of Merina spoken by descendants of Indonesian immigrants.

In 1975 the government changed hands four times. Some one hundred forty thousand French professionals, managers, and farmers left. United States and French military bases were closed. Strong ties were established with communist nations. A new one-party constitution was adopted, threatening severe punishment for anyone caught "opposing the objectives of the revolution." By the end of the year, Comdr. Didier Ratsiraka was invested as head of state and the military junta dissolved itself.

As blood purges continue, persecution of Christians in the Malagasy Republic could be resumed at any time.

CENTRAL AFRICAN EMPIRE – "STANDING IN THE NEED OF PRAYER"

Another major potential trouble spot in former French Africa, the Central African Empire (formerly Central African Republic) is one of the poorest nations in Africa. Fifteen per cent Protestant and twenty per cent Roman Catholic, it is served by 138 evangelical missionaries.

The first president outlawed opposition parties and established strong ties with communist China. He was ousted by Col. Jean–Bedel Bokassa in 1966. President Bokassa nationalized many industries and opened the country's first university. In 1975 he appointed Elisabeth Domitien as premier, the first woman to serve in that office in any African nation.

Another Idi Amin?

In 1976 Bokassa escaped an attempted assassination plot. He executed his son-in-law and seven others for leading the attempted coup. Three months later he dismissed the woman premier, took on dictatorial powers, and announced he had converted to Islam.

Later he renamed the country the Central African Empire and had himself crowned as emperor in a lavish bacchanalian ceremony. Two foreign news reporters were imprisoned for filing stories about the coronation. After his release one of the newsmen claimed that he had been beaten by Bokassa himself.

Bokassa is being compared to Uganda's Idi Amin for cruelty. At the time of his takeover, Bokassa had the eyes of the former security chief torn out before the officer's family. He had another political opponent hauled before a cabinet meeting where he himself slashed the man with a razor. Another time he led a band of soldiers armed with clubs to the central prison. He watched gleefully as the soldiers beat forty-five convicted thieves and left them critically wounded to roast for six hours under the equatorial sun. When UN Secretary–General Kurt Waldheim protested the brutality, Bokassa called him a "colonialist pimp" for daring to intervene.

The future of the Central African Empire and its large Christian population is not bright. Trouble for Christians could erupt at any time.

THE KINGDOM OF BENIN – LATEST MARXIST PRIZE

The latest Marxist prize in former French Africa is Benin (formerly Dahomey), a long Tennessee-sized stretch of poverty lying between Nigeria and Togo. After thirteen years of political turmoil, the small country fell under the control of Marxist dictator Mathieu Kerekou in 1972. An attempted coup, allegedly engineered by five neighboring countries, failed the following year.

Fifteen per cent of Benin's people are listed as Christians. Catholics apparently outnumber Protestants more than ten to one. Some Catholics, including at least one priest, have been among those killed in attempts to topple the Marxist strongman.

About fifty evangelical missionaries are allowed to work in Benin with some restrictions. The largest mission, SIM, is concentrating on Scripture translation to prepare the national church for any eventuality.

Dark Days May Be Ahead

The political future of Benin, the Central African Empire, Chad and some other nations which belonged to France does not look especially promising. Militant Marxists and fanatical Muslims threaten the minority of Christians. New persecutions could occur, resulting in more martyrdoms, at any time.

LIBERIA, NIGERIA, GHANA, SIERRA LEONE, CAMEROON:

Former British West Africa

The libertine John Newton traded for slaves along these swampy shores before he was "preserved, restored, pardoned and appointed to preach the faith he long had labored to destroy." His hymn "Amazing Grace" is sung today by thousands of descendants of the Africans he bought and sold.

Some two centuries after Newton, American author Alex Haley visited the village of Juffre, ancestral home of Kunta Kinte of Haley's epochal book *Roots*. Juffre was declared a national monument of Gambia, a former British colony on the coastal bulge of West Africa.

In the years separating "Amazing Grace" and *Roots*, hundreds of missionaries sailed into the calm harbors of Africa's Atlantic coast, bringing the gospel of Christ to black tribal peoples steeped in ancestor worship, fetishism, and witchcraft. Today in five new nations once controlled by Britain—Gambia, Sierra Leone, Ghana, Nigeria, and Cameroon—as well as in Liberia, millions of black believers sing praises to the Savior whose love was brought to them by brothers and sisters, both black and white, from Europe and North America.

LIBERIA – COLONY FOR FREED SLAVES

The impetus for missionary work in Liberia came in a Baptist meeting in Richmond, Virginia, in 1812, before the tribal area was set apart as a colony for freed slaves by the American Colonization Society. Members of Richmond's First Baptist Church gathered to hear Reverend Lott Carey, a black freeman, preach from Romans 8:32: "He spared not his own Son, but delivered him up for us all, how shall He not with him also freely give us all things?" After the sermon, Carey, Colin Teague, and five others organized themselves into a sister church, the other members of the Richmond church pledging prayer support. They sailed on the S.S. *Nautilus* the next day to transplant the first Baptist church to West Africa. The church continues today as the Providence Baptist Church of Monrovia, Liberia.

Lott Carey was elected acting governor of the small colony. Year after year the colonists experienced numerous hardships and frequent threats from slave ships and wild tribesmen. In November, 1828, they were attacked by a Spanish slaver. Lott Carey and others were loading shells in their fortress when a child accidentally knocked over a candle. The gunpowder blew up and Carey and seven associates were killed.

But the Liberian colony prospered. On July 26, 1847, Liberia became an independent republic, the first black African colony to gain independence. The Liberians patterned their constitution after that of the United States under the motto, "The Love of Liberty Brought Us Here."

The missionary losses to deadly fevers were staggering. Forty–four of seventy–nine workers sent by the Church Missionary Society before 1830 died during their first year. Thirty–one of seventy–five sent out by the American Presbyterian Mission perished. The Methodists suffered also. They went in the spirit of Melville B. Cox, the first foreign missionary of the American Methodist Church. "Let a thousand fall before Africa be given up," he challenged. Within four months he was dead.

It was apparent that blacks could survive in the damp Liberian forests better than whites. In 1856 the (Northern) Baptist Convention (now known as American Baptist Churches in the U.S.A.) adopted a policy of sending only Negro missionaries to the new country. The larger Southern Baptist Convention, which had split from its northern counterpart over slavery in 1845, could not follow suit. In southern states it was against the law for blacks to be taught to read and write, even in Sunday school.

Liberia's "Prophet" Harris

In the twentieth century Liberian Christians began taking the gospel to neighboring territories. The most famous Liberian missionary was William Wade Harris, a Methodist convert. Obeying a vision, in 1913 he moved to the Ivory Coast. Clad in a white gown and turban and carrying a large cross and Bible, he preached against idolatry, and urged repentance and faith in Christ. By the time Methodist missionaries reached him, he had won nearly one hundred thousand converts. Hundreds of congregations from "Prophet" Harris's ministry exist today in the Ivory Coast.

NIGERIA—TRIALS AND TRIUMPHS

In the twentieth century Nigeria, the most populous nation in Africa today, has been one of the most fruitful mission fields in the world. The influence of Christianity in Nigeria is immeasurable. Practically all of Nigeria's leaders were educated in mission schools. The smoothness with which Nigeria attained independence, the efficiency of its government in contrast to some of the other new African nations, and the prosperity of its economy are due in large part to the ministries of foreign missionaries and the leadership of astute national church leaders.

The nation became a favorite mission field of Southern Baptists. But during the first fifty years, thirteen of forty-five missionaries died on the field and several others were sent home for health reasons.

The Southern Baptists were plagued by racial prejudice, both at home and among some of the missionaries. One of their pioneers to Nigeria was Reverend W.J. David, a native of Mississippi, who believed that white Christian civilization was superior to African culture. He set about to build an imposing "back home" church in Lagos, importing Mississippi pine for pews, stained glass for the windows, and even a bell. David was a stern taskmaster, so much so that he whipped "lazy" Nigerian workmen. He also had a falling out with his first native pastor, Moses Stone, over Stone's low pay and the Nigerian's belief that blacks should control their own churches. Stone cited the deaths of so many white missionaries from disease as evidence that it was God's will for Africans to command their own destinies. The American and African parted company. The African established the dissident Native Baptist Church. Only eight Nigerian Baptists stayed with the missionary.

Reverend David and his work crew completed the building. But his joy was interrupted by the sudden illness of his wife. He started home with her. She died a few days out at sea and was buried just off the coast. Her dying words to him were, "Don't give up Africa."

After a furlough home, David and his daughter returned to the field. In the years to come he came to better understand the Nigerian point of view. The breach among Nigerian Baptists was healed. The church in Lagos became a landmark house of worship in Nigeria.

Besides the Southern Baptist work in Nigeria, the Sudan Interior Mission, the Christian Reformed Church, the Church of the Brethren and over fifty other missionary agencies established churches.

Disease Is a Constant Threat

Missionaries were as safe in Nigeria as in their western homelands except for the constant peril of disease. Despite the advancements of modern medicine, many missionaries succumbed to the dread fevers. Some were caught in epidemics in which thousands of Nigerians likewise perished.

In 1937 a deadly yellow fever epidemic hit Ogbomosho. Among the hundreds who died were two Southern Baptist missionaries. Lucille Reagan died while nursing others. She was buried beside Frances Jones, who perished during her first year of service. Their epitaphs indicated their devotion to Christ. Of Miss Reagan it was said, "Her life was the measure of her gift." Of Miss Jones: "She has done what she could for Nigeria. She gave her best for Christ the Lord."

A Sacrifice for Lepers

The constant risk of deadly disease never stopped the steady flow of new missionaries to Nigeria. Young Dr. W.G.R. Jotcham arrived in January, 1937. A Canadian of rare promise, he had completed his course in medicine at McGill University in Montreal, Quebec with honors at age twenty-two, the youngest ever to be granted a Doctorate of Medicine at that institution. A Baptist, he applied for service with SIM, anticipating a ministry to lepers at the Katsina Leprosarium in a Muslim area of Nigeria.

After six months study of the Hausa language, he was placed in charge of the leper colony at Katsina. Two hundred lepers greeted him at the settlement outside the leprosarium. Some had ugly patches on their faces and bodies. Some bore lumpy and distorted features. Some tottered about on stumps of legs and clutched at him with mangled hands. He described his feelings in a letter home:

> Behind these faces who knows what thoughts were racing? But we who were facing them had thoughts. We could not but think of who when He walked among men viewed lepers with peculiar pity and healed them. These hungry hearts had never been fed upon the bread of heaven, these cold lives had never warmed themselves before the fire of God's eternal love, nor upon these aching ears had the sweet story of the Gospel ever fallen. What a privilege it is to be one of those who first break the glad tidings of salvation to such as these.

Young Dr. Jotcham threw himself into the work of restoring "the buried hopes of blighted youth, loveless old age, the blind, the crippled, the voiceless. . . ." Unflagging, he gave himself without measure in the spirit of a poem he had written six years before:

> You may have to sacrifice pleasure—small loss
> Compared with the blessings that flow from the Cross
> The world's vain attractions are worthless to me
> Since I followed the Master, who calleth for thee.

Early in 1938, barely a year after Jotcham's arrival, a dread epidemic of spinal meningitis hit the leper colony and surrounding villages. Hundreds died as Dr. Jotcham worked himself to exhaustion. He finally fell prey to the disease he was fighting. Wracked with excruciating pain, he whispered through cracked and feverish lips, "It's all right. I pray God will be glorified whether by my life or by death." A few minutes later he slipped into the presence of his Master.

The Mystery of Lassa Fever

The causes of the deadly epidemics which continued to strike regions of Nigeria and other African countries were usually marked down to yellow fever, cerebral malaria, and typhus. But missionary doctors often felt that the diseases

needed more extensive diagnosis. This need for better understanding was tragically illustrated in the discovery of a new
virus in 1969.

In January of that year a critically ill nurse of the
Church of the Brethren mission was brought to SIM's Binham
Hospital in Jos, Nigeria. SIM's Dr. Jeanette Troup and nurse
Charlotte Shaw tried vainly to save her life. She died the
next day.

A week later Miss Shaw came down with similar symptoms. Dr. Troup and nurse Lily Pinneo worked valiantly
around the clock, but this second missionary victim died ten
days later.

Dr. Troup had kept frozen blood specimens from both
patients and had made careful notes. When a third missionary, Miss Pinneo, fell ill, Dr. Troup immediately flew with
her to New York. Dr. John D. Frame, a medical consultant
for SIM, met them at the New York airport. He quickly obtained the aid of top specialists to treat Miss Pinneo. Though
her fever rose to 107°, she recovered.

Dr. Frame sent the blood specimens supplied by Dr.
Troup to the Yale Arbovirus Research Unit in New Haven,
Connecticut. Virologists Dr. Sonja Buckley and Dr. Jordi
Cassals successfully isolated the virus from the blood samples and established that the surviving nurse, Miss Pinneo,
had developed antibodies. They studied the mystery virus
under an electron microscope and determined that it was different from over one hundred other viruses from Africa, and
viruses from eight other world regions. They called it Lassa
Virus, after the town where the first missionary victim had
worked.

In June Dr. Cassals, the virologist, became ill. His associates suspected Lassa Fever. Nurse Pinneo was flown back
to the states so that blood could be withdrawn from her and
given to Dr. Cassals. The antibodies in her blood saved his
life.

The following November a Yale lab technician succumbed. Because he had not worked directly on the Lassa
project, his physicians had not suspected the disease. An investigation revealed that he too had been infected with the
disease that had claimed the two missionary nurses.

After her return to Nigeria, Dr. Troup reported a new
outbreak of Lassa Fever in the Jos area. Ten Nigerians died,
including four of the hospital's medical staff. She was searching for clues from autopsy results when she suffered a small

cut on her hand while performing an autopsy on one of the Nigerian victims. Ten days later she was stricken.

The courageous missionary physician was buried in the SIM cemetery near Jos. Reverend Byang Kato, then General Secretary of the Evangelical Churches of West Africa, recalled that she was only one of many missionaries who had died while serving Africa. "Every missionary grave is an addition to the debt we owe," he said. "These deaths are not in vain."

The discovery of the Lassa Virus created world-wide excitement among medical researchers. Reported Dr. Frame, the SIM consultant:

> This fever likely explains many mysterious deaths of missionaries in West Africa over many years. These deaths were vaguely ascribed to fever, typhus, and cerebral malaria. We are trying to evaluate Lassa Virus in relation to large-scale epidemics of a mysterious fever that have been reported from time to time in the areas along the southern borders of the Sahara. This germ may be also related to certain epidemics of a fever with bleeding tendencies reported from the Middle East.

The researchers searched diligently for the carrying agent. After they determined the disease was not transmitted by insects, mouse droppings became the most likely suspect. Identifiable cases popped up in other African countries. Some survived; some did not. It appeared that some Africans had built up a sort of immunity to the disease.

For a long time only plasma antibodies from Lily Pinneo were available to known victims. Then as the dedicated laboratory sleuths were able to positively identify the fever in other persons, more plasma became available. Many lives were saved.

Almost nine years after the first missionary casualty, SIM lab technician Elsbeth Lenherr became ill in Benin (formerly Dahomey). The Swiss missionary's sickness was first diagnosed as hepatitis and she was flown to Jos for further treatment. She died the day after arriving. Samples of her blood shipped to the National Communicable Diseases Center in Atlanta, Georgia "proved conclusively" that the cause of death was Lassa Fever.

The search for more information and a substance for mass inoculation for Lassa Fever continues.

The Biafra Tragedy

Nigeria, like other African countries, is a babel of tribes and languages. Following a long period of relative peace, religious, tribal, and political differences led to a coup and then a counter-coup. This was followed by the breakaway of the eastern region into a self-proclaimed state called Biafra. Bloody civil war raged from 1967 until 1970 when the Biafrans surrendered.

Many Nigerian Christians were killed in this war, though their faith was not a primary factor. Missionaries did not take sides and were able to participate in a mammoth relief effort that saved thousands of Biafrans from starvation.

A Missionary Church

The Nigerian church emerged from the war with honor, and during the 1970's has continued to grow rapidly. The two largest groups are the Nigerian Baptist Convention and SIM-related Evangelical Churches of West Africa (ECWA). Both bodies have mounted extraordinary mission efforts to reach Nigerians and Africans in neighboring countries.

ECWA's Nigerian Evangelical Missionary Society now has 254 Nigerian missionaries and expects to have 300 soon. Fully supported by ECWA churches, they work in unevangelized areas. Additionally, over five hundred trained ECWA evangelists spread the gospel to still unreached peoples of Nigeria.

Not surprisingly, today over a third of Nigeria's population professes Christianity. This includes most of the nation's top political leadership.

GHANA—BORN IN SACRIFICE

Christianity in Ghana (formerly the Gold Coast), as in Nigeria, was born in sacrifice. Four pioneer missionaries of the Basel mission landed at Accra in 1827. Three died within a few weeks. The fourth survived until 1831. Three more arrived, but again in a few weeks there was only one man left alive.

The first Methodist missionary, Joseph Dunwell, arrived in 1836 and lived six months. Two couples followed, the Wrigleys and Harrops. The Harrops and Mrs. Wrigley died within a month. Stricken himself and in agony, Mr. Wrigley sent a last plea for help. "Come out to this hell," he begged, "if it is only to die here." He did not live out the year.

Successors of both missions and representatives of later agencies did succeed in planting a solid core of Christianity on Ghanian soil.

The Dark Shadow of Marxism

In 1957 Ghana became the first black African colony granted independence by Britain. Political firebrand Kwame Nkrumah was elected president. Nkrumah had studied in a Roman Catholic mission school, as well as in France, Britain, and the United States. While living in Philadelphia, he had become embittered at racial segregation and discrimination.

Although Nkrumah termed himself a Marxian socialist, he also called himself a non-denominational Christian and not a communist. By 1961 he had made himself into a cultic messiah "equal to Moses, Christ, Marx, Lenin, and Ghandi." He fostered guerrilla warfare in neighboring countries and conducted purges of political opponents. The Christians who perished in these purges died primarily because of their identification with groups opposed to the dictator.

Nkrumah's Christian profession to the contrary, Ghanian church leaders did feel threatened. Several leading missionaries, including the Anglican bishop of Accra, were expelled. Church attendance plummeted.

In 1966, while Nkrumah was visiting in Peking, Ghanian military officers took power. Seven of the eight coup leaders were practicing Christians. Unable to return home, Nkrumah landed in Guinea where dictator Sekou Toure proclaimed him his co-ruler. Nkrumah's popularity waned in socialist Guinea. He was never able to return home.

Ghana today continues under military rule. But it is not regarded as a subversive threat to neighbors. Over forty per cent of the population is classified Christian.

REPUBLIC OF SIERRA LEONE—THE "HUT TAX REBELLION"

This South Carolina-sized colony that became known as "the white man's graveyard" was the earliest Protestant mission field in West Africa. The first two missionaries were sent by the Baptist Missionary Society in 1795.

Christians in Sierra Leone were never a target for intensive persecution. However, there was one tragic missionary massacre in a violent tribal rebellion against British assumption of authority over tribal lands in the interior.

In 1896 the British governor at Freetown arbitrarily proclaimed the hinterland region a British protectorate. Administrators were appointed and members of the Frontier Police Force sent into areas where hitherto only missionaries and traders had gone.

The chiefs of the various tribal domains felt humiliated. Slave owners themselves, they had long resented the colony of freed slaves established at Freetown. Many had lost runaways to the colony. Now former slaves were coming back as Frontier Police to harass and arrest their former owners.

The chiefs had been unhappy with the missionaries for a different reason. Some of the young people educated in the mission schools had come to despise their illiterate and pagan elders. And Christian converts were questioning the custom of polygamy. Some of the chiefs claimed as many as three hundred wives.

The last straw was a British property tax based on the size of native huts for administration of the "protected" areas. Chief Bai Bureh, a chief of the Temne people in the north, refused to pay. The Frontier Police began forcibly collecting the taxes, plus sizable commission fees. Temne warriors sprang on the police and the fight was on. A few weeks later the Mende chiefs in the south joined the rebellion, vowing to push the whites into the sea.

Bai Bureh and neighboring chiefs protected missionaries and traders in their territories on the grounds that they were guests. But they could not prevent the killing of Reverend W. J. Humphrey, the principal of Fourah Bay College in Freetown which had been established to train Africans for the Anglican priesthood.

The Rotifunk Massacre

No European was safe in Mende country. Friendly chiefs, knowing of the danger, had to force some reluctant missionaries into canoes. However, the concerned chiefs were unable to get to the American United Brethren's Rotifunk station in time.

An African who escaped told the grim story:

> We started to walk to Sierra Leone [the original colony at Freetown], but had gone only half a mile when we met warriors who blocked the way. The Reverend Mr. Cain tried to frighten them by firing a revolver over their heads, but seeing they were deter-

mined to do mischief, he cast his revolver away and said that he would not have anybody's blood on his hands.

The natives then seized the party and Misses Hatfield, Archer and Kent, stripped them of their clothing, dragged them back to the mission home in front of which the "war boys" cut down the Reverend Mr. Cain and hacked him to death, and then treated Miss Archer and Miss Kent the same way. Miss Hatfield, who was very ill, was thrown on a barbed wire netting, and finally her throat was cut. Mrs. Cain escaped to the bush with a native girl, but the warriors went out seeking for them and afterwards killed them.

Before the year's end British forces, with their superior fire power, had put down the "Hut Tax Rebellion" as it was called. They imprisoned Bai Bureh and hung twenty-nine other dissident chiefs. Bai Bureh and those chiefs are national heroes in Sierra Leone today.

Partly because of conflicts with British colonists and partly because of Islam's close identification with tribal customs, only six per cent of Sierra Leone's population is Christian today, compared to twenty-eight per cent Muslim. However, Christian mission agencies have been giving more attention to Sierra Leone in recent years. About 165 missionaries are now in the country. The Wesleyan Church has the largest representation.

CAMEROON—NO MARTYRS UNTIL 1978

Cameroon, lying just south of Nigeria, has a checkered history of colonialism but has experienced less violence than any of its neighbors. It belonged to Germany before World War I, then after the German defeat, was apportioned between victorious Britain and France. French Cameroon became independent in 1960. Part of British Cameroon voted to join Nigeria. The remainder joined independent Cameroon.

Baptists, Lutherans, and Presbyterians built up strong constituencies in Cameroon. But it was during World War I, while the missionaries were absent, that the church grew most rapidly. Today about thirty-five per cent of the 7.6 million people scattered among a melange of two hundred tribes, are Christians. The North American Baptist General Conference has the largest missionary force—about sixty—in the struggling country.

Missionaries and national evangelists have pushed steadily into the interior taking the gospel to tribes who still practice witchcraft and make animal offerings to dead ancestors. There has always been the risk of confronting fanatics steeped in ancient pagan rituals such as human sacrifice. Yet not until May, 1978, did the first martyrdoms occur.

The victims were fifty-nine-year-old Ernest Erickson and his wife Miriam. Natives of Minnesota, they had served in Cameroon for thirty–four years as representatives of the small nine thousand member Lutheran Brethren Church of America. Details of their deaths are still not known. But from the condition of their bodies, other missionaries speculated that they might have been victims of spirit worshipers.

Whatever the dangers and the consequences to health, missionaries and African Christians will continue ministering in West Africa. They are spurred on by brave pioneers of the past who risked all for the sake of the gospel.

MOZAMBIQUE AND ANGOLA:

Former Portuguese Possessions

The trail of martyrs' blood widens in Angola and Mozambique. In these two former Portuguese possessions, thousands upon thousands of Christians have perished in the twentieth century.

Seeds of Trouble

Portugal was the first of the European colonial powers in Africa and among the worst. Tiny Portuguese Guinea on the western bulge of Africa was claimed in 1446, Mozambique in lower east Africa in 1483, and Angola in lower west Africa in the 1500's. Portugal hoped to exploit rich lodes of gold and silver. These and other metals were found, but the greatest riches came from slaves. The cruel traffic in human cargo persisted long after foreign pressure forced Portugal to pass a law abolishing slavery in 1869. Only the name was changed. Under a new "contract labor law" African adult males were required to work for Portuguese employers who could deduct from their paycheck the cost of fines, rent, overdue taxes or any other cleverly devised charge. Employers could also send their contract laborers to neighboring countries. In this way hundreds of thousands were sent to toil in South Africa's sweltering mines. They were given no choice. Any African not under contract could be arrested for vagrancy.

After World War II, Portugal defined her African colonies as "provinces" to which citizens could immigrate and buy land. On paper, any African could become a Portuguese citizen by learning the Portuguese language and adopting the culture of the mother country. In reality, few Africans could. Portuguese settlers always ended up with the best land.

So it was that disease, immorality, drunkenness, and ignorance pervaded the colonies. For instance, as late as 1955 there were only six secondary schools for almost five million people in Angola, which covers an area nearly twice the size of Texas.

In all of this, church and state were intertwined. At the height of the slave trade, Catholic bishops blessed cargoes of chained Africans departing for Portuguese Brazil. Catholic institutions were provided labor pools. A single monastery in Luanda, the capital of Angola, had at one time twelve thousand slaves.

Catholic authorities tried to block the entry of Protestant missionaries. Not until 1939 were the first evangelical workers allowed to enter Portuguese Guinea. Today only a half dozen serve there. Missionaries managed to enter Angola (1878) and Mozambique (1880) earlier. The evangelical witness met with huge success in these colonies. But in both countries the Church developed through chafing restrictions and, at times, bitter persecution.

MOZAMBIQUE — FREEDOM CRIES OUT

Mozambique was stirred by the independence fever that swept Africa in the 1950's and 1960's. Mozambique nationals pressed Portugal for promises of freedom. But the Portuguese dictator felt the African provinces were too valuable to relinquish.

Mozambiquan freedom fighters asked western democracies for help. But the United States and Britain had commitments to Portugal through the NATO alliance in addition to heavy investments in apartheid South Africa which supported Portugal. To their chagrin, the nationalists saw western arms going to Portugal. They turned to communist countries for arms.

The Mozambique independence movement was backed by Protestants who had suffered under the Portuguese. Some pastors joined the Mozambique Liberation Front (FRELIMO), the leading organization crusading for freedom. But while most Protestant missionaries sympathized, their denominations and agencies in the United States and Britain adopted a hands-off policy. The World Council of Churches did provide some aid and was accused of helping the communist cause in Africa.

The Vatican had a concordat with Portugal and until 1970 the Catholic hierarchy gave no official attention to the rebels in Mozambique, Angola, and Portuguese Guinea. Suddenly in June, 1970, Pope Paul received in special audience, the leaders of the movements. Portugal instantly protested, but the die was cast. A year later members of the White Fathers Catholic missionary order denounced their church in Mozambique for its identification with Portuguese rule. Portuguese authorities immediately ordered them out of the country.

From this time on the Portuguese government began arresting church leaders, Catholic and Protestant, suspected of rebel sympathies.

Presbyterian Leaders Are Arrested

On June 13 and 14, 1972, the Portuguese security police arrested several hundred Mozambiquans. Among them were about twenty members and leaders of the Presbyterian church in Mozambique, including its president, Reverend Zedequias Manganhela. No official cause was given for the surprise arrests. Prisoners picked up at their homes were given no chance to take warm clothing for the cold nights of the southern African winter. Some of the Presbyterian church leaders were aged and in need of medical attention, but were denied permission to take any medicines with them. They were ferried to an infamous detention camp for political prisoners near Lourenco Marques, the capital.

When news of the arrests reached the general secretary of the World Alliance of Reformed Churches, the Rev. Edmond Perret, he expressed "disquiet at the serious situation created for the Presbyterian church in Mozambique by the arrest of its leaders." Police authorities responded that their target was not the Presbyterian church, but individuals involved in "certain liberation movements." Portuguese officials later told a group of visiting Swiss clergymen that one charge related to "the subversive way in which one of the Presbyterian church leaders had interpreted the autonomy of his church." By the end of November, however, official charges still had not been announced.

Suicide or Murder?

On December 12 the wife of Jose Sidumo, an arrested church elder over sixty years old, went to the camp to try to locate her husband. She was told to come back the next day. Then she was told he had hung himself in his cell on July 21. But prison authorities refused to disclose where he had been buried. A few days later the Portuguese governor-general of Mozambique denied the suicide story and claimed the elder had died of natural causes.

A few days later a report leaked out that the President of the Presbyterian church in Mozambique, Pastor Manganhela, age sixty, had committed suicide on December 11 following six months of isolation and interrogation by the security police. People who knew him refused to believe the story, and some Portuguese authorities agreed with them.

World-Wide Protests

Verification of this second death brought world-wide indignation upon the Portuguese. The director of Portugal's cabinet, writing on behalf of the prime minister, replied quickly that an investigation had "confirmed" that the suicide "was entirely due to a state of nervous depression."

More protests followed from international agencies. Demands were made for an independent investigation of the clergyman's suicide with the understanding that "human rights" would be "henceforth respected in Mozambique" and that "legal assistance" be given to the "prisoners." United States Presbyterian leader, Dr. William P. Thompson, seconded these concerns. He also deplored the fact that Portuguese authorities in Mozambique had long been "impervious to world opinion which called for an end to their anachronistic and harsh rule in Africa."

A Belgian radio commentator opined that only two conclusions were possible regarding the church leader's death: "Either he was murdered in prison by persons unknown, or the six months of total isolation and the pressure of the kind of interrogation, for which the white authorities there are known, had become so unbearable that he laid hands on himself."

Catholic Missionaries Speak Up

Pressure came on the Vatican when, in an open letter to the pope, a former Portuguese Catholic missionary in Mozambique, Father Luis Afonsoda Costa, expressed "sorrow and apprehension" over the death of Pastor Manganhela. The shock came when Father Costa disclosed that he had earlier sent to the Vatican secretary of state a dossier detailing "the conditions under which hundreds of political prisoners live [in Mozambique], of torture, massacres of civilians, the destruction of villages, and the creation of concentration camps in which people are interned by the colonial authorities." He had accused the Vatican of "not having come to the defence of these people and their legitimate aspirations," and appealed to the pope "to break the silence in order to defend our African brethren against the injustices of colonial oppression."

On New Year's Eve, 1972, Presbyterian church authorities announced the release of thirty–seven of their churchmen from the dread prison. They regretted that no information was available about the fate of the several hundred other prisoners arrested with the Presbyterians.

The furor among Catholics continued. In July, 1973, news leaked that Catholic priests in Mozambique had presented their bishops with documented evidence, including pictures, of massacres of whole villages by Portuguese soldiers in 1971 and 1972. The bishops had taken no action. The priest courier who had delivered the evidence had been arrested by Portuguese police. Another priest who had been speaking in Europe about Portuguese massacres and tortures was suddenly transferred to Peru.

Behind-the-scenes maneuvering by Vatican officials and Portuguese bishops failed to silence the former missionaries. Father Jose Roman, for example, told *The Observer* of London:

> The present state of affairs in Mozambique is no
> more than the explosion and unleashing of a long
> history of oppression, repression and violence against
> the black population by Portuguese colonialists
> under the pretence of Western and "Christian" civilization. The Church has also been involved in this
> history, either through its collaboration or through
> its silence. The Church . . . is now suffering in its
> own flesh what the blacks of Mozambique have been
> suffering for a very long time.

A Coup in Lisbon

Bitter fighting continued until a military coup in Lisbon overthrew the government of Portugal. The new Portuguese government quickly granted Mozambique provisional independence in 1974. A year later Mozambique gained full independence. The head of FRELIMO, Samora Machel, age forty-one, became the country's first president.

For awhile there was cheering by Mozambiquan Christians. The jubilation faded when President Machel called for development of a Marxist state and announced that the government was taking over even the private ownership of homes.

Martyrs in the Future?

Further government actions cast a deeper pall. Several Catholic priests were deported. Members of ten Mozambique denominations, including members of the Church of the Nazarene, who were associated with the largest mission in the country, were arrested and charged as plotters against the state. Infant baptism was banned.

Government spokesmen claimed that the policy of the new regime was equal treatment of all denominations and a guarantee of religious freedom. Observers viewed this religious freedom as "a nebulous thing" without the "rights of Christians to share beliefs, pass them on to children, or express them in regular worship with others." Further analysis indicated that the new country under President Machel might be constitutionally neutral on religious practice but ideologically and factually antireligious, and especially anti-Catholic. It was noted that Machel had been born of poor Protestant parents and had been forced to become a Catholic to continue his education.

As the debate continues, some missionaries and church leaders are reported to be in jail. None are known to have been martyred by the new Marxist government.

How have Mozambique Christians been reacting? One evangelical leader said to a Marxist government official, "I will share what I have, I will give what I have, I will help you all I can, and sacrifice all I can, not because there is a rifle in my back, but because I love you, and because we love God."

PEOPLE'S REPUBLIC OF ANGOLA – OPPRESSION AND EVANGELISM

Angola is the tragedy of Mozambique and much more: it is a history of more than four centuries of oppression by Portugal, seen in seventy per cent illiteracy, rampant disease, abject misery and discrimination, and religious intolerance by the state-aligned Catholic Church.

But Angola was blessed with more evangelical mission work than Mozambique. English Baptists arrived in 1878 and by 1961, when guerrilla warfare began, they had opened 250 preaching-stations. The American Board of Commissioners for Foreign Missions arrived in 1880, but won fewer than three hundred converts in the first twenty–five years. After 1914 the growth rate picked up and by 1961 they had fourteen hundred places of worship and thirty thousand members. Methodists attained about the same growth during this period. The Plymouth Brethren opened 145 assemblies and 350 preaching places. Canadian Baptists, the United Church of Canada, the African Evangelical Fellowship, and the South African General Mission came later than the three largest mission groups, but also found Angolans responsive.

The Cost of Pioneering

One of the most remarkable missionary pioneers to Angola was Frederick Arnot. Inspired by Livingstone, Arnot went to Africa in 1881 without the backing of any mission board.

In his first journeys across Angola he frequently saw the bleached bones of slaves beside the trail. People he met recalled that when slaves became sick their hands were hacked off to facilitate removal of their shackles and they were thrown into the bushes to die. If a woman with a small child happened to die, the child was killed by swinging its head against a tree. Realizing he could never evangelize such a vast area alone, he went home for recruits.

Trouble and tragedy hit Arnot's return party before they reached the African coast. Robert J. Johnstone died of yellow fever. Two other men died in one night, twelve days' inland from the coast. When the survivors finally reached the first mission station, a fourth recruit was bitten by a mad dog and died from rabies. These were only the first to die along "The Beloved Strip"—the chain of preaching stations and schools across Central Angola. Arnot, who survived, died in 1914.

The Mysterious Death of an Angolan Believer

Plymouth Brethren missionary T. Ernest Wilson, who provided many details about Frederick Arnot, shares these circumstances about twentieth-century martyrdom in Angola. One of the first Angolan Protestant martyrs was a former witch doctor named Chiteta. A member of the wild Chokwe tribe, Chiteta built a grass hut near the house where the

Wilsons lived. After attending services for several weeks, Chiteta and his wife Chambishi publicly announced they had accepted Jesus as Savior.

A few days later one of Chiteta's legs suddenly became swollen for no discernible reason. Also a piece of bone broke through his five-year-old daughter's hand. He took this for the power of witchcraft and immediately removed some hidden fetishes from his hut. The next Sunday he carried the bundle to church and publicly dumped them in the flames. He told the missionary, "There is a saying among the Chokwes, 'Throw away the honeycomb and the bees will leave you.' "

Missionary Wilson left on a trip. When he returned, Chiteta and his family were gone. Neighbors told Wilson that they had taken sick and some men had carried them back to their home village.

The next morning Wilson and three African believers walked the twenty-four miles to the village. When he asked the old men in the palaver house about Chiteta, they pointed to a grass hut. There the missionary found the ex-witch doctor. His body was naked and mutilated and he had been dead for several days. Through further questioning, Wilson learned he had been poisoned.

When villagers refused to help make a coffin, Wilson and his African companions tenderly wrapped the decaying corpse in a blanket and buried it in a grave in the forest. The village headman would not even accompany them to the grove. "The dead man followed the teaching of the white man and this is what has become of it," he declared.

Where were the dead man's wife and children? Again, Wilson inquired and was told she had been married off to a crippled pagan as payment for an unredeemed debt. One of the children, a four-year-old girl, had been poisoned. Others would die, the villagers predicted, because they had insulted the spirits of their ancestors and become Christians. Before the affair was over, several other members of Chiteta's family did die under mysterious circumstances.

Portuguese Were Unfriendly to Protestants

Portuguese administrators and police tended to treat the Protestant missionaries as if they were invaders. Young men frequently disappeared from the mission school and the missionaries would later learn they had been "drafted" for contract labor. In one case, Wilson made a respectful and diplomatic plea to the nearest Portuguese administrator for a young man who was the sole support of his mother. The missionary was sharply rebuffed. "If you ever interfere again in government affairs," the administrator warned, "you will be expelled from the country."

Portuguese "Justice"

But all previous trouble was child's play when compared to the sufferings experienced by Angolan Christians after guerrilla fighting began in the 1960's. Any Angolan who showed the slightest inclination to disobey a government order or who could be linked to a guerrilla band, was an immediate candidate for arrest and perhaps execution.

Sakaya, a gifted Chokwe evangelical teacher, and his wife had one cherished son whom they named Samuel. He was educated in mission schools and later became the school teacher in the village where his preacher–father was the headman. In the early days of the guerrilla fighting, Samuel heard that Portuguese soldiers were on their way to the village. He became frightened and ran away. A little later a jeep loaded with soldiers drew up and asked for the headman. Upon learning that the headman's son had run away, they took Sakaya out and shot him.

Full-Scale War Begins

The first big uprising came in Luanda, the capital, on February 4, 1961. A crowd of frustrated, poorly armed Angolans stormed a hated jail and police post. They were driven off and seven were killed. The next day they attacked again, suffering even greater casualties.

Portuguese police and troops, reinforced by armed Portuguese civilians, began killing Africans wherever they could find them. Trucks rumbled behind the revenge seekers, picking up bodies like garbage for dumping in a mass grave. After the killings tapered off, frightened Angolans secretly sought out missionaries to give details of the massacre.

The Angolans responded on March 15 when sullen, angry Africans, who had been hiding in the forests of northern Angola, took bloody revenge. They burst into the homes of Portuguese planters and officials, killing and mutilating some two hundred men, women, and children. From this time there was no peace in Angola.

Most Protestants, who numbered twelve per cent of Angola's population, sympathized with the revolutionaries.

Thousands of young men joined the guerrilla armies. Most pastors gave moral support. Some encouraged their parishioners to give material aid. Some who did not believe Christians should take sides in war and politics were persecuted by both the Portuguese and guerrillas.

The Guerrilla Leaders Were Protestants

As the fighting intensified, the revolutionaries broke into three factions centered around three leaders. Each leader had a strong Protestant background and had received backing from his particular denominational constituency.

Holden Roberto, head of the National Front for the Liberation of Angola (FINLA), was a Baptist, grandson of a minister, and once taught in a British Baptist mission school.

Jonas M. Savimbi, leader of the National Union for Total Independence of Angola (UNITA), was an active member of the United Church of Christ and had close ties with American Board missionaries. He had studied medicine in Lisbon and earned a doctorate in political science in Switzerland through the support of church scholarships.

Agostinho Neto, head of the Popular Movement for Liberation of Angola (MPLA), was the son of a Methodist minister, and also a product of Methodist mission schools. Neto studied medicine on a Methodist scholarship in Portugal and later served as secretary to Angola's Methodist bishop.

Marxism and Methodism

Roberto and Savimbi worked together in FINLA before Savimbi split off to form UNITA. Even after that, they both looked to the western democracies for aid. Neto and MPLA depended on the help of the Soviet Union and Cuba. Accordingly MPLA ideology took on a more Marxist tone. Some observers felt Neto had been influenced by certain Methodist missionaries schooled in "liberation theology." The Soviets provided massive arms aid to MPLA and Cuba airlifted troops. Zaire, South Africa, China, and a few other nations provided aid to FINLA and UNITA. But the United States, wary of another Vietnam, gave little more than moral support to the non-Marxist movements.

Christian Casualties

While world headlines played up potential big-power nuclear war over Angola, the people suffered. Most Protestant suffering resulted from Portuguese repression.

Over two hundred thousand Angolan refugees, fleeing Portuguese repression in the north, flooded into western Zaire. British Baptist missionaries, who established relief centers, heard harrowing tales of civilians being strafed and bombed by Portuguese planes and attacked by soldiers who showed no mercy to the aged, the infirm, or children.

A Protestant pastor was killed for no other reason than that he was a minister in the Cuanza Norte District. "Before killing him," his horrified daughter reported, "they tortured him by cutting off his limbs." She had escaped by hiding in the bush.

A nineteen-year-old girl told British Baptist missionaries that her father, Vemba Mateus, a teacher–evangelist in the village of Kidilu, and many other church leaders and teachers had been arrested in March, 1961. Her mother and ten children, she said, escaped into the forest and had had no word of her father since.

T. Ernest Wilson recalls that a disgruntled native teacher, who had been dismissed from his post in a mission school for misconduct, had spitefully told Portuguese authorities the Christians in his village favored Angolan independence. Eight church leaders were arrested, beaten, and tortured to extract confessions. When it was clear they could not be made to submit, they were lined up on the edge of a pit and shot, one by one, through the neck. As the shots rang out, one of the younger men started to sing in his tribal language,

> Be not dismayed whate'er betide,
> God will take care of you...

Methodists were made special targets. For example, Reverend Filipe Antonio de Freitas, an Angolan clergyman, was slain at his home near Quessua Mission Station. In reporting his death, the Methodist bishop said he did not know how many Angolan Methodist workers had lost their lives in the fighting in the area.

The Communist-Backed Faction Won

After fifteen years of savage fighting, while western countries refused to intervene, the communist-backed MPLA faction gained the upper hand and won control of the capital, Luanda, as well as other major cities. But the war did not stop. FINLA and UNITA soldiers mounted a guerrilla war against MPLA. The quarter million Angolan refugees that had been in Zaire returned, only to face starvation. Christian relief groups were unable to obtain agreements from the three revolutionary movements to bring in supplies.

Christianity Under Marxism

Before the communist MPLA had captured the capital, a veteran Protestant missionary had predicted: "If the Communist MPLA wins out, missions will get rough weather."

He was apparently right. Declared Neto, named president by the dominant MPLA: "No [Communist] Party member can be a church member, and no church member can be a member of the Party." Neto also forecast: "Twenty years from now we expect no churches to exist in Angola."

Nevertheless, Neto has permitted a surprising amount of religious freedom "in this period of transition to scientific socialism." Churches function freely, except in areas where bush fighting continues. Hundreds of people are reportedly being baptized every Sunday. Bibles are still being sold. Church leaders can travel and hold conferences. Some of the foreign missionaries expelled by the Portuguese have been allowed back in. Others are hoping to enter.

The Methodists, who are the most favored religious group in the country, and the World Council of Churches are promoting an MPLA-favored Angola National Council of Churches. Conservative evangelicals have countered with their Angola Association of Evangelicals, which represents forty per cent of Angola's Protestants. Baptists decline to join either group.

Cuban troops remain in Angola. Neto's MPLA government strongly backs Soviet–Cuban policies in the rest of Africa. If MPLA is successful in holding off the rival groups, Angola could become as repressive as the Soviet Union toward evangelical Christianity. Angolan believers watch, pray, and work, knowing that many who are living now may be the martyrs of the future.

TANZANIA, KENYA, UGANDA:

Former British East Africa

Legendary land of Livingstone and Stanley; safaris and big game hunts; cockney accents under pith helmets; British administrators in tailored white suits shuffling papers under high ceilinged fans; four o'clock tea on shaded, expansive lawns, served by immaculate house servants; and Sunday morning church services with croquet in the afternoon. This was British East Africa for most whites before black revolutionaries unceremoniously rang down the curtain on colonialism forever. This vast area of mountains, lakes, and steaming jungles, twice the size of Texas, became Tanzania, Kenya, and Uganda.

THE UNITED REPUBLIC OF TANZANIA — STRONGHOLD OF LUTHERANS

Tanzania is the largest of the three nations. Bordered on the east by the Indian Ocean and the west by beautiful Lake Tanganyika and the tiny countries of Rwanda and Burundi, Tanzania is steeped in antiquity. Greek mariners visited the coast before Christ was born. Arabs from the Persian Gulf established city-states in the eighth century. After the fifteenth century, Portugal, Germany, and Britain claimed the territory successively, before independence in 1961.

The Arabs brought Islam; the Portuguese, Catholicism; and the Germans and British, Protestantism. The earliest missions were inspired by Livingstone's visit to Oxford and Cambridge in 1857. He said: "I beg to direct your attention to Africa. I know that in a few years I shall be cut off in that country, which is now open; do not let it shut again. . . . I leave it with you."

The first to go was the indomitable German Johann Ludwig Krapf, who established the first station on the coast at Mombasa, Kenya, slightly northeast of the present Tanzania border. After burying his wife and only child, Krapf wrote his home supporters with fevered fingers, "The hour is approaching when you will be called to convert Africa, beginning from the east coast."

Today there are about two hundred fifty missionaries in Tanzania. The population of sixteen million is about equally apportioned between Christians, Muslims, and tribal animists. The country is the second largest Lutheran mission field in the world, with a Lutheran community of three hundred thousand. Over twenty more missions are active in Tanzania, the largest being the Southern Baptists and the Africa Inland Mission.

There have been no Christian martyrs to violence in mainland Tanzania. Unlike many other new African nations, Tanzania was birthed in relative peace. The founding president, Julius Nyerere, is still in power. Both a mystic and a pragmatist, Nyerere once taught in a Catholic mission school. An avowed socialist who preaches a stern work ethic, Nyerere has managed to keep strong links with the Soviet Union, China, and the United States.

"Sowing in Tears"

Tropical disease is another matter. Scores of foreign missionaries are buried in cemeteries in Dar es Salaam, the beautiful harbor capital of Tanzania. A historian wrote of them: "One generation of missionaries after another have stuck to their sweltering stations in faith and out of [the] sowing in tears has blossomed a noble springtime of God's."

Typical of such persevering missionaries was Reverend Ralph Hult, a Lutheran minister, who was first a missionary to Nigeria, then Tanzania. When German Lutherans had to leave Tanzania during World War II, Pastor Hult was home in Missouri. He left his family and took a ship back to Africa "to carry out John Krapf's vision." The vessel *Zamzam* was sunk in midocean by German raiders on May 19, 1941. Hult and other missionaries on board were picked up by German ships. Returning to New York, he immediately took passage on another vessel.

Hult had hoped to be joined by his wife and the youngest of their ten children. After Pearl Harbor, he had to be satisfied with letters, and the mail was never reliable. Once after having not received a letter for five months, he wrote his beloved Gertrude, "At times I am almost sick with my longing to see you."

In March, 1943, the family received a terse telegram stating that their loved one had died from malaria.

Daughter Ingrid, a student at Wahoo Luther Academy in Nebraska, was the first to know. Her father was an alumnus of the school and had been a frequent subject of student prayer. The academy pastor called the older students together and told them of his death. "Who will carry on where he left off?" he asked. Ten young men came forward. Of the ten, seven eventually became foreign missionaries and the other three, pastors in the United States.

The family named their home in Missouri "Dar es Salaam" (meaning "Haven of Peace") and in the living room hung a picture of the harbor city where their father had died. After three years, the mother, now a grandmother, volunteered to serve in Bolivia as matron of a home for missionaries' children. When friends wondered about her decision to go and take her younger children, she said, "I'm convinced that this business of carrying the gospel to all the world is so important that even we grandmothers have to go."

All ten children became outstanding Christians. Two became missionaries to Africa. Ingrid married a young German pastor, Walter Trobisch, and served in Cameroon. She later wrote the story of her family in *On Our Way Rejoicing!* (Harper & Row). Her husband, Walter, wrote the best seller, *I Loved a Girl,* based on his marriage counseling with young Africans.

Several years after arriving in Africa, Ingrid was able to visit Dar es Salaam and her father's grave. The African pastor who knew him best recalled for her his passing. "He died because of love. It was love that prompted him to make that last safari to the outstations after he got malaria. If there was a heavy load to carry," the African continued, "he always picked up the heaviest end. He never dictated to us. He set us an example."

Beside Pastor Hult's grave Ingrid noticed the stone of

young Pastor Bryson. He had lived only a few months after coming to succeed her father.

Island of Terror

The coastal island of Zanzibar, which federated with Tanzania in 1963, has been less peaceful than the mainland. From 1964 to 1972 the tyrant Sheikh Abeid Amani Rashid Karume was allowed to rule the former haven of pirates in the fashion of a despot. He slaughtered thousands of people, mostly Arab Muslims, while releasing hundreds of common criminals. Any teen-age girl that caught his fancy was game for his harem. Protesting male relatives were flogged, imprisoned, or deported. The despot was assassinated while playing cards in 1972. Zanzibar is quieter now.

KENYA — CRUCIBLE OF CONFLICT

The story of Kenya is tragically different than that of mainland Tanzania. The clashes between Europeans and Africans have been violent and bitter. Christians have suffered immensely, although only one missionary has died.

The gospel was pioneered in Kenya, as in Tanzania, by missionaries challenged by Livingstone, and later, Krapf. The sacrifice of the pioneers is amply illustrated by the toll taken of the first workers of the Africa Inland Mission. AIM entered Kenya in 1895 with the landing of Peter Cameron Scott and seven other workers. Scott survived only fourteen months. One by one the others fell prey to African diseases until only one was left. Finally he gave up and returned home. A second force landed a few years later and survived. Today AIM has over two hundred missionaries in Kenya and is the largest mission in the country.

The Circumcision Controversy

As in other African countries, there were tribal rebellions against European domination from time to time. Revolts in 1905 and 1908 by the Gusii people ended disastrously. Tribal spears were no match for European rifles. Disappointed Africans turned to a movement known as the Mumbo cult which advocated a return to the old ways and forecasted the departure of the Europeans and the coming of a golden millennial age when the lost glory of the tribes would shine again.

The Christian teaching that wives and daughters were equal to men before God and deserved respect as individuals was bound to clash with one of the most barbaric of the old ways—female circumcision. From a humane perspective there could be no defense for the coming-of-age rite. Older women, using crude, unsterilized instruments operated on the young girls. When the wound healed, hard scar tissue formed at the opening of the birth canal. This made subsequent childbirth hard and dangerous and resulted in many deaths at first births. There were also risks of infection and complications. Not to mention the agony the young girls suffered, which was excruciating. Every missionary in a tribal village had heard their cries.

The missionaries first tried to get girls to come into the mission hospital where the village circumciser could perform the rite under the supervision of a trained doctor. But it increased the workload and made no sense to the doctors, who began to crusade against performing the rite for medical reasons. Opposition also grew rapidly in Protestant missions and churches. Government reports called the rite "horrible mutilation," but the British administrators took no legislative actions.

The Protestants pressed on. In March, 1929, a conference of representatives of African churches among the Kikuyus, Kenya's largest tribe, pronounced the custom "evil" and resolved "that all Christians submitting to it should be suspended by churches everywhere."

Elders of the Kikuyu Central Association (KCA), the dominant national political group in Kenya, immediately condemned the conference action. Opposition also rose within the churches, prompting the purging of some church elders. The missionaries took a hard line, demanding that all African teachers on mission payrolls accept the church rule on female circumcision and resign from the KCA until the association stopped its anti-Christian propaganda. Twelve teachers refused to comply and were fired.

In October, 1929, a scurrilous song aimed at the churches swept through the villages. Christians, known to be against the rite, were threatened. Schools were boycotted, school buildings raided, and some African parents abused for not surrendering their daughters. All the while, unappointed circumcisers roved around villages looking for girls who had not been circumcised.

A Brutal Missionary Murder

It was bound to happen. An elderly, deaf AIM missionary, Hilda Stumpf, was found choked to death. First reports said she had been killed by a thief. Then the real facts came out. She had been brutally mutilated in a fashion that pointed to the work of circumcision fanatics.

Miss Stumpf's shocking murder caused some of the tribal zealots to back off. But the deeper conflict between Africans and Europeans dragged on and culminated in the bloody Mau Mau rebellion of the 1950's.

What Caused the Mau Mau Rebellion?

The major issue which fueled the Mau Mau revolt was white ownership of land. In the early twentieth century white settlers had been allotted about one-fourth of the best land in the country on leases running for 999 years. Any European could receive up to 640 acres. An African could only hold a temporary occupation license on five acres for one year.

Africans resented the continuing political and economic control by the British and the system of forced labor under which thousands of Kenyans had been "drafted" into virtual slavery. Discontent had been rising rapidly since World War II. The Kenyan African National Union (KANU), successor to the banned KCA, was pressing for equal rights for all Kenyans.

The head of the KANU was Jomo Kenyatta, a witch doctor's son who had been educated in Scotch Presbyterian schools, then disciplined by his home congregation for impregnating an unmarried girl. Kenyatta had gone to England for further study. He had visited Moscow three times and returned to Kenya in 1946. Kenyatta and the KANU had sympathizers among some missionaries. Indeed, many said quietly that Kenyans had the right to control their own destiny.

The immediate incident which provoked the Mau Mau insurgency was the eviction in 1949 of sixteen thousand Kikuyu squatters from "British" land. Stories spread of a secret Mau Mau society, in which members took an oath to expel Europeans from the country.

The Violence Begins

Fights erupted in the villages between Mau Mau organizers and more conservative Kenyans. Cattle belonging to whites were found mutilated. Twenty-one Kikuyu rioters were killed outside a police station in Nairobi, the capital.

In October, 1952, the colonial government proclaimed a state of emergency. British troops were flown in from the Suez Canal Zone. Kenyatta and 182 other Africans were arrested and detained. Late in the month a European settler was found murdered, the first victim of the Mau Mau.

Before the violence was over nearly eight years later, some twelve thousand persons were dead. Some overseas press reports gave the impression that Europeans were being massacred. Actually, only thirty–two settlers and sixty–three other Europeans in armed units were killed. The rest were Africans, and most were killed by British military and the Kenyan police.

The Christian Martyrs

The Mau Maus claimed that ninety per cent of all male Kikuyus took the oath. Pressure was put on all to join the antiwhite, anti-Christian crusade. Mau Mau organizers swept into the villages rounding up the men. They ordered them to swear on the sacred oath-stone that if called upon, they would join in the killing of Europeans. Many professing Christians yielded. Many did not. Some of those who refused were beaten and their houses torched. Some were martyred. Many more cut ties with churches and missionaries for fear they would be killed.

A respected Christian chief was shot while traveling in his car. Another chief, who tried to break up a Mau Mau meeting, was hacked to pieces. Still another was assassinated as he lay in a hospital bed. Altogether, almost one thousand Christians lost their lives for standing against the Mau Maus.

Evangelism in the Prison Camps

Barbed wire barricades and volunteer guards of missionaries and African Christians helped British soldiers protect mission stations and homes. Not a single missionary was killed.

Before the trouble was over, seventy thousand Mau Maus were incarcerated in concentration camps. The British government recognized that force of arms could never overcome the movement. Missionaries and loyal national leaders were encouraged to provide special ministries for the prisoners. Thousands were converted, including a number of admitted Mau Mau killers.

As terrible as it was, the Mau Mau Rebellion forced Britain to grant self-government to Kenya in 1960. Kenyatta's party won the first election, but members refused to take office until Kenyatta was released. He was freed and became prime minister in 1963.

Kenyatta: Villain or Statesman?

Kenyatta's Africanization policy forced thousands of Asian shopkeepers and businessmen to leave Kenya. Many Britishers departed also. When Kenya was hit by drought in 1794, Kenyatta refused offers of United States aid.

Yet the "Burning Spear," as Africans called Kenyatta, pursued good relations with the missions and churches. His government did ban Jehovah's Witnesses and six smaller sects on grounds of endangering state security. But mainline denominational and faith missions operated with few restrictions. By the 1970's only Zaire and Nigeria had more foreign missionaries than Kenya. Fifty–eight per cent of the Kenyans termed themselves "Christian"; most said they were Protestants.

Belief that Kenya would go communist proved unfounded. Kenya, Kenyatta often said, was a free enterprise nation with Africans in control.

The old revolutionary lived into his eighties. The personality cult around him was so great that the Kenyan attorney general said even imagining his death could be punishable by execution. He died in August, 1978, leaving only six surviving African leaders who had led their nations to independence. He was succeeded by Daniel Moi, his vice president and a professing evangelical Christian. The martyrdom of Christians in the future is not expected here.

REPUBLIC OF UGANDA—NERO'S ROME REVISITED

Rivers of blood. Bodies floating like logs amidst hungry crocodiles. Execution cells littered with human eyes and teeth, the gory residue from the sledge-hammering of prisoners. Innocent civilians, whose only crime was to belong to an unfavored tribe, screaming in agony as their sex organs are ripped away.

This is Uganda, dark domain of "Big Daddy" Idi Amin, the "Nero" and "Hitler" of Africa, who is credited with killing one hundred thousand people in six years out of a population of only twelve million. The victims include political opponents; members of tribes that he sees as a threat to his despotic rule; residents of any city or village viewed with the slightest suspicion; and Christian lay leaders and clergy who dare criticize misuse of authority and suggest that the fat, swaggering dictator will one day be judged by God.

How the Gospel Came to Uganda

The story of how the gospel came to Uganda and the martyrdoms that resulted is familiar to Ugandan Christians. It
helps explain their joy and courage during the present tribulations under Idi Amin.

Henry Stanley, the newspaper man who found Livingstone and was converted to Christianity, was the first em-
issary of the gospel to enter the area. He reached Buganda,
the principal tribal kingdom, after a five month's journey
from the East African coast. As his boat touched the northern shore of Lake Victoria, a welcoming party from the Bugandan capital of Rubaga fired a salute, waved flags, and
shouted greetings, while suspicious Arab traders glared from
afar. After proper introductions from court officials, he was
quickly ushered to the king's house by two royal pages.

Stanley met a tall, thin, smiling black man, dressed in a
long, white, gold-embroidered tunic worn under a handsome
black robe. King Mutesa I was a type of emperor, with kings
of other tribes under him. He had the power of life and death
over his subjects and a sizable army and fleet of war canoes
to back up his royal commands.

Stanley announced that he had come with a book that
told about a Savior. Through an interpreter, King Mutesa responded that visitors from the north—Muslim Arabs—had
already come with their book, the Holy *Koran.* "They say
their book is best," the king declared. "How are we to know
yours is better?" When Stanley presented his arguments, the
king said, "I am like a man sitting in darkness. All I ask is
that I be taught how to see."

Stanley sent a letter to England quoting the king's plea.
It was published in the London *Daily Telegraph* in 1875.
"Oh, that some pious, practical missionary would come
here," Stanley exclaimed. "What a harvest ripe for the sickle
of civilization!"

Within eight days thousands of English pounds were do-
nated for the first mission advance. The Church Missionary
Society quickly commissioned twenty-seven-year old Alexander Mackay, a bachelor and a Scottish engineer, to head a
party of eight. Their plans were to land in Zanzibar and hire
an escort that would take them to Uganda. But they had
hardly reached the coastal island when Mackay was seriously injured by a wagon that fell on his leg. He encouraged
the seven others to go on and said he would follow when his
leg healed.

The First Missionary Martyrs

Only C.T. Wilson and Shergold Smith of the seven reached the court of Mutesa on January 30, 1877. Two others had given up and returned to England because of illness. Another had been murdered before crossing into Bugandan territory. Still another had come down with a raging fever and at the last minute had stayed in Zanzibar. The seventh, a man named O'Neil, stayed behind at the south end of the great lake to complete repairs on a boat.

Wilson and Smith received a festive welcome from Mutesa. When the celebrating died down, King Mutesa asked them earnestly, "Did you bring the Book?"

A short while later Shergold Smith decided to return for their colleague who had remained with the boat. He located O'Neil and the two started back to Mutesa's capital. Contrary winds forced them to put in at the village of Ukerere in present Tanzania. There they went to the rescue of an Arab and were killed by a tribal chief.

Wilson, alone at the court, began Sunday worship services at the palace and English lessons for the king and members of his court. Mutesa showed interest in the gospel, but refused to make a personal commitment. After hearing of the murders of his two colleagues, Wilson asked the king's permission to go to find Mackay. He linked up with the Scotsman and brought him back to Rubaga. King Mutesa, impressed with Mackay's mechanical skills, soon banished his Muslim instructor from the court to give full attention to Christianity.

Four months later Wilson and Mackay were joined by three other missionary–priests of the Church of England. But the king remained noncommittal, and not until 1882 did the Anglicans baptize their first convert, a slave boy.

The King's Puzzlement

Mutesa was just becoming comfortable with Mackay when a party of French Catholic priests landed on the lake beach. The following Sunday, Mackay went to the king's court as was his custom. One of the priests was there. Mackay shook hands with him and then sat down to await the wish of the monarch. Shortly, Mutesa asked Mackay to pray and read the Bible. The king knelt with Mackay, but the priest did not. When the priest failed to participate on succeeding Sundays, Mutesa asked why. The priest replied frankly, "We do not join Mr. Mackay's Protestant religion because it is false."

Mackay disputed this and a debate ensued in the royal court. The puzzled king could only grunt, "Every white man seems to have his own religion."

As the months passed, the Catholics won their own converts and acquired friends in the court, just as Mackay did. The king vacillated. One week he seemed to favor Protestantism; another week, Catholicism; and another week, Islam.

While the missionaries felt safe enough, they never knew which one of his subjects the king would execute next. Once Mackay heard a sharp cry in the road outside his hut, then an agonizing scream, followed by loud laughter. At this, one of Mackay's servants remarked, "They have cut that fellow's throat, ha, ha, ha." Another victim. Mackay knew that others died at the king's whim every day. Some had their throats cut. Some were slowly tortured, with noses, ears, lips, and sinews from arms and thighs sliced off and roasted before they died. Mackay begged the king to be merciful and remember the Fifth Commandment of the Bible. Each time the king listened, then as soon as Mackay was diverted, the senseless killings began again.

The King Is Dead

Suddenly, in 1884, Mutesa died and was buried in a coffin built by Mackay. One of his sons, Mwanga, succeeded him. Still a teen-ager, he had been catechized by one of the Catholic priests. But Christian hopes for him were rapidly dashed. Coming under the influence of the degenerate Arab traders, he proved to be worse than his father. Like his father, he also kept a harem of concubines, but the harem included young men as well as women.

The Arabs had watched the number of Protestant and Catholic converts increase along with the growing influence of the European missionaries in the royal court. Now they began persuading young Mwanga that the missionaries were agents in a plot by France and England to take over his empire.

The First Martyrs

Mwanga struck. His targets were a group of young Christians who had accompanied Mackay across the lake, a trip for which they had official permission. They were seized by one of Mwanga's petty officials on the pretense that they were leaving the country. All but three escaped. Mwanga's warriors cut off their arms and bound them to scaffolding. A fire was lit underneath and as the flames rose around them, the executioners stood around the fire jeering. "Pray to your Isa Masiya [Jesus Christ]," they shouted. "See if He will help you now." In response the young Ugandans raised their voices in a hymn which Mackay had taught them in their language:

> Daily, daily, sing to Jesus
> Sing my soul His praises due
> All He does deserves our praises,
> And our deep devotion, too.
>
> For in deep humiliation
> He for us did live below;
> Died on Calvary's cross of torture,
> Rose to save our souls from woe.

The missionaries could do nothing. Mwanga raged that he would burn alive anyone else who went to the English church. Only a few stopped going. Mwanga carried out his threat by burning thirty-two Ugandans to death in one day. One of the executioners was so moved by the conduct of the Christians in their martyrdom that he went to Mackay for spiritual instruction. Nor were the Catholics exempt. The cruel Mwanga had scores of their converts killed. (In 1964, twenty-two of the Catholic martyrs were canonized as saints by the Roman Catholic Church.) Some of the young men, Protestants as well as Catholics, were put to death because they refused to submit to Mwanga's perverted sexual passions.

Brave Bishop Hannington

In the midst of this persecution was Anglican bishop James Hannington and five other missionary volunteers who had come from England to eastern Africa. When Mackay learned that Bishop Hannington was coming, he sent a warning, but the message never reached the bishop. Hannington and all his bearers were hideously slaughtered by fanatical Muslims acting under orders from Mwanga. Before the spears were run through his body, the bishop said, "Tell your king that I have purchased the road to Buganda with my death." After plunging their spears through his body, the callous executioners cut off Hannington's head and feet and left his torso for the hyenas. Such mutilation, they believed, would keep the missionary from rising from the dead and avenging his murder.

Intrigue, Disease, and Church Growth

The killings continued. The Protestant and Catholic missionaries were under house arrest and no longer had influence in the king's court.

Between 1888 and 1894 the political situation swung back and forth between Christian and Muslim, until the Imperial British East India Company moved in. There was a period of confused fighting—by Ugandans against Sudanese mercenaries, by Ugandans against Ugandans, by Catholics and Protestants against Arabs, and Catholics and Protestants against one another. The British won out and declared Buganda a protectorate in 1900. The name was later changed to Uganda to include other tribal kingdoms in the area.

By this time there were more missionary graves. Bishop Henry Parker, who had come to succeed James Hannington, perished from malaria within the year. Three years later, in 1890, Alexander Mackay, who had been translating the Gospel of John into the Bugandan language, died from malaria in the same bed where Bishop Parker had breathed his last. The pioneering Catholic missionaries were also in their graves.

Their labor was not in vain. By 1890 there were twelve thousand Anglican Christians and an equal number of Catholics. Under the benevolence and protection of British rule, the proportion of professed Christians rose to seventy per cent of Uganda's population.

A Revival of Paganism

The British permitted the Bugandan head of state to remain as figurehead ruler of the dominant tribe. But the pervasive influence of paganism did not die. As late as 1955 there was a brief revival of the worship of the old Bugandan gods.

Mathias Kibuka Kigaira, a twenty-year-old trucker, declared himself a prophet of Kibuka, the Bugandan god of war. Thousands flocked to hear him preach from a tree top. "Neither Jesus nor Muhammed can help you," he told the Bugandans. "You must return to the spirits of our ancestors." Worshipers piled money at the foot of his tree and brought cattle and other gifts to him. After he urged Bugandans not to pay taxes, the government tried three times to arrest him. The third attempt to arrest him was successful and his movement soon collapsed for lack of leadership.

Independence and the Rise of Idi Amin

In 1962 Uganda became an independent sovereign country within the British Commonwealth. The titular Bugandan ruler was named president, but the real power was Prime Minister Milton Obote. A member of the Lango tribe, Obote came to power by forming a political coalition of minority tribal leaders with Bugandans anxious to break with old traditionalists of their tribe. His ascendancy was bitterly resented by many of the old chiefs.

After a rebellion in 1966, Obote assumed full executive authority of Uganda for five years. One of his first acts was to repeal the special status of Buganda. The Bugandan figurehead monarch fled to Britain where he died in poverty three years later. Obote took the title of president. The unrest continued. An assassination attempt on the president failed in 1969. The second most senior army officer was murdered the next year.

Obote was overthrown in 1971 while attending the Commonwealth of Nations Conference held in Singapore. General Idi Amin took power. He quickly suspended parts of the constitution, dissolved the Uganda Parliament and forbade political activity. Obote fled into exile in Tanzania.

Tall and beefy, Amin had been the heavyweight boxing champion of the Ugandan army for almost ten years. He had fought with the British in Burma during World War II and in Kenya during the Mau Mau rebellion. For five years before overthrowing the Obote government, he had been chief of staff of Uganda's armed forces.

After taking over, Amin promised free elections and invited Obote home to participate if he desired. Obote sensed a trap and declined.

Playing on tribal pride, Amin scored a political coup by bringing home the remains of the last Bugandan king for a ceremonial burial. Then to divert concern over acute economic problems, he threatened to invade Tanzania.

A Reign of Terror

Ugandan exultation over Amin's stratagems soon froze into national fear. The army, under his direct command, began raiding private homes, seizing property and arresting anyone suspected of disliking Amin. Dissenting senior army and police officers were murdered. Hundreds of soldiers from the Lango and Acholi tribes were killed in their barracks in July, 1971.

Two of Amin's July victims were Americans—Nicholas Stroh, a free-lance writer, and Robert Siedle, a sociologist who was researching a book about missionaries in Uganda. Two top-level defectors from Amin's inner circle later related that the two were hacked to pieces with machetes. Their testimony and other evidence were factors in the United States decision to cut off foreign aid to Uganda.

Amin's troops were empowered to shoot "armed robbers" on sight. Many more Ugandans were killed. Amin ordered the expulsion of Uganda's fifty-five thousand Asians, most of whom were small businessmen and shopkeepers, as well as fifty-eight European missionaries.

Erratic and Cruel

In the months ahead Amin's behavior became even more unpredictable and malicious. He praised Hitler and pledged to build a memorial to the Nazi fuehrer. Following the lightning Israeli raid on July 3 and 4, 1976, to rescue Jewish hijacked hostages at Kampala's Entebbe Airport, he ordered the execution of air-traffic controllers, policemen, and other airport officials on duty at the time of the rescue.

The Israelis had once been his allies. Now he turned on Israel with a vengeance, saying Hitler's only failure was that he had not killed enough Jews. He accused Ugandan Christians and foreign missionaries of helping his Jewish enemies. For himself, Amin said he was now a Muslim and would welcome aid from Muslim countries.

Christian Martyrs Under Amin

All along, many devout Christians had been killed. One of the first was Chaplain Ogwang of the Ugandan army, murdered in the coup that overthrew Obote. Another well-known Christian killed was Francis Walugemebe, mayor of the fourth largest town in Uganda. Walugemebe was dragged from his house by Amin's hired killers on September 22, 1971. When he asked to call the president, a soldier mutilated him, then dumped him in the back of a jeep and drove him away to be finished off.

Still another Christian leader murdered was Benedictor Kiwanuku, whom Amin had made chief justice in June, 1971. The respected judge was literally butchered in 1973. Still alive, he was thrown in his car and burned to death.

An evangelist was killed in 1972 for innocently reading over the radio a reference to Israel from the Psalms. The chairman of an evangelical church, Joseph Kiwanuka, after escaping to Kenya, was kidnapped by Amin's agents and brought back to Kampala for execution. According to Dr. Kefa Sempangi, a Christian leader who eluded Amin's agents and emigrated to the United States, Kiwanuka "died with hands lifted to Jesus, refusing to deny his Lord as the murderers demanded."

Witness of the Widows

Dr. Sempangi recalls a touching experience at his church before he escaped:

> After our church's Easter service in 1973 . . . five of Amin's killers followed me back to the vestry. They told me their mission and asked if I had anything to say. I assured them I was not going to plead with them to spare my life, for my life was already dead and hid in Christ (Colossians 3:3).
>
> What struck the tallest of the men, who had killed more than two hundred people, was that the widows of some of his victims were in the church that day, singing with hope and joy.
>
> "Why are they not grief-stricken?" he asked.
>
> "Because they have been transformed by the Gospel. They have the joy and the hope which no man can take away," was my reply.
>
> To my utter amazement, the man asked if I could pray for him and for his friends. One of these men later became very instrumental in my escape from Uganda and also became an effective worker in our church. (Now a church in hiding.)

After his escape, Dr. Sempangi deplored the silence of the world evangelical community about the murders in Uganda. "Is there no room in the church for such a cry?" he asked. "Is the church an ivory tower that cannot be touched by the needs of the people? The church should have been outraged at the very word go, when Amin started on his present course."

A Month of Horror

Amin's bloodiest month, February, 1977, merited a *Time* cover story, "The Wild Man of Africa." News media around the world joined in reporting the most shocking massacre yet. Typical was a grisly cartoon in *The Des Moines News and Register* showing a smiling Amin, beribboned with a row of clinking skeletons.

The so-called provocation for the massacre was a short-lived army rebellion in which seven men had been killed and another wounded. Before the month was over, Amin's trusted hirelings had killed thousands of soldiers and civilians. In the village of former president Milton Obote, Amin's men reportedly killed every civilian they could find.

But the most sensational act was the killing of Anglican archbishop of Uganda Janani Luwum along with two former cabinet ministers. It was the archbishop's death and Amin's clumsy cover-up that aroused the loudest outcry in many world capitals.

The macabre bloodletting sent thousands more Ugandans fleeing across the eastern border into Kenya to join refugees from Amin's previous bloody tantrum. Among those escaping were the martyred archbishop's widow and children, three black Anglican bishops, and thousands of other Christians. Best known of the three bishops was Festo Kivengere, an evangelical leader of world renown. Bishop Festo went on to New York and told the terrible story to trusted church leaders and editors.

Bishop Festo's Story

On Sunday, January 30, Bishop Festo had preached to a crowd of thirty thousand in a western Ugandan city. His topic: "The Preciousness of Life." In the audience were Ugandan governors, Muslim sheiks, and officers of Amin's dread State Research Bureau—killers in sport shirts with authority to kill as they desired. The bishop concluded his sermon with a direct speech to government authorities. "God entrusts governments with authority," he declared. "But authority has been misused in our country by force."

"When I sat down," he later recalled, "every Christian was trembling, thinking that I was going to be whisked away. I wasn't."

Instead of coming for Bishop Festo, Amin's operatives in Kampala, the capital, roused Anglican Archbishop Janani Luwum out of bed at 1:30 A.M. the following Saturday. While eight soldiers pointed guns at his stomach, others ransacked every room of his house. Amin would later claim arms had been found near the Anglican prelate's house. The real reason for the shakedown were the calls from Archbishop Luwum, Bishop Festo and other churchmen for morality and decency in government.

The invasion of the Anglican archbishop's residence resulted in a long, signed protest to Amin. The archbishop and fifteen bishops said:

We are deeply disturbed. In the history of our country such an incident in the Church has never before occurred. . . . Now that the security of the archbishop is at stake, the security of the bishops is even more in jeopardy.

This is a climax of what has been constantly happening to our Christians. We have buried many who have died as a result of being shot and there are many more whose bodies have not yet been found; yet their disappearance is connected with the activities of some members of the Security Forces. Your Excellency, if it is required, we can give concrete evidence of what is happening because widows and orphans are members of our Church.

The archbishop delivered the letter to Amin in person on February 12 and told him he had not been involved in any overthrow plot. Amin countered by summoning the prelate to hear the reading of a document attesting his guilt.

After exchanging pleasantries over afternoon tea, Amin charged that the document had been written by ex-president Obote. He read the fabricated evidence before the archbishop and a carefully selected audience of supporters. When he came to the archbishop's name, the audience shouted on cue, "Kill!" Amin replied that the archbishop and two accused cabinet officers would be given military trials.

A few hours later, Uganda Radio announced their deaths in an automobile accident. Newsmen were shown pictures of a wrecked car, which Amin claimed was the death vehicle.

Bishop Festo and other refugees told the true story. Archbishop Luwum and the two cabinet members, both devout Christians, were led through an underground passage to the torture chamber. In the torture room they met four other condemned prisoners, awaiting their execution. The guards permitted the archbishop to hold a short prayer meeting. He laid his hands on each prisoner, prayed for them, and encouraged them in Christ.

Then the archbishop and the two cabinet ministers were roughly shoved into a Land Rover and driven to a private lodge outside the capital. They were never seen alive again. The next day, February 17, the official announcement was made that one of the cabinet members had tried to subdue the driver of the vehicle. The Land Rover spun out of control and the three prisoners were killed in the crash. The severely injured driver was taken to a hospital in Kampala. The story was widely disbelieved. The alleged driver, a Major Moses, was seen walking around in apparent good health the next day. Further leaks and rumors gave a strange twist to the incident.

The Bizarre Murder

According to the pieced-together accounts, Amin came to the lodge and asked Archbishop Luwum to sign a prepared confession stating that he had plotted to overthrow the dictator. After several refusals, the archbishop was stripped and forced to lie on the floor.

At Amin's orders, two soldiers began whipping the archbishop mercilessly. Instead of agreeing to sign the confession, the archbishop prayed for his tormentors. Amin flew into a frenzy. Screaming obscenities, he struck the archbishop, then ordered the soldiers to perform certain obscene and sacrilegious sex acts with the churchman. When Amin grew tired of watching, he drew his pistol and shot the archbishop twice in the heart. Death occurred instantly.

Family members and church officials were denied the archbishop's body. They were not even permitted to view his corpse. Instead, Amin's soldiers took the remains to Luwum's native village for burial. Relatives there were told to bury him immediately, but they insisted on summoning a pastor to officiate. When the Anglican priest arrived, the coffin was opened and the bullet holes discovered.

Bishop Festo's Escape

Bishop Festo had been among those trying to get the body. On Saturday, February 19, he was warned by friends that Amin intended to get him next. Festo and his wife drove to their home town in eastern Uganda. There they were told that Amin's agents had checked on their house four times that day. Festo had planned to preach in his home church the next day, but after a tearful prayer meeting, he and his wife decided they should try to get across the border into Kenya. They drove to the end of the road, then followed a guide on foot five miles through the mountains. At 6:30 A.M. they stepped across the border.

Meanwhile, a story spread in Kampala that Amin had prohibited services in Uganda on Sunday. Nevertheless, forty–five hundred worshipers packed the Anglican cathedral in Kampala for a thanksgiving service. Afterwards, they went outside and gathered around the open grave that had been dug for the martyred archbishop next to the plot of Bishop Hannington who had been martyred in 1885.

The archbishop's grave had been purposely left open. His appointed successor began reading about the resurrection of Christ. When he voiced the assurance of the angels to the women on the day of Christ's resurrection, "He is risen," the crowd burst into a song of spontaneous praise. In Nairobi, Kenya, a crowd estimated at ten thousand participated in a second memorial service for the murdered archbishop of Uganda.

Selective Condemnation

One of the participating bishops at Archbishop Luwum's memorial service in Nairobi blasted the selective condemnation of the World Council of Churches in Africa. "It is very well to condemn white regimes in southern Africa and turn a blind eye elsewhere. But the time has come for the church to be the church, otherwise we are doomed." Kenyan church leaders subsequently declared in a statement: "We confess that we have too often kept quiet when we should have identified ourselves with the suffering and persecuted peoples of the Continent of Africa and Uganda in particular."

Archbishop Luwum's murder and sweeping purges that followed in the Lango and Acholi tribes did bring widespread condemnation on the erratic Amin. The Vatican found Amin's wrecked-car story "unswallowable." The World Council of Churches' executive committee lashed the Ugandan dictator for "inhuman behavior." Billy Graham deplored the "cold-blooded murder" of the archbishop. President Jimmy Carter said Amin's actions had "disgusted the entire civilized world."

Amin reacted to Carter by ordering Americans in Uganda not to leave and to appear before him on February 28, 1977, bringing their chickens and goats. When they came, Amin praised them and asked them to keep up their good work for Uganda. Fearful that Amin might again reverse himself, many left the country anyway.

The "Martyrs" Who Became Martyrs

During that bloody month of February, the Protestant churches had been preparing for the June centennial celebration of the coming of Christianity to Uganda. As part of the celebration, a group of talented young Ugandan Christians were producing a play about the first martyrs of Uganda. A week after the archbishop's death, they themselves became martyrs. Their bodies were found a few miles outside Kampala.

The celebration went ahead as planned. Twenty-five thousand Ugandan Christians came into the capital in June for two days of festivities. Most camped outside the Kampala Cathedral at night, singing, praying, ignoring Amin's agents who circulated through the crowd. On June 30 they formed a procession behind church leaders and gospel bands. Singing and holding crosses aloft, they marched through the streets of Kampala as a testimony that the Ugandan church could not be silent. In the procession were many reclaimed backsliders who had renewed their commitment to Christ after the death of Archbishop Luwum.

The Future of the Church in Uganda

On September 20, 1977, Amin banned twenty-seven religious organizations whose activities "are not conducive to the security, peace, and welfare of Uganda." Besides the Islamic, Anglican, Roman Catholic and Uganda Orthodox churches were allowed to continue services.

Although apprehension over the possibility that Amin might order the selective killing of missionaries has never been realized, the indiscriminate killing of Ugandans continues. Most missionaries left the country before 1977, although a few have trickled back to minister outside the churches to the Ugandan people. Before the bloodletting began, 114 foreign evangelical workers were in Uganda, with the Southern Baptists having the largest representation. One missionary planning to return after furlough in the United States says, "I'm happy to go back. The safest place to be is in God's will and if Uganda is where God wants me, then I'll be safe there."

With or without missionaries, the Ugandan church is expected to keep growing. When asked how long he thought the church in his country could keep going, Bishop Festo Kivengere replied, "Until Jesus comes back. You can persecute, you can kill some, but there is no possibility of removing the church. It is going to remain, with suffering, under pressure, and sometimes maybe with oppression."

And Idi Amin, the monster of Africa? Bishop Festo, who talked with Amin many times before fleeing Uganda, replies: "He's a complicated person. He can be very amicable, very social. He can also be destructive. His anger becomes almost ritualistic and sadistic many times. I can't explain his erratic ways. He can roll out the red carpet. He can give a party. All while two hundred Ugandans are in the darker chambers having their ears chopped off."

Is he now purposely persecuting Christians? "It has reached a state where you can say it is Christian persecution because he has singled out Christian leadership by replacing them with Muslims who don't qualify. Muslims are not enemies of Christians in Uganda, but President Amin has been using them for his own purposes."

Festo holds little hope for Amin changing. "I don't think he now has the ability to change politically because of the forces which surround him. If he can't change, the very machinery which he has created will one day get rid of him. There have been attempts from the people who are so fed up and bitter because of the murders."

Will Christians participate in a plot to rid Uganda of their dictator? Festo cannot accept violence as the answer. "I love Idi Amin (the title of a book by Festo Kivengere). I pray for him. I want to see him saved."

ZIMBABWE/RHODESIA, ZAMBIA, MALAWI:

Former British Central Africa

Friday night, June 23, 1978. British Pentecostal missionary Ian McGarrick slept soundly in his quarters at the Emmanuel Christian School in the Rhodesian town of Vumba, near the western border of Mozambique. The two hundred fifty black students rested uneasily in their dormitories. They knew something McGarrick did not know. A short while before, about twenty black guerrillas had crept onto the school grounds. They wore knitted caps, spoke English and the Shona tribal language, and identified themselves to the students as members of Robert Mugabe's outlawed Zimbabwe African National Union (ZANU). "The school is being closed," they said. "Stay in bed and no harm will be done you."

The students later claimed they heard nothing from their dorms. Not until the next morning did they alert McGarrick. He quickly began looking for the other missionary personnel at the school — four children and nine adults. All were missing.

A Grisly Discovery

McGarrick was walking anxiously past the soccer field when he saw the horribly mutilated bodies. Three of the children, all under nine years of age, lay in a cluster, pajamas stiff with dried blood, faces bloody and disfigured. One of the little girls had the purple imprint of a boot on her face and

440

neck. Nearby he came upon the parents of two of the girls. Robert Evans, his hands tied behind his back, was dead. Thirty-six-year-old Joyce Evans, her face battered beyond recognition, lay with her left hand touching the battered head of their three-week-old infant, Pamela. The baby had apparently been killed by a single blow to the head. A short blood-stained log lay nearby.

McGarrick spotted the bodies of another missionary couple, Peter and Sandra McCann, both only thirty. A few feet away he found the ravaged corpses of two single women missionaries, Elizabeth Wendy Hamilton and Catherine Pickens, and a little farther on, two other single women. One woman, her hair in curlers and clutching a scarf, had an ax embedded in her back. Some of the women were only partially clothed and presumably had been raped. Only Mary Fisher was missing.

Stupefied by grief and horror, McGarrick ran to call the Rhodesian police. They drew up in a cloud of dust, leaped out and followed the missionary to the soccer field. A trail of blood took them to the cricket field where they located Miss Fisher. Still alive, she was taken to a hospital in Salisbury, the capital, one hundred twenty miles away. She later died of her injuries.

The Rhodesian government flew in troops and reporters. The troops crossed the border into adjoining Mozambique and searched the scenic Vumba mountains for the killers of the Britons. Reporters came and took pictures of the carnage and hastily interviewed McGarrick and some of the students. McGarrick, who by this time was beyond tears, noted that the missionaries and the children had been scheduled to move to the fortified town of Umtali on Sunday.

A Toy on a Coffin

Five days later the funeral of the martyrs was held in Umtali municipal hall. Some five hundred mourners, mostly whites, crowded into the building. They saw the eight oak coffins of the adults and three small white ones of the children. Each coffin bore a single wreath. Tiny Pamela Lynn shared a coffin with her mother. The mourners watched Rachel Evans, age eight, place a yellow toy owl on the coffin of her sister, Rebecca. Rachel and her ten-year-old brother Timothy had been in a boarding school in Salisbury.

Leaders of the Elim Pentecostal Church, which has headquarters in Cheltenham, England, presided at the services. One of them, Reverend Ronald Chapman, declared, "We do pray God will be merciful to those who perpetrated such an act of shame, that they might know grief and repentance and God's mercy."

Denials and Charges

Already a bitter controversy was raging. Guerrilla leader Robert Mugabe, a former teacher in a Roman Catholic mission school, strongly denied that his men were responsible. He claimed to have witnesses that would implicate black soldiers of the Rhodesian army in the murders. A World Council of Churches magazine came to Mugabe's defense, charging that Rhodesian soldiers had previously dressed like guerrillas to attack defenseless civilians. The Rhodesian government called such claims "completely without foundation" and blamed the guerrillas. The hunt went on for the alleged murderers.

The slaying of the nine missionaries and four children marked the worst atrocity of the recent Rhodesian guerrilla war. Altogether during the previous two years, thirty-six European and American missionaries and children had been killed, along with hundreds of white and black civilians.

Confused, "Christian" Rhodesia

At this writing the situation in Rhodesia is confused, unpredictable, and gloomy. Rhodesia is one of the most Christianized countries in Africa. Over five hundred missionaries from North America alone are in the country. Twenty-four per cent of the seven million people are avowedly Christian. Another twenty-four per cent are animist and follow tribal religions. Fifty-one per cent are classified by World Vision International as "Christo-pagan." The remaining one per cent are linked with Muslim and non-Christian sects. The ruling white minority is almost solidly Christian in profession. And all of the major black political leaders, including the commanders of the two major guerrilla groups, are products of mission schools.

The Rhodesian problem, with its resultant missionary martyrs, has divided church groups in Rhodesia and in Europe and North Africa as well. The most acrimonious debate centers on the legitimacy of the two outlawed guerrilla movements led by Joshua Nkomo and Robert Mugabe, and the role they should play after black majority rule becomes a reality. Mugabe has said plainly that if he obtains power,

Zimbabwe (Rhodesia) will be a Marxist state. Yet the World Council of Churches made an eighty-five thousand dollar grant to his Patriotic Front in 1978. Methodist Bishop Abel T. Muzorewa, leader of the strongest legitimate political party in Rhodesia, has condemned the grant. The grant has further factionalized United Methodists who sponsor over fifty missionaries in Rhodesia. Critics of the World Council's act charge that the international church agency is subsidizing a political organization which kills missionaries.

Europeans Pursued Gold and Souls

Political and religious quarrels have divided Rhodesia, named for the European colonizer Cecil Rhodes, and the other two countries which made up British Central Africa (Zambia and Malawi—formerly Northern Rhodesia and Nyasaland) for over a century.

The two great archetypal colonial figures who dominate white history in Central Africa came with different motives. David Livingstone, whose heart is buried in Zambia, came to free Africans from ignorance, disease, famine, and the slave trade. Cecil Rhodes, son of an Anglican priest, saw that Central Africa was strategic to Britain's growing colonial empire and also ripe for exploitation. Rhodes and associates chartered the British South Africa Company to prospect for gold, diamonds, and other valuable minerals. This company controlled Northern Rhodesia (Zambia) and Southern Rhodesia until 1923. Livingstone brought missionaries to evangelize and educate Africans. Rhodes brought white settlers to take over the best tracts of land and employ Africans at slave wages. Most of the whites settled in fertile Southern Rhodesia where their rule over a ninety-six per cent black majority was never seriously threatened until the late 1960's.

The missionaries divided over social issues from the beginning. First was the question of what to do with runaway slaves. Pioneer Anglican Bishop Charles Mackenzie and a few others took them in and incurred the wrath of slave hunters and plantation owners. Other missionaries turned them away to avoid trouble with the white power structure. In Nyasaland some Scotch Presbyterian missionaries reportedly "sentenced" rebellious African employees to floggings.

The Scotch Presbyterians in Nyasaland were allied closely with the colonial administration and received subsidies for their schools. (In Rhodesia today, mission schools still enjoy partial government support.) The preachers and teachers accepted the prevalent European belief in segregation and white superiority.

The Seeds of Revolt

The thorn in their side was Joseph Booth, a British Baptist businessman and farmer who practiced equality and planned a string of self-supporting Baptist churches and schools. Booth's ideas would inspire a tragic, bloody rebellion against the unyielding European establishment.

Booth arrived in 1892 and set up the Zambezi Industrial Mission a few miles from the Blantyre station of the Presbyterian Church of Scotland. His goal from the beginning was African leadership and he soon attracted a small following of young black men. His most devoted disciple was John Chilembwe, a former student of the Scottish missionaries.

The Africans practically worshiped Booth. He criticized the comfortable life led by European missionaries amidst African poverty. He paid his African employees higher wages than did the Scottish mission or the colonial government. But what really excited their passions was Booth's call for an African Christian union to lead Africans into equal political, social, and economic rights beside Europeans, develop African education along the lines of European technology, secure land reform, build a pro-African press and literature, and establish independent African churches. In this, Booth was one of the first whites to proclaim the doctrine of "Africa for Africans." Unfortunately, he was far, far ahead of his time.

Seeking more financial support, Booth wrote the Negro National Baptist Convention in the United States. In 1897 he and Chilembwe traveled to Virginia where both spoke in black Baptist churches and Chilembwe enrolled in the black Virginia Theological College and Seminary. Black Baptists in Virginia received the two men with aplomb and enthusiasm. White response was something else. In Richmond, white mobs frequently followed and stoned the Britisher and African for walking together, sitting on the same public park benches, and living in the same black household. The impressionable African gained both a theological education and an understanding of racial discrimination in "Christian" Virginia. He heard about lynchings. He read about black rebellions. He listened to the impassioned longings of Virginia blacks to be free. When he returned to Africa, the seeds of revolt against white domination had been planted.

Booth's African dream blossomed. Soon there was a large church led by blacks, a chain of schools taught by blacks, and impressive model farms. His black colleagues worked hard and prospered. All this was quite upsetting to European neighbors who believed Africans were condemned to servitude and poverty.

A Quest for Black Power

Booth's crowning achievement came when Joseph Chilembwe took over the renamed Providence Industrial Mission in 1900. It was the first mission and church under African control. As Booth had predicted, the work expanded rapidly under African leadership. But instead of accepting this success, European administrators and some missionaries became fearful of the new display of African power.

Booth and Chilembwe believed that blacks should organize and work together. In 1909 Chilembwe established the Natives' Industrial Union "for the promotion and protection of Negro Christian work in the country, the collecting and recording of commercial information and . . . the establishment of a Court of Arbitration, and communication with the public authorities on subjects affecting the commercial and planting community, or such other things as occasion may require." Plainly and simply, the black Baptists wanted justice and an end to European mistreatment which often involved cheating, flogging, and imprisoning blacks.

The black Baptists did not want something for nothing. Wrote Chilembwe to a friend: "Our pathway must be up through the soil, up through swamps, up through forests, up through the streams and rocks, up through commerce, education and religion!"

Five years passed and conditions remained the same. Chilembwe was now almost blind and afflicted by asthma. He sent a list of African grievances to the British administrators with a plea that they respond before it was too late. Nothing happened.

The Tragedy of Taking Vengeance

For several years Chilembwe had been preaching principally from the Old Testament. In his mind, the Africans were the oppressed children of Israel in bondage to the Europeans. God had commissioned him to lead his people to freedom. "It is better for me to die than to live," he declared. "I hear the crying of my Africans."

His mind undoubtedly became affected by his failing health. Passion turned to a steely determination to execute justice against the European overlords; to make them listen to the cries of Africans who were then being drafted to help fight England's war against Germany, while the governor was preparing to deport Chilembwe at the first chance.

In 1915 the demented African pastor led a revolt. One raiding party marched on the home of William Livingstone, a planter notorious for mistreating Africans and for destroying some of the mission's "prayer houses." The rebels killed Livingstone and a white employee with spears, then cut off Livingstone's head. They did not harm the women and children. Other contingents of Chilembwe's ill-armed corps attacked elsewhere, killing European men, while sparing their dependents.

The whites counterattacked. Within two months the uprising had been put down and forty rebels, including the pastor, executed and some three hundred others imprisoned. The angered whites claimed Chilembwe had wanted to make himself a king. Africans and their sympathizers said the pastor had acted out of mental anguish and despair, believing that his martyrdom might bring about a change of heart among the European masters.

The tragedy caused the Providence Mission to be closed. It was reopened in 1926 and continues today with support from the National Baptist Convention of America.

The Fight for Independence

The seeds which Booth and Chilembwe had planted did not die. The Nyasaland African Congress (NAC), founded in 1944, kept pushing for independence. In 1953 Britain forced Nyasaland into the Central African Federation with Northern Rhodesia and Southern Rhodesia. The NAC opposed the Federation because it was governed by whites in Southern Rhodesia. They implored the respected Dr. Hastings Banda to return home to lead the opposition. A Presbyterian elder, Dr. Banda had earned degrees in history, political science, and medicine in the United States and had practiced medicine in England. When the summons came to help his people, he was practicing medicine and writing articles from Ghana against the Federation.

In 1958 he returned to a rousing welcome and stepped up the anti-Federation campaign. The British governor declared a state of emergency and imprisoned Banda and his associates on charges that they had plotted a massacre of whites.

Mass protests continued until Dr. Banda was released in 1960. In elections the following year, he won control of the territorial government. In 1963 Nyasaland became the independent state of Malawi within the British Commonwealth. Dr. Banda was elected prime minister. The hated Federation was dissolved.

The "Persecution" of Jehovah's Witnesses

Through the years African-controlled congregations had proliferated in Malawi. Among them were the zealous Jehovah's Witnesses who refused to salute the national flag. After persuasion failed, Dr. Banda's government banned their activities. When they disregarded the order, soliders rounded up thirty thousand of the sect and placed them in prison camps. In December, 1975, officials of the Witnesses in other countries protested that adherents in Malawi were being beaten, tortured, and raped with official approval. Malawi is now, in effect, a police state. Dr. Banda is firmly in power for "life." No foreign reporters are allowed in the country, making facts about the persecution of the Witnesses hard to determine. However, twenty evangelical foreign missions enjoy freedom of operation under the Banda regime. The Presbyterian Church of Zambia, to which the President belongs, has over six hundred thousand members.

"Holy War" in Zambia

Northern Rhodesia (Zambia) also bitterly resented the Federation and the rule from white dominated Southern Rhodesia. When the Federation was dissolved, the country moved toward independence. The transition to majority African rule led to the election of Kenneth Kaunda, son of an evangelical pastor and a former mission school teacher, as the first president. Like Banda in Malawi, Kaunda outlawed opposition parties. He also nationalized privately owned land, theaters, hospitals, and newspapers.

Kaunda welcomed evangelical missionaries from abroad. About three hundred are serving in the country today. Some thirty per cent of the population is Christian.

But the Kaunda government does not feel as warmly about the Christo–pagan Lumpa Church, launched by a former United Church lay preacher, Alice Nulenga Lubusha (also known as Alice Lenshina), in 1953. Mrs. Lubusha's followers believe that during a three-day disappearance she died and was raised from the dead with divine instructions to preach against "sorcerers." In 1964, the year before Zambian independence, the "Prophetess Alice" led her devotees in a bloody "holy war" against government troops. During the battle, she kept assuring her followers that the cry of "Jericho!" would turn enemy bullets to water and give them "passports" to heaven. Over seven hundred Lumpas were slaughtered and some twenty thousand fled into neighboring Zaire.

In 1975 the Lumpas tried to revive their holy war in Malawi. Before they could organize, police swooped down on a gathering and arrested about one hundred persons. The "Prophetess Alice" was not among them. She had been restricted to a remote security area since 1971.

The Tragedy of Rhodesia

Of all the British possessions, Rhodesia was the most promising for white settlers. The first pioneers came in the 1890's to help Cecil Rhodes and the British South African Company conquer the area from tribal chiefs. The settlers were awarded thousands of fertile acres around the present capital of Salisbury. More whites arrived. The colony prospered. By the 1960's white Rhodesians enjoyed a standard of living comparable to Americans, while black employees and neighbors barely subsisted as farmers.

Rhodesia welcomed foreign missionaries. In the 1970's some thirty agencies were represented in the country with over five hundred adult workers. The Methodist Church acquired over two hundred thousand members. But like it or not, black Rhodesians identified most missionaries with the white majority government from which they received land grants and financial subsidies for their schools and hospitals.

Because of their great investment in Rhodesia, whites held on to power more tenaciously here than anywhere else in British Africa. They liked the Central African Federation. As the dominant Federation power, they could keep back trouble from Northern Rhodesia and Nyasaland.

Early in the 1950's some saw the "handwriting" of growing black power on the wall. Garfield Todd, a missionary-turned-politician from New Zealand, saw the future clearly. Elected prime minister in 1953, he tried to steer Rhodesia away from a white enclave mentality and toward shared rule with Africans. After Todd's ouster in 1958, Rhodesia's white power structure moved deeper into separation and apartheid (apartness).

Out On a Limb

The British foreign office also saw trouble ahead and tried to move the white Rhodesians toward majority rule. In 1965, the Rhodesian white nationalist party won a decisive election among franchised white voters. Rather than surrender to British demands of representative government, the Rhodesians under white supremacist Ian Smith, declared independence. Britain and many other nations condemned the move and withdrew diplomatic recognition. The white Rhodesian government was now out on a dangerous limb, with black nationalist firebrands sawing away behind them.

Smith's party kept winning elections. The United Nations called for a trade embargo. Newly independent Zambia and Mozambique closed their borders and gave Rhodesian guerrillas sanctuary. Communist countries provided arms. Some guerrillas took military training in China, Algeria, and Tanzania.

By 1976 black-ruled African nations were threatening all-out war against Rhodesia. Fearing a blood bath, the United States pressured the white government to agree to turn over the reins to black majority rule within two years. Smith invited black political leaders to join in an executive council and prepare for the change of power. Joshua Nkomo and Robert Mugabe, head of two dissident political parties, refused and called the plan a sellout. They vowed to keep raiding white settlements from sanctuaries in Zambia and Mozambique.

The First Missionary Martyrs

The first missionary killings occurred near Bulawayo in southwestern Rhodesia. The retired Catholic bishop of Bulawayo, seventy-five-year-old Adolph Schmitt, and two nuns were shot to death on a lonely road.

Hitherto, missionaries and black church leaders had experienced more trouble with the white government than with dissident African political groups. Some missionaries, mostly Catholics and Methodists, had been deported for speaking against white minority rule and other policies of discrimination. There was little fear of the black guerrillas. Many of the guerrillas had attended mission schools and received medical aid from mission hospitals. There seemed no reason for an attack on the hands that had educated and cared for them.

This attitude began to change after the Bualwayo killings and similar tragedies that followed. In February, 1977, for example, two Jesuits, four Dominican nuns and one lay brother were murdered at St. Paul's Mission, thirty–five miles north of Salisbury. Government investigators blamed terrorists from Joshua Nkomo's Zimbabwe African People's Union (ZAPU). Ironically, the slaughter came just after Prime Minister Smith had announced plans to deport Irish-born Roman Catholic bishop Donald R. Lamont. The bishop had been convicted of aiding guerrillas by failing to report a rebel request for aid at a mission.

In a second raid about this same time, guerrillas marched four hundred students from the Manama Swedish Evangelical mission school across Rhodesia's southern border into Botswana where many were put on planes for training camps in Zambia. Black Lutheran leaders from southern Africa, meeting in Botswana, "thanked" that nation for receiving the young "refugees."

Through the rest of 1977 and into 1978 guerrilla attacks increased. Some six hundred civilian whites and two thousand blacks were killed. Frightened whites began leaving Rhodesia at the rate of one thousand a month, while thousands of blacks fled into slum camps around Salisbury. Most missionaries at rural stations remained at their posts.

Bloody June

Then came bloody June, 1978, when twenty missionaries and dependents died violent deaths in Rhodesia, compared to sixteen killed during the previous eighteen months.

The June victims included, besides the thirteen Pentecostal casualties already mentioned, two German Jesuits, two Catholic Marianhill brothers, two Salvation Army workers, and a Southern Baptist missionary.

The German Jesuits, Fathers Gregor Richert and Bernhard Lisson, were located at St. Rupert's, a remote mission hospital in central Rhodesia. Black staff members reported that three gunmen came to the station and took the foreigners away. The black staffers heard gunfire but did not see the shooting. Afterward the gunmen returned and told them, "We have shot the two whites." The gunmen were presumed to be from Joshua Nkomo's Zimbabwe African People's Union. St. Rupert's is one of sixteen stations operated by German Jesuits in Rhodesia. Monsignor Helmut Reckter, leader of the group, said after the killings, "All our stations have white personnel. We have no plans to withdraw anyone."

The Catholic Marianhill brothers, one Swiss and one German, were shot while sleeping on the veranda of the Embakwe Mission near the Botswana border.

The young Salvation Army workers, twenty-five-year-old Sharon Swindells from Northern Ireland and twenty-eight-year-old Diane Thompson from London, were killed at the Usher Institute, a World Vision-sponsored boarding school for girls, about one hundred miles from the Botswana border.

Southern Baptist missionary Archie G. Dunaway, the only American to die during the month, was a veteran of over thirty years of service in Nigeria and Rhodesia. A maintenance supervisor of the Baptist hospital at Sanyati, he was also a well-known and well-liked area evangelist. He was bayoneted to death by four intruders and his body carried or dragged to the spot where it was found. The guerrillas took his wallet, glasses, boots, pen and watch, but left his wedding ring.

Fellow missionaries brought the ring to Mrs. Dunaway at the Salisbury airport as a gesture of support when she was departing for home. She blamed her husband's death on "outside terrorists, Communists who wanted to make an example of Archie, to scare us away." His murder, she said, "does not represent the feelings of the Christian Africans. The only thing that sustains us now is our love of the Lord. It's such a loss. Archie and I were together thirty–three years."

Dunaway's body was flown to Nashville, Tennessee, where he was buried beside the remains of another Baptist missionary, eighty-one-year-old Mansfield Bailey who was a medical missionary in China until forced out by the Japanese war in 1937.

The loss of so many personnel in one month forced some missions to tighten security to minimize future risks. Southern Baptists, for example, began traveling only between eight A.M. and four P.M. Some went out from Salisbury in the morning to their rural posts and returned at night. After guerrillas shot down a Rhodesian passenger plane and brutally murdered some of the injured survivors, safety precautions were further tightened.

The Missionaries Carry On

The majority of missionaries are remaining in Rhodesia. Many fear that the communist-backed guerrillas, especially the Mugabe forces, are out to destroy law and order by closing down the mission schools and hospitals in the unprotected countryside. Some say, however, that Rhodesian government soldiers have committed atrocities as bad as the guerrillas.

Missionaries, along with national Christian workers, are

caught in a dilemma between the government and the guerrillas. People who deny aid to the guerrillas have been shot and sometimes burned alive in their homes. But if they do help the rebels, they are in danger of arrest and possible beatings by government soldiers.

In 1979 Rhodesia voted for black majority government. But the outlawed rebels have vowed to keep fighting, no matter what the outcome of the elections.

How Do the Missionaries See the Future?

"We know things are going to get a lot worse," Southern Baptist Linda Coleman conceded in an interview while on furlough. "But our intent is to return. You cannot live in fear. You either have to conquer it or you have to leave."

The missionaries will stay as long as possible and serve beside their African brothers and sisters in sharing God's love for the building of a new and better Rhodesia, which the Africans have renamed Zimbabwe.

SOUTH AFRICA AND NAMIBIA:

Southern Africa

On December 5, 1956, one hundred fifty-six South Africans were charged with treason by their government. About two-thirds were black. They were teachers, lawyers, shopkeepers, laborers and many from other walks of life. Most had been educated in mission schools. A few were Communists, but the great majority were sincere Christians.

The chief evidence against them was their participation in a "Defiance Campaign," and their signing of a "Freedom Charter," which began: "We, the people of South Africa declare for all our country and the world to know: that South Africa belongs to all who live in it, black and white, and that no government can justly claim authority unless it is based on the will of all the people." It went on to ask equality for all races in voting, legal status, employment, landownership, education, and government. It called for the abolition of the hated apartheid laws which regulate segregation among the races and establish white South Africans as the superior race.

The legal process ran on for four years. During this time most lost their means of earning a living. Some of the wives had to take in washing to buy food. Some mothers saw their babies starve to death because they could no longer feed them. A trickle of charity from abroad helped a little and kept some of the defendants free on bail.

The Trial of Simon Mkalipi

One of the last to come to trial was a half-blind black man named Simon Mkalipi. A black laborer with a long history of involvement in "illegal" black political groups, he carried a well-worn Bible to the witness stand. He was not ashamed of belonging to the African National Congress (ANC), which had issued the Freedom Charter. He had proudly worn the movement's green, yellow and black armband to his church until his minister rebuked him. Fearing trouble from white superiors, the minister had told him not to wear it in church. "This is as much a thing of the Church as are the things you call spiritual," replied Simon. He never returned to that church.

Now on August 2, 1960, he faced the possibility that he might be sentenced to death. The prosecution pressed him about violence.

Prosecution: "Did you think that the ANC struggle would become more bitter as the government sought to suppress it?"

Simon: "Yes, but I did not think blood would flow as though there was a war. I expected that if we were strong, the government would turn and repent, as Nebuchadnezzar did."

Then he asked to read from the Bible. The judges consented. Holding the Book close to his eyes, he read from Daniel, Chapter three about the three Hebrew youths who refused to bow down and worship Nebuchadnezzar and were cast into the fiery furnace.

Simon: "Now, my lords, these three men defied a commandment by their king who had set up an image on the plain of Dura to be of gold and to be worshiped as God. Now, according to the Hebrew belief, although they were under captivity, they did not deem it fit to ignore the living God through an idol."

Prosecution: "Do you place the Defiance Campaign on a par with what those people did in defying the law?"

Simon: "Yes."

Neither Simon nor any of the other defendants were sentenced to death. Most were acquitted with the implicit warning that the next time they might not be so fortunate. But all were stigmatized for life in a society which does not brook rebellion against laws covering racial discrimination which are written into the South African Constitution.

An Embarrassment to Christianity

This is South Africa, the most prosperous and most Christianized nation in black Africa, and the last nation to be ruled by a minority white regime. It is the embarrassment of black and white evangelicals elsewhere in Africa, as well as abroad. For along with apartheid, the government officially espouses Christian doctrine and requires that the Bible be taught in public schools and military camps with the object "that young people may come to know Jesus Christ as their Lord and Savior."

In this "Christian" country, larger than Texas and California combined and populated with almost twenty-three million people, hundreds, perhaps thousands, have died as the result of riots and strikes and government attempts to put down rebellions and enforce the apartheid laws. And, as in Rhodesia, a number of missionaries who have taken bold stands against apartheid have been deported or warned that they will be expelled if they continue to make trouble.

The Sharpeville incident in 1960 and the more recent riots in Soweto, a teeming black suburb of Johannesburg, have been well reported. In the latter over six hundred blacks were killed and hundreds injured, hundreds more imprisoned without trial, and hundreds of thousands thrown out of work.

Babies Die in Jail

Much is also known about the treatment of "political" prisoners in South African jails. After the 1960 "Defiance," some twenty African infants reportedly died of dysentery while they were with their mothers in prison. Eyewitnesses claim that torture, assault, and even murder of African prisoners are common occurrences. The murder of Stephen Biko, for example, shocked the world after proof was established that he had been beaten to death by guards or police.

Michael Scott, an Anglican priest, described what life in South African jails is like for Africans:

At night the floor space was entirely covered with the forms of prisoners lying alternately head to foot with room only for a pail of drinking water and a latrine bucket. . . . Many of the warders took an obscene delight in the searches that were made at each parade for tobacco or anything else that could be concealed on the person. The non-European pris-

oners were made to strip naked in view of all of us
and perform the most grotesque antics. . . . Worst of
all were the days when corporal punishment was
inflicted. . . . Those due for this barbaric treatment
were made to undress and stand naked. . . . Then one
by one the prisoners would enter the shed to be tied
to a triangular frame and undergo their sentence.
Sometimes there were screams, sometimes there
were not; but always when the victim emerged from
the shed, he would hardly be able to stand.

Death in Pondoland

Other tragic incidents related to apartheid in South Africa
rarely make headlines abroad. Take the police "action" in
1960 near the Anglican Holy Cross mission hospital in Pon-
doland, one of South Africa's many tribal reserves. The Pon-
dos were upset over new agricultural laws which had been
decreed without consultation with tribal elders. They
objected to an arbitrary tax increase. They were angry over
bribery and corruption among "chiefs" appointed by the federal government. As a symbol of protest, they talked of burning down the empty house of one of the hated officials who
had fled. Before taking any action, they decided to hold
another meeting.

About three hundred Pondo men met at the foot of a
hill. Many belonged to various Christian churches in the
area. Some worked at the Holy Cross mission station. They
were not expecting police trouble and went unarmed to the
meeting, although they knew an unauthorized meeting to
discuss their own affairs was against the law.

Suddenly a police helicopter clattered overhead. Behind
it came two small planes dropping tear gas bombs. This was
a signal for about a hundred policemen to move into position
on surrounding hillsides. The police opened fire while the
Africans were waving a white flag and running to escape the
gas. The police later claimed the Africans fired first. But it
was established that not one policeman was touched, let
alone hit with a gun.

The police left without counting or identifying the dead
or trying to aid the injured. The white missionary doctors at
the Holy Cross hospital did all they could, operating for
twelve hours and saving all but eleven of the victims.

Just after the missionaries fell asleep exhausted, two
tearful Pondo girls came asking about their father, a tribal

pastor, sixty years of age. He was not among the dead or wounded. Reverend Vaughn Jones, the hospital adminis- trator, phoned the jail. The preacher was there an attendant said. He and twenty–one others had been arrested. The white missionaries pooled their money to get the pastor out of jail.

The "Martyr" Question

So it goes. Are the Pondo victims "Christian martyrs?" Should Stephen Biko and the many others who have died in protests against apartheid be so classified?

Most members of the Dutch Reformed Church, largest denomination in the country, say no. Powerful politicians and some clergy say separation of the races is a part of God's plan. To tamper with apartheid is to impugn God's sover- eignty. Many hold that African blacks are inferior to whites because of the curse on Canaan as recorded in Genesis 9:25. Communists, they claim, are behind the riots and rebellions.

Members of the second most influential denomination, the Anglican Church, will not cloak apartheid under such interpretations. Some Anglicans make noises about the evils of racial segregation and discrimination, but for business or social reasons will not actively fight to eliminate apartheid. Others oppose it and take the consequences.

Why Thoughtful Christians Oppose Apartheid

Writer Alan Paton, a devout Anglican, is the most vocal op- ponent of apartheid. Paton has written, "Because I am a Christian, I am a passionate believer in human freedom, and therefore, in human rights." Paton has called members of the National Party, which established and continues to defend the apartheid laws, "outraged believers in that heretical Christianity which has made racial separation the highest of all gods, and racial difference a God-given gift which no ordi- nary man could set aside." South Africa's most renowned in- tellectual, Paton has written many books on his country's problems and in 1960 went to New York to receive the Free- dom Award. Upon returning home, Paton's passport was can- celed for blackening his country's reputation abroad.

Hundreds of foreign missionaries work in South Africa, over five hundred from North America alone. Missionary so- cieties with work in South Africa are not as reticent to speak against apartheid as they once were. But missionaries tend to keep a low profile on the subject. To speak out publicly can result in expulsion from the country. So they hold their tongues, believing their hospitals, schools, and evangelistic ministries to be more important than mounting a do-or-die crusade against apartheid.

Of course some evangelical missionaries believe it is their duty to uphold the law in a country where they are guests, including apartheid. And a substantial number still maintain that their calling is restricted to evangelism of individuals, not to social change.

The Races of South Africa

South Africa has the highest percentage of whites of any black African nation. About ten per cent of the population is of Dutch descent and speaks Afrikaans, a language developed from Dutch. Around seven per cent are mostly of British descent and speak English. The colored (mixed race) comprise another nine per cent, and three per cent are Indians (Asians). The remaining seventy per cent are blacks, divided into eight tribal subgroups. Afrikaners control the government.

Afrikaners argue that they are "natives" of South Africa and were there before the blacks. Their ancestors did arrive in 1652, but the unpopulated region where they settled on the Cape was small. There were thousands of native Africans then in the vast area now controlled by South Africa.

Missionaries Tangled with Dutch Clergy

In 1705 Moravian missionaries from Denmark stopped at the Cape on their way to India. They were so shocked by Dutch treatment of native Hottentots that they appealed for missionaries to come from Europe. The first one arrived in 1737 and had trouble with the Dutch from the start.

The Dutch thought the Hottentots were little better than animals. Missionary George Schmidt pressed on, and after six years, six Africans were ready for baptism. The local Dutch Reformed Church clergy objected that he was not qualified to baptize them since he was not ordained. Schmidt wrote home and received ordination credentials from his home church by mail. The Dutch parsons still said no; he had to be ordained in person. Disgusted with the nit-picking, Schmidt went ahead and baptized the Hottentots privately. The incensed clergy pronounced the baptisms invalid, defrocked Schmidt, and expelled him from the colony. The disillusioned missionary died shortly after returning home.

The next missionaries also had problems with the Dutch. Missionary John Vanderkemp, affiliated with the

London Missionary Society, riled them by founding a settlement for runaway slaves. Some of the slaves came from the households of the good burghers. To add insult to injury, Vanderkemp married a freed African girl. Some of his bachelor colleagues also married Africans. This was mixing the races, the Dutch ranted, a violation of God's Old Testament commandments not to intermarry with heathen. No matter that some of the burghers were themselves mixing European and African blood on the sly. From such illicit unions came the present "colored" race of South Africa.

As a result of the Napoleonic wars, Britain took possession of the Cape colony in 1814. English missionaries could now teach as they pleased. To the consternation of the Dutch, most taught racial equality. John Philip, for example, said that given the same advantages, blacks would not be inferior to whites. Philip won emancipation for slaves in South Africa in 1828.

Battle with the Zulus

Abolition of slaves was the last straw. Many Dutch, then called Boers, migrated to the interior in the Great Trek of 1835–1843. Along the way they met African Zulus in battle at a river. The Afrikaner Voortrekkers (Pioneers) wheeled their wagons into a circle, loaded their guns, and cut down thousands of Zulus. Only three Voortrekkers were killed. The "Battle of Blood River" is sacred to the history of Afrikaners today.

The Voortrekkers founded two independent territories and each was annexed by the British in successive years. Dutch resentment against British expansion led to the Boer War, which Britain won in 1902. Eight years later the British joined the colonies in the Union of South Africa.

As in other colonies, the British welcomed foreign missionaries. Preachers, teachers, doctors, and nurses flooded into the interior, setting up stations among black tribes where whites had never been seen. Hundreds of congregations were formed at the dreadful price paid by missionaries elsewhere in disease-plagued black Africa.

Racial Discrimination — A Way of Life

In 1934 the Union of South Africa became a sovereign nation within the British Commonwealth, the first British colony in black Africa to win independence. Fourteen years later a coalition of English and Dutch segregationists took power. Apartheid became official policy.

Apartheid, as it has developed under the ruling National Party, demands that the four racial groups be kept strictly separated, politically and socially. Apartheid laws affect every part of life, specifying where a person may live, attend school and even church, what jobs he may hold, and where he may be buried. South African whites and nonwhites may not eat in the same restaurants, stay in the same hotels, or ride on the same buses. White women are addressed as "madam" in stores; black women as "nanny." News stories list the names and other pertinent information about whites involved in accidents. Blacks involved in accidents are described typically as "two natives were killed." It is not unusual to come upon an auto with whites in the front seat and the back seat empty, while a black passenger occupies the half-open trunk.

The centerpiece of apartheid is a "homeland" policy under which two–thirds of the blacks live on tribal reserves that cover about thirteen per cent of the country's land area. Thousands of blacks have been forcibly removed from other areas to these intended "homelands." Some of the homelands are a crazy quilt of widely separated "islands" scattered across the country. The government purports to grant the black homelands independence, as it did to Transkei in 1976 and Bophuthatswana (Tswana) in 1977. These new entities are not recognized by the world community of nations today.

Three other new nations in the area were administered by Britain apart from South Africa. The Kingdom of Swaziland, the Kingdom of Lesotho, and the Republic of Botswana are given diplomatic status by other countries, although their economies are heavily dependent upon South Africa.

The Guerrilla War in Namibia

The hotspot at the moment is South West Africa, called Namibia by other African states. A former German colony, Namibia was put under South African mandate by the League of Nations after World War I. In 1966 the United Nations resolved that South Africa had lost jurisdiction and should withdraw its administration. South Africa disagreed and a guerrilla war for Namibia has been raging since.

The Marxist-oriented guerrillas receive assistance from Zambia, Marxist Angola, and Communists abroad. A beautiful virgin land, the size of Texas and Louisiana, Namibia is one of the richest corners of Africa in diamonds, copper, and other minerals. A plan for UN supervised elections is going ahead. South Africa has reluctantly agreed to grant independence to Namibia in 1979.

As in guerrilla wars in Angola and Mozambique, many Christians have been killed. One of the latest casualties is Namibian Lutheran evangelist Abraham Kandjibi. The father of ten, he was apparently shot and killed by guerrillas.

South Africa's Dangerous Stand

The South African government has yielded on Namibia. It has further informed neighboring Rhodesia's white minority government to expect no military help if they renege on the adopted plan for black majority rule. But inside South Africa apartheid supporters are drawing up their "wagons" as the Voortrekkers did at Blood River. They will not heed UN resolutions nor urging from the United States and Britain, both of which have large investments in the country, that South Africa move toward racial equality and majority black rule. As at Blood River, they are well-armed—possibly with nuclear weapons—and are determined to hold out. With angry black African states pressing, war becomes more of a likelihood every day.

The Dilemma of Christians

Meanwhile, sensitive missionaries and national Christians continue in a quandary. Vocal missionaries can be forced out of the country with only a month or less notice. National Christians can be arrested and imprisoned without warrants. White Christians, taking a stand, may be ostracized in society at least and jailed at worst. Black believers are in the worst bind of all. To stand up means being called a Communist and facing possible arrest by police. Failure to stand means rejection by fellow blacks.

The Frightening Future

The fuse is burning. Call them martyrs or not, it is likely that many more South Africans, of all races, will die before the fire is quenched.

As things stand now, South Africa is in a desperate position, says Stuart Briscoe, an American evangelical leader who recently spent two months there. "It's a nation divided," Briscoe wrote in *Christianity Today*, "with a church divided, in desperate need of a mighty touch of God."

BURUNDI AND RWANDA, AND ZAIRE:

Former Belgian Possessions

THE REPUBLIC OF BURUNDI AND THE KINGDOM OF RWANDA – THE HUTUS AND TUTSIS

A war between Hutus and Tutsis? The few westerners who read about it in 1972 tended to snicker over the bloody quarrel in Burundi, a little land-locked African country they had never heard of. Yet it was no joke to the families of the two to three hundred thousand killed in less than three months, and to the missionaries who saw the leadership of hundreds of congregations decimated.

The Anglican Church lost thirteen of thirty–five national pastors. All but one of fourteen members of the Baptist executive committee were killed. And in some congregations there were more widows than wives with living husbands. Yet this massacre and other lesser genocides in Burundi and Rwanda was not a religious purge, but the bitter fruit of hatred centuries old.

Adjoining Burundi and Rwanda are together less than two-thirds the size of Maine. But their combined population is almost eight times that of Maine, while their economies are among the lowest in the world. Per capita income is around sixty dollars a year. Increase in the gross national product hovers at zero. This is an area billed as the Switzerland of Africa with enormous potential for tourism.

Setting the Stage for Conflict

It was Ruanda–Urundi before the territory was split by Belgium and the United Nations into two independent nations in 1962. Belgium got the territory from Germany through a League of Nations mandate at the close of World War I. Germany had had possession only since 1890. Before that it had been an independent Tutsi monarchy for almost a thousand years. Tall and slender and skilled in warfare and dancing, the Tutsis moved down from Ethiopia. They took over the land for their cattle and made the shorter Hutus their serfs. The "Short Ones" paid tribute to the "Tall Ones" until modern times.

Missionaries Prepared the Way for Revolution

Catholic missionaries came in with Belgian administrators. Danish Baptists arrived in 1928. Anglicans, Free Methodists, Quakers, Swedish Pentecostals, and Adventists followed. By 1968 Anglicans had 85,000 members and Adventists 77,000 adherents in Rwanda alone. In Burundi to the south, the Swedish Pentecostals won 160,000 converts. Other groups reached smaller numbers. Most congregations were comprised of persons of only one ethnic group. A minority included both Hutus and Tutsis in their fellowship.

The Germans and Belgians administered Ruanda–Urundi from afar and permitted the feudal system to rule fifteen per cent of the population. The seeds for change were planted in the mission schools where Hutus learned the biblical teaching of equality and acquired skills and trades. After World War II this long trodden-upon majority began asking for equal rights.

Belgium was willing to grant independence. But the restless Hutus in Rwanda could not wait. In November, 1959, they massacred thousands of Tutsis and took over the government. Thousands more Tutsis fled to Burundi where their people still ruled. The Hutu Emancipation Movement proclaimed Rwanda a republic in 1961. Belgium granted independence the following year to Hutu rule in Rwanda and the Tutsi-dominated government in Burundi.

This same period was marked by a rising antiwhite spirit and a passion for a higher standard of living. Many missionaries left. Some national church leaders resigned. A number of pastors, of both ethnic groups, lapsed into old vices. All the while, bitterness increased between Hutus and Tutsis.

Hutus Kill a Brave Pastor

In 1963 an unsuccessful Tutsi invasion from Burundi provoked the Rwandan Hutu army to go on a rampage against Tutsis in Rwanda. Tutsi pastors did not escape the wrath.

One of the bravest pastors was Reverend Yona Kanamuzeyi who ministered to a camp of Tutsi refugees whose homes had been destroyed in previous purges. He had developed a string of twenty–four village churches, centered around a large mother church, to help six thousand people.

On January 24, 1964, a jeep loaded with soldiers drew up in front of his house. They ordered the pastor and a friend, Andrew Kayumba, into the jeep. The pastor anticipated what was coming and told his friend, Kayumba, "Let us surrender our lives into God's hands."

When they reached a military camp, Pastor Kanamuzeyi asked permission to write in his diary. He inscribed, "We are going to heaven" then asked the senior sergeant to please see that his wife was given the diary and the money in his possession. The sergeant replied, "You had better pray to your God."

The pastor stood up and prayed. As his friend Kayumba later recalled, he said, "Lord God, You know that we have not sinned against the government, and now I pray You, in Your mercy, accept our lives. And we pray You to avenge our innocent blood and help these soldiers who do not know what they are doing. . . ."

The two prisoners were then tied. One soldier came to take the pastor away, but before leaving, he asked his friend, Kayumba, "Do you believe, Brother?" Kayumba replied, "Yes."

Then the pastor was taken to a bridge. As he walked, Kayumba heard him singing:

There's a land that is fairer than day
And by faith we can see it afar:
For the Father waits over the way,
To prepare us a dwelling place there.

Shots rang out. The pastor fell, and they threw his body in the stream.

The soldiers told Kayumba to get in the jeep. "We're taking you home," they said. "But remember, if you tell anyone about the killing of the pastor, you, too, will be killed." After the soldiers dropped him off, Kayumba escaped to a neighboring country where he told the story of his pastor's martyrdom.

A Calamity Occurs

In Burundi a coup brought a new Tutsi government into power, which was pledged to progress for all citizens. A Hutu politician was appointed prime minister and other Hutus were installed in some lesser offices. But the bloom of cordiality quickly faded. The Hutu prime minister was assassinated in 1965 and a coup attempt by disgruntled Hutu leaders failed. In the confusion, the Tutsi king's nineteen-year-old son Ntare V usurped the throne and made Capt. Michel Micombero, a fanatical Tutsi, the premier. Micombero then deposed the new king, declared himself president, and ruled as dictator.

More disorder followed. Hutu discontent increased until in 1972 a rebel faction tried to overthrow the Tutsi ruler. The Tutsis quickly put down the revolt, then began a systematic slaughter of Hutu leaders and university students. Half of the country's eight thousand Hutu teachers were eliminated. Sixty of one hundred thirty teacher-training students died. Over a third of three hundred fifty university students were lost. Two thousand of ten thousand Hutu secondary school students perished. Typically, Tutsi police came to schools demanding lists of Hutu students and teachers. These were pushed into trucks and taken away to be shot.

Time's African correspondent wrote, ". . . Hundreds of bodies lie in tangled clusters, rotting in the sun. . . . In one village only five people are still alive; an army patrol shot down the women and children and pushed the men over a cliff. . . ."

Hutu pastors and lay leaders were likewise hunted down like wild animals. In some instances, Tutsi Christians were ordered to kill Hutu members of their own congregations, with the ultimatum, "If you don't kill them, we'll kill you." At one school, Christian students were beaten with their own Bibles, then finished off with rifle butts.

"Jesus, I Come"

Many Hutu Christians went to their death expressing peace and asking forgiveness for their executioners. One was Abel Binyoni, the principal of a Quaker mission school and the lay leader of a local church. Before Friends missionaries left

Burundi, he wrote them a farewell of thanks and appreciation: "We have nothing that we could return to you for all that you have done to help us. But we know well that our Lord, who is also your Lord Jesus, will not fail to repay you abundantly over and above what you have done for us. . . ."

Abel Binyoni was one of those marked for death in the 1972 carnage. A Christian soldier later reported the details of his death. After he stood up to be shot, he asked if he could sing. Permission was granted and he began,

> Out of my bondage, sorrow and night,
> Jesus, I come, Jesus, I come;
> Into Thy freedom, gladness, and light,
> Jesus I come to Thee

When he finished the fourth stanza the order came to fire. Deeply affected by his testimony, the squad hesitated for a suspenseful moment, then obeyed.

The killings tapered off after a few weeks, with selective executions continuing. In 1973 the Tutsi government launched a new reprisal. More Hutus were killed, but not before substantial numbers of Tutsis died also in bloody fighting. In Rwanda, where Hutus continued in power, reprisals were taken against smaller numbers of Tutsis.

A Blessed Revival

After the storm came a rainbow of beautiful revival in churches that had been torn asunder. Hutu and Tutsi Christians trooped to pastors, confessing sin, begging forgiveness of one another, and offering to make restitution wherever possible. Sensing the opportunity, Burundi church leaders invited in Dr. Vergil Gerber and a team of missionary specialists on evangelism and church growth.

In the aftermath of the blood baths, "Tall Ones" and "Short Ones" sat side by side in the *uruganda*—"a place to sharpen your tools"—and discussed how to heal their churches and win more Burundians to Christ. Before the workshop ended, representatives of five evangelical bodies set a goal of ninety-three per cent increase in membership within the next four years. One of the missionary specialists reported:

> It was a week of miracles! Tutsi and Hutu tribesmen
> praying and planning together in a Church Growth
> Workshop! We didn't just sing "Amazing Grace"—
> we felt it! Only the grace of God could produce this
> kind of victory and vision in a land gripped by the

mutual fear of two large tribes, a fear which had erupted into a genocidal conflict.

Two years after the workshop the Burundi Tutsi dictator was overthrown by a coalition of moderate Tutsi military officers. The leader, Lt. Col. Jean-Baptiste Bagaza, a Belgian-educated political scientist, declared his intention to end the strife between Tutsis and Hutus. One of his first actions was to appoint several Hutus to his cabinet.

Relations remain tense between the governments of Burundi and Rwanda, where Hutus continue in power. Each country accuses the other of atrocities. Christianity appears to offer the only real hope for peace.

THE REPUBLIC OF ZAIRE – THE BELGIAN CONGO

"We will make our fetishes with the hearts of the Americans and Belgians, and we will clothe ourselves in their skins." So thundered Christophe Gbeyne, president of the rebel forces that in 1964 took over Stanleyville (now known as Kisangani) the second largest city of Belgium's former possession. This was no idle threat from the communist-supported, hate-crazed rebel leader. Before the bloody debacle was finished, hundreds of foreigners were dead, including 179 Catholic priests and nuns and thirty Protestant missionary personnel in southeastern Congo. Ten thousand Congolese also fell before the spears, arrows, and guns of the rebels who called themselves Simbas (lions).

The Congolese massacres occurred less than twenty years ago. Over a dozen books have been written about the martyred missionaries, some by wives whose husbands were killed. Hundreds of articles about the faith and conduct of missionary and Congolese victims have been published. The "Congo Crisis" has likewise been well aired in the secular media. Yet the circumstances under which so many Christians died in the Congo are still not widely understood. Westerners especially are not fully aware of the role which "Christian" Belgium played in setting up the Congo for bitter division and anarchy. Nor has the incendiary role played by communist nations in fostering subversion and fomenting chaos in an unstable new African country been adequately told.

The Portuguese Connection

The Portuguese discovered the Congo in the fifteenth century and built forts at the mouth of the mighty river named for the Congo kingdom which flourished the century before. Under Portuguese rule, thousands of Congolese were converted to the Catholic faith. At the opening of every court session in the Congo, the judge announced, "Let not the money become black; let not Christ the Redeemer be overturned! Speak but the truth; do not shame Christ. We, the chiefs, will not overturn the crucifix. We swear to deliver a just judgment." Relics of the Congo's "Golden Age" indicate a highly advanced artistic civilization from the Middle Ages.

"Black ivory" (slavery) pulled down a curtain of darkness over the Congo for over four centuries. The slave trade revived tribal hatreds and promoted continual warfare. Battles meant slaves. Slaves meant geegaws (baubles) and rum from shrewd European traders. Rum meant drunkenness, more fighting, and more slaves. More slaves meant increased profits which spurred increased rivalries between Portuguese and other European merchants.

Abolition of slavery in the nineteenth century brought an end to the era of easy money. Explorers began trekking into the interior searching for gold, diamonds, white ivory, rubber, and other treasures.

Leopold's "Treasure"

Enter Leopold II, the profligate, playboy king of Belgium. Leopold saw the potential for riches in the Congo. He craftily formed the Association Internationale du Congo and hired explorer Henry Stanley as his chief agent. Stanley obtained from friendly tribal chiefs, over nine hundred thousand square miles for his employer. Leopold got his claims recognized at the Berlin West Africa Conference of 1884–1885 which divided up Africa.

Leopold's "Congo Free State" proved to be a veritable private treasure house for its owner. He broke up tribal domains by dividing the area into zones. He sold concessions to European and American businessmen. The capitalists hired Congolese for pittances and earned up to three hundred per cent profit a year. The businessmen made fortunes and paid Leopold enough royalties for him to keep his stable of European mistresses in high style.

Leopold's Horrors

Leopold saw to it that the Congolese chiefs got a share of the booty. They could collect taxes. In lieu of money a family head had to work a period of time for his assessment. This system kept the companies supplied with workers, and the chiefs got paid and were happy.

Congolese commoners got the boot end of Leopold's bonanza. Always in debt, they were subject to a system as cruel as slavery. For not making his quota, a man might be flogged or have his hand chopped off. Or his wife and children might be kept as hostages.

Not that Leopold was a heathen. He was a Catholic with high standing at the Vatican. He invited Catholic missionaries into the Congo, giving them land and subsidies for schools and churches, and bestowing on priests civil authority. He admitted Protestants also, but denied them subsidies. Leopold himself never visited his private kingdom.

By 1904 news of the abuses and atrocities in Leopold's African kingdom reached Europe. Returning Protestant missionaries and "ungrateful" Catholics told tales of horror. Some said they had seen hands stacked like cordwood in places where rubber workers had failed to meet their quotas. Social reformers in Britain and the United States branded Leopold a tyrant, more pagan than any Congolese demon worshiper. Leopold denied everything. The companies were only trying to bring Christian civilization to the Congo, he said. The criticism continued. Belgium was embarrassed. Grumblings emanated from the Vatican. Finally Leopold decided the Congo was too much trouble and deeded his private domain over to Belgium in 1908.

Belgian Paternalism

Under the beneficent rule of Belgian civil servants, missionary activity increased, until the Congo led all other countries and colonies in Africa in the number of missionaries. The Belgians yielded to criticisms of religious favoritism in the 1950's by providing some subsidies to Protestant schools.

American Catholic missionaries were not welcome. The Belgian administrators were afraid they might introduce democratic ideas and encourage Congolese involvement in politics. Nor did the Belgians want Congolese being educated abroad as hundreds of Africans from other European colonies were doing. At independence there was not a single trained Congolese lawyer in the country.

Not that the Belgians did not feel charitable toward their "children," as they spoke of the Congolese. They bragged of having fifty per cent of the school-age children in school, the highest percentage in black Africa. They were also proud of having the most comprehensive system of worker training and social welfare in Africa. As a Belgian in Stanleyville put it, "Give a Congolese a bicycle and bread in his stomach and he won't care about politics."

"We Are No Longer Your Monkeys"

Political associations began forming anyway. The Congolese had radios. They knew what was happening elsewhere in Africa. The British and French were giving up their colonies. Why shouldn't Belgium? In 1959 Belgium banned the most prominent associations. A riot ensued and fifty were killed. "Ungrateful wretches!" the colonial rulers snorted. "And after all we've done for them."

Also in 1959 a young Congolese firebrand named Patrice Lumumba went to Ghana and met Kwame Nkrumah. A former postal clerk, Lumumba had served two years for embezzling postal funds. While in prison he had written a book outlining a new Congo. A visit to the All-African People's Conference meeting in Accra, Ghana, convinced him to press for independence. Nkrumah and other black African leaders assured him that Third World nations would be supportive.

Alarmed, the Belgians offered to hold elections of rural and municipal councils, with the promise to look at the situation again in four years. Congolese politician Joseph Kasavubu boycotted the elections. Lumumba received eight per cent of the vote in some areas, placing more pressure on the Belgians.

Suddenly the Belgians stopped pushing gradualism. It was almost as if they said, "Let's get done with it." They called a Round Table Conference in Brussels and there in January, 1960, agreed to grant full independence to the Congo in June. And yet they knew all too well that the Congolese were woefully unprepared.

In hurried elections Lumumba's party led, but did not get a majority. He was quickly installed as premier, with runner-up Joseph Kasavubu named president. At independence, Lumumba told Belgium's King Baudouin I, "From today we are no longer your monkeys!" Lumumba demanded that Belgians leave immediately. Thousands began packing. Within days most of the civil servants who had held the government together were gone.

The Army Mutiny

The Congolese army mutinied and began attacking whites. Bands of undisciplined soldiers prowled the capital looking for colonialist "spies." Lumumba tried to calm them by agreeing to sack the army's white officers and replace them with Congolese. He also promised pay increases and a step up in rank to every soldier. When the disorder continued, Belgium flew in paratroops to "protect" remaining civilians.

Lumumba asked the United States for troops to put down the revolt in his army and to get the Belgian soldiers out. Fearing that military intervention might bring Russians in on the side of the rebels, since there was evidence that the Russians and Czechs had fomented the mutiny, the United States refused and supported United Nations involvement.

The UN sent in technicians and troops. But the infant nation was bereft of the Belgian infrastructure that had held the Congo together and was reeling toward catastrophe.

Troubles Increase

Mineral-rich Katanga and Kasai Provinces seceded from the Congo. Moise Tshombe, leader of the Katanga insurrectionists and a strong anti-Communist, asked Belgium for military aid.

Lumumba expected the UN would bring Katanga and Kasai back into the Congo. Dag Hammarskjold, UN Secretary–General, feared another Korea and told the UN forces to keep the conflict from spreading to involve major world powers. The United States supported Hammarskjold. Russia did not. Lumumba asked for communist military aid and the Russians and Czechs immediately sent planes and trucks. Lumumba tried but failed to take back Kasai Province. Thousands of people died in the fighting.

Angered by Lumumba's special deal with the communists, President Kasavubu dismissed him as premier. When Lumumba refused to resign, Colonel Joseph Mobutu took over command of the tattered army. Lumumba was jailed, but escaped and then was recaptured and mysteriously murdered. Russian propaganda turned Lumumba into a martyr for Congolese freedom. A university in Moscow was named for the dead African revolutionary and his supporters were offered "scholarships" to study in the Soviet Union.

Meanwhile, Dag Hammarskjold tried to deal with Tshombe in Katanga. The United Nations official was killed in a plane crash in September 1961 enroute to meet with Tshombe. Failing to bring Tshombe to terms, the UN sent troops from Ethiopia, India, and Sweden to invade Katanga. Some of the UN troops were as undisciplined as the Congolese. Running amuck in the city of Elisabethville (present Lubumbashi), they raped European women, shot unarmed whites on sight, fired on ambulances, and bombarded a hospital marked with Red Cross flags. Two of those who died were the director of the International Red Cross and a Catholic priest, Father Alexandre Ferdinando Gagna. Protestant churches and missions and forty-six civilian doctors in Elisabethville protested the slaughter.

Finally in January, 1963, the central government at Leopoldville, with UN military aid, took over Katanga. The following year, Tshombe was invited back from exile to become premier of the Congo. He immediately called in white mercenaries, who had supported him in Katanga, to solidify control of the country.

The Communist Plan for the Congo

Pierre Mulele and other key followers of Patrice Lumumba returned from "study visits" to China and other communist countries. They recruited other dissatisfied Congolese for training by Chinese officers in neighboring Tanzania. Schooled in techniques of guerrilla warfare, they came back to help the rebel leadership recruit an army to aid in the overthrow of the new Congolese government.

Youths from age ten and up were recruited by promises of adventure and revenge on whites who had persecuted their forefathers. Old stories of Belgian atrocities—some true, some exaggerated—incited young passions. Agitators told them that Christianity was the tool of Belgians and Americans to bring them back into slavery. They promised the youngsters wealth and tickets to anywhere once the "imperialists" in the Congo were defeated. They plied them with whiskey and narcotics to keep them in a stupor, then witch doctors poured a "magic" potion over their bodies to make them "invincible" to bullets so long as they did not wash or "touch" a woman. The ringleaders knew that stories of rape and the killing of female civilians could turn world opinion against them. It was one of the cruelest and most diabolical schemes ever concocted for a communist takeover of a country unprepared for independent government.

When the wave of attacks began in January, 1964, the United States provided only paltry amounts of aid to Tshombe's central government. Missionaries had been warning that communist-backed rebels were priming for battle. But the State Department thought missionaries politically naive. Unable to get further help from abroad, Tshombe hired white mercenaries for his army. The sight of whites leading Congolese troops added credence to the communist propaganda line that the central government in Leopoldville was the tool of western colonialists.

The First Attacks

From guerrilla hideouts, the young Simba rebels struck defenseless villages and government posts, looting, burning, and killing selected persons. Isolated attacks were also made on mission stations.

One morning in Kwilu Province, rebels dragged Mr. and Mrs. Auguste Eicher of Baptist Mid-Missions from their house before sunrise. They beat Auguste and forced him to kneel. One of the crazed, grinning youths fingered a sledge hammer. "Aren't you afraid?" another asked Auguste. And to his wife, "Aren't you scared of what will happen to you after we kill your husband?"

"No, I am not afraid," each declared. Their courage touched some of the rebels. A Simba intervened and after four more hours of threats, the invaders permitted villagers to take the Baptist workers into the forest. They hid for a week and were flown out to safety by a Missionary Aviation Fellowship pilot.

The Catholic mission of Kilembe in the same province was hit about the same time. The Belgian priest who answered a midnight pounding on the door was beaten to death. A second priest came to see what was happening and was also killed. Then the attackers entered and found a third Belgian father immobilized by a hip cast. They slashed him to death with butcher knives.

It was believed that the rebels were only killing men until the attack at Irene Ferrel and Ruth Hege's Baptist Mid-Mission station in the Kwilu bush. Ruth's story of Irene's murder and how she escaped dispelled any doubts that women were also vulnerable.

Death in the Moonlight

The two missionary teachers had retired for the evening at their school and dispensary in the Kwilu bush. They had heard that Simbas were moving into their area, burning villages, shooting and spearing every person with ties to Americans or Europeans, seizing and torturing foreigners in unspeakable ways. A few hours earlier they had held a farewell worship service with faithful African workers. In the morning they were anticipating the landing of a helicopter to snatch them away.

Shortly past midnight a gang of young Simbas, crazed from drinking alcohol and smoking hemp, some barely fourteen years old, invaded the lonely station. Hurling rocks through windows and screaming for blood, they rushed into the house, jerked the women from their beds, and dragged them to a grove of trees outside. There was no pleading with them. Dancing wildly about under the bright moon, they began shooting arrows at the Baptist women. A teen-ager shot an arrow into Irene's neck. Ruth saw her pull it out, take a few steps, and collapse. Also hit, Ruth fell to the ground feigning death, not even moving when a Simba jerked out a handful of her hair. Finally the attackers ran away into the forest, permitting Ruth to escape and tell the story.

Cruelty Beyond Measure

About fifty Protestant and Catholic missionaries were herded into a Catholic mission compound at Buta in the northeast. The arms of thirty-one priests were tied and crossed in back with elbows pressed together. Their feet were bound and their bodies arched. The arm and foot ropes were looped together. The tight bonds evoked cries of agony.

Denied food and water, the entire group of priests was untied, stripped, and inspected under a scorching sun. Then they were retied and marched to the river bank where the Simbas cut them to pieces and threw the parts of their bodies into the river. When the job was done, one Simba returned to the mission with a priest's leg. Extending it on a spear, he forced each captive, including the children of the Protestants, to hold it.

"They Won't Hurt Us"

The raids continued into the summer. On August 4, 1964, the rebel Simbas took the new nation's second largest city, Stanleyville, some six hundred miles northeast of Leopoldville. Their People's Republic of the Congo regime, led by Christophe Gbeyne and Pierre Mulele was quickly recognized by the Soviets as the legitimate government of the Congo. By September the rebels controlled a wide arc of territory extending south and west from their stronghold in the northeast. Many missionaries had left. Those remaining took comfort that there had been no more missionary casualties since early in the year. "They know we're nonpolitical and are only here to help the people," the holdouts reassured themselves. "They won't hurt us."

"I'll See You in Heaven"

How wrong they were. Early in September the Simbas struck the Unevangelized Fields Mission (UFM) station at Ekoko, some three hundred miles north of Stanleyville. William and Dorothy Scholten and their five young children were there, along with two nurses, Pearl Hiles from Pennsylvania and Betty O'Neill, a native of Northern Ireland. Bill Scholten was well known in the area. He had trained many African teachers. He led a corps of the *Flambeau*, a Boy Scout type of organization, taking frequent treks with his students through the jungle. When the rebels arrived, Bill was suffering from malaria, parasites, and dysentery.

The Simbas tore the station apart. They found only an out-of-order transmitter that had been used for communicating with other UFM stations. One fired his pistol five times near Bill's throbbing head. They forced him and the women to sit for hours under the blazing sun. They made him drive them on trips to nearby villages.

On September 13 malarial chills sent Bill into convulsions. That day an order came from rebel headquarters in Stanleyville to arrest him. "I'll see you in heaven," he told his family as the young men shoved him into a truck. Along the road they picked up a group of Catholic priests and took them with Bill to the prison in Aketi. The next day the other prisoners were herded into the truck for transport to Stanleyville. Bill was so sick they left him in his cell.

Somehow he managed to write his wife: "Dearest Dorothy, The Lord will not allow you to go through more than you can bear." On Wednesday morning, the sixteenth, his body convulsed in a final spasm and he passed into eternity. His wife and children and the two nurses were not harmed.

"Get Out While You Can"

Dr. and Mrs. Carl Becker and the staff at the African Inland Mission Hospital at Oicha stayed close to their radios. In 1961 the United States Consul in neighboring Uganda had radioed missionaries in the northeastern Congo provinces to leave. American intelligence, he said, had intercepted a message from Moscow inciting Lumumba's supporters to start massacring whites until Lumumba was released from prison. The missionaries at Oicha were crossing the border into

Uganda when overtaken by Lumumba's men. Dr. Becker and four other missionaries agreed to return to the hospital if their colleagues would be permitted to seek refuge in Uganda.

In 1964 Dr. Becker and the staff heard radio speeches from Stanleyville claiming Americans were killing Congolese and inciting the rebels to take revenge. As they listened over the area missionary network, one by one the transmitters of the Unevangelized Fields Missions fell silent. One night Dr. Becker heard the last UFM station warn, "Get out while you can; you don't know how bad it is."

On August 22, the staff received a message from their embassy in Kampala, Uganda: "We strongly advise all Americans to leave the Congo immediately. Pack lightly, as you may have to . . . walk through the bush to Uganda."

The AIM people at Oicha and their colleagues at other stations debated leaving. Dr. Becker wanted to stay. Those who thought it best to go argued, "If the rebels come, we will endanger the national Christians by our presence. We will be killed not because of the gospel but because we are white." Dr. Becker consented to evacuate. That evening Congolese officials from the nearby town of Beni interrupted a prayer meeting at the Beckers. "We heard you are leaving. What will happen to the hospital?" Dr. Becker assured them that national workers would continue to help the sick and injured. The Congolese were adamant that Dr. Becker must stay. "We will die with you," they said. Not until the rebels were nearing the hospital did the Congolese consent for Dr. Becker to go. Yonama Angondia, the Congolese medical director, was left in charge of the staff.

The Raid on Dr. Becker's Hospital

On September 23, 1964, Simbas moved into the area. At Yonama's urging, some of the staff and many of the stronger patients fled into the forest. The next day the Simbas surrounded the hospital. Yonama and some of those remaining hid in some tall elephant grass. Bullets whistled over their heads as they prayed for protection upon themselves and those unable to leave the hospital. The shooting stopped before nightfall, but Yonama waited all night before sending back a scout. He returned to report that seven patients and workers had been killed. Dr. Becker and Yonama had been at the top of the rebels' "kill list." Rebels, the scout said, had split open the skulls of some patients and taken their brains.

The surviving staff urged Yonama to get away before he was killed. He started toward the border of Uganda stopping for shelter with people he knew along the way. Finally he reached the other refugees who had fled on September 23. They were waiting at a rest camp just inside Uganda. Dr. Becker and the missionaries, they said, were safe.

A Missionary "Spy" Is Captured

Young Dr. Paul Carlson and his wife Lois served at an Evangelical Covenant Church hospital in the northern Congo. Their station at Wasolo was called "the forgotten corner" because it was so remote. Dr. Carlson had come out to help in Congo relief for a few months during 1961. Later he and his family returned as permanent missionaries.

Dr. Paul kept Congolese Christians abreast of what was happening. At the annual church conference he told them at communion time that Pierre Mulele had been taught by the Chinese to hate Christians and shown how to wage war. "He returned in 1963 to the Congo to begin doing just what others did long ago in China. . . . Our missionaries worked there for Jesus, but when the Communists took over the government, they sent away all the missionaries." Then he gave reports radioed by other missionaries about the burning of churches and Bible schools. "We do not know what will happen in 1964 — and in 1965 — until we meet together again. We do not know if we will have to suffer or die during this year because we are Christians. But it does not matter. Our job is to follow Jesus." Then he urged, "My friends, if today you are not willing to suffer for Jesus, do not partake of the elements. . . . To follow Jesus means to be willing to suffer for him."

In August the Carlsons heard that rebels were coming toward Wasolo. They waited until after the wedding of two missionaries at the hospital. Then in early September Paul escorted Lois and their two children across the Ubangi River into the Central African Republic and returned to the hospital alone. Before leaving his loved ones, he assured them he had several escape routes mapped out just in case.

They stayed in touch by radio. Wednesday morning, September 9, Paul reported a "little disturbance" in the town near the hospital. "I'm going to check it out." That afternoon he came on again. "I must leave this evening," he said.

Lois and a woman colleague waited up and watched the stream of refugees pour across the river. Dr. Paul was not among them. Lois remembered a message he had recently taped for their church in California. He had asked prayer for revival in the Congolese church and for wisdom to help the Congolese Christians with their problems. "They do not realize," he had said, "that in this century more people have died for their witness for Christ than died in the early centuries, which we think of as the days of martyrs."

Saturday morning Lois picked up his voice again. "I'm all right. I'm all right," he repeated. "I love you all. Take the children to a school. This may take a long time. I love you."

She hung by the radio. Another missionary came on, calling for Paul. "Where are you? Everyone is gone." Lois heard him answer back, then the other missionary asked, "Can we send a plane or a 'copter?" Paul replied, "Please don't. I am all right now. . . . The Lord is very near."

Once more, on September 18, she heard him say again, "I'm all right." The next report was that he and three Catholic priest friends had been captured by rebels who had burned the hospital and taken them away.

She received a brief letter dated September 24 in which he said, "Where I go from here I know not, only that it will be with Him. If by God's grace I live, which I doubt, it will be to His glory." And another dated October 21 assuring, "I know I'm ready to meet my Lord, but my thoughts for you make this more difficult. I trust that I might be a witness for Christ. . . ."

Five days later the rebel radio announced that a "Major" Carlson, a mercenary, had been captured and brought to Stanleyville and would be tried for spying.

"You Will Please Come with Us"

UFM missionaries were scattered all over the northern Congo. Britisher Margaret Hayes and Virginian Mary Baker were at Bopeke. Through the spring and early summer of 1964 they were so busy teaching and nursing that they seldom thought of danger. But the pastor of the village church, Bo Martin, often suggested that missionaries and Congolese Christians would soon see much bloodshed.

Margaret became very tired. "Go to Banjwadi and take a rest," Mary urged. "I'll carry on here." Reluctantly, Margaret left on August 1 for the larger station where UFM had a hospital. Her first evening there, she enjoyed fellowship and worship with several colleagues. The next morning Dr. Ian Sharpe and his wife, Audrey, an English doctor–nurse team, their children and a first-term Irish nurse, Robina Gray, left on a trip.

About noon the UFM Field Secretary came on the radio to warn of rebel advances. "Have a bag packed for emergencies," he urged missionaries in the southeastern bush. The group at Banjwadi stayed near the radio. Several days later Mary Baker called. Simbas had come to Bopeke, she reported and were asking about her radio.

One quiet Saturday afternoon a carload of Simbas drove into Banjwadi and asked if any Americans were there. Charles Davis stood up proudly and announced, "I am an American."

"You will please come with us," the officer then said. "We must take you and your family to the American Consul in Stanleyville." He displayed a paper which he claimed was signed by the Consul. The Davises believed him and went along willingly.

In Stanleyville they were driven to the airport hotel where the Consul and four of his staff were being held hostage. A few minutes later a rebel officer ordered the Davises to line up against an outside wall. Muriel Davis prayed they would all die together. It was just a scare, for the rebels permitted Muriel and the children to join other missionaries at a mission center in the suburbs known as Kilometer Eight.

"Please Tell Me How to Become a Christian"

At Banjwadi, Margaret Hayes was feeling very concerned about her partner Mary Baker at Bopeke when a French doctor showed up. The British Consul in Stanleyville, he said, had asked him to escort Margaret back to Bopeke. When Margaret arrived, Mary burst into tears. The Simbas were still there. They told the two missionaries to go ahead with their work.

In September they grieved to hear of Bill Scholten's death from malaria. Later in the month they rejoiced when a local chief was converted.

In October a rebel captain came and asked if he could be baptized. "I know I will die in battle," he said. "I want to be ready to meet God." Margaret and Mary gave him instructions, and asked him to wait.

A few evenings later a truck rumbled up at 11:30 P.M. Six half-naked Simbas, their bodies decorated with palm leaves, jumped out shouting, "You are under arrest." They let Margaret and Mary go back to bed. Then after extensive "inspections" the next day, they ordered the women to walk with a Simba escort to the town of Banalia. Upon arriving, they were told that other Simbas had been dispatched to pick up the Dennis Parry and Dr. Ian Sharpe families and nurse Robina Gray at other locations.

They were put in a house and watched day and night, and were often subjected to taunts and threats. One night a young Simba crept up to Margaret and knelt beside her head. "Please, tell me how to become a Christian," he begged. Quietly she led him to give his life to Christ.

"We'll See You . . . in Glory"

In November the other missionaries were brought in. Dennis and Nora Parry had been severely beaten. Nora's leg and arm were broken. But otherwise they and the others were in reasonably good shape.

The missionaries were permitted to talk and pray and read their Bibles together. One day Margaret read a promise about deliverance. "That's for you," Mary murmured. "It's not for me." Another day, Nora Parry said substantially the same about herself.

There were now about thirty Catholic missionaries with the Protestant prisoners at Banalia. They all noticed that their guards were growing increasingly edgy about anticipated American intervention. "If your planes come," the Simbas told the missionaries, "we will kill all of you."

On November 23 Margaret was called out alone and put on a truck. "Reserve a seat for the rest of us on the plane," Dr. Ian requested lightly. Then more seriously: "We'll see you either on the plane or in Glory."

"You Americans Are the Cause of All Our Trouble!"

Missionaries and other foreigners continued to be rounded up by rebel soldiers in the northeastern Congo. Usually they were first put under house arrest and watched, then later the men, and in some instances women, were imprisoned in a more secure place.

J.W. and Angeline Tucker were in Paulis (now Isiro), a bustling town about three hundred fifty miles northeast of Stanleyville. Since late summer "Jay" Tucker and seventy–one other foreigners had been in and out of prison.

The Tuckers were with the Assemblies of God. Jay had come to the Congo in 1939 and married Angeline on the field. For a quarter century they had preached, baptized, established churches, translated Scripture, and dispensed medicines. Almost everyone in Paulis knew them. Jay was the only American man in the town.

After their capture, Jay was ushered into the office of a rebel colonel who sat beside his witch doctor, an obese mulatto woman. The missionary noticed that the colonel, who seemed to be on drugs, never answered a question or gave an order without first getting her concurrence. When Jay said that he was an American, both went wild. The colonel pushed a revolver against Jay's jaw, swinging his face from side to side, while shouting, "You Americans are the cause of all our trouble. You gave our enemies planes and guns and mercenaries. I'm going to kill you." Seizing on inner strength, Jay stared until the rebel officer dropped the gun and told him to go home and not mix in politics. The missionary returned to his wife and children.

Early in November Jay and a number of priests were sequestered in a new Catholic boarding school for European children. It was a comfortable jail. They had individual rooms, and Catholic sisters were allowed to prepare their meals. The only discomfort was the frequent beatings by Simba soldiers.

Around November 10 about half the men were freed. Word went around that Jay and the rest were being held as hostages against the day when the national government might try to retake Paulis. They did not know how near that day of reckoning was.

"Smiling Bill"

Between Paulis and Stanleyville the rebels sealed off a large area around the Worldwide Evangelization Crusade's station at Ibambi. The six WEC missionaries there were allowed to continue their work with only minor harassments.

The sunbeam of the group was twenty-eight-year-old bachelor William McChesney. "Smiling Bill," as everyone called him, was only five foot two and weighed a hundred ten pounds. He more than made up for his size with cheer. The son of a Free Methodist minister, Bill was on his first term as an evangelist.

Bill's commitment had been expressed in a poem written shortly before embarking for the Congo and published in the WEC news publication. Titled "My Choice," it bespoke the reason for other missionaries coming to the Congo as well:

I want my breakfast served at eight,
With ham and eggs upon the plate;
A well-broiled steak I'll eat at one,
And dine again when day is done.

I want an ultramodern home
And in each room a telephone;
Soft carpets, too, upon the floors,
And pretty drapes to grace the doors.

A cozy place of lovely things,
Like easy chairs with inner springs,
And then I'll get a small TV—
Of course, "I'm careful what I see."

I want my wardrobe, too, to be
Of neatest, finest quality,
With latest style in suit and vest:
Why should not Christians have the best?

But then the Master I can hear
In no uncertain voice, so clear:
"I bid you come and follow Me,
The lowly Man of Galilee."

"Birds of the air have made their nest,
And foxes in their holes find rest,
But I can offer you no bed;
No place have I to lay My head."

In shame I hung my head and cried.
How could I spurn the Crucified?
Could I forget the way He went,
The sleepless nights in prayer He spent?

For forty days without a bite,
Alone He fasted day and night;
Despised, rejected—on He went,
And did not stop till veil He rent.

A man of sorrows and of grief,
No earthly friend to bring relief;
"Smitten of God," the prophet said—
Mocked, beaten, bruised, His blood ran red.

If He be God, and died for me,
No sacrifice too great can be
For me, a mortal man, to make;
I'll do it all for Jesus' sake.

Yes, I will tread the path He trod,
No other way will please my God;
So, henceforth, this my choice shall be,
My choice for all eternity.

"I Wonder What Is Ahead"

On October 30 the WEC missionaries and other foreigners at Ibambi were carted into Paulis. The rebel commander there was not too happy to see them. "I have no orders from Stanleyville for them to be brought here. Take them back." So the trucks turned around and returned them to Ibambi. When the Congolese Christians at the station saw the missionaries coming, they burst into joyful shouts and singing. Yet they knew their friends were still not out of danger. "If the Simbas try to force you to deny the Lord," one old deacon pledged, "we are ready to die with you."

The next weeks were hard as the rebels put the missionaries through staged trials, threatening to kill them for crimes they knew nothing about.

On November 14 the rebels came for Bill McChesney. Though he was ill with malaria, they took him to the neighboring WEC station at Wamba where four other missionaries were under house arrest. One of the four, James Rodger, a forty-two-year-old Scot, was a solemn, staid opposite to the smiling McChesney. Bill and Jim Rodger knew each other, but during the next ten days they became bosom companions. Their fellowship ran deep as they talked about the sufferings of Christ and what might be in store for them. "I wonder what is ahead," Jim mused. "I'll guess we'll know pretty soon."

"I Put My Hand to the Plow"

At Boyulu, directly south of Paulis, eight UFM personnel had been anticipating a rebel advance into their area. They continued teaching, preaching, training, and caring for the physical ills of Congolese neighbors, believing that it was God's will for them to remain. The group included four single women and two married couples, John and Elizabeth Arton and Chester and Dolena Burk. The Arton's sixteen-year-old daughter Heather was visiting from school in England, making nine foreigners at the station. Heather took her turn with the others in leading daily prayer sessions.

The first truckload of Simbas roared onto the grounds in August. Brandishing long, sharp spears, the young warriors looked fierce in their palm leaf coverings and white paint.

"Tie them up," one Simba commanded as they leaped from the trucks.

"Why us?" Chester Burk asked.

"We always tie government officials."

"But we're not officials."

"Isn't this the government station of Bafwasende?"

"No. This is Boyulu, a missionary station."

"Oh, we are very sorry. Forgive us." And with that the rebels jumped back in their trucks and drove away.

Harassment continued, though, and in mid-November the Boyulu missionaries and Heather were put under house arrest. Armed Simbas lounged outside their house day and night, never coming inside but often staring through the windows. In spite of the tense situation, they were kept in good spirits by Laurel McCallum, an Aussie girl, who never seemed to have a down moment.

The Boyulu nine were plucky, sturdy people. The Burks, for example, had farmed in Alberta, Canada, before answering the call to missionary work. After studies at Prairie Bible Institute, they had come to the Congo where Chester acquired fame among the Congolese as an elephant hunter. He used illustrations from farming and the jungle in his preaching and teaching.

The Burks had been harassed at gunpoint during the 1960–1961 troubles. Afterwards Chester became seriously ill. After a furlough in Canada, he seemed to be his old self and they returned to Africa. He did admit to UFM friends Hector and Ione McMillan of a dread in returning. But there was no flinching. "I put my hand to the plow, and I'll not look back," he said.

"Do You Believe in God?"

While being held under guard, Chester and John Arton heard Simba officers telling young recruits about "people with different white skins and with different eyes" who "will come next year." Obviously, Chinese. "They will buy your crops and give you a good price," the officers promised. Another time they overheard the officers tell young Simbas, "Don't be fooled when these missionaries say they love you. They are only in the Congo to cheat you."

The suspense-filled days passed slowly until November 24 when two rebel officers drove up in a small automobile. "Why aren't these foreigners in prison?" they shouted to the guards. "Take them to Bafwasende at once."

The eight missionaries and young Heather Arton hurriedly packed and climbed into a truck. At Bafwasende, only five miles away, they were ordered into a room in a house confiscated from a Belgian businessman. The small room was already crowded with seven Catholic priests and eleven Italian nuns.

Young Simbas ordered them all to kneel. Then the guards began pressing lighted cigarettes against the foreigners' mouths. Once a guard barked to a nun, "Do you believe in God?" When she replied, "Yes," he struck her with his stick and snarled, "There is no God!"

No one could be sure what would happen next.

In "Limbo" At Kilometer Eight

Among other missionaries trapped behind rebel lines were four men and their wives, four other women, and a flock of children at the UFM station known as Kilometer Eight—so named because it was eight kilometers from Stanleyville. It consisted of only two houses and a group of small cottages. In better times African pastors had come here for spiritual life conferences. The missionary refugees occupied the two houses now.

Charles and Muriel Davis were here, Charles having been permitted to rejoin his wife after a short imprisonment in Stanleyville. Dr. Paul Carlson was still being held in a hotel as a spy. The rebel radio kept announcing his imminent execution, but he was still alive. The senior missionary at Kilometer Eight was Al Larson. The other two men there were Hector McMillan and Bob McAllister. The McMillan's six sons, ranging in age from ten to seventeen, were with them.

Since the rebel capture of Stanleyville on August 4, the missionaries at Kilometer Eight had been under house arrest. Young Simba guards were lounging informally around the premises, fingering their rifles as if they were toys, asking questions of the missionaries, scowling when any of the children laughed, and reporting to officers who came by periodically. As at other stations where missionaries were held, those at Kilometer Eight kept up a work routine. The women nurses were even permitted to bicycle into nearby villages for medical emergencies.

Kilometer Eight was on a main road leading to Stanleyville. Bands of Simbas straggled along the road daily. One day a group told the missionaries that the United States had dropped an atomic bomb on a village to the north, killing six thousand innocent women and children. Authorities of the People's Republic of Congo regime had ordered two days of mourning, they said.

At night the missionary couples gathered for quiet fellowship and Bible study. They were living in limbo, waiting for something to happen. They both feared and looked forward to anticipated foreign intervention. The rebels had also threatened them with death if there was an invasion or parachute drop of rescue troops.

Challenged By Martyrs of the Past

The group recalled events that had touched their lives in the past. Charles Davis had been challenged by the five Auca martyrs in Ecuador and the testimony of German martyr Dietrich Bonhoeffer. Muriel had been touched by the sacrificial deaths of John and Betty Stam in China. Ione McMillan said she had offered her life to God as a missionary when the Stams had been killed in China.

Ione had attended Moody Bible Institute. Her husband, Hector, a Scotch-Canadian, was a graduate of the Prairie Bible Institute. They were married in the Congo, with Chester and Dolena Burk "standing" in their wedding. The McMillans had given twenty–three years to the Congo. Hector had a booming voice. The other missionaries could easily hear him reading to his six sons each night. Besides chapters from the Bible, he read the life of Hudson Taylor, founder of the China Inland Mission, books by A.W. Tozer and V. Raymond Edman, and even a history of the Reformation. He "claimed" a Bible verse for each son every day and prayed for each individually.

In November the men at Kilometer Eight were taken to Stanleyville. Because Hector McMillan and Bob McAllister were Canadians, the British Consul was able to arrange for their return to their families at Kilometer Eight. Hector seemed to have a harbinger of his death. After he came back, he began handing over the spiritual nurture of the boys to Ione. He also talked with Ione about the unimportance of a

Christian's body, for "one who dies is with Christ immediately," he said.

The Hostages in Stanleyville

By mid-November hundreds of foreigners were trapped in Stanleyville. But only the Americans and Belgians were held as hostages.

"Major" Paul Carlson was the most talked-about captive. Rebel propaganda had made the mild, unassuming missionary medic a monster to the minds of impressionable Congolese. Almost every day he was marched out for execution to the monument erected in memory of Patrice Lumumba. He was cuffed and kicked around before jeering mobs, but never shot.

Public facilities had broken down. Young gun-toting Simbas were everywhere, each a law unto himself it seemed. But it was the near prospect of intervention that kept nerves on razor's edge.

On Friday, November 20, Paul Carlson, five United States diplomats, and two young American conscientious objectors who had come to help in relief work were moved to the Victoria Hotel. Here they joined Charles Davis and Al Larson along with an assortment of other prisoners.

In the four days they were together, the little group enjoyed a close fellowship. They laughed and kidded one another a little, but underlying everything was the feeling that each day might be their last. "I can't think about the future," Paul Carlson said. "I can just live one day at a time, and trust the Lord for that day."

But they did talk about the future. Paul said he would like to come back to the Congo if his wife was willing. He wanted an airstrip built at the Wasolo hospital. (Less than a year later children in vacation Bible schools of the Evangelical Covenant and Evangelical Free churches collected money to buy a plane for Wasolo. An airstrip was subsequently built.)

Saturday night, November 21, the men prisoners were ordered downstairs. A Simba officer appeared and gave a long harangue about American and Belgian atrocities. He claimed that planes had bombed the town of Banalia, killing most of the women and children there. Then he said, "You're all going to prison tomorrow to be shot. Go back to your bedrolls and wait in the hallway."

Sleep was impossible. Simbas roamed the hallways,

frequently stopping to point a rifle at a prisoner and stare. If a man stared back, the Simba would turn away. Sunday morning came and nothing more had happened. The Simbas had only been playing another cruel game.

Or had they? That afternoon the male prisoners were herded into two trucks and a bus. "You're going to Banalia," an officer said. Seven miles outside Stanleyville the bus broke down and the passengers were brought back to the hotel.

Day of Doom and Deliverance

Tuesday morning, November 24. The prisoners in the hotel were awakened about 6:00 A.M. by the roar of plane engines. "Outside! Outside!" a Simba screamed through the halls. "Run! Run! Hurry!"

At the sound of the planes, missionary hostages and prisoners held elsewhere in Stanleyville were also herded into the streets. Among them were WEC's Muriel Harman, the Cyril Taylor family and Miss Phyllis Rine who was with the African Christian Mission.

At age twenty-five Miss Rine was one of the youngest missionaries in the Congo. A teacher from Cincinnati, she had signed up in 1960 for missionary service. Before the rebels took over Stanleyville, she had been planning to ride her bicycle into outlying areas of the city and teach Jesus Christ.

Silver-haired Muriel Harman had been in the Congo thirty-seven years, during which she had taken only three furloughs. A native of British Columbia, Canada, she had spent many of those years with a co-worker among the isolated Wandaka people who had been completely unreached by the gospel. Another missionary would later remember how she had once taken the sheets off her own bed to bind up the wounds of lepers.

Cyril Taylor, forty-five was a New Zealander. A gifted linguist, he had opened a Bible school just the year before. His wife, two sons and two daughters were with him in Stanleyville when the American planes dropped the rescue force.

The Belgian paratroopers were floating down like giant snowflakes when the Taylors and Muriel Harmon were pushed into the street and ordered to get into a line. Moments later a nervous Simba sprayed the line with an automatic rifle. Cyril crumpled to the ground—dead. His sons, fourteen and twelve, escaped by falling down and feigning death. Mrs. Taylor and two daughters, three and five, were attacked by a rebel soldier with a machete. They received severe gashes across their heads, but all survived.

Phyllis Rine was among some two hundred fifty white hostages driven into the public square near the Lumumba monument. She was fatally hit by a machine gun blast.

"Paul Died That I Might Live"

Charles Davis ran beside Paul Carlson. "What's happening, Paul?"

"They may be planning to use us as a shield."

They were in the street now and still running. They heard a machine gun cut loose about a block away. Suddenly they were halted at the corner and ordered to sit on the ground. The firing was closer now.

They recognized a Simba colonel named Opepe. He looked like a wild man. "Haven't I been your friend and protected you?" he yelled. "Why are your brothers coming to attack us now?"

The machine gun kept firing. Closer. A Simba guard at the rear of the crowd panicked and fired his rifle. Other guns began firing, shooting into the crowd. The prisoners fell flat on the street and waited for the end. The guns fell silent. About ten prisoners ran for a house. They had to climb over a masonry wall to reach the porch. Paul Carlson was behind Charles Davis and motioned for Charles to go first. Charles leaped and dove over the wall. He turned to grasp the doctor's outstretched hand. A gun cracked five times. Dr. Paul fell back into the street . . . dead.

Some of the other hostages were hit and killed or wounded. Among the missionaries, only the doctor was shot fatally. Charles Davis ran on into the house and huddled among seven other men on the floor of a closet. A Simba ran by and did not see them. Ten minutes elapsed. They heard an American voice. "They're in here." Then two Belgian paratroopers. "You're safe! You're safe!" they called. "Come out."

Charles Davis ran back to the porch and saw his friend's bullet-riddled body. "Paul's dead! Dead!" he sobbed. "I must have cried for fifteen minutes," he later recalled. "By letting me go first, Paul died that I might live."

"You Shot My Friend"

The missionaries at Kilometer Eight were also awakened by the planes. They ran outside to see. Then they went back for breakfast and devotions as usual.

Two armed Simbas burst into the house while they were praying and turned the breakfast tables upside down. One grabbed a slide projector and shouted accusingly, "Radio transmitter!" Another ordered, "Everybody outside."

The Simbas lined their prisoners up, separating the men from the women. Then they sent the women and children back inside one of the houses, telling the two men, Hector McMillan and Bob McAllister, to stay where they were.

The Simba who escorted the women inside turned back to the door, and then whirled and sprayed the room with bullets. Two of the McMillan boys were hit, but not hurt seriously. The younger children were crying; the rest were praying.

Guns blazed in the yard. Hector McMillan fell, dying instantly. "You shot my friend!" Bob McAllister yelled at a Simba. The Simba shot again. Bob fell to the ground and lay there playing dead. The Simbas left, apparently thinking they had killed both men. Bob got up, and he and some of the women tenderly carried Hector's body into the living room. Ione McMillan called her six sons. "Your father has gone to be with the Lord," she announced. Those in the room knelt with her in prayer.

Some of the women and children fled into the forest behind the station. Others remained to care for the injured boys. Those in the forest waited until almost noon, when suddenly they heard heavy shooting. Abruptly the shooting stopped. Al Larson, who had escaped from Stanleyville, called out that the siege was over.

The Massacre at Banalia

Before the parachute drop, the prisoners at Banalia had been permitted to do medical work. Dr. Sharpe was too valuable, the rebels said, to be kept in confinement.

The Simbas there waited until the day after the parachute drop into Stanleyville. At 4:00 P.M. they pulled Dr. Sharpe from the midst of an operation. "We will kill your family and allow you to keep helping us in the hospital," they offered.

The British medic shook his head. "We will die together. You may kill me first."

A Simba threw a spear. Others beat the doctor with guns and arrows until he died. Then they killed Audrey Sharpe and their three young children. The Parrys and their two children were next. Then Mary Baker and Robina Gray. The Catholic missionaries were the last to die.

The Simbas threw their bodies into the river.

"He is in Heaven"

Angeline Tucker was still separated from her husband in Paulis. She heard via Voice of America that paratroopers had landed in Stanleyville and rescued about a thousand Europeans. Shortly afterwards, the Mother Superior phoned her from the Catholic school where J.W. Tucker and other prisoners had been held. The nun assured her that J.W. was well and in good spirits. There were seventy-two prisoners at the school, she said.

At 9:00 A.M. the next morning, November 25, she called the Mother Superior back. "How are things?" she asked.

"Oh—so-so," the nun replied in a tight voice. Angeline knew something had happened.

"How is my husband," she asked hopefully.

"*Il est au Ciel*—He is in Heaven," the nun replied softly. "May God comfort your heart to know he was ready to die."

Angeline was still crying when her daughter Carol Lynne appeared. "Mummy, what happened?"

"Honey, I'm afraid the rebels have killed Daddy." The little girl and her younger brother, "Cricky," burst into tears.

The phone connection had been broken. Somehow Angeline managed to call the nun back. "Sister, how did it happen?"

"I don't know all the details, Madam. Only that the rebels came about nine-thirty last night and dragged the men from their rooms. We think they killed about thirteen. We know your husband was among them and some of the priests." Angeline later heard that J.W. and the priests had been stomped and clubbed to death and thrown in the Bomokandi River, twenty-five miles away.

The next morning they heard planes, then after awhile gunfire. An hour or so after the planes landed, Cricky looked out the front window. "Mummy," he squealed, "Soldiers in the street. They're white!"

One of the Belgian soldiers saw them and several ran into the yard. "Come quickly! Quickly!" they called in

French. The grieving family climbed into a truck for the trip to the airport. An officer asked who they were.

"We're Protestant missionaries," Angeline said. "Americans."

"Mrs. Tucker's husband was killed by the rebels two nights ago," the woman beside her whispered.

The Belgian gently put his arm over Angeline's shoulder. "I'm so sorry, Madam. I wish we could have come in time to save him."

"We Will All Die Together"

On November 27 the Protestant and Catholic women prisoners at Bafwasende were ordered into the yard and made to pick grass. Then the Simbas marched them barefoot to the nearby river to bathe. "Sing," a Simba ordered Dolena Burk and Olive McCarten, who were leading the procession. They began, "Onward, Christian Soldiers." Louie Rimmer, an elderly missionary woman, Laurel McCallum, Jean Sweet, Elizabeth and Heather Arton, and the nuns joined in.

After they got back to the house, fighter–bombers of the Congolese air force, piloted by anti-Castro Cuban mercenaries, buzzed the station. The Simba guards panicked and ran in every direction. "If one of us dies today, ten of you will be killed," one Simba yelled as he ran for cover.

When the planes were past, several rebel soldiers ran into the house screaming, "We've got to kill you now." "Disrobe! Disrobe!" shouted another.

Helpless before pointed guns the eighteen Catholic missionaries and the eight Protestants began undressing. Before they had finished, some of the rebels were already prodding the men toward the river.

"Chester!" Dolena Burk called. "Chester!" The Simbas pushed him ahead, refusing even to let him turn his head.

On the veranda the Simbas separated three nuns from the other sisters. "You nursed in the hospital, so you will not be killed," they told them.

The three refused. "If one dies, we will all die together." But by beatings and sheer force the Simbas kept the three nurses back.

The Simbas pointed at the Protestant women. "You and you and you," they said, indicating Dolena, Louie, and Olive. "Follow the sisters and the men to the river."

They walked a few steps, then the apparent leader of the Simbas yelled for them to come back. The other nuns, also, were brought back.

Dolena stumbled back to the house. At the doorway she heard shots from the river. She looked back at the path to the river bank. Laurel McCallum, Jean Sweet, and Betty Arton and Heather were disappearing from sight. No one was calling them back.

Nothing more happened until evening when Simba guards brought back clothing to the nuns and the three Protestant women who had been spared.

"When will we be killed?" one of the nuns wanted to know.

"Oh, we're done," a Simba replied.

"Did you shoot my husband and the others?" Dolena Burk pressed. The Simba refused to answer.

A couple of days later the survivors saw Congolese women in the area wearing the clothing of those who had been marched to the river. Then the wife of the rebel colonel who commanded Bafwasende stopped at the house and verified that Chester and the others were dead. "My husband told me," the woman reported. "He said the teen-age girl could have lived if she had let the soldiers do what they wanted. She was so stubborn."

During the next two weeks the survivors were kept in suspense. Some were slapped around and cursed. Only the intercession of a young rebel captain, Jean Pierre, kept them from being killed. They knew he was risking his life by protecting them.

On December 18 the government mercenaries came and rescued them. The women signed a letter attesting to Jean Pierre's bravery and asked that he be spared. "We'll not kill him," the mercenary officer promised. "But the national army is something else."

That afternoon the women were flown to liberated Stanleyville. While there Dolena Burk heard a radio newscaster say a young rebel captain from Bafwasende had been turned over to the national army and executed.

"Brother, I'll Die With You"

Bill McChesney, Jim Rodger, and their colleagues faced the final wrath of the Simbas on the evening of November 24 at Wamba. An arriving rebel officer turned livid when he saw Bill McChesney. "Why is this man still free?" he demanded. "Take him to prison at once!"

When Bill was pushed into a truck, Jim Rodger jumped in to accompany his sick friend. During the short trip, Simba soldiers beat Bill mercilessly. Still weak from malaria, Bill could not stand up under the abuse. Jim had to carry him into the prison where they were pushed into a tiny, fetid cell, already jammed with some forty prisoners, including several foreign priests. The Simbas had ripped Bill's clothes from his back. The priests gave him their clothes to contain the malarial chills that wracked his body.

The next morning a glowering rebel colonel came and ordered the prisoners to be moved into the courtyard where local Congolese swarmed around them, screaming for their deaths. After a while the colonel began separating the prisoners by nationality.

Eight Belgian priests and a bishop were put in one group. The bishop had been beaten so badly that he was hardly recognizable. The Colonel turned next to Bill and Jim. "You, American?" he snarled at Bill. Bill nodded weakly. The colonel glared at Jim. "What are you?"

"British."

The officer motioned for Bill to stand apart. From signs made to his men, it appeared that he was about to order Bill's death. Jim Rodger stepped beside his friend. "If you must die, brother, I'll die with you."

"He's an Englishman," one of the priests shouted to the colonel. The colonel turned to face Jim. "What is your nationality?" No reply. "Doesn't matter. American—British— they're all alike."

The frenzied mob was permitted to move forward. Clubs and fists rained on the two WEC missionaries. Bill McChesney was probably killed by the first blow. Jim Rodger caught him as he fell and gently laid him on the ground. The mob knocked Jim down and trampled on his body until he was dead. The Belgian fathers were next. Like crazed jungle beasts, the rebel-incited mob beat, kicked, and trampled them until life had fled their bruised bodies. The mob also killed sixteen other foreign civilians before the massacre was over.

Cooler Congolese carted the bodies to the Wamba River and tossed them into the yellow, swirling water to be eaten by crocodiles.

"Burleigh Law's Last Flight"

The Congo missionary martyrs were all killed in groups except pilot Burleigh Law. The genial Methodist might have lived had he not insisted on trying to help colleagues in difficult circumstances.

Law dropped a note to missionaries at the Wembo

Nyama station, requesting a landing signal. Trapped by rebels, they did not respond, hoping he would fly on. He landed anyway to check on them and was seized. When he refused to turn over his plane key, he was shot by a trigger-happy guard.

Burleigh Law was known and loved in the area. The rebel commander was displeased at the rash action of the guard. One of the young Simbas talked sadly about him. "He was *our* pilot, you know."

The rebels permitted two missionary doctors to operate with the hope of saving his life. "Why did you land?" his friends asked. He replied, "I just couldn't leave you folks in this situation." Despite transfusions from fellow missionaries, he died on the operating table.

The missionaries he had tried to help later escaped.

The Last Missionaries Are Rescued

With the loss of Stanleyville, the rebel capital, the insurrectionists in other major northeastern cities surrendered quickly to government troops led by the white mercenary officers hired by Premier Tshombe. Anxious missionaries and families at home followed news of the advance with breathless concern for the scores of rebel hostages not yet accounted for. One by one, the missing were established as dead or alive. The bodies of those thrown into rivers were never found. Eyewitnesses verified their deaths, however.

Seven months after the parachute drop on Stanleyville, British nurse Margaret Hayes was still missing. Finally, in late June, 1965, she and a group of Catholic nuns were rescued by mercenaries. They were bedraggled and in poor health, but none were seriously ill. "Until the last we had expected to be killed any day," Margaret said. "The Lord gave me Mark 5:36, 'Be not afraid, only believe.' I knew that whether I lived or died, the Lord had everything in hand."

Margaret told how Congolese Christians had brought them food and other aid, sometimes at the risk of their lives. In her published account of her experiences as a *Captive of the Simbas* (Harper & Row, 1966), she recalls being marched through a village when a voice called, "Mama Margarita, Mama Margarita!" Having had her glasses taken, she could not identify the person. He came nearer, boldly taking her hand. Now she knew. He was Ndimu Gaspar, a UFM evangelist, the first Protestant she had seen in three months. He asked her to stop and talk. She whispered, "We're prisoners and must keep going."

"Then, I'll follow and find where you'll be," he insisted.

Later, Ndimu burst into the hut where they were lodged, boldly explaining to the guards, "It's all right, I am an evangelist and she is one of our missionaries." He brought a large bowl of hot sweet potatoes, a three-pound tin of powdered milk and welcome news that the churches in his area were carrying on. He noticed that she was having trouble with her eyes and asked why. When told that the Simbas had taken her glasses, he immediately extended his own. "I was very touched by this magnificent gesture," Margaret wrote, "for to own a pair of glasses was to the Congolese practically a status symbol, and I knew he had bought them fairly recently."

A Brave Prayer

Missionary remembrances of their time in Simba captivity were replete with such incidents of kindness. Many also related thrilling accounts of death-defying bravery by Congolese Christians.

Rebels invaded the Sunday worship services of the local Africa Inland Church in Bunia. One stood up and began extolling his leaders. The people sat grim-faced until the man finished. Then the pastor called on Miss Fitenia Papalaskalis to lead in prayer.

Miss Papalaskalis was the daughter of a Greek man and a Congolese woman. Mulattos were the object of special ridicule from rebels. Nevertheless, she stood and prayed audibly in the presence of the gun-toting Simbas: "Lord, we ask you to help us in our hour of great need. You know that Congo is in need of you at this time. You know that we have evil men who have come into our area recently. Many of them are thieves and murderers. They beat and kill our people for no reason. Lord, judge these evil men. Bring your wrath down on these terrible men. Put the fear of God into them. Save us from these people and bring us peace and freedom once more we pray. In Jesus' name. Amen."

She sat down. The Christians looked on her with admiration. The rebels looked, too, but did not move or speak. The pastor preached. At the benediction the rebels filed out silently.

Preaching to the Doomed

Simbas had terrorized hundreds of villages. In one hamlet they had shot every man who was not wearing a loin cloth. More typically they would pick out one man and shoot him as an example of what would happen to anyone who did not give them aid.

In one village, the terrorist commander had pointed to two brothers. "One of you must die. Who will it be?" The villagers gasped in shocked horror. The Udubre brothers were Christian leaders.

Lazaro Udubre, their aging father, stepped up. "Please, don't kill either of my boys. Their families need them desperately." The rebel leader shoved the old man away. But the father cried, "You said someone must die. Let me be that one. I am old and have lived my life. I am a Christian and I know that I will go to a far better place. Kill me!"

The commander was moved. He directed his men to put Lazaro in the lorry with instructions to kill him later.

The sobbing sons embraced their father. "Don't worry about me," he assured. "I'll see you in heaven."

The rebels drove a few miles down the road and stopped in a clearing. Lazaro saw bodies strewn around. He was thinking that this was where he would be killed when a line of men and boys was marched into the clearing. "We're going to kill them," the Simba leader told Lazaro. "But since you're a Christian, you can preach to them for a minute before we shoot them."

The old man looked at the ragged prisoners. Some were sobbing, begging for their lives. Briefly he told them of how the thief on the cross had been saved a few minutes before death. "Bow your heads and ask Jesus to forgive you," he urged. "Take Him into your heart. Now." Some of the men were bowing when the rifles cracked and the line pitched to the ground.

The next day brought more prisoners, another opportunity to preach and more executions. Every day Lazaro thought he would be pushed into a lineup and shot. But perhaps the drunken rebels had forgotten that the preacher had once been selected to die. Finally, a messenger came with word that government troops were close by. The rebels scrambled into their vehicles and fled. Lazaro stood alone in the clearing, free to return home!

Comparisons with the Boxer Rebellion

Not since the Boxer Rebellion had so many foreign missionaries been killed in one year. Indeed, the Congo massacres of 1964–1965 bear striking parallels to the Chinese Boxer uprisings in 1900. The assailants were whipped into a frenzy by their political superiors bent on controlling the country. The attacks were motivated, at least in part, by a burning hatred of western foreigners and a drive to stamp out Christianity. There was even a Chinese connection, for some of the rebel leaders had been trained and armed by Chinese Communists in the forests of bordering Tanzania. And some had been to China, and to other communist countries as well, for indoctrination in Marxism. On a different note, missionaries held captive by Congolese rebels were encouraged by reading of the courage of the martyrs in communist China.

"No Greater Love"

After the massacres came the funerals and memorial services. Most of the slain missionaries, whose bodies were retrieved, were buried in the Congo. Lois Carlson felt that her husband would have wanted to be buried at Karawa in a little cemetery in the northeast where other missionary personnel were interred. His body was flown there for burial.

Hundreds and hundreds of Congolese, along with many foreigners, flocked to Karawa for the funeral. As Lois and the children approached Palm Lane which led to the church, they saw that flowers and bright-colored leaves had been tied to the trunk of each palm tree. All along the way children stood holding flowers. Still more flowers decorated the arches of the doors. A single bundle of native flowers graced the plain wooden casket. Lois placed beside it a bouquet of red and pink carnations that she and her children had picked for the occasion. A large white bow held the carnations together, and on it was the word "BELOVED," in large, gold letters.

Pastor Zacharie Alengi, president of the Evangelical Church of the Ubangi, gave the funeral message. He recalled the last time he had seen Dr. Paul: "He told us, 'If I have to leave, I won't go far, and I will return to you as soon as possible.' I saw this was love, and I asked myself, 'Why did this doctor choose a place like this?' It came from love and joy."

Later the funeral procession wound to the cemetery, where other missionaries and missionary children who had given their lives to the Congo lay. An honor guard of Congolese soldiers stood at attention. The soldiers presented arms and played "Taps." Palm branches were laid reverently across the coffin. Then the body of "Monganga Paul,"* as the people knew him, was lowered into the ground.

*The title of the biography of Dr. Paul Carlson, written by Lois Carlson and published by Harper & Row, 1966.

The simple grave marker placed under a plain cross, said:

DR. PAUL E. CARLSON
THERE IS NO GREATER LOVE THAN THIS,
THAT A MAN SHOULD LAY DOWN HIS LIFE
FOR HIS FRIENDS. JOHN 15:13

Revival!

Besides the loss of so many missionaries, the Congolese church had been depleted of some of its finest pastors and evangelists. The missionary survivors did not desert their African brothers and sisters in the aftermath of the massacres. They began returning in the spirit of Margaret Hayes' last letter, smuggled through rebel lines, before her rescue: "We can't leave our field high and dry. We must have workers, and if God wills it, when and if I am released, I would like to return. Think of the poor scattered flock of Christ! My heart breaks whenever I think of it."

The church was scattered and decimated by many deaths, but it was still alive. In one congregation after another there was revival as professing Christians who had done the rebels' bidding came back to ask forgiveness, and members who had remained loyal pledged new commitments. Hundreds of other Congolese accepted Christ and asked for baptism.

Trouble Over Church Divisions

The political situation had improved, but the government still lacked stability. In October, 1965, Premier Tshombe was ousted and replaced by Evariste Kimba. When Kimba was unable to firm up the government, General Mobutu proclaimed himself president and took total power. Kimba and other opponents were hung.

In 1967 white mercenaries, who had spearheaded Premier Tshombe's defeat of the Marxist rebels, staged an unsuccessful revolt in Katanga Province. Tshombe, suspected of planning to return from exile, was kidnapped by Algerians. He reportedly died in an Algerian prison in 1969.

President Mobuto launched an Africanization crusade. He changed the country's name to Zaire, took for himself the tribal name Mobutu Sese Seko, and renamed cities which had been named for Europeans. Leopoldville became Kinshasa and Stanleyville was changed to Kisangani.

There were now almost fifty Protestant missions in Zaire serving a constituency of five million. Most were related to denominations which their missionaries had developed. Some of the national church leaders, with encouragement from President Mobutu's government, formed an ecumenical council called the Church of Christ of Zaire. The organizers stated that they did not want Zairians to further suffer from the "shameful" denominational divisions created in the West and replicated by missionaries in the Congo. They encouraged believers not to think of themselves as Baptists or Methodists or Presbyterians, but as communicants of the one Church of Christ in Zaire. The idea was appealing and the ecumenical union was voted into official existence on March 8, 1970. The government announced that it would now be working through the Church of Christ, the Catholic Church (nine million strong), and the Kimbanguist Church of Zaire (an independent blending of Christian and native African beliefs).

Some Congolese church leaders and missionaries feared stifling bureaucratic control from officers of the new church. The ecumenical body was not a member of the World Council of Churches, but some of the leaders were active in the Council, and the dissidents in Zaire feared the spread of liberal theology. They organized eight denominations into the Council of Protestant Churches in Zaire.

President Mobutu's Decrees

Further extension of President Mobutu's "authenticity" campaign was more alarming. The government seized all mission-owned elementary and secondary schools and prohibited religion classes. The schools were told to teach Mobutu's political philosophy, "Mobutism," and to replace photographs of religious figures on school walls with pictures of him. Though a baptized, mass-attending Catholic, Mobutu increased worries by banning religious youth organizations, church periodicals and radio programs, and the national holiday of Christmas. Some newspapers even printed hymns that substituted Mobutu's name for that of Jesus. Was Mobutu trying to make himself a messiah. "No," an official press release said. "Mobutu does not think he is God."

Then in a stunning reversal in late 1976, Mobutu's government announced that the schools would be returned to church control and the ban on religious instruction would be dropped. Why the turnaround? Observers cited economic problems and government alarm over widespread moral laxity under nationalization.

Another Missionary Is Killed

March, 1977 brought trouble from a new source. Ex-Katangese rebels, trained by Cubans in Marxist Angola, invaded Zaire's copper-rich Shaba Province (formerly Katanga). Seven Methodist missionaries at Katanga were put under house arrest, but allowed to continue their medical and teaching work.

On April 18, the rebels ordered one of the missionaries, Dr. Glenn Eschtruth, to face trial at their headquarters in Angola for "capitalistic crimes." He spent his last night at home setting family and financial matters in order with his wife Lena, and writing messages to their three daughters. The next morning—his forty-ninth birthday—he wrote on the flyleaf of Lena's Bible, "And we know that all things work together for good to them that love God" (Romans 8:28).

That afternoon the rebels came for him. They ordered the mission hospital and school to be closed and the remaining missionaries to stay in their homes.

Six weeks later government forces recaptured Katanga. Mission planes landed to evacuate the Methodists.

Lena Eschtruth asked about her husband and was told he had never reached Angola, but had been shot about thirty miles from Katanga. Africans led a missionary friend to Glenn's body which was identified by his watch and khaki bag. The Asbury Seminary graduate was buried at the Katanga station.

"I Say to God: 'You Lead' "

In June, 1978, the Katangese rebels returned from Angola and captured the town of Kolwezi. Methodist missionary Kenneth D. Enright was in Lubumbashi (formerly Elisabethville) on church business when the invaders came. The welfare of his wife, daughter, missionary son and daughter-in-law and other foreigners in Kolwezi was unknown until his son John radioed: "They've bombed our house. The war has broken out. Mortars have hit the room. . . . What do we do?"

Shortly rebels came to the house and took John off to a makeshift jail for questioning. Along the way they met an African Methodist district superintendent who convinced them they should release the American.

Before the rebels were driven out by a drop of French paratroopers, six hundred Africans and some one hundred thirty whites were killed. No missionaries died in this rebellion. Rebel stragglers faded back into Angola.

The senior Enright returned to his family. When told that he was on the rebels' death list, Enright remarked, "I don't worry about that because I am on another list—God's. I say to God: 'You lead; you take over; I'm yours.' That is the kind of God I walk with and fly with."

That is the spirit of other missionaries and national church leaders who continue to serve in Zaire, a nation that is one-fourth the size of the United States and rich in natural resources, and that is still coveted by Marxist strategists.

Africa, O Africa

Africa, with its diverse millions, is no longer the "Dark Continent." To world watchers it is the "Dangerous Continent" where possibilities of devastating, genocidal war loom with every outbreak of fighting. Zimbabwe, South Africa, Angola, Somalia, Zaire, are only some of the nations threatened with mass warfare. Some of these nations are already wracked with revolts and civil strife. Peace, short of Christ's return, will not come soon. Communism, tribalism, racism and greed for power among politicians will keep the lands in turmoil. Islam and a resurgence of pagan religions will make Christian work and further witness difficult.

So many missionaries and national Christians have already died in Africa. So many western Christians have given their sons and daughters and millions upon millions of dollars for Africa.

Missionaries in the nineteenth century nailed the coffin lid shut on legalized slavery. The seed they and their converts planted has blossomed into the fastest-growing church on any continent in this century. The Sudan Interior Mission reports that the Protestant church in Zaire grew from less than one million to more than six million persons between 1968 and 1978.

By the year two thousand, Christians in black Africa will, at present growth rates, outnumber those in the West. By then there will doubtless be many more martyrs in this fast-developing, churning, and troubled area of the world.

MARTYRS OF THE CARIBBEAN AND LATIN AMERICA

CATHOLIC BY CONQUEST:
The Caribbean and Latin America

Christian martyrs in "Christian" nations such as Mexico, Colombia and Brazil? Yes, though there have not been as many as in "pagan" Africa.

Until recent times, in the southern hemisphere the name "Christian" signified little more than adherence to traditional rituals in the Catholic church—baptism, marriage, and burial. The Catholic hierarchy claimed over ninety–eight per cent of the population in countries where spiritual ignorance, poverty, immorality, and political oppression reigned. Astute and honest Catholic leaders now say five to ten per cent may be a more accurate figure.

The story of how Latin America and most of the Caribbean islands became Catholic by conquest is well known. Little changed after these colonies of Spain, Portugal and France gained independence. Concordats with the Vatican were retained, making governments, in effect, subservient to intolerant Catholic hierarchies. Inquisitions continued. In Peru alone one hundred twenty thousand "heretics" were tortured and 189 dissenters burned at the stake.

Early Protestant missionary thrusts were beaten back. Five of the first Protestant preachers in Brazil were killed. In Argentina hostile Indians drove the first missionaries back to their ship, where they starved to death. A pioneer missionary in Peru was imprisoned, then released only after a sensational trial brought international criticism on the government. The first Baptist worker in Cuba, when that nation was still a Spanish colony, was imprisoned and threatened with death.

Reaction to heavy-handed clerical intolerance, leading to the rise of liberal parties, brought some relief in the nineteenth century. But in most countries Catholic opposition to Protestant ministries continued.

Political-clerical alliances representing the rich and powerful, fought every movement towards civil, political, and religious freedom. The ruling oligarchies opposed Bible translation in the vernacular, banned Bible distribution, and encouraged fanatics to stone, flog, and sometimes murder Bible colporteurs. They even blocked Protestant orphanages and schools for poor children, who otherwise would not receive an education. Such religious and political repression, accompanied by rampant disease and poverty, drove many intellectuals into agnosticism and atheism, and some into communism. In most Latin American countries this persecution persisted into the 1950's with sporadic outbursts still recurring in remote rural areas.

A new twist to the violence involves the peasant revolts against the conservative governments, resulting in the deaths of a number of Catholic priests who became allied with the Marxist left. Then there is the other end of the spectrum in Cuba where many Catholics have been killed or imprisoned by Castro's Marxist government.

The great majority of evangelical missionaries and national pastors have not been involved in volatile political conflicts, choosing instead to pursue evangelism, church-building, and healing and teaching ministries. Their service in the name of Christ has not been without great sacrifice. Some have been martyred by hostile mobs acting at the behest of fanatical Catholic priests and politicians; some have been speared to death by hostile Indians or killed by bandits; others have been mysteriously slain and their assailants never identified.

COMMUNISM IN THE WESTERN HEMISPHERE:
Cuba

"Fidel is a reformer, a revolutionary, maybe a socialist, but not a Communist." So ran the line that issued from Havana to Castro apologists and liberal clergymen all over the world when Castro and Argentine "Che" Guevara were trying to overthrow Cuban dictator Fulgencio Batista.

The deception was still being repeated in 1959 by thousands of foreign clergymen and other Castro defenders. But Cuban patriots knew Fidel had betrayed the revolution. He was no more than a left-wing dictator.

A Sad Awakening

The previous year the Cuban Catholic hierarchy had turned down a priest's request for an investigation of "communist trends" in the new government and had rebuked the priest. Now they were aroused. The evidence was too compelling to deny the rapid drift towards communization of Cuba.

While the hierarchy had slept, Castro and his minions had been busy arresting political opponents and putting them on trial with trumped-up evidence. Many had fought in the Cuban Revolution with Castro. Their only crime was objecting to the leftist turn. Hundreds of these political prisoners had either been executed or were in Morro Castle, the fortress turned into a prison at the entrance to Havana Harbor. Thousands of Cubans had been tried on lesser charges.

Some lost their property and went to prison simply because their last name happened to be the same as someone in the deposed Batista government.

"Cuba, Yes! Russia, No!"

The big explosion came November 29, 1959, at the first National Catholic Congress in Havana. To avoid trouble, the leadership had chosen the speakers carefully and censored their speeches in advance. One incendiary statement got through. Dr. Jose Ignacio Lasaga, a psychologist and leader of the Catholic Youth Movement, declared, "The Catholic attitude toward the revolution can be summed up in this phrase, 'Social Justice, Yes! Communism, No!' " The crowd roared back its agreement. Then the people began chanting: "Cuba, Yes! Russia, No!" It was the first loud outcry against communism in Cuba. Castro denounced the protest angrily as "dishonest and unjust."

But no member of the hierarchy said anything publicly until the following May. Seventy-six-year-old Monsignor Enrique Perez Serantes, the archbishop of Santiago de Cuba, who had saved Castro's life in 1953, now issued a pastoral letter denouncing communism. "The enemy is already within our gates," he warned. This was the signal for concerned priests to begin preaching openly about Cuban parallels to the communization of Eastern Europe.

The Communists Strike Back

The head of the Cuban Communist Party came out fighting. "Catholics have nothing to fear so long as they remain in their temples adoring their images," he stated. "But if they work in the counter-revolution, they will find us in the front line fighting against them."

On July 17, 1960, a mass was celebrated in the Havana Cathedral for victims of communism. Cuban Catholics in attendance sang, "Viva Cristo Rey" (Long Live Christ the King) and waved handkerchiefs. Outside a communist mob was waiting for mass to end. Fights and beatings ensued, with scores of worshipers picked up by the police. Three weeks later the Catholic bishops signed a collective message stating, "Catholicism and communism . . . are totally opposed and can never be reconciled. . . . The majority of the Cuban people, which is Catholic, is against materialistic and atheistic communism. Only by deceit or coercion could the Cuban people be led into a Communist regime. . . . "

Castro's militiamen responded by raiding churches, convents and schools. Soldiers profaned altars, smashed statues and relics, stole chalices and jeweled crucifixes. Some got drunk on sacramental wine, staged mock weddings, then danced through the streets, holding up sacred vessels. Others donned clerical cloth and consorted with known prostitutes in public.

The ill-fated Bay of Pigs invasion took place April 17, 1961. The anti-Castro Cubans equipped by the United States CIA were quickly routed with many of them taken prisoner. Acting on advance intelligence, Castro's militia had already started rounding up Catholic priests, including four of the country's six Catholic bishops, and others suspected of opposing the regime. In Havana alone twenty thousand were arrested from April 15 to 20.

A Catholic Leader Is Killed

The government had prohibited religious processions, but on September 10, 1961, a crowd burst out of the Church of Our Lady of Charity in Havana and began shouting for a march. A guard of militiamen were overwhelmed. Reserves were rushed to the church under the command of the Minister of Interior. They wore a Russian military cap adorned with the hammer-and-sickle insignia.

The militiamen charged into the Catholic crowd, firing machine guns and swinging clubs. Dozens were wounded. Arnaldo Socorro, a leader of the Young Catholic Workers' Association, was killed. The next day Castro declared him a "Hero of the Revolution" and announced that he had been shot down by priests.

Priests and Nuns Are Deported

Castro decreed that religious demonstrations would never again be allowed in Cuba. Any priests who did not pledge loyalty to the government would lose their citizenship and be deported. The pastor of Our Lady of Charity Church was one of the first to go. Father Diego Madrigal was pulled out of bed and shoved aboard a ship with over one hundred other priests. They landed in the United States, and from there they proceeded to countries of their choice. None were permitted back in Cuba.

Over two thousand nuns also left Cuba during this time. Few went voluntarily. Most were expelled. The forced ex-

odus left only about four hundred priests and nuns to serve
Cuban Catholics.

Later in the year Castro quit pretending. "I am a Marxist–Leninist and I will be a Marxist–Leninist to the last day
of my life," he declared in a five-hour telethon.

Most Protestants Had Favored the Revolution

Until this time the religious struggle had been mainly carried by Catholics. The Protestant minority were mostly
lower class workers and farmers. They had not been identified with Batista, as Catholics had been. Protestants had
been persecuted in Cuba when the island was a colony of
Spain. After independence, which followed the defeat of
Spain in the Spanish–American war, they enjoyed more freedom than Protestants were experiencing in most Latin
American countries. Church and state were separate in
Cuba.

In a society which favored the rich, Protestants sympathized with the announced aims of the revolution. Many
cheered Castro's land redistribution policies. But when it became obvious that Cuba was becoming a communist state,
the seeds of discontent were sown. As the government tightened controls, thousands of Protestants joined the Catholics'
flight to Florida.

Still the Protestants did not experience overt persecution. They were small and divided. Their churches did
not operate large institutions or own large sections of land,
as did the Catholics. There was little that Castro's commissars could confiscate from them.

The Hammer Falls on Protestants

Late in 1963 Dr. John A Mackay, a prominent leader in the
National Council of Churches, visited Cuba and returned
saying he saw no religious persecution. His itinerary had
been cleverly drawn.

The following March 13 Castro openly attacked certain
"Protestant sects" for the first time. This signaled a wave of
persecution and government legislation over church affairs,
not unlike what had happened in Eastern European satellites
of the Soviet Union.

The law limited religious activities to church buildings
and to traditional schedules. Special services could not be
held on weekday nights with the exception of Wednesday,
the customary prayer meeting time. Churches were also or-

dered to register as associations. Those that refused were fined. Only persons above legal age could become church members. Youth under fifteen, unless accompanied by parents, were forbidden to enter churches. Government spies began appearing in church meetings.

Church construction was stopped and some buildings were confiscated. Around one hundred churches were closed, their furniture and pews confiscated. The Pentecostal Bible Institute of Manacas was closed. The Baptist Seminary in Santiago de Cuba was denied a food quota. Theological students were drafted into the military or sent to labor camps.

Radio preaching and distribution of literature was outlawed. The last shipment of Bibles was confiscated. Circulation of other Bibles and hymnals was forbidden. House to house proselytizing was banned.

Protestant preachers fought back. Baptist pastors were especially bold in condemning state interference in church affairs. Using a spy network that included children, the government began amassing a list of the most troublesome Baptists. In 1965 police arrested fifty-three Baptists simultaneously. Thirty-four were tried and sentenced for offenses ranging from espionage to "twisting biblical texts for the purpose of ideological diversionism."

Executions and Imprisonment

Among those arrested and sentenced were two Americans, David Fite and his father-in-law Dr. Herbert Caudill. Dr. Caudill was superintendent of the Baptist seminary and Fite was pastor of a Havana church and a faculty member at the seminary.

Convicted of espionage, which they vehemently denied, they were held for four years. Their release largely resulted from a crusade by Fite's pastor-father among American, Canadian, Mexican, Cuban, and Russian diplomats to persuade Castro to let them go.

Fite told of "witnessing more than two hundred executions about one hundred meters from my cell." The firing squad would march into the area, he said, and tie the condemned person to a stake. After the sentence was read, "we could occasionally hear a cry of desperation and then the volley of shots . . . and then the shot of grace."

Another pastor, Benjamin Valdez, was kept in a Cuban prison for twelve years. He told reporters in Atlanta in 1978 that only one Baptist pastor still remained in prison. He indicated some government relaxation against church activities. "The church is able to work from house to house. But in a careful way, you know," he added with a wry smile. Cuban pastors, he said, were not making "big propaganda. But as long as a minister speaks only on religious matters, the government isn't going to interfere." Valdez said he was never physically abused in prison and was able to witness to fellow prisoners. "We won several to the Lord," he recalled.

Behind the Communist Mask

An uneasy detente now exists between Christians in Cuba and the Castro communist government. Some Protestants are eager to take advantage of a relaxation in the enforcement of anti-religion laws. They are quietly trying to arrange for permission to hold an evangelistic crusade led by a prominent Latin American preacher. Billy Graham's preaching excursions to Yugoslavia, Hungary, and Poland, they feel, have set a precedent in the communist world that Cuba can follow.

The Catholic clergy is quiet. The papal nuncio, Monsignor Zacchi, is known to be a friend of Castro's. He has said that young Catholics may join the Communist Youth Organization, since there is only one political party in Cuba and Catholics have a right to participate in politics. He has further stated that Cuban Catholics can adopt Marxist economic theory, so long as it is separated from atheism.

Meanwhile, the Cuban government is busy sending troops to support Marxist revolutionary movements in Africa while agitating for the overthrow of noncommunist governments in its own hemisphere. Thus, Cuban communism is responsible for much more violence.

Castro and other Cuban communists vigorously deny that they are enemies of religion. However, the policies of international Marxism, which they have adopted, indicate that this is mere propaganda intended to deceive a naive public. Their ultimate objective is to stamp out religious faith. At the present time, it is not in their best interests for advancing communist doctrine to violently oppose religious activities or to make martyrs of those who will not submit.

THE ISLAND OF HISPANIOLA:

Haiti and The Dominican Republic

The word Haiti arouses images of frolicking tourists, quickie divorces, casino gambling, cockfighting, and backyard voodoo at midnight. Shadowy secret police wearing dark glasses and gray fedoras, telltale bulges at their hips, whispers of revolution, palace intrigue, and rumors of a torture room painted dark brown so the walls and floor will not reveal the blood splotches—these imaginative pictures contrast harshly with the grinding poverty and wasting disease that abounds in the back alleys and remote countryside of Haiti.

A History Bathed in Blood

Haiti and the Dominican Republic share the island of Hispaniola—the land Columbus "loved most." French settlers on the western side of the island imported thousands of black slaves from Africa to work on sugar plantations. A century later, in 1791, the blacks rebelled and murdered most of the whites. French troops sent to establish order were crushed by black defenders and wiped out by disease. With independence in 1804 came a long reign of political terror marked by palace purges and power plays between whites and mulattoes. From 1915 to 1934 the United States fully controlled the country. More recently, Haiti has been the private fiefdom of the despotic Duvaliers. First was the father, Francois "Papa Doc" Duvalier, who died in 1971. He was succeeded by young Jean-Claude "Baby Doc" Duvalier. Like his father he serves as "president for life." The Duvalier government has been one of the most repressive regimes in the world—torturing, murdering, and forcing political dissidents including many clergymen, into exile, while effectively blackmailing Washington for financial aid against the threat of a communist takeover.

Life Under the Duvaliers

Under the Duvaliers, no Haitian has felt safe. "Papa Doc," especially, was known for turning on family members, long-time friends, and loyal members of his government at the slightest suspicion. Often the wives and children of suspected rebels were killed first to enrage the men. Children were sometimes hacked to death in their mother's arms.

Before "Papa Doc" became president, he was sheltered by Catholic Father Jean-Baptiste Georges from political foes for several months. Duvalier later dismissed the priest from his cabinet and forced him into exile.

Another cleric driven out by "Papa Doc" was Bishop Jean-Marie Paul Robert. His crime, in 1962, was instructing his priests to omit the customary prayer for the president at the end of mass. As an expression of contempt, Duvalier's militia chief held a voodoo ceremony on the steps of Bishop Robert's church and sacrificed pigs to the voodoo gods. Haiti's 4.7 million people are sometimes said to be ninety per cent Catholic and one hundred per cent voodoo.

An Episcopalian Clergyman Disappears

The previous year, an Episcopalian clergyman, Father Yvon Emmanuel Moreau, joined with five other senators in opposing dictatorial powers for Papa Doc, while speaking for constitutionality, rights, and the dignity of man. Duvalier accused the six of advancing a communist plot and declared them immediately impeached. Two fled the country. Three took refuge in the Mexican embassy. Father Moreau refused to run, replying,

> I am a believer in democracy and I thought I was doing my job when I criticized what should be criticized to protect the welfare of the people and the country. . . . I have never been involved in any subversive activities and I don't intend to be used now by any group of politicians. Despite the action taken against me, I will continue a normal life.

Moreau was arrested and disappeared, as so many Haitians have, never to be heard from, or of, again.

Evangelical Silence

Over three hundred evangelical missionaries, representing some forty–six North American agencies, are in Haiti. Protestant work dates to 1816 when two Wesleyan Methodists were invited in by the president of the country.

Protestant missionaries and pastors generally keep quiet about Haitian politics. They have complete religious freedom so long as they stick with the gospel. A missionary falling into government disfavor can be expelled in twenty–four hours. A Haitian pastor can be picked up by the secret police.

An Evangelical Leads Opponents of the Dictator

Interestingly, the most influential Haitian opposition leader-in-exile is an evangelical. Raymond Joseph is the son of a leading Baptist pastor who worked with the West Indies Mission in Haiti. Young Joseph attended Moody Bible Institute and Wheaton College with the goal of returning to translate the Bible into contemporary Haitian Creole, the language of Haiti's masses.

Joseph's "awakening" came in 1964 when he learned that the late "Papa Doc" had forced young children to watch executions. He took up residence in New York and became the leader of the Haitian Coalition which numbers about forty thousand exiles. Joseph edits a weekly newspaper and broadcasts daily to Haiti. He says he wants only to see a democracy in Haiti. He is critical of revolutionaries, especially communists. Should a change of government come to Haiti, he could be elected president.

The Dominican Republic — Haiti's Next-Door Neighbor

The terror is over in the D.R., as Haiti's next-door neighbor is known, although adult Dominicans still look around cautiously when the name Rafael Trujillo is mentioned. The "Hitler of the Caribbean" was assassinated in 1961. For thirty years previous he and his relatives practically ran the D.R. like a concentration camp. Motorists had to show identification every few miles. Phones were tapped, hotel rooms bugged, and informers seemed to be everywhere, even in families. Each week the balding dictator's procurers selected a group of young girls for the president's bed. Young women and families that resisted sometimes lost their jobs, were beaten, or if they made a big fuss, simply disappeared.

The "Benefactor of the Fatherland," as he termed himself, kept up a front of respectability. He milked the economy to build showplace monuments, jailed communists, and cultivated United States politicians. When Batista was being overthrown, he funneled money to the Cuban dictator. After Castro won, Batista took up temporary exile with his friend Trujillo.

Protestant Policy

Trujillo, like other Caribbean and Latin dictators of his time, was a Catholic and tried to appease the local hierarchy. He did not bother with Protestants, except for individuals caught in police dragnets for espousing liberty. As a two per cent minority, Protestants followed a policy recalled by a missionary: "We minded our own business and stayed out of politics. Trujillo didn't bother us." No missionaries were ever arrested.

When Trujillo fell, the impoverished little country almost came apart. Conflicts between left and right wing groups flared into full-scale war in 1965. Fearful of a Castro-like takeover, the United States sent in troops to help defeat leftist forces. The fighting left hundreds dead. The bitterness sticks to this day.

A Tall Texan

About one hundred foreign missionaries were then in the D.R. Most had been in the country less than a decade even though the first missionary, a Free Methodist, had arrived back in 1889. Of the missionaries, best known to the Dominican people was rangy Howard Shoemake, a tall Southern Baptist from Texas. He had been in the country only three years.

Shoemake introduced a television ministry and a unique medical aid program credited with saving thousands of Dominican children from deadly gastroenteritis. Shoemake had a powerful ham radio and during the war sent hundreds of mercy messages for desperate Dominicans. He and his wife also welcomed into their home various political refugees.

The medical program featured clinics at churches in Santo Domingo, the capital, where patients paid a dollar for a doctor's services and received needed medicines free. The medicines came from United States drug companies through

Medical Assistance Programs in Wheaton, Illinois. Shoemake and other missionaries also cooperated with medical projects by visiting Christian physicians under the auspices of the Christian Medical Society.

After the fighting ended, other clinics were set up around the country and staffed by Dominican Christian doctors. One was in Santiago, the D.R.'s second largest city, under the direction of Paul and Nancy Potter, newly arrived Southern Baptist missionaries from Missouri.

The First Missionary Martyrs

Paul, age thirty-three, had been a seminary-trained pastor. He had heard a missionary home on furlough ask, "Why has God called so few to serve the rest of the world and so many to serve the United States?" When a challenge was given for five thousand new missionaries at the Southern Baptist Convention in Atlantic City, he and Nancy offered themselves for service. Nancy was a warm, outgoing young woman who had sensed God's leading through teaching mission study courses at their church. At Cottey College in Nevada, Missouri, she had been selected by the faculty as the student who most nearly approached "the ideal of intellect and spirituality" and who had exerted "the most wholesome influence upon her associates." Paul and Nancy brought with them two lively youngsters, Susan, seven, and David, five.

In their first evangelistic effort in Santiago they won eleven young Dominicans to Christ. When these came to the Potter home for instructions, they brought four friends who wanted to accept Christ.

They soon organized a church. Four hundred Dominicans came to the dedication of the new sanctuary. By 1970, when they left for their first furlough, they had two flourishing churches and three mission chapels.

Near the end of their year at home, Nancy was asked why they wanted to return to such a troubled, impoverished country. "We have seen God's power at work and human lives changed," she said. "Nothing can be more thrilling."

They returned in June 1971, to find that the work had continued to grow under the leadership of fellow missionaries. The clinic was handling almost two hundred patients a week, each patient receiving a Christian witness. They began to think of the possibility of establishing five churches by the end of their next term.

The Potters never reached that goal. Early on the morning of July 7, ten-year-old David discovered their bloody bodies. While the son and daughter had slept, Paul and Nancy had been beaten and stabbed to death.

Why Were the Potters Killed?

The first martyrdom of missionaries provoked editorials in all the leading newspapers demanding an immediate investigation. The papers took note of their medical services to the poor.

Robbery was one motive considered by investigators. The possibility that they had been killed by anti-American political terrorists was also weighed. A reporter noticed that "Death to the Yankees" had been scrawled on their car. Another theory later surfaced that some members of the Dominican medical establishment had paid to have the Potters killed and their deaths blamed on leftists. These upper-class Dominicans were losing money in patient fees and pharmaceutical sales to the missionary clinic and wanted the clinic closed. The investigation continued for months, but no one was ever arrested. The case is still open.

The churches begun by Paul and Nancy Potter continue to grow. The medical clinics continue to serve thousands of poor Dominicans. With the murders still unsolved, missionary Shoemake expressed the feelings of the Potters' missionary colleagues. "Regardless of the cause of the death of Paul and Nancy," he said, "our attitude must be that of Christ who said from the cross, 'Forgive them for they know not what they do.' The work which they began must be carried on."

A Harvest of Converts

The commitment of Paul and Nancy Potter and other evangelical missionaries, pastors, and lay Christians in the Dominican Republic has contributed to a rich spiritual harvest during the last two years. The highlight of this harvest was the 1977 Luis Palau evangelistic crusade in Santo Domingo — 3,984 Dominicans came forward for spiritual counsel. The significance of such response is obvious when it is noted that only one in fifty of the D.R.'s five million population is an evangelical believer.

SOUTH OF THE BORDER:
Mexico

Mexico today is a warm, friendly country where thirteen hundred North American missionaries work in cooperation with a body of more than a million evangelicals.

Mexico yesterday was far different. As in other Latin American countries, Mexico's native Indian population was forced to renounce their pagan religions and submit to Catholic baptism. It was convert or die in "New Spain" during the sixteenth century. The corrupt church, in league with the Spanish oligarchy, was not challenged for three centuries. Bible colporteurs and later missionaries met with immediate opposition. Evangelical workers risked their lives every time they preached the gospel. They were often cursed, spat upon and stoned, then chased out of town by a mob. Many were killed by mobs incited by Roman Catholic priests who feared evangelicals as their worst enemy.

Two Missionary Martyrs

In 1872 the American Board of Commissioners for Foreign Missions sent two preachers, J.L. Stephens and D.F. Watkins, to Guadalajara. Their preaching was well received. Within a few months they had a church of seventeen members and several Mexican evangelists.

All along they had been heckled, stoned, and threatened by fanatics at the behest of local priests. Then a mob formed

521

and attacked Stephens where he was preaching. He and one of his Mexican assistants were killed. Watkins refused to leave and asked for reinforcements. New missionaries were sent and a strong new church arose at the very place the murders had occurred.

Early Baptist, Methodist, and Presbyterian missionaries were treated no better. In town after town they were welcomed by rocks, mud, and curses.

One of the first Baptists was James Hickey, an Irish convert who had once studied for the Catholic priesthood. Hickey was a Baptist pastor in Texas when the Civil War broke out. Favoring the Union cause, he moved across the border into Mexico for his own safety. In Monterrey he became associated with Thomas Westrup, a Spanish-speaking Englishman who worked for the American Baptist Home Mission Society of New York. He and Westrup organized the first Baptist church in Mexico in 1864 with five members.

Thomas Westrup urged his brother John to join them. John Westrup came as the first Southern Baptist missionary to Mexico. A few weeks after arriving, he took a mission trip into Indian territory and was murdered either by Catholic fanatics or Indians.

The Southern Baptists sent William D. Powell, their Sunday school director in Texas, to investigate the murder. He traveled by stagecoach to the younger Westrup's home in Progreso, Mexico, where some of John's converts met him. One handed him a bloodstained coat. In the pocket was the missionary's diary with notes about four small churches he had organized and the names of seventy-five members. The last entry said: "Four baptisms today. Go back and teach them next week." Powell felt that this was God's call for him to serve in Mexico. He wrote his mission board and was appointed in 1882.

Powell proved to be an outstanding missionary. He started a church in Saltillo, began a newspaper, and obtained the help of Governor Francisco I. Madero in establishing a school in which orphans could be educated free. The school was named the Madero Institute in honor of the governor.

Evangelicals Died in the Mexican Revolution

Mexico was ruled at this time by the oppressive dictator Porfirio Diaz. Foreign investors paid huge sums to the dictator for control of major industries. Wealthy ranchers purchased land for as little as nine cents an acre from Diaz, who had taken the property from the peasants. The peasants had to work as peons on the huge haciendas from daylight to dusk.

Diaz stayed in power for nearly thirty–four years through bribery and election frauds. In 1910 Governor Madero, with the support of evangelicals and liberal Catholics, ran for president in opposition to the dictator. Diaz kept him in jail for most of the campaign, then allowed him only 168 votes. Students in Mexico City sounded a call to arms. The world's first full-scale national revolution of the twentieth century was on.

Diaz was backed by the Catholic hierarchy and by big business in the United States. Andrew Carnegie, the steel magnate, called him, "the Moses and Joshua of his people." The revolutionaries had the support of most Mexicans, including the Protestants who had suffered intense religious persecution under the Diaz regime. The chief of staff of the revolutionary forces at the close of the war was a young Presbyterian, Aaron Saenz. Before the dictator finally surrendered, one of every fifteen Mexicans had died. Many of those who gave their lives were evangelicals.

Religious Persecution – Revolutionary Style

The victory resulted in a massive land reform program and stiff antireligion laws aimed at curbing the power of the Catholic hierarchy. Clergymen were denied the right to vote or hold public office. Foreign missionaries could not pastor churches in Mexico. Churches could not have primary schools. Church buildings became state property. Religious periodicals were prohibited (a law later repealed). Religious garb was forbidden in public. The laws were aimed at checking Catholic power, but evangelicals suffered also.

Anti-Catholic mobs roamed the countryside, burning and pillaging churches, threatening priests with execution. Most Protestant missionaries living in Mexico before the revolution had already left the country. Those remaining kept in the background. Americans were not popular because of past Yankee support for the dictator.

The fiercest religious persecution raged in the zone of Tabasco. The governor there ordered all church services stopped, images of saints buried, and Bibles burned. He also closed all saloons and gambling halls. Tabasco's Catholic churches were badly hurt. Protestants went underground and increased in number while the antireligion laws were enforced.

Mexico's Era of Martyrs

The revolutionary fervor was waning by 1940. Easing of restrictions brought an upsurge in evangelical activity and hundreds of new missionaries. The Catholic hierarchy, which had regained much of its old power, became alarmed.

In 1944, the archbishop of Mexico, Luis Maria Martinez, issued a harsh pastoral letter to all priests in the country. "We oppose the continual extension of the Protestant campaign," he said. "We will fight it until we finish. God wills it." Then he called on the priests to "place their efforts at the service of the faith" in vanquishing the "hellish serpent" of Protestantism.

This signaled the beginning of the most intense Catholic persecution against evangelicals ever seen in Latin America, with the exception of Colombia. Scores, perhaps hundreds, of evangelical pastors, evangelists, and lay leaders were murdered by Catholic fanatics. The worst incidents occurred in small communities and rural areas where Catholics controlled law enforcement and the courts. Little protection was provided for the embattled Protestants, and newspapers feared to publish the truth.

The fanatics were careful not to kill foreign missionaries. The missionaries agonized with their Mexican brothers and sisters. But all they could do was write letters to the State Department, which ignored their protests. At that time the State Department opposed the sending of Protestant missionaries to Catholic Latin America.

The Murderers Are Exposed

A few small stories about the persecution were printed in Mexico City newspapers. But it was not until February 8, 1952, that a major publication, *Tiempo*, published a long documentary covering eight years of savagery.

Tiempo called the Catholic war on evangelicals "an unprecedented violence, whose extremes have been murder, rape, pillage, and the extermination of small communities." Among cases "which have come to the knowledge of the Federal authorities," the following were cited in *Tiempo:**

November 25, 1944, the evangelical church house of La Gloria, Veracruz, was burned as well as nine houses of Protestants. Seven people, among them five children, died in the disaster. A little later the Catholics expelled from the vil-

---

*Translation provided by Orvil W. Reid, then a Southern Baptist missionary to Mexico.

lage, sixty families who were affiliated with the Church of God.

May 27, 1945, in Santiago, the Catholic priest led an assault on the homes of Protestant pastors Feliciano Juarez and Vicente Garita. The preachers were lynched and quartered and their homes dynamited.

June 1, 1945, the parish priest of Caulote, Michoacan, burned the Lutheran temple. [Lutheran was used to mean any evangelical church; this congregation was Pentecostal.] Urged on by him, the Catholics abused the women and beat up the men. The evangelicals who succeeded in escaping fled to the mountains. One hundred five arrived in Mexico City seeking protection.

January 15, 1946, in Neblinas, Hidalgo, various Sinarquistas [a fanatical religious–political organization] led by Candido Munoz and Julio Bautista and spurred on by the local priest, attacked the evangelicals who were gathered there. Many were wounded and others expelled from the village. They beat the pastor, then hung him from a tree.

On July 31, 1946, agents of the federal police, Marcelo Fernandez Ocano and Leopoldo Arena Diaz, arrived at San Felipe de Santiago to investigate atrocities committed by the Catholics. The priest, Pedro Juarez, had the mob take them to the mayor's office. Both were tortured. Fernandez Ocano was scalped alive with a machete and his eyes were plucked out with a nail. Afterwards they clipped off his ears, broke his teeth with blows and clubbed him until his bones were broken. When he was dead, his body was cut in pieces and thrown to the dogs. Arena Diaz succeeded in escaping. Perhaps this is the only time that justice acted to punish the monstrous crime. Some of the fanatics who took part in the offense were detained in the Toluca jail. However, the priest, Pedro Juarez, was still at liberty to spur further violence.

March 8, 1947, in Ameca, Jalisco, the Catholic priest, after a scuffle that he himself provoked, kidnapped several Protestants, carried them to his church and, using inquisitional methods, obliged them, under threat of death, to be baptized according to the rite of the "Holy Mother."

April 13, 1949, in Rioverde, San Luis Potosi, the body of Samuel Juarez was found with eighty–five knife wounds in it. This heinous crime was attributed to the vengeance of the priest, Jose Maria Rosales, whose abuses against the people had been halted by the Protestant minister.

On December 7, 1950, for the second time in the same year, the Catholics attacked the church building of the Presbyterian Church in Tixtla, Guerrero. At the cry of "Long live Christ the King" they broke the furniture, raped the women and wounded the men, according to the exhortation of the priest, Adalberto J. Miranda.

Sunday, January 27, 1950, in the town of Mayoro, twenty–one people gathered in the home of Francisco Garcia to dedicate themselves to their prayers. Soon afterward the bells of the Catholic church began to sound, and a few minutes afterward a mob of fanatics armed with clubs, machetes, axes and hoes, fell upon the Protestants. All of them received wounds and blows. The pastor, Agustin Corrales, was dragged with a rope from the saddle horn and left for dead at Kilometer No. 115 on the highway to Queretaro.

January, 1952, in Zacamitla, Veracruz, two individuals shot and killed the Protestant catechist, Miguel Martinez. This occurred three days after the priest, Jose Perez, had said in the pulpit: "I promise you, my children, that I will go to the front with you to finish off these evangelicals with clubs."

Tiempo quoted the archbishop of Mexico as responding, "We lament the happenings, . . . but we do not have any control over the people in this respect. It is to be regretted that the Protestant ministers go to Catholic people to diffuse their faith. We have always tried to avoid these embarrassing acts; but the people have their beliefs and, good or bad, we cannot take them away from them."

Tiempo called his response "insincere, false and contradictory," nothing that Article Twenty–Four of the Mexican constitution establishes complete religious freedom in one's church building or in his private home.

The *Tiempo* report and subsequent articles in leading Mexico City newspapers exerted strong pressure upon the Mexican Catholic hierarchy. The attacks and atrocities tapered off. News reports of similar Catholic persecutions in Colombia provoked disgust among United States Catholics. Word went out from the leadership that the violence was counter-productive and had to cease. Except for infrequent attacks in remote areas, the persecution in Mexico was halted.

An Otomi Miracle

By the mid-1960's Wycliffe Bible Translators were working in about one hundred Mexican Indian dialects. The translators had the endorsement of high officials in the Mexican government and none were ever attacked in the villages.

However, Indian believers in some remote villages did become targets of violence.

One persecution hit the Mesquital Otomis living in a desert area near Ixmiquilpan, Hidalgo. Otomi believers were accused of insulting tribal elders by studying a book written by "lying spirits" (the Bible), refusing to take food to the graves of the dead, declining to hang skulls in their gardens to frighten away evil spirits, and failing to give their share to purchase beer for the annual fiesta.

Driven from their cactus huts at gun point, the believers relocated on a bare hill overlooking Ixmiquilpan. One afternoon, they noticed people in the town below gathered in clusters. They feared an attack. Pastor Venancio Hernandez was away. His wife, Isidra, ran barefoot from hut to hut, asking the Christians to pray. They prayed and slept in peace that night, not knowing of the apparent miracle that had kept them from harm.

This story later leaked from embarrassed enemies. On the chosen night several hundred townspeople massed back of the hill armed with dynamite, guns, and machetes. At a signal from the leader, they started up the hill. Part way up, the forward marchers saw the little church outlined in a glaring light and soldiers positioned in a circle around the church, holding guns in firing position. Suddenly they heard a loud trumpet blast. The would-be-attackers turned and ran in fright.

Martyrdom Among the Chamulas

Christians have been martyred in other Mexican tribes where elders opposed converts of Bible translation ministries. The most noteworthy martyrdoms occurred in the zone of Chiapas, near the Guatemala border.

The Chamula Indians were catechized and baptized by priests after the conquest. Like most other Mexican Indians, they simply absorbed Catholic symbols and rituals into their pagan belief system. Around 1850 the elders drove out the foreign priests and announced they were returning to the faith of their fathers. In a form of mockery, they impaled a young boy on a cross and declared that he was their savior.

The Chamulas were not again threatened with change until the late 1960's when Wycliffe translators Ken and Elaine Jacobs moved to the market town of Las Casas near Chamula territory. A young Chamula named Domingo showed up at their door seeking work. They agreed to hire him for garden work if he would teach them their language.

In the process of language study and Bible translation Domingo became a believer. He then told the Jacobs that he wanted to return home.

When he saw them again, he asked if they would come to dedicate his new house. "Chamulas have always dedicated their new houses to evil spirits," explained Domingo. "I want to dedicate my house to the true God and His Son, Jesus." The Jacobs made the trip into Chamula territory and participated in the dedication. They felt it wise not to spend the night and returned to Las Casas about midnight.

Domingo next reported nine families "trusting in Jesus and meeting for worship and Bible study" at his house. "Enemies have tried to kill us and burn my house down," he told the Jacobs. "But we will go on following Jesus."

A few weeks later Domingo brought forty Chamula refugees to the Jacobs. "The elders ran us out," he said sadly. "We have nowhere to go and nothing to eat."

The Jacobs took the crowd in. Then Ken and Domingo went to the local police. An official went into the tribe and demanded that the elders allow the evangelicals to come back. "If you resist," he warned, "we will send in soldiers."

Most of the Chamula Christians returned home. One evening a band of Chamula men surrounded the house of a Christian family. Inside were four young sisters and an eighteen-year-old babysitter. They tossed gasoline on the thick, thatched roof and set the house on fire. When the girls ran out, they opened fire. The babysitter was hit, but escaped to the house of her uncle and was saved. One of the young sisters was burned to death. The other three were wounded running from the house. One died on the way to the hospital in Las Casas.

The killers were not apprehended. The persecution continued. At one point the Chamula elders held one hundred sixty believers in their crude jails. When the Mexican army threatened to intervene, they let the prisoners go.

More threats and harassment followed. The Chamula Christians stood firm, never resorting to violence themselves. They grew to a thousand strong and today worship in small chapels all over Chamula territory. They look forward to having the New Testament in their own language.

Missionary Martyrs

Only two missionaries, Ancel Allen and Nyles G. Huffman, are known to have been martyred in Mexico in this century. Both were affiliated with a small United States-based mission called "Air Mail From God" which has since merged with Trans World Missions. Huffman was director of the mission; Ancel Allen was a new recruit.

Fresh from Moody Bible Institute, Ancel and his wife Naomi began work in August, 1956. They would fly low over villages, dropping Gospels which contained invitations to write for a free Bible correspondence course. Ancel flew the plane and Naomi dropped the Gospels to excited people below. During the first five weeks they dropped 55,000 Gospels.

Ancel was looking forward to seeing the first responses from the Gospels he had dropped. The first letters came on September 21, 1956, the date of his last flight.

This time he flew alone, never expecting to be hit. When he did not return at the expected time, 3:30 P.M., Naomi went to her room and prayed especially for him. "The answer the Lord gave me," she recalls, "was, 'everything is all right.' "

Later news came that his crashed plane had been found with his body inside. The attackers had tried to hammer over the bullet holes in the fuselage without success. They had also tried to dig the bullets from his body with a knife in an effort to disguise the cause of death.

No one was ever charged with the crime nor was any motive ever proven. Naomi was not bitter. "The people who shot at Ancel did so because they had never received the Word," she wrote.

> They didn't know that Christ died for their sins. The Christian villagers who took such wonderful care of Ancel's body and were such a help to me, did so because they had received and believed the Word. They purchased the casket, the plot in the cemetery, and took care of the service. . . . After the service, the native Christians accompanied us to the cemetery, and just as the sun was going down, the women of the church sang songs and lovingly placed over the grave flowers gathered from the mountainside. It is for such a transformation as this in the lives of the Mexican people that Ancel gave his life, and it is for such a transformation as this that I am continuing in the work that Ancel and I began together.

Air Mail From God continued flying. About two years later Director Huffman's plane was shot down. His attackers were never caught either.

More recently, in 1977, an independent Mexican Protestant evangelist was hacked to death in the plaza of Ejutla, Oaxaca, a state with a large Indian population. The Catholic Mother Superior in Ejutla subsequently warned evangelicals never to come back. They continue to evangelize there.

Martyrdoms have also recently occurred in another Oaxacan town, Santa Rosa Matagallinas, where four Baptists have reportedly been murdered, others wounded, and still other evangelicals harassed by local people acting at the behest of their parish priest.

Christianity Today (March 2, 1979) quoted Presbyterian Nicolas Fuentes, head of the Mexico City-based National Committee for Defense of Evangelicals: "Our evangelical chapels are destroyed, we are forbidden to preach, and our pastors are persecuted. In this committee, we receive a minimum of twenty cases per year of flagrant violations against evangelicals by Catholic mobs."

The martyrdom of the Air Mail From God missionaries and other evangelicals does not mean that Mexico is as dangerous for evangelical workers as in past decades. Overall, there is probably less violence in Mexico per capita than in New York City or Chicago. Pockets of fanaticism still exist, however, where it is not safe for Protestant evangelists to remain overnight.

Looking to the Future

Population has quadrupled to sixty-four million since the 1910 Revolution. Mexico faces grave economic problems. Students, fanned by Marxist propaganda, are restive. Attacks by Marxist terrorists on the wealthy and on national leaders are increasing. Still, a Marxist takeover, such as occurred in Cuba, appears unlikely in the foreseeable future.

Spared from Marxist terrorism and widespread religious fanaticism, evangelical work should keep growing in Mexico. Memories of the sacrifices of their martyrs in past years will spur them on.

CENTRAL AMERICA:
Panama, Guatemala, Honduras, El Salvador, Nicaragua, and Costa Rica

Central America, like Mexico, was conquered and Catholicized by Spain in the sixteenth century. For three hundred years no religious dissent was tolerated. In the old Guatemalan capital of Antigua, relics of the Inquisition can still be seen. One niche formed a straight jacket where heretics were chained while water dripped on their heads until they either recanted or went mad. More troublesome heretics were reportedly roasted alive in a huge oven. Other dissenters were hung from metal rings attached to the ceilings.

The breakup of Spain's Central American Federation in 1838 produced five independent nations—Guatemala, Honduras, El Salvador, Nicaragua, and Costa Rica—and weakened the power of the Catholic hierarchy. One by one the countries adopted constitutions guaranteeing religious freedom and separation of church and state. Panama, which broke off from Colombia in 1903, became the sixth nation in what is now Central America.

The First Evangelicals

The first evangelical missionaries arrived in the latter half of the nineteenth century. German Moravians came first, then Presbyterians (at the personal request of the president of Guatemala), then the Central American Mission (CAM), which today has the largest number of field workers of any mission.

The pioneer missionaries were welcomed with volleys of curses and stones. Wrote Miss Eleanor M. Blackmore, an early CAM worker in Nicaragua: "I'm stoned and cursed and hooted in every street. I don't know one road in the whole city where I can walk in which there are not houses where they lie in wait to stone me. . . . We don't want pity. We count it an honor thus to be trusted to suffer, but we do covet your prayers." Their converts experienced more persecution. Many were beaten and some were threatened with death for identifying with the evangelicals.

Earthquakes and Revolutions

Central America is one of the most earthquake prone areas in the world. Superstitious Catholics once blamed evangelical missionaries for causing the quakes, even while the missionaries were risking their lives in relief operations. In recent disasters, such as the 1976 quake in Guatemala in which 22,934 persons were killed, evangelical and Catholic relief workers worked side by side.

Armed rebellions and revolutions have taken more lives than earthquakes. Yet not one evangelical missionary has lost his life in such violence. One of the closest calls came in 1918 when the CAM headquarters in Guatemala City was peppered by more than four thousand bullets in a crossfire between rebels and government forces.

The First Missionary Martyrs

The deadliest peril for the pioneers was yellow fever. In 1894 Mr. and Mrs. H.C. Dillon and bachelor Clarence Wilbur were crossing Nicaragua enroute to El Salvador when all three became violently ill, suffering fever, chills, and congestion of the eyes, gums and tongue, and vomiting dark blood—symptoms of yellow fever. Wilbur died in the town of Granada and was buried in an isolated grave since public cemeteries were reserved for Catholics and could not be profaned by Protestant remains.

The Dillons reached a ship and started for home. They were hardly out to sea when Mrs. Dillon died. Mr. Dillon recovered and eventually remarried. Three years after his first wife died, he was stricken again in the tiny village of El Paraiso in western Honduras. After several weeks at the brink of death, he passed away and was buried by the local believers in a board coffin – a great honor, since the impoverished nationals customarily buried their own dead in a simple grass mat.

Dillon's second wife, Margaret, remained at El Paraiso, living in a small shack and sleeping on a hard straw mattress. She trained Honduran evangelists who ministered in area villages. Fifteen years passed without a furlough. Visiting missionary colleagues noticed how pale she was and insisted she take a rest. The dread fever hit her while she was packing. Unable to walk, she was carried in a hammock thirty-six miles by Honduran men to a mission station. They arrived Friday, June 6, 1913. She died the following Sunday morning.

Yellow fever was conquered. Persecution cooled. Evangelicals became more accepted. There are now substantial evangelical communities in all the Central American countries. Evangelist Luis Palau, called "the Billy Graham of Latin America," predicts that evangelicals will be in the majority in Guatemala by the year 2,000.

A Family Is Murdered

Many evangelicals have paid a heavy price for their commitment to Christ in Central America.

The Juan Campos family lived in a village a few miles from Managua, Nicaragua. From a visit to the capital, their daughter brought home a little red book she had found in a garbage heap. Senora Campos was using a page to roll a cigarette when Juan grabbed up the book and began to read. A loud, swaggering man given to bouts of drinking, he had never before shown interest in religion. What he read in the New Testament so intrigued him that he went into Managua and hunted up the address of the publisher listed on the flyleaf. CAM missionaries led him to Christ.

Juan Campos became one of the most effective evangelical preachers in the country. Several years later, in 1957, a young man became infatuated with the Campos's granddaughter. Since Juan was her guardian, the youth asked his permission to marry her. "Are you a believer?" the preacher asked. The youth shook his head. "Then until you become one of us, I cannot give her to you. It is written in God's Word that a believer should not be unequally yoked together with an unbeliever."

The suitor stormed off in a rage and returned with his machete. Catching the family unaware, he hacked the preacher and his wife and granddaughter to death. Then he vandalized the house to give the appearance of robbery.

News of the brutal crime stunned the small country. The president of Nicaragua expressed his dismay and said, "We need more pastors like Juan Campos."

A Recent Missionary Martyr

Only one evangelical missionary is known to have been murdered in Central America during this century. The circumstances and motives surrounding his death are still murky.

In the summer of 1974 Canadian Gilbert Reimer, one of eighteen missionaries of the Gospel Missionary Union serving in Panama, returned to Panama City after leading a Christian youth camp in the country. He never reached home. His body was found floating in a canal.

He had been stabbed and beaten to death, but no valuables had been taken from his body. A police investigation led nowhere. Neither the identity of the murderers nor their motives is yet known.

One theory circulated that the killing was a case of mistaken identity. Another story spread that he was counseling a drug addict and the supplier became angry over losing a customer and took revenge. Whatever the reason, the fragrance of Gil Reimer's concern for Panamanian young people lingers in Panama today.

"Martyrs" for Social Justice

The situation of Catholics in Central America has been quite different since 1968 when Latin American bishops called for their church to become identified with the cause of the poor and oppressed. As a result of this pronouncement and the influence of "liberation theology," many Catholic clergy have backed movements for social justice. Because Central America's poor are so desperate and the wealthy landowners so resistant, these crusades have triggered violent clashes between peasants and soldiers. The involvement of revolutionary Marxists on the side of the peasants has brought charges that the activist clergy are siding with communists.

Several Catholic missionary priests and at least one evangelical pastor have been killed—or "martyred," as the advocates of social justice would say.

Honduras: June 25, 1975, Honduran army troops stormed a Catholic training center for peasant leaders in the town of Juticalpa. The peasants were demanding that the government speed up promised land redistribution. They had previously blocked bridges and invaded several large estates, and were now planning a hunger strike. In the June melee six Catholic lay workers were killed.

That same day two Franciscan foreign missionaries, Frs. Michael Cypher of Wisconsin and Ivan Betancourt of Colombia, disappeared. A special squad of government investigators, set up as a result of pressure from the Catholic hierarchy, found the bodies of the two priests and seven others at the bottom of a well in front of the hacienda of rancher Jose Manuel Zelaya.

Further investigation uncovered these facts: Fr. Cypher was walking into Juticalpa with a man who needed medical treatment when overtaken and arrested by soldiers. Fr. Betancourt was stopped while taking three women visitors to town. Both priests and the three women were taken to rancher Zelaya's home where they and four others were interrogated, beaten, shot, mutilated and then thrown into the well. The murderers dropped dynamite into the well to destroy the evidence, but the powder failed to ignite.

The rancher, the provincial army commander, and two accomplices were indicted for murder. The government ordered all Catholic priests, monks, and nuns to leave the area. Bishop Nicholas D'Antonio, a United States citizen, left only after ranchers offered a five thousand dollar bounty for his head.

The Honduran Catholic hierarchy gave the slain priests a martyr's funeral. A spokesman noted that the peasants had been promised land in the spring by a previous president, Oswaldo Lopez Arellano. He had been deposed after disclosure by the United States Securities and Exchange Commission that the American-owned United Brands Company (formerly United Fruit) had paid Honduran officials $1.25 million in bribes for lowering of export taxes on bananas.

El Salvador: March 12, 1977, Father Rutilio Grande left his home in the town of Aguilares El Sol with an older man and a boy to celebrate mass in an outlying rural church. Their car was ambushed and all three were killed.

Fr. Grande was perhaps the best-known priest in tiny El Salvador. He was president of the Priests' Senate and headmaster of the Jesuit high school as well as being pastor of a rural parish. He had recently protested the beating of peasants by soldiers and had joined with other Jesuits in supporting land reform. Big landowners in the area claimed he had incited the peasants.

Following his murder, townspeople crowded a midnight mass held at the Aguilares church to express their sorrow. Salvadoran archbishop Oscar Romero called him "Salvador's first Christian martyr, a dedicated man of God who worked for the very poor." The archbishop then pronounced excommunication on all who would commit violence against a priest.

After the funeral, a landowners' group called the White Warrior Union announced that it would begin assassinating other Jesuits in El Salvador on July 21. The government also denounced social activist priests as a tiny minority in league with Marxists.

Throughout 1977 and 1978 attacks on peasants continued, but no more priests were killed. A Catholic investigator claimed to have heard at least forty separate stories of murders, disappearances, or jailings of persons against whom no charge was made. Several Catholic religious communities reported terrorism to Archbishop Romero that included killings, kidnappings and gang rapes of women and young girls by soldiers. They said the terrorism was aimed directly at Catholic leaders and teachers in rural areas.

Guatemala: In the summer of 1978 a priest was killed by vigilantes for defending peasant rights. About the same time, according to *Christianity Today,* the army massacred more than one hundred peasants protesting seizure of their land by well-to-do ranchers.

In contrast to bishops in neighboring El Salvador and Nicaragua, the Guatemalan Catholic hierarchy has said virtually nothing about attacks, assassinations and torture of peasants and political prisoners. In response to this silence, "Padre Chemita," one of the most popular priests in the country, has accused the hierarchy of siding with the rich and powerful against the landless poor, and has led a small faction of priests out of the church.

Nicaragua: The Capuchin Catholic fathers reported in 1976 that Pastor Hernandez, minister of the Evangelical Chapel of Sofana, members of his family, and sixteen other persons disappeared or were shot in 1974 by the Nicaraguan

National Guard. Their crime, according to the priests, was supporting land reform.

The reputable Amnesty International published a long report August 15, 1977, documenting the arrest without warrants, of 303 peasants in Northeast Nicaragua, all of whom have not been heard from since. Amnesty International also cited the shooting of four men, eleven women and twenty-nine children "in cold blood" by National Guardsmen in the village of Varilla in January, 1977.

The subsequent bloody war between the Nicaraguan government and the Marxist-backed Sandinistas has been widely reported. Many Nicaraguan evangelicals supported the Sandinistas call for the overthrow of long-time multi-millionaire dictator Anastasio Somoza whose family has virtually run Nicaragua as a private fiefdom since 1936.

The Future

One Catholic priest martyr, Fr. Hector Gallejo, a native of Colombia, is claimed in Panama. No priests are known to have been recently martyred in Costa Rica, which has been the most democratic and least troubled of all the Central American countries in the twentieth century.

The great danger in Honduras, El Salvador, Guatemala, and Nicaragua is that Marxists could come to power if the enormous gap between rich and poor is not narrowed. The greatest suffering for both evangelicals and Catholics may be ahead.

THE WORLD'S LEADING MISSION FIELD:
Brazil

Since the doors of China closed, Brazil has become the leading mission field for evangelical mission agencies. Over three thousand foreign missionaries serve in Brazil today. The Southern Baptist Convention alone has 269 workers scattered over this huge country that ranks seventh in the world in population and is larger than the United States in area, excluding Alaska.

Almost all evangelical groups are growing rapidly, especially Pentecostals. Twenty–five thousand Brazilians crowd into a single Pentecostal church in Sao Paulo each Sunday. Brazil, which had a Lutheran president from 1974 to 1979, is also the most populous Catholic country in the world. The Vatican claims ninety-three per cent of Brazil's one hundred fourteen million people.

The First Protestant Martyrs

The Catholic stake in Brazil dates to 1500 when Pedro Alvares Cabral, a Portuguese admiral, claimed the vast region for his country. As in Africa, the Portuguese baptized all the native inhabitants they could round up.

The first Protestants arrived in 1555 when a band of Huguenots, fleeing Catholic persecution in France, settled on an island in Rio de Janeiro Bay. Their governor was Admiral Nicolas Durand de Villegaignon. Actually a Catholic, he had

538

passed himself off as a Protestant. He was not happy when John Calvin sent two pastors and fourteen students for the Christian ministry to serve the spiritual needs of the colonists and to proclaim the gospel to jungle Indians. On a pretense of returning to the "true faith," Admiral Villegaignon killed five of the preachers and set the other ministers adrift in a leaky vessel. Then he banished the original settlers in favor of Catholics.

Persecution Resumed When Protestants Returned

Almost three centuries elapsed before Protestants returned to Brazil. American Methodists arrived in the 1830's, then Presbyterians, Baptists, and Lutherans.

The pioneer missionaries were treated roughly. Catholic mobs often gathered outside church buildings and private homes where Protestants worshiped and threw stones through the windows. One such missionary was Baptist pioneer W.G. Bagby who was hit while preaching and fell to the floor unconscious with blood streaming down his face. He bore the mark to his grave. Arrests, stonings, and jailings were common for missionaries in the late nineteenth and early twentieth centuries. The record for imprisonments was probably attained by Solomon Ginsburg, a fiery Baptist evangelist known as "the wandering Jew."

As in Spanish countries, native converts suffered more than the missionaries. One entire congregation was driven into the forest. The sister of a pastor in Pernambuco (now known as Recife), a center of intense persecution, was attacked while lying in a hammock and cut to pieces. Her mother was beaten and forced to run practically naked among jeering men.

Jose Clodoaldo de Souza, a lay evangelist from the First Baptist Church of Bahia (now Salvador), was hauled from his home by a mob led by a local policeman. He was severely beaten and left bound all night at the riverside to be tormented by mosquitoes. The persecutors then sent telegrams to newspapers in Bahia accusing the layman of destroying Catholic images, marrying brothers and sisters, and hiding firearms. After he was released, it was learned that a priest had given the equivalent of one hundred dollars to the mob for their work.

In another instance, two groups of persecutors vowed to kill Baptists meeting in the home of Primo Fonesco. Neither group knew of the other's plans. The first group, led by Jose

Cabral, a Catholic farmer, reached the house first. The second group, directed by police inspector Manuel Joaquim, saw these men, presumed they were the Baptists, and opened fire. The farmer–hooligans thought they were being attacked from behind by the Baptists and fired back. While their enemies were shooting at one another, the Baptists escaped from the rear of the house. Not until the next day did the attackers realize what had happened. Three men had been killed.

The two groups joined in falsely accusing the Baptists of killing the three men. Twelve Baptists were rounded up in the nearby town of Bom Jesus. Four had not even been in Primo Fonesco's house. The twelve were beaten, tortured, and forced to sign confessions. They were kept in jail four years until Solomon Ginsburg paid their heavy legal fees.

Eventually the crude mob attacks and frame-ups began backfiring on the priests. Newspaper editors wrote editorials condemning religious persecution of "the best citizens of Brazil." Courageous judges dispensed justice instead of yielding to mob demands. The federal government demanded that freedom of religion be respected. Today mob attacks on Protestants are extremely rare in Brazil.

The persecutions drew evangelicals closer and made them more bold in witness. The attacks also made thousands of Brazilians curious about the message of the despised Protestants. Many came to evangelistic meetings and were converted.

Martyrs to Indians

Only five evangelical missionaries have been martyred in Brazil in this century. They were killed in two groups by hostile Indians.

From the sixteenth century to present times, the treatment of Indians is one long saga of cruelty and horror. Portuguese settlers took Indian lands for farming, women for concubines and household servants, and men for field hands. Rubber and gold hunters used and abused Indians as desired and sometimes shot them for sport. Some immigrants to Brazil became millionaires through the exploitation of Indians.

It is no surprise that Brazil's Indian population has been decimated from several million to little more than two hundred thousand. Nor is it any wonder that Indians whose hearts have not been changed by the gospel have attacked missionaries venturing into the jungle with the noblest of motives.

The Nhambiquara Massacre

Protestant efforts to reach and evangelize the mysterious tribes of Amazonia began shortly after World War I. In May, 1924, three Americans set out from Cuiaba in south central Brazil to contact the untamed devil-worshiping Nhambiquara Indians. The group included Arthur F. Tylee and Alexander Hay, two young missionaries with the Inland South American Missionary Union, and Rev. L.L. Legters, a rough-and-ready United States evangelist who had longed for the evangelization of South American Indian tribes.

Tylee, a wiry young intellectual who had studied six languages, was from Worcester, Massachusetts. He had made a profession of faith in Christ at fifteen, but in college had drifted away. His experiences in France during World War I showed him that education was no substitute for Christian faith. After the war he enrolled at Harvard Law School, but soon became dissatisfied and transferred to the Moody Bible Institute. At Moody he learned about the pioneer work of the Inland South American Missionary Union. He and his fiancee, Ethel Canary, also a Moody student, were accepted by ISAMU shortly after graduation. They were to be married as soon as he located a permanent station.

There was no road into the interior from Cuiaba. The three Americans and their mule drivers followed an old telegraph line that had been built in 1909 to warn of a possible military invasion from Bolivia. Day after day the explorers pushed along in the sweltering heat and clouds of mosquitoes. After weeks of debilitating travel through soggy forests and swampy marshes, they reached Juruena. No mecca for tourists, it was only a relay station staffed by Brazilian employees who occupied a few pole houses in clearings.

They asked the telegraph operator about Nhambiquaras. "They come in to trade now and then," he said. "We keep our guard up. They're wild fellows and have a reputation for killing anybody who crosses their path." The first Nhambiquaras showed up a few days later, stark naked and slender with bronze skin and straight black hair.

Arthur Tylee recorded his impressions:

> ... Here was the raw article; the Indian; the wild Indian; the absolutely uncivilized Indian. Instead of repulsion or fear, such a feeling of love toward them rose within me that it seemed as though I must tell them how much I loved them, and how God loved them even to the giving of His Son for them. ...

The three moved on to the next telegraph station and then turned back, stopping at a Nhambiquara village. The chief received them cordially and in broken Portuguese invited them to return. "As soon as possible," Tylee assured.

A week after their marriage, Arthur and Ethel were on their way to Juruena where they planned to build a house. The Brazilians remembered Arthur. "You can live in the station until you build your house," the operator told them. It was only one room and the only piece of furniture was a canvas chair, but the Tylees welcomed his offer gladly.

At the time the Brazilians were fearful of an Indian attack. Four months before, the station's food supply had run short. Six Brazilians had gone to a Nhambiquara village to buy food even though they were warned not to go. The chief was said to be angry over the killing of his brother by a Brazilian. When the six did not return on schedule, a search party was sent out. The searchers found only the graves of their friends.

The Tylees noticed that no Brazilian ever stepped outside his house without carrying a gun and long knife. "You'd better be prepared," they warned the missionaries. "These Indians can look friendly one minute and the next minute kill you." The missionaries had brought guns only for protection against snakes and wild animals. "Better that we die," Arthur told Ethel, "than ever shoot a Nhambiquara in self-defense. Otherwise, all our preaching will come to an end."

They decided to build their house at a Nhambiquara campsite about a kilometer northeast of the station. They wanted to avoid any trouble between the Brazilians and the Indians.

Every day the Tylees looked for Indian visitors. Five months later they saw seven coming over a hill. They were armed with bows and arrows but appeared friendly and claimed they had not killed the six Brazilians. They stayed an hour, then left after promising to return and bring some wild honey. The next day fifteen came and stayed for several hours.

The Indians were hard to predict. Most days they were friendly. Other times they seemed to be testing the missionaries. Twice, Arthur felt the cold steel of a long knife at his throat. Each time he merely smiled and pretended that the Indian was joking.

The health of both Tylees deteriorated. Their temperature went up and down from fevers. Food supplies often ran short and they had to live off *mandioca*, a kind of jungle potato. Once Ethel almost died from beriberi.

After bachelor Albert McDowell came to help in the work, they took an extended furlough. They returned two years later in glowing health, bringing a registered nurse, Mildred Kratz, whom they had known at Moody, and a fair-haired, brown-eyed baby. Little Marian Tylee quickly charmed the Indian visitors. The Indians tried to teach her words, which she parroted back with a lisp that sent them into convulsions of laughter.

Nhambiquaras were now coming regularly. Some worked for wages in a model garden. During the furlough Arthur had had soil samples analyzed and was trying to introduce new crops to the Indians. Groups often stayed for supper and overnight, joining the missionaries in prayers and hymn singing.

The Nhambiquaras built huts near the Tylees where they stayed on extended visits. Everything continued to go well. Arthur's language notebook filled up with Nhambiquara words and phrases. Nurse Kratz did medical work and helped Ethel with teaching. Albert McDowell also treated the sick.

In 1929 a flu virus was brought in by Brazilian visitors and quickly spread among the Indians. The missionaries were kept busy treating patients. One Nhambiquara, Manoel, died at their house. His friends immediately tied his body to the back of an Indian for transport back to his village and burial.

Ten months passed. Late in the evening of October 27, 1930, three Indians came with news that some of their friends had died from the flu—a story later discovered to be untrue. Saturday, four days later, ten Indians came. Sunday, more Indians arrived. They acted morose and sullen. When Ethel asked one if he wanted to spend the night, he replied angrily, "No. It is too dangerous. Manoel died here."

Early Monday morning the crowd increased. Still the missionaries sensed no trouble. The Indians were only a little quieter than usual.

Suddenly Ethel heard a weird call. She looked and saw an Indian grasp Nurse Kratz in a tight grip. When she tried to go to Mildred's aid, another Indian, who had always been friendly before, pinned her arms back. "Let me go!" she shouted, and he did.

The Indians were murmuring in low tones and it was impossible to catch what they were saying. Instinctively,

Ethel ran toward the bedroom where baby Marian was still asleep. A hoe handle crashed against her head. She fell, tried to get up, and was hit twice more. Afterwards she recalled seeing a revolver on a table and remembering what Arthur had said, dismissed the idea of using it.

Dazed and with blood streaming from her nose and mouth and wounds on her head, Ethel crept to Marian's bed. The baby seemed to sigh. She turned around and saw Mildred Kratz lying on the dirt floor. Instinctively, she pulled an arrow from the nurse's body. She crawled across the room and found Arthur. Three Brazilians were lying nearby. Ethel later recalls:

> It was perhaps the blackest hour of all. Up to this time it seemed only a question of bearing the pain patiently until I would be released from all suffering forever and be with my Lord and loved ones. But now—could I pick up the broken threads of my life and go on without the one who had been more than life to me? The brain was too numb to even think of what it would be like but I was conscious of a Presence and Strength with me far greater than my own and out of the blackness of human despair spoke the voice of One who had gone that way before: "The cup which my Father hath given me, shall I not drink it?" With the question came also the reply, "Even so, Father, for so it seemed good in thy sight." Then Romans 12:1 came to my mind: "I beseech you . . . by the mercies of God, that you present your bodies a living sacrifice, holy, acceptable unto God." I thought, "It will be harder to be a living sacrifice than a dying sacrifice, but I must be."

Somehow she managed to get to the telegraph station. The operator telegraphed for Albert McDowell who was at another station down the line. Albert arrived at 9:00 P.M. and cleansed and bandaged her deep scalp wounds. The next morning, Albert and the Brazilians laid the bodies to rest under trees across from the mission house. Baby Marian was buried in her father's arms.

The Brazilians at Juruena wanted to punish the Indians. "My loved ones are already with the Lord," Ethel said. "I want no revenge." Years later, one of the Brazilian workers at the telegraph station told another missionary, "Her faith brought me to the Savior."

After a period of recuperation, the widow went back to

the United States. For the next twenty-five years she was a "living sacrifice," speaking in churches, Bible conferences, Bible schools and colleges, presenting the challenge of the lost tribes. It is a reasonable guess that hundreds of young Christians heard the call of God through her impassioned pleas and volunteered for foreign missionary service. She never remarried and died September 7, 1955, in West Branch, Michigan, at the age of sixty-one.

And the Nhambiquaras?

In 1937 a missionary went back to Juruena and found only a few charred posts and a pile of ash-covered rocks to mark the site of the massacre. "But we found another building which will never perish," he wrote, "erected by the testimony of His servants—a living temple of living stone— hearts that are open to the gospel and lives that are bearing faithful witness to Christ." He referred to the Brazilians converted through the witness of the missionaries there.

The year before, missionary work had been reopened among the Nhambiquaras at an outpost called "Campos Novos." The Indians were slow in responding, but after several years they came to trust the missionaries fully. In the years since, intertribal fighting and disease have wiped out large segments of the tribe on the Brazilian side. But a ministry at two stations continues to this day.

The Kayapo "Big-Lips"

In the 1920's north central Brazil was just as trackless as the state of Mato Grosso in the south. The only highways were the yellow tributaries of the Amazon that drained a basin over three times larger than Texas. Life in scattered white settlements at the mouths of rivers consisted of long periods of boredom shattered by moments of terror. Brazilians attacked Indians. Indians took revenge, usually killing Brazilian males and taking the women and girls captive. Then the cycle of terror started all over again.

In the Xingu-River area the Kayapo "Big-Lips" were most feared. The deformity resulted from a tribal custom of stretching out the lower lip an inch or more by a wood disc inserted into the flesh. Just the sight of a Big-Lip warrior, his body painted jet black, sent a white running for his gun.

The first missionary to attempt to reach the Big Lips was Ernest Wotton, a member of the Heart of Amazonia mission, then affiliated with the Worldwide Evangelization Crusade and later absorbed into The Unevangelized Fields

Mission. Wotton had been challenged by Fenton Hall, a young English bachelor who had died from malaria while trying to Christianize the Guajajara Red Indians.

Wotton hired a young civilized Indian couple, Jacinto and Caroline, as guides and set out from the outpost town of Nova Olinda at the confluence of the Xingu and the Rio-zinho rivers. With a crew of rowers, they started up the Rio-zinho in a long canoe, looking for Kayapos.

Rounding a bend, they surprised an Indian fishing. The protruding lower lip told them he was from the tribe they were seeking. But upon sight of the visitors, he ran back into the jungle. The missionary ordered the rowers to swing into a sand bar. Leaping out, he and Jacinto waded ashore. The young woman Caroline followed.

"We want to be your friends. Come," Jacinto called. About a dozen Big-Lips crept cautiously out of the jungle and stopped near the men. While Wotton and Jacinto's attention was diverted, others grabbed Caroline and carried her screaming into the jungle. Jacinto yelled for a rifle. The frightened rowers announced they were leaving. The missionary and guide could come if they wished. There was no choice. The sobbing husband waded to the canoe, leaving his wife at the mercy of the wild Kayapos.

Ernest Wotton made several more tries. Eventually his health broke and he had to give up.

In 1928 a young Australian couple, Fred and Mabel Roberts, came to Brazil. Before the year was out, Mabel contracted malaria. "I have done all I can," she whispered to Fred. The young husband conducted her funeral service and buried her beside the grave of Fenton Hall.

After Mabel's death, Fred felt God wanted him to pick up the mantle of Ernest Wotton. Two other young missionaries volunteered to go with him. Fred Dawson, a fellow Australian, said, "If the Lord calls me to lay down my life for Christ and the Indians, I am willing." Fred Wright, an Irish athlete, was also ready to die if necessary.

The Three Freds, as they came to be called, went to Nova Olinda in 1935. There they stored most of their belongings and bought a boat and motor, eliminating the need for a crew. Fred Wright's last letter to his home prayer–partners indicated the depth of their commitment:

> I do not know when you will receive this, or even if
> you receive it at all. . . . Once we leave civilization,
> it may be months or even years before we can come

down with mail. It may be that we shall never get down again; God only knows.

As far as we can ascertain, the Kayapos are very numerous. We are quite aware that, humanly speaking, we are as good as dead men, but brethren, stand by us as one man. Do not criticize. We are beyond criticism as we go forward in the Name of the Lord and under His command, after having fully counted the cost.

Finally, it is well to remember that Calvary was and is the greatest victory of all times. Death to the Christian is not defeat. Should the Lord will that we be taken, our prayer is that more men and more money be rushed out to follow up this advance. Let our generalship be greater than that of our arch-enemy, the devil, and set aside all sentiment for the sake of the spread of the Gospel of our Lord Jesus Christ in that day.

They were never seen alive again.

Months later, missionaries Horace Banner and Jock Johnstone reached Nova Olinda. They hired two Brazilian youths and started up the Rio-Zinho. They came to some long impassable rapids and found where the Three Freds had made wheels from a large tree trunk to apparently make a cart for portaging the canoe past the rapids. In the woods nearby they came upon a straw-thatched shack and beyond that a large abandoned village. When they found a charred piece of wood, with a round two-inch hole, the Brazilians refused to go further. The wood was evidently from the cart built to carry the canoe.

The two missionaries stuffed a brief record of their trip into a bottle and tied the bottle to a tree hoping that the missing men might find it. They returned to Nova Olinda, hired other boatmen, and came back to the village. The bottle was gone and there were tracks of Indians all around.

This time they had brought three canoes. Leaving one canoe and a crew at the rapids, they pushed further upriver. On the eighth day they reached a giant cataract, which they called Smoke Falls. At the foot of the falls they recovered the Three Fred's boat and motor. The prow of the boat was smashed and the motor had been stripped of some parts. They searched the riverbank nearby and found a heap of blood-stained, ant-eaten clothing.

Banner and Johnstone reported to their home office in

London that the three Freds could be considered dead. The story was picked up by newspapers throughout the British Commonwealth. It was discussed and prayed over in hundreds of missionary groups and churches. A book about the three Freds aroused more interest. The Heart of Amazonia Mission received hundreds of letters pledging prayer. Many writers, including Christians in Africa, sent money. Some volunteered for service in Amazonia.

Two years later hundreds of wild Kayapos swarmed into Nova Olinda. These Big-Lips were not attacking but seeking refuge from tribal enemies. Horace Banner got the news and hurried back. Stepping ashore, he was surrounded by the naked Indians from the very tribe for which the three Freds had given their lives. Among the group was the woman Caroline who had been kidnapped years before. She now had a new husband and conducted herself as one of the wild ones.

The missionary found another kidnapped woman, Magdalena, willing to talk. She recalled a party of warriors returning to the camp with revolvers, felt hats, and sport shirts. They bragged of killing three strange white men, she said.

The Indians at Nova Olinda were anxious to revenge their defeat. Night after night the men held war dances. Then they began leaving in relays. The women, children, and old men stayed behind.

About a week later the warriors began trickling back. Many burned with fever. Some had died. None had found the enemy. Banner and Frank Houston, a new missionary, felt God had intervened and brought them back.

The government Indian Protection Service put the Indians in the hands of the missionaries. Then, in 1938, all of the Indians left.

Banner and Houston went upriver and built a mission house praying that the Indians would settle there. Within a month the first contingent came out of the jungle and built a communal house next to the missionaries. Other groups came and built more houses. The missionaries began language studies and taught the Indians new ways to grow crops.

The missionaries were hesitant to ask about the fate of the three Freds, believing that the Indians might fear reprisals. One day an Indian asked if they had heard "about three white men like yourselves" who were killed. "Yes," Banner replied, "but tell us what you know." The informant said he had only heard about the killings from others.

Horace Banner passed around a photo of the Three Freds. Various Indians volunteered details until the sad story was pieced together. The missionaries used the opportunity to explain their purpose in coming to the Indians and God's love for them.

The killers were named, but the Indians said none were in the camp. A few weeks later a party of strange warriors arrived. Among them were two of the alleged murderers. The missionaries befriended them and invited them to attend Sunday services. One evening as Horace Banner played a hymn on his concertina, one of the men came and handed over his war club. Then he sat down and listened attentively to the music.

No More Martyrs

The sacrifice of Arthur Tylee and his baby, nurse Mildred Kratz, and the Three Freds spurred other missionaries to push deeper into the Amazonian jungles of Brazil. The frontier was pushed further and further back. Yet there are still many tribes that have not been reached, even today.

There have been no more martyrs in Brazil's Amazonia. Thousands of Indians have become model Christian citizens. Still, missionaries have had to work under a constant barrage of criticism, first from Catholic clergy and more recently from non-Christian anthropologists. The anthropologists argue that the missionaries are destroying the Indian cultures. The missionaries counter that they are preparing the Indians to face onrushing civilization by giving them the Bible in their own languages and helping them build a viable morality that will save them from extinction. "Whether we stay or not," the missionaries plead, "change is certain." Change is now accelerating as the government builds a trans-Amazonian highway westward to the border of Peru.

In 1977 the Brazilian government ordered the Wycliffe Bible Translators, the largest mission in the country, out of their tribal locations. The decision was influenced by the critical anthropologists and possibly also by resentment of criticism by the Carter administration of human rights violations in Brazil. Wycliffe translators are continuing their work outside the tribes at regional centers.

Brazil's Catholic Martyrs

Recent clashes between Roman Catholic priests and Brazilian authorities are concentrated in economically depressed northeast Brazil where priests are participating in land reform movements and protests by impoverished peasants.

The situation here is similar to that in Nicaragua, El Salvador, Honduras, and Guatemala. Powerful land owners are allied with the government, the military, and conservative bishops of the Catholic hierarchy. A new breed of Catholic clergy, supported by a few Protestants, preach social change through revolution if necessary. Skillful Marxist agitators eagerly capitalize on discontent.

The Catholic activists look to Archbishop Helder Camara of Recife (formerly Pernambuco), Brazil, for leadership. He has powerful links to many world Catholic figures, yet this has not prevented alleged murders, imprisonments under false pretenses, and torture of priests and nuns.

Archbishop Camara's "Justice and Peace" movement claims three priests have been martyred since 1975. Father Rudolf Lunkenbein was killed July 15, 1976, while defending the rights of Indians against encroaching land grabbers. Father Joao Bosco Penido Burnier was gunwhipped and shot in the state of Mato Grasso after he came upon four military policemen torturing two women and protested. Bishop Adriano Hipolito da Costa was mutilated by "hoodlums" representing a group of wealthy Brazilians.

The movement also cites the arrest of Sister Maurina Borges da Silveira, a forty-three-year-old Franciscan nun, for allowing a group of young people to meet at her orphanage and discuss politics. After being forced to strip, she was beaten and given electric shocks, then told to stop praying and renounce Christ for he could not help her. Her archbishop, who had been silent on politics, excommunicated her torturers.

Altogether, the Catholic social activists claim that seventy-nine persons fighting for social justice have died under torture in the past nine years.

The small minority of Protestants who have participated include Paul Wright, the son of United States missionaries, and United Methodist missionary Fred Morris. Young Wright was arrested in 1973 and has not been heard from since. Morris was seized and tortured, allegedly for sending reports to *Time* magazine on problems in northeastern Brazil and for associating with supposed communists.

Brazil's Future

Brazil continues under military rule, although there are signs that the government is easing restrictions on civil liberties.

At the same time, the nation's economy booms while multitudes in northeast Brazil and other pockets of poverty exist at near-starvation levels. By the year 2,000 Brazil could be a world superpower, barring depression, internal revolt or a Marxist revolution.

Evangelicals see the future of Brazil in a deeper dimension, as a nation ripe for spiritual harvest. They hold that most Brazilians are only baptized Catholics and are committed more to secularism or voodoo worship than to the church of Rome. If they can be reached by the gospel, Brazil will be one of the strongest Christian nations in the world.

THE SOUTHERN
STRETCH:
Uruguay, Argentina
and Chile

Argentina and Chile occupy the long southern tail of South
America; Uruguay is tucked between Argentina and Brazil
on the north. These countries were settled and Catholicized
by Spanish soldiers and priests in the sixteenth century.
They threw off the shackles of Spain in the early nineteenth
century. They permitted limited Protestant missionary work
years before other nations to the north. The first Protestant
church on the west coast of the Western Hemisphere, south of
California, was opened in Chile in 1856. At that time missionaries were allowed to evangelize only non-Spanish
speaking foreign immigrants. Spanish work was prohibited
for many years in both countries by intolerant Catholic
hierarchies allied with civil and military authorities. Early
evangelicals suffered the same stonings, beatings, imprisonments, and family and social pressures that Protestants
experienced elsewhere in Latin America before the 1950's.

The First Martyrs
No evangelical missionaries have died in connection with
their service in Uruguay, Argentina and Chile during the
twentieth century. However, fifteen were martyred in the
preceding century. Their story, which has inspired national
believers ever since, deserves telling.

552

In 1842 Captain Allen Gardner, who had resigned from the British Royal Navy to serve God full time, sailed into the Strait of Magellan. Unfriendly Indians kept him moving along until he finally found a group who said he might build a church for them.

The pioneer went home and tried to interest mission boards in the work. When they all turned him down, he organized the Patagonian Missionary Society.

Seven years and two more trans-Atlantic voyages later, the mission had seven members, including the founder. Before leaving England the last time, he arranged for a vessel to bring supplies periodically from the Falkland Islands. Then he and his six associates put to sea in a tiny ship with six months of stores.

On December 5, 1850, they went ashore on the coast of the remote island of Tierra del Fuego. The Indians they had hoped to evangelize drove them back to their ship, and they took refuge in Spanish Harbor. The first supply ship did not arrive until January, 1852. By then it was three months too late. The crew found all seven dead of starvation. Captain Gardner's last diary entry read: "Great and marvelous are the loving-kindnesses of my gracious God unto me. I neither hunger nor thirst, though five days without food."

The tragedy awakened English Christians to the need for evangelizing the Indians in southern South America. A party of eight sailed six years later. Seven of the eight were massacred by aborigines while conducting a worship service on shore. Others took their places. The mission's name was changed to the South American Missionary Society. There are churches in southern Chile and Argentina today which have connections to the pioneer work.

Church Growth in Dark Times

Evangelicals have made great gains in Uruguay, Argentina and Chile in recent years. The most rapid growth has been among indigenous Pentecostals in Chile. One of every twelve Chileans is a Pentecostal or Methodist Pentecostal. In 1974 the president of Chile participated in the dedication of a Methodist Pentecostal cathedral in Santiago that seats 15,000. Nothing like this had ever happened before.

Church growth has spiraled alongside inflation, political terrorism and turmoil. Argentina has been in almost daily crisis since the fall of strongman Juan Peron. One military

government has succeeded another, each failing to stop rightist and leftist killings and to curb the world's worst
inflation.

The Catholic church is split. Many priests and laymen
with leftist ties have been arrested and reportedly tortured.
Some have been killed in alleged revenge of leftist terrorism
against political leaders and security forces.

The worst violence against priests apparently was in retaliation for a leftist bomb explosion that killed twenty policemen. A wave of killings followed the murders, climaxed
by the assassination of three priests and two seminarians in
a parish residence in Buenos Aires. The priests belonged to
the Irish Pallottine order and were shot in the back of the
head. None had engaged in political activities.

The killing of the five clerics in July, 1976, brought the
wrath of the Catholic hierarchy down on Argentine officials,
but did not stop the bloodshed.

Protestant missionaries and national pastors have thus far
not been targets of terrorists in Argentina. In recent years Protestant leaders have enjoyed more public favor than Catholics
because of their charitable works and avoidance of politics.

Terrorism in Uruguay

Little Uruguay (population 2.7 million), long a haven of
political liberalism, was hit by terrorism in the late 1960's.
In succeeding years many foreign diplomats and businessmen
were abducted by the leftist, urban Tupamaros guerrillas.
However, no missionaries were attacked or kidnapped. Since
1973 the tiny country has been controlled by a rightist military
dictatorship which has clamped down hard on leftist subversives. Evangelical missionaries continue to be welcomed
and some one hundred thirty foreign Protestant workers are
in the country, representing about thirty mission societies.
Churches are reported to be growing.

Marxism in Chile

Chile, according to leading evangelicals there, came to the
brink of disaster in 1973. Only an "act of God in answer to
our prayers," they say, brought the downfall of the Marxist
government and prevented a massacre of middle and upper
class leaders.

The basic facts of what happened in Chile are well
known. Marxist Salvador Allende, head of Chile's Socialist
Party, won the presidency in 1970 by a narrow plurality, re-

ceiving 36.3 per cent of the vote in a three-man race. Allende became the first Marxist president of a nation ever freely elected.

Chile became a mecca for leftists all over Latin America. Allende quickly established diplomatic relations with communist states, including Cuba. He expropriated many banks, industries and large farms, and nationalized the properties of four large United States corporations. Chile's economy fell into a tailspin. Inflation skyrocketed. Production declined. Food became scarce.

In the 1973 election Allende's opposition, the Democratic Confederation, retained control of both the senate and the chamber of deputies. Subsequently, the Chilean Congress and Supreme Court declared Allende's expropriation of property illegal under the nation's constitution. Allende refused to retreat. His communist allies, according to evangelical sources, stockpiled quantities of Russian and Chinese arms.

The Marxist government virtually ignored church organizations except for welcoming support from leftist priests. Evangelicals, however, saw a storm of persecution ahead. Many pastors began secret prayer meetings asking for divine intervention.

A "Miracle" or a Tragedy?

September 11, 1973, the "miracle," as it was called later by many evangelical leaders, happened. Chilean military commanders surrounded and bombarded the presidential palace. Allende died in the successful coup. Afterwards it was announced that the military had acted after learning of Plan Zeta, which the Marxists planned to initiate on September 17. The military leaders said the plan called for liquidation of thousands of Chileans in the initial purge (a thousand influential people were to be killed in one city alone), with expectations that as many as ten per cent of Chile's population might have to be killed before a classless Marxist society was formed.

The new government under Army General Augusto Pinochet began rounding up leading leftists. Thousands of foreign leftist refugees fled the country with assistance from the UN and the World Council of Churches. Reports were leaked to newspapers claiming brutal torture and killing of political prisoners inside Chile. Supporters of the new government countered that the stories were vastly exaggerated by communist propaganda mills. Nevertheless, the new government was criticized and condemned, both in the United

States and elsewhere. The censure became heavier after it was learned that the United States Central Intelligence Agency had worked for Allende's downfall.

Some Protestant churchmen abroad came down hard against the new government. A number of American evangelical leaders abhorred the coup, but most waited to hear from their brothers and sisters in Chile. The answer came in a formal declaration by representatives of practically all the evangelical bodies in Chile:

> Chile fell without fear into the clutches of international Marxism whose national leaders, in spite of not representing the majority, knew how to deceive with false promises many Chileans who desired needed changes. . . . Once in power, they brought about chaos and the breakdown of the institutional structures, leading the country to a slow death, poisoned by hatred and divested of our most cherished spiritual values.
>
> The pronouncement of our Armed Forces in the historical process of our country was God's answer to the prayers of all the believers who recognized that Marxism was the expression of satanic power of darkness in its highest decree. . . . We, the Evangelicals, . . . recognize as the maximum authority of our country the Military Junta, who in answer to our prayers freed us from Marxism.

Rev. Rogelio Aracena, a Chilean Methodist pastor and district leader of Campus Crusade for Christ in Chile, came to the United States to present the evangelical viewpoint. He said inflation had exceeded one thousand per cent under three years of Allende. University students, he noted, had been ordered to spread Marxism in public surveys. Christian students who refused to participate had been forced to leave their schools.

Missionaries wrote their home constituencies to explain what had happened. One pointed out that "some Chilean priests" along with "quite a few French and other European priests . . . were frankly favorable" to Allende. "To these must be added a goodly number of ex-priests who were openly Marxists." He conceded that the new government had jailed "a few evangelical pastors," but "not for preaching the gospel. They were directly involved in Marxist politics though they may not have been aware of where this philosophy would lead them eventually."

Chile's right-wing military regime continues under heavy pressure abroad for alleged human rights violations. Evangelicals there continue to insist that the downfall of the Marxist president was a miracle. Had he stayed in power, they add, Chile would have become a Marxist dictatorship and a base for inciting and abetting Marxist revolutions in neighboring nations.

INLAND COUNTRIES:
Paraguay and Bolivia

Landlocked Paraguay has never recovered from a nineteenth century war against Brazil, Argentina, and Uruguay that took the lives of almost every able-bodied male in the country. Still abysmally poor, Paraguay is today a police state in the iron grip of dictator Alfredo Stroessner who has ruled since 1954.

Most of the 2.7 million people are *mestizo*, of mixed Indian and Spanish ancestry. Fifty thousand or more pure Indians still survive in the jungled, swampy Chaco (hunting ground). The British Anti-Slavery Society accuses the Paraguayan government of practicing a policy of extermination towards many of these Indians, charging that most men have been killed and the women and children sold into slavery.

A Mennonite Martyr

Missionaries with the New Tribes Mission (the largest mission in Paraguay) and Mennonite workers have hazarded their lives in trying to evangelize the wild Indians of Paraguay. The only martyr has been Mennonite Cornelius Isaak. The Mennonite knew that Ayore Indians in Bolivia had killed five New Tribes missionaries in 1943 (see next section). Nevertheless, he set out in the summer of 1958 to contact Ayores in Paraguay. He died of a spear wound received in his first contact with the wild Indians.

The missionaries in Paraguay's Chaco have continued trying to tame the wild forest dwellers with love and the gospel. They, too, are grieved at cruelty shown toward the Indians by civilized Paraguayans. But they make their protests known in quiet, personal diplomacy, scrupulously avoiding political involvements to which the government might object.

Most other evangelical missionaries in Paraguay also avoid political entanglements. The dictator regards their work favorably and years ago permitted Billy Graham to hold an eight-day crusade in Asuncion, the capital. It was the first evangelical meeting ever held on public grounds in this country.

"Martyrs" for Land

One and one-half per cent of the wealthy elite own eighty-nine per cent of all land. To promote a fairer distribution of farmlands, a group of priests set up the Christian Land League. A story soon surfaced that the Paraguayan government intended to liquidate leaders of the League.

Seven foreign Jesuit priests and two Disciples of Christ missionaries were arrested and deported. Three Paraguayan priests were seized, then released. Seven Paraguayan workers for the Friendship Mission of the Disciples of Christ were also taken into custody and of these three remain in prison.

The Committee of Churches for Emergency Aid, headed by a Catholic bishop and two prominent Protestants, claims the government is holding around six hundred political prisoners. Three "Christians" fighting for social justice, they say, have been martyred in prison and many others tortured. The government denies this and blames the trouble on Marxist subversives. M. Frisco Gilchrist, a twenty-five year Disciples of Christ missionary veteran and one of those expelled, replies that in Paraguay it has become a crime to help the poor. The Disciples' Friendship Mission which the government closed, calling it an "arsenal . . . and resistance center," was only developing self-help projects and encouraging poor people to organize cooperatives, the ex-missionary claims. Charges of communism, he adds, are often an excuse to arrest and mistreat rivals to the Stroessner regime.

Relations between the government and the Roman Catholic hierarchy have deteriorated. The archbishop of Asuncion refuses to attend meetings of the Council of State, explaining that his conscience forbids him to participate in the "institutional violence" that plagues Paraguay.

Is there more bloodshed ahead for Paraguay, both among

the Catholic and Protestant social activists and among the evangelicals who devote themselves to the spiritual needs of the people?

BOLIVIA — TARGET OF COMMUNISTS

Bolivia has long been a special target for Marxists. Che Guevera was killed there in 1967 while leading a guerrilla band. Slightly smaller than Texas and Colorado combined, Bolivia is strategically bordered by five other nations coveted by Marxists. It has a history of clerical domination, genocidal wars, military rule, an imbalance between extreme wealth and grinding poverty, and ethnic and economic conflicts between the Indian underclass (sixty–five per cent of the population) and the ruling Spanish oligarchy.

Another "Miracle?"

The Marxists nearly captured Bolivia in 1971, evangelical missionaries say. Only a "miracle," similar to that which happened in Chile, prevented the country from becoming another Cuba and experiencing a purge of anti-Communists, which would have included many evangelical leaders.

The year before, 1970, leftist General Juan Jose Torres had captured the presidency. In August, 1971, the Torres government suddenly began arresting prominent noncommunist leaders in Santa Cruz, the nation's second largest city. A young evangelical, Oscar Velasquez, discovered the plot and ran from one Catholic church to another ringing church bells, the traditional means of summoning the populace to the plaza. When the people came and were told what was happening, they thundered an ultimatum for the arrests to stop and the prisoners already taken to be released. Massive demonstrations quickly spread across the country and after a short period of fighting, the leftist government fell.

John G. Palmquist, a Canadian Baptist missionary, called the overthrow of the leftists "an answer to our prayers. How close this man Torres came to repeating the betrayal of a nation as his counterpart Castro had done!" In a follow-up report to evangelical media in the United States, Palmquist said that after the noncommunist leadership had been put away, Castro would have flown in from Cuba and pronounced Bolivia "a socialist republic." He noted that after the coup, Cubans had been discovered in a Catholic cathedral with a stockpile of arms. The Cubans and the arms, the Canadian Baptist said, had been brought there by six foreign leftist Catholic priests. The priests were taken to the bishop who turned them over to the army to "do with as you like." They were expelled from the country.

A Million New Testaments

The new president was Colonel Hugo Banzer Suarez, a fervent anti-Communist and a warm friend of evangelicals. How he came to back evangelical causes is a story worth telling.

When he was a colonel in the army, Banzer was befriended by missionary David Farrah, Wycliffe's liaison with the Bolivian government. Farrah visited Banzer in prison after the army officer was arrested by the leftist regime. He gave him a Bible and, according to Farrah, "God touched his heart." The friendship continued after Banzer became president. At Farrah's suggestion, Banzer invited evangelist Luis Palau to speak on Bolivian television. Palau offered Spanish New Testaments to all who would call or write. When the president saw the huge response, he asked Farrah to help him get a million copies for required reading in all the schools in Bolivia. The United States-based World Home Bible League supplied the Testaments.

In 1978 Palau held a full-length evangelistic crusade in Bolivia, resulting in almost twenty thousand professions of faith. This was an unprecedented response in "Catholic" South America.

Mountain Indians Die for Christ

The ministry to isolated rural Indians is another story. Ten million Quechua Indians, speaking a variety of related dialects, populate cold, barren plateaus and hidden mountain valleys in western South America. One and a half million of these live in Bolivia. Only one in twenty is literate. Quechuas have been among the most difficult people in the world to reach with the gospel. Only a small percentage are believers today. The majority are in bondage to the angry gods of their ancestors.

In Bolivia hundreds of Quechua evangelicals have been ostracized from their communities, blamed for crop failures, and severely persecuted. Many believers have had their homes burned. Some have been killed or stoned.

Missionaries and national church leaders believe the key to Quechua evangelization is Scripture translation. Wycliffe personnel in Bolivia are already translating for six Quechua groups, and plan to produce eighteen editions of the New Testament to meet the needs of all Quechuas whose languages vary from village to village.

Martyrs in the Jungle

Wild Bolivian Indians roam the eastern jungle bordering Brazil and Paraguay. They have long been the concern of Wycliffe, the South American Mission, and the New Tribes Mission.

Six New Tribes missionaries have been martyred in heroic attempts to take the gospel to tribesmen who have long suffered inhumane abuse from traders, rubber hunters, and white adventurers.

The first five martyrs were among the first members of the mission founded by Paul Fleming in 1942. A missionary to Malaysia, Fleming had returned to Michigan weak from malaria. He shared with a young pastor, Cecil Dye, his dream of taking the gospel to remote tribes that other missions had not yet reached. From their talks evolved an interdenominational mission to *new tribes*, hence the name.

Two years later Cecil and Dorothy Dye and their three children, Cecil's younger brother Bob and his wife Jean, newlyweds Dave and Audrey Bacon, George Hosbach, and Eldon Hunter arrived in Bolivia. The goal of the five men was to establish a mission with the Ayores, a tribe that a Bolivian official called "impossible to tame. They attack any civilized person who comes near them," he warned. "Slip up and club their victims in their hammocks. You'll never come back alive." Other Bolivians made the same predictions.

The married men moved their families to remote Santo Corazon in the heart of a jungled area where several nomadic tribes roamed at will. From here the five men planned to launch their first missionary journey looking for Ayores and pushing their base camps further and further into the wilds.

The men went without guns. An American reporter had planned to accompany them, but backed out upon learning they were going in unarmed. "I don't know God that well," he said.

They left November 10, 1944, after telling two colleagues, Clyde Collins and Wally Wright, "If you don't hear anything inside a month, come and make a search for us." The married men did not mention that to their wives.

The month passed. Clyde and Wally and four Bolivian men followed their trail over a hill and along a rocky river.

They came upon a group of Ayores. The frightened Indians ran away. A little farther on they found a cracked camera lens, one of Cecil's socks, George's machete, and some other personal items, but no bodies. While they were camped, Wally was wounded by an arrow. They gave up and went back.

A second and larger search party of Bolivians moved into the jungle. They picked up the missionaries' trail and followed it to an abandoned Ayore plantation. There they found more personal belongings.

An army commander wanted to send in troops on a revenge raid. The wives pleaded, "Don't go. We want to reach them for Christ." The soldiers did not go.

More months passed, then a year. Jean Dye and other missionaries moved to a railway camp deeper into Ayore's country. Dorothy and Audrey went home on furlough. One day in 1948 a band of naked Ayores suddenly appeared at the camp. The missionaries gave them gifts and tried to make friends. The Indians took the gifts and melted back into the jungle. Six weeks later the Indians returned and spent the night. Some remained. They told of another clan who had killed five whites years before and had thrown their bodies into the river.

The following year, Degui, a friendly Ayore, brought an Indian boy to Jean. The boy told of five tall white men coming to his village. "Your countrymen are dead," he told Jean. "Our warriors killed them and buried their bodies."

Jean came down with malaria and went home to see a doctor. She now believed the five were dead. Among the survivors, only Audrey held out hope. Six months later Jean returned to Bolivia. Dorothy and her three children, and Audrey and daughter Avis also went back.

Degui brought another Ayore who added more to the previous story. In time still others would add more details until the wives had a fairly accurate account of what had happened to the men.

How the Five Were Killed

A man named Ejeene was hoeing his crops when he saw the five men coming. They were extending knives and clothing as gifts. Ejeene ran to the village shouting, *"Conjnone! Conjnone!* (Civilized! Civilized!)

The women and children darted into the jungle. The men came running from their gardens and hid behind their huts. They armed themselves with spears, clubs, and bows and arrows. From their hiding place they watched the five walk into the center of the circle of huts and place gifts on the ground. An impatient Ayore, Ajarmane, suddenly released an arrow. It hit one man in the shoulder. A companion pulled it out, then all five began walking rapidly away.

After the five left, the Ayore men rushed for the gifts. One, Upoide, was angry because he did not get a machete. "I'm going after the Conjnone and get me a machete," he shouted.

He found them sitting on a log. They motioned him near, holding out more knives, machetes, and pointing to heaven. Upoide walked up to the smallest man (Dave Bacon) and extended his hands. Dave gave him a machete and hugged him.

Upoide was still angry. He pulled back, whirled and pierced Dave with a spear. As Dave struggled to pull the weapon out, other Ayores ran up. One named Aburasede struck him on the head with a club and killed him.

The other Ayores now felt they must follow suit, or the dead man's companions would take vengeance. They closed in on the missionaries, hurling spears and wielding clubs. In the confusion of the melee, one missionary managed to run through the crowd. Datide, another warrior, overtook him and struck him down.

The shouts brought other Indians running. Ejeene, the man who had spotted the missionaries first, yelled, "They are descendants of our ancestor, *Corabe* [White Butterfly]. You shouldn't have killed them. They were not bad." The war chief, Amajane, who had been away, arrived. He agreed that the missionaries must have been descendants of the legendary white woman who at one time had lived with the Ayores. He lectured the killers sternly but did not punish them.

The Fate of the Killers

Relatives of the killers who became Christians told the missionary widows, "We're sorry our men killed your husbands. They didn't know better."

"We understand," the wives assured them. Audrey added, "It was worth my husband's death to see you come to know Christ."

What happened to the killers? Four died in the jungle before having a chance to hear the gospel. Two of these were killed by tribal enemies. Upoide, the one whose anger triggered the massacre, was the first to come to the mission station. When assured that the three widows had forgiven him, he became the first of the killers to accept Christ. Ajarmane, the one who had shot the arrow, was next. The remaining killers also heard the gospel but made no profession of faith.

And the widows? Jean Dye married Larry Johnson, an instructor at New Tribe's language school, thirteen years after her husband's death. She serves with him at the school in Camdenton, Missouri. Dorothy Dye also serves here. One of her children, Paul, is a missionary to the Guica Indians of Venezuela. Audrey Bacon married Rollie Hoogfhsagen. They serve at New Tribe headquarters in Sanford, Florida.

As for the rest of the Ayores—a permanent Christian Ayore settlement was established. The community became a base for other missionaries launching advances into jungle areas never before penetrated. No further missionary killings have been charged to Ayores in Bolivia.

Another "New Tribes" Martyr

One dark January evening in 1944 Bruce Porterfield sat down in his home in Lansing, Michigan, to read the paper after a hard day's work. The story of how five missionaries had presumably been killed by Stone-Age Indians in Bolivia caught his attention. That evening he committed himself to follow in their footsteps.

Six years later he and his wife Edith arrived in Bolivia in the midst of a revolution. They survived the shooting that blazed around them and joined other missionaries at a backwoods river town named Cafetal. Here they heard of the wild Nhambiquaras who had attacked the Tylee family and Mildred Kratz in Brazil.

In January, 1951, they were joined by a big, ambling bear of a bachelor named Dave Yarwood. A farm boy from Washington State, Dave loved the outdoors and was anxious to join the expedition to reach the Nhambiquaras.

The next month, Bruce, Dave, and colleague Jim Ostewig began their hunt. Meeting no success, they returned to Cafetal. August came and they were still no closer to making contact. Then on a turtle egg hunt they ran smack into four naked Indians. Nhambiquaras! The Indians took some gifts and vanished into the jungle.

In September they met up with eight Nhambiquaras.

These Indians came right up and gave them bear hugs. Then they began touching the missionaries all over.

Other encounters followed. The Indians indulged in painful horseplay, suddenly seizing one of the missionaries around the neck and almost choking the breath from him.

The dangerous game of hide and seek continued. Sometimes the missionaries were able to eat meals with the Indians. Sometimes they learned a few Nhambiquara words.

After one stay of several days at an outlying camp, Dave suggested that the others go back to Cafetal and stock up on supplies. "I'll hang around here and keep up the contact," he said. Bruce did not want to leave him alone. But Dave insisted.

Bruce was glad to spend a few days with his wife. But he could not get his mind off Dave. He visualized him lying in his bunk reading his Bible. He recalled the time Dave had put his arm around a Nhambiquara and told him in English of God's love. The Indian put his lips to Dave's ear after each sentence and whispered back, in precise English, every word Dave told him. The Nhambiquaras were remarkable mimics. The Indian thought it was a joke.

Before Bruce could go back, a riverboat captain stopped to tell him that Dave was dead. Three Brazilian tax collectors looking for rubber hunters had come across Dave's body. By the description Bruce knew that it really was his friend.

Bruce and Jim went back and found Dave's remains. The shafts of two arrows trimmed in turkey feathers were sticking out of his back. Two more were in his chest. They buried the body, gathered up the few personal effects which the Indians had not taken and went back to Cafetal. Dave's diary told part of the story. December 4, the day before he was killed, nine Nhambiquaras came to see him. He learned some more words. "On the whole . . . the atmosphere was friendly," he wrote. "We'll see what happens tomorrow." That was the last entry.

The shock of Dave's murder drove Bruce into a deep depression. It was two months before he emerged from his "Dunkirk of the soul" and accepted an invitation from another missionary to help reach the wild Macurapis. They made a contact, then he joined another New Tribes' man in search for wild Yuquis. These efforts led to some hair-raising incidents, but his faith was renewed and he continued the quest for more lost tribes.

In his book *Commandos for Christ* (Harper and Row)

Bruce Porterfield has expressed the New Tribes Mission's purpose.

> It is for us to furrow the ground. It is for others to plant the seed and reap the harvest. And as surely as day follows night, the harvest will come. And it will be rich, the result of all the hard plowing, sowing, and watering that has been done, in tears, heartaches, suffering, and blood. . . .

LAND OF THE INCAS:
Peru and Ecuador

The same sacrificial purpose has motivated missionaries to risk their lives in reaching tribes in Peru and Ecuador. Besides the mountain Quechuas, about fifty jungle groups have challenged the evangels of the gospel on the eastern side of the snow-capped Andes in these two countries.

The gold-seeking Spaniards baptized the mountain Indians then robbed their Inca rulers of precious treasures at sword point. But the conquistadors stopped short of the forbidding jungle east of the Andes. Only a few intrepid traders and priests dared to cross the rugged mountains and search for the mysterious brown denizens of the forest. Many never returned.

Dawn Over Amazonia

The first evangelical missionaries ventured into the vast Amazonian forests early in the twentieth century. First in Peru were the Church of the Nazarene and the Christian and Missionary Alliance. The Nazarenes began work among the headhunting Aguarunas; a tribe that had massacred an entire settlement of white farmers around 1900. First in Ecuador was the Gospel Missionary Union (GMU) which established a station among the feared Jivaro headhunters on an upper Amazon tributary.

The pioneer missionaries faced unimaginable hardship in the rain forests of Peru and Ecuador. Some walked overland for two to three weeks, then canoed down swift, often flooded rivers to reach their stations in uncharted tribal territories ruled by powerful chiefs. It seems a miracle that none were killed by Indians who knew whites only as enemies. However tropical diseases left many missionaries with broken health and shortened life expectancies.

Jungle Base Saves Lives

By 1946 only a half dozen tribes in Peru and Ecuador had been entered. Reaching the remainder appeared impossible until the Wycliffe Bible Translators developed a central jungle base in Peru. It was the idea of Wycliffe's founder, Cameron Townsend, to have a dispensary, commissary, radio communication center and an airline at the hub of operations in an area larger than Texas. Missionaries in trouble could get help fast. Under Townsend's direction, Wycliffe also established ties with the Peruvian government, bringing the umbrella of national protection over Bible translators at their far-flung posts.

Wycliffe began work in Peru in 1946 and today has workers in forty-four tribes. Not one translator has been killed by Indians, although there have been some close calls.

Two single women, Lorrie Anderson and Doris Cox, entered Shapra territory when it was ruled by Chief Tariri, the most feared headhunter in Peru. Tariri later told Cam Townsend, "Had you sent two men we would have killed them. Had you sent a man and wife we would have killed the man and kept the woman for a wife. You sent two young women, calling me 'brother.' I had to protect them." Since his dramatic conversion, Tariri has been a sensation in Peru and a celebrity to Christians in Europe and the United States.

The Mayorunas were feared more than the Shapras. By 1969 they had killed hundreds of Peruvians and kidnapped many white women for wives in raids on government outposts. A peaceful entry was made that year by seventeen-year-old Ronald Snell, who had grown up in another tribe, and translator Harriet Fields. Miss Fields and her partner Harriet Kneeland live among the Mayorunas today.

No missions have lost missionaries to tribal violence in Peru.

ECUADOR—MISSIONARY STORY OF THE CENTURY

In Ecuador occurred the most publicized missionary massacre of the twentieth century, when five young stalwarts representing three mission societies, were killed by Auca Indians in January, 1956.

Jim Elliot was from Portland, Oregon. At Wheaton College he was president of the Student Foreign Missions Fellowship. A perceptive thinker and writer, he wrote in college: "He is no fool who gives what he cannot keep to gain what he cannot lose." He was married to Elisabeth Howard, from a prominent Christian publishing family in Philadelphia. The Elliots had an infant daughter.

Pete Fleming was from Seattle, and at twenty-seven was a year younger than his friend Jim Elliot. Pete had recently received his M.A. in literature. He was married to his childhood sweetheart, Olive, and they had three young children.

Ed McCully, the oldest son of a Milwaukee bakery executive, attended Wheaton and starred on the football team. He had won the National Hearst Oratorical Contest in San Francisco in 1949 and studied at Marquette University Law School. He and his wife Marilou had an eight-month-old son.

Roger Youderian was raised on a Montana ranch. He attended Northwestern Schools in Minneapolis where he met his wife, Barbara. They joined the Gospel Missionary Union and were working with Mr. and Mrs. Frank Drown among the headhunting Jivaros when the Elliots, Flemings, and McCullys arrived.

Nate Saint, the most animated of the lot, had been flying missionaries in and out of stations in the Ecuadorean jungle since 1948 for Missionary Aviation Fellowship. Builder, inventor, and skilled pilot, Nate had devised an alternate fuel system for single-engine planes and an ingenious method of lowering a bucket by using a spiraling line to the ground. "During the last war, we had to be willing to be expendable," he wrote. "A missionary constantly faces expendability." Nate was married to a nurse, Marj, whom he had met in the service. They had three children.

The Challenge of the Aucas

None of the five came to Ecuador anticipating the Auca project. Once in Ecuador they kept hearing about these feared Indians who had never been tamed by soldiers or missionaries. The first Jesuit priest to enter Aucaland, Pedro Suarez, had been murdered in 1667. After the Jesuits gave up, they were left alone for over two hundred years. Then the rubber hunters came, burning Indian homes, raping, torturing, killing, enslaving; and later the oil companies, searching for black gold.

Missionaries often talked about how the Aucas might be reached. Nate Saint had flown all around their territory and longed and prayed for the day when they might know of his Savior.

Nate's older sister, Rachel, a Wycliffe member, learned of a young Auca girl named Dayuma, who had fled to the outside after her father had been killed by the tribe. In 1955 Rachel began studying the language with her at a hacienda.

"We Decided It Was the Lord's Time"

While Rachel was learning the Auca language, Jim Elliot, Ed McCully, and Nate Saint studied maps and talked about how entry might be made. One evening they pored over the maps for several hours before adjourning for midnight cocoa. "We decided it was the Lord's time," Nate wrote on October 2.

Pete Fleming joined up. Nate then thought of Roger Youderian, not knowing that Roger was discouraged over his work among the Jivaros. When Nate asked if he would help with the Auca project, he volunteered. Roger made five.

All knew the danger. Jim Elliot had told his wife Betty: "If that's the way God wants it to be, I'm ready to die for the salvation of the Aucas."

They made careful plans. Their main base would be at Shell Mera where the World Radio Missionary Fellowship, sponsors of the missionary radio station HCJB in Quito, had a hospital. For an advance base, they cleared off an old air strip at Arajuno, a camp abandoned by Shell on the very edge of Auca territory. From here they would fly out and look for an Auca clearing to make gift drops. If the Indians responded favorably, a ground contact would be attempted.

The Operation Gets Underway

After flying over the area for several days, Nate located a large thatch house in a clearing. Using Nate's invention, they let down a gift machete, wrapped in canvas and decorated with colored streamers. When they flew back over, the gift was gone. The next time Nate passed over "Terminal City" Ed McCully spotted three Aucas through binoculars. They dropped more gifts. On succeeding passes, Nate flew lower, calling through a loudspeaker Auca phrases learned from Dayuma: "We like you! We like you! We have come to visit you." Each time they dropped a bucket of gifts, with Nate circling to keep the drop spiraling down towards the drop zone. The people on the ground smiled and waved, and one day they put a live parrot in the bucket as a reciprocal gift. Another day, December 23, they put in squirrels, another parrot, and a smoked monkey tail.

The next step was to find a landing place as close to the clearing as possible. The Curaray River was nearby and they went looking for a sand bar. They christened the site selected "Palm Beach."

D-Day

Tuesday, January 3. They huddled at Arajuno for a final prayer meeting, then sang a favorite hymn:

We rest on Thee, our Shield and our Defender
Thine is the battle, Thine shall be the praise
When passing through the gates of pearly splendor
Victors, we rest with Thee through endless days.

Johnny Keenan, another MAF pilot, flew in. He would stand by to see if the first landing turned out okay.

About 8:00 A.M. Nate began ferrying in the men and supplies to Palm Beach. After the last landing he buzzed Terminal City calling to the Aucas, "Come tomorrow to the river!" The Indians looked puzzled.

He flew back to Arajuno, leaving the others to sleep on the beach, and returned the next morning. He and Pete checked out Terminal City again. Some of the Indians seen the day before were missing. They must be on their way to the river, the two decided.

When Nate and Pete got back, the others had a tree house up and were walking along the beach holding up gifts and shouting welcomes across the river. Nate got on the radio to Shell Mera and brought Marj up to date.

The "neighbors" did not show on Wednesday. The five spent a second night in the tree house. The next morning Nate and Pete went up for reconnaissance. They saw only women, children, and an old man at Terminal City. While they were gone Jim and Roger hiked downstream and found Auca footprints. They judged them to be at least a week old. Nate and Pete took another look at Terminal City. This time they saw an Auca kneel and point in the direction of Palm Beach. They flew back to the sand bar rejoicing.

Aucas!

Nothing else happened until 11:15 A.M. Friday when three naked Aucas suddenly appeared on the far bank of the river—a young man, a woman about thirty, and a girl around sixteen. Jim waded across, seized the hands of the man and woman, and led them back to the spot where the plane was parked. The girl splashed across on her own.

The missionaries used all the phrases they could remember. The Aucas jabbered and smiled. The men took pictures and displayed a copy of *Time*.

The Auca man, "George," kept touching the plane. Nate opened the passenger door and with little urging George jumped in. Nate took off and flew over Terminal City with George shouting gleefully all the way. When they landed back on the beach, the Auca leaped out clapping his hands in delight.

At 4:15 P.M. Nate radioed Marj reporting their favorable progress.

The girl, "Delilah," and George left. The woman stayed by the beach fire. When the missionaries came down from the tree house the next morning, she was gone. But the fire was still warm.

Saturday, no neighbors came to visit. Nate and Pete flew low over Terminal City. The people they saw looked afraid. The women and children ran to hide. "Come, come, come to the river," Nate invited. Pete tossed some gifts. A man looked up and smiled. It was George.

"Pray for Us. This Is the Day!"

Sunday morning, Nate went up alone and spotted a group of Auca men walking towards the camp. He flew back to the beach with the good news and radioed Marj. "A commission of ten is coming. Pray for us. This is the day!" He set the next scheduled transmission at 4:30 P.M. and signed off.

At 4:30 P.M. Marj switched on the radio at Shell Mera. Nothing. She kept trying. The radio must be out, she thought. The wives prayed and tossed and turned that night.

Monday, January 9, Johnny Keenan took off for Palm Beach. A few minutes later he radioed that the plane had been stripped of fabric. There was no sign of the men. Obviously, something was wrong.

Bodies Are Sighted

Wycliffe pilot Larry Montgomery, an American reserve officer, was at Shell Mera. He contacted Lt. General William K. Harrison, commander in chief of the Carribean Command in Panama, to report the five missing. Radio station HCJB broadcast the news and asked for prayers. Newspapers headlined around the world: FIVE MISSIONARIES MISSING IN ECUADOR.

A search party led by missionary Frank Drown, started overland. Johnny Keenan made his fourth flight over Palm Beach and saw a body he could not identify. Johnny made another pass and sighted a second body in the river.

The big United States Air Force planes roared in. They could not land at Palm Beach. Wednesday night, rain fell in torrents. Thursday, two Navy fliers went in with a chopper. They found four bodies in the river. All had been speared to death.

Major Nurnberg, one of the chopper pilots, flew to Shell Mera and described the clothing to the wives. Pete, Roger, Jim, and Nate were identified. The Major speculated that the first body seen by Johnny was Ed and it had been washed away by the rain.

The overland search party arrived Friday and buried the four. *Life* magazine photographer, Cornell Capa, landed in a chopper in a heavy downpour just as the last body was being dropped into the grave. His photos and the accompanying story in *Life* made the Auca massacre the missionary story of the century.

The next day the United States Air Force flew the five widows over to see the common grave. Peering down at the scar of white sand, Olive Fleming thought of II Corinthians 5:1: "For we know that if our earthly house of *this* tabernacle were dissolved, we have a building of God, an house not made with hands, eternal in the heavens."

Why had the Indians attacked after the initial friendly encounter? Frank Drown noted that Indians are naturally curious about something new and will accept it. But after thinking about it, they may feel threatened and attack in fear.

Life had to go on for the wives. Barbara Youderian returned to work among the Jivaros. Betty Elliot helped with Quechua ministries, then wrote the first book about the martyred five, *Through Gates of Splendor* (Harper and Row). Marj Saint took a new missionary job in Quito. Marilou McCully went home to have her second child, then returned to work with Marj. Olive Fleming's plans were undecided.

Why Did God Let It Happen?

Response from the civilized world came swiftly. Some church leaders thought the men had died needlessly. Others felt God had allowed the men to die for a great purpose.

Part of that purpose seemed evident immediately. An American naval officer was shipwrecked shortly after reading the story. As he floated alone on a raft he recalled a sentence from Jim Elliot which a reporter had quoted: "When it comes time to die, make sure that all you have to do is die." He prayed for salvation, spiritual and physical. Both prayers were answered. From Iowa, an eighteen-year-old boy wrote that he had turned his life "over completely to the Lord." He wanted to take the place of one of the five. Indeed, in succeeding months, missions were deluged with offers to "take the place" of the Auca martyrs.

The work with the Aucas was only beginning. The Auca girl Dayuma, now a Christian, went back to her people. Her family greeted her with joyful amazement. They thought she had been eaten by a foreign cannibal. She said the missionaries had come in friendship to tell them about a Savior. "Just as you killed the foreigners on the beach, Jesus was killed for you," she told them.

Matchless Love

One month later Rachel Saint and Betty and little Valerie Elliot hung their hammocks with the Aucas. Valerie played with the children of her father's killers.

Rachel and Betty gradually learned the reason for the murders and the identity of the six killers. "We thought foreigners would kill and eat us," one Auca said. Another confessed that he had cried after the killings.

An older man, "Uncle Gikita," admitted that he had advanced on Nate Saint as the pilot held his hands high, pleading for mercy. "I speared him," he said. When the others shot in the air, the other Auca men had run. The old man called them back and they killed Ed, Pete, Roger, and Jim.

Gikita accepted Christ, then Kimo, another of the killers. "Jesus' blood has washed my heart clean," Kimo told Rachel. "My heart is healed." The other four killers—Nimonga, Dyuwi, Minkayi, and Tona—soon believed also.

Betty Elliot returned to the States. Wycliffe's Dr. Catherine Peeke came to help Rachel with the tedious language analysis and translation of the New Testament into Auca. Nine years after the killings, the first published copies of the Gospel of Mark in Auca were dedicated at "God's Speaking House." Kimo, now the Auca pastor, prayed, "Father God, You are alive. This is Your day and all of us have come to worship You. They brought us copies of Your Carving, enough for everybody. We accept it, saying, 'This is the truth.' We want all of your carving."

Special guests for the dedication were Wycliffe's Ecuador Director, Don Johnson, his wife, Helen, and Steve and Phil Saint. Steve, fourteen, had visited his Aunt Rachel several times and was a beloved friend to the Aucas. He read a verse in Auca during the service.

Auca Killer Baptizes Nate Saint's Son and Daughter

Steve stayed on after the other visitors left. Later he received a letter from his sister Kathy, fifteen, saying that she would like to show her faith by being baptized by the Aucas. Steve decided that he would be baptized at the same time.

Marj and Phil, the younger brother, came for the occasion. The baptisms were held on Palm Beach at dawn. Kimo talked to Steve and Kathy and two Auca teen-agers who were to be immersed about the meaning of baptism as a witness of resurrected life in Christ. Then he baptized them.

Afterwards, Kimo and Dyuwi led the group to the site of the missionaries' graves. The two forgiven killers, Marj and Rachel, and the four teen-agers sang the hymn which the five men had sung just before leaving to meet the Aucas: "We rest on Thee, our Shield and our Defender. . . ."

The First Auca Martyr

Still there is more. The Christian Aucas felt compelled to reach a long-time enemy clan downriver. The missionaries helped them locate the group and flew over and dropped gifts, using Nate's invention. Tona, one of the six killers, volunteered to take the gospel to his downriver brothers. Axed from behind, he cried, "I'm not afraid. I'll die and go to heaven." "We'll help you go," his attackers shouted. In his dying breath, Tona whispered, "I forgive you. I'm dying for your benefit."

These downriver Aucas later came to the Christian community where Rachel and Catherine were staying. Many became Christians.

Auca Update

The rippling effect of the Auca incident continues. More Aucas are coming to Christ. More people are being won by missionaries who initially felt God's call at the news of the massacre of the five. The Auca killers have traveled abroad to tell what God has done. Kimo and his friend Komi were a sensation at the World Evangelism Congress in Berlin. Uncle Gikita and others joined Rachel for a series of missionary rallies in major cities in the United States.

Seven books, including *Through Gates of Splendor*, and hundreds of newspaper and magazine follow-up articles have been written about the Aucas and the five missionaries they killed. The most recent book is *The Diary of Jim Elliot*, compiled and edited by Elisabeth Elliot (Fleming H. Revell).

The "Auca incident" is enshrined in the missionary history of the church and in the past of Ecuador as well. The president of the predominantly Roman Catholic country flew to Wycliffe's jungle base at Limoncocha to meet the forgiven Auca killers personally. On the tenth anniversary of the five martyrs' death, Ecuador issued commemorative postage stamps honoring each man.

And the widows today? Four are remarried. Olive Fleming is wed to a professor at Trinity Evangelical Divinity School in Chicago. Betty Elliot, after losing her second husband, Addison Leitch, to illness, was recently married to an institutional chaplain in Georgia. She has become one of the most respected and best-known Christian writers on the evangelical scene. The former Marilou McCully is living in quiet privacy with her Christian husband. Marj Saint is the wife of Dr. Abe Van Der Puy, president of World Radio Missionary Fellowship. They live in Quito. Barbara Youderian, who chose not to remarry, also lives in Quito where she is hostess at the Guest House of the Gospel Missionary Union.

Revival Follows the Storm

The Auca experience has eclipsed persecution of evangelical Christians in Peru and Ecuador. Many missionaries and nationals among Quechuas and Spanish-speaking people have been beaten, stoned, and spat upon. Some have lost their jobs and been alienated from families and old friends for the sake of the gospel, though none are known to have been killed. As recent as the late 1960's, Gospel Missionary Union medic, Dr. Donald Dilworth, was beaten so severely by a mob of crazed Quechuas that nearly one hundred stitches were required to close his wounds.

Overreaching all of the persecution is news from GMU missionaries of an unprecedented turning to Christ by Quechuas in Ecuador. In one province alone the Christian community has grown to around sixteen thousand. Ecuadorian Christian Quechuas are now going as missionaries to mountain Indians in Colombia, Peru, and Bolivia. Great things are happening as Christ is proclaimed in areas where evangelicals once witnessed at risk of severe persecution.

BANQUET OF HOPE:
Colombia

With Colombia we have traveled almost full circle around
South America, omitting only Venezuela, which borders Colombia on the northeast, Guyana, French Guiana, and Suri-
nam (formerly Dutch Guiana). No missionaries or national
Christian workers are known to have been martyred in these
countries, although evangelicals in Venezuela experienced
Catholic persecution before the 1950's.

Colombia, however, is uniquely a land of martyrs to fanaticism and intolerance. No other Latin American nation
approached the persecution heaped upon evangelicals there
in the 1940's and 1950's. Not even Mexico experienced widespread violence of such intensity upon godly pastors and
Christian believers.

Conservatives Versus Liberals

Of all the Spanish American countries, Colombia was closest
to Spain until the rise of the Liberal Party. In contrast to the
Conservative Party which stood for a centrally governed
church–state, the Liberals believed in decentralized federal
government, separation of church and state, and religious
freedom. The Liberals excommunicated the Jesuit order three
times and once banished the powerful archbishop of Bogota
for declaring that the church was over the state. Rivalry between the two parties caused nearly a hundred civil wars be-

fore 1899 when the War of a Thousand Days took over one hundred thousand lives.

Conservatives took control until 1930 when Liberals were swept back into office. The Liberals trimmed clerical power and removed from the constitution a concordat with the Vatican giving the Catholic Church power over education, marriage, morality, family life, and religious activities. The Catholic hierarchy was incensed and worked constantly to get back the presidency.

"False Prophets" and "Devouring Wolves"

In 1944, when evangelicals were coming under attack all over the continent, sixteen Colombian bishops ordered a letter read in every Catholic church in the country to incite attacks on Protestants. The epistle called Protestant ministers "false prophets" and "devouring wolves." "Protestants," the bishops said, "come to our country to carry out a work of destruction; they come not only to steal our faith . . . but to ruin our national and social structure." Opposition to Protestant "propaganda" was both a religious duty and "an act of true patriotism," and Catholics should avoid Protestants and give complete devotion to "Our Lady . . . who has always killed off all heresies."

The following year Pope Pius XII urged Colombian Catholics not to permit "the sacred deposit of your faith . . . to be contaminated by that propaganda, as audacious as it is cunning, which wishes to convert into a mission land, a people who count in their glorious history four centuries of irreproachable Christianity."

Passions Are Inflamed

The storm kept building. A Colombian priest published a book, *Protestantism in Colombia*, in which he called Protestants "undesirable foreigners," a "virus," and an "infection." He asked Colombians to strive for "the final extirpation of Protestantism from our midst." The required religious text in most public high schools justified persecution of Protestants and defended the infamous Spanish Inquisition and the Massacre of St. Bartholomew's Day.

Attacks on Liberals escalated. As a result of a Liberal split, a Conservative was elected president in 1946 with only forty-one per cent of the popular vote. In 1948 the most popular Liberal leader, who would undoubtedly have been elected the next president, was assassinated. Riots flared in

Bogota and spread across the country. The Conservative president dissolved Congress and claimed dictatorial powers. Before the undeclared civil war was over, two hundred thousand Colombians were dead.

The Great Persecution Begins

The Conservative politicians and their allies in the church hierarchy set out to destroy the Protestant "scourge." Mobs and vigilantes, sometimes led by priests, attacked practically at will while town officials looked the other way. Local police often joined in the attacks.

Every accusation imaginable was thrown against Colombian Protestants and missionaries. They were destroying national unity by damaging religious uniformity. They were agents of international communism. They were trying to legalize divorce. Missionaries were paying poor Catholics to apostatize. Protestant schools were infecting the nation with moral disease. Protestant pastors were helping revolutionaries trying to overthrow the government.

From 1944–1958, at least one hundred twenty evangelicals or members of evangelical families were killed. Five martyrs were under age four. Eighty–eight Protestant churches and chapels were destroyed by fire or dynamite. An additional 183 houses of worship and 206 Protestant primary schools were closed by official orders. Over fifteen thousand evangelicals were driven from their homes. Protestant children were shut out of public schools.

In the Department (state) of Huila Pastor Perez and his twelve-year-old son Bernardo were arrested in November, 1953, when the violence was at its peak. Soldiers hung the boy by a thumb and demanded a confession that his family were bandits. When he denied this, the tormentors asked if they were evangelicals. "Yes," he gasped, "but we don't hurt anyone."

They turned to the agonized father. "How many people have you killed?"

"I have killed no one," he answered. "I follow God's Word which does not permit us to kill or do evil against anyone."

Having no witnesses, the soldiers had to let the two go. "If we arrest you again," they warned, "you and your entire family will be killed. Not a seed of this wickedness will remain."

Around midnight the following May 19, an armed mob burst into the Perez home without warning. They shot both parents and attacked the seven children with machetes. One boy, David, was slashed on the arm and neck but managed to drag a younger sister across the yard and over a fence. An enraged man caught up with them and literally severed the little girl's hand from her brother's grasp. David was the only one who escaped alive.

Christian and Missionary Alliance missionaries Lee and Ruth Tennies became David's second parents. Five years later he graduated from the Alliance Bible Institute in Armenia, Colombia, and became a pastor.

More Colombian Martyrs

Pedro Moreno, a young preacher, was arrested for evangelizing around Saboya, Colombia. The police promised to release him if he would sign a statement pledging to stop spreading the evangelical message. He refused and was thrust into a cell.

Only one evangelical family lived in Saboya. The father, Juan Coy, brought food and encouragement to Pedro and tried to obtain his release. One night a trusted friend warned Juan, "Be careful. The police have a plot to leave Pedro's cell door open. If he walks out, he'll be shot on the spot for escaping." Sure enough, the prisoner did find his door open. He stayed inside.

Then they learned of a second plot. Pedro would be released and shot as he left the jail. The release came through. Juan went to the jail and talked to Pedro. They decided to trust God for protection. Pedro cautiously stepped from his cell, dashed out the jail door, and leaped into a passing truck. The driver took him out of the city and today Pedro Moreno is an evangelical pastor in Colombia.

After failing to kill the preacher, the fanatics decided to take revenge on Juan Coy. They went to his farm and waited until he had finished his evening milking. When he appeared on the path, they opened fire and killed him. But the evangelical witness survived. Today there is an evangelical church in Saboya attended by three hundred people.

One of the worst atrocities occurred in July, 1951, in the state of Meta. A priest issued orders for all Protestants in a town to be exterminated. Ten policemen and four civilians, armed with rifles and submachine guns, burst into the home of Carlo Arturo Gahona, an evangelical connected with the Worldwide Evangelization Crusade. "Long live the Holy Catholic Church!" they shouted. "Down with the Protestants!" Turning their guns on the helpless family, they martyred three sons, a daughter-in-law, and three grandchildren. One of the three grandchildren, four-month-old Carlos Arturo, was pitched across the patio onto a pile of broken bottles and died vomiting blood.

Children Were Abducted

Ironically, Colombian officials and Catholic clergy who accused Protestants of abetting Marxism were following the procedure used in the Soviet Union in taking children from evangelical parents for "proper" training.

In Manizales, capital of the state of Caldas, the eleven- and twelve-year-old sons of martyred Obdulio Moralies, a member of a Christian and Missionary Alliance church, were taken from school and given to a Jesuit priest who put them in a Catholic orphanage. The broken-hearted mother appealed to a judge, the National Police, the army, and the state governor. Each told her the law could not interfere. The family was apostate Catholics. The children had been baptized in infancy and according to law were required to be reared in the Catholic faith. Not until the Evangelical Confederation of Colombia publicized the case did authorities yield to public pressure and return the children to their mother.

A Missionary Is Rolled in Hot Ashes

The national Christians bore the brunt of the persecution. No missionaries were killed, although some were jailed, some fired upon, some stoned, and one was tortured. The worst missionary incident involved Rev. William C. Easton of Worldwide Evangelization Crusade in the state of Tolima.

On June 15, 1951 he was leading a youth service in a church. The police crashed through the doors and grabbed and beat him and three young men with the broadside of a sword and rifle butts. The officers then took them outside and beat and kicked them around before marching them to the station and booking them as Communists. There the four were clubbed, kicked, whipped, and dunked in a tank of cold water. They were made to sing hymns, preach sermons (which brought more beatings), and burn their Bibles and hymnbooks. Once the missionary was asked, "Are you really the Devil in the flesh?" He replied, "I am only a humble servant of Jesus Christ."

As time wore on, the torture became worse. They were stripped naked and forced to roll in hot ashes of rice chaff.

Then they were forced to fight each other while the police stood around wielding clubs and whips. Other tortures were too obscene and perverted to be described here.

When they were released the next morning, the missionary extended his hand to the police sergeant. "I forgive you in the name of Jesus Christ," he said. The policeman turned away.

Justice Is Denied

Evangelicals were helpless before the mobs that burned and dynamited churches and schools. Local officials scoffed at their complaints and pleas for justice. Some officials replied in effect, "You got what you deserve. Don't bother us." Pleas for the reopening of evangelical schools or the readmission of children expelled from public schools likewise went unheeded.

Catholics Tried to Control the American Press

News accounts of the persecution embarrassed the Roman Catholic hierarchy both in Colombia and abroad. They claimed the reports were grossly inflated and blamed the violence upon Protestant revolutionaries trying to overthrow the government.

The American National Catholic Welfare Conference lambasted press wire services and other United States media for printing erroneous reports. The National Association of Evangelicals (NAE) countered by inviting professional media organizations to inspect documents on file in the Washington NAE office.

In Colombia the fighting did not taper off until 1957 when the two political parties agreed to alternate the presidency between themselves until 1974. A Liberal was elected to serve the first term.

Shock Waves from Pope John

Close on the heels of political change came the election of Pope John XXIII. He called Catholic–Protestant bickering "no longer tolerable," and said "many points of doctrine" were open to theological debate. He "hoped" for the reunion of all who "agree on the most memorable fact of human history—the Incarnation of Christ." He desired "the return of the spirit of friendliness and of amiable brotherliness" among those who loved the cross.

Nowhere did the shock waves hit harder than in Colombia where only months before Catholics were being told to stamp out Protestant heresy. But Catholics respected the authority of the Pope and if the primate said it was time to open the windows to change, then it was time. Wonder of wonders, priests began calling evangelical missionaries and pastors to propose dialogues and ask them to lead Bible studies in Catholic churches.

A Spiritual Revolution

Along with the opportunities to teach the Bible to their former persecutors, evangelicals could now build new churches, hold open-air meetings and evangelize from door to door without undue fear.

Colombians poured into evangelical churches. Some were hungry to know God in a more personal, vital way. Some were curious to know what the once hated Protestants taught from their Bible. Some came to relieve guilt for what had happened in their country during the past fifteen years. Thousands met the living Christ.

The country was open to evangelical witness as never before. But persecution still persisted in remote, backwoods villages where law enforcement was limited. Reports of beatings and stonings continued to come in during the 1960's, particularly from Indian territories long closed to evangelicals and now open.

Colombia's First Evangelical Missionary Martyr

The veteran evangelical missionaries were greatly loved and respected by Colombian evangelicals. One of the most honored was Ernest Fowler, who had served thirty-two years in Colombia with the Gospel Missionary Union and the Latin American Mission. The product of a devout Methodist couple, Ernie had grown up on a Montana ranch. He had made many trips through the rugged Colombian Andes training national evangelists and encouraging churches. Once threatened with death during the persecution, he had the courage of a Daniel and the compassion of a Barnabas.

In 1966 Ernie was looking forward to reducing the language of the Yupka Indians to writing and translating the Bible. But first he felt his family deserved a summer vacation high up in the mountains near the Venezuelan border. Another missionary couple loaned them their home; and Ernie, his wife Eva, three children—Valerie, John, and Alison—and a Colombian girl friend of Valerie's, Elvira, moved in. A few days later two other missionary kids, Peter Clark and David Howard, Jr., arrived to enjoy the summer with them.

On Wednesday, August 3, Ernie took Valerie and Elvira for a hike and met seven strangers on the trail. "We're policemen looking for communists," they said. At their request, Ernie handed over his shotgun and machete. But when he asked for a receipt, two of the "policemen" drew their guns and shot him dead. Surprisingly, the bandits did not harm the horrified girls. They made a few obscene remarks then headed down the trail. The stunned girls rushed to Ernie's body and turned him over. His mouth was full of blood and his eyes were rolled back.

The girls ran back to the house with Valerie shouting, "They shot Daddy!" The house was in a shambles. "Oh, they've killed mother and the boys, too," Valerie moaned. A frightened whisper came from behind a wall. "Quiet. Are there any bandits around?" When assured that the men had left, the others came out of hiding.

The seven men had come by the house first and told Eva the same story. Suddenly they drew guns and demanded money and jewels. When she handed over the few pesos she had, one tried to tear her wedding band off her finger, while the others vandalized the house. After forcing the family into a side room, they left.

Eva and the children spent the night in some bushes near Ernie's body. It took them all day Thursday to dig a grave in the rocky, mountain soil. A Christian neighbor came by and took the news to other missionaries who came and helped with the burial. Soldiers pursued the bandits without success.

Scores of tributes came to the Fowler family. A Catholic priest sent "brotherly greetings" and spoke of Ernie's death "not as a bereavement but rather as a departure to the Lord."

Banquet of Hope

Two years after Ernie Fowler's martyrdom an Evangelism-in-Depth campaign trained thirty thousand evangelicals in personal witness and follow up. These believers visited one hundred forty-three thousand Colombian homes and distributed half a million gospel tracts. That same year the Roman Catholic hierarchy invited evangelicals to participate in the Church's thirty-ninth International Eucharistic Congress held in Bogota. The congress included hundreds of neighborhood Bible studies in which evangelicals participated with joy.

Miracles kept recurring in the seventies as evangelicals grew in number and respect. The most significant event came on October 19, 1977 when evangelicals sponsored a Banquet of Hope, similar to the National Prayer Breakfast of Washington, D.C. The top leaders of both political parties were invited as guests of honor to hear a message by Evangelist Luis Palau.

The celebration began about noon in the courtyard of the national government building. Hundreds of evangelicals participated in the prayer and praise service. Some knelt while others fell prostrate on the concrete shouting, "Glory to God!" There were short testimonies. "Many were killed for this day," declared a pastor, "now we are the church victorious." "If they put a bullet through my chest, that will not stop the power of the gospel," vowed another.

The formal banquet was scheduled that evening in the Red Room of posh Hotel Tequendama in downtown Bogota. Would the president and other high leaders come? At precisely 8:30 P.M. President Alfonso Lopez Michelsen, the four major candidates for the next year's presidential election, the heads of the four major labor unions, judges, ambassadors, and many other high officials walked in. They heard Evangelist Palau declare, "Christ is Colombia's only hope. Only He can solve the moral crisis in this nation." The entire program was broadcast to the nation.

There were pastors sitting near the president who had been in jail twenty years before. Some had lost loved ones in the great persecution. Tears flowed freely. One pastor summed up his feelings: "The road to evangelization of our nation is paved with the blood of our martyrs."

Looking to the Future

Conflicts between radicalized priests and ex-priests with governments continue in many Latin and Caribbean countries today. But religious persecution by Catholics, such as was experienced in the first half of the twentieth century, now occurs only occasionally and is seldom incited by Catholic clergy. To the contrary, Catholic clergy in many areas now welcome evangelical missionaries and some give tacit approval to evangelistic crusades. A rural bishop in Colombia even proposed to a Baptist missionary, "Let's buy a plane and share its use and expenses." Some members of the Catholic hierarchy now candidly admit that the continent is hardly Christianized at all.

However, leftists and Marxists are now pressuring government agencies in some countries to block the admission of new missionaries and deny visas to those returning from furlough. As yet, Latin American and Caribbean Marxists, except in Cuba, have hardly dared physical violence against missionaries or national church workers. Should certain countries be captured by Marxists, then arrests and perhaps executions might follow.

Meanwhile, opportunities for evangelical growth have never been greater. The crusades of Evangelist Luis Palau are producing results comparable to the Billy Graham Crusades in United States cities. Palau thinks three countries — Colombia, Guatemala, and the Dominican Republic — could have evangelical majorities by the end of this century. Even if this does not happen, and even if Marxist influence grows, evangelicals are likely to increase faster than population growth in the Carribean and Latin America.

In these areas and elsewhere, the people of God will be spurred on by the heritage of their martyrs and other believers who risked life, loved ones, and property for the sake of Christ and the gospel.

EPILOGUE

This edition of "Christian Martyrs of the 20th Century" is ended. Research and writing required twice as much time as planned. As we progressed from country to country, more martyrs kept coming to light. And still we have not included them all — certainly not all the national believers who have died in connection with their witness for Christ in this century.

It appears likely that Dr. Paul Carlson was correct when he told Congolese believers before his martyrdom, that more believers have died for Christ in this century than in all the previous centuries combined. Of course, there is no hard evidence to prove this, since the records of most martyrdoms before the twentieth century are lost, and the names of countless martyrs in this century (those who died in the Soviet Union and China, for example) are not available for scrutiny.

This book will not be the final word on martyrs, no more than *Foxe's Book of Martyrs* was of those who died in a previous era.

We have not reached the end of the twentieth century. Should Christ not return before 2000 A.D., another edition of this book may include martyrs in the 1980's and 1990's from countries which have not yet been torn by religious persecution. Christians in nations which have religious freedom now should thank God every day for this blessing which is denied their brothers and sisters elsewhere.

Some of the martyrs of the next two decades may be the children of previous martyrs. No count has been made, but the number of martyrs' children now preparing for missionary service or who are already on their chosen fields appears to be high. Dr. David and Rebecca Thompson, for instance, are now serving with the Christian and Missionary Alliance in Africa. Dr. Thompson's father and mother were killed at Banmethuot, Vietnam, in 1968. Mrs. Thompson's father, Archie Mitchell, was captured by Communist Viet Cong in Vietnam in 1962, and is still unaccounted for, and her mother endured almost a year's communist captivity in 1975. And five of six sons of Hector McMillan, martyred in Zaire, in 1964, are either already missionaries or under appointment to go. The remaining son has spent six months helping missionaries in Africa. Their mother died from cancer in 1976.

But there will come an ending, an ending with triumph and victory when that "great multitude, . . . of all nations, and kindreds, and people, and tongues," stands before the throne and worships God, saying, "Blessing, and glory, and wisdom, and thanksgiving, and honor, and power, and might, *be* unto our God for ever and ever" (Revelation 7:9, 12). At that time, which no one can now predict, those "that were slain for the Word of God, and for the testimony which they held" will be honored before the throne of the King of kings and Lord of lords (Revelation 6:9).

Persecution may increase and more martyrs fall. But God's messengers, free or fettered, will keep proclaiming their Redeemer, Reconciler, and Resurrected Savior until that great Day of the Lord.

ASSISTANCE AND SOURCES

This is no ivory tower book. During the past thirteen years, as free-lance evangelical religion writers, we have written over a dozen missionary books based on research trips to Latin America, Asia, and the Middle East. James was the first writer on the scene after the communist massacre of six Christian and Missionary Alliance missionaries at Banmethuot, Vietnam, in 1968. Marti was recently in embattled Beirut, Lebanon, to cover the story of Christian sacrifice and service there amidst war. James, again, stayed with Paul and Nancy Potter, who were later martyred in the Dominican Republic. We have shared the burdens, joys, and some of the fears of missionaries and national evangelicals caught in life-threatening situations. During the first of two trips to Vietnam, James and three Wycliffe missionaries were thrust into the midst of a blazing gun battle. Two of these Wycliffe members, John and Carolyn Miller, were later captured and imprisoned by the Communist North Vietnamese for about nine months.

We must recognize at this point the inestimable contribution of Diane Zimmerman, Editor of Mott Media. As it happened, on the very day we were thinking of submitting a query about a book on Christian martyrs to another publisher, an inquiry came from Diane, through her father and our good friend Eldon Schroeder, asking if we would be interested in doing a book on this subject. Through the long months of preparation, Diane has been a faithful counselor, critic, and prayer supporter. She and her staff have double-checked literally hundreds of names, places, and events cited in the book. No book of ours has ever had the advantage of such intense editorial scrutiny and for this we are grateful.

We are also appreciative of the faithful secretarial work of Jane Wilson who often went beyond the call of duty and press of motherhood to keep the sections of the book moving to the publisher.

It would be impossible to name all of the missionaries and national believers who shared recollections and information with us, as well as mention survivors and loved ones of the martyrs who gave us first-hand reports on what happened and why. They, more than any others, made this book possible.

Beyond personal experiences and interviews, we owe an incalculable debt to the many mission societies who opened their files and private libraries to us. Some loaned rare out-of-print books. We will simply list the agencies we can recall who gave assistance in varying degrees:

Africa Evangelical Fellowship; Africa Inland Mission; African Enterprise, Inc.; American Baptist Foreign Mission Society; American Board of Commissioners for Foreign Missions; Assemblies of God, Division of Foreign Missions; Association of Baptists for World Evangelism (ABWEY); Bibles for the World; British and Foreign Bible Society; Central American Mission (CAM International); The Christian and Missionary Alliance (C&MA), Foreign Department; Christian Missions in Many Lands; Church of the Nazarene, Department of World Missions; Conservative Baptist Foreign Mission Society; The Evangelical Alliance Mission (TEAM); Evangelical Covenant Church of America, Board of World Mission; Free Methodist Church of North America, General Missionary Board; Gospel Missionary Union; Independent Board for Presbyterian Foreign Missions; Inter-Varsity Christian Fellowship; Jesus to the Communist World; Medical Assistance Programs (MAP International); Mennonite Central Committee; Missionary Aviation Fellowship (MAF); Navigators; New Tribes Mission; North Africa Mission; Overseas Crusades, Inc.; Overseas Missionary Fellowship; Slavic Gospel Association, Inc.; South America Mission, Inc.; Southern Baptist Convention, Foreign Mission Board; Sudan Interior Mission; Trans World Missions (incorporating Air Mail From God); Unevangelized Fields Mission; United World Mission; World Radio Missionary Fellowship, Inc.; World Vision International; Worldwide Evangelization Crusade; and Wycliffe Bible Translators, Inc.

Informational and background material came also from many other missions through their missionaries or other sources with personal knowledge of martyrdoms, and from the Evangelical Missions Information Service, a service arm of the Evangelical Foreign Missions Association (EFMA) and the Interdenominational Foreign Missions Association (IFMA).

Three knowledgeable evangelical leaders, not connected with missionary sending agencies, were extremely helpful: Arthur F. Glasser and Donald A. McGavran, Dean and Dean Emeritus respectively of the School of World Mission at Fuller Theological Seminary, and Edward E. Plowman, Senior

Editor of *Christianity Today*, long-time personal friend, and the best investigative religion reporter on the world evangelical scene.

Besides books, reports, and articles from missions and individuals, we used libraries at three Christian colleges in the Chattanooga area, the Dargan–Carver Library of the Historical Commission of the Southern Baptist Convention, and the Chattanooga–Hamilton County Public Library. The Christian schools were Bryan College, Covenant College, and Tennessee Temple College and Seminary. Bryan holds the personal collection of the late evangelical leader Dr. Harry Ironside, who amassed many out-of-print missionary books.

To list the hundreds of reports, entries from diaries, and newspaper and magazine articles would be too formidable a task for two independent writers. We consulted, for example, hundreds of old copies of *China's Millions* at Overseas Missionary Fellowship's (formerly China Inland Mission) United States headquarters, which covers this pioneer mission's long tenure in China. Anyone doing research on Christianity in China before 1950 will find the China Inland Mission's records essential. We read volumes of raw reports from old-time missionaries of the Christian and Missionary Alliance at C&MA headquarters in Nyack, New York. These and many other nonbook resources are available only to trusted persons at the headquarters of various missions.

We are listing a bibliography of books by sections of the world where there have been Christian martyrs in this century. Many of these books are out of print and rare. A large number provide good background reading on the political and religious situations in various countries where martyrdoms occurred. Some are documentaries which cover various massacres. Researchers will find a wealth of information on certain martyrs in recent documentaries, particularly about the Congo massacres in 1964 and the killing of five American missionaries by Auca Indians in 1956. Unfortunately, the martyrdoms of many other missionaries and thousands of nationals who died with equal courage and commitment have not been documented with equal balance.

Our bibliography does not list standard reference books, such as the indispensable *Mission Handbook: North American Protestant Ministries Overseas* by World Vision's MARC. These are readily available in most Christian college libraries. Reference books of more limited circulation are listed only in the section under which they were first used.

BIBLIOGRAPHY

CHINA:

Anderson, John A. "By Faith. . . ." London: China Inland Mission, 1950.

Baker, Richard T. *Methodism's First Century in China.* New York: Board of Missions and Church Extension of the Methodist Church, 1947.

Barr, Pat. *To China With Love.* Garden City, N.Y.: Doubleday & Co., 1972.

Bianco, Lucien. *Origins of the Chinese Revolution, 1915–1949.* Stanford, Calif.: Stanford University Press, 1971.

Bosshardt, ——. *The Restraining Hand.* London: Hodder and Stoughton, 1936.

The Boxer Uprising, 1900. Reprinted from the Shanghai *Mercury.* New York: Paragon Book Reprint, 1967.

Broomhall, Marshall. *The Chinese Empire.* London: Marshall, Morgan and Scott, n.d.

——. *The Jubilee Story of the China Inland Mission.* Philadelphia: China Inland Mission, n.d.

——, ed. *Last Letters and Further Records of Martyred Missionaries of the China Inland Mission.* London: Marshall, Morgan and Scott, 1901.

——, ed. *Martyred Missionaries of the China Inland Mission and Perils of Some Who Escaped.* London: Marshall, Morgan and Scott, n.d.

Brown, Arthur J. *The Chinese Revolution.* New York: Student Volunteer Movement for Foreign Missions, 1912.

Bull, Geoffrey T. *When Iron Gates Yield.* Chicago: Moody Press, 1950.

Caldwell, John C. *China Coast Family.* Chicago: Henry Regnery Co., 1953.

Cauthen, Baker J., et al. *Advance: A History of Southern Baptist Foreign Missions.* Nashville: Broadman Press, 1970.

Chang, Lit-Sen. *Strategy of Missions in the Orient.* Nutley, N.J.: Presbyterian & Reformed Publishing Co., 1970.

Christian and Missionary Alliance Foreign Dept. *Missionary Atlas.* Harrisburg, Pa.: Christian Publications, 1964.

Christian Missions in China. Boston: D.C. Heath & Co., 1965.

Clark, Elmer T. *The Chiangs of China.* Nashville: Abingdon–Cokesbury Press, 1943.

Encyclopedia of the Southern Baptist Convention, vol. I. Nashville: Broadman Press, n.d.

Fifty Wonderful Years. Chicago: Scandinavian Alliance Mission, 1940.

Fisher, Welthy. *To Light a Candle.* New York: McGraw–Hill Book Co., 1962.

Fletcher, Jesse C. *Bill Wallace of China.* Nashville: Broadman Press, 1963.

Forsythe, Sidney A. *An American Missionary Community in China, 1895–1905.* East Asian Monograph ser. no. 43. Cambridge, Mass.: Harvard University Press, 1971.

Glover, Archibald E. *A Thousand Miles of Miracle in China.* London: Hodder and Stoughton, 1904.

Goforth, Rosalind, and Goforth, Jonathan. *Miracle Lives of China.* New York: Harper & Brothers, 1931.

Haldane, Charlotte. *The Last Great Empress of China.* Indianapolis, Ind.: The Bobbs–Merrill Co., 1965.

Hamilton, E.H., and Hamilton, Mrs. E.H. *China Diary.* Honolulu: Crossroads Press, 1976.

Hawes, Charlotte E. *New Thrills in Old China.* New York: George H. Doran Co., 1913.

Hawks, F.L. *The Emergency in China.* New York: The Presbyterian Department of Missionary Education, 1913.

The Haystack Centennial. Boston: American Board of Commissioners for Foreign Missions, 1912.

Headland, Isaac T. *China's New Day.* West Medford, Mass.: Baptist Central Committee on the United Study of Missions, 1912.

Hipps, John Burder. *History of the University of Shanghai.* n.p.: Board of Founders of the University of Shanghai, 1964.

Hunter, Edward. *The Black Book on Red China.* New York: The Bookmailer, 1958.

Inglis, James. *Blind Chang, Missionary Martyr.* New York: Evangelical Publishers, 1943.

Johnston, Julia H. *Fifty Missionary Heroes Every Boy and Girl Should Know.* Old Tappan, N.J.: Fleming H. Revell, 1913.

Jones, Francis Price. *The Church in Communist China: A Protestant Appraisal.* New York: Friendship Press, 1962.

Kuhn, Isobel S. *Green Leaf in Drought Time.* Chicago: Moody Press, 1957.

Latourette, Kenneth S. *Christianity in a Revolutionary Age.* vol. IV: *The 20th Century in Europe.* vol. V: *The 20th Century Outside Europe.* New York: Harper & Row, 1962.

——. *History of Christian Missions in China.* New York: The Macmillan Co., 1929.

Lawrence, Una Roberts. *Lottie Moon.* Nashville: Sunday School Board of the Southern Baptist Convention, 1927.

Lipphard, William B. *Out of the Storm in China: A Review of Recent Developments in Baptist Mission Fields.* Valley Forge, Pa.: Judson Press, 1932.

Lockyer, Herbert. *The Man Who Changed the World*, vol. II. Grand Rapids: Zondervan Publishing House, 1966.

Lyall, Leslie T. *A Passion for the Impossible: The China Inland Mission 1865–1965*. Chicago: Moody Press, 1965.

———. *Red Sky at Night*. Chicago: Moody Press, 1969.

Martinson, Harold H. *Under the Red Dragon*. Minneapolis: Augsburg Publishing House, 1956.

The Modern Crusade. Athens, Ga.: Laymen's Missionary Movement, Presbyterian Church in the U.S., 1909.

Monsen, Marie. *The Awakening — Revival in China 1927–1937*. London: Lutterworth Press, 1961.

Monsterleet, Jean. *Martyrs in China*. Chicago: Henry Regnery Co., 1956.

Moon, Lottie. Unpublished Collection of Letters. Richmond, Va.: The Foreign Mission Board of the Southern Baptist Convention, n.d.

Mooneyham, Stan, and Ballard, Jerry. *China: The Puzzle*. Monrovia, Calif.: World Vision, 1971.

Moore, Raymond S. *China Doctor*. New York: Harper & Brothers, 1961.

Neill, Stephen. *Colonialism and Christian Missions*. New York: McGraw–Hill Book Co., 1966.

O'Connor, Richard. *The Spirit Soldiers: A Historical Narrative on the Boxer Rebellion*. East Rutherford, N.J.: G.P. Putnam's, Sons, 1973.

Oldfield, W.H. *Pioneering in Kwangsi*. Harrisburg, Pa.: Christian Publications, 1936.

Outerbridge, Leonard M. *The Lost Churches of China*. Philadelphia: Westminster Press, 1952.

Pollock, John. *A Foreign Devil in China: The Story of Dr. L. Nelson Bell*. Grand Rapids: Zondervan Publishing House, 1971.

Saunders, A.R. *A God of Deliverance*. London: Marshall, Morgan and Scott, n.d.

Smith, Arthur H. *The Uplift of China*. New York: Young People's Missionary Movement, 1907.

Speer, Robert E. *The Church and Missions*. New York: George H. Doran Co., 1926.

Students and the Modern Missionary Crusade. New York: Student Volunteer Movement for Foreign Missions, 1906.

Students and the World-wide Expansion of Christianity. New York: Student Volunteer Movement for Foreign Missions, 1912.

Taylor, Howard, and Taylor, Mrs. Howard J. *"By Faith . . .": Henry W. Frost and the China Inland Mission*. Philadelphia: The Bingham Co., 1938.

———. *Hudson Taylor and the China Inland Mission*. London: The Religious Tract Society, 1918.

Taylor, Mrs. Howard J. *Borden of Yale '09*. Philadelphia: China Inland Mission, n.d.

——. *The Triumph of John and Betty Stam*. Chicago: Moody Press, 1935.

Timperley, Harold J., ed. *Japanese Terror in China*. New York: Modern Age Books, 1938.

Tuchman, Barbara W. *Stilwell and the American Experience in China, 1911–1945*. New York: The Macmillan Co., 1971.

Welch, Robert. *The Life of John Birch*. Chicago: Henry Regnery Co., 1954.

Wiley, Elizabeth Ellyson. *Three Pairs of Hands*. Nashville: Broadman Press, 1948.

Williamson, H.R. *British Baptists in China 1845–1952*. London: The Carey Kingsgate Press, 1957.

Wong, Molly. *They Changed My China*. Nashville: Broadman Press, 1970.

World-wide Evangelization: The Urgent Business of the Church. New York: Student Volunteer Movement for Foreign Missions, 1902.

ASIA (EXCLUDING CHINA) AND THE PACIFIC ISLANDS:

Awe, Chilho, and Webster, Herbert F. *Decision at Dawn (The Underground Christian Witness in Red Korea)*. New York: Harper & Row, 1965.

Barlow, Sanna. *Mountains Singing*. Chicago: Moody Press, 1952.

Blan, Norah. *Heroes of the Conquest*, no. 8. Springfield, Mo.: The Foreign Missions Department of the Assemblies of God, n.d.

Bringing It All Together: A Current View of Alliance Missions. Harrisburg, Pa.: Christian Publications, 1974.

Brown, George Thompson. *Mission to Korea*. Nashville: Board of World Missions, Presbyterian Church in the U.S., 1962.

Buckingham, Jamie. *Into the Glory*. Plainfield, N.J.: Logos International, 1974.

Burke, Todd, and Burke, DeAnn. *Anointed for Burial*. Plainfield, N.J.: Logos International, 1973.

Cable, Mildred, et al. *The Challenge of Central Asia*. London: World Dominion Press, 1929.

Campbell, Arch. *For God's Sake*. Philadelphia: Dorrance & Co., 1970.

Chisholm, William H. *Vivid Experience in Korea*. Chicago: The Bible Institute Colportage Association, 1938.

Chung, Henry. *The Case of Korea*. Old Tappan, N.J.: Fleming H. Revell, 1921.

Clark, Marjorie A. *Captive on the Ho Chi Minh Trail.* Chicago: Moody Press, 1974.

Cowles, Robert H., comp. *Operation Heartbeat.* Harrisburg, Pa.: Christian Publications, 1976.

Crane, Allan. *Fierce the Conflict.* London: Lutterworth Press, 1960.

Dowdy, Homer E. *The Bamboo Cross.* New York: Harper & Row, 1964.

Early History of New Tribes Mission. Wordsworth, Wis.: Brown Gold Publications, n.d.

Fletcher, Grace Nies. *The Fabulous Flemings of Kathmandu.* New York: E.P. Dutton & Co., 1964.

Gaither, Ralph E. *With God in a POW Camp.* Nashville: Broadman Press, 1973.

Gale, James S. *Korea in Transition.* New York: Young People's Missionary Movement of the United States and Canada, 1909.

Gardner, Brian. *The East India Company: A History.* New York: McCall Books, 1971.

Glover, Robert H. *The Progress of World-Wide Missions,* rev. ed. New York: Harper & Row, 1960.

Goldsmith, Elizabeth. *Batak Miracle.* London: Overseas Missionary Fellowship, 1967.

Harris, Stephen R., and Hefley, James C. *My Anchor Held.* Old Tappan, N.J.: Fleming H. Revell, 1970.

Haskin, Dorothy C. *In Spite of Dungeon.* Grand Rapids: Zondervan Publishing House, 1962.

Hefley, James. *By Life or By Death.* Grand Rapids: Zondervan Publishing House, 1969.

_____. *No Time for Tombstones.* Wheaton, Ill.: Tyndale House Publishers, 1974.

Hefley, James, and Hefley, Marti. *Christ in Bangladesh.* New York: Harper & Row, 1973.

_____. *God's Tribesman: The Rochunga Pudaite Story.* Philadelphia: A.J. Holman Co., 1974.

_____. *Prisoners of Hope.* Harrisburg, Pa.: Christian Publications, 1976.

Heimbach, Mertis B. *At Any Cost.* London: Overseas Missionary Fellowship, 1964.

Hitt, Russell T. *Cannibal Valley.* New York: Harper & Row, 1970.

Horne, Shirley. *An Hour from the Stone Age.* Chicago: Moody Press, 1973.

Kuhn, Isobel. *Ascent to the Tribes: Pioneering in North Thailand.* Chicago: Moody Press, 1956.

Lamott, Willis. *Suzuki Looks at Japan.* New York: Friendship Press, 1932.

Lee, Robert. *Strangers in the Land.* London: Lutterworth Press, 1967.

Moffett, Samuel Hugh. *The Christians of Korea.* New York: Friendship Press, 1962.

Olsen, Viggo, and Lockerbie, Jeanette. *Daktar: Diplomat in Bangladesh.* Chicago: Moody Press, 1973.

Paik, L.G. *The History of Protestant Missions in Korea,* 2d ed., rev. Seoul, Korea: Yonsei University Press, 1971.

Pape, Dorothy. *Captives of the Mighty (Christ and the Japanese Enigma).* Chicago: Moody Press, 1959.

Pittman, Richard. *Elwood Jacobsen.* Grand Forks, N.D.: Summer Institute of Linguistics, 1969.

Pollock, J.C. *Earth's Remotest End.* New York: The Macmillan Co., 1961.

Read, Katherine L., and Ballou, Robert O. *Bamboo Hospital.* Philadelphia: J.B. Lippincott Co., 1961.

Richardson, Don. *Peace Child.* Glendale, Calif.: Gospel Light Publications, Regal Books, 1974.

Rijnhart, Susie Carson. *Tibet.* Cincinnati, Ohio: Foreign Christian Mission Society, 1901.

Royer, Galen B. *Christian Heroism in Many Lands.* Elgin, Ill.: Brethren Press, 1915.

Rutledge, Howard, and Rutledge, Phyllis. *In the Presence of Mine Enemies.* Old Tappan, N.J.: Fleming H. Revell, 1973.

Sheetz, Paul H. *The Sovereign Hand.* Wheaton, Ill.: The Evangelical Alliance Mission, 1971.

Shelton, Albert L. *Pioneering in Tibet.* Old Tappan, N.J.: Fleming H. Revell, 1921.

Smith, Mrs. Gordon H. *Farther into the Night.* Grand Rapids: Zondervan Publishing House, 1954.

——. *Victory in Vietnam.* Grand Rapids: Zondervan Publishing House, 1965.

Soltau, T. Stanley. *Korea: The Hermit Nation and Its Response to Christianity.* London: World Dominion Press, 1932.

Steven, Hugh. *The Measure of Greatness.* Old Tappan, N.J.: Fleming H. Revell, 1976.

Sunda, James. *Church Growth in New Guinea.* Lucknow, India: Lucknow Publishing House, 1963.

Thompson, Phyllis. *Minka and Margaret.* London: Hodder and Stoughton, and Overseas Missionary Fellowship, 1976.

Through Shining Archway: In Memoriam to Missionaries of the American Baptist Foreign Mission Society and of the Woman's American Baptist Foreign Mission Society, Who Died in the Custody of the Japanese. New York: American Baptist Foreign Mission Society and Woman's American Baptist Foreign Mission Society, 1953.

Tong, Hollington K. *Christianity in Taiwan: A History.* Taipei, Taiwan: *China Post,* 1961.

Torbet, Robert G. *Venture of Faith, The Story of the American Baptist Foreign Mission Society and the Woman's American Baptist Foreign Mission Society 1814–1954.* Valley Forge, Pa.: Judson Press, n.d.

Twenty-Five Wonderful Years, comp. for the Christian and Missionary Alliance. Harrisburg, Pa.: Christian Publications, n.d.

Whitzel, Randall, and Whitzel, Dorothy. *Yet There Is Room.* Privately published, 1946.

Wilson, Dorothy Clarke. *Granny Brand, Her Story.* Chappaqua, N.Y.: Christian Herald Books, 1976.

Young, John M.L. *The Two Empires in Japan.* Nutley, N.J.: Presbyterian & Reformed Publishing Co., 1961.

GERMANY, THE SOVIET UNION, AND EASTERN EUROPE:

Andrew, Brother; Sherrill, John; and Sherrill, Elizabeth. *God's Smuggler.* Old Tappan, N.J.: Fleming H. Revell, 1968.

Area Handbook for Albania. Washington, D.C.: U.S. Government Printing Office, 1971.

Bain, ——. *The Reluctant Satellites.* New York: The Macmillan Co., 1960.

Barth, Karl. *The Church and the War.* Translated by Antonia H. Froendt. New York: The Macmillan Co., 1944.

Basansky, Bill, and Manuel, David. *Escape from Terror.* Plainfield, N.J.: Logos International, 1976.

Beeson, Trevor. *Discretion and Valour.* Glasgow: Fontana Books, 1974.

Blumit, Oswald A., and Smith, Oswald J. *Sentenced to Siberia.* Washington, D.C.: Privately published, 1947.

Blunden, Godfrey, and the Editors of Life. *Eastern Europe, Czechoslovakia, Hungary, Poland.* New York: Life World Library, Time, Inc., 1965.

Bosanquet, Mary. *The Life and Death of Dietrich Bonhoeffer.* New York: Harper & Row, 1969.

Bourdeaux, Michael. *Faith on Trial in Russia.* New York: Harper & Row, 1971.

Bourdeaux, Michael; Hebly, Hans; and Voss, Eugene, eds. *Religious Liberty in the Soviet Union.* Kent, England: Keston College, Centre for the Study of Religion and Communism, 1976.

Brant, Stefan. *The East German Rising.* Translated and Adapted by Charles Wheeler. New York: Frederick A. Praeger, 1957.

de Grunwald, Constantin. *The Churches and the Soviet Union.* New York: The Macmillan Co., 1962.

Dellin, L.A., ed. *Bulgaria.* Praeger Publications in Russian History and World Communism, vol. 47. New York: Frederick A. Praeger, 1957.

——. *Christians in the Shadow of the Kremlin.* Elgin, Ill.: David C. Cook Publishing Co., 1974.

Deyneka, Anita, and Deyneka, Peter, Jr. *Christians in the Shadow of the Kremlin.* Elgin, Ill.: David C. Cook Publishing Co., 1974.

——. *A Song in Siberia.* Elgin, Ill.: David C. Cook Publishing Co., 1977.

Deyneka, Peter. *Much Prayer—Much Power!.* Grand Rapids: Zondervan Publishing House, 1958.

Falconi, Carlo. *The Silence of Pius Twelfth.* Translated by Bernard Wall. Toronto: Little, Brown and Co., 1970.

Fejto, Francois. *Behind the Rape of Hungary.* New York: David McKay, Co., 1957.

Fetler, William. *How I Discovered Modernism Among American Baptists and Why I Founded the Russian Missionary Society.* Chicago: Russian Missionary Society, 1924.

——. *The Marvelous Results of Work Among Russian War Prisoners and the Greatest Missionary Challenge of the Christian Era.* Chicago: Russian Missionary Society, n.d.

Forster, Thomas M. *The East German Army.* Translated by Markus-Verlag Koln. London: George Allen & Unwin Ltd., 1967.

Fotitch, Constantin. *The War We Lost: Yugoslavia's Tragedy and the Failure of the West.* New York: Viking Press, 1948.

Friedlander, Saul. *Pius XII and the Third Reich: A Documentation.* Translated by Charles Fullman. New York: Alfred A. Knopf, 1966.

Gallo, Max. *The Night of Long Knives.* Translated by Lily Emmet. New York: Harper & Row, 1972.

Gibney, Frank. *The Frozen Revolution: Poland, A Study in Communist Decay.* New York: Farrar, Straus and Cudahy, 1959.

Goddard, Donald. *The Last Days of Dietrich Bonhoeffer.* New York: Harper & Row, 1976.

Gumkowski, Janusz, and Kazimierz, Leszczynski. *Poland Under Nazi Occupation.* Warsaw: Polonia Publishing House, 1961.

Hanfstaengl, Ernst. *Unheard Witness.* Philadelphia: J.B. Lippincott Co., 1957.

Harris, Rosemary, ed. *Christian Prisoners in Russia.* Wheaton, Ill.: Tyndale House Publishers, 1972.

Hefley, James C. *Heroes of Faith.* Chicago: Moody Press, 1963.

Hirschmann, Maria Anne. *Hansi, The Girl Who Loved the Swastika.* Wheaton, Ill.: Tyndale House Publishers, 1973.

Hominuke, J. *A Century of Ukranian Baptists, 1852-1952.* Detroit: Ukranian Evangelical Alliance, 1952.

Jesus to the Communist World. Bound volume of newsletters 1967-1977. Glendale, Ca.: Jesus to the Communist World, 1978.

Karev, Alexander. *The Russian Evangelical Baptist Movement or Under His Cross in Soviet Russia.* Typewritten Manuscript, n.p.: n.d.

Kohout, Pavel. *From the Diary of a Counter Revolutionary.* Translated by George Theiner. New York: McGraw-Hill Book Co., 1969.

Korbel, Josef. *The Communist Subversion of Czechoslovakia, 1938-1948: The Failure of Coexistence.* Princeton, N.J.: Princeton University Press, 1959.

Korbonski, Stefan. *Warsaw in Chains.* New York: The Macmillan Co., 1959.

Lasky, Melvin J., ed. *The Hungarian Revolution: A White Book.* New York: Frederick A. Praeger, 1957.

Levy, Alan. *Rowboat to Prague.* New York: Grossman Publishers, An Orion Press Book, 1972.

Littell, Franklin Hamlin. *The German Phoenix.* Garden City, N.Y.: Doubleday & Co., 1960.

McCaig, A. *Grace Astounding in Bolshevik Russia.* London: Russian Missionary Society, n.d.

Mikolajczyk, Stanislaw. *The Rape of Poland.* New York: Whittlesey House, McGraw-Hill Book Co., 1948.

Polsky, Archpriest Michael. *The New Martyrs of Russia.* Montreal: Monastery Press, n.d.

Popov, Haralan. *I Was a Communist Prisoner.* Grand Rapids: Zondervan Publishing House, 1966.

——. *Tortured for His Faith.* Grand Rapids: Zondervan Publishing House, 1970.

Rauschning, Anna. *No Retreat.* Indianapolis, Ind.: The Bobbs-Merrill Co., 1942.

Rohrer, Norman B., and Deyneka, Peter, Jr. *Peter Dynamite—Twice Born Russian.* Grand Rapids: Baker Book House, 1975.

Schlamm, Vera, and Friedman, Bob. *Pursued.* Glendale, Calif.: Gospel Light Publications, Regal Books, 1972.

Settle, Arthur, ed. *This Is Germany.* New York: William Sloane Associates, 1950.

Skendi, Stavro, ed. *Albania.* Praeger Publications in Russian History and World Communism, vol. 46. New York: Frederick A. Praeger, 1956.

Solzhenitsyn, Aleksandr I. *The Gulag Archipelago.* vols. 1 &

2. Translated by Thomas P. Whitney. New York: Harper & Row, 1974–1975.

Some Interesting Facts Concerning Baptists in Russia. Typewritten Manuscript. n.p.: Christian Baptist Convention, n.d.

Stillman, Edmund, and the Editors of Life. *The Balkans.* New York: Life World Library, Time, Inc., 1964.

Stransky, Jan. *East Wind Over Prague.* New York: Random House, 1951.

Ten Boom, Corrie. *Prison Letters.* Old Tappan, N.J.: Fleming H. Revell, 1975.

Ten Boom, Corrie, and Buckingham, Jamie. *Tramp for the Lord.* Old Tappan, N.J.: Fleming H. Revell, 1974.

Ten Boom, Corrie; Sherrill, John; and Sherrill, Elizabeth. *The Hiding Place.* Old Tappan, N.J.: Fleming H. Revell, Spire Books, 1971.

Thayer, Charles W., and the Editors of Life. *Russia.* New York: Life World Library, Time, Inc., 1965.

Tornquist, David. *Look East, Look West: The Socialist Adventure in Yugoslavia.* New York: The Macmillan Co., 1966.

Vins, Georgi. *Georgi Vins: Testament from Prison.* Edited by Michael Bourdeaux. Translated by Jane Ellis. Elgin, Ill.: David C. Cook Publishing Co., 1975.

The Voice of Soviet Christians. Translation Services 6, 9, 11, 12, 13, 14, 23. n.p.: Publisher Requests Anonymity, 1974–1975.

Wurmbrand, Mihai. *Between Hammer and Sickle.* Glendale, Calif.: Diane Publishing Co., 1972.

Wurmbrand, Richard. *If That Were Christ, Would You Give Him Your Blanket?.* Waco, Tex.: Word Books, 1971.

——. *My Answer to the Moscow Atheists.* New Rochelle, N.Y.: Arlington House Publishers, 1975.

——. *Tortured for Christ.* Glendale, Calif.: Diane Publishing Co., 1967.

Wurmbrand, Richard, and Foley, Charles. *Christ in the Communist Prisons.* New York: Coward–McCann, 1968.

Zimmermann, Wolf-Dieter, and Smith, Ronald Gregor, eds. *I Knew Dietrich Bonhoeffer, Reminiscences by His Friends.* Translated by Kathe Gregor Smith. New York: Harper & Row, 1966.

THE MIDDLE EAST AND AFRICA:

Abboushi, W.F. *The Angry Arabs.* Philadelphia: Westminster Press, 1974.

The Arab World. New York: Time, Inc., 1962.

Area Handbook for the United Republic of Cameroon. Washington, D.C.: U.S. Government Printing Office, 1974.

Area Handbook for Chad. Washington, D.C.: U.S. Government Printing Office, 1972.

Area Handbook for People's Republic of the Congo. Washington, D.C.: U.S. Government Printing Office, 1971.

Area Handbook for Ethiopia. Washington, D.C.: U.S. Government Printing Office, 1971.

Area Handbook for Ghana. Washington, D.C.: U.S. Government Printing Office, 1971.

Area Handbook for Guinea. Washington, D.C.: U.S. Government Printing Office, 1975.

Area Handbook for Ivory Coast. Washington, D.C.: U.S. Government Printing Office, 1973.

Area Handbook for Kenya. Washington, D.C.: U.S. Government Printing Office, 1976.

Area Handbook for Liberia. Washington, D.C.: U.S. Government Printing Office, 1972.

Area Handbook for Malawi. Washington, D.C.: U.S. Government Printing Office, 1975.

Area Handbook for Mauritania. Washington, D.C.: U.S. Government Printing Office, 1972.

Area Handbook for Nigeria. Washington, D.C.: U.S. Government Printing Office, 1972.

Area Handbook for Senegal. Washington, D.C.: U.S. Government Printing Office, 1974.

Area Handbook for Sierra Leone. Washington, D.C.: U.S. Government Printing Office, 1976.

Area Handbook for Somalia. Washington, D.C.: U.S. Government Printing Office, 1977.

Area Handbook for Southern Rhodesia. Washington, D.C.: U.S. Government Printing Office, 1975.

Area Handbook for the Democratic Republic of Sudan. Washington, D.C.: U.S. Government Printing Office, 1973.

Area Handbook for Zambia. Washington, D.C.: U.S. Government Printing Office, 1974.

Barton, James L. *Daybreak in Turkey.* Boston: The Pilgrim Press, 1908.

Bayly, Joseph T. *Congo Crisis.* Grand Rapids: Zondervan Publishing House, 1966.

Best, Alan C., and de Blij, Harm J. *An African Survey.* New York: John Wiley & Sons, 1977.

Boutros, Allison D. *The Soul of Egypt.* London: Marshall, Morgan and Scott, n.d.

Bradt, Charles Edwin, ed. *Men and the Modern Missionary Enterprise.* Chicago: The Winona Publishing Co., 1907.

Bradt, Charles E.; King, William R.; and Reherd, Herbert W. *Around the World: Studies and Stories of Presbyterian Foreign Missions.* Wichita: The Missionary Press, 1912.

Brain, Belle M. *From Every Tribe and Nation.* Old Tappan, N.J.: Fleming H. Revell, 1927.

Brockelmann, Carl. *History of the Islamic Peoples.* New York: Capricorn Books, 1967.

Brown, Arthur J. *Rising Churches in Non-Christian Lands.* New York: Missionary Education Movement, 1915.

Bryant, Cyril E. *Operation Brother's Brother.* Philadelphia: J.B. Lippincott Co., 1968.

Campbell, Alexander. *The Heart of Africa.* New York: Alfred A. Knopf, 1954.

Camphor, Alexander P. *Missionary Story Sketches: Folk-Lore from Africa.* Cincinnati: Jennings & Graham; New York: Eaton and Mains, 1909.

Carlson, Lois. *Monganga Paul.* New York: Harper & Row, 1966.

Churchhill, Rhona. *White Man's Gold.* New York: William Morrow & Co., 1962.

Coates, Austin. *Basutoland.* London: Her Majesty's Stationery Office, 1966.

Coles, Samuel B. *Preacher with a Plow.* Boston: Houghton Mifflin Co., 1957.

Cornwall, Barbara. *The Bush Rebels.* New York: Holt, Rhinehart & Winston, 1972.

Coughlan, Robert, and the Editors of Life. *Tropical Africa.* New York: Life World Library, Time, Inc., 1966.

Cragg, Kenneth. *The Call of the Minaret.* New York: Oxford University Press, 1964.

Crowder, Michael. *A Short History of Nigeria.* New York: Frederick A. Praeger, 1962.

Darlington, Charles, and Darlington, Alice. *African Betrayal.* New York: David McKay Co., 1968.

Davidson, Basil. *The African Awakening.* New York: The Macmillan Co., 1955.

_____. *In the Eye of the Storm: Angola's People.* Garden City, N.Y.: Doubleday & Co., 1972.

Davis, Raymond. *Fire on the Mountains.* Grand Rapids: Zondervan Publishing House, 1966.

Debenham, Frank. *Nyasaland, Land of the Lake.* London: Her Majesty's Stationery Office, 1955.

Deering, Alma E. *Leopold's Spots or God's Masterpiece—Which?* Privately published, 1916.

Diamond, Stanley, and Burke, Fred G., eds. *The Transformation of East Africa: Studies in Political Anthropology.* New York: Basic Books, 1966.

Dowdy, Homer E. *Out of the Jaws of the Lion.* New York: Harper & Row, 1965.

Dugan, James, and Lafore, Laurence. *Days of Emperor and Clown: The Italo-Ethiopian War 1935-1936.* Garden City, N.Y.: Doubleday & Co., 1973.

Eller, Paul Himmel. *History of Evangelical Missions.* Harrisburg, Pa.: The Evangelical Press, 1942.

Elliot, Elisabeth. *Furnace of the Lord.* Garden City, N.Y.: Doubleday & Co., 1969.

Eprile, Cecil. *War and Peace in the Sudan, 1955-1972.* North Pomfret, Vt.: David & Charles, 1974.

Fahs, Sophia Lyon. *Uganda's White Man of Work: A Story of Alexander M. McKay.* New York: Missionary Education Movement, 1912.

Farwell, Byron. *Prisoners of the Mahdi.* New York: Harper & Row, 1968.

Fletcher, Lionel B. *South African Jewels.* London: Marshall, Morgan and Scott, n.d.

Forsberg, Malcolm I. *Land Beyond the Nile.* New York: Harper & Brothers, 1958.

Fraser, Donald. *The New Africa.* New York: Missionary Education Movement, 1927.

Fried, Ralph. *Reaching Arabs for Christ.* Grand Rapids: Zondervan Publishing House, 1947.

Fuller, Frances, ed. and trans. *Flowers from the Valley of Terror.* Beirut, Lebanon: Baptist Publications, 1977.

Fuller, W. Harold. *Run While the Sun Is Hot.* Chicago: Moody Press, 1967.

Furbay, Elizabeth Dearmin. *Top Hats and Tom-Toms.* Chicago: Ziff-Davis Publishing Co., 1943.

Gann, L.H., and Duignan, Peter, eds. *Burden of Empire: An Appraisal of Western Colonialism in Africa South of the Sahara.* New York: Frederick A. Praeger, 1967.

Grubb, Norman. *After C.T. Studd.* London: Lutterworth Press, 1939.

Gwyn, David. *Death-Light of Africa: Idi Amin.* Boston: Little, Brown and Co., 1977.

Hall, John. *From Cannibalism to Christ.* Toronto: Evangelical Publishers, 1944.

Harr, Wilber C., ed. *Frontiers of the Christian World Mission Since 1938: Essays in Honour of Kenneth Scott Latourette.* New York: Harper & Brothers, 1962.

Hatch, John. *Nigeria: The Seeds of Disaster.* Chicago: Henry Regnery Co., 1970.

Hayes, Margaret. *Captive of the Simbas.* New York: Harper & Row, 1966.

Hefley, James, and Hefley, Marti. *Arabs, Christians, Jews.* Plainfield, N.J.: Logos International, 1978.

Hefley, Jim, and Hefley, Marti. *Where in the World Are the Jews Today?* Wheaton, Ill.: Scripture Press, Victor Books, 1974.

Hefley, Marti, and Hefley, James. *The Liberated Palestinian.* Wheaton, Ill.: Scripture Press, Victor Books, 1975.

Hennessy, Maurice N. *The Congo: A Brief History and Appraisal.* New York: Frederick A. Praeger, 1961.

Heroes of the Cross. London: Marshall, Morgan & Scott, n.d.

Hoagland, Jim. *South Africa: Civilizations in Conflict.* Boston: Houghton Mifflin Co., 1972.

Hughes, John. *The New Face of Africa South of the Sahara.* New York: Longmans, Green and Co., 1961.

Hunting, Joseph. *Israel—A Modern Miracle.* vol I: *Prophecies Fulfilled in the Land.* Murrumbeena, Australia: The David Press, 1969.

Hussein, King, of Jordan. *Uneasy Lies the Head.* New York: Bernard Geis Associates, 1962.

Ingrams, Harold. *Uganda, A Crisis of Nationhood.* London: Her Majesty's Stationery Office, 1960.

Kane, J. Herbert. *Faith, Mighty Faith.* New York: International Foreign Missions Association, 1956.

————. *A Global View of Christian Missions.* Grand Rapids: Baker Book House, 1975.

Kiernan, Thomas. *Arafat: The Man and the Myth.* New York: W.W. Norton, 1976.

Kwast, Lloyd E. *The Discipling of West Cameroon.* Grand Rapids: William B. Eerdmans Publishing Co., 1971.

Lane, Margaret. *A Calabash of Diamonds.* New York: Duell, Sloan and Pearce, 1961.

Latourette, Kenneth S. *Christianity in a Revolutionary Age.* vol. III: *The 19th Century Outside Europe.* New York: Harper & Row, 1962.

Lemarchand, Rene. *Political Awakening in the Congo.* Berkeley and Los Angeles: University of California Press, 1964.

Lewis, Roy. *Sierra Leone.* London: Her Majesty's Stationery Office, 1954.

Lindsey, Hal, and Carlson, C. C. *The Late Great Planet Earth.* Grand Rapids: Zondervan Publishing House, 1970.

Mabie, Catharine L. *Congo Cameos.* Philadelphia: Judson Press, 1952.

Marsh, Charles R. *Share Your Faith With a Muslim.* Chicago: Moody Press, 1975.

Mason, Alfred D., and Barny, Frederick J. *History of the Arabian Mission.* n.p.: The Board of Foreign Missions, Reformed Church in America, 1926.

Mason, Carolina A. *Wonders of Missions.* New York: George

H. Doran Co., 1922.

McCave, Mrs. Alexander. *Congo.* Harrisburg, Pa.: Christian Publications, 1937.

McGavran, Donald A. *Understanding Church Growth.* Grand Rapids: William B. Eerdmans Publishing Co., 1970.

Melady, Thomas Patrick. *Profiles of African Leaders.* New York: The Macmillan Co., 1961.

Melady, Thomas, and Melady, Margaret. *Idi Amin Dada: Hitler in Africa.* Mission, Kans.: Sheed Andrews and McMeel, 1977.

Menhun, Moshe. *The Decadence of Judaism in Our Time.* Hicksville, N.Y.: Exposition Press, 1965.

Miller, Charles. *The Lunatic Express: An Entertainment in Imperialism.* New York: The Macmillan Co., 1971.

Miller, William M. *Ten Muslims Meet Christ.* Grand Rapids: William B. Eerdmans Publishing Co., 1969.

Moorhouse, Geoffrey. *The Missionaries.* Philadelphia: J.B. Lippincott Co., 1973.

Murray-Brown, Jeremy. *Kenyatta.* New York: E. P. Dutton & Co., 1973.

Naylor, Wilson S. *Daybreak in the Dark Continent.* New York: Laymen's Missionary Movement, 1905.

Olsen, Hal. *African Heroes of the Congo Rebellion.* Kijabe, Kenya: Kesho Publications, 1969.

Olson, Gilbert W. *Church Growth in Sierra Leone.* Grand Rapids: William B. Eerdmans Publishing Co., 1969.

O'Meara, Patrick. *Rhodesia: Racial Conflict or Coexistence?* Ithaca, N.Y.: Cornell University Press, 1975.

Paton, Alan. *Apartheid and the Archbishop: The Life and Times of Gregory Clayton, Archbishop of Cape Town.* New York: Charles Scribner's Sons, 1973.

——. *Hope for South Africa.* New York: Frederick A. Praeger, 1959.

——. *The Long View.* Edited by Edward Callan. New York: Frederick A. Praeger, 1968.

——. *South African Tragedy: The Life and Times of Jan Hofmeyer.* New York: Charles Scribner's Sons, 1965.

Petersen, William J. *Another Hand on Mine: The Story of Dr. Carl K. Becker of the Africa Inland Mission.* Grand Rapids: Zondervan Publishing House, 1967.

Questing in Galilee. Richmond, Va.: The Foreign Mission Board of the Southern Baptist Convention, 1937.

Reed, Jane, and Grant, Jim. *Voice Under Every Palm.* Grand Rapids: Zondervan Publishing House, 1968.

Report of World Missionary Conference. Commissions I, II, III, IV, V, VI, VII, and IX, 9 vols. Edinburgh and London:

Oliphant, Anderson, and Ferrier, 1900–1910.

Richardson, Kenneth. *Garden of Miracles: A History of the Africa Inland Mission.* London: Victory Press, 1968.

Richter, Julius. *A History of Protestant Missions in the Near East.* Old Tappan, N.J.: Fleming H. Revell, 1910.

Rodwell, J.M., ed. *The Koran.* New York: E. P. Dutton, Co., Everyman's Library, 1909.

Rotberg, Robert I., and Mazrui, Ali A., eds. *Protest and Power in Black Africa.* New York: Oxford University Press, 1970.

Sales, Jane M. *The Planting of the Church in South Africa.* Grand Rapids: William B. Eerdmans Publishing Co., 1971.

Scott, J.F. *The Man Who Loved The Zulus.* Pitermaritzburg, South Africa: Shuter and Shooter, n.d.

Seats, V. Lavell. *Africa ... Arrows to Atoms.* Nashville: Convention Press, 1967.

Shaloff, Stanley. *Reform in Leopold's Congo.* Richmond, Va.: John Knox Press, 1970.

Sheetz, Paul H. *The Sovereign Hand.* Wheaton, Ill.: The Evangelical Alliance Mission, 1971.

Signs and Wonders in Rabbath–Ammon. Amman, Jordan: S. B. Kawar, n.d.

Smith, Oswald J. *Tales of the Mission Field.* London: Marshall, Morgan and Scott, 1965.

Stanley, Henry M. *How I Found Livingstone.* New York: Scribner, Armstrong and Co., 1872.

Stewart, James. *Dawn in the Dark Continent.* Old Tappan, N.J.: Fleming H. Revell, 1903.

Stone, Elaine M. *Uganda: Fire and Blood.* Plainfield, N.J.; Logos International, 1977.

Students and the Present Missionary Crisis. Addresses delivered before the International Convention of the Student Volunteer Movement for Missions. New York: Student Volunteer Movement for Foreign Missions, 1910.

Students and the World-Wide Expansion of Christianity. Addresses before the International Convention of the Student Volunteer Movement for Missions. New York: Student Volunteer Movement for Foreign Missions, 1914.

Taylor, S. Earl. *The Price of Africa.* Cincinnati: Jennings and Rye, 1902.

Thielicke, Helmut. *African Diary.* Waco, Tex.: Word Books, 1974.

Trobisch, Ingrid H. *On Our Way Rejoicing.* New York: Harper & Row, 1964.

Tucker, Angeline. *"He Is In Heaven".* New York: McGraw–Hill Book Co., n.d.

Van Den Berghe, Pierre L. *South Africa: A Study in Conflict.*

Middletown, Conn.: Wesleyan University Press, 1965.

Vleurinck, T., ed. *Forty-Six Angry Men.* n.p.: *American Opinion,* n.d.

Ward, W.E.F. *A History of Ghana.* 2d ed., rev. London: George Allen and Unwin Ltd., 1958.

Watson, Charles R. *The Sorrow and Hope of the Egyptian Sudan.* Philadelphia: The Board of Foreign Missions of the United Presbyterian Church of North America, 1913.

Wattenberg, Ben, and Smith, Ralph Lee. *The New Nations of Africa.* New York: Hart Publishing Co., 1963.

Webster, J.B.; Boahen, A.A.; and Idowu, H.O. *History of West Africa: The Revolutionary Years—1815 to Independence.* New York: Frederick A. Praeger, 1970.

Weissman, Stephen R. *American Foreign Policy in the Congo 1960–1964.* Ithaca, N.Y.: Cornell University Press, 1974.

Welensky, Roy. *Welensky's 4000 Days: The Life and Death of the Federation of Rhodesia and Nyasaland.* New York: Roy Publishers, 1964.

Wiedner, Donald L. *A History of Africa South of the Sahara.* New York: Random House, 1962.

Willis, Colin. *Who Killed Kenya?* New York: Roy Publishers, 1953.

Wilson, T.E. *Angola Beloved.* Neptune, N.J.: Loizeaux Brothers, 1967.

Wingert, Norman. *No Place to Stop Killing.* Chicago: Moody Press, 1974.

World-Wide Evangelization. Addresses delivered before the International Convention of the Student Volunteer Movement for Foreign Missions. New York: Student Volunteer Movement for Foreign Missions, 1902, 1906.

Your Muslim Guest. Toronto: Fellowship of Faith for Muslims, n.d.

Ziegler, Philip. *Omdurman.* New York: Alfred A. Knopf, 1974.

Zogby, James J., ed. *Perspective on Palestinian Arabs and Israeli Jews.* Wilmette, Ill.: Medina Press, 1977.

Zwemer, Samuel M., and Brown, Arthur J. *The Nearer and Farther East: Outline Studies of Moslem Lands.* New York: The MacMillan Co., 1908.

THE CARIBBEAN AND LATIN AMERICA:

Area Handbook for Argentina. Washington, D.C.: U.S. Government Printing Office, 1974.

Area Handbook for Bolivia. Washington, D.C.: U.S. Government Printing Office, 1974.

Area Handbook for Colombia. Washington, D.C.: U.S. Government Printing Office, 1977.

Area Handbook for Cuba. Washington, D.C.: U.S. Government Printing Office, 1976.

Area Handbook for the Dominican Republic. Washington, D.C.: U.S. Government Printing Office, 1973.

Area Handbook for Mexico. Washington, D.C.: U.S. Government Printing Office, 1970.

Banner, Horace. *The Three Freds and After.* Philadelphia: Unevangelized Fields Mission, n.d.

Beach, Harlan P. *Renascent Latin America.* New York: Missionary Education Movement of the United States and Canada, 1916.

Birns, Laurence, ed. *The End of Chilean Democracy: An IDOC Dossier on the Coup and Its Aftermath.* New York: Seabury Press, 1963.

Bodard, Lucien. *Green Hell.* Translated by Jennifer Monaghan. New York: E. P. Dutton & Co., 1971.

———. *Massacre of the Brazilian Indians.* Translated by Jennifer Monaghan. New York: Outerbridge, 1972.

Bosch, Juan. *The Unfinished Experiment: Democracy in the Dominican Republic.* Translated by C. Zapata. New York: Frederick A. Praeger, 1965.

Brandenburg, Frank R. *The Making of Modern Mexico.* Englewood Cliffs, N.J.: Prentice–Hall, 1964.

Brazil. New York: Life World Library, Time, Inc., 1967.

Brown, Hubert W. *Latin America.* Old Tappan, N.J.: Fleming H. Revell, Student Missionary Campaign Library, 1901.

The Call of God to Men. Addresses of the Laymen's Missionary Movement of the Methodist Episcopal Church, South. Nashville, 1908.

Cardenal, Ernesto. *In Cuba.* Translated by Donald D. Walsh. New York: New Directions Publishing, 1974.

Caute, David. *Cuba, Yes!.* New York: McGraw–Hill Book Co., 1974.

Clark, Francis E., and Clark, Harriet A. *The Gospel in Latin Lands.* New York: The Macmillan Co., 1909.

Clark, Gerald. *The Coming Explosion in Latin America.* New York: David McKay Co., 1962.

Clark, James A. *The Church and the Crisis in the Dominican Republic.* Westminster, Md.: The Newman Press, n.d.

Cook, Frank S. *Seeds in the Wind.* Miami: World Radio Missionary Fellowship, n.d.

Crabtree, A.R. *Baptists in Brazil.* Rio de Janeiro: Baptist Publishing House, 1953.

Crassweller, Robert D. *Trujillo.* New York: The Macmillan Co., 1966.

Cunningham, Rosemary. *Harvest Moon on the Amazon.* Grand Rapids: Zondervan Publishing House, 1958.

Dame, Lawrence. *Maya Mission*. Garden City, N.Y.: Doubleday & Co., 1968.

Daniels, Josephus. *Shirt-Sleeve Diplomat*. Chapel Hill, N.C.: University of North Carolina Press, 1947.

Diaz del Castillo, Bernal. *The Discovery and Conquest of Mexico*. Edited by Gerano Garcia. New York: Farrar, Straus and Cudahy, 1956.

Diederich, Bernard, and Burt, Al. *Papa Doc: The Truth About Haiti Today*. New York: McGraw–Hill Book Co., 1969.

Dix, Robert H. *Colombia: The Political Dimensions of Change*. New Haven, Conn.: Yale University Press, 1967.

Dominican Action—1965: Intervention or Cooperation?. Washington, D.C.: The Center for Strategic Studies, 1966.

Dowdy, Homer E. *Christ's Witchdoctor*. New York: Harper & Row, 1963.

Edman, V. Raymond. *Not Somehow, But Triumphantly*. Grand Rapids: Zondervan Publishing House, n.d.

Elliot, Elisabeth. *Through Gates of Splendor*. New York: Harper & Brothers, 1957.

Ferguson, J. Halcro and the Editors of Life. *The River Plate Republics: Argentina, Paraguay, Uruguay*. New York: Life World Library, Time, Inc., 1965.

Fite, Clifton Edgar. *In Castro's Clutches*. Chicago: Moody Press, 1969.

Freyre, Gilberto. *The Mansions and the Shanties: The Making of Modern Brazil*. Edited and Translated by Harriet De Onis. New York: Alfred A. Knopf, 1963.

Glass, Fred C. *Through the Heart of Brazil*. Liverpool, England: South American Evangelical Mission, n.d.

Grubb, Norman P. *Modern Crusaders: The Challenge of Colombia*. London: Worldwide Evangelization Crusade, 1936.

Gruening, Ernest H. *Mexico and Its Heritage*. New York: D. Appleton–Century Co., 1968.

Halliwell, Leo B. *Light in the Jungle*. New York: David McKay Co., 1959.

Hawthorne, Sally Reese. *Cloud Country Sojourn*. London: Marshall, Morgan and Scott, The Bolivian Indian Mission, n.d.

Hay, Alex Rattray. *Our Line of Advance*. n.p.: The Inland South American Missionary Union, 1920.

Hefley, James C. *Aaron Saenz, Mexico's Revolutionary Capitalist*. Waco, Tex.: Word Books, n.d.

——. *Intrigue in Santo Domingo*. Waco, Tex.: Word Books, 1968.

——. *Peril By Choice.* Grand Rapids: Zondervan Publishing House, 1968.

——. *A Prejudiced Protestant Takes a New Look at the Catholic Church.* Old Tappan, N.J.: Fleming H. Revell, 1972.

——. *Uncle Cam: Founder of Wycliffe Bible Translators.* Waco, Tex.: Word Books, 1974.

High, Stanley. *Looking Ahead with Latin America.* New York: Missionary Education Movement of the United States and Canada, 1925.

Horowitz, Irving Louis. *Revolution in Brazil.* New York: E. P. Dutton & Co., 1964.

Horowitz, Irving Louis; de Castro, Josue; and Gerassi, John, eds. *Latin American Radicalism.* New York: Random House, 1969.

Howard, David M. *The Costly Harvest.* (Originally Published as *Hammered as Gold,* New York: Harper & Row, 1969.) Wheaton, Ill.: Tyndale House Publishers, 1975.

Johnson, Jean Dye. *God Planted Five Seeds.* New York: Harper & Row, 1966.

Kane, J. Herbert. *The Progress of World Wide Missions.* rev. ed. New York: Harper & Row, 1970.

Knechtel, Dorothy. *Land of Dry Rivers.* Randolph, N.Y.: Register Publishing Co., 1972.

Kurzman, ——. *Revolt of the Damned.* New York: Van Rees Press, 1965.

Lavine, Harold, and the Editors of Life. *Central America.* New York: Life World Library, Time, Inc., 1964.

Logan, Rayford W. *Haiti and the Dominican Republic.* New York: Oxford University Press, 1968.

Loya, Diego Garcia. *Mosaic of Mexican History.* Mexico D.F.: Editorial Cultra, T. G., S. A., 1958.

MacEoin, Gary. *Revolution Next Door: Latin America in the Nineteen Seventies.* New York: Holt, Rinehart & Winston, 1971.

Manning, Helen. *To Perish for Their Saving.* Minneapolis: Bethany Fellowship, 1971.

Martin, John Bartlow. *Overtaken by Events.* Garden City, N.Y.: Doubleday & Co., 1966.

Martz, John D. *Colombia: A Contemporary Political Survey.* Chapel Hill, N.C.: The University of North Carolina Press, 1962.

McGavran, Donald. *Church Growth in Mexico.* Grand Rapids: William B. Eerdmans Publishing Co., 1963.

McLean, J.H. *The Living Christ for Latin America.* n.p.: The Board of Foreign Missions and the Woman's Board of Foreign Missions of the Presbyterian Church, U.S.A., 1916.

Mexico. New York: Life World Library, Time, Inc., 1964.

Monahan, James, and Gilmore, Kenneth O. *The Great Deception (The Inside Story of How the Kremlin Took Over Cuba).* New York: Farrar, Straus and Co., 1963.

Nicholson, Joe, Jr. *Inside Cuba.* New York: Sheed and Ward, 1974.

Oliver, A. Ben. *Baptists Building in Brazil.* Nashville: Broadman Press, 1942.

Patterson, Frank W. *Caribbean Quest.* Nashville: Convention Press, 1960.

Porterfield, Bruce E. *Commandos for Christ.* New York: Harper & Row, 1963.

Quirk, Robert E. *The Mexican Revolution 1914–1915.* Bloomington, Ind.: Indiana University Press, 1960.

Reid, Orvil W. *The Challenge of Mexico to Missions.* Guadalajara, Mexico: Baptist Student Home Print Shop, 1952.

Rodman, Selden. *Haiti: The Black Republic.* Old Greenwich, Conn.: The Devin–Adair Co., 1973.

Sheetz, Paul H. *The Sovereign Hand.* Wheaton, Ill.: The Evangelical Alliance Mission, 1971.

Spain, Mildred W. *"And in Samaria"—The Story of the Central American Mission.* Dallas: Central American Mission, 1954.

Steven, Hugh. *They Dared to Be Different.* Irvine, Calif.: Harvest House Publishers, 1976.

Steven, Hugh, and Hefley, James C. *Miracles in Mexico.* Chicago: Moody Press, 1972.

Stevens, Dorothy A. *Neighbor Voices.* Philadelphia: Judson Press, 1958.

Strong, William M. *God's Irregulars.* Westchester, Ill.: Good News Publishers, 1974.

Swanson, J.F. ed. *Three Score Years . . . and Then.* Wheaton, Ill.: The Evangelical Alliance Mission, n.d.

Tannenbaum, Frank. *The Struggle for Peace and Bread.* New York: Alfred A. Knopf, 1950.

Taylor, W.C. *Sharing with Neighbor America.* Richmond, Va.: The Foreign Mission Board of the Southern Baptist Convention, 1935.

Thiessen, John C. *A Survey of World Mission.* Chicago: Moody Press, 1961.

Torres, Camilo. *Revolutionary Priest.* Edited by John Gerassi. New York: Random House, 1971.

Townsend, William Cameron. *Lazaro Cardenas, Mexican Democrat.* Ann Arbor, Mich.: George Wahr Publishing Co., 1952.

Tylee, Mrs. Arthur F. *The Challenge of Amazon's Indians.* Chicago: Moody Press, 1931.

Veliz, Claudio, ed. *The Politics of Conformity in Latin America.* New York: Oxford University Press, 1967.

Wagner, C. Peter. *The Defeat of the Bird God.* Grand Rapids: Zondervan Publishing House, 1967.

Wallis, Ethel E. *The Dayuma Story.* New York: Harper & Brothers, 1960.

Wallis, Ethel E., and Bennett, Mary. *Two Thousand Tongues to Go.* New York: Harper & Row, 1964.

The West Indies. New York: Life World Library, Time, Inc., 1963.

Willems, Emilio. *Followers of the New Faith (Culture Change and the Rise of Protestantism in Brazil and Chile).* Nashville: Vanderbilt University Press, 1967.

Woodward, Ralph L., Jr. *Central America: A Nation Divided.* New York: Oxford University Press, 1976.

INDEX